The Glory of Kings

The Glory of Kings

A Festschrift in Honor of James B. Jordan

edited by
PETER J. LEITHART
and
JOHN BARACH

PICKWICK *Publications* · Eugene, Oregon

THE GLORY OF KINGS
A Festschrift in Honor of James B. Jordan

Copyright © 2011 Wipf and Stock Publishers. All rights reserved. Except for brief quotations in critical publications or reviews, no part of this book may be reproduced in any manner without prior written permission from the publisher. Write: Permissions, Wipf and Stock Publishers, 199 W. 8th Ave., Suite 3, Eugene, OR 97401.

Pickwick Publications
An Imprint of Wipf and Stock Publishers
199 W. 8th Ave., Suite 3
Eugene, OR 97401

www.wipfandstock.com

ISBN 13: 978-1-60899-680-3

Cataloging-in-Publication data:

The glory of kings : a festschrift in honor of James B. Jordan / edited by Peter J. Leithart and John Barach.

xxx + 336 p. ; 23 cm. Includes bibliographical references.

ISBN 13: 978-1-60899-680-3

1. Jordan, James B., 1949–. 2. Bible — Criticism, interpretation, etc. 3. Theology. 4. Liturgics. I. Leithart, Peter J. II. Barach, John. III. Title.

BV600 G62 2011

Manufactured in the U.S.A.

Unless otherwise noted, Scripture quotations in chapters 1 and 3 are the authors' own translations.

Scripture quotations in chapter 2 are either the author's own translation or his modification of *The Holy Bible, English Standard Version* (ESV), copyright © 2001 by Crossway Bibles, a division of Good News Publishers. Used by permission. All rights reserved.

Unless otherwise indicated, Scripture quotations in chapters 4, 6, 8, and 10 are from *The Holy Bible, New King James Version* (NKJV). Copyright © 1979, 1980, 1982, Thomas Nelson, Inc. All rights reserved worldwide.

Unless otherwise indicated, Scripture quotations in chapters 5 and 12 are from the *NEW AMERICAN STANDARD BIBLE®* (NASB). Copyright © 1960, 1962, 1963, 1968, 1971, 1972, 1973, 1975, 1977, 1995 by The Lockman Foundation. Used by permission.

Scripture quotations in chapters 7 and 13 are from *The Holy Bible, English Standard Version* (ESV), copyright © 2001 by Crossway Bibles, a division of Good News Publishers. Used by permission. All rights reserved.

Scripture quotations in chapter 14 are from the *King James Version*.

Scripture quotations marked (NIV) are taken from the *Holy Bible, New International Version®*, NIV®. Copyright © 1973, 1978, 1984 by Biblica, Inc.™ Used by permission of Zondervan. All rights reserved worldwide.

Scripture quotations marked (RSV) are taken from the *Revised Standard Version of the Bible*, copyright 1952 [2nd edition, 1971] by the Division of Christian Education of the National Council of the Churches of Christ in the United States of America. Used by permission. All rights reserved.

Italics within Scripture quotations indicate emphasis added.

It is the glory of God to conceal a matter,
But the glory of kings is to search out a matter.

Proverbs 25:2 (NASB)

Contents

List of Contributors / ix
Foreword by R. R. Reno / xiii
Editors' Acknowledgements / xvii
James B. Jordan's Acknowledgments / xix
Introduction—Peter J. Leithart / xxi

PART ONE: Biblical Studies

1. The Glory of the Son of Man: An Exposition of Psalm 8—*John Barach* / 3
2. Judah's Life from the Dead: The Gospel of Romans 11—*Tim Gallant* / 35
3. The Knotted Thread of Time: The Missing Daughter in Leviticus 18 —*Peter J. Leithart* / 57
4. Holy War Fulfilled and Transformed: A Look at Some Important New Testament Texts—*Rich Lusk* / 75
5. The Royal Priesthood in Exodus 19:6—*Ralph Allan Smith* / 93
6. Father Storm: A Theology of Sons in the Book of Job—*Toby J. Sumpter* / 113

PART TWO: Liturgical Theology

7. On Earth as It Is in Heaven: The Pastoral Typology of James B. Jordan —*Bill DeJong* / 133
8. Why Don't We Sing the Songs Jesus Sang? The Birth, Death and Resurrection of English Psalm Singing—*Duane Garner* / 147
9. Psalm 46—*William Jordan* / 163

PART THREE: Theology

10. A Pedagogical Paradigm for Understanding Reformed Eschatology with Special Emphasis on Basic Characteristics of Christ's Person —*C. Kee Hwang* / 185
11. Light and Shadow: Confessing the Doctrine of Election in the Sixteenth Century—*Jeffrey J. Meyers* / 203

Contents

PART FOUR: Culture

12   James Jordan, Rosenstock-Huessy, and Beyond—*Richard Bledsoe* / 249

13   Theology of Beauty in Evdokimov—*Bogumil Jarmulak* / 275

14   Empire, Sports, and War—*Douglas Wilson* / 289

Afterword—John M. Frame / 301

The Writings of James B. Jordan, 1975–2010—John Barach / 305

Contributors

John Barach (Bachelor of Biblical Studies, Peace River Bible Institute, 1994; MDiv, Mid-America Reformed Seminary, 1997) is the pastor of Covenant Presbyterian Church (CREC) in Sulphur, Louisiana and a faculty member at the Martin Bucer Institute for Biblical Studies in Monroe, Louisiana. Previously, he pastored Trinity Reformed Church (URCNA) in Lethbridge, Alberta, Covenant Reformed Church (URCNA) in Grande Prairie, Alberta, and Christ Church (CREC) in Medford, Oregon. He and his wife Moriah have three children.

Richard Bledsoe (MDiv, Westminster Theological Seminary, Escondido, CA, 1984; DMin, Urban Missions, Bakke Graduate University, 2009) is a minister in the Presbyterian Church in America and served for twenty years as pastor of Tree of Life Presbyterian Church (PCA) in Boulder, Colorado. He currently pursues ministry to various city, county, and university officials in Boulder, serves as a chaplain at the local hospital, and teaches Bible and Theology at Rivendell College in Boulder. He and his wife Carla have been married for thirty-four years.

Bill DeJong (BA, Redeemer University College; MDiv, Mid-America Reformed Seminary, 1996) is the pastor of Cornerstone Canadian Reformed Church in Hamilton, Ontario, and is a student in a PhD program at McMaster Divinity College. He previously pastored Covenant Reformed Church (URCNA) in Grande Prairie, Alberta, and Covenant Reformed Church (URCNA) in Kansas City, Missouri. He and his wife Kim have four sons.

John M. Frame (AB, Philosophy, Princeton University, 1961; BD, Westminster Theological Seminary, 1964; MPhil, Yale University, 1967; DD, Belhaven College, 2003) is Professor of Systematic Theology and Philosophy at Reformed Theological Seminary (Orlando). Previously, he taught theology, apologetics, ethics, and philosophy at Westminster Theological Seminary (Philadelphia) and Westminster Theological Seminary (Escondido, California). He has published thirteen books, including the *Theology of Lordship* series, *Apologetics to the Glory of God* (P&R, 1994), *Evangelical Reunion* (Baker, 1991), *Cornelius Van Til* (P&R, 1995), and *Salvation Belongs to the Lord* (P&R, 2006). He and his wife Mary have five children.

Tim Gallant (MDiv, Mid-America Reformed Seminary, 2000) is an elder of Christ Covenant Church (CREC) in Grande Prairie, Alberta, where he preaches frequently, and runs a small graphic design and web development business. Previously, he pas-

Contributors

tored Conrad Christian Reformed Church. He is the author of *Feed My Lambs* (Pactum Reformanda, 2002) and *These Are Two Covenants* (Pactum Reformanda, 2010).

Duane Garner (Bachelor of Biblical Languages, Oxford Baptist Institute) completed four years of study at the Dabney Center for Theological Studies, Monroe, Louisiana, and is the associate pastor of Auburn Avenue Presbyterian Church (CREC) in Monroe, Louisiana. He is the author of *Why the End Is Not Near: A Refutation of End Times Hystera* (Athanasius Press, 2008). He and his wife Sarah have two children.

C. Kee Hwang (MAR and ThM, Westminster Theological Seminary, Philadelphia; ThD, Potchefstroom University) is the former President and Professor Emeritus of New Testament at Kosin Christian University in Busan, South Korea, and the founder and President of Korea South East Bible Institute. He is the author of *Jesus, the Church and I: A Redemptive Historical Interpretation of New Testament in Light of the Person of Jesus Christ* and *Christocentric Interpretation of the Bible*(both in Korean).

Bogumil Jarmulak (BA, Biblical Seminary of Theology, Wroclaw, Poland; MA, Lutheran Faculty of Theology, Warsaw, Poland) is the pastor of the Evangelical Reformed Church (CREC) in Poznan, Poland. Previously, he pastored the Evangelical Reformed Church in Wroclaw, Poland. He is the chief editor of Reformation in Poland Publishing House. He and his wife Eva have three children.

William Jordan (BMus, Georgia, 1971; MA, Pennsylvania, 1973; PhD, Florida State, 1976) is Professor of Composition and Musicology at the University of Calgary. He has composed over two hundred works for diverse ensembles. He is the recipient of over twenty commissions from sources such as the Canada Council and the Alberta Foundation for the Arts, as well as individual sponsorships from both private supporters and organizations such as the Calgary Philharmonic, the Cathedral Church of the Redeemer, the Windsor Symphony Orchestra, New Works Calgary, and the Land's End Chamber Ensemble. His commissioned orchestral compositions from the 1980s—*Symphonic Fantasy* (1980), the *Second Concerto for Piano and Orchestra* (1986) and *Variations for Orchestra* (1990)—were recorded and broadcast nationally by the CBC. In recent years he has turned to chamber music, choral music, and songs. Principal works since 2000 include the oratorios *City of Peace* and *Prince of Peace,* the *Concerto for Organ, Violin, Strings and Continuo*, and *Four Ambrosian Hymns* for soprano and organ.

Peter J. Leithart (AB, Hillsdale College, 1981; MA, Religion, Westminster Theological Seminary in Philadelphia, 1986; ThM, Westminster Theological Seminary in Philadelphia, 1987; PhD in Systematic Theology, Cambridge, 1998) is Senior Fellow of Theology and Literature at New Saint Andrews College, Moscow, Idaho, and serves as a pastor at Trinity Reformed Church (CREC), also in Moscow. He has written a number of books, including *Against Christianity* (Canon, 2003), *Deep Exegesis* (Baylor, 2009), and *Defending Constantine* (IVP, 2010), and is a regular contributor to several periodicals. He and his wife Noel have ten children and four grandchildren.

Contributors

RICH LUSK (BS, Auburn University; MA, Philosophy, University of Texas) is the pastor of Trinity Presbyterian Church (CREC) in Birmingham, Alabama. Prior to that, he was on staff at Auburn Avenue Presbyterian Church in Monroe, Louisiana, and Redeemer Presbyterian Church (PCA) in Austin, Texas. Rich is the author of *Paedofaith: A Primer on the Mystery of Infant Salvation and a Handbook for Covenant Parents* (Athanasius Press, 2005), as well as numerous articles, papers, and essays. He and his wife Jenny have four children.

JEFFREY J. MEYERS (BS, University of Missouri–Columbia; MDiv, Covenant Theological Seminary; STM and PhD studies, Concordia Theological Seminary) is Senior Pastor at Providence Reformed Presbyterian Church (PCA) in St. Louis, Missouri, and is a member of the board of the Slavic Reformation Society. He is the author of *The Lord's Service: The Grace of Covenant Renewal Worship* (Canon, 2003) and *A Table in the Mist: Meditations on Ecclesiastes* (Athanasius Press, 2006). Jeff and his wife Christine have four children.

R. R. RENO (PhD, Yale) is Senior Editor at *First Things* and Professor of Theology, currently on leave from Creighton University. His most recent books include *Genesis* (Brazos, 2010), *Sanctified Vision: An Introduction to Early Christian Interpretation of the Bible* (Johns Hopkins, 2005), and *Fighting the Noonday Devil* (2010).

RALPH ALLAN SMITH is the pastor of the Mitaka Evangelical Church (CREC), Tokyo, Japan, and the director of the Covenant Worldview Institute. He has written several books, including *Trinity and Reality* (Canon, 2004) and *The Baptism of Jesus the Christ* (Wipf & Stock, 2010).

TOBY SUMPTER (BA, Liberal Arts and Culture, New St. Andrews College, 2002; MA, Theological Studies, Erskine Theological Seminary, 2008) serves as a pastor of Trinity Reformed Church (CREC) in Moscow, Idaho. Previously, he pastored Holy Trinity Church (CREC) in Greenville, South Carolina. He is writing a commentary on Job, to be published by Athanasius Press. Toby and his wife Jenny have four children.

DOUGLAS WILSON (BA, Philosophy, University of Idaho, 1977; BA, Classical Studies, University of Idaho, 1988; MA, Philosophy, University of Idaho, 1979) is the minister of Christ Church (CREC) in Moscow, Idaho, where he has served over thirty years, and Senior Fellow in Theology at New Saint Andrews College. He is the author of several books, including *Reforming Marriage* (Canon, 1995), *The Case for Classical Christian Education* (Crossway, 2003), and *Heaven Misplaced* (Canon, 2008). He and his wife Nancy have three children, and the roster of their grandchildren keeps increasing.

Foreword

R. R. RENO

JAMES B. JORDAN IS remarkable. There are plenty of Bible preachers in America who know the Scriptures well. Lots of professors read books in philosophy, history, and literature and have all sorts of interesting things to say about culture. Pundits cultivate a sharp, pungent, and readable style. But Jim is perhaps unique. Who else writes detailed interpretations of the Book of Daniel and quotes Allen Tate's poetry? Who else can give a lecture on echoes of Leviticus in the apocalyptic vision of Zechariah and then chat over cigars about Friedrich von Hayek and Richard Weaver? Moreover, who can cover such a range with vivid images, punchy tag lines, and memorable turns of phrase? Not many, which is why I've come to think of Jim Jordan as one of the most important Christian intellectuals of our day.

Jim knows a great deal, but I have no doubt that the electricity in his writing and conversation come from his biblical vision. He does something remarkable. He takes the cultic core of the Old Testament—Temple and Priesthood, altar and sacrifice—and reads it into the full sweep of the biblical witness. The result is not the usual sort of "theological" interpretation we're all familiar with: Christ's fulfillment of the Old Testament explained by way of warmed-over theologies of substitutionary atonement or observations that really amount to little more than restating New Testament passages. Instead, Jim takes texts such as Leviticus seriously on their own terms. He brings to life the intense concreteness of tabernacle and sanctuary, and he allows the prophets a retrospective restoration as well as a prospective anticipation. As Jim has helped me see, the Scriptures are forever reaching back and renewing even as they reach forward to fulfillment in Christ.

We live in space and time. Our lives have a concrete and quotidian reality. Precisely because Jim's reading of the Old Testament takes its bearings from the point of maximal particularity—the cultic focal point that is the most enduring and transparent anticipation of the Incarnation—his reading of the larger biblical witness is saturated with immediacy. Take a look at any of his writings on worship. The life of God's people has a particular shape in Israel. The tabernacle and temple have a specific architecture. The sacrifices involve discrete patterns of action. As a result, we do not encounter nebulous theological concepts. The immediacy of the cult of Israel is accessible to us today. Indeed, it is more accessible and more immediate, because in Christ we have been brought into the inner sanctuary.

Foreword

Any particular detail of Jim's biblical theology is up for debate, but the larger project is compelling—and much needed today. Many of us have limited biblical imaginations. We have stock phrases and favorite passages. We think of ourselves as biblical, but our friends recognize that nine times out of ten we're quoting from Paul's Letter to the Romans or the Book of Revelation or the Gospel of John. The Old Testament functions as a hazy background. The Psalms have no living power. Although we would vigorously deny it, we are functionally allied with Friedrich Schleiermacher, who notoriously set aside the Old Testament, or Immanuel Kant, who rejected the "Jewish" parts of the Old Testament as unusable.

Should we be surprised, therefore, that our preaching and teaching remains "spiritual" or "theological" in an abstract and theoretical way? Nothing we say is heretical. Orthodoxy carries the day. But it all floats a few feet above the ground. The gears of faith never seem to do what Jim's biblical theology does: mesh with the gritty realities of life.

If we diagnose ourselves honestly, then perhaps we can see that, unlike Jim, there are no biblical actualities at the center of our preaching and teaching, things to be seen and entered and touched. Perhaps, for example, we imagine ourselves agreeing with him because we endorse a "sacramental" view of the church. But there is a world of difference between "sacramental" and Jim's trenchant reading of the Book of Revelation as a handbook for Christian worship, a reading that depends upon his interpretation of the cultic core of the Old Testament. Again, one can debate the details, or the biblical typology, or Jim's assumptions about how to understand biblical inerrancy, or his conception of biblical history, or any number of other different technical questions. But of this I am certain. Jim does something few achieve, even (perhaps especially!) those who make loud claims about their biblical fidelity. He puts the living realities of the Bible at the center of his thought.

By my reckoning, our intellectual culture has come to a dead end. Concepts are powerful and necessary tools for uniting and intensifying our grasp of reality, but they have come to be super-eminent. As evidence, consider the fact that "critical thinking" now supersedes any particular body of knowledge as the goal of humanistic education. Thinking about culture—having the conceptual sophistication to identify and analyze cultural practices and patterns—has taken the place of participating in a culture and arguing about what is right and wrong, what is true and false. We have been romanced by Hegel's dream of absolute knowledge, which turns out not to be knowledge at all, but instead a knowingness about how knowledge is produced, disseminated, and preserved in all cultural systems. The result? A deracinated intellect skilled at debunking but increasingly incapable of sustaining substantive beliefs.

The church in the West does not just participate in this trend. To a great degree the church herself has fueled our collective movement away from substance. As Richard Popkin observed decades ago and Ephraim Radner more recently and with more richly detailed theological evidence, the division of the church in the sixteenth century threw the substance of the Christian faith into doubt. Faced with contradictory beliefs, it became tempting for Western intellectuals to try to adjudicate between the differences by shifting attention away from the *what* of belief to the *how*. From Descartes onward, western philosophy has been in the grips of arguments more focused on the *how* (epistemology) of belief than *what* (metaphysics). Hegel represents a desire to mediate rather than adjudicate. After Hegel, by and large our interest in the *how* of belief shifts from epistemology to historical or cultural analysis, allowing us to talk about how Protestants and Catholics have developed different ways of expressing the common sacramental or Incarnational or Trinitarian genius of Christianity. The result? An increasingly abstracted faith that tends to affirm doctrines or theologies or "faith dispositions," always at one or two removes from the concreteness of scripture and worship.

I'm very much a stranger to Reformed theology. I can't distinguish a "Bucerian" from a "Zwinglian" or a Kuyperian from a "Vantillian." But even as an outsider, I can see that Jim senses movement in modern theology, often unconscious, away from animating particularity—even in modern conservative theology. He inveighs against a common phenomenon: using a confessional affirmation as the criterion for Reformed identity without regard to its role within a functional biblical theology. Confessional standards grew out of a sustained engagement with the vast and heterogeneous sweep of biblical details, and the living authority of these confessions depends upon their continued immersion in living exegetical practice. Taken in isolation, confessional standards easily become deracinated. They become "theological" in the bad sense of floating free from the anchoring concreteness of the Bible. They become instruments for bureaucratic boundary marking rather than instruments for guiding the faithful toward orthodoxy.

Not surprising, our often de-scripturalized theological vocabulary tends to be culturally impotent as well as spiritually ineffective. Modern Lutheranism has shown that the *sola gratia* principle, which has been operative for many centuries in Western Augustinian Christianity, can be levered out of the living context of exegesis and worship and then turned into a justification for *affirming* the antinomian spirit of modern secular individualism. Jim has a great deal to say about contemporary culture that is interesting and fresh, in large part because he does not traffic in the usual modern tools of mediation; he does not commerce in theological abstractions. In his work, the *realia* of the Bible run up against the *realia* of contemporary life, and as a consequence Jim is in a position to make observations that lend themselves to wisdom and insight rather than an abstracted critical knowingness.

Nearly twenty years ago, I read *Mimesis: The Representation of Reality in Western Literature* by Erich Auerbach. It is a great and strange book, written by a secular German Jew who had fled to Istanbul just before the outbreak of World War II. In a series of close readings of only a few pages of twenty classic texts from Homer through the New Testament and the Song of Roland all the way to Virginia Woolf, Auerbach sets himself against Hegel and the Triumph of the Concept, which he saw as the taproot of Fascism and the murderous ideological brutality of the twentieth century. Auerbach does not argue. He does not analyze. Instead, in loving attention to textual detail, he lifts up the tradition of realism in Western literature that was born, he suggests, on the pages of the Scriptures. When words serve the concrete particularity of the human condition, Auerbach observes in one of the few general statement in this very long book, we find

Foreword

an intellectual humanism that surrenders itself to "the wealth of reality and the depth of life."[1]

I'm not sure if I met Jim before or after reading Auerbach, but it was around the same time, and it had a similar galvanizing effect. There was something about the immediacy of the Bible in his thinking, an immediacy entirely at home with many levels of intellectual sophistication. I was attracted to something in Jim's biblical vision akin to Auerbach's devotion to literary realism. The Scriptures serve divine reality, and because God is love, the sacred pages serve human reality as well. With every conversation I become more and more convinced that it is not Van Til or Rushdoony or any other grand synthesizer that gives Jim's ideas their sparkling allure (even the ideas I think are wrongheaded). To be sure, the Big Picture guys of years past add those layers of sophistication. But to my mind it's a scriptural realism (if you will permit me the formulation) that gives an electrical charge to Jim's ideas.

For too long I thought that the key to being a Christian intellectual was on the "intellectual" side—reading smart books in philosophy, literature, political theory, and so forth. Jim has taught me otherwise. We need to read those smart books. The intellectual engine needs fuel to burn. But the key element is on the "Christian" side. We need something like Jim's scriptural realism. The concreteness and historical density of the Bible is alive with human reality betrothed to God's purposes, always already on the way to being "heavenized" as Jim puts it.

Today our culture seems capable of neither humanizing nor "heavenizing." As I have suggested, this is the legacy of the Triumph of the Concept. The now postmodern equipoise of understanding without commitment, of thinking without allowing oneself to feel the power of something commandingly concrete and real stems from the deracinating effect of our tendency to favor meta-reflection on the problems of life. Jim's scriptural realism guides us in a very different direction: toward the Triumph of God Incarnate. God does not raise us up to the dignity of a concept. He hurls the spear of His love—He hurls Himself—into the irreducible, mute, and otherwise transient particularity of life. The Lord comes to us in the realities of life, most directly in the bread and wine of the Eucharist, but also in the relentless concreteness of the sacred Scriptures: the dusty streets of Jerusalem, royal intrigue, temples built and destroyed, the blood-stained altar of sacrifice attended to by priests in their elaborate vestments. We need to serve this concreteness in our intellectual work, and Jim's scriptural realism gives us guidance about how to do so. If we follow Jim's lead, then perhaps we will also have something to say that can humanize and heavenize.

---

1. Erich Auerbach, *Mimesis: The Representation of Reality in Western Literature* (Garden City, NY: Doubleday/Anchor, 1957), 488.

Editors' Acknowledgments

The editors would like to acknowledge the help of Jeffrey Meyers, who helped to launch this project but later had to back out because of heavy pastoral commitments. Special thanks are due to John Frame and Rusty Reno, neither a typical member of the "Biblical Horizons" group, who graciously contributed the Foreword and Afterword to this volume. We are grateful, too, for the patience of K. C. Hanson and others at Wipf and Stock as they awaited the completion of this long-overdue volume. Above all, we are thankful to God for James Jordan, whose work has inspired us for decades and whose friendship we all deeply value.

James B. Jordan's Acknowledgments

I WISH TO TAKE this opportunity to thank Peter Leithart and Jeffrey Meyers for dreaming up this honor and John Barach for working so hard editing it and doing the bibliography. I'm not worthy of this, and it both surprised me and humbles me.

I also wish to thank Rusty Reno and John Frame for their gracious words at the beginning and end of this book. I am happy to count both of these brilliant Christian men as my friends.

Finally, I thank all the contributors. I was constrained to "reply" to each essay, and in some cases I have perforce taken issue with various matters. But then again, that's what it means to hold to a biblical view of history. We have a long way to go before all nations have been discipled as Jesus commanded, and so theology is a conversation about the Bible and what it means. It is a privilege to be part of God's conversation, especially with all of you.

Introduction

PETER J. LEITHART

JAMES B. JORDAN IS unclassifiable. He is virtually unknown outside a small but enthusiastic band of friends and admirers. He has never held a teaching position in an American college or seminary, and has never held a full-time academic position anywhere. For the past two decades he has lived in Niceville, Florida, a sleepy town near the buzzing white-sand resort of Destin, hardly one of the intellectual centers of the universe. Yet Jordan has been called (by R. R. Reno) one of the leading Christian intellectuals of his generation, and I, along with much of his fan base, consider Jim to be one of the most profound biblical scholars in the history of the church. Though I have been listening intently to him for twenty-five years, I have never listened to Jim lecture without gaining some fresh insight into Scripture. Several of us who have been Jim's close associates say jokingly that we learned everything we know from him. For myself, it is too nearly true to be entirely a joke. Did I mention that we are Jordan enthusiasts?

From a distance it may be difficult to grasp what he is on about. Long ago, he taught many of us to be more catholic in our Protestantism, introducing us to Louis Bouyer and Alexander Schmemann and finding some good things to say about the Church of England, all quite heady stuff in the small Reformed world where Jordan is rooted. It is the same Jordan, though, who has published sharp diatribes against the Marian doctrines of the Roman Catholic church, calling the dogma of perpetual virginity an "abysmal notion." Jim taught, or re-taught, many of us the value of the historic liturgies, yet he is a powerful opponent of iconolatry in any form and criticizes the liturgical renewal within evangelicalism for its romantic traditionalism. He is old right, hard right, in his politics. He ostentatiously wears ostentatious Rush Limbaugh ties. Yet it was from Jim that I first heard the suggestion that conservative Christians care little about justice for the poor because they refuse to sing Psalms. Jordan was ordained in 1982 in a small and now extinct Reformed denomination, and he has spent his ecclesiastical life in the conservative backwaters of the North American Reformed world. Yet many Reformed theologians wonder, not without reason, whether Jordan counts as a "Reformed" theologian at all. There is more than a little of the perfectionist in him, yet he is generous enough to encourage the very imperfect efforts of less exacting thinkers. He is a prolific writer and lecturer, with a two-hundred-plus lecture series on Revelation and another hundred-plus on the life of Jacob. Yet he is at his best in an intimate informal setting, relaxed and off the record.

Introduction

Jordan is an unclassifiable thinker because he is an unclassifiable person, as those of us privileged to become his friends have again and again discovered. An evening with Jordan will include wine or something stronger, especially single malt Scotch, in copious amounts and, until recently, large cigars. He closes his eyes in ecstasy listening to Messiaen or Rachmaninoff, but in the next moment will tell or laugh riotously at an off-color joke. His knowledge of science fiction is vast, he enjoys television and movies, but he prefers to teach in Saint Petersburg during the ballet and opera season. He can give a sophisticated, and seemingly spontaneous, semiotic analysis of a film, novel, or Shakespeare play, but when he visits my house he spends part of the evening wrestling with the kids, telling stories of space bears, and reciting *Where the Wild Things Are*. With age, he has cultivated a curmudgeonly demeanor that enhances his natural-born Southern cussedness. He knows his gifts, but those who know him well know him as self-effacing, accommodating, and humble. He will be deeply embarrassed by this introduction.

James Burrell Jordan was born on December 31, 1949, in Athens, Georgia. His father taught French language and literature at the University of Georgia, and Jim, along with his brother Bill, grew up in an environment saturated with literature and music. He finished his undergraduate studies in comparative literature at the University of Georgia, served in the Air Force as a military historian, attended Reformed Theological Seminary in Jackson, Mississippi, and graduated from Westminster Theological Seminary in Philadelphia. Jim grew up a believing Lutheran, but, like many, he experienced a "conversion" of sorts during his college years. He began reading Reformed "world-and-life" literature, and for a number of years contributed to publications of the Chalcedon Foundation founded by R. J. Rushdoony, the granddaddy of Christian Reconstruction, and wrote for the economist Gary North, another leading Reconstructionist. During the 1980s, Jim served as a pastor of Westminster Presbyterian Church in Tyler, Texas, and directed Geneva Ministries and Geneva Divinity School, both ministries of the church. As the church moved toward Anglicanism, Jordan resigned his position and eventually moved to Niceville, where he set up his own biblical studies ministry, Biblical Horizons. "BH" is billed as a study center and think tank, but it is basically Jim, along with his library, his computer, and a photocopier. Drop into BH "headquarters," and you will likely find Jim sorting or stapling papers, preparing books and articles for mailing. In the background will be the strains from one of his hundreds of classical music CDs or the latest audio book from Stephen King, Dean Koontz, or Alexander McCall Smith.

All great theologians are, at bottom, fairly simple-minded. The greatest questions and most Byzantine answers all arise from a childlike adherence to the gospel. Jim Jordan is a great theologian, and I believe the driving impulses behind his work can be reduced to two. The first is biblicism. Jim is an unreconstructed inerrantist who believes that the words of Scripture are, down to their details, the words of God. Since the words of Scripture come from the Spirit, and the Spirit does not waste His breath, we ought to attend to every twist of grammar and syntax and also to every resonance of allusion and every turn of structure. Jim has little time for high-falutin' theologies, traditional or modern, that smother Scripture under alien categories. Wherever the Bible leads, Jordan wants to follow, because the words of Scripture are the words of life, the words of the eternal Word, Jesus Christ.

Introduction

Jordan's biblicism leads to the second main impulse of his theology, which is his remarkable openness to new disclosures from the text. Jordan has changed his mind about some early convictions, and at some point during nearly every lecture he assures his hearers that he does not claim to offer the "final" word but only a "helpful" word. Typically, his hearers have a different experience; his interpretations are so rich, so closely linked to the text, so *beautiful* that they seem to possess a kind of inevitability. But Jim's humility is genuine. Jordan believes that the Christian church is still in her infancy and that we have thousands of years of maturation before the resurrection and final judgment. During that time, God will continue to show new things in His Word, because He is the God who does all things new.

Jordan's interests and insights range too widely to give them full representation in a single volume, and the editors decided early on that the book would not be a set of essays evaluating Jordan's work but instead a collection that attempts to apply Jordan's themes and insights to various subjects. Above all, the editors have hoped to produce a collection that would interest Jim and show the love and respect that we all have for him. In the following comments, I briefly summarize each essay and tie it to Jordan's work. Several of the essays take issue with Jordan's views, but the editors, believing that Jordan is often at his best in vigorous but cordial debate, concluded that these essays strengthen rather than weaken the volume.

We have divided the essays into four categories. Following Jordan's claim that a simple division of Old Testament and New Testament is highly problematic, we have assembled all the biblical studies in one section, and this is followed by essays on liturgy, preaching, and music; then theology; and finally culture.

BIBLICAL STUDIES

At least since his 1988 *Through New Eyes*, Jordan has displayed a fascination with angels. In that book, he pointed to biblical passages that indicate that God employs angels to rule creation, leading Jordan to the whimsical thought that gravity is not an impersonal force but the pressure of angels pushing things down.[1] For Jordan, angelology is part of the worldview of "cosmic personalism" developed by Cornelius Van Til and John Frame, and his interest in the subject is also no doubt influenced by Jim's long tutelage in SciFi. Through his detailed studies in Genesis 2–4[2] and in Revelation,[3] Jordan's insight into the role of angels in the cosmos and in history deepened. He has argued that angels were created to be humanity's "drill sergeants" who teach and train until humanity matures to become greater than the angels. The angel Satan fell when he enviously refused that subordinate calling, and the fall of Adam subjected humanity to a long old covenant that amounted to a covenant under angelic guardianship. In his careful reading of Psalm 8, co-editor John Barach shows how this Psalm expresses the subordination of Adamic

---

1. *Through New Eyes: Developing a Biblical View of the World* (Brentwood, TN: Wolgemuth & Hyatt, 1988; reprint, Eugene, OR: Wipf & Stock, 1999), 110–11.
2. *Trees and Thorns: Studies in Genesis 2–4*, draft ed. 1.1 (Niceville, FL: Biblical Horizons, 2005).
3. *Revelation in Detail*, 204 lectures (Niceville, Florida: Biblical Horizons).

Introduction

man "for a little while" to angels, as well as celebrates the exaltation of humanity in the new Adam, Christ. Barach's essay also summarizes Jordan's work on the chiastic structure of Genesis 1,[4] and applies it to the structure of Psalm 8.

Jordan is a postmillennial theologian who believes that the gospel will triumph in history and that through the gospel cultural and political life will be transformed. Jordan's postmillennialism is, however, of a somewhat revisionist sort. His eschatology is more ecclesio- and liturgico-centric than some historic forms of postmillennialism, and he departs also from earlier postmillennial theologians in his understanding of the future of the Jewish people. In classic postmillennialism, the future conversion of the Jewish people, prophesied by Paul in Romans 9–11, is the spark that sets the flame of millennial glory. Reading the New Testament in the light of Jesus' prophecies about the destruction of Jerusalem (Matt 24 and parallels), Jordan argues that Romans 9–11 describes a process that is already taking place in the first century and that Paul's hope for the conversion of the Jewish people is fulfilled in the harvest depicted in Revelation 14. In the time leading up to the Jewish War that ended with the destruction of Jerusalem and its temple, Jordan argues, many Jews became convinced that Jesus was a true prophet and turned to Him.[5] Tim Gallant challenges Jordan's "preterist" reading of Romans 9–11 and defends the traditional postmillennial view that Paul predicts a conversion of Jews that is still in the future for us.

During his years at Reformed Seminary, Jordan studied with Greg Bahnsen, best known for his "theonomic" thesis that Old Testament law applies to modern societies "in exhaustive detail." Jordan wrote his Master's thesis at Westminster on the biblical view of slavery,[6] and his first published book was *The Law of the Covenant*, a detailed examination of the "case laws" of Exodus 21–23.[7] Though Jordan later became critical of Bahnsen's particular formulation of "theonomy,"[8] he has remained a theocratic small-t theonomist who believes that the Bible deals with all of life and that the Old Testament law should be the foundation of Christian reflection on public justice.

More than the theonomists, however, Jordan has given detailed attention to the "ceremonial" laws of Leviticus, plundering them for their symbolic significance as well as for their liturgical and practical implications.[9] Leviticus has been high on his agenda for several decades. Around the same time Jim moved to Niceville, Florida, in the late 1980s, I accepted a call to a Presbyterian church in Birmingham, Alabama. I had met Jim

---

4. Most fully developed in *Creation in Six Days: A Defense of the Traditional Reading of Genesis One* (Moscow, ID: Canon, 1999).

5. "The Future of Israel Reconsidered: A Preterist View of Romans 11," Biblical Horizons Occasional Paper 18 (Aug. 1994).

6. *Slavery in Biblical Perspective* (Th.M. Thesis, Westminster Theological Seminary, 1980).

7. *The Law of the Covenant: An Exposition of Exodus 21–23* (Tyler, TX: Institute for Christian Economics, 1984).

8. *Theonomy: A Preliminary Theocratic Critique*, 3 lectures (Niceville, FL: Biblical Horizons); "The Death Penalty in the Mosaic Law: Five Exploratory Essays," Biblical Horizons Occasional Paper 3, rev. ed. (Niceville, FL: Biblical Horizons, 1989).

9. He has done this most thoroughly in his studies of the dietary laws. See his *Studies in Food and Faith* 1–13 (Niceville, FL: Biblical Horizons, 1989–90).

Introduction

several years before, and was writing for newsletters published by Geneva Ministries, which Jim directed. With our respective moves, we were only five hours from each other, and Jim began to organize annual summer conferences where Jeff Meyers, Rich Bledsoe, and I would be regular speakers. Jim was always eager to tackle the forgotten byways of Scripture, and so one of our first conferences was devoted to detailed study of the sacrificial system of Leviticus.[10] It was not the kind of study that makes a conference popular, but those studies in Leviticus provided a foundation for much of Jim's future work in liturgics and biblical theology as well as my own. At the time, I promised Jim that I would devote myself to a study of the sexual legislation of Leviticus 18 and 20. That was in the early 1990s, and my essay in this volume is a long-overdue fulfillment of that promise. After sketching the logic and structure of the incest rules of Leviticus 18, my essay focuses on the question of the missing daughter: Why is father-daughter incest never explicitly prohibited? I answer by offering a Trinitarian account of Yahweh's strange Father-and-Husband relationship with Israel (cf. Ezekiel 16).

Jordan spent four years in the U.S. Air Force, mainly as a military historian, and this experience has contributed to a lifelong interest in military matters. He has written on militias and military tactics in the Bible and frequently has recourse (as the Bible does) to military metaphors for describing the Christian life and the church's mission.[11] "God's War Against Humanism" was the subtitle of his 1985 commentary on Judges.[12] One of his favorite science fiction writers is Cordwainer Smith, the pseudonym of Paul Linebarger, a trailblazer in psychological warfare. Jordan recognizes that theology is a ministry of the church militant. Rich Lusk's contribution to the volume focuses on holy war in Scripture. Following Jordan's lead, he demonstrates that the Old Testament distinguishes between the specifics of *herem* warfare against the Canaanite peoples and "normal war," mostly defensive warfare against other nations. Lusk traces the theme of holy war from the Old to the New Testament. By attending to several passages in the gospels and the overarching structure of Acts, he shows that Jesus is the new Joshua, whose conquest of the world is carried out by preaching the gospel in the power of the Spirit.

Though Jordan is best known, and often attacked, for his creative interpretations of Scripture, he is at one with tradition in insisting on the reality of the letter. A recent essay on the early chapters of Genesis, "Getting Real in Genesis,"[13] urged pastors and commentators to take the Bible's historicity seriously. No Bible scholar in recent years has done as much detailed work on biblical chronology as Jordan or given as thorough a defense of the literal sense of Genesis 1–2.[14] His emphasis on the literal sense produces

---

10. Jim's lectures are available on tape as part of the 1992 Biblical Horizons Conference on Worship and Sacrifice.

11. "The Israelite Militia in the Old Testament," in *The Militia in Twentieth-Century America: A Symposium*, ed. Morgan Norval (Falls Church, VA: Gun Owners Foundation, 1985).

12. *Judges: God's War Against Humanism* (Tyler, TX: Geneva Ministries, 1985), reprinted as *Judges: A Practical and Theological Commentary* (Eugene, OR: Wipf & Stock, 1999).

13. "Getting Real in Genesis," *Biblical Horizons* 203 (May 2009).

14. See *Creation in Six Days*. Jordan wrote the monthly *Biblical Chronology* newsletter published by the Institute for Christian Economics from 1989 to 1999.

Introduction

significant theological and practical results. By paying attention to the chronologies of Jeremiah and Daniel, for instance, Jordan noticed that Jeremiah's exhortation to the people of Jerusalem to submit to Nebuchadnezzar (Jer 29) occurred after Daniel was already a leading adviser to the Babylonian king (Dan 2). That sheds a completely new light on Jeremiah's program: Surrender to Nebuchadnezzar is not a leap into the dark but an act of confidence in Yahweh who has placed Daniel, as He had placed Joseph, to prepare a place for His people. Ralph Smith's contribution to this volume focuses attention on Jordan's work in this area. Setting Jordan into opposition with the recent work of Peter Enns,[15] Smith argues that the "problems" Enns addresses are problems of his own making. Once we take the literal sense of Scripture seriously, many of the problems evaporate. Smith's main goal in the paper, however, is to explain the character of Israel's "royal priesthood" and to show how that priestly status is rooted in the priesthood of Adam and Noah, which is the priesthood after the order of Melchizedek to which Jesus and His people belong.

Toby Sumpter's rich reading of Job accomplishes a number of things. He shows the narrative integrity of the whole book, linking the prologue and epilogue tightly to the dialogue. He also finds important parallels between Job and Jacob and highlights the sacrificial language of Job. On Sumpter's reading, Job is about maturing sonship, about the growth of a *perfect* son of God into a *perfected* son of God. By careful attention to the book's use of the word *ruach* and various stylistic devices, Sumpter shows that Yahweh's appearance in the whirlwind provides the fitting climax to a war of windy words between Job and his "comforters." In highlighting these themes, Sumpter is illustrating the fruitfulness of several of Jordan's characteristic insights. Though a radical postmillennial thinker who believes that the gospel will penetrate human life and culture until human life as a whole is devoted to Jesus, Jordan also recognizes the fundamental place of the cross in the church's progress through history. Human beings are created to be transfigured from glory to glory, but that process, even in an unfallen world, would have been a process of death and resurrection. As Adam moves through deep sleep and division to receive the glory of his bride (1 Cor 11), so Job is cut and burned in God's sacrificial fire as he moves toward an encounter with Yahweh, God of the storm. Further, in *From Bread to Wine*,[16] Jordan has offered a paradigm of maturation that works with a revised understanding of Christ's triple office. Human beings move from priestly to kingly to prophetic stages of life, and this is also the sequence of maturation for Israel, for Jesus, for the church. It is, finally, the ritual sequence of the Old Covenant sacrifices and of the Eucharist. Sumpter shows how Job's progress follows that same sequence.

---

15. *Inspiration and Incarnation: Evangelicals and the Problem of the Old Testament* (Grand Rapids: Baker, 2005).

16. *From Bread to Wine: Toward a More Biblical Liturgical Theology*, draft ed. 1.1 (Niceville, FL: Biblical Horizons, 2001).

LITURGICAL THEOLOGY

Jordan's work in liturgical theology has been wide-ranging and important.[17] Drawing on his own liturgical heritage, he has sought to "Lutheranize" the Reformed tradition by giving greater emphasis to liturgy and sacraments, and he has also sprinkled in insights from Orthodox theologians such as Alexander Schmemann and Catholic liturgists such as Louis Bouyer along the way.

In several fundamental ways, however, Jordan has highlighted liturgical practices that reflect his roots in the Reformed tradition. Far more than most liturgical theologians, he has made an effort to ground his liturgical theology and his suggestions for liturgical practice in biblical norms and patterns. Though the term is not unique to his work, Jordan has offered a distinctive version of "covenant-renewal worship," worship that draws on sacrificial patterns of Leviticus and the sequence of liturgical actions evident in historical accounts such as 2 Chronicles 29.[18] Jordan has charged that the Reformed "regulative principle of worship" is often a form of "liturgical Nestorianism" because it separates God's word from human judgments about liturgy, but at heart he is a regulativist: He believes that God tells us how to worship and that we should worship in obedience.

For Jordan, hermeneutical and liturgical concerns are closely connected. He advocates and, more importantly, practices a rich form of typological interpretation. Yet, in Jordan's hands, hermeneutics is not just about methods for reading texts but is tied up with the practical use of the Bible, the shape of Christian liturgy, the maturation of humanity in history, the Adamic and new Adamic project of "heavenizing earth," and glory. Bill DeJong's contribution provides a summary of Jordan's approach to Scripture, focusing attention on the "vertical" (heaven-to-earth) dimension of Jordan's typology as it is revealed in Jordan's studies of the development of the sanctuary from Eden to the new Jerusalem. Comparing and contrasting Jordan with recent work by Gregory Beale, DeJong highlights the fact that Jordan's typology is deeply pastoral in that it aims to train students of Scripture in discerning not only the *telos* but the repeating rhythms of history. For Jordan, typology has a musical shape: It not only moves toward a satisfying resolution, but moves toward the eschaton in revolving, complexly repetitive patterns.[19]

Psalm-singing, another distinctively "Reformed" liturgical emphasis, has been of great importance in Jordan's work.[20] Duane Garner summarizes some of Jordan's work on this theme and reviews the history of Psalm-singing in early English Protestantism.

---

17. Liturgical themes permeate Jordan's work, but three brief books summarize some of his main emphases: *Theses on Worship: Notes Toward the Reformation of Worship*, 2nd ed. (Niceville, FL: Transfiguration, 1998); *Liturgical Nestorianism and the Regulative Principle: A Critical Review of Worship in the Presence of God*, 2nd ed. (Niceville, FL: Transfiguration, 2000); *The Liturgy Trap: The Bible vs. Mere Tradition in Worship*, 3rd ed. (Monroe, LA: Athanasius Press, 2008).

18. See Jeffrey J. Meyers, *The Lord's Service: The Grace of Covenant Renewal Worship* (Moscow, ID: Canon, 2003), which provides a thorough introduction to the Biblical Horizons "school" of liturgical theology.

19. See, for instance, "Music and Hermeneutics," *Biblical Horizons* 89 (Nov. 1996).

20. See, for instance, "Music and Life: The Benefits of Psalm Singing," *Geneva Review* 37 (Apr. 1987); "How to Chant the Psalms," *Rite Reasons: Studies in Worship* 61 (Jan. 2000). Jordan has also translated and arranged music for many Psalms.

Introduction

He shows how Separatist Puritanism corroded Psalm-singing, leaving a vacuum that was eventually filled by the lighter Psalm paraphrases of Isaac Watts and then by the sentimental gospel hymns of revivalistic Christianity. Garner ends with a powerful exhortation to sing Psalms on behalf of the oppressed of the world.

Jim's brother, William, a composer who teaches at the University of Calgary, reinforces this portion of the book with an original setting of Psalm 46.

THEOLOGY

Though Jordan's work has often been ignored or attacked by Reformed theologians in the United States, he has gotten a warmer reception in some other countries. Over the past two decades, he has been on the faculty of Biblical Theological Seminary in St. Petersburg, Russia, and has taught frequently in Eastern Europe. His influence also extends to Asia. C. Kee Hwang, former President of Kosin University in Busan, South Korea, read Jordan's work while on sabbatical at Calvin College, and when he returned to Korea he began teaching his students biblical theology of a Jordanian stripe. Hwang's contribution to this volume is a review of Reformed eschatology. In contrast to American fundamentalist obsession with newspaper exegesis and eschatological timetables, he argues that the New Testament's eschatology focuses on "who" rather than "when" or "what." The central person in Christian eschatology is Jesus Christ, and Hwang shows that a focus on Christ's role as the head, not only of the body, but also of all things produces a comprehensive and victorious eschatology.

When I first began studying Jordan's work in the 1980s, one of the things that intrigued me was his recovery of themes from the early Reformation. Cutting through the "Baptist" culture of American Reformed churches and reaching even past the Puritan tradition, Jordan recaptured some of Calvin's original emphases that had gotten muted during the intervening centuries. In particular, Jordan was a Calvinist who embraced Book IV of Calvin's *Institutes* (on church and sacraments) with as much passion as he embraced Calvin's teaching on election, depravity, grace, and perseverance. Here was a Calvinist who did not blush when Calvin quoted Cyprian's classic formula, "You cannot have God as your Father unless you have the church as your Mother." Here was an *American* Calvinist comfortable with Calvin's breathless conclusion regarding the real presence: "I rather admire than understand." Jordan highlighted those aspects of Calvin's theology that were inspired by Calvin's Strasburg mentor, Martin Bucer. Jordan sometimes describes himself as a "Bucerian," a term that picks out Bucer's liturgical theology, his biblicism, and his theocratic political outlook. Bucer was also notably ecumenical, striving to hold together a Reformation that threatened to fracture into Lutheran and Reformed factions. Jeff Meyers's essay in this volume is inspired by this Bucerian vision. Through a detailed comparison of early Lutheran and Reformed confessional statements on election, Meyers shows that Lutherans and Calvinists confessed essentially the same doctrine and that the early Reformed doctrine of election was neither a speculative determinism nor a nominalist voluntarism. As Meyers shows, the early Reformed confessions treat the doctrine of election evangelically, that is, as the ultimate ground of the Protestant battle cry, *sola gratia*.

CULTURE

Jordan has always done his biblical theological work within a much wider horizon of cultural and political concerns. For Jordan, typological exegesis is not a kind of decorative poetry but an effort to discern the recurring patterns of human history, as revealed in the recurring patterns of Scripture. During the past twenty years, Jordan's cultural and political reflections have been influenced by the work of the German-American thinker Eugen Rosenstock-Huessy. Rosenstock-Huessy wrote on many subjects—language and speech, social theory, calendars and time-keeping—but Jordan has been most deeply influenced by Rosenstock-Huessy's effort to organize his immense historical and legal knowledge into a remarkable and deeply Christian scheme of Western and universal history and revolutionary change. Jordan discovered that many of his own biblical insights into the movement of history snugly matched Rosenstock-Huessy's theories, and in *Crisis, Opportunity, and the Christian Future* he offered a brief synthesis of his work and Rosenstock's.[21] In his contribution to this volume, Richard Bledsoe summarizes Rosenstock's important study, *Out of Revolution: The Autobiography of Western Man*, which examines the "revolutionary moments" of Western history from Gregory VII to the Bolshevik Revolution. Picking up on Rosenstock's prescient observation that late modernity would be an age of simultaneous imperial expansion and neo-tribalism, Bledsoe argues that Protestants have been attempting to address a novel situation with the out-dated theological and pastoral tools of the sixteenth century. Instead of focusing on Romans, ethical law, and justification, the need of the hour is to proclaim a gospel that inflames and glorifies people who have all but turned to dust.

Bogumil Jarmulak, a pastor in Poznan, Poland, is another international contributor to the volume. His essay deals with the intersection of liturgy and the arts that has been a recurring interest in Jordan's work from the beginning.[22] Jarmulak begins with a summary of Paul Evdokimov's theology of beauty, which feeds into a theology of the icon. Drawing on Jacques Ellul, Jarmulak criticizes Evdokimov for stressing the visual to the exclusion of the audible and for an over-realized eschatology. As Jarmulak shows, Jordan's work on the Second Word (Second Commandment) repeats some of Ellul's criticisms of Orthodox iconodulism but goes further to stress the fact that the prohibition of icons is rooted in the nature of God as "Pure Language," the God who makes Himself visible but who *is* Word.[23]

---

21. *Crisis, Opportunity, and the Christian Future*, 2nd ed. (Monroe, LA: Athanasius Press, 2009).

22. See, for example, Jordan's "Sophomoric Theologians Versus the Mystery of Art," *Open Book* 12–13 (Nov. 1992, Jan. 1993). Jordan's most arresting insights into aesthetics are found in studies of the tabernacle and temple, such as "Thoughts on Jachin and Boaz," Biblical Horizons Occasional Paper 1 (Niceville, FL: Biblical Horizons, 1988) and "From Glory to Glory: Degrees of Value in the Sanctuary," Biblical Horizons Occasional Paper 2, rev. ed. (Niceville, FL: Biblical Horizons, 1994). He has explored the aesthetic dimensions of money in "Paper Money," *Biblical Economics Today* 9.5 (1987).

23. "The Second Word," *Rite Reasons: Studies in Worship* 33–36, 57–59 (June–Dec. 1994, May–Sept. 1998).

Introduction

As a theologian working in the context of the work of the Dutch-American philosopher and apologist Cornelius Van Til, Jordan is deeply hostile to Hellenistic and gnostic corruptions of Christianity. That hostility is manifested in many ways, perhaps most pointedly in a 1997–98 series of essays entitled "The Case Against Western Civilization" in which Jordan critically assesses the rise of classical Christian education.[24] In that essay, Jordan attacks the dominance of sports in modern education, arguing that in place of sports schools should provide military exercises or training in martial arts. Taking up Jordan's challenge, Doug Wilson's contribution to this volume offers a biblical and practical defense of sports. He notes the frequency of athletic metaphors in Scripture, and points also to passages that draw parallels between sports and warfare. Both sports and warfare are agonistic, both require self-discipline and training, both involve striving for the prize of victory. Christian defenses of just warfare, he claims, should entail a defense of sports.

CONCLUSION

Jordan's biblicism and his striking openness to the new things God is doing and showing are drawn together in another of Jordan's major themes. He has described his life project as the exploration of a theology of "glory." Glory is a constant category of his biblical work, a central theme in Jordan's typological interpretation. The eternal glory of God is revealed in the glory of the Shekinah, which imprints itself on the sanctuary and the priest, and then imprints itself anew as the sanctuary is dismantled and rebuilt. Humanity and the world mature from glory to glory, approximating the glory of God who always infinitely exceeds created approximations.

This, finally, is the burden of our title for this *Festschrift* volume. "It is the glory of God to conceal a matter; but the glory of kings is to search out a matter," Solomon tells us (Prov 25:2 NASB). For Jordan, that proverb summarizes an essential pattern of history and a basic principle of hermeneutics. The glorious God glorifies Himself by concealing things in His creation, in His word, in history, and then inviting us, children of Adam and brothers of the Last Adam, to grow in maturity as we wrestle with Scripture and the world, searching out what God has concealed so we can bathe in its beauty. For the contributors to this volume, Jordan is a king and a maker of kings, a scholar and friend whose work has encouraged us, and others, to mimic him in searching out what the God of glory has concealed.

---

24. "The Case Against Western Civilization," *Open Book* 36–42 (Oct. 1997–Oct. 1998).

Part 1

Biblical Studies

1

The Glory of the Son of Man

An Exposition of Psalm 8

JOHN BARACH

PSALM 8 IS SURELY one of the most familiar and best loved psalms. The New Testament cites it more than once. Theologians draw on it for evidence of both man's lowliness and his exaltation. Add that the psalm is joyful and short enough to be memorized and that it seems relatively simple and straightforward, and its popularity is not surprising.

Its simplicity, however, is only apparent, as a look at the New Testament use of this psalm reveals. In its few lines, Psalm 8 brings together themes that stretch from man's creation in the beginning to the incarnation and glorification of Jesus, shedding light on the transition from the Old Creation to the New Creation, from mankind created under the angels to mankind exalted over them to rule the world.[1]

THE STRUCTURE OF PSALM 8

^aFor the director.
^bOn the *gittith*.
^cA Psalm.
^dBy David.

A   ¹Yahweh, our Lord, how supreme is Your name in all the earth,
²Who have set Your splendor upon the heavens!

    B ³From the mouth of children and infants
       You established strength,
       because of Your oppressors,
    ⁴To silence enemy and avenger.

---

1. Although James Jordan has not written or lectured on Psalm 8 at length, its themes have been foundational to much of his thinking. It is an honor to present this essay to him and, in it, to bring together matters that he has touched on here and there throughout his essays, books, and lectures.

PART ONE: BIBLICAL STUDIES

C   ⁵When I consider Your heavens, the works of Your fingers,
    ⁶Moon and stars, which You have set firm,
      ⁷What is needy-man (*enosh*) that You remember him,
        ⁸And the son of Adam that you visit him?
      ⁹And You made him lower a little while than the gods,
    ¹⁰And with glory and honor You will crown him.
  ¹¹You will make him ruler over the works of your hands.

B' ¹²All things You have put under his feet:
    ¹³Sheep and oxen—all of them,
      ¹⁴And also beasts of the field,
    ¹⁵Bird of heaven and fish of the sea,
  ¹⁶Whatever passes through the paths of the seas.

A' ¹⁷Yahweh, our Lord, how supreme is Your name in all the earth!²

The psalm begins and ends with an identical line (A–A'), an obvious inclusio. There are two "x and y" phrases in B ("children and infants," "enemy and avenger") and in B' ("sheep and oxen," "bird and fish"), and that structural parallel invites us to consider the thematic parallel between Yahweh's use of children to silence the enemy and avenger (B) and Yahweh's placing all things under man's feet (B'). At the center of the chiasm is David's consideration of Yahweh's intention to exalt needy man over all His works.³

It may also be possible, however, to view Psalm 8 as a heptamerous chiasm, tracking with the seven days of creation.⁴ The seven days in Genesis 1 themselves form a chiasm:

Day 1: creation of heavens and earth; light (from Spirit) on earth (Gen 1:1–5).
  Day 2: firmament-heavens between earth and heaven (Gen 1:6–8).
    Day 3: dry land ("*earth*") and seas; plants and trees (Gen 1:9–13).
      Day 4: firmament lights to rule (Gen 1:14–19).
    Day 5: *sea* creatures swarm; birds multiply on *earth* (Gen 1:20–23).
  Day 6: land animals; man, promised dominion over creatures (Gen 1:24–31).
Day 7: Sabbath and rest (enthronement) (Gen 2:1–3).

This is not the place to discuss this chiasm in detail, let alone defend it,⁵ but a few features call for comment. The parallel between Day 3 and Day 5 is perhaps the clear-

---

2. While there are minor differences, my translation of Psalm 8 is very close to James Jordan's in *Studies in the Psalter 2* (Niceville, FL: Biblical Horizons, 2005), 2.

3. Each of these central sections (B, C, and B' is also chiastic in structure, and these chiasms will be discussed in more detail in the exposition later on. In *Studies in the Psalter 2*, Jordan does present the chiasm in C, but does not structure the psalm as a whole as a chiasm.

4. A relationship between Psalm 8 and Genesis 1 is suggested by the references to earth and the heavens as well as to man's dominion over the beasts (cf. Gen 1:28) as well as by the *seven*ness of the psalm's structure: there are seventeen lines and a total of 77 words in Hebrew, and the first and last lines each contain seven words. James Jordan has suggested that there is a connection between Psalms 1–7 and the seven days of creation (*Studies in the Psalter 1* [Niceville, FL: Biblical Horizons, 2004], 17–18), so that Psalm 8 picks up the theme of the first day again (*Studies in the Psalter 2*, 1). Given the symbolism of the eighth day in the Bible, Psalm 8 would have something to do with new creation, which is, in fact, what we will see.

5. Cf., e.g., James B. Jordan, *Creation in Six Days: A Defense of the Traditional Reading of Genesis One* (Moscow, ID: Canon, 1999), 60–61 and *Trees and Thorns: Studies in Genesis 2–4*, draft ed. 1.1 (Niceville, FL:

est: both deal with the *seas* and the *earth*. The parallel between Day 1 and Day 7 is not obvious until we notice that the parallel is *by way of* Day 4: Light (Day 1) is delegated to the firmament lights (Day 4); those lights rule, and rule links up with God's rest (Day 7), since rest in the Bible is associated with enthronement.[6] God rests enthroned over His creation.

The chiastic outline also suggests that man's exaltation over the creatures (Day 6) is parallel in some way to the firmament heavens that mediate between heaven and earth (Day 2). Again, that parallel seems to be by way of Day 4: the firmament-heavens (Day 2) are where the lights are placed to rule (Day 4), and rule over the earth is what is delegated to man on Day 6.[7]

Psalm 8 appears to follow this seven-day pattern, although it switches the fifth and sixth sections:

Day 1: [1]Yahweh, our Lord, how supreme is your name in all the earth.
   Day 2: [2]Who have set your splendor upon the heavens.
      Day 3: [3]From the mouth of children and infants
         you established strength,
        because of your oppressors,
       [4]To silence enemy and avenger.
        Day 4: [5]When I consider your heavens, the works of your fingers,
          [6]Moon and stars, which you have set firm,
           [7]What is needy-man that you remember him,
            [8]And the son of Adam that you visit him?
          [9]And you made him lower a little while than the gods,
         [10]And with glory and honor you will crown him.
        [11]You will make him ruler over the works of your hands.
   Day 6: [12]All things you have put under his feet:
      [13]Sheep and oxen—all of them,
     [14]And also beasts of the field,
   Day 5: [15]Bird of heaven and fish of the sea,
     [16]Whatever passes through the paths of the seas.
Day 7: [17]Yahweh, our Lord, how supreme is your name in all the earth!

Biblical Horizons, 2005), 160ff. In the latter book, Jordan shows how the seven-point chiasm of Genesis 1 recurs and snowballs all through Genesis 2–4.

6. Cf. Meredith G. Kline, *Images of the Spirit* (Grand Rapids: Baker, 1980; reprint, Eugene, OR: Wipf & Stock, 1999), 111; Meredith G. Kline, *Kingdom Prologue: Genesis Foundations for a Covenantal Worldview* (reprint, Eugene, OR: Wipf & Stock, 2006), 34–38; James B. Jordan, *Sabbath Breaking and the Death Penalty: A Theological Investigation* (Niceville, FL: Biblical Horizons, 1986), 46–51.

7. In a chiasm with a central hinge (e.g., A B . . . X . . . B' A'), there may be a parallel not only between the two A sections, but also between them and the middle hinge (X). But there may also be a parallel between the two B sections and that middle hinge (X), and so on, so that all the parallel sections have some relation to that hinge. That seems to be the case here.

PART ONE: BIBLICAL STUDIES

Table 1

Genesis 1:1—2:3	Psalm 8
1. Creation of earth; light	Yahweh's name supreme in earth (1)
2. Firmament called "heavens"	Yahweh's splendor set on heavens (2)
3. Dry land and seas	Children and enemy (3-4)
4. Heavenly lights to rule	Heavenly lights and rule (5-11)
5. Sea creatures and birds	Birds and sea creatures (15-16)
6. Land animals and man's dominion	Man's dominion over land animals (12-14)
7. God enthroned in Sabbath rest	Yahweh's name supreme on earth (17)

Table 1 shows the parallels. As God created the earth and caused light to shine on it (Day 1), so here Yahweh's name is supreme in all the earth (line 1). As God completed His work and rested from it, enjoying it in Sabbath enthronement (Day 7), so here Yahweh's name is supreme in all the earth (line 17), this time specifically as a result of the narrative of the psalm. The "six days" development of the psalm leads to a "seventh day" enthronement-rest in supreme majesty.

On Day 2, God created the firmament and called it "heavens," and so too in Psalm 8 we hear about the "heavens" (line 2). On Day 6, God created land animals and man, giving man dominion over the animals. In Psalm 8—though the order of Day 6 and Day 5 is reversed, perhaps for reasons discussed below—we hear about man's dominion over the land animals (lines 12-14). The parallel with Day 2 in Psalm 8 is seen most clearly in connection with the hinge section in the middle of the chiasm: the splendor of the heavens (Day 2, line 2) is related to the moon and stars in the heavens (Day 4, lines 5-6). The heavenly lights are rulers (Day 4), and so man is exalted to rule (Day 6; lines 12-14).

On Day 3, God formed the dry land and the seas. In Psalm 8 we have a distinction between children and infants on the one hand and the enemy and avenger on the other (lines 3-4). On Day 5, God created the sea creatures and the birds, which fly "above the earth" and "across the face of the firmament-heavens" (Gen 1:20). In Psalm 8, we are told that man has dominion over both the "bird of heaven" and the sea creatures (lines 15-16).

The center of the chiasm, again, has to do with the heavenly lights and rule (lines 5-11), both of which are Day 4 themes.

A PSALM, NOT A PUZZLE

At the heart of Psalm 8 is the question: "What is man?" That question, asked by philosophers and thinkers throughout history, is often posed as a puzzle to be solved, in the hope that understanding who man is will help us make sense of our lives. "What is man?" leads to "Who am I?" and then to "What should I be doing with my life?"

But valuable as this question can be—and important as its answer is—Psalm 8 does not ask the question in this way. Psalm 8 does not give us a puzzle to solve. Rather, it gives us a song to sing in the context of joyful worship, and in that context "What is man?" is not so much a question to answer as an exclamation of joy and wonder.

That context is indicated already by the four-part title: "For the director. On the *gittith*. A psalm. By David."[8] "For the director" tells us that Psalm 8 is a song for the Levitical choirs to sing on Israel's behalf and in the assembly of God's people—and therefore for Israelites to learn and take up on their lips. It is a song for the church to sing as we draw near to God, and that assembly is the context in which we are invited to meditate on who man is and what God's purpose for him is. If you are not in church to worship God, you will not understand man.

Commentators do not agree on the meaning of the second part of the title ("On the *gittith*").[9] *Gittith* may be derived from Gath, the Philistine city in which David took refuge and which then converted and became allied with Israel.[10] If *gittith* refers to an

---

8. While some commentators dispute the validity of the titles of the psalms, Joseph Addison Alexander rightly points out that the titles are "found in the Hebrew text, as far as we can trace its history, not as addenda, but as integral parts of the composition" (*The Psalms Translated and Explained* [Grand Rapids: Eerdmans, 1864], 3). There is no reason to believe they are not original.

9. There is even some question about which title fits which psalm in the Bible. James William Thirtle points out that the only clear case outside the Psalms of a song with a title is Habakkuk 3. There, we have a title at the beginning ("A prayer. By Habakkuk the prophet. On *Shiggionoth*," v. 1) and a postscript providing musical information at the end ("For the director. With my stringed instruments," v. 19). Thirtle argues that the postscripts to several psalms have mistakenly been identified as parts of the titles of the following psalms. The title proper, he says, begins with "A psalm" or "By David" or something like that. Cf. James William Thirtle, *The Titles of the Psalms: Their Nature and Meaning Explained*, 2nd ed. (London: Henry Frowde, 1905); E. W. Bullinger, *The Chief Musician: Or, Studies in the Psalms, and Their Titles* (1908; reprint, New York: Cosimo, 2007); and, more recently, Bruce K. Waltke, "Superscripts, Postscripts, or Both," *Journal of Biblical Literature* 110 (1991) 583–96.

If Thirtle and his followers are correct, "For the director. On the *gittith*" is actually the postscript to Psalm 7 and Psalm 8's title is simply "A Psalm. By David." But then the words usually taken as the first lines of Psalm 9's title are actually Psalm 8's postscript: "For the director. On *Muth-Labben*."

While *muth-labben* is often rendered "death of a son," Thirtle takes it to mean "death of the champion" and understands it as a reference to Goliath, who is described in 1 Samuel 17:4, 23 as *ish-habbenayim* ("the man of the two betweens," i.e., "the man between the two sides"). Compare the way this title is rendered in the Targum: "To praise, regarding the death of the man who went out between the two camps" (Thirtle, *Titles of the Psalms*, 71), though note that the Targum includes the Philistines and Goliath explicitly in Psalm 9:6, which suggests that the editors of the Targum saw *muth-labben* as the title of Psalm 9, not the postscript to Psalm 8 (cf. *The Targums of Psalms*, ed. and trans. David Stec, The Aramaic Bible, vol. 16 [Edinburgh: T. & T. Clark, 2004], 38).

David would then be presenting himself as the "child" who had dominion over the beasts of the field (lion and bear) and who then "silenced the enemy and avenger"—namely Goliath (1 Sam 17:45–47). Cf. Thirtle, *Titles of the Psalms*, 70–75. Note, too, that Psalm 144 (143 LXX), which echoes Psalm 8—"What is man that you acknowledge him, the son of man that you think of him?"—has as its title in the Septuagint: "By David. On Goliath." Cf. Bullinger, *Chief Musician*, 29.

On the other hand, if *muth-labben* means "death of a son," it is harder to see how it fits with Psalm 8, which does not seem to deal with death at all—though Psalm 9, to which this title is usually affixed, clearly does (v. 13).

Perhaps Psalms 8 and 9 provide a test-case for the Thirtle thesis. Can *ben* really be a defective form of *beyn* and can *beyn* by itself mean what the whole phrase *ish-habbenayim* means in 1 Samuel 17 ("the one who stands in between")? If not, and if *ben* must mean "son," then is it more likely that Psalm 8 or Psalm 9 is the psalm "on the death of a son"?

10. David takes refuge in Gath (1 Sam 27). Later, when he flees from Absalom, he is accompanied by "all the Cherethites, all the Pelethites, and all the Gittites, six hundred men who had followed him from Gath"

instrument from Gath (NJKV) or to a tune associated with Gath, the title may already hint at a theme of the psalm, namely, man's exaltation, coronation, and dominion: an instrument associated with a Philistine city is now used by David to worship Yahweh.

There is another possibility. The word *gath* refers to a wine or oil press,[11] and so *gittith* may mean something like "wine pressings," that is, what is produced by the wine press. Hirsch thinks in this connection of afflictions, which crush God's people only to "ennoble" them.[12] But, while the psalm does mention oppressors, does it really speak of the "ennobling effect" of their oppression?

Others note that the wine press (*gath*) produces wine for celebration.[13] Still others, noticing that all the psalms with this title (Pss 8, 81, 84) are joyful,[14] suffice with saying that, whatever *gittith* itself means, the songs "on the *gittith*" are joyful. Certainly that is the case with Psalm 8, which opens and closes with a burst of praise and sustains a joyful tone throughout.

"A Psalm" may also point toward joyful celebration, since the verb behind this noun is used for singing praise to God accompanied by instruments, though there are certainly examples of psalms with this title that are *not* primarily praise (e.g., Pss 6; 88).

Finally, the title tells us that Psalm 8 is "by David." None of the psalms appear to have been written prior to David's anointing as king. As the anointing as king leads to Saul prophesying, accompanied by instruments (1 Sam 10:5–13), so the anointing as king appears also to have led to David's prophetic psalmody.

Though the title does not link the psalm specifically with any event in David's life,[15] it may alert us to a connection between David's exaltation as king and the coronation of the son of Adam and his dominion in this psalm. It is David, exalted as king, who teaches Israel to praise God by singing this joyful song about what God has done and will do for man, even for the son of Adam. In this context, "What is man?" is not a puzzle to solve but an exclamation of wonder.

(2 Sam 15:18 NKJV), including Ittai the Gittite (15:19, 22). In Zephaniah 2:4, woe is pronounced on four of the Philistine cities, but not upon the fifth, Gath. Cf. James B. Jordan, "Five Cities and Isaiah 19," *Biblical Horizons* 116 (April 1999).

11. E.g., Isaiah 63:2, 3; Lamentations 1:15; Joel 3:13; cf. "Gethsemane," which means "oil press."

12. Samson Raphael Hirsch, *The Psalms*, trans. Gertrude Hirschler, 2nd ed. (New York: Feldheim, 1997), 48.

13. Willem A. VanGemeren, "Psalms," in *The Expositor's Bible Commentary*, ed. Frank E. Gaebelein, vol. 5 (Grand Rapids: Zondervan, 1991), 36, mentions the suggestion that the *gittith* is a festival song associated with the wine press. James Jordan (*Psalter Book 3*) suggests that it might be "for singing at the Feast of Booths during the pressing of the wine," which, he says, would fit well with Psalms 81 and 84 (6).

14. F. Delitzsch, *Psalms*, trans. Francis Bolton, 3 vols. (Peabody, MA: Hendrickson, 1989), 1:148.

15. But see footnote 9 for the suggestion that this psalm is connected with the defeat of Goliath.

YAHWEH'S SUPREME NAME (8:1A)

¹*Yahweh, our Lord, how supreme is your name in all the earth . . .*

Psalm 8 focuses on Yahweh's plan for man, but it does not start or end with man. It starts with an exclamation of praise to Yahweh.

The first seven psalms use the first person singular ("I," "me," "my"), but now, for the first time, we have the plural ("*our* Lord"). The reason cannot be that this psalm is meant for corporate worship while the previous seven were not. After all, some of those psalms were also written "for the director" (Pss 4, 5, 6) and therefore for the Levitical choirs to sing corporately. So why does David use the plural here?

The answer likely has to do with the content of the psalm, namely God's purpose, not just for David, but *for mankind*. As the Levitical choirs represent and lead Israel in praise to God, so Israel, as the priestly nation, represents the whole of mankind in proclaiming the greatness of Yahweh. "Yahweh, our Lord" is the master and king who rules over Israel but also over all the earth.[16] His name—His manifestation of Himself, of His character[17]—is so supreme in all the earth that the singers do not attempt a description but simply exclaim.

If we are right in seeing a relationship between Psalm 8 and the days of creation, line 1 parallels Day 1, the day on which God created the earth and then caused light to shine upon it, light that appears, in context, to come from the Spirit hovering over the deep (Gen 1:1–5). When Psalm 8 describes Yahweh's name as "supreme (*addir*) in all the earth," we may think first of God's glorious revelation of Himself and His power in creating and lighting the world.

But while it is true that all of creation displays God's greatness and power, the word *addir* is used in the Bible primarily in connection with victory and rule.[18] In Exodus 15:6, Israel sings, "Your right hand, Yahweh, has become supreme (*addir*) in power; your right hand, Yahweh, has beaten down the enemy." The same term is applied to the waters in which the Egyptians sank (15:10 NKJV: "mighty [*addir*] waters") and then once more to Yahweh, who is called incomparable, "supreme (*addar*) in holiness." Here, for Yahweh to be *addir* means that He has power over His enemies.

In 1 Samuel 4:8, the Philistines cry out as the ark comes near because they fear Israel's God, because he is supreme (*addir*). He overcame the Egyptians by His power, and they are afraid He will do the same to them. In Psalm 76:4, the term is again used for God's greatness in battle. Psalm 93:4 applies the term to the power of the waves of the sea, and then says that Yahweh is more *addir* than the noise of many waters and the waves of the sea.

---

16. It might be possible to take *erets* here as "land," so that the psalm is proclaiming that Yahweh's name is supreme in *Israel*. But given the connection between this psalm and creation (cf. Gen 1:1: "the heavens and the earth [*erets*]") and the psalm's emphasis on man's dominion, which is not limited to Israel but extends to all the works of God's hands, it is best to take *erets* as referring to the whole earth.

17. Alexander identifies Yahweh's *name* as his "manifested excellence" (*Psalms*, 38).

18. Cf. Van Gemeren, "Psalms," 110.

Again and again, for Yahweh to be *addir* involves not just glory but supremacy. Yahweh has incomparable power over all His creation, and specifically over all His enemies. So when Psalm 8 proclaims His name to be *addir* in all the earth, it is inviting us to think not just of creation but also of salvation, not so much of natural revelation as of God's mighty works in history. The God who caused light to shine in the darkness in creation continues to cause the light of His most powerful name to shine in salvation by overthrowing enemies and rescuing and exalting His people. So powerful is His name that His enemies tremble before Him (Josh 2:9–10; 1 Sam 4:8).

YAHWEH'S SPLENDOR UPON THE HEAVENS (8:1B)

²Who have set your splendor upon the heavens!

From the earth, Psalm 8 moves to the heavens. In Genesis 1, the creation of the heavens, which are God's throneroom, precedes the creation of the earth (Gen 1:1). Then, God makes the firmament and calls it by the name of His throneroom: "Heavens" (Gen 1:6–8), thereby indicating that these heavens represent His throneroom. The heavens created *before* the earth are God's throneroom heavens; the heavens created *after* the earth are the firmament-heavens.

Since "earth" precedes "heavens" in Psalm 8 and since Psalm 8 seems to parallel the creation account, it is most likely that the firmament-heavens, created on Day 2, are in view here.[19] Certainly the "heavens" of lines 5–6 are the firmament-heavens, since they contain the moon and stars (cf. Gen 1:14).

But what does it mean that Yahweh has set His splendor *upon* (*al*) the heavens?[20] Often, the preposition here is translated as "above," so that this line declares that Yahweh is enthroned in splendor, either above the firmament-heavens or even above the throneroom heavens.

But other passages in Scripture use this phrase—"set splendor on" (*nathan hod al*)—for putting authority and glory upon someone. In Numbers 27:19–20, Moses is told to take Joshua, lay his hand on him, set him before the priest and the congregation, inaugurate him, and "set some of your splendor upon him." The result will be that "the whole congregation of the sons of Israel will hear"—that is, obey. Likewise, in 1 Chronicles 29:25, we are told that "Yahweh made Solomon great . . . in the eyes of all Israel and set upon him splendor." And in Psalm 21:5, though a different verb is used, the psalmist says, "Splendor and honor you have placed upon him."

---

19. *Contra* Jordan (*Studies in the Psalter 2*, 1), who takes these to be the heavens created on the first day.

20. The meaning of *tenah* (here translated "set") is disputed. Derek Kidner suggests changing a vowel so that this phrase means "chanted above the heavens" (*Psalms 1–72*, Tyndale Old Testament Commentaries [Downers Grove, IL: InterVarsity Press, 1973], 66n1). But for a defense of seeing it as a form of the verb *nathan* ("to give, set"), see E. W. Hengstenberg, *Commentary on the Psalms*, 4th ed., vol. 1 (Edinburgh: T. & T. Clark, 1869), 128–29. Online: http://faculty.gordon.edu/hu/bi/Ted_Hildebrandt/OTeSources/19-Psalms/Text/Books/Hengstenberg-vol1/Hengstenberg-Vol1.pdf.

In all of these cases, setting "splendor" on someone entails giving him *authority*, the personal greatness to which one responds (or ought to) with awe and obedience. It is best to understand the phrase in Psalm 8 accordingly: It is not that Yahweh has set his personal splendor *above* the heavens; rather, He has set it *upon* the heavens so that they represent His royal authority.

We look *up* to the heavens, which already implies that we are *under* them and therefore *under* Yahweh, and what we see in the heavens—the lights Yahweh set there—are His delegates, ruling for Him and representing His rule to us.[21] Our king's name is supreme in all the earth, and He has ordained the firmament-heavens to display His glory and represent His authority.

BATTLING BABIES (8:2; LINES 3–4)

³From the mouth of children and infants
  you established strength,
  because of your oppressors,
⁴To silence enemy and avenger.[22]

Having started with Yahweh's supreme greatness, the psalm suddenly switches to focus on virtual nothingness, on "children and infants." Or is that the wrong way to look at it? These are not, after all, mere babies. They are battling babies, and it is precisely through them that Yahweh "establishes strength"[23] so that His name is supreme in all the earth, not least through the silencing of those who speak against Him.

The word translated "oppressors" (*tsorar*) is frequently used for enemies, but it has to do especially with *pressing in*.[24] These people want to limit Yahweh's work and so they press in upon Yahweh's people. They are described, furthermore, as "enemy and avenger." The enemy attacks Yahweh's people, while the avenger thinks he has been wronged by them and wants vengeance.

Ever since Psalm 2, we have heard about enemies, and in particular about their *words*.[25] These enemies do not always attack with physical weapons; often they attack through verbal troublemaking. They lie and deceive; they backbite; they use their words to turn people against Yahweh and against His anointed, David.

---

21. "God has clad the heavens with His glory, in that He has set in them the sun, moon, and stars, as monuments of His almighty power and greatness" (Hengstenberg, *Commentary on the Psalms*, 129). Cf. Alexander, *Psalms*, 38.

22. These verses display something of a chiastic structure. They begin and end with a pair of nouns: "children and infants" and "enemy and avenger." In the center, we have Yahweh: *He* establishes strength and He does so because of *His* oppressors. The structure is significant. On the one hand, there are the "children and infants" and on the other the "enemy and avenger," but "between the contrasted parties is God" (Peter C. Craigie, *Psalms 1–50*, Word Biblical Commentary 19 [Waco, TX: Word, 1983], 107).

23. The phrase here might mean "founded a bulwark." Cf. Kidner, *Psalms 1–72*, 67.

24. Hirsch, *Psalms*, 50, takes the root verb to mean "to confine, to limit in space." The related noun refers to a well, a tightly enclosed space. The verbal form here, then, has to do with pressing or oppressing.

25. Cf. e.g., Psalms 2:2–3; 3:2; 5:4–6, 9–10; 10:7; 12:1–4, and especially the title of Psalm 7: "Concerning the words of Cush."

In doing so, they look strong. Goliath's boasts are designed to reveal his own strength and the weakness of the "servants of Saul" (1 Sam 17:8). Goliath forgets that these "servants of Saul" are "the armies of the living God" (17:26), but so do Saul and all the men of Israel until David comes along to silence the blasphemer, who exalts his own strength over the name of Yahweh of hosts (cf. 17:45–47).

And who is David? "The youngest" son of Jesse (17:14), despised by his own eldest brother (17:28), a "young man" in contrast to Goliath who has been a warrior since he was young (17:33). But Yahweh uses "children and infants" to "establish strength"—that is, to make His strength manifest in spite of all these oppressors—and to "silence enemy and avenger." And in particular, Psalm 8 says, He uses their *mouths*.

From their earliest years,[26] the mouths of the children of Yahweh's people begin to speak in a way that silences the wicked. They may not be able to *do* much, but they can *speak*. Instead of asserting themselves and their own strength as Goliath did, children praise Yahweh, thereby confessing His strength and relying on it.

We may be inclined to say, "They don't even understand what they are saying," but what does that matter? We are not called to critique their speaking, let alone to shush them, but rather to join in their song. As Douglas Wilson has said, "Who shuts down the railing atheist? The answer of this psalm is the jabbering baby in the back of the sanctuary. *He* is the one who silences the foe and the avenger."[27]

Too often, though, we admire what we regard as power, the sort of authority that the lords of the Gentiles display (cf. Mark 10:42). But God uses the weak to overcome the strong, the foolish to thwart the wise (1 Cor 1:27–29; cf. Matt 11:25).

So in Matthew 21, children cry out *the Name*: "Hosanna to the son of David" (21:15). When the chief priests and scribes want to silence them, Jesus replies by quoting this line of Psalm 8, deliberately altering the last words, in accordance with the Septuagint, to bring out their meaning: "Out of the mouth of babes and nursing infants, you have perfected praise" (21:16 NKJV).[28] The praise of children—singing the majesty, not simply of Yahweh, but of Jesus—establishes Yahweh's strength over against oppressive priests and scribes.

But Psalm 8 applies not only to literal children.[29] In Luke 10:21, the seventy are described as "babies," who know what the wise do not. Jesus Himself came as a baby and already then began to establish Yahweh's strength and silence the enemy and avenger, and so His disciples, though just "babies" compared to the wise and mighty, win the victory.[30]

---

26. The word for "children" here is used even for the unborn (Job 3:16).

27. Douglas Wilson, *Christ and His Rivals: Hebrews Through New Eyes* (Monroe, LA: Athanasius, 2008), 32.

28. "Since the outcome of this praise is the enemy's defeat, as in the Heb., the LXX wording is probably a paraphrase to show what the psalm means by its unusual metaphor of an audible bulwark. *Cf.* 2 C. 20:22; Ne. 8:10" (Kidner, *Psalms 1–72*, 67n1).

29. Charles Spurgeon ("Psalm 8," in *The Treasury of David*. Online: http://www.spurgeon.org/treasury/ps008.htm) identifies the children as (1) man in general, (2) David in particular, (3) Jesus especially, (4) the apostles, (5) the children in Matthew 21, and (6) all who follow Christ. Interestingly, he does not focus on the *literal* children of the Church.

30. While Matthew 21 points us in the direction of *praise*, it is worth considering the possibility that

LOWER, THEN HIGHER (8:3–6A; LINES 5–11)

⁵*When I consider Your heavens, the works of Your fingers,*
⁶*Moon and stars, which You have set firm,*
⁷*What is needy-man that You remember him,*
⁸*And the son of Adam that You visit him?*
⁹*And You made him lower a little while than the gods,*
¹⁰*And with glory and honor You will crown him.*
¹¹*You will make him ruler over the works of Your hands.*

Structure

Lines 5–11 are the heart of Psalm 8, as both chiastic outlines above suggest, and they are themselves structured as a chiasm.³¹ "Works of your fingers" (line 5) parallels "works of your hands" (line 11). "Moon and stars" (line 6) parallels "glory and honor" (line 10), not only in syntax but also in that the moon and stars are lights and rulers in heaven and therefore are symbolically associated with glory and honor. The question about "needy-man" (line 7) is balanced by the statement that Yahweh "made him lower . . . than the gods" (line 9). At the center of the chiasm is the question about "the son of Adam," whom Yahweh "visits" (line 9), and on this "visit" everything hinges.

Man and the Heavens

This central section of Psalm 8 begins with the psalmist considering the heavens, which he speaks of as "the works of [Yahweh's] fingers." The heavens in question are the firmament-heavens, since in them Yahweh has "set firm" the "moon and stars." Thinking about the lights in the night sky raises the question: "What is needy-man that you remember him?"

Right here, however, we easily get things backwards. We tend to think immediately of vast and largely empty space, of stars as balls of fire, light years away. And when we think of man in relation to the immensity of outer space, we think of him as puny, insignificant, nothing in comparison.

But David's focus here is not on man's insignificance—a tiny speck of dust in an immense universe—but on man's exaltation, glory, and rule. His exclamation is not the result of humiliation but rather of wonder at man's greatness in this universe.

Perhaps the problem is that when we consider the heavens, we think primarily of astronomy. But David thinks of Scripture, and in particular of the symbolism of Scripture, starting in Genesis 1 where the lights are placed in the firmament-heavens to

---

the battle in Psalm 8 may be fought by *lamentation*, as well, that is, that Yahweh overthrows the enemy in response to the cries of His people, including the cries of their little babies. Robert Southwell's poem "New Heaven, New War" (perhaps best known as the Christmas carol, "This Little Babe") speaks of Jesus' suffering as an infant this way: "With tears he fights and wins the field, / His naked breast stands for a shield; / His battering shot are babish cries, / His arrows made of weeping eyes . . ." (online: http://www.luminarium.org/renlit/newheaven.htm).

31. Cf. Jordan, *Studies in the Psalter 2*, 2.

replace the Spirit light of Day 1, shedding light on earth and ruling. Yahweh has set His splendor upon the firmament-heavens (line 2), and when David looks at them, he sees a representation of Yahweh's glory and authority.

But he might also think about what these lights mean for man. From Genesis 1 on, the heavenly lights are associated with rule, and rule was promised to man at creation (Gen 1:28). Thus, the delegating of the light of Day 1 to the lights of Day 4 foreshadows Yahweh's delegating of rule to man.[32] The moon and stars represent man enthroned as a lightbearer in and ruler over God's world. Looking up at the night sky ought especially to remind us of who we are and who God intended us to be.

If we want to bring astronomy in, however, we should view it this way: The vaster the universe, the greater man's glory and dominion. After all, when David views "the works of [Yahweh's] fingers," he goes on to say that man will rule "over the works of [Yahweh's] hands." Whatever immense reaches of space there might be, the Son of Man will rule over them—and the bigger the universe is, the greater man's rule.

Nevertheless, David does speak of man as *enosh*, a term that often indicates weakness and neediness. When he views the heavens, seeing them as a manifestation of Yahweh's splendor and seeing pictured in them man's own future exaltation and rule, he is amazed that Yahweh would "remember" someone who is, after all, only *enosh*, a needy man.

In the Bible, when Yahweh remembers, He acts, and His action here is described with the pregnant verb "visits" (*paqad*): "And the son of Adam that you visit him" (line 8). Adam's sons deserve death because of sin, but instead, Yahweh visits "the son of Adam."

While the word "visit" (*paqad*) can mean "take care of, provide for," it can also refer more narrowly to ordination or appointment to a special calling (Gen 39:4; 40:4; Num 27:16).[33] Given the context, it is likely that Psalm 8 is using the word in this more specialized sense: David is not just exclaiming over the way in which Yahweh cares for and provides for "the son of Adam" in general, but rather is marveling over His ordination and appointment of "the son of Adam" to a position of "glory and honor."

Creation and Exaltation

Man's position, however, is not static. His status at creation is temporary; a change is coming, and man will be crowned with "glory and honor." This shift in position is often overlooked, and we will discuss it at greater length below. But first, we must understand what is meant when David says that Yahweh "made him lower a little while than the gods" (line 9).

Commentators often point out that the word *haser*, translated here "made lower," can mean "to withhold, deprive, make someone lack,"[34] and certainly that is how the

---

32. On the sun, moon, and stars in connection with *rule*, see James B. Jordan, *Through New Eyes: Developing a Biblical View of the World* (Brentwood, TN: Wolgemuth & Hyatt, 1988; Eugene, OR: Wipf & Stock, 1999), 53–67.

33. Hirsch, *Psalms*, 53. It is intriguing to note that Numbers 27, which uses the verb *paqad* to refer to ordaining Joshua (27:16) is the same passage that speaks of *setting splendor upon* Joshua (27:20), and both of these phrases are echoed in Psalm 8.

34. Cf., e.g., Van Gemeren, "Psalms," 113; Alexander, *Psalms*, 39; Hengstenberg, *Commentary on the Psalms*, 133; Hirsch, *Psalms*, 55.

verb is used in the only other passage in which it appears in this form, Ecclesiastes 4:8: "deprive my soul of good" (cf. Eccl 6:2). But the parallel is far from exact. In Psalm 8, the direct object ("him") is not deprived of "gods" (or of God). Rather, according to these commentators, he lacks some of the qualities or characteristics or glory or status of God or the gods—but that way of taking this verb is unattested elsewhere in Scripture.

Hebrews 2 renders this verb with the word *elattoō*. While *elattoō* can refer to a lack or a need (1 Sam 2:5; 21:15; 2 Sam 3:29; Ps 33:11 LXX; cf. 2 Cor 12:13), it does so only when one thing lacks another. Never is it used for a lack of the qualities or characteristics of something else. Instead, in Hebrews 2, as in traditional translations of Psalm 8, it has the sense of being or becoming less than, lower than, or inferior to something else.[35] It is best to read Psalm 8 accordingly: Yahweh has made man lower than or inferior to "the gods."

But who are "the gods"? *Elohim*, translated "gods" here, often refers to God Himself, and some translations and commentaries take it that way in Psalm 8.[36] Man is made in the image of God but nevertheless he is still just a man, still "lower than God." On this view, "lower than God" describes man's *permanent* status, and "little" must refer to a *degree* of difference from God rather than to the length of time that man is lower.

Others take "gods" here to refer to the *pagan* gods.[37] Surely God did not *create* man lower than—let alone subject to—the false gods, but perhaps He *made* man lower than these gods as a consequence of man's rebellion. After all, Scripture does speak of men being under the authority of demonic princes (e.g., Dan 10:13, 20; Eph 2:2).[38]

A third option is to see the "gods" here as angels, who, as heavenly beings, may be called "gods,"[39] and this is the interpretation that Scripture itself gives. Hebrews 2 quotes Psalm 8 this way: "You made him lower . . . than the *angels*."[40] God Himself is not in view.[41]

---

35. Walter Bauer, Frederick W. Danker, W. F. Arndt, and F. W. Gingrich, *A Greek-English Lexicon of the New Testament and Other Early Christian Literature*, 3rd ed. (Chicago: University of Chicago Press, 2000), s.v.

36. E.g., ASV, NASB, New Living; cf. Craigie, *Psalms 1–50*, 105, 108; and John Calvin, *Commentary on the Psalms*, vol. 1, trans. James Anderson (Grand Rapids: Christian Classics Ethereal Library, n.d.), online: http://www.ccel.org/ccel/calvin/calcom08.xiv.iv.html. Hirsch takes the word to refer more generally to the divine attributes, few of which have been withheld from man (*Psalms*, 55).

37. Van Gemeren mentions this view: "Man's position is to be compared to the place the pagans give to their gods. Yahweh is above the gods (cf. 86:8), and man is a little below them" ("Psalms," 113). He cites J. Ridderbos as an exegete who holds this position, but Van Gemeren himself does not comment on it.

38. On the identity of the "princes" in Daniel 10, see James B. Jordan, *The Handwriting on the Wall: A Commentary on the Book of Daniel* (Powder Springs, GA: American Vision, 2007), 528–30.

39. The versions of this psalm found in the Septuagint, Syriac, Targum, and Vulgate all render this word as "angels," though some other early versions translate it as "God" (cf. Craigie, *Psalms 1–50*, 108).

40. Similarly, when Hebrews 1 quotes Psalm 97:7, it changes "Worship him, all gods" to "Let all the angels of God worship Him" (Heb 1:6 NKJV). Van Gemeren points to Psalm 82:1, 6 as another example of angelic beings being called "gods" ("Psalms," 113, 533–35), but in light of John 10:34–36, it is best to take the gods in that psalm as *human* judges and rulers.

41. Calvin (*Commentary on the Psalms*) argues that Psalm 8 is speaking of God, but that Hebrews 2 is drawing an implication from Psalm 8. He says he does not "disapprove" of the Septuagint's use of "angels," but prefers to take Psalm 8 as referring to God. Then he adds: "Nor is it any sufficient objection to this view, that the apostle, in his Epistle to the Hebrews (Hebrews 2:7) quoting this passage, says, *little less than*

PART ONE: BIBLICAL STUDIES

Nor are the fallen angels, as a survey of how the term "angels" is used in Hebrews 1 and 2 makes clear.

There is a third element in this line in Psalm 8 that we must consider, and that is the word *meat*, which is translated here as "a little while." As an adverb, as it is here, *meat* may be used of place (2 Sam 16:1 NKJV: "a little past the top"), of degree of action (cf. 2 Kgs 10:18 NKJV: "Ahab served Baal a little, Jehu will serve him much"), or of a short period of time (e.g., Job 24:24 NKJV: "They are exalted for a little while"; Hos 1:4 NKJV: "For in a little while I will avenge . . .").[42]

So which is it here? Is Psalm 8 saying that Yahweh made man lower than the angels in *degree*? Or is it saying that Yahweh made man lower than the angels for a little *time*? The latter is most likely. But to see why, we need to consider what Psalm 8 says next ("And with glory and honor you crown him," line 10) and how these two lines are related.

"Glory and honor" (*kabod wehadar*) are terms used elsewhere "to express royal dignity" (e.g., Pss 21:5; 45:3; Jer 22:18; 1 Chr 29:25).[43] They are, in fact, terms used to describe Yahweh's majesty as King (Pss 29:1; 104:1).[44] As a king, man shares in Yahweh's royal "glory and honor."

But *when* does Yahweh "crown" man with this regal majesty? Many commentaries assume that Psalm 8 is speaking of man's *creation* here.[45] Yahweh created man lower than the angels, and at the same time Yahweh also crowned man with glory and honor, making him ruler over everything. After all, doesn't God bless man at his creation with dominion "over the fish of the sea and the birds of the heavens and every beast that creeps upon the earth" (Gen 1:28)?

Hebrews 2, however, does not take Psalm 8 as a reference to creation, but rather applies it to Jesus' exaltation: "We do not yet see all things put under [man]. But we see Jesus . . . crowned with glory and honor" (2:8b–9 NKJV).[46] Man does not have the dominion

---

the angels, and not *than God*; for we know what freedoms the apostles took in quoting texts of Scripture; not, indeed, to wrest them to a meaning different from the true one but because they reckoned it sufficient to show, by a reference to Scripture, that what they taught was sanctioned by the word of God, although they did not quote the precise words. Accordingly, they never had any hesitation in changing the words, provided the substance of the text remained unchanged."

But Calvin's argument is not compelling. If Psalm 8 is really speaking of God, then a reference to it would *not* show that man is lower than the angels. After all, one might be lower than God and yet be *higher* than the angels. If Hebrews 2 is citing Psalm 8 to "show, by a reference to Scripture, that what [is] taught was sanctioned by the word of God," as Calvin says, then there can be only one conclusion: the writer of Hebrews took Psalm 8 to be speaking about man in relation to the angels, not to God.

42. Cf. William L. Holladay, ed., *A Concise Hebrew and Aramaic Lexicon of the Old Testament* (Grand Rapids: Eerdmans, 1993), s.v.; Francis Brown, S. R. Driver, and Charles A. Briggs, *Hebrew and English Lexicon of the Old Testament* (Oxford: Clarendon, 1907), s.v. The Greek word used in Hebrews 2:7, *brachus*, is similar: It may be used of something short in space (Acts 27:28), low in quantity (Heb 13:22), or brief in duration (Luke 22:58; Acts 5:34; cf. Isa 57:17 LXX) (BDAG, s.v.).

43. Alexander, *Psalms*, 39. Hengstenberg calls them "the common designations of kingly state and majesty" (*Commentary on the Psalms*, 135).

44. Cf. Van Gemeren, "Psalms," 113.

45. E.g., Alexander, *Psalms*, 39; Craigie, *Psalms 1–50*, 108; Hengstenberg, *Commentary on the Psalms*, 134–35; Van Gemeren, "Psalms," 113.

46. Philip Edgcumbe Hughes argues that the first clause is not speaking of man but of Christ: We do not

that Psalm 8 speaks of, but Jesus does.[47] The Hebrews themselves are still awaiting their coronation, but because *the* "Son of Adam" has at last been "crowned with glory and honor" as Psalm 8 promised, they can be confident that He will also bring "many sons to glory" (Heb 2:10 NKJV).

Notice, too, that Jesus' coronation "with glory and honor" involves exaltation over the angels, so that He is no longer "lower than the angels." Hebrews 1 tells us that "Having by Himself made cleansing for our sins, [He] sat down on the right hand of the Majesty on high, having become as much greater than the angels as he has inherited a more excellent name than theirs" (Heb 1:3b–4).

He is the Son and they are not (Heb 1:5). He is the firstborn, and the angels are to bow to Him (Heb 1:6). They are servants (Heb 1:7), but He is God enthroned (Heb 1:8–9). To Jesus—and not to the angels—has God said, "Sit at my right hand until I make your enemies a footstool for your feet" (Heb 1:13). Furthermore, "the world to come" has not been made subject to angels but to Jesus (Heb 2:5–9) and to man united with Him (2:10, 14–16). No longer is Jesus "lower than the angels." Now, as a result of His coronation, He is enthroned above them.

Hebrews 2, therefore, does not take "You made him . . . lower than the angels" as a permanent description of man's status. Instead, it understands this status to have been temporary, followed by a transition from lower to higher, from being "lower than the angels" to being "crowned with glory and honor."

Now we can return to the word *meat* ("a little"). Does it refer to a degree of status ("a little lower than the angels")? Nothing in Hebrews 2 hints at that interpretation. The issue is not whether man was just a wee bit lower or a great deal lower than the angels in status until the coming of Christ. Rather, the focus in Hebrews 2 is on the change that has taken place: Jesus was lower for a while, but now He is exalted above the angels. It is best, therefore, to understand *meat* (Greek: *brachus*) temporally: "You made him lower *for a little while* than the angels."[48]

When David wrote Psalm 8, man was still "lower than the angels." But he sang in hope because this status was not permanent. One day, Yahweh would crown the son of Adam "with glory and honor." The "lower than the angels" stage is temporary and short-lived. Afterward comes exaltation.[49]

---

yet see all things under Christ, but we do see that He has been crowned and so He is beginning to exercise what will eventually be universal dominion (*A Commentary on the Epistle to the Hebrews* [Grand Rapids: Eerdmans, 1977], 86–87). His argument is plausible. But even if he is correct, my point still stands: If we do not yet see all things subject to *Christ*, then how much less are they subject to *man* in general or even to *godly men*?

47. Perhaps one could argue that man originally did have that dominion but that he lost it at the fall. Psalm 8, on that argument, would be speaking of man *as he was at creation*, not as he is after his rebellion. But then David would be celebrating something that is no longer the case, ever since the Fall. Furthermore, this argument does not do justice to the text of Psalm 8, which uses the perfect tense for Yahweh's making man lower than the angels ("made lower") but the imperfect here, which most naturally refers to the present ("Yahweh crowns him") or the future ("Yahweh will crown him"). Since Hebrews 2 indicates that Yahweh does not continually crown man with this glory, it is best to take the verb here as a future: "Yahweh *will* crown him with glory and honor."

48. Cf. Kidner, *Psalms 1–72*, 67; Hughes, *Hebrews*, 85.

49. That Psalm 8, followed by Hebrews 2, speaks of a transition from being "lower than the angels" to

That exaltation involves not only kingly "glory and honor," but also rule. Line 11—using an imperfect tense, which again is best understood as future—adds, "You will make him ruler over the works of Your hands." The verb *mashal*, here used in the Hiphil ("make . . . ruler"), appears also in Genesis 1, where the lights in the firmament-heavens are appointed to *rule* the day and the night.[50] The echo of Genesis 1 may remind us that these lines in Psalm 8 correspond to Day 4 in the creation account. But here the "heavenly light" who is made into a glorious ruler is the son of Adam, who was once "lower than the angels" but now is exalted over them.

In fact, he is exalted over *everything* that Yahweh has made, over "the works of Your hands." Remember that this central section of Psalm 8 is chiastically structured, so that "glory and honor" in line 10 parallels "moon and stars" in line 6, and "the works of Your hands" here in line 11 parallels "the works of Your fingers" in line 5.

When we hear about man as "ruler over the works of [Yahweh's] hands," we might be inclined to rush immediately to the next verses and to focus on all the earthly creatures who are under man's authority. But the parallel with line 5 indicates that we ought to think first of all of something even greater, of man's rule over *the heavens*. They are "the works of [Yahweh's] fingers," and man will be exalted to rule over them, even over the moon and stars set in the firmament-heavens.[51] Man's dominion will extend not just to the earth but also to the heavens.

---

being exalted over them sounds the death knell for the "chain of being" view held by so many throughout history. In this view, God is at the top of the chain, with angels—as spiritual beings or pure intelligences—below him, human beings—who are a blend, both spiritual and material—lower still, the beasts beneath them, and so on. Though there might be the possibility that man might rise in glory, the angels too would be continually rising above him, so that the order of the chain never changes. But if man, created "lower than the angels," is then exalted over them, the chain is no longer static, with each creature in the place "rationally" assigned to it. Furthermore, if man can be exalted over the angels, the idea that matter is inherently lower than spirit must also give way, since Jesus is fully human, with a human body, and yet is exalted over the angels. For a discussion of the "chain of being," see Arthur O. Lovejoy, *The Great Chain of Being: A Study of the History of an Idea* (1936; reprint, Cambridge: Harvard University Press, 1964), and E. M. W. Tillyard, *The Elizabethan World Picture* (New York: Vintage, n.d.), 25–52.

50. Hirsch, noting that a related word is used in Genesis 24:2 for Abraham's eldest servant, who was "ruler" over all that was his, suggests that the word refers to *stewardship*. As Abraham's servant "assigned to everything its own proper purpose and task in accordance with Abraham's will," so man also serves as a steward in God's world. "Man must not enforce his own proud will upon his fellow-creatures; it is his task merely to rule them in accordance with the purposes revealed to him by God" (*Psalms*, 55). Attractive as this suggestion may be, however, it goes beyond the *lexical* evidence. Certainly every ruler under God has delegated authority and is therefore a steward. But we cannot conclude that this particular word refers strictly to a steward, since it is used also for God Himself (Judg 8:23), who is nobody's steward.

51. We might ask why Psalm 8 mentions the moon and stars, but not the sun. Surely the sun is the first thing that comes to mind when we think of the firmament-heavens sharing Yahweh's splendor. Perhaps we can approach an answer by considering, first, that Yahweh Himself is associated with the sun (e.g., Ps 84:11), so by leaving the sun out Psalm 8 avoids any hint that man will be exalted over Yahweh. But the close association between angels and stars in Scripture (e.g., Rev 9:1, 11; 12:4) suggests that rule over the moon and stars implies rule over the angels as well.

Second, we should bear in mind that moon and stars are associated with night. Night is the time of transition, the time of waiting for the new day (or new creation) to dawn (e.g., Ps 130:6; Isa 60:1–3). Passover, for instance, happens at night; the new day brings the Exodus. In a sense, the whole period of the Old Creation up to the coming of Jesus is nighttime. When Jesus comes, it is a new dawn, as the "Sun of Righteousness"

Angels and the Old Creation

To understand the transition presented in Psalm 8 better, we ought to go back to Genesis 1 and 2. In Genesis 1:28, God promises man dominion over the earth: "And God blessed them and God said to them, 'Be fruitful and multiply and fill the earth and subdue it, and govern over the fish of the sea and the bird of the heavens and every beast that creeps upon the earth.'" From the beginning, man was intended to rule over all of these earthly creatures.

But when we read Genesis 2, we find that man did not start out exercising this dominion. Yahweh creates man and then plants a Garden and brings Adam into it "to serve it and to guard it" (Gen 2:15). The Garden is not *man's* garden; it is *God's* garden. Adam is there as a servant. In fact, the language of "serving" and "guarding" is associated in Scripture with *priests and Levites* (Num 3:7–8; 8:25–26; 18:5–6).[52]

At this point Adam is not exercising dominion in the world. Naming an ox is not the same thing as taming an ox. It is one thing to give a dog a name; it is another thing to teach the dog to come when you call. Adam is not yet working; he is assembling his tools. He is in training, learning to serve the Garden so that later, when he leaves the Garden, he can serve the earth. He is to be a king, but he starts his life as a priest—that is, as a servant[53]—in God's Garden.

Eventually, however, Adam (or his sons) would go out into the world to subdue it and increasingly to rule over it. The transition from service in the Garden to rule in the world is associated in Genesis 2 with the Tree of the Knowledge of Good and Evil. In the Bible, knowing or discerning good and evil is associated with maturity (Deut 1:39; Heb 5:14) and especially with kingly judgment (2 Sam 14:17; 1 Kgs 3:9)

All that God created, including this tree, was very good (Gen 1:31); Adam needed this knowledge to rule wisely and well; and God promised Adam that "every tree" would be "for food to him" (Gen 1:29), including this one. For a time, the tree was forbidden (Gen 2:16–17) and Adam would have to wait. But eventually, he would be allowed to eat this tree, would gain kingly wisdom and glory, and would be exalted to rule.[54]

---

arises "with healing in His wings" (Mal 4:2 NKJV; cf. Rev. 1:16b NKJV, where Jesus' face is "like the sun shining in its strength"). When the Sun rises, the glory of the moon and stars fades away and disappears. The Old Creation night has passed away, and now it is New Covenant day (Jordan, *Through New Eyes*, 54, 56–57).

Finally, the exaltation over "moon and stars" has liturgical significance. The heavenly lights were for "seasons" (Gen 1:14), and that term refers to festival times. There were new moon festivals (e.g., Num 29:6); Passover, Pentecost, and Tabernacles were all on a certain day of the month, counting from the new moon (Lev 23:5–6, 34; Num 28:11–14; 2 Chr 8:13; Ps 81:3). One result of being exalted over the moon and over the Torah given by angels is that our worship times are no longer governed by the heavenly lights. "In the New Covenant, we are no longer under lunar regulation for festival times (Colossians 2:16–17). In that regard, Christ is our light" (Jordan, *Through New Eyes*, 54).

52. William J. Dumbrell, *The Faith of Israel*, 2nd ed. (Grand Rapids: Baker, 2002), 21–22; Gordon Wenham, *Genesis 1–15*, Word Biblical Commentary 1 (Waco, TX: Word, 1987), 67, 87.

53. On priests as palace servants, see Peter J. Leithart, "What Is a Priest?" *Biblical Horizons* 33 (Jan. 1992) and *The Priesthood of the Plebs: A Theology of Baptism* (Eugene, OR: Wipf & Stock, 2003), 48–86.

54. For more discussion, see James B. Jordan, "Merit Versus Maturity: What Did Jesus Do for Us?" in Steve Wilkins and Duane Garner, eds., *The Federal Vision* (Monroe, LA: Athanasius, 2004), 151–200.

PART ONE: BIBLICAL STUDIES

So Adam's life was designed to have (at least) two stages: a *priestly* phase, serving and guarding the Garden, followed by a *kingly* phase, exalted in glory and exercising dominion in the world outside the Garden.[55] Given that the second phase involves glory and rule, we might expect that the first phase would entail being "lower than the angels." And that is exactly what we find.

When Adam was in the Garden, the serpent entered (Gen 3:1), the serpent who is later identified as "the devil and Satan" (Rev 12:9), which means that this serpent is to be identified not only as a "beast of the field" but also as an angel.[56] We are not told *when* this angel rebelled, but given that his punishment—the crushing of his head—is connected with his behavior in the Garden (Gen 3:14: "because you have done this"), not with some previous sin, it seems best to conclude that Satan's fall happened in the course of his conversation with the Woman in Genesis 3—and certainly by the time he directly contradicted God's warning: "*Not* 'dying you will die'" (Gen 3:4).[57]

The serpent's presence in the Garden is thus the presence of an angel and likely an unfallen angel. What was he doing there? It turned out that he deceived the Woman, but his temptation came in the form of instruction and tutoring. And even though this temptation was a perversion of the angel's task, it still gives us some indication of what that task ought to have been. The serpent was crafty, which is not a bad trait (Matt 10:16); he was crafty, not to lead man astray but to make man crafty, in a good sense, too.

This angel was therefore to be man's chief tutor. From the beginning, even before Adam sinned, his growth to maturity was related to angelic instruction. From the beginning, then, man was "lower than the angels."

James Jordan offers an illustration to help us understand this angelic role.[58] When you enlist in the army to be trained as an officer, you do not start out as an officer. Instead, you are under a drill sergeant, who makes you do things you would rather not do. He makes you hike for miles when you are already bone weary from the previous day's hike. He makes you do pushups early in the morning. And even though you are one day

---

55. For a fuller discussion of priest, king, and prophet as phases in maturation—with implications for our own maturation—see James B. Jordan, *From Bread to Wine: Toward a More Biblical Liturgical Theology*, draft ed. 1.1 (Niceville, FL: Biblical Horizons, 2001).

56. We are not told how "the serpent," who is clearly a "beast," could also be an angel, but *how* is not our concern here. That Satan is a (rebellious) angel is evident from Revelation 9:11, where he is called "the angel of the bottomless pit." He is said to appear as "an angel of light" (2 Cor 11:14). He is closely associated with angelic followers (Matt 25:41; 2 Cor 12:7; Rev 12:7, 9), who are spoken of as "demons" and "unclean spirits," and he is their ruler (Matt 9:34). Cleansing people from unclean spirits is plundering Satan's house (Matt 12:28–29). Furthermore, he appears before God when the angelic "sons of God" assemble (Job 1:6; 2:1). For a helpful discussion, see Greg L. Bahnsen, "The Person, Work, and Present Status of Satan," *Journal of Christian Reconstruction* 1.2 (1974) 11–41.

57. "The first part of the serpent's conversation with Eve is unobjectionable. Arguably, he is no more than seeking to help her understand God's command. Satan, however, understands that the meaning of the Tree of the Knowledge is that mankind will go from being a little lower than the angels to being over the angels. . . . Evidently this was what he was trying to prevent. It may be that his decision to undermine God's plan for humanity happened precisely between Genesis 3:3 and 3:4" (Jordan, "Merit Versus Maturity," 200).

58. I do not recall where Jordan uses this illustration.

going to be an officer, above that drill sergeant in rank, you must obey him during basic training.

But when you graduate, what happens? He salutes you. Is he jealous of you because you are higher in rank than he is? Not if he's a good drill sergeant. Far from being frustrated by your promotion, he is proud. "Look at him," he says. "When I first got him, he couldn't shine his shoes for anything. But look at them shine now."

Satan was a bad drill sergeant, eager to prevent man's future promotion. But his plot did not thwart God's plan. When Satan rebelled, God provided a new chief drill sergeant, a new chief tutor to guide man—who, until the coming of Jesus, was a child (Gal 4:1–3)—to full, grown-up maturity.[59] Often in the Old Testament, we hear about "the Angel of Yahweh," who is Yahweh Himself (e.g., Gen 16:10–13; 22:11–12; Judg 2:1–3; 6:11–24; 13:15–23; Zech 3:1–2), the Second Person of the Trinity.

He leads Israel through the wilderness to the Promised Land (Exod 32:34). He is the Commander of Yahweh's army, who ensures Israel's victory in the land (Josh 5:13–15). Nor does He work alone. He is not only the Angel of Yahweh; He is the leader of Yahweh's angels, who accompany Him on His mission (e.g., Gen 18; 19:1, 15) or perform various tasks under His authority.

From Adam on, God's people are "lower than the angels." They are led and directed and visited and taught by angels. Even the Torah was "appointed through angels" (Acts 7:53; Gal 3:19; cf. Heb 2:2).[60] The Torah was given to be a *paidagōgos* (Gal 3:24–25), a child-custodian, which suggests that guarding and overseeing and caretaking were also the prominent tasks of the angels by whom the Torah was given.

The angels are also referred to as "principalities and powers"—whether good or bad.[61] The former term may be related to the angelic "princes" we hear about in Daniel: Gabriel, who is the (good) angelic prince of the Oikumene, and the (wicked) princes of Persia and Greece (Dan 10).[62] The titles given to these angelic rulers emphasize their authority over man and remind us that, in this period from creation to Christ, man was "lower than the angels."

Nevertheless, throughout this period God did begin to exalt man, giving to him (or giving *back* to him) some tasks that were being performed by angels.

After casting Adam out of the Garden, Yahweh set cherubim at the entrance to the Garden, with a sword and fire. But when the Tabernacle is built as a new Garden-Sanctuary, there are woven cherubim on the veil but the guardians are men, priests and

---

59. "The chief tutor originally was Lucifer, but he betrayed his calling in the Garden. So the Son of God entered as the Angel of the Lord to guide humanity toward maturity. Before He was the Second Adam, Jesus was the Second Lucifer. Throughout the Old Creation, we see the Angel of the Lord and His spirit angels supervising and judging humanity" (James B. Jordan, *The Vindication of Jesus Christ: A Brief Reader's Guide to Revelation*, 3rd ed. [Monroe, LA: Athanasius, 2008], 9).

60. That the Torah was given by angels gives added significance to Paul's statement in Galatians 1:8: "Even though we, *or an angel from heaven*, should preach to you a gospel contrary to that which we have preached to you, let him be accursed" (NKJV).

61. The "principalities and powers" in Ephesians 6:12 and Colossians 2:15 are clearly enemies, but the phrase is used more broadly elsewhere in Scripture (Eph 1:21; 3:10; Col 1:16; 2:10).

62. Cf. Jordan, *Handwriting on the Wall*, 526, 528–32.

Levites. Moreover, given that the Tabernacle is a world model with the Holy Place and Most Holy Place representing the heavens and the highest heavens, the priests in these places are symbolically parallel to the angels in the heavenly places.[63]

Similarly, we can trace the development in messengers from the Exodus to the coming of Christ. At the Exodus, it was the Angel of Yahweh who led Israel to the Promised Land (Exod 23:20, 23; 33:2; Num 20:16).[64] In Malachi 3:1, Yahweh says, "I send My messenger [or: angel], and he will prepare the way before Me" (NKJV). And in Mark 1:2, drawing on both Exodus and Malachi, we find this: "I send My messenger [or: angel] before Your face, who will prepare Your way before You" (NKJV). But that messenger is identified as John the Baptizer.

What has happened? The role associated with the Angel of Yahweh has now been given to a man, John the Baptizer—another indication of Israel's growth in maturity. While still "lower than the angels," men begin to take on the tasks of angels, even in the time of the Old Creation and Old Covenant. In fact, as we progress from creation to the coming of Christ, we see fewer and fewer messages brought by angels—including the Angel of Yahweh—and more and more messages brought by men, and particularly by the prophets.[65]

Angels and the Son of Man

At various points in Jesus' life, we hear about angels. An angel announces His conception (Matt 1:20; Luke 1:26–38). Angels announce His birth (Luke 2:9–15). An angel warns Joseph to flee and then tells him to return (Matt 2:13, 19). Angels minister to Jesus in the wilderness (Matt 4:11; Mark 1:13). An angel strengthens Him in Gethsemane (Luke 22:43). Angels appear to the women after His resurrection (Matt 28:2, 5; Luke 24:23; John 20:12).

The frequent involvement of angels reminds us that Jesus was born "lower than the angels." As Paul puts it, He was "born of a woman, born under the law"—that is under the Torah given by angels—"to redeem those who were under the law, that we might receive the adoption as sons" (Gal 4:4 NKJV; cf. 3:19). Jesus came under the Torah and under the angels in order that we might be exalted, as full-grown sons of God, to receive our inheritance, the dominion promised to man in Genesis 1 and Psalm 8.

---

63. Cf. James B. Jordan, *Through New Eyes*, 207–11. Arthur Kay, "Saul's Nakedness Exposed," in *Christendom Essays*, ed. James B. Jordan (Niceville, FL: Transfiguration, 1997) points out that Israelites wore garments with four "wings" (Deut 22:12) and that elsewhere in the Bible the creatures that have four wings are the cherubim (Ezek 1:3, 6–11; 10:15–22; Exod 25:20; 37:9; 1 Kgs 8:27; 1 Chr 28:18; 2 Chr 3:11–13). "So when the LORD clothed Israel in four-winged garments He was saying they were like the cherubim. This clothing represented a restoration to a role of guardianship or priesthood for Israel. . . . Now being clothed with vestments like the cherubim, Israel was being, once again, invested with the office of guarding the holiness of God" (120).

64. This Angel is identified with Yahweh Himself (compare Exod 13:21 and Exod 14:19) and was the Second Person of the Trinity. But He is referred to as an "Angel," as is fitting for the time when man was "lower than the angels" and in which the angels served as man's tutors.

65. Cf. Kline, *Images of the Spirit*, 58–59, 78–79. Kline notes that in 2 Chronicles 36:15–16; Haggai 1:13, where *malak* ("angel, messenger") is used for prophets.

Hebrews 2 makes a similar point:

> We see Jesus, who for a little while was made lower than the angels, because of the suffering of death crowned with glory and honor, so that by the grace of God He might taste death for everyone, because it was fitting that he, for whom and by whom all things exist, in bringing many sons to glory, should make the pioneer of their salvation perfect [or: mature] through suffering.[66]

Being made "lower than the angels" leads to Jesus suffering death.[67] He is, after all, the "son of Adam," and the death-sentence pronounced on Adam in Genesis 3 is echoed again and again throughout the account of Adam's sons (Gen 5: "And he died"). What must "the son of Adam" do? He must die.

But death is not the end of the end of the story. Precisely because He suffered death, Hebrews says, he was "crowned with glory and honor" (2:9). His suffering was the way in which He was made perfect or fully mature—and that as the "pioneer" of the salvation of the "many sons" He was to bring "to glory" with Him (2:10).[68]

Now Jesus has been exalted above the angels (Heb 1:3–13) and the whole world has been placed under Him. Hebrews 2 says that God "has not put the world to come, of which we speak, in subjection to angels" (2:5 NKJV). Rather, it goes on to say, quoting Psalm 8, God has "put all in subjection under" man, and specifically under Jesus (2:8b–9). This is what it means for Jesus to be "the son of man," as Jesus so often calls himself: it means to be *the* "son of Adam" of Psalm 8, to be lower than the angels for a while, in order to suffer death, and by that route to be exalted and glorified and given dominion over all.

What is this "world to come" of which Hebrews speaks? It is not heaven or a future millennium or the new heavens and new earth after the general resurrection. Rather, it is the world of the New Creation and of the New Covenant, which was established through Jesus' suffering, death, resurrection, ascension, and outpouring of the Spirit at Pentecost, but which overlapped for a time with the Old Creation and the Old Covenant. James Jordan explains:

> The New Creation began at Pentecost, when the ascended and enthroned Jesus sent the Spirit to enable us to disciple the nations and in that sense to rule the world. The Old Creation did not end at that time, however, because God gave the Jews and God-fearing Gentiles a period of time to make the transfer from the Old to the

---

66. This is my slight modification of the translation offered by Hughes, *Hebrews*, 87, 97. For an explanation of the chiastic structure of this verse—which accounts for why Jesus' tasting death here comes *after* His being crowned with glory and honor, when it actually happened *before*—see the discussion in Hughes, *Hebrews*, 90–91.

67. On "tasting death," which means nothing less than fully experiencing death, see Hughes, *Hebrews*, 91–92.

68. Earlier, we noted that Hirsch takes *gittith* in the title of Psalm 8 as a reference to wine pressing and thus to oppression leading to joy. At first glace, that interpretation does not seem to fit Psalm 8. But interestingly, it does fit the fulfillment of Psalm 8, for the transition from "lower than the angels" to "crowned with glory and honor" is precisely Jesus' suffering, death, and resurrection. Mind you, someone who takes *muth-labben* (from Psalm 9) to be Psalm 8's postscript and understands it to mean "Death of the Son" might argue that it fits just as well.

PART ONE: BIBLICAL STUDIES

> New. According to Matthew 23:34–38, all the sins and crimes of the Old Creation were to be rolled up and judged with the destruction of Jerusalem, which happened in AD 70.[69]

Jesus receives dominion at His ascension, and Christian tradition has wisely taken Psalm 8 as an Ascension Day psalm.[70] Ephesians 1 alludes to Psalm 8, when it says that God raised Christ

> from the dead and seated Him at His right hand in the heavenly places, far above all principality and power and might and dominion, and every name that is named, not only in this age but also in that which is to come. And He put all things under His feet, and gave Him to be head over all things to the church, which is His body, the fullness of Him who fills all in all. (Eph 1:20–22 NKJV)

Jesus, Paul says, has been exalted over "all principality and power," titles given to angels in the Bible. He is enthroned over everything, "not only in this age but also in that which is to come"—that is, not only in the time Paul is writing but also in the age after AD 70, after the end of the Old Creation and Old Covenant.

The first exercise of Jesus' exaltation over the angels is a war in heaven. Revelation 12 presents Jesus' birth and ascension back to back and then tells us how Michael and his angels defeated the dragon and his angels. Michael here is Jesus in His role as Angel of Yahweh.[71] Jesus is exalted over the angels, including over the angelic serpent Adam could not defeat, and now the serpent and his hosts are cast out of heaven to earth.

This casting out is the firstfruits of Jesus' exaltation. But throughout Revelation, we hear about the further outworkings of His exaltation, specifically in connection with His vindication—and the vindication of His people—over against apostate Israel and the Judaizers.

All the way through Revelation, we hear about *angels* administering Jesus' judgments upon His enemies. Remember that it is the Old Creation, from Adam to Christ, that is under the angels' superintendence. James Jordan points out what the presence of these angels in Revelation implies: "since angels are bringing the judgments, they must be judging the world that was committed to their charge. This cannot be the world of the New Creation; it must be the world of the Old Creation."[72]

---

69. Jordan, *Vindication of Jesus Christ*, 9. Cf. Wilson, *Christ and His Rivals*, 71. Wilson's commentary helpfully shows that Hebrews as a whole is concerned with the coming end of the Old Covenant era.

70. Cf. Craigie, *Psalms 1–50*, 106.

71. Jude 9 quotes Michael as saying, "The Lord rebuke you," a phrase that appears in only one other place, on the lips of the Angel of Yahweh in Zechariah 3:1–2. This Angel is Yahweh Himself, the preincarnate Second Person of the Trinity. So if Michael ("He who is like God") is the name of the Angel of Yahweh and the Angel of Yahweh is the preincarnate Jesus, then we ought to conclude that Michael in Daniel and in Revelation 12 is Jesus in His role as Angel of Yahweh. Cf. Jordan, *Handwriting*, 530–31.

72. Jordan, *Vindication of Jesus Christ*, 9. Jordan sees Revelation 4–5 as a preview of the replacement of the angels by the saints: "We are told in 4:10 that the twenty-four archangels will fall down and worship God and cast their crowns before Him. This forecasts the drama of Revelation, for we shall find exactly twenty-four actions by archangels in the book. Each archangel in his turn comes before the Throne, removes his crown of ruling the Old Creation, and then goes forth to perform his last act of judgment against that Creation. This pile of crowns is then picked up by the saints, who enter heaven to replace the archangels as co-rulers with Jesus (20:4)" (37–38).

In other words, the fact that these judgments are administered by angels is another indication that Revelation is not about the end of the world at Christ's last coming but rather about the end of the Old Covenant and Old Creation world, that is, about the judgments that culminate in the destruction of Jerusalem in AD 70.

But before the culmination of "this age," Paul can already say that the saints are seated "in the heavenly places in Christ Jesus" (Eph 2:6 NKJV), which implies that because Jesus is in heaven the saints themselves begin to share in His rule on earth. He tells the Corinthians to judge themselves, knowing that they will judge angels (1 Cor 6:3). Already during this period, the gospel begins to go out to the nations. And already, as Revelation shows, the Church is involved in ruling the world, not least through her prayers.

But the Church of Paul's day could also look forward to something greater, to the "age to come" (Eph 1:21), to the "world to come" (Heb 2:5), to the time when, having suffered with Jesus as they followed in His steps, the "many sons" of Hebrews 2 would enter into their kingly glory and honor together with Jesus in an even greater and more obvious way than they had during the interim period when Old and New overlapped.[73]

What was once the "world to come" is now the world in which we live, the fullness of the New Creation and New Covenant. Unlike the old world, this new world is not subject to angels. Instead, it is subject to King Jesus and to His people, who are enthroned not only over the earth but even over the heavenly realms and over the angels.

Now the judgments and blessings that angels administered in the previous era are administered by men. As Jordan says, speaking of the application of Revelation to today's situation, "the spirit-angels who blow the trumpets of God's word in Revelation translate into Christian preachers and evangelists today."[74] It is through the Church, not through angels, that Jesus sends out His gospel—but also His judgments—to the four corners of the world. Now the Church rides forth with Jesus to conquer all nations (Rev 19:11–21).[75]

Christ—the *totus Christus*, head and body—rules heaven and earth, all the works of Yahweh's fingers, and He is extending His dominion—and ours—until all enemies fall and everything in heaven and earth is under His feet (1 Cor 15:24–27).

---

73. The exaltation of the saints and their fully receiving the kingdom *after* the slaying of the beast in Daniel 7 seem to be related to the glorification of Jesus and the subjection of the "world to come" to the "many sons," not to mention the theme of rule over the beasts later in Psalm 8, but I cannot discuss Daniel 7 here. See Jordan, *Handwriting on the Wall*, 327–408, and especially 390–95, 405–6.

74. Jordan, *Vindication of Jesus Christ*, 10.

75. Our own experience is different but also similar to that of Jesus and of these first century saints. The only path to glory is the path of the "son of Adam," the path of death and resurrection (cf. Hughes, *Hebrews*, 88). Although we do not now move from being "lower than the angels" to being "crowned with glory and honor," as Jesus did, and though the transition into the fullness of the New Creation in AD 70 was a once-for-all event, we do continue to move—by way of death and resurrection—from glory to glory, as Paul makes clear throughout 2 Corinthians.

PART ONE: BIBLICAL STUDIES

WORLDWIDE DOMINION (8:6B–8; LINES 12–16)

> [12]*All things you have put under his feet:*
> [13]*Sheep and oxen—all of them,*
> [14]*And also beasts of the field,*
> [15]*Bird of heaven and fish of the sea,*
> [16]*Whatever passes through the paths of the seas.*

Under Man's Feet

Line 12 is, of course, closely related to line 11: "You will make him ruler over the works of your hands." Both have to do with rule. But we must also note the differences between these lines.

For one thing, line 12 begins a new subsection of the Psalm, detailing the things Yahweh has put under man's feet. This subsection, like the previous ones, is roughly chiastic in structure, though the chiasm is not as obvious and not as obviously significant as some of the others. Line 12 speaks of "feet" and line 16 of "paths," creating something of a parallel. Both line 13 and line 15 involve pairs: "sheep and oxen" and "bird . . . and fish." At the center of the chiasm are the "beasts of the field."

There is another difference between line 12 and line 11. Where line 11, like line 10, uses an imperfect tense verb, best taken as referring to the future, line 12 uses one in the perfect tense: "You *have* put all things under his feet."

The change in verb tense in line 12 alerts us to the possibility that focus of this section is not primarily on the future dominion of man in Christ, though it certainly foreshadows it. Instead, David seems to be speaking about what is already the case, the dominion man received already on Day 6, when he was created (Gen 1:28).[76]

As we have already discussed, Adam did not start out as a king, but rather began his life serving in God's Garden as a priest. After eating rebelliously from the Tree of Knowledge, Adam did go out into the world to rule, though he was still under the angels and was not "crowned with glory and honor" to rule over everything in heaven and earth.

Nevertheless, God allowed man, after the fall, to begin the task of subduing the earth, taming the animals, turning them into helpers, and ruling over them—and thereby bringing to fuller expression their potential as the sorts of creatures they are.[77] It is pos-

---

76. As the structural outline at the beginning of this essay suggests, this section of Psalm 8 corresponds to Day 6 and Day 5, which are closely linked even in Genesis 1 (cf. Jordan, *Creation in Six Days*, 196). Note, too, that *six* sets of creatures are listed here.

77. The question of man's relationship to the animals is far too complex to explore here, and unfortunately few theologians have dealt with it at any length. Some comments by C. S. Lewis may help provoke further thought: "Let us here guard against one of those transmuted lumps of atheistical thought which often survive in the minds of modern believers. Atheists naturally regard the co-existence of man and the other animals as a mere contingent result of interacting biological facts; and the taming of an animal by man as a purely arbitrary interference of one species with another. The 'real' or 'natural' animal to them is the wild one, and the tame animal is an artificial or unnatural thing. But a Christian must not think so. Man was appointed by God to have dominion over the beasts, and everything a man does to an animal is either a lawful exercise, or a sacrilegious abuse, of an authority by divine right. The tame animal is therefore, in the

sible that the order in which the creatures are listed here in Psalm 8 reflects the expansion of man's dominion from sheep to sea creatures.[78]

While Adam only names the animals, Abel becomes a keeper of sheep (Gen 4:2). The word "sheep" (*tsoneh*) refers to smaller domesticated herd animals and can also include, for instance, goats. Later on, though we are not told when, men domesticated larger herd animals, such as cattle (*alaphim*).[79] It is here that man's dominion begins. Both Moses and David learn to rule Israel by serving first as shepherds.

After the Flood, God puts the dread of man "on every beast of the earth and on every bird of the heavens, on everything that creeps on the ground and on every fish of the sea" (9:2). It may have been the case, as James Jordan has suggested, that before the Flood, when wickedness was abounding, the wild beasts hunted and attacked men freely.[80] Now, however, the animals will fear godly Noah and his offspring. God gives the animals into Noah's hand, allowing him to eat them—which is an increased form of dominion—and also to kill animals and men that shed man's blood (Gen 9:1–7).[81]

We have thus moved from tame animals to the "beasts of the field" (*bahamoth saday*),[82] a category that may include animals such as camels or even elephants, but might

---

deepest sense, the only 'natural' animal—the only one we see occupying the place it was made to occupy, and it is on the tame animal that we must base all our doctrine of beasts. Now it will be seen that, in so far as the tame animal has a real self or personality, it owes this almost entirely to its master. If a good sheepdog seems 'almost human' that is because a good shepherd has made it so" (C. S. Lewis, *The Problem of Pain* [London: Geoffrey Bles, 1940; reprint, London: Collins, 1977], 126–27.

Pet owners are sometimes charged with "anthropomorphizing" their pets, in the sense of treating them as if they were human. But if Lewis is correct—and it seems to me that he is—loved pets do develop personalities that are, in some ways, human-like; animals that are loved by humans are, in some sense, anthropomorphed. To what degree could this development reach? Perhaps the story of Balaam's donkey gives us a glimpse of the potential of animals. It is not God (or an angel) who speaks *through* the donkey. The donkey herself speaks, reminding Balaam of her history with him: "Am I not your donkey on which you have ridden, ever since I became yours, to this day? Was I ever disposed to do this to you?" (Num 22:30 NKJV).

78. "The list moves outward from domestic animals, which are near the feet of human dominion, to wild beasts and then to those farthest from the seat of human rule—but all are under man" (Jordan, *Studies in the Psalter 2*, 1–2). Perhaps this organizational principle accounts for the reversal of Day 5 and Day 6 in the seven-day structure of Psalm 8: The creatures made on Day 5 are the ones farthest from man, while the ones created on Day 6 are closer, designed to be his primary helpers.

79. *Alaphim* is related to a verb that means "to learn" and to an adjective meaning "tame" (BDB). Hirsch, however, points out that Genesis 25:16 uses the word "for leaders among men" and takes it to refer to "those beasts that assume leadership in the herd by virtue of their superior strength and larger size." "Sheep and cattle" thus has the sense of "the tame and the strong" (*Psalms*, 55–56).

80. James B. Jordan, "Rebellion, Tyranny, and Dominion in the Book of Genesis," in *Tactics of Christian Resistance*, ed. Gary North (Tyler, TX: Geneva, 1983), 48.

81. It is important to recognize that it is not *all* men who enjoy this dominion over wild beasts. Genesis 9:1–7 is addressed to the godly—to Noah and to his sons—and not to "mankind in general." Cf. James B. Jordan, "Who Rules the Land? The Meaning of the Noahic Covenant (Part 1)," *Biblical Horizons* 19 (Nov. 1990).

82. Hirsch describes these animals as "the beasts of the great outdoors, which do not attach themselves to men of their own accord." Man tames them, too, Hirsch says, "so that they become pedestals for his might and dominion," noting the relationship between *behemah* and *bamah* ("high place") (*Psalms*, 56; cf. Hirsch, *The Pentateuch: Genesis*, trans. Isaac Levy [1963; reprint, Gateshead: Judaica, 1989], 29).

also include wild animals. Some wild animals can be tamed so that they serve man; others are subdued by being defeated. David kills lions and bears to rescue his sheep (1 Sam 17:34–37), a foreshadowing of what he would later do to Goliath and the other enemies of God's people. David could say that he had sheep and oxen, as well as the beasts of the field, under his feet.

Next in Psalm 8 we come to the more distant creatures, "bird of heaven and fish of the sea." Birds may be caught and may even be tamed and made serviceable to man. Think of songbirds, talking parrots, homing pigeons, or hunting falcons. But in general, while sheep and cattle tend to stay close to man and even beasts share the earth with man, birds are "of the heavens." They are associated with a different realm, and their ability to fly makes them harder to catch or tame.

There may be another sort of distance as well. The longer you live with *and love* a cat or a dog, the more human it seems in many ways. Some birds may develop personalities as well. But do they develop the sort of close bond with their owners that we associate with dogs or cats? I suspect not.[83]

As for fish, the distance from man is even greater, both literally and psychologically. Go to sea and you leave the land animals behind; go farther to sea and you will reach a point where you no longer see birds. When you see a bird again, you will know that you are nearing land. Fish go where beasts and birds cannot.

But there is a psychological distance, too. I suspect that, no matter how long you keep a goldfish, it will not come to seem more human the way a dog will. Fish are likewise less tameable, less easily trained. Though a dolphin—which, in the Bible, would fall into the general category of "fish"—can be trained to some degree, few other fish can. A goldfish in a bowl may be tame—it will not attack you—but it has not really been *tamed* by man; it is simply docile. You may keep it in a bowl, but you cannot communicate with it and it will not do your bidding.

Finally, Psalm 8 comes to the most distant creatures of all, the ones we know the least about: "whatever passes through the paths of the seas." What are these creatures? *Who knows?* But whatever might be out in the depths of the seas would also come under man's sway.

But we can go a bit farther. In Genesis 1, on Day 5, God makes not only the fish and the birds, but also the *tanninim*, the great sea creatures or "dragons."[84] These creatures are not included explicitly in the dominion promised to man in Genesis 1:28, and it is clear from what God says about one of them, Leviathan, that man cannot rule them (Job 41).[85] God made them to play in the seas (Ps 104:26), and they do so as a demonstration of God's almighty power and as a reminder that man does not have full dominion over

---

83. But I am not a bird owner. Perhaps someone who owns a cockatiel will tell me that I am mistaken and that he has as close a bond with his bird as another person does with her cat. Still, it seems to me that it would be *harder* to develop that close bond with a bird than it would be to develop a bond with a dog or cat. It would be for me, at least.

84. Cf. Exodus 7:9, 10, 12; Deuteronomy 32:33; Nehemiah 2:13; Job 7:12; Psalms 74:13; 91:13; 148:7; Isaiah 27:1; 51:9; Jeremiah 51:34; Lamentations 4:3. In the Septuagint, this word is sometimes translated as *drakōn*. James Jordan refers to these creatures as "aquatic dinosaurs" (*Creation in Six Days*, 195).

85. Ibid., 199.

every creature—at least, not in the time of the Old Creation. They are God's pets; they will not be man's.

The tannins, while they themselves are good as creatures made by God and are summoned to praise Him (Ps 148:7), sometimes represent evil or hostile forces. Satan is a dragon (Rev 12),[86] and as such could not be subdued by God's people until the death and resurrection of Christ. As well, large Gentile powers are sometimes described as Leviathan (e.g., Ps 74:14; Isa 27:1) or as sea monsters (Jer 51:34; cf. Jonah1:17—2:10); while God does sometimes defeat these Leviathans, they do not become subject to Israel.[87]

But Psalm 8 hints that that situation will not hold true forever. While the tannins are not included explicitly in the dominion mandate in Genesis 1:28 and while Job 41 suggests that the Leviathan cannot be tamed by man, Psalm 8 proclaims that "whatever passes through the paths of the seas" has been placed under man's feet—at least, in the sense that the other creatures have.[88] Not every bear has become fully subservient to man. Not even every goat has. But the dominion over them has nevertheless been given *in principle*, though it remains for man to extend his dominion to these creatures *in fact*.

So, too, with whatever is actually in the sea and whatever it symbolizes. Dominion over the tannins is not something that man has achieved (and, in fact, it seems that most of the tannins are gone, except perhaps in a certain Loch in Scotland). But in that he was ruling over Israel, the royal priesthood, the people set apart from the world for the sake of the world and in whom all nations would be blessed, David really did have at least a shadow dominion over all the tannins, over all the world empires of his day—a dominion that began with him crushing the head of Goliath, who was dressed like a serpent in "scales" (*qasqassim,* 1 Sam 17:5) and who represented the serpent of old (Gen 3:15). Already, David could sing that (symbolically, at least) "whatever passes through the paths of the seas" was already put under his feet.

He could sing that song in hope, looking forward to a further extension *in fact* of the dominion already given to man on earth. More and more sheep and cattle will be domesticated. More and more beasts will be made subservient. Man's rule will extend so that even birds of the heavens who normally fly above man and the fish and other creatures—whatever they may be—who inhabit the seas will be under man's feet. Do not lose sight of the significance of the word "paths" here in line 16: the *feet* of line 12 will one day walk those *paths*, as it were, as they now walk over the earth.[89] One day, the whole world will be under man's rule.

---

86. Jordan suggests that "In Job, the fire-breathing Leviathan ruled by God at the end of the book relates to the fire-sending Satan at the beginning of the book" (ibid.). On the basis of this association between angels (e.g., Satan) and the tannins (e.g., Leviathan), Jordan writes: "Let me suggest that the tannins no longer exist in the earth precisely because angels no longer rule humanity" (199).

87. Ibid.

88. The Targum makes explicit what Psalm 8 only hints at, dropping the word "whatever" and substituting "Leviathan," so that this line in Psalm 8 reads "Leviathan that passes in the paths of the seas" (*Targums of Psalms*, 38).

89. In the light of Psalm 8, Jesus' walking on water suggests that He is the "son of Adam" who will have dominion even over "whatever passes through the paths of the seas." As the sea is literally under His feet, so too will be all the Gentile nations around Israel that the sea often symbolizes in Scripture.

PART ONE: BIBLICAL STUDIES

The Expansion of Man's Dominion

How will this extension of man's dominion take place? It is important to read Psalm 8 both as a *chiasm,* paying attention to the relationships between the corresponding sections, and as a *narrative*.

If we read Psalm 8 as a *chiasm*, we notice that this section is parallel to the earlier section about the battling babies. In lines 3 and 4, we have two sets of pairs: "children and infants" and "enemy and avenger." Here, in lines 13 and 15, we have another set of pairs: "sheep and oxen" and "bird . . . and fish."

That structural parallel alerts us to the thematic parallels and helps us understand how man achieves his dominion over all the creatures and over the people and powers they represent. It is not a matter of hamfisted mastery or lording it over others, after the example of the rulers of the Gentiles (Mark 10:42). It is not through Goliath-like or Saul-like reliance on one's own strength, armor, and weaponry (1 Sam 17). Rather, it is through humility.

It is the "children and infants," and those who become like them, who receive the kingdom of God (Mark 10:13–15). It is the ones who, like David, are concerned for Yahweh's honor who crush the head of Goliath. It is the meek who inherit the earth (Matt 5:5). It is by Christlike humility, by the way of the cross, that we become those who "silence enemy and avenger," who put the beasts under their feet and who extend their dominion to "whatever passes through the paths of the seas."

But if we read Psalm 8 as a *narrative*, we recognize that this section (lines 12–16) *follows* the central section about man's being "crowned with glory and honor" to rule over the works of Yahweh's fingers, including the heavens, the moon and stars, which share in Yahweh's splendor.

While man was promised dominion over the earth already in Genesis 1 and while godly man began to exercise that dominion before the coming of Christ, it was not until Jesus was born "lower than the angels," died and rose again and ascended to glory above the heavenly realms, that God's kingdom was established on earth and man began more fully to enter into and expand the dominion of Psalm 8.

First came exaltation over all things in heaven; now comes exaltation over all things on earth. The serpent is been cast down from heaven to earth (Rev 12) and now "the kingdoms of this world have become the kingdoms of our Lord and of His Christ" (Rev 11:15). Now at last, a man—Jesus Christ—has put the tannins and what they symbolize under His feet. And if even the tannins have become and are becoming His footstool, will not all the sheep and oxen, the beasts of the field, the birds of heaven and the fish of the sea?

That is the future Paul expects. In Ephesians 1, he cites this passage from Psalm 8, as we have seen above, emphasizing that God "put all things under His feet" (Eph 1:22). But in 1 Corinthians 15, he alludes to this passage again, combining it with Psalm 110: "Then comes the end, when He delivers the kingdom to God the Father, when He puts an end to all rule and all authority and power. For He must reign till He has put all enemies under His feet. The last enemy that will be destroyed is death. For 'He has put all things under His feet'" (1 Cor 15:24–27a NKJV).

God *put* all things under Jesus' feet—that is what Paul says in Ephesians 1. God *will* put all things, and especially all enemies, under Jesus' feet—that is what Paul says in 1 Corinthians 15. They are under His feet already: Jesus *is* already Lord over heaven and earth. And therefore they will not be able to persist in their enmity. The enemy and avenger will be silenced and will fall under His feet.

And who are His feet? We are, for we are the body of Christ.[90] It is to the Church that Paul promises: "The God of peace will crush Satan under your feet shortly" (Rom 16:20).

YAHWEH'S SUPREMACY REAFFIRMED (8:9; LINE 17)

[17] *Yahweh, our Lord, how supreme is your name in all the earth!*

At the close of Psalm 8, we come back to the affirmation that opened the psalm: Our Lord Yahweh's name is supreme in all the earth. But this is not simple repetition.

In fact, in a text as in music there is no such thing as mere identical repetition. You may play two G notes in a row, but when we hear the second one we also *remember* the first one so that the second one does not give us exactly the same experience the first one did. The last sentence of a story may be word for word the same as the opening sentence, but now we read it in light of all that has happened in between—and as a result a line that meant little to us at the outset of the story can shock us at the end.[91]

So it is here. Pull line 1 and line 17 out of the psalm and lay them alongside each other and you will spot no differences between them. The same words appear in the same order. But what a difference the intervening material makes.

When we first heard the acclamation in line 1, we did not know in what way Yahweh's name was supreme in all the earth. We knew that He was our Lord, our Master, and our initial inclination—which we followed above—was to think of other references in the Scriptures to His supreme power in creation and in particular in His conquest of our enemies.

But then Psalm 8 describes how Yahweh set His splendor upon the firmament-heavens so that they reflect and represent Him and how He demonstrates His superiority on earth by using the weakest of His servants to defeat His foes. His victory through their weakness makes His name supreme in all the earth.

The story continues however. The night sky is full of the lights appointed to reflect Yahweh's glory and rule on His behalf, but they also remind David of God's plans for man. The Son of Adam is a needy man, lower than the angels, but Yahweh will exalt Him to rule even over the heavens that share Yahweh's splendor and therefore also over the earth, as Yahweh puts all creatures under His feet and silences all His foes.

The narrative thus starts with Yahweh's supremacy, centers on Yahweh's exaltation of man, and culminates in Yahweh's supremacy again—but now we see that Yahweh's name

---

90. Wilson, *Christ and His Rivals*, 35, 75.

91. See the discussion of texts as music in Peter J. Leithart, *Deep Exegesis: The Mystery of Reading Scripture* (Waco, TX: Baylor University Press, 2009), 144–48.

is supreme because of what He has done for Jesus Christ, *the* Son of Adam, and for us in Him. The "six days" of the psalm lead to this "sabbath" rest, with Yahweh enthroned supreme and with man exalted to share in His glory and honor.

It is important to stress that Psalm 8 is not about *everyone*. Not everyone is crowned with "glory and honor" (cf. Rom 2:5–10) to rule over all the works of Yahweh's fingers. But Jesus is. And we are, as members of His body. As Douglas Wilson has written: "Jesus Christ is not the *isolated* perfect man. Jesus Christ is the new mankind, he is the new Adam, he is the new race of man. And all who are in him are included in this glorious new dominion."[92]

Hengstenberg is right when he says that the theme of the psalm is "The greatness of God in the greatness of man"—not man in general, but man in Christ. The glory of Jesus, the son of Adam and the new Adam, to which this psalm looks forward, does not threaten Yahweh's glory, because glory is not a zero-sum game. Rather, Yahweh is exalted even more—His name is even more supreme in all the earth—as a result of His exaltation of Christ, of the *totus Christus*, Jesus and His Church, to the highest place, above the angels, above the heavens, above all principality and power and every name that is named.

~

Dear John,

This is great stuff, and I certainly don't have anything to add. You've persuaded me at every point where you correct my initial brief foray into this psalm. But what can I add? Here are some remarks on Psalms 8–15 from my ongoing studies, to which you referred in your essay, amended in the light of your essay.

Recalling that Psalm 9–10 is one psalm, our seven psalms range from Psalm 8 to Psalm 15. Psalm 8 is clearly concerned with creation, and Psalm 15 is clearly concerned with who is fit to ascend to God's house to join with Him. Hence, the brackets of this second set of seven psalms seem again to arise from Genesis 1.

Beyond that, is there any kind of overall structure to these seven psalms? At the center is a chiastic psalm, Psalm 12, which moves basically: wicked—God—wicked. On either side are two psalms that are roughly parallel, Psalms 11 and 13. Both move from the wicked to God. Both mention the heart in the first part ("upright in heart," Ps 11; "sorrow in my heart," Ps 13). Both speak of looking and inspecting/judging in the second half ("eyes observe, eyelids examine," Ps 11; "Look! . . .enlighten mine eyes," Ps 13).

While there is a rough chiasm in Psalms 11–13, there seems no link between Psalm 9–10 and Psalm 14. With Genesis 1 as background, however, it is clear that Psalm 14 is a reflection on the sin of Adam, the "fool." Adam is mentioned four times in this set of seven psalms (Pss 8, 12 [2x], 14), but not once in the first set of seven. In Psalm 14, God examines the sons of Adam, thus providing a link with the sixth day.

It requires a bit more "advanced" understanding to recognize the second day in Psalms 9–10, but it is there. Psalm 9–10 is an alphabetical acrostic. The alphabet is the

---

92. Wilson, *Christ and His Rivals*, 34.

Word of God, the (Greek) Alpha-through-Omega, the (Hebrew) Aleph-through-Tav (or Urim-through-Thummim, which words begin with Aleph and Tav respectively). This is the "firmament" between God and man: language, the word—or Word—of God. This is why there are so many alphabetic acrostics in the Bible, and why the "oracle" used to consult God consists of Aleph (Urim) and Tav (Thummim). When two persons communicate, they use language as the go-between, as the medium, as the "firmament." Similarly, God employs language, which ultimately is the Second Person of Himself (John 1), to communicate with us. This is what is "behind" Psalm 9–10 and is what relates this psalm to the firmament between heaven and earth.

How does Psalm 8 shed light on this sequence of psalms? In *Studies in the Psalter* for 2004, I showed how meditating on the Teaching of God "day and night" introduces the first set of seven psalms, all of which are about evening and morning, day and night. Psalm 8 begins with God's supreme name over all, which is what Psalm 8 is about. That statement repeats at the end of Psalm 8, after man has been elevated and glorified, and man's ascending to join God is what Psalm 15 is about.

"Day 2" in Psalm 8 tells us God has enthroned His splendor upon the firmament heavens. If I am right, this connects with the firmament-alphabet of Psalm 9–10, that God's Word is His enthroned splendor.

It seems to me that it is the "Day 3" sentence in Psalm 8 that sets up the rest of this second cycle of seven psalms. God intends to deal with oppressors, enemies, and avengers. Such enemies are found not only in Psalms 11–14, but also in the alphabetical Psalm 9–10. In the "Day 4" position in Psalm 8 we find man enthroned above the stars, while in Psalm 12 (the fourth in this cycle) it is the wicked who "strut about on every side when vileness is exalted among the sons of Adam."

Hence, at present I would see Psalm 8 as introducing man as the one to be glorified, but this is followed by five psalms about the wickedness and folly of man, which must be defeated by God. At the end, however, God being victorious, the righteous is indeed able to ascend to join God in glory upon His holy hill.

Jim

2

Judah's Life from the Dead

The Gospel of Romans 11

Tim Gallant

James Jordan's work is marked by a very strong partial preterist hermeneutic.[1] He understands many texts as referring to AD 70 that even fellow partial preterists refer to the future. One such text is Romans 11, frequently taken to refer to a mass future conversion of the preponderance of Israel. Jordan suggests that the promise in this passage was fulfilled by the time Jerusalem fell and that thereafter there is no ongoing significance for Israel as a people. Her identity has been taken up fully into the Church.[2]

My task here is one of appreciative dissent. We will work not only with Romans 11 itself, but also with prophecies, types, and motifs (hallmarks of Jordan's own work) that I believe lend themselves to the more traditional view.[3]

PAUL'S ARGUMENT IN ROMANS 11:11–32[4]

In Romans 11, Paul is wrestling with the place of Israel. Has God rejected His people (Rom 11:1)? Paul, identifying himself among a remnant, bears witness that God has not rejected His foreknown people (11:1bff.). But nonetheless, while the elect remnant has obtained the salvation Israel sought, the rest of the nation was hardened (11:7).

Some go no further with the entire chapter: the remnant are saved, and the rest do not really count. No significant alteration of this situation is to be expected.

---

1. *Partial preterism* generally takes many texts considered by others to be prophecies of the future as referring to events which are now past to us and, in particular, to the events surrounding the destruction of Jerusalem in AD 70.

2. James B. Jordan, "The Future of Israel Reconsidered: Another Look at Romans 11," Biblical Horizons Occasional Paper 18 (Aug. 1994).

3. I am not here reproducing or interacting with all of Jordan's bases for rejecting the traditional reading of Romans 11. For a cursory point-by-point response, see my essay, "Salvation of Gentile and Jew." Online: http://www.biblicalstudiescenter.org/interpretation/Israel2JordanResponse.pdf.

4. For additional treatment of this passage, see my essay, "All Israel: The Saved in Romans 11.26." Online: http://www.biblicalstudiescenter.org/interpretation/rom11_26.htm.

PART ONE: BIBLICAL STUDIES

Romans 11:11–15

But Paul indicates otherwise. In Romans 11:11, Paul denies that the mass of Israel stumbled "in order that [*hina*] they might fall." Surely they *did* fall, but that was not *the stated purpose* of the stumble. "Rather through their trespass salvation has come to the Gentiles" (ESV)—and even this in turn aims to make them jealous, indicating that God has a further purpose for them.[5]

And then, in verse 12, Paul says something that appears rather enigmatic: "Now if their trespass means riches for the world, and if their failure means riches for the Gentiles, how much more their fullness?"

Although Christ's crucifixion resulted in salvation for Gentiles, Israel's "trespass" here is not simply her role in that. Paul has been stressing a *continued* hardening, "down to this very day" (11:8). Although the rejection of Christ and giving Him up to crucifixion was doubtless definitive, Israel's ongoing hardness somehow favors the Gentiles.

In verses 13–14, Paul gives, in the example of his own ministry, a further hint of the mysterious interplay between Israel and the nations. Just as Israel's fall means *present* riches for the world and her promised rescue means *future* riches, so there is a dynamic at work between Jew and Gentile in the apostolic mission. Paul the Jew, himself demonstration of God's commitment to Israel (11:1), is the apostle to the Gentiles, and yet even here part of his purpose is to make his kinsmen jealous, that some may be saved.

But *some* is Paul's rather modest hope for his *own* ministry. Ultimately, he anticipates much more. He has already connected both Israel's fall and her prospective blessing with great riches (11:11); in 11:15, he expands: "For if their rejection means the reconciliation of the world, what then their acceptance, except *life from the dead*?"

Various attempts have been made to understand this verse in *metaphorical* fashion.

Some, limiting Romans 11 to an account of scattered individuals being added to the remnant, take 11:15 *subjectively*: When individual Israelites believe, they are raised up from spiritual death. The problem with this take is at least twofold: (1) It overlooks the parallelism with verse 12, where the blessing of Israel's "fullness" implies great riches for *all*, including the Gentiles—indeed, a blessing that outshines the amazing salvation already granted to the Gentiles. (2) It creates an *anticlimax* to the first part of the verse: their rejection means the reconciliation of the world, but their acceptance means subjective life for individuals. This letdown is again at odds with verse 12, where the recovery in view entails a "how much more."

John Murray envisions a future conversion of Israel and suggests that this will be a great trigger that involves *even greater blessings in history for the Church*, including more mass conversions around the world.[6] But if Murray is correct that "fullness" here means "Israel as a whole," then does not "the fullness of the Gentiles" in verse 25 refer to "the world as a whole"? And if that is the case, since verse 25 says that the conversion of

---

5. This jealousy is not predicated upon Israel retaining some form of the old covenant religion or cult; Paul is drawing on Deuteronomy 32:21, where Israel's putative condition is outright idolatrous.

6. John Murray, *The Epistle to the Romans*, 2 vols. in one, New International Commentary on the New Testament (Grand Rapids: Eerdmans, 1968), 2:80–84.

Israel *follows upon* the "coming in" of the fullness of the Gentiles, what worldwide "mass conversions" would be possible? The nations as a whole would be already converted.

For his part, Jordan thinks that the "fullness" here refers to extensive conversions that took place among Jews prior to the destruction of the temple in AD 70. "Life from the dead" he takes as referring to the Church, which emerged triumphant despite widespread martyrdom in and around Jerusalem as the Roman armies were about to strike.[7] All of Jordan's evidence appears to be drawn from assumptions based upon the book of Revelation. He takes the 144,000 Israelite saints (Rev 7, 14) to refer to Paul's "remnant."[8] The only plausible conversion text he references is Revelation 11:13: seven thousand people in Jerusalem were killed in the earthquake, and "the rest were terrified and gave glory to the God of heaven" (ESV).

This evidence is slight and depends upon a particular understanding of how Revelation fits together. An in-depth reading of the the book lies well beyond our scope at present and is in any case unnecessary. Jordan's view depends upon the entire conversion taking place within Jerusalem. But this means "all Israel" excludes not only the remainder of Jews living elsewhere in Palestine, but also the masses throughout the Diaspora (the worldwide "Dispersion")—who were in fact the overwhelming majority of Israelites.[9] Therefore, even on the most generous reading of Revelation 11:13, it does not depict the salvation of a preponderance of Israel just before AD 70. (As we will see, the upshot of Paul's argument is that the preponderance of a particular generation of Israel will be re-engrafted, i.e., converted.)

Leaving Revelation aside, there is no record (biblical or extrabiblical) of mass Israelite conversions just prior to AD 70. As Paul writes Romans in the mid-to-late 50s, the initial wave of Jewish conversions has largely run aground. Whatever conversions may have occurred in the following decade could not have brought up the number of Jews in the Christian Church to something appropriate to describe as "the fullness" of Israel (11:12) or "all Israel" (11:26)—particularly when we consider that these phrases stand in stark contrast to the modest "remnant" language that typified believing Israel when Paul wrote Romans (11:7).

But the problem for Jordan's position is more serious. As with the other two positions we have mentioned, Jordan's view also fails to explain why Israel's present hardness serves as salvation, riches, and reconciliation for the Gentile world (Rom 11:11, 12, 15).

Admittedly, given Paul's principle of "to the Jew first, and also to the Greek," Jewish rejection of the gospel meant earlier Christian witness to the Gentiles—obviously a blessing. Yet regardless, the issue cannot simply mean a *delay*, as on that view, the gospel would *still* go to the world at some point. But as 11:11–12, 15 speak of Israel's fall and hardness as *life for the world*, these verses remain unaccounted for.

---

7. Jordan takes the harvest of Revelation 14:14–20 to refer to a mass martyrdom of believers ("Future of Israel," 21).

8. Ibid.

9. Exact numbers are not possible. Most Israelites did not return to Canaan following the Babylonian captivity. Estimates I have seen indicate that in the first century there were approximately three times as many Israelites in the Diaspora as in Palestine, and maybe more.

When we abandon the metaphorical interpretation of 11:15's "life from the dead," a way is opened up for the pieces of the puzzle to come together.[10] If "life from the dead" refers to *the general resurrection*, then Israel's "acceptance" (11:15's parallel to "fullness" in 11:12) is tied to the consummation, and this conversion will "trigger" the resurrection of the dead.

The implication is that had Israel not been hardened, there would have been no historical "space" for the salvation of the world.[11] Had Israel turned to Christ *en masse* at the start, the gospel would not have gone out to the ends of the earth; the resurrection would have occurred, and the eternal kingdom would have been populated by Israelites and relatively few scattered God-fearers. And yet Israel's restoration will mean the ultimate blessing: resurrection and eternal glory.

Excursus: Life from the Dead

But is Paul using the term "life from the dead" literally? Surely, yes. The full phrase is unique here, but *ek nekron* ("from the dead") is used throughout the New Testament to refer to bodily resurrection. Only once in well over thirty instances is it used metaphorically—and that usage is individual (being raised to life with Christ), not a reference to some sort of corporate revivification.[12] Lexically, literal resurrection is the most natural referent in Romans 11:15.

Moreover, a little consideration of Paul's historical context shows that the thought world of which he was a part readily associated a faithful Israel with the consummation of the messianic kingdom. The Pharisees were intent on making first century Israelites better lawkeepers, in part because they thought the messianic kingdom would arrive only when the people of the land were faithful, when Israel was serving Yahweh properly. Even the sectarian Essenes saw themselves as a reconstituted Israel working toward a faithfulness that would be acceptable enough for the ancient promises to come to fruition.[13]

We frequently ignore that sort of data, because we assume that these are simply the misguided notions of people legalistically attempting to earn God's favor. In addition, we are accustomed to what we already know: the arrival of the Messiah did *not* immedi-

---

10. Although I have many disagreements with him, I owe the initial spark for this insight to Terence L. Donaldson, *Paul and the Gentiles* (Minneapolis: Fortress, 1997), in particular, chapter 8 on Israel (215–48).

11. This is a much better explanation than the one that suggests that Israel's fall resulting in riches for the Gentiles is due to the severed branches making room for Gentiles in the covenant tree. This fails, because the tree is not limited in size, such that there must not be room for both the Gentiles and the fallen Jews. Indeed, this conclusion is implicit in Paul's statements that God can and will re-engraft the severed branches (11:23ff.), quite aside from the fact that Paul envisions the salvation of ever-increasing numbers of both Jews and Gentiles.

12. The other uses in Romans are in 4:24; 6:4, 9; 7:4; 8:11; and 10:7, 9. The metaphorical usage is at 6:13. Note that the literal meaning does not require the verb *raise* or related nouns in context (see, e.g., Heb 13:20).

13. For a New Testament analogy to this line of thought, cf. 2 Peter 3:11–12, where the Day of the Lord is apparently hastened by the holiness and godliness of believers.

ately result in the general resurrection; the establishment of the new covenant took place within what we would call "normal history," and a whole lot of time has transpired since with no bodily resurrection.

But this is not what Israel expected from the Old Testament. Many promises make sense only when we see how God has in fact acted in Christ; no first century Jew was likely to be expecting the Messiah to come twice. Even John the Baptizer, having identified Jesus as the Coming One, apparently became confused when things didn't unfold as expected (e.g., Luke 7:19). He too supposed that big things associated with the consummation of all things would occur on the heels of Jesus' unveiling. That a believer like John, Spirit-filled from the womb, assumed such things indicates that they are not merely to be dismissed as the vain imaginings of legalistic Pharisees. The last days blessings of Israel were seen—not only by Pharisees and Essenes, but also by the best of the faithful—to belong to a complex of events within which the general resurrection also belongs.

Examining things from this perspective clarifies other data in the Scripture, as well.

Note first the question the disciples ask immediately prior to Christ's ascension (Acts 1:6): "Lord, will You at this time restore the kingdom to Israel?" (ESV). We customarily treat this as a bad and wrong-headed question, and then we are forced to assume that Jesus' answer is evasive because He is exasperated with their continuing ignorance. But when the disciples' questions elsewhere are misguided, Jesus may not answer them directly, but He at least indicates that their thinking is wrong (e.g., Matt 16:5–12). Not so here: "It is not for you to know times or seasons which the Father has placed in His own authority" (1:7). This is not an answer that derides their foolishness nor an evasion of the question. Rather, the answer presupposes the validity of the assumption—that the kingdom will be restored to Israel (cf. Ezek 37:24)—while denying that the timing of the event is going to be made known to them.

This exchange occurs in the context of the ascension and the angelic affirmation of a like return. Is there the slightest hint of association between the promise of "restoration of the *kingdom*" to Israel and the return of *King* Jesus (which is bound up with the general resurrection)?

Peter's sermon in Solomon's portico makes such a connection explicit. He addresses his hearers as "men of Israel" (Acts 3:12) and exhorts them "Repent therefore, and return, that your sins may be blotted out, *in order that* times of refreshing may come from the presence of the Lord, and that He may send the Christ appointed for you, Jesus, *whom heaven must receive until the time for restoring all the things about which God spoke* by the mouth of His holy prophets long ago" (Acts 3:19–21).

Notice that Peter ties "times of refreshing" to the repentance and return of the men of Israel. We might suppose that this is an individual promise, but Peter ties these times of refreshing together with the promise of the sending of Christ, who will return at the time for the restoration of all things (cf. Acts 1:6 again) spoken of by the prophets. This suggests that, although Peter is obviously concerned with individual salvation, he believes that if Israel as a whole repents and turns, eschatological blessings will be *the result* ("in order that").

Another interesting feature here is that the Greek word "refreshing" may also have the idea of reviving or recovery of breath, giving Peter's speech resurrection overtones.

These observations point us back to the Old Testament. Paul's language of "life from the dead," the disciples' question about the restoration of the kingdom, and Peter's speech in Acts 3 all evoke the great prophecy of Ezekiel 37. Indeed, Paul's "life from the dead" language is perhaps paralleled nowhere more closely than by Ezekiel 37:9 (LXX).[14] Like Jeremiah 31, this is a new covenant prophecy. And like Jeremiah 31, Ezekiel 37 also finds adumbrations ("small fulfillments," we might say) in earlier history. Part of the promise of Ezekiel 37 is that God will place Israel in her own land (37:14), and we find a form of fulfillment of that at the time of the return from Babylon.

Yet first century Jews did not regard this chapter as a whole as fulfilled. Yahweh had promised resurrection; He had promised to put His Spirit within Israel (36:26–27) and to gather the whole of Israel into one people under David His servant as king (37:24). This did not reflect the situation at the end of exile nor of the first century. The Spirit had not come upon Israel after the manner seen in earlier days, much less in an eschatological sense. The whole of Israel was not gathered; indeed, the overwhelming majority were scattered across the nations even more than was the case during the exile. Moreover, where was the son of David?

If Ezekiel 37 was not simply fulfilled with the Cyrus-era return from exile, was it fulfilled with the life, death, resurrection, and ascension of Christ, along with Pentecost? Certainly, here the new covenant has definitively arrived, not simply by way of adumbration, but in reality. Christ does rule. The Holy Spirit has been sent.

Still, the promise of Ezekiel 37 is addressed to *the people* Israel, not to a scattered few. Even in Acts, the promised blessings of the new covenant have not come upon them as a whole. And the gathering of which Yahweh speaks has only begun; it is not completed.[15]

Ezekiel 37 cannot be completely satisfied in its fulfillment until Israel as a whole serves the Messiah. Its full force will not be in place until the revivification of the bones means, not simply a metaphorical new giving of life but literal *life from the dead*.[16] Israel's reconciliation to Yahweh under the rule of the Messiah, on the one hand, and the general resurrection, on the other, belong together not only in later first century Jewish thought; the connection is already quietly present in Old Testament prophecy, and it is *that* fact which explains why the connection is so prevalent in later Jewish thought.

The hardening of Israel, then, is a prerequisite for the triumph of the gospel throughout the nations. Apart from Israel's hardening, there is no "space" for Gentile conversion. And thus, as Paul says, Israel's failure and rejection meant riches and reconciliation for the world, and Israel's fullness and acceptance will mean life from the dead.

---

14. *Emphysēson eis tous nekrous toutous kai zēsatōsan*: "Breathe upon these *dead*, and they will *live*."

15. Note that this is true even if we take the promise to refer, not specifically to Israelites, but more generally to the gathering of believers.

16. This is supported by the use of Ezekiel 37:27 in the eschatological promise of Revelation 21:3.

Romans 11:16–24

Verse 16 looks back at the expectation of the preceding section and grounds it in the patriarchal promises: "If the firstfruits are holy, so also the lump; and if the root is holy, so also the branches."

The first metaphor alludes to Numbers 15:17–21. Upon Israel's entrance into Canaan, they were to bring the first of their dough made from the grain of the land as an offering to Yahweh. This reminded them that their whole livelihood was His gift and holy to Him, just as Israel herself was a holy nation to Him. Paul's point may be that Yahweh's choosing of the fathers impacted, not only them, but the whole of Israel—a thought that underlies 11:16's other metaphor. However, Paul has a tendency to use the firstfruits imagery to refer to early converts to the Christian faith (Rom 16:5; 1 Cor 16:15) and, given the remnant imagery earlier, his point here likely is that the present believing remnant serves as a sign and guarantee that the "lump"—the mass—of Israel remains God's special possession. This gives weight to the hope Paul has just expressed in verses 11–15.

The other image is that of the olive tree and is less ambiguous. The olive tree as a whole is something that contains "natural" branches (11:21) and "wild" branches that have been grafted in (cf. 11:24). By inferring the holiness of the branches from the holiness of the root, Paul is saying that the branches are God's holy possession on account of the fathers.[17] God remains committed to their offspring precisely because of the binding words of promise He pronounced to the patriarchs. Again, all of this grounds the hope articulated in 11:11–15.

In what follows, Paul explains that although Gentiles do not naturally have a part in Abraham, yet in grace God has engrafted these wild branches and made them partakers of the riches provided by the root of the cultivated olive tree (11:17). Meanwhile, "some" of the natural branches have been broken off; the inclusion of Gentiles and the cutting off of Israelites display both the kindness and severity of God (11:22).

This situation is not static, however. Although we can look at the cutting off of the natural branches as judgment due to Israel's fall (cf. 11:11), yet Paul makes it clear, not only that Gentiles likewise can be cut off if they fail to stand fast in faith, but also that these severed branches can be re-engrafted. Indeed, they remain "the natural branches," and therefore if God has engrafted Gentiles into Israel's root, much more will He re-engraft the natural branches (11:23–24).

There is thus *no suggestion of a "second way" of salvation for Israel*. Her fall was a stumbling over Christ (9:32–33) and, as with Gentiles, (re-)engrafting will be by way of faith in Him.

Romans 11:25–27

Paul now returns to the matter of future prospects. Even as he has already told the Gentile believers not to be boastful against the fallen branches (11:18–20), he again warns against an ignorance of God's purpose, an ignorance that will engender conceit

---

17. Cf. Romans 11:28: unbelieving Israelites are presently enemies of God, yet are beloved *for the sake of the fathers*.

(11:25a). God has hardened Israel *in part* until the fullness of the Gentiles has entered, and in this way—by means of the re-engrafting process just described—*all* Israel will be saved (11:25b–26a).

The mention of Israel's hardening refers back to 11:7: "the elect" obtained what Israel sought, but "the rest" were hardened. This hardening, depicted as a spirit of stupor, blindness, and deafness (11:8–10), has prevented the mass of Israel from obtaining what they were seeking. Paul says the *terminus ad quem* for this hardening is the entrance of "the fullness of the Gentiles."

This "fullness" in 11:25 is parallel to Israel's "fullness" in 11:12. The term is quantitative—fittingly, given the recurring contrasts between part and whole Paul has been working with throughout the chapter (e.g., firstfruits and lump). The fullness of the Gentiles is thus a form of the ancient promise that the knowledge of the Lord would fill the earth as the waters cover the sea (Isa 11:9; cf. Hab 2:14). In Scripture, *earth* (Heb. *erets*) can mean either the *land* of Israel or the inhabitable *world* as a whole. There is an implicit promise to the world in the Old Testament promises to Israel; indeed, Paul himself earlier asserts that the promise to Abraham (which in its original context gave him the land of Canaan) was that he would be "heir of the *world*" (Rom 4:13). It is thus no surprise that there is a parallel between the fullness of Israel enjoying eschatological blessings and the fullness of the Gentiles doing so.

The *Israel* in "all Israel" (11:26) maintains the referent it has carried throughout the passage. Paul does not equivocate here and turn "Israel" into "the people of God made up of Jew and Gentile," as some claim. To the contrary, the relationship of 11:26 both to the preceding and to the succeeding makes that claim impossible. The *all* of 11:26 stands in direct relationship to the *partial* hardening of 11:25, and the insistent "how much more" of 11:24 finds its natural resolution in the promise of the salvation of all Israel in 11:26. Moreover, it is this very Israel as a whole (*presently* largely made up of unbelieving, severed branches) that is the antecedent of the "they" in 11:28 ("they are enemies on your account"). It is therefore utterly impossible to make "all Israel" mean something other than Israel in distinction from Gentiles.

What then does the "all" convey? The earlier "fullness" terminology provides a good hint. In Scripture, "all Israel" is frequently used rather broadly to refer to the nation as a whole, without necessarily including every Israelite without exception. Israel is taken substantially but not exhaustively (e.g., Judg 8:27; 1 Sam 13:20; 2 Sam 3:37; Acts 4:10; 13:24). More specifically, given the thematic context of Romans 11, the promise here echoes Ezekiel's prophecy of restoration to "*all* the house of *Israel*" (*pas oikos Israēl*; Ezek 37:11 LXX) or "*all* the sons of *Israel*" (*pantas tous huious Israēl*; 37:16).

In 11:26b–27, Paul indicates that this restoration also accords with the prophecy of Isaiah 59:20–21: "The Deliverer will come from Zion; He will turn back ungodliness from Jacob. And this to them [is/will be] My covenant, when[ever] I take away their sins."

Since elsewhere in the New Testament, similar prophecies are taken to be fulfilled, it seems unlikely that Paul can be referring to a future event. Has Christ not yet come to forgive sins?

It must be observed that the promise is concerned, not merely with *individuals* being relieved of guilt, but with *the restoration of Israel as a whole*. There will be global fear of Yahweh as His glory will be revealed over the whole earth (Isa 59:19). The point is not merely that forgiveness of sins will suddenly be *available* to *individuals* (that was always available), but that *in actuality* not merely individuals, but *"Jacob" as a whole* will be restored to a full relationship with Yahweh through His Redeemer, with all the eschatological blessings that entails. Christ *has* come to *accomplish* that, but the *application* still largely awaits.

Romans 11:28–32

Speaking still with reference to "all Israel," which at this point is predominantly made up of those who remain hardened and whose sins are not yet forgiven, Paul continues, "in terms of the gospel, indeed they are enemies on your account, but in terms of the election they are beloved on account of the fathers" (11:28).

The mention of "the election" here is related, but not identical, to the mention of "the elect" in 11:7. The relationship is that between the part and the whole, the remnant and the all, the firstfruits and the lump of dough. The two groups explicitly differ, since in the case of 11:7, the elect are those who *have obtained* what Israel was seeking, whereas "the election" here is predicated of those who even now are enemies of God.[18] There are thus two elections that must be kept distinct but also must be understood in their mutual relationship. The election of the remnant is not merely for its own sake; it bears witness to the election of the whole, just as the firstfruits bear witness to the holiness of the whole lump (cf. 11:16a).

Paul says that this election means that the Jews are beloved on account of the fathers. We have already noted that the image of the root of the olive tree (11:16b) refers to the fathers, but Paul has additional reason to mention them here, as he has just quoted a passage in which Israel is summed up as "Jacob." The point could scarcely be clearer: although taken as a whole, Israel is largely at war with Christ's Church at present and is therefore an enemy, yet they remain beloved on account of the fathers. They are still seen as "Jacob."

This idea of beloved enemies should ring a bell: "while we were enemies, we were reconciled to God by the death of His Son" (5:10, ESV).

So, while individual rejection of Christ entails judgment, nonetheless the love for "Jacob" stands firm—even while "Jacob" remains at war against God's Messiah. Even after the crucifixion and nearly a generation of hardness, Israel as a whole is still considered in relation to the fathers and loved.

And not even AD 70 can alter that. Paul adds in 11:29, "for the gifts and the calling of God are unrepentable." God brings judgments, but the promises to the fathers cannot be undone.

18. Note that *the election* here is set in contrast to *the gospel* in the first part of the verse. The elect in view here are a people taken corporately who, as a whole, presently reject the gospel. The choice (election) of the people transcends their current relationship to the gospel, but nonetheless, it guarantees their future reception of it.

The irrevocability mentioned here brings to mind the great new covenant promise of Jeremiah 31. God promises a new covenant that He will make with Israel and Judah (Jer 31:31–32), that He will put His law within them and write it on their hearts (31:33), that *each of them will know Him, from the least to the greatest* ("all Israel"!), and that their iniquities and sins will be forgiven and forgotten (31:34).[19]

Then comes the sturdiest statement of irrevocability ever made: If the fixed order of the sun, moon, and stars comes to an end, "then shall the offspring of Israel cease from being a nation before me forever" (Jer 31:35–36, ESV). In short, *Israel will exist throughout history*, and will do so "before Yahweh." And in case we are tempted to read the cessation of the order of the heavenly lights as a metaphorical reference to the powers of Israel falling (which wouldn't leave much significance to the promise at all), Yahweh restates unambiguously: "If the heavens above can be measured, and the foundations of the earth below can be explored, then I will cast off all the seed of Israel for all that they have done" (31:37). The promises cannot be revoked; nor can the recipients simply be redefined. The promises are for *Jacob*, for Israel. Yes, Gentiles are made *partakers* of Israel's promises—but they remain *Israel's promises*, irrevocably.

Paul continues: "For just as you once disobeyed [or *disbelieved*] God, but now have received mercy because of their disobedience, so also they now have disobeyed, that through the mercy to you, they also may [now] receive mercy" (Rom 11:30–31).

Just as in 11:11 and 15, the disobedience and unbelief of Israel has become the occasion of the salvation of the Gentiles. That is the meaning of "you" receiving mercy because of "their" disobedience." But once again, that is not the end of the story. The fall of Israel was for the sake of the Gentiles; yet the mercy shown in the salvation of the Gentiles ultimately becomes the instrument by which Israel too will receive mercy. The final "now" in v. 31, not present in all manuscripts, perhaps reflects the fact that the eschatological salvation is already underway—the ultimate restoration belongs to this history, not another epoch. Yet one must not forget that the ultimate removal of hardness from most Jews occurs after "the fullness of the Gentiles" has come in (11:25).

In 11:32, Paul sums up the dynamic of much of Romans by saying, "For God shut up all unto disobedience, in order that He might show mercy upon all."

In Romans 5:12ff., Paul has said that death spread to all men through Sin, adding that through the law, Sin increased. Yet where Sin increased, grace abounded all the more, so that as Sin ruled in death, so also grace would rule through righteousness unto eternal life, through Jesus Christ our Lord (Rom 5:20–21). In Romans 11, we have an outline of the history of that triumph of grace, unfolded more fully in terms of the Jew-Gentile dynamic. Death had spread to all the nations through the Adamic trespass, but that shutting up of the nations unto disobedience was not an end in itself; its ultimate aim was that God would "show mercy upon all."[20]

---

19. On the appropriateness of taking this new covenant prophecy to refer to still-future events, see the comments on Paul's use of Isaiah 59 above.

20. Here we find resolution of the difficulty raised by Paul's statements in Romans 5:18–19 that righteousness, justification, and life are to come to "all men." The "all" is not distributive, head for head; it refers to the salvation of the preponderance of mankind at a particular point at the climax of history. Paul is not

Similarly, even among God's chosen people, the law became the agent of Sin's dominion, to the point that, like Adam, Israel herself fell in unbelief (cf. 11:11; also 3:1–8), stumbling over Christ (9:32ff.). But here too, this shutting up in disobedience, still a present reality during this time when the preponderance of Israel remains hardened, is not an end in itself either. Here too, the ultimate aim is that God will "show mercy upon all."

The narrative of Romans is a narrative of postmillennialism. That is, it is a narrative that promises that the death that has come upon all through two parallel falls—that of Adam stumbling at the beginning, and that of Israel stumbling at the new beginning, the advent of the last Adam—will ultimately issue in glorious life that comes upon all at the end. First, the life of communion restored between God and men, both Gentiles and Jews, and then the life of bodily resurrection, giving final and ultimate rescue from death.

YES AND AMEN PROMISES *FOR ISRAEL*

Underlying Paul's argument in Romans 11 is the fact that the gifts and calling of God are "without repentance" (*ametameleta*: 11:29). Israel's restoration is a divine commitment that will not be shirked. As we have already seen from prophecies such as Isaiah 59, Jeremiah 31, and Ezekiel 37, God has committed Himself to an eschatological revivification of all Israel.

The biblical prophecies are formulated in a way that forbids us from radically redefining the recipients of the promises. The promises given to Israel are far too frequently intertwined with promises to the nations, with Israel and the nations made distinct, to allow that.

For example, in Genesis 12 (and the reiterations in Gen 15 and 17), God promises Abram that He will make of him *a great nation*, that He will bless those who bless Abram and curse those who curse him, and that all *the families of the earth* will be blessed *in* him (Gen 12:2–3). Both the "great nation" (Israel) and "the families of the earth" (Gentiles) are in view.

The eschatological anticipation of the later prophets fits the same matrix, portraying the widespread eschatological salvation of Gentiles *alongside* of Israelites. The nations (= Gentiles) are repeatedly distinguished from Israel. In the prophecies of Isaiah 49, 60, and 66, we find that the eschatological salvation entails the calling of "peoples from afar" *and* the regathering of Jacob (e.g., Isa 49:1, 5). The Servant restores Jacob and *also* serves "as a light for the nations, that My salvation may reach to the end of the earth" (Isa 49:6, ESV). The coming in of the nations will be a coming to Israel, upon whom the glory of Yahweh will be seen (Isa 60:1ff.). The nations that survive Yahweh's historical judgments will see Yahweh's glory and they will declare it—and they will bring Israel as an offering to the Lord (Isa 66:18ff.).

In short, every eschatological hope of the nations is first of all the distinct eschatological hope of Israel herself. That is the universal witness of Old Testament prophecy.

---

teaching universalism; rather, he is proclaiming the eschatological triumph of the gospel: as sin reigned in death, grace also will reign through Jesus.

PART ONE: BIBLICAL STUDIES

But Who Is Israel?

But who is the Israel that qualifies as the recipients of these promises?

Israel was never a purely and strictly "ethnic" people determined solely by bloodlines; outsiders could come into the assembly (Exod 12:38) and apparently become full Israelites *via* circumcision (cf. Ex 12:48).[21] Thus "Israel" has always had an ethnic core, but with "soft edges," since new members could be added who were not blood relatives.[22]

Throughout the New Testament, and in Romans itself, Israel remains so. Israel is the nation to whom the patriarchs belong (Rom 9:5) and is marked out by circumcision (e.g., Acts 10:45). These mutually-determinative aspects are highlighted shortly, when Paul says that Christ came as a servant of the *circumcised* on behalf of the truth of God, to confirm the promises to the *fathers* (Rom 15:8). Israel remains a people that is largely ethnic, but for whom circumcision remains partially constitutive.

It is objected that circumcision marked out the seed people, until the ultimate Seed (Christ) was born; thereafter, circumcision is meaningless. After all, Paul himself says that neither circumcision nor uncircumcision count for anything, but a new creation (Gal 6:15). And do not the Gospels depict Jesus Himself as the true Israel, the fulfillment of Israel's purpose?

For reasons of space, I must be succinct:

1. It is not true that circumcision marked out the seed simply for the purpose of identifying the line of Christ, such that it becomes utterly meaningless after His advent. Otherwise, circumcision would have been unnecessary for eleven tribes after it became clear that Christ would be from the tribe of Judah.[23] Moreover, circumcision would already be meaningless altogether immediately following the birth of Jesus. There would be no Israel at all for Jesus to save. That clearly was not the case.

2. It is not true that circumcision is meaningless apart from the many temple-based identity markers that were obliterated by the destruction of the temple in AD 70. Circumcision predated the temple and the sundry rituals of Torah by over four centuries, and the Israelite people were also marked out sufficiently during the time of the exile when the temple had been destroyed.

3. Care must be given to Paul's negative comments about circumcision. These all refer in context either to the undesirability of circumcision of *Gentiles* (e.g., Gal 6) or to the fact that circumcision will not save Jews or make them superior to believing Gentiles. Not only does Paul never hint that Jews should not be circumcised; he goes out of his way to prove that he teaches no such thing (Acts 21:21ff.).

21. Note however that the edges were never so soft that all believers were considered "Israelites." Indeed, not all those *circumcised* at God's command were Israelites: Esau and Ishmael were circumcised, but did not belong with Israel as a people, even when walking faithfully. Something similar could be said regarding the men of Abram's household, who were also circumcised along with him (Gen 17:23, 27).

22. The "soft edges" go the other way as well: those not circumcised are cut off from Israel (Gen 17:14).

23. Something similar could be said regarding the genealogies, which were never limited to the Messianic line.

4. While Jesus is revealed as the true Israel and fulfills her calling perfectly, it is misguided to conclude that Israel herself becomes meaningless or nonexistent thereafter. Paul writes Romans 11 long after the earthly ministry of Christ has concluded but clearly uses "Israel" to refer to his kinsmen. Moreover, Christ has also been revealed as the last Adam, the true Man, and yet that does not mean that men become meaningless or nonexistent thereafter—even unbelieving men. To the contrary, just as the postmillennial promises refer salvation to the mass of such men, so Romans 11 refers salvation to "all Israel." Christ's fulfilling role does not negate either mankind or Israel, but it does mean that, for men generally and Israel specifically, genuine purpose and calling will be found only when they turn to Christ, in whom is the new creation in its totality.

Paul has no difficulties speaking of Israel after Christ's advent. And even today, no people group is more identifiable than Israel. God has promised the salvation of all Israel, and if we dare not admit that Israel obviously exists, He dares to sustain that existence, throughout the generations.

What About "Neither Jew nor Gentile"?

Paul insists that in Christ there is neither Jew nor Gentile (Gal 3:28). Doesn't a distinct, special future for Israel undercut that?

But what is meant by a "distinct, special future for Israel"? Paul does not envision a future for Israel *different* from the future promised for Gentiles. The meek, Gentile and Jew, will inherit the earth: Abraham is promised the land (Israel) and the world (the nations). Every promise to Gentile and Jew finds its answer in Christ, in whom every promise is "Yes and Amen."

Second, in terms of the Pauline statement, it is *in Christ* where there is neither Jew nor Gentile. It is completely wrong to say, "Since there is no Gentile or Jew, it's impossible for Israel to exist other than as the Church. And since no Israel exists, there can be no promise to Israel of future salvation." To the contrary, *Gentile and Jew do exist*. That fact is evident *everywhere* in Paul's writings. The gospel is *to the Jew first, and also to the Greek* (Rom 1:16), a statement that would be incomprehensible if Jew and Gentile were simply meaningless terms. Saying that *in Christ* there is neither Jew nor Gentile does not imply in the least that the division is erased *outside of Christ*.

Third, even in Christ, "neither Jew nor Gentile" is not an absolute statement, any more than "not male and female" (which parallels the Jew-Gentile phrase in Gal 3:28) is an absolute statement. We can indeed distinguish Jew and Gentile within the Church; that is, as we have seen, necessary to answer to prophecies that Paul himself cites as central to the purpose of Christ (see again Rom 15:8–12). Indeed, the significance of Paul's great collection task depends precisely upon the distinction between Jew and Gentile (e.g., Rom 15:27).[24] The point of Galatians 3:28 is not to obliterate all distinctions such

---

24. Paul undertakes a massive collection for the saints in Judea. Were there no poor Christians elsewhere? Certainly there were. But he places special significance upon Gentiles providing for Israel out of their material things while sharing in Israel's spiritual things. These are not the actions of one for whom Jew and Gentile are indistinct.

as Jew and Gentile, or male and female, but to place them all within the context of one united body of members equal in Christ, whether Jew or Gentile, slave or free, male or female. In Christ, all of these *distinct* members are free and full heirs of grace, so that there is no need for Gentiles to become circumcised in order to get on equal covenantal footing with Jews, just as Christian women share fully in Christ, equally with Christian men, through baptism and, unlike their old covenant counterparts, enter fully into congregational life without worries about all sorts of ritual impurities.

Far from destroying all distinctions, the apostle glories in the triumph of the gospel precisely in terms of Gentile and Jew, as the necessary denouement for both the history and the promises that precede. It is precisely as uncircumcised Gentiles that the nations must be incorporated into Abraham; nothing else suffices (Gal 3:8–9). And it is precisely as familial recipients of the Abrahamic promises that believing Jews find those promises fulfilled in them. For just so may it be said that the Gentiles rejoice *with* Yahweh's people Israel: "Christ became a servant *to the circumcised* (lit., "of circumcision") for the sake of God's truth, *in order to confirm the promises given to the fathers*" (Rom 15:8).[25] The Gentiles are full partakers with Israel in her blessings (11:17; 15:10), but nonetheless those blessings are distinctly *hers* (15:27).

This is the pattern into which Romans 11 so comfortably fits, a pattern further confirmed by a number of Old Testament stories and motifs.

A PATTERN THAT FITS

Secondborn Brothers and Firstborn Sons

One of James Jordan's contributions to biblical theology has been his accent on believing Gentiles during the Old Testament period: the repentant Ninevites, leaders in Egypt during Joseph's time, and numerous other God-fearers.

In *Primeval Saints*, Jordan devotes an entire chapter to Esau, Jacob's older twin, arguing that the form of exclusion he endured was not from salvific blessings altogether; Scripture gives strong indication of faith and righteousness at work in his later life. To be sure, in Romans 9:13 (citing Malachi), God says, "Jacob have I loved, but Esau have I hated." But such contrasts are not as absolute as we might think:

> Jacob loved Rachel and hated Leah, but this only means he treated her as second-wife instead of as first-wife (Gen. 29:30–31). Jacob's "hatred" of Leah did not mean he divorced her and cast her out. Quite the contrary: He had many children by her, and Jacob honored her by burying her in the patriarchal tomb (Gen. 49:29–32). "Hate" in this case does not mean pure abiding hatred; it means to count as second, to prefer someone else as first. The same thing is meant when Jesus says we must hate our parents in order to love Him (Luke 14:26). It means we place them second.[26]

---

25. This passage refutes the notion that the Israel of promise is unidentifiable. Israelites—precisely as bearers of the promise!—are marked out by circumcision (Rom 15:8). As a people, Israel was never strictly "ethnic"; yet it was always identifiable and remains so today.

26. James B. Jordan, *Primeval Saints: Studies in the Patriarchs of Genesis* (Moscow, ID: Canon, 2001), 101.

In the case of Esau, Jordan argues, the meaning of God's hatred is explained by the preceding verse: the elder will serve the younger.

True, in early life, Esau acted both recklessly and wickedly. He sold his birthright (an error for which he could not repent), married badly, and plotted against Jacob's life. But that is not the last word on Esau; he later accepted his lot, took possession of the land God had given him outside of Canaan, and was reconciled to his brother.[27] A number of Esau's descendants, such as Job and Caleb, were faithful believers.[28]

The "younger brother" theme continues in the Joseph story. He is not merely the second brother, as with Isaac and Jacob; but the second youngest of twelve. And yet, he receives a dream that he will rule over the family. Not only his brothers, but also his parents, will bow before him.

Joseph is not only a junior brother; he is the son of the second sister. The common theme of the younger brother being chosen over the older is customized in the story of Jacob's romance: he chooses the younger Rachel over her older sister Leah. And even after he is tricked into marrying Leah, Rachel remains his first choice, the woman he loves. By comparison, as we have already seen, Leah is "hated." She is "second-wife."

If Jordan's take on Esau is correct, it fits with what we know of these other stories. God indeed passes over the eldest in favor of the younger, but not in order simply to destroy or abandon them. Rather, God uses the younger to bring His purposes for the elder to fruition. Often this means deliverance and protection: Joseph becomes God's agent for preserving the whole host of Israel alive during a great famine; David becomes the instrument through which Yahweh liberates Israel—including his own family—from the Philistines. And then too, there are other forms of blessing passed from the younger to the elder; it is probable that at least some of the biblical revelation passes from Israel into the hands of Edomites such as Job.

Going further, there is a more radical, mysterious biblical thread wherein God sacrifices one son for the sake of others, a son who is in fact central to His purposes.

Abraham was commanded to take Isaac his son—his beloved son, as God reminded him—and make of him an offering on an altar. God of course relented, providing another offering, but Isaac was nonetheless figuratively resurrected—and hence, sacrificed (Heb 11:19).

There are much less obvious stories about God's sacrifices. We might conclude from the story of the destruction of Egypt's firstborn on the first Passover that Yahweh hates Egypt. He is destroying its future. And yet ultimately, God not only tells Israel to be kind to generic strangers, because "you were strangers in Egypt" (e.g., Exod 22:21), but He also ends up promising that Egypt itself will be a redeemed nation like Israel herself (Isa 19:18–25).

---

27. Indeed, as Jordan notes (ibid., 103), Esau's reunion with Jacob strongly resembles the father's reunion with the prodigal son in Luke 15:20.

28. Jordan notes that Job's home, Uz, was in Edom (cf. Job 1:1; Lam 4:21), as was Teman, where his friend Eliphaz was from (Job 2:11; Gen 36:11), while Caleb is listed as a "Kenizzite," arguably a descendant of Esau's grandson Kenaz—a name shared by Caleb's younger brother and his own grandson.

But without question, the most powerful story of all is when God gives up *His* firstborn for the sake of others. Like Israel, Jesus is identified as God's firstborn Son, and it is this firstborn Son that He offers for the life of the world, so that He will become the firstborn of many brothers (Rom 8:29). He makes the sacrifice that, ultimately, He was unwilling to force Abraham to make.

It is within this context that Romans 11 must be understood. In Exodus 4:22, Yahweh instructs Moses to tell Pharaoh, "Israel is My son, My firstborn" (NKJV). The threat that He will slay Pharaoh's firstborn is Yahweh's response to Pharaoh's refusal to let His firstborn go (Exod 4:23). In the remainder of Exodus, the firstborn of man and beast become set apart: for sacrifice, for service.

This is what the giving up of Israel (cf. Deut 32:30b) for the sake of the Gentiles is about. It was well within God's power to draw that very first generation of Israel to Christ. But instead, by and large, He hardened them. He gave up His firstborn son—again!—for our sake, so that there would be time for us Gentiles to be saved—not because He has stopped loving that son, any more than He stopped loving His eternal Son when He gave *Him* up for the sake of our salvation. This giving up *is* a costly sacrifice. This son He loves dearly for the sake of the fathers He has given up for a time, that we may be rescued. But just as He did not leave His eternal Son in Sheol, but raised Him up (Acts 2:24–31), so He will not leave this son in death, but will raise him up, as well.

This is the way God works.

Preliminary and Final Judgments

One of Jordan's recurring themes is the third day/seventh day pattern of preliminary and final judgment. In these terms, it makes some sense to take the rejection and trial of Jesus as Israel's preliminary judgment and the destruction of Jerusalem in AD 70 as Israel's final judgment.

Such evidence, however, is not decisive. The destruction of Jerusalem under Nebuchadnezzar and the ensuing exile were a sort of "final judgment," to the degree that Ezekiel 37 depicts Israel as utterly dead, a valley of dry bones. And yet God was not done with Israel.

Deuteronomy 32 underscores this. Yahweh depicts a future when Israel will be rebellious to the point of rank idolatry and will suffer something that sounds much like AD 70: "For a fire is kindled in My anger, and shall burn to the lowest hell [Sheol, Hades]; it shall consume the land with her increase and set on fire the foundations of the mountains" (32:22 NKJV). Yet after that unspeakable disaster, Yahweh promises to judge His people and save them when they are powerless (32:36) and, in a passage that sounds reminiscent of the new covenant promises of the later prophets, He concludes in verse 43: "Rejoice, O Gentiles, with His people; for He will avenge the blood of His servants, and render vengeance to His enemies; *He will provide atonement for the land of His people*" (NKJV, modified).[29]

---

29. We have already seen Paul's use of this passage in Romans 15:10.

The Gospels do frame things dramatically (e.g., the ax being laid to the root of the trees). But the promise of resurrection in Ezekiel 37 is no less dramatic, and the promise of Israel's continuance found in Jeremiah 31 is unshakable. Beyond Israel's judgment is her restoration.

JUDAH AND JOSEPH

Let's be Jordanian and allow typology to lead us to our conclusion by revisiting the Joseph story. The primary acting culprit was not the eldest brother; Reuben tried to restrain his siblings. While the specific conspirators thinking to kill Joseph (Gen 37:18–20) are not named, we are explicitly told that they sell the dreamer because of Judah's influence. Even though Judah says that Joseph ought to be sold rather than slain because he is their own flesh and blood (Gen 37:27), we nonetheless get no sense of nobility from him. Brotherly love would not have allowed him to urge that Joseph be sold into slavery.

And yet, it is Judah who voluntarily becomes surety for Benjamin when the brothers must make a second trip to Egypt to purchase food (Gen 43:9). And he follows through and begs (the unrecognized) Joseph to keep him as a slave and let Benjamin go free (44:33). Indeed, it is this very act that finally leads Joseph to relent and reveal himself to his brothers.

Joseph is the Christ figure, the innocent one unjustly accused, the faithful servant, and the deliverer. And at the key moment of the story, it is the repentance of the one who sold him that triggers the climactic revelation of the Christ figure and the culminating outflow of blessings.

As with the type, so with the antitype. Yes, "the Jews" sold Jesus—indeed, instigated His death. The blessings under the true Joseph have spread to the nations, largely without much blessing for Israel, even as Joseph's wisdom was initially enjoyed by Egypt but not the Israelites.

But notwithstanding the significance of His judgments upon them in AD 70, the true Joseph did not simply destroy them. Judah is yet destined for repentance, which will be the trigger point for the final and full revelation of the Christ, and Jew and Gentile—unlike the Hebrews segregated in Egypt—will be fully one as all believe together.

But what is the point of one final generation being saved if the majority of Israel was apostate through the preceding generations? If the goal is the salvation of all Israel, how can this answer to the promise? But as postmillennialists, we hold to something similar regarding the world as a whole. The promise that God will save the world is not a guarantee that the preponderance of people throughout history will be saved; rather, it is an eschatological promise that at some point the knowledge of the Lord will fill the earth as the waters cover the sea. To return to the Joseph framework: yes, generations of Jews have "not known Joseph." But that is no contradiction to God's promise, which is not that all Israel *is* saved, but that all Israel *will be*. All Israel will come to Joseph, the Savior of the world, both Jew and Gentile.

PART ONE: BIBLICAL STUDIES

CONCLUSION

In Romans 11, Paul deals with the critical question of whether God has forsaken His people. Contrary to the frequent notion that Romans 9–11 is an excursus, virtually accidental to the point of the letter, this question is at the very heart of Paul's argument, because throughout his concern has been with the faithfulness, truth, and righteousness of God. If God is not faithful to Israel, neither can He be counted on to be faithful to the nations. If God is not faithful to Israel, there is no gospel for anyone. In truth, the gospel to the Gentiles is tightly bound up with the gospel to Israel.

And so Paul proves that faithfulness to Israel with a twofold argument: God has remained faithful throughout by maintaining an elect remnant, of which Paul himself is a part. And God remains faithful by staying the course, by remaining committed to what He yet will do. Even as He has not abandoned the nations to their fate of death, neither will He abandon Israel to hers.

"Boasting against the branches" in Romans 11 means, in part, failing to come to terms with God's purposes: that the present hardened state of Israel has come about for *our* sake. God has set aside the bulk of His people Israel, not because He is done with them, but because in mercy He is creating space for Gentiles to repent before the end of all things. All Israel *will* be saved; her election is not done away with or even reconfigured, for the gifts and calling of God are irrevocable (11:29). God is faithful, and therefore we can believe the gospel He brings.

~

Dear Tim,

Thank you for your essay. I have to say I remain unpersuaded. Let me make a few conversational rejoinders.

The majority read of Romans 11 by most of the Reformers and virtually all within the "Calvinistic" world for a couple of centuries thereafter was this: The gospel would go to all nations and eventually all nations would be converted: the fulness of the gentiles. At that point, the Jews, as the last nation, would be converted: the fulness of Israel. This event would be like a corporate international resurrection, "life from the dead," and would usher in a period of time often called the "latter-day glory," after which Jesus would return. Your interpretation is the same, save that you take "life from the dead" to mean physical resurrection of individuals, so that the conversion of Israel brings about the end of history and the return of Jesus.

A small minority of Puritans argued that Romans 11 was fulfilled in the first century, particularly John Lightfoot, who was followed by Cotton Mather in his *Triparadisus*. The notion, however, was stillborn.

I and others today believe Lightfoot and his comrades were correct. The promises made to Israel are fulfilled in Jesus, the True Israel, and then in the Church, His body. As Jeremiah 31:36 says, the *offspring* of Israel will not cease to be a nation. The offspring of Israel, through Jesus, is the Church/Kingdom, the holy nation of which Peter speaks (1 Pet 2:9).

The history of the Old Creation reveals a racial and geophysical bifurcation of the human race. In Genesis 2, we have the Foodland of Eden and the Stoneland of Havilah. This bifurcation continues: in the days of Solomon produce from Foodland was exchanged with the Stoneland of Tyre in order to build the Temple (1 Kings 5). This geophysical bifurcation continued until AD 70 and no longer exists nor will ever again. The state of Israel today is not a Foodland that exchanges food for other things from Stonelands.

Similarly, from the beginning the human race was bifurcated into a priestly people and a cultural people. Abel and Cain were the first instances of this, and Abel became a sacrifice. Thereafter the line of Seth were the "sons of God" who led in worship (Gen 4:26). This continued until the apostasy of the Sethites brought the Flood. After the Flood, the priestly people were those from Shem, while the sons of Japheth and Ham were cultural people. The apostasy of the Shemites at the Tower of Babel (Gen 10:30 + 11:2; and see my *The Handwriting on the Wall*, chap. 5) was followed by the call of Abram to issue forth a new priestly nation. This call was enhanced by the later addition of the rite of circumcision, and later still by the feast of Passover and Unleavened Bread and the imposition of the law of clean and unclean (life and death) at Mount Sinai. The division of labor continued into the Oikumenical period, with the priestly people spread out in the oikumene as "the four winds of heaven" in a Jerusalem without walls (Zechariah 2).

The genealogy of Jesus in Matthew 1 shows us the addition of four Gentile women into Jesus' line. I assume Bathsheba was a Gentile for reasons I won't go into here. Even without her, there are three Gentile women. Jesus, then, was both Jew and Gentile. In Him both come together. In His death under condemnation by both Jew and Gentile courts, He dies as both, and in His resurrection there is One New Man.

The New Age is not an age of lands. The geophysical bifurcation has been replaced by City. In Israel, both Israelite and gentile lived together in the cities of Israel, which were not under the land laws of the Jubilee (Lev 25; Deut 13:12–18; 23:16). This arrangement is now fulfilled, for there are no more lands. There are no feasts of the land, only the feast of the New Jerusalem.

According to Matthew 23:35, the destruction of physical Jerusalem and of the "Jerusalem without walls" of first century Jewry—of the navel of the world—was the destruction of the Old Creation. As Paul argues in Colossians and elsewhere, the old times marked out by sun and moon, the old land feasts, the old rules of circumcision and cleanness, are gone. The racial bifurcation is gone.

One has to ask then: What is the purpose for there to be a continuing people of Israel distinct from the rest of the Kingdom? And the answer is that there is no purpose at all. Post-biblical Jews are simply one people group among all the rest.

The Apostolic Age was an age of overlap, with "Isaac and Ishmael" in one house, but this was shortly to end (Gal 4). While the Temple stood, the Old Creation had not been yet removed. After AD 70 it has been removed, and with it the division of humanity into priestly and cultural peoples, into "Jew" and "Gentile." Today there are no Israelites in the biblical sense, and there are no Gentiles. There are only people, in Christ or not in Christ.

Well, there's my view. A few specifics:

PART ONE: BIBLICAL STUDIES

1. I cannot see that "life from the dead" implies physical resurrection. Death and resurrection are all over the Bible in many ways, starting with the evenings and mornings in Genesis 1, then the death-sleep of Adam in Genesis 2, the death and resurrection of Israel in the book of Numbers, every story in the book of Daniel, and so forth. Since Romans 11 is speaking of cultural affairs, it seems to me that the traditional view is correct: this is cultural resurrection.

2. The conversion that takes place in "Jerusalem" in Revelation 11 is not in a physical city. Revelation is written in symbols. This is the "Jerusalem without walls" of Zechariah 2, and refers to Jewry throughout the oikumene.

3. You note that no first century Jew is likely to have thought of the Messiah's coming twice. I'm not at all sure of that. Every time a Jew became unclean he was resurrected on the third and again on the seventh day (Numbers 19). If this double resurrection were not in their conscious minds, it was surely in their subconscious. Moreover, the prophecies about the Messiah were that he would usher in a new age, not that he would end the world.

4. And I think you are wrong about John the Baptist. He was not at all confused about Jesus' being the Messiah; he had known that from his infancy. Nothing indicates that he expected great things and was disappointed. What John wanted to know was if Jesus were also That Prophet Like Moses, something that he and others had not linked with the Messiah. I imagine John's disciples were telling John that he himself was That Prophet. Jesus replies by telling John that He is doing the things the prophets Elijah and Elisha did: raising the dead, and so forth. John had identified Jesus as the Lamb of God, and he knew full well that Jesus was going to die.

5. In Acts 1:6 the disciples ask if Jesus was at that time going to restore the kingdom to Israel. This came after forty days of instruction about the kingdom (Luke 24:45; Acts 1:3). Jesus answered "Yes." He told them that some times were in the Father's hand, but that in a few days they would receive power. Just so, on the day of Pentecost Peter proclaims that Jesus is David and that the kingdom has come to Israel. Jesus had told them that in the "regeneration" they would rule the twelve tribes (Matt 19:28). We see this right away in that people bring gifts to the apostles as new Melchizedekal kings (Acts 4:35ff.), who pass judgment on sinners (e.g., Acts 5, 8). More than that, though, Jesus as King was enthroned on a cross, and the apostles also ruled through martyrdom.

Restoring the kingdom of David to Israel raises a question: Did this Davidic Israel kingdom last forty years, down to AD 70, and then become transformed fully into the worldwide rule of the Last Adam? That makes the most sense to me. Jewish apostles ruled down to AD 70, but not afterward. The specifically Davidic/Jewish phase of the New Creation lasted a Davidic forty years. That makes the most sense to me.

6. Ezekiel 37: Surely this refers to the restoration of the nation of Israel after the exile. The bones in view are those of the idolaters of Ezekiel 6. I readily grant that Romans 11's "life from the dead" alludes to this, but as such it is speaking of a cultural resurrection.

This is a vision. The physical resurrection at the end of history will not happen anything like what is described here, for the bones of the vast majority of human beings will have rotted and been eaten eventually into the people by that time.

Well, I'll stop here. I'm certain that the last word has not been said about Romans 11 and the issues involved there, so let the conversation continue! Thanks again for a stimulating challenge.

Jim

3

The Knotted Thread of Time

The Missing Daughter in Leviticus 18[1]

PETER J. LEITHART

> When fathers love daughters and daughters love fathers, it is like tying up into a knot the thread that runs into the future, it's like a stream wanting to flow backwards.
>
> —Simone de Beauvoir, *The Mandarins*

Though it is typically not a topic for polite conversation, incest has been a major theme of twentieth-century intellectual culture.[2] Freud's "Oedipal complex" is the best-known incest theory, and Freud has permeated not only psychology but many other disciplines as well, most notably literary studies, and has left his mark on the popular imagination. Feminists have charged that Freud's theorizing is driven by a patriarchal bias that obscures the more common form of incest—father-daughter, not mother-son—and have argued more generally that incest is not a pathological aberration but an expression of the sexual exploitation inherent in a male-dominated social order.

Since Durkheim, anthropologists have puzzled over the universality of incest prohibitions, and the central importance given to kinship systems in structuralist anthropology locates incest prohibitions at the boundary between culture and nature. Post-structuralists have picked up that thread: Derrida explains how Rousseau's essay on the origins of language deconstructs on the shoals of the incest prohibition. Rousseau's theory about the festal origins of society implies that the "festival *itself* would be incest *itself*," since the festival is a Saturnalian moment without boundaries or restrictions. Because the festival is the pre-social origin of society, however, incest cannot yet ex-

---

1. I presented the core of this paper at the Biblical Horizons Summer Conference in July 2009 and received much assistance from many of the conferees, especially from Rich Bledsoe and James Jordan. It is appropriate that my paper should consist of repeating Jordan's own insights back to him. Such, in large measure, is my theological life.

2. Helpful summaries are available in the introductions to Vicki Bell, *Interrogating Incest: Feminism, Foucault, and the Law* (London: Routledge, 1993) and Ellen Pollack, *Incest and the English Novel, 1684–1814* (Baltimore: Johns Hopkins University Press, 2003).

ist: "before the prohibition, it is not incest; forbidden, it cannot become incest except through recognition of the prohibition." Incest prohibitions thus highlight Rousseau's inability to discover the origin of society and more broadly disclose the reality of what Derrida describes as the "supplement at the origin." As he says, "we are always short of or beyond the limit of the festival, of the origin of society," and the festive origin is not a process but "a point, a pure, fictive and unstable, ungraspable limit."[3]

Incest has also become a motif of popular culture, explicitly in *Chinatown* and in Freudianized films, plays, and Shakespearean remakes, implicitly in the displaced father-daughter incest of *Lolita* and *American Beauty*.[4] Clinical psychologists study controversial claims about repressed memories of childhood sexual abuse, and at least since the 1950s sex researchers, sociologists, and historians of sexuality have insisted that incest is far more common than anyone likes to imagine.

All this attention to incest might appear to be a sign of late modern decadence, but in fact we are only beginning to recapture the frankness of Leviticus and of medieval Christianity. Incest was a common motif in medieval cautionary tales; for medieval clerical writers, "incestuous desire was not regarded as a rare and barbaric perversion but rather as a constant danger for all, rich and poor, powerful and humble, male and female."[5] Scripture, for its part, includes not only the incest rules of Leviticus, but also many tales of incest—from (perhaps) Ham's incest with his mother (Gen 9); through Lot and his daughters, mothers of Moab and Ammon (Gen 19); through Judah and his daughter-in-law, Tamar (Gen 38); to the brother-sister incest of Amnon and Tamar, which shattered the house of David (2 Sam 13). If filmed unexpurgated, the Bible could not escape at least an R rating.

I glancingly address some of the wider cultural and philosophical aspects of incest below, but I can best honor Jordan's contributions to theology by first paying close attention to the text itself. Initially, I provide a structural analysis of Leviticus 18, then expound on key phrases that capture the theo-logic of Leviticus's incest rules, and finally examine one of the often-discussed anomalies of the passage: There is no explicit prohibition against uncovering the nakedness of a daughter.[6] I demonstrate below that daughters *were* excluded, but in a passage that explicitly excludes aunts, sisters-in-law,

---

3. Jacques Derrida, *Of Grammatology*, trans. Gayatri Chakravorty Spivak (Baltimore: Johns Hopkins University Press, 1976), 267.

4. Robert M. Polhemus's *Lot's Daughters: Sex, Redemption, and Women's Quest for Authority* (Stanford: Stanford University Press, 2005) examines the "Lot complex" from Genesis through the Brontes, Freud, and Joyce, to Woody Allen and Monica Lewinsky. This complex is not necessarily strictly incestuous, but involves sexual desire between older men and women young enough to be their daughters.

5. Elizabeth Archibald, *Incest and the Medieval Imagination* (Oxford: Oxford University Press, 2001), 7.

6. It can be argued that Leviticus 18:17 excludes daughters by prohibiting uncovering nakedness of a woman and her daughter. The scenario in view is of a man taking a woman and her daughter from a previous marriage, but a *qal wahomer* ("how much more?") line of reasoning suggests that one's own daughter is even more certainly prohibited: If my stepdaughter is "flesh of flesh," how much more my own daughter? That is a valid line of reasoning. While it resolves the practical question (may I marry my daughter?), it still leaves the textual question open, though in a somewhat weakened form: In a text that *explicitly* prohibits marriage with one's aunt, why is the prohibition of sex with a daughter merely *implied*?

daughters-in-law, step-daughters, and granddaughters, the absence of a direct prohibition of father-daughter incest is so startling that it must be deliberate and meaningful.[7] By exploring the structure of excluded sexual relationships and this anomaly, I grope my way back to broader concerns raised by incest prohibitions—questions about the socio-religious order of Israel, time, and, inevitably, Trinity.

STRUCTURE

The most obvious structuring device for Leviticus as a whole is the phrase "Yahweh spoke to Moses," with variations like "Yahweh said to Moses." Following these markers, we discover that there are thirty-seven speeches in Leviticus. This is numerologically unpromising, but it does provide a center for the book, the nineteenth speech found in chapter 16, which describes the rites for the Day of Atonement or the "day of coverings."[8] The day of coverings thus stands at the center of the book in the same way it stood the center of Israel's system of holiness and offerings. From this structuring device, too, we discover that Leviticus 18 is a self-standing section of the book, opening with the formula "Yahweh spoke to Moses."

The late Mary Douglas argued that the two narrative portions of Leviticus also function as dividers for the book.[9] Chapter 10 records the story of Nadab and Abihu, whom Yahweh burns for offering unauthorized ("strange") fire in the sanctuary, and chapter 24 concludes with the narrative of the half-Egyptian stoned for blasphemy. These incidents stand out as narratives in a book devoted almost exclusively to law, and they match and contrast in various ways. Both narratives involve two men, both involve sin, both end in death. More subtly, they form contrasting narratives that recall stories of Genesis and broader themes of Leviticus: Sin of Adam *v.* sin of Cain (a struggle in the "camp" precedes the blasphemy); a sanctuary sin *v.* a land sin; a priestly *v.* a kingly incident; Yahweh's direct punishment *v.* punishment carried out by Israel; fire *v.* stone as the means of punishment.

Douglas uses these narratives to establish a tripartite division of the book (1–10; 11–23; 24–27), and points out that this structure is reinforced by the distribution of the word "Sinai." As a continuation of Exodus, Leviticus begins with an implicit reference to Sinai, but the first explicit reference to Sinai occurs in Leviticus 7:38, just before the first

---

7. A second oddity is the exclusion of marriage between brothers and sisters and between half-brothers and half-sisters. If one takes the early chapters of Genesis as a record of early human history, as both Jordan and I do, brother-sister marriage was obviously necessary in the early life of humanity. Cain and Abel both married sisters, and neither was condemned. More difficult to explain is the fact that Abraham and Sarah were half-siblings (Gen 20:11–13), and the problem is intensified by the prohibition of this relation in Leviticus 18:9, 11. Had they lived under Moses, Abraham and Sarah would have been "cut off in the eyes of the sons of their people" and would have "borne their guilt" (Lev 20:17). In fact, many of the degrees of incest prohibited in Leviticus 18 are exemplified in the lives of the patriarchs. For an interesting but unconvincing exploration, see Calum M. Carmichael, *Law, Legend, and Incest in the Bible: Leviticus 18–20* (Ithaca, NY: Cornell University Press, 1997).

8. Wilfried Warning, *Literary Artistry in Leviticus* (Leiden: Brill, 1999). The fact that there are 18 speeches (3 x 6; 6 + 6 + 6) on either side of the center is perhaps more promising as a numerological structure.

9. Mary Douglas, *Leviticus as Literature* (Oxford: Oxford University Press, 2001), passim.

PART ONE: BIBLICAL STUDIES

narrative describes both the ordination of priests and the death of Aaron's sons. Between chapters 11 and 24, there is no mention of Sinai, but as soon as the stoning scene is out of the way, "Sinai" reappears, framing the final three chapters (25:1; 26:46; 27:34). When we combine the thirty-seven speech structure with Douglas' tripartite structure, we can discern a chiastic structure for the entire book:

    A. Offerings, chs. 1–7
        B. Priestly ordination; fall and fire-punishment, chs. 8–10
            C. Laws of uncleanness: defile sanctuary, chs. 11–15
                D. Day of coverings, ch. 16
            C'. Laws of society: defile land, chs. 17–20[10]
        B'. Priestly regulations; fall and stone-punishment, chs. 21–24
    A'. Jubilee and things consecrated, chs. 25–27

Chapters 18–20 form a subunit within Leviticus 17–20. Chapter 16 is addressed to Aaron's sons the priests, and chapter 17 addresses both Aaron and his sons and all Israel (17:2). In chapter 21, Yahweh returns to addressing the priests (21:1). Nestled within these priestly addresses, chapters 18–20 consist of three long discourses, each of which begins with Yahweh telling Moses to "speak to the sons of Israel" (18:2; 19:2; 20:2), that is, to all Israel.

As Jordan has pointed out in a number of places, Leviticus retells the early chapters of Genesis in a new form. Structured by a heptamerous arrangement reminiscent of Genesis 1:1—2:4, Exodus 25–40 describes the "new creation" of the tabernacle, which is also an architectural garden. Following that, the early chapters of Leviticus outline the system of offerings, protocols for approaching Yahweh in His house. Leviticus 8–9 describes the formation of a new Adam, Aaron, and his assistants, the helpers suitable to him, his sons. A fall scene immediately follows the creation of "Adam" and "Eve" (Lev 10), and the next several chapters present laws of uncleanness, all forms of death and curse that can be traced to the curses of Genesis 3: Unclean animals, like Satan, crawl in the contaminated dust (Lev 11); a woman who bears a child is unclean because childbearing has been cursed (Lev 12); skin disease is a form of the sweat that appears on Adam's brow as he works to overcome the thorns and thistles that come from the earth (Lev 13–14); uncleanness from the "flesh" is uncleanness from the sexual organs (Lev 15). Leviticus 16

---

10. Jordan has suggested that 17–24 forms a section but, for various reasons, I think the section begun in 17:1 ends with chapter 20. 20:25 clearly links back to the regulations regarding priestly distinctions of unclean and clean, holy and profane (10:10) and especially to the rules about unclean foods (ch. 11). That suggests that chapter 20 is the conclusion of a unit that reaches back to chapter 11. As a result, chapters 11–20 are set off as a separate section, which is bisected by the day of coverings passage in chapter 16.

Further, chapters 17–20 share vocabulary not found elsewhere in Leviticus. The phrase "blood on them" (or "him"), sometimes translated as "bloodguiltiness on them," is used seven times in the book of Leviticus. It appears first in 17:4 and then is used six more times in chapter 20. Since the phrase is used for the last time in 20:27, Leviticus 17–20 is enclosed by this phrase. Additionally, the phrase "I will set my face" in combination with "I will cut off" is also unique to this section. The first phrase is used five times in Leviticus, initially in 17:10 and elsewhere only in chapter 20 (vv. 3, 5, 6, 17). The phrase "cut off" is used throughout Leviticus, often in the passive ("shall be cut off"). Only in chapters 17 and 20, though, do we find the Lord Himself threatening to cut off: "I will cut off" (17:10; 20:3, 5–6).

brings us to Genesis 3:21, the original "day of coverings" (*yom kippurim*) when Yahweh provided tunics of skin to veil the nakedness of Adam and Eve.[11]

According to this scheme, Leviticus 18 is connected with the expulsion of Adam and Eve from Eden's garden into the land beyond. Appropriately, at this point, Leviticus's interest turns from defilements of the sanctuary to pollutions of land (18:24–30). Yet, Leviticus 18 and its companion, chapter 20, also hearken back to the opening narratives of Genesis 1–3. As we will see below, the rules of incest in Leviticus are rooted in Genesis 2:24's requirement that a man leave his father and mother and cleave to his wife. Leviticus 18 and 20 use the word "nakedness" frequently (twenty-four times in chapter 18 alone), especially in the phrase "uncovering nakedness," recalling Adam's and Eve's recognition of nakedness after they ate from the tree. Given the chiastic outline suggested above, Leviticus 17–20, though continuing the story of Genesis in one sense, also turns back to the concerns of Genesis 1–3.

Internally, Leviticus 18 forms a chiasm:[12]

0. Address to sons of Israel, v. 1
A. I am Yahweh (keep statutes), vv. 2–5
    B. Do not approach flesh of flesh, vv. 6–14
        C. Do not uncover relatives-by-marriage, vv. 15–19
    B'. Do not give seed, vv. 20–23
A'. No defilement, no abomination; keep statutes; I am Yahweh, vv. 24–30

RULES OF INCEST

Leviticus 18:6 is the key to the system of excluded relations: "Each man to any flesh of his flesh shall not approach to uncover nakedness. I am Yahweh." Explaining the key phrases of this verse will help make sense of the logic of excluded relations and will begin to expose some of its wider implications.

"Approach"

The verb "approach" (*qarab*) is employed three times in chapter 18 (vv. 6, 14, 19). It is a key term in the Levitical system of offerings. The opening instructions of Leviticus 1 use the word repeatedly: "When any adam of you brings a *qorban* to Yahweh, you shall cause-to-*qarab* your *qorban* of animals from the herd or the flock. If an ascension is his

---

11. Jordan has argued that the *kpr* root means "cover" rather than "purge" or "atone." The rite of Leviticus 16 confirms this: the (Adam) priest puts aside his garments of glory and beauty for the day and is reinvested at the end of the rites. See also the suggestive, if overstated, discussion of sinful self-hiding, covering, and atonement in N. Kiuchi, *Leviticus*, Apollos Old Testament Commentary 3 (Downers Grove, IL: InterVarsity, 2007), *passim*. Kiuchi has attempted a rigorous exegetical defense of his claims in *A Study of Hata and Hatta't in Leviticus 4–5* (Tübingen: Mohr/Siebeck, 2003). I have drawn on Kiuchi's work, and offered a few criticisms, in "Stripped and Re-Clothed: The Meaning of Sacrifice," forthcoming in a book on liturgy edited by Gregg Strawbridge.

12. I have given a much more detailed structural analysis of this chapter on my blog: http://www.leithart.com/2009/07/31/structure-of-leviticus-18/.

qorban from the herd, an unblemished male he shall cause-to-*qarab*. To the doorway of the tent of meeting, he shall cause-to-*qarab* it" (1:2–3). The system of Levitical offerings offers a way of "approach." Bringing-near an animal was the means for the worshiper to draw-near to the house of Yahweh.

By the time we get to chapter 18, therefore, *qarab* is charged up with liturgical significance (1:13–15; 2:1, 4, 8, 11–14; 3:1, 3, 6–7, 9, 12, 14; 4:3, 14; etc.), and that charge remains when the word is used in the sexual context of chapter 18. At least, the use of *qarab* points to an *analogy* between liturgical and sexual approach: To approach a woman for sexual intimacy is *like* drawing near to Yahweh's secret place. Both forms of approach must be done in accord with Yahweh's statutes and ordinances. Leviticus 1–7 describes how to approach Yahweh's inner sanctuary rightly, while Leviticus 18 and 20 legislate about how not to approach a woman, or, more accurately, which women may not be approached. This verb may also be a faint acknowledgment of the fact that much of the sexual activity prohibited (including sodomy and bestiality) was part of Egyptian and Canaanite cults (18:3).[13]

If sexual approach is like liturgical drawing-near, then, conversely, liturgy is analogous to sexual union. The Bible does not sanction sex in worship and does not treat sex itself as an act of worship. Still, Israel's offerings are described in sexual/marital terms. In worship, Israel the bride draws near to her Lord and husband, seeking union in one spirit through animals turned to smoke. The offerings that mediate the worshiper's approach are "bridal food" (*isheh*, often translated as "fire offering," from *ishah*, "woman"; cf. Lev 1:9, 13, 17; 2:2, 3, 9–11; 3:3; 4:35; etc.).[14]

"Flesh of Flesh"

Liturgical and sexual motifs are also intertwined in the second phrase. Leviticus 18:6 prohibits Israelite men from approaching any "flesh of his flesh" to uncover nakedness. Two different words for "flesh" are used. The first and rarer is *she'er* (cf. 18:12, 13, 17), used sometimes to describe the musculature of a human body but also in contexts where it is best translated as "meat" (cf. Exod 21:10; Ps 78:20, 27). In two passages, *she'er* describes human flesh consumed by cannibalistic rulers:

> For thus says the LORD of hosts, the God of Israel: "The daughter of Babylon is like a threshing floor at the time it is stamped firm; yet in a little while the time of harvest will come for her." "Nebuchadnezzar king of Babylon has devoured me and crushed me; he has set me down like an empty vessel; he has swallowed me like a monster; he has filled his stomach with my delicacies; he has washed me away. May the violence done to me and to my flesh (*she'er*) be upon Babylon," the inhabitant of Zion will say; and, "May my blood be upon the inhabitants of Chaldea," Jerusalem will say. (Jer 51:33–35 NASB)

---

13. The phrasing of the prohibition of bestiality in 18:23 is also suggestive of a cultic setting. Women are forbidden to "stand before" an animal to mate with it, and that is the terminology used to describe the duties of the Aaronic priests before Yahweh (Deut 10:8).

14. At the 2009 Biblical Horizons Summer Conference, Jordan offered a brilliant meditation on the epithalamion Psalm 45 as sacrificial approach.

> And I said, "Hear now, heads of Jacob and rulers of the house of Israel, is it not for you to know justice? You who hate good and love evil, who tear off their skin from them and their flesh (*she'er*) from their bones, who eat the flesh (*she'er*) of my people, strip off their skin from them, break their bones and chop them up as for the pot and as meat in a kettle." (Mic 3:1–3 NASB)

The use of this word in Leviticus 18:6 suggests, first, a link between uncovering forbidden flesh and seizing forbidden food,[15] and, second, that forbidden sexual approaches are a form of violence, an assault and transgression, a "cannibalism" of the woman.[16]

The second word for "flesh" is the more usual word, *basar*. Literally, the word describes the muscle that covers the bones and organs and is itself clothed by skin. "Flesh" is in the intermediate position in the human body; it is the "holy place" between the veil of the skin and the "inner sanctuary" of the heart and kidneys. Elsewhere, "flesh" implies weakness, frailty, mortality ("all flesh is grass"; "flesh and blood cannot inherit the kingdom") in contrast to the Spiritual body promised in the eschaton. In the purity laws of Leviticus 15, "flesh" refers specifically to the sexual organs, from which defiling issues flow.

What counts as a "flesh of flesh" relation in Leviticus 18? Most obviously, the phrase describes strictly biological/genetic relations. Verse 7 prohibits uncovering the nakedness of a mother, who is the same "flesh" as her son because she is a direct biological ancestor. Sisters (v. 9) are explicitly described as "flesh of flesh," horizontally related to a brother through parents or a parent (v. 11). "Flesh of flesh" relations exist between myself and siblings of my immediate ancestors. An aunt is not a direct ancestor, but she shares flesh with my father or mother, and so she is flesh of my flesh (vv. 12–13).

Fictive "flesh of flesh" relations also exist where there is no biological connection at all. Verse 8 prohibits uncovering nakedness of one's father's wife, presumably not a mother. Though I share no genetic link with a stepmother, she is counted as my "flesh," and excluded. At a further remove, verse 14 prohibits uncovering nakedness of a father's brother's wife. My father has no direct blood relation with this woman—she is his sister-in-law—and she certainly has no blood relation with me. Yet she is prohibited because she is counted as "flesh of flesh." In addition to the direct biological flesh relations, Leviticus 18 acknowledges what we might call "covenant flesh" relations and requires that these be honored as fully as biological relations. Yahweh, in short, sanctions and protects "socially constructed" kin relations.

From the explicit regulations, we can begin to draw some more general rules. First, however, we should note that Leviticus 18 and 20 imply a distinction between horizontal and vertical flesh relations. Maternal incest is a capital crime (20:11) and so is incest with a daughter-in-law (20:12), but brother-sister incest is punished by "cutting off"

---

15. Jordan's extended treatment of the parallels of sexual and festive "incorporation" are relevant here. See his study, "The Meaning of Eating in the Bible," *Studies in Food and Faith* 7 (Jan. 1990).

16. In medieval Western and other political systems, rulers are conceived of as political "fathers," and their exploitation and oppression of their children is sometimes characterized as incestuous rape. See Archibald, *Incest in Medieval Imagination*, 145–46. The biblical phrases "daughter Jerusalem" and "daughter Zion" point to a similar conception: Rulers who pillage their cities are rapists and incestuous fathers.

(20:17; *karet*), perhaps an act of Yahweh (cf. 20:2–3) or a punishment like banishment or excommunication.

Leviticus 18 treats horizontal and vertical relations differently as well. Any vertical relation, no matter how distant, is a "flesh of flesh" relation and therefore excluded; horizontally, however, "flesh," we might say, *dissipates* at a certain point, so that along the horizontal axis of flesh relations, some women eventually become available. At what point does flesh dissipate sufficiently to make a woman accessible? Who stands *outside* the "flesh of flesh" relation?

We can answer that question by penetrating beneath the explicit prohibitions to the system of rules that govern the system, summarized by Figure 1.

Figure 1: Rules of Incest

    I. Notation.[17]

        F^1 = Blood relation
        vF^1 = Vertical blood relation (e.g., mother, daughter)
        hF^1 = Horizontal blood relation (e.g., sister)
        F^2 = Relation by marriage (e.g., spouse, sister-in-law, daughter-in-law)

    II. Rules.

1. Primary F^1 relations are prohibited (no intercourse with or marriage to mother, sister, [implicitly] daughter).

2. Secondary F^1 relations are prohibited (no intercourse with or marriage to father's sister or mother's sister).

3. Primary F^1 relations of my spouse (F^2) are prohibited (no intercourse with or marriage to my wife's or my wife's sister).

4. Relations of spouses (F^2) of my blood relations (F^1) may be permitted.

    4a. If the blood relation to me is vertical (vF^1), the relation is prohibited (e.g., the wife of my father's brother).

    4b. If the blood relation (F^1) to the spouse (F^2) of my blood relation is vertical (vF^1), the relation is prohibited (e.g., the daughter of my brother's wife, my brother's mother-in-law).

    4c. If the blood relation both to me and to the spouse is horizontal (hF^1), the relation is permitted (e.g., the sister of my brother's wife).

---

17. Anthropologists typically use the terms consanguinity (brother-sister), affinity (spouse), and descent (parent-child) to describe these basic kin relations. I use variations on "F" to reflect the fact that for Leviticus, all of these qualify as "flesh of flesh" relations.

III. Rules in symbolic form.
 1. Me – F^1: Prohibited.
 2. Me – F^1 – F^1: Prohibited.
 3. Me – F^2 – F^1: Prohibited.
 4a. Me – vF^1 – F^1 – F^2: Prohibited.
 4b. Me – F^1 – F^2 – vF^1: Prohibited.
 4c. Me – hF^1 – F^2 – hF^1: Allowed.

Three prohibited categories are involved here. Vertical blood relations—whether ancestors or descendants—are always prohibited and violations are punished with death. Horizontal blood relations are prohibited but not punished with death. "Covenant kin" are treated as flesh relatives, so that women related to me by marriage to a direct blood relative are not available.

A chain of flesh relations may be broken if it is a certain length or if it consists of a combination of vertical and horizontal steps. My first cousin is available.[18] Even though it consists entirely of blood relations, the chain of vF^1 (father) – hF^1 (brother) – vF^1 (daughter) is long enough to open up access. One operative principle is that flesh dissipates at the third degree, when F^1 relations are involved; my father's brother counts as "flesh of flesh," but his daughter does not:

$$\begin{matrix} 1 & 2 & 3 \\ \text{Me}^{\wedge\wedge}\text{Father}^{\wedge\wedge}\text{Brother}^{\wedge\wedge}\text{Daughter} \end{matrix}$$

A second principle is that the chain is broken because there is more than one vertical relation (mine to my father, my uncle's to his daughter). The zigzag of vertical relations dissipates "flesh of flesh" relations.

If a cousin is permitted, can I have my aunt, my uncle's wife (vF^1 [father] – hF^1 [brother] – F^2 [wife])? She also seems to be three degrees separated from me, and she is not even a blood relation:

$$\begin{matrix} 1 & 2 & 3 \\ \text{Me}^{\wedge\wedge}\text{father}^{\wedge\wedge}\text{brother}^{\wedge\wedge}\text{wife} \end{matrix}$$

Yet, she is explicitly prohibited (18:14). Why? There are two answers to this: My uncle and his wife are considered "one flesh," so there are, by Leviticus's reckoning, only two degrees separating me from my aunt:

$$\begin{matrix} 1 & 2 \\ \text{Me}^{\wedge\wedge}\text{father}^{\wedge\wedge}\text{brother/wife} \end{matrix}$$

Further, there is no vertical break in the chain, as there is with my cousin.

Could I marry my uncle's mother-in-law? The chain looks like this:

---

18. Several cousin-marriages appear after Leviticus 18 without condemnation or even comment. The daughters of Zelophahad marry their "uncles' sons" (Num 36:11), and Caleb gives his daughter Achsah to the son of his brother Kenaz (Josh 15:16–17; Judg 1:12–13).

PART ONE: BIBLICAL STUDIES

$$\text{Me}\overset{1}{\wedge\wedge}\text{father}\overset{2}{\wedge\wedge}\text{brother/wife}\overset{3}{\wedge\wedge}\text{mother to aunt}$$

The answer is Yes. My aunt's mother is three degrees separated from me.

Finally, chains of flesh relations may also be broken, and broken sooner, by the intervention of F^2 relations than by the zigzags of F^1 relations. By the same line of reasoning, I could marry my brother's wife's sister, even though the chain is only two links long:

$$\text{Me}\overset{1}{\wedge\wedge}\text{brother/wife}\overset{2}{\wedge\wedge}\text{sister}$$

In sum, along the horizontal axis of relation, F^1 flesh "dissipates" at the third degree when the chain zigzags between vertical and horizontal relations; F^2 flesh dissipates at the second degree (counting spouses as "one flesh," that is, one degree).

With these details before us, we can draw some conclusions about the theological rationale for this system of prohibited sexual relations. We can begin by noting the analogy between the system of incest prohibitions and the system of graded holiness[19] that organizes the entire world of the Levitical system. This chart lays out the scheme in a simplified form:

Space	Personnel	Incest
Most Holy	High Priest	vF^1
Holy	Priests	hF^1
Court	Israelites	F^2

These analogies help to explain why incest rules are introduced in detail at the same time as the tabernacle system, and they call attention to the common theme of exclusion (from holy space, from "flesh of flesh" relatives) that is a central feature of the Mosaic order. Just as a veil separates Israel from Yahweh's presence, so the veils covering a close female relative ought not be drawn back. To seize the flesh of my flesh is a kind of sacrilege, analogous to treading on Yahweh's holy ground.[20]

Genesis 2:24 also provides key background. A man is prohibited from taking a wife from his father's house; marriage must be exogamous, ex-static.[21] Translated into the

---

19. The term is from Peter Philip Jenson, *Graded Holiness: A Key to the Priestly Conception of the World*, JSOT Supplement (Sheffield: Sheffield Academic, 1992).

20. This doesn't mean that the incest prohibitions were discontinued with the coming of the New Covenant. The decision of the Jerusalem Council (Acts 15) indicates that the sexual legislation of Leviticus remains in place, applicable to Gentiles.

21. Rosenstock-Huessy plays with the link between the passions of sexual ecstasy and the need for marriage to be exogamous. Brides *become* sisters (Song 4:9—5:1), and a husband's recognition of the non-sexual sisterly dimensions of marriage is essential to marriage, but the first name of the bride must be "beloved" or "sweetheart" rather than sister. A woman whose *initial* love-name is "mother" or "sister" cannot arouse the ecstasy of first encounter that is the passionate ground of marriage. On this basis, Rosenstock suggests that elementary schools have a quasi-incestuous effect, since they link pre-pubescent boys and girls who may later marry in brother-sister relations and thus make the ecstatic moment impossible ("Tribalism," in *I Am An Impure Thinker* [Norwich, VT: Argo, 1970], 133–34).

terms of Leviticus 18, Genesis 2 requires that a man cut off "flesh of flesh" relations in his father's house (mother, sister, half-sister, aunts) in order to become one flesh with his wife. Marriage is thus analogous to circumcision: Proper marriage requires a stripping of flesh. And marriage is also analogous to the procedure for animal offering, which is fundamentally a sequence of uncovering and transformative re-covering. In the ascension offering (Lev 1), the animal's skin is removed so that its flesh can be vested, like Yahweh Himself, in fire and smoke. Symbolically, representatively, that happens to the worshiper as well; he is stripped of his old, decayed, unclean skin and transfigured to approach the presence of Yahweh. Marriage likewise strips a man's "flesh of flesh" so that he can become a new flesh in union with his wife, so that he can assume a new skin.

Marriage is thus creative, a replication of the division and reunion that was the pattern of the original creation. In building Eve, Yahweh follows the same procedure of division and reunion: He tears Adam asunder and then commands him to form one flesh with his bride. As a creative movement of cutting off and uniting, of discarding old flesh and taking on new flesh, the family is an institution of generational renewal, constant creativity, movement of wealth and power. Marriage, like animal offerings, marks a new beginning. Incest, as Leviticus 20 implies, is the way of death, producing a static social world that never changes, cannot mature.

"Uncover Nakedness"

The third key phrase of 18:6 is "uncover nakedness," used throughout the chapter to describe illicit sexual sin, particularly incest. The Bible's theology of nakedness begins in the early chapters of Genesis. Prior to sin, Adam and Eve are naked yet unashamed (Gen 2:25), but as soon as they sin, they recognize their nakedness and attempt to cover it. Nakedness becomes associated with shame, and this shame is concentrated in the sexual organs: Adam and Eve make loin coverings from fig leaves (Gen 3:7), covering their genitals from one another.

Shame in the Bible is not only embarrassment but defeat, whether in legal conflict or in war. Bodies of the slain were literally "stripped," exposed to public shame, and a man defeated in court was exposed to retribution.

In Genesis, Yahweh provides covering to hide the shame of Adam and Eve, but also to vest them in robes of office. Yet the first moment of sacrifice is a further shame, stripping the fig leaves, exposing to Yahweh's presence and judgment. Only when Adam and Eve have been fully exposed does Yahweh invest them with glory, a tunic that covers shame and prepares them for rule and ministry outside the garden. This was the effect of the first sacrifice and the first and main purpose of all subsequent sacrifice. The sacrificial sequence is the sequence of divestiture and reinvestiture, of stripping and recovering, a removal of false or corrupted glory and bestowal of renewed glory.

From this angle, sexual sins that "uncover nakedness" constitute a de-sacrifice. Marriage, as we have noted, involves a sacrificial "cutting off" and "union," and sexual sin, especially incest, is an assault on the marriage that seeks to undo the sacrificial origins of the one-flesh relation.

PART ONE: BIBLICAL STUDIES

Leviticus 18 emphasizes that incest shames people who are to be honored. The command to "honor" father and mother in the law uses the verb *kabad*, to "give glory" or "to make weighty." Honoring father and mother is to give weight to their words, actions, discipline. Honor to parents also means "covering" them with the glory of praise, of respectful speech, of obedient action, of deferential protection of their reputation. A wise son is the glory of his father because the father is "covered over" with glory-clothing by the wisdom of his son. A son can shame a father by words or actions, but in Leviticus 18:7 a son brings shame by stripping the covering from the father, the covering that hides the father's nakedness. This helps to explain how 20:9 sneaks into these chapters.

Of course, the exposure of the father's shame is not literally the exposure of his *own* sexual organs. Rather, a son uncovers his father's nakedness and exposes him to shame when he takes his father's wife, the wife who *is* his glory (1 Cor 11:7).[22] In marriage, a man spreads the wing of his garment over his wife as a sign of taking her into a one-flesh relation, and the covering is a covering of covenant authority and protection. Husband and wife thus share flesh and are covered with a single robe or covering, so that uncovering the mother equally uncovers the father (cf. Deut 22:30; Ruth 3:9; Ezek 16:8). A woman who willingly throws off that covering is throwing off her husband; likewise, a man who has sex with a close relative strips off another man's covering, flouts her husband's authority, and penetrates a barrier, and a man who approaches his mother for sex strips his father of the glory of his bride. Again we see analogies between sexual and liturgical concerns: Uncovering nakedness is a sacrilege, a trespass on "holy space." Drawing back the cover of a father's nakedness is analogous to pulling back the veil of the Holy Place.

In some prophetic passages, Yahweh warns that He will punish harlot Israel by stripping her bare and exposing her nakedness (Isa 47:3; Ezek 16:36–37; Nah 3:5). Exposing nakedness is her sin; she offers herself to every passerby on every high hill and under every green tree. In retribution, the Lord gives her more of the same, an eye-for-eye retribution: "You want to expose yourself," Yahweh says. "I'll expose you. You want to be uncovered; I'll give you uncovering."

The threat of "uncovering nakedness" links subtly with the threat of exile. Throughout Leviticus 18, the verb for "uncover" is *galah*, the word most commonly used for exile (2 Kgs 15:29; 16:9; 17:6, 11, 23, 26–28; 24:14–15; 25:11, 21; cf. "nakedness of the land" in Gen 42:9, 12). Exile is an "uncovering" of the land. People are the glory-covering of a land, and if the people are removed, then so is the glory and dress. When people leave the

---

22. This, perhaps, is what is going on in Genesis 9. Jordan has interpreted this story as an assault on Noah's authority, an attempt to seize the robe (most recently in *Primeval Saints: Studies in the Patriarchs of Genesis* [Moscow, ID: Canon, 2001], 51–54). It is possible that the specific form of assault may have been incestuous. Seeing or exposing nakedness is used in Leviticus to refer to incestuous sex. Though Leviticus 18 typically uses "uncover nakedness" to refer to incest, Leviticus 20:17 does use "see nakedness." Arguably, we are to understand that Ham raped or seduced his mother and the son of that union was cursed, just as Lot's incestuous sons also later became. See John Sietze Bergsma and Scott W. Hahn, "Noah's Nakedness and the Curse on Canaan (Genesis 9:20–27)," *Journal of Biblical Literature* 124 (2005) 25–40. Against this interpretation, the response of Seth and Japheth, who refuse to *look* at their father, suggests that Ham's fault was literally to see his father's nakedness.

land, there is no one to plant, cultivate, or harvest; the land is stripped of the glory-robe of crops and instead reverts to naked dust, crowned with thorns rather than wheat, olive trees, vines. Exiles themselves are uncovered as they are taken from the land. Slaves went about naked, or virtually so, and people are driven into exile stripped of their clothing and glory and possessions. Symbolically, the exile is a stripping of the covering of Yahweh's protection and covenant. Exile is an eye-for-eye punishment: Yahweh's bride has not obeyed Him; she has thrown off His robe, and so Yahweh removes the vestiges of covering that remain.

The notion of "uncovering" also has a sacrificial dimension. Sacrifice, as explained above, provides covering, but only for "inadvertencies" or if confession of sin accompanies sacrifice. High-handed sins are uncovered sins, shameful, exposed, unforgiven, uncovered. When Israel attempts to hide her sins by some means other than Yahweh's ordained sacrifice, she is engaged in self-hiding, self-covering. Fig leaves are not coverings for sin but are emblematic of the state of sin. Yahweh punishes this self-hiding and self-covering, this rejection of sacrificial covering, by removing the protection of sacrificial covering. Literally, when Israel goes into exile, Yahweh puts an end to covering sacrifice until a temple is built; theologically, exile is a denial of sacrificial covering because the Lord's patience ends and He refuses to cover over sin and shame and instead determines to expose it.

Scripture never describes licit marital sex as "uncovering nakedness." Biblically, marital sexuality takes place "under cover," under the cover of a marital covenant, a marital tent or robe. Sexual activity done under the single covering of a marriage bed is not an exposure of nakedness; the wedding night is a sacrificial moment, as the husband and bride strip off their clothes and lie together under a single covering in their common bed. Sexual fidelity is sexual activity under the cover of Yahweh's favor.

The use of the phrase "uncover nakedness" thus emphasizes the complex paradoxes of covering and uncovering that this chapter points to. Sexual sin, in practice, takes place under cover. An unfaithful woman meets her lover at a hotel room, at night, in secret. Yet, Scripture describes this kind of sexual sin as "uncovering." In the very effort to cover, sinners are exposed to shame. Redemption from sexual sin, or any other, is first of all the death of stripping skin, an exposure, which leads to the resurrection of new vestments.[23]

One last observation, of a more pastoral character: The sexual union of husband and wife is at the heart of marriage, but Leviticus 18 makes it clear that the "unashamed nakedness" of husband and wife is only half the story of a healthy household. Even within the husband-wife relationship, Leviticus sets up a veil, prohibiting sexual union with a wife during her menstrual period (Lev 18:19; 20:18). A man who does not see his wife

---

23. The pastoral import of this line of thought is enormous. Families where incest has occurred are understandably reluctant to bring the dirty family secret to the surface. By the logic of sacrifice, however, the only hope for healing lies in exposure. Adam would find no redemption hiding among the trees; he had to be drawn out, stripped of his leaves, and judged before he could be clothed with new robes. The same logic holds for metaphorical incest: A pastor is a father figure to his congregation, and a pastor who sexually abuses the "sons and daughters" of his church has committed a kind of paternal incest. An abusive church cannot be healed until the wrong is brought to the surface, repented of or disciplined. These thoughts were sparked by comments by Rich Bledsoe at the 2009 Biblical Horizons Summer Conference.

as a sister, who does not recognize that he has both a sexual and non-sexual relation with his wife, cannot be a husband.[24] Leviticus likewise erects impenetrable veils between other family members, between sons and mothers, fathers and daughters-in-law, between brother and sister. It is a sign of family sickness when members of a family are, literally or metaphorically, naked to one another.[25] Like Yahweh's house, the tabernacle, the home envisioned by Leviticus 18 is articulated into private spaces. While the father is seen as head of the home in certain respects, Leviticus does not envision him spreading the wing of his garment over his entire home. He does *not* have sexual rights over his daughter, a fairly drastic limitation on patriarchal authority.

THE MISSING DAUGHTER

I have just said that a father does not have sexual rights over his daughter. That is clear from the logic of the system examined above: Fathers are in an F^1 relation to daughters, with only a single degree separating them. My guess is that father-daughter incest was a capital crime, since it involved sexual violation of a vF^1 relation (cf. 20:12). Yet, the text does not state this prohibition explicitly.[26] The gap is arresting, and opens up broader theological perspectives on incest.

We can go some way toward explaining this anomaly by noting that Leviticus 20:12 calls incest with a daughter-in-law *tebel*. The word is very rare in the Hebrew Bible, and lexicons generally link it with the word *balal*, "confuse," the verb used for the confusion of lips in Genesis 11.[27] The only other use of this word in the Old Testament is in Leviticus 18:23, where it describes bestiality.[28] Bestiality is more obviously a form of "confusion," a confusion of created kinds and a transgression of boundaries between man and other

---

24. Rosenstock-Huessy, "Tribalism," 130.

25. Of course, very young children need to be changed and bathed and so must be exposed to their parents. After children are potty-trained and capable of bathing themselves, their nakedness should be covered from parents and siblings. There may be complications and exceptions, but the general rule should be that, apart from husband and wife, the members of the family are veiled to one another.

26. Jacob Milgrom (*Leviticus 17–22*, Anchor Bible #3A [Garden City: Doubleday, 2000], 1527) claims that father-daughter incest is excluded by Leviticus 18:6 and that the rest of the passage focuses on incest that is not directly condemned by that general rule. This is unconvincing: The rule does prohibit father-daughter incest, but the general rule also prohibits mother-son incest and yet the text explicitly prohibits the latter but not the former.

27. Hirsch intriguingly links *tebel* with *balah*, defining the latter as "the gradual accomplishment of the non-existence of the hitherto existing," and points to its use "in reference to mechanical or physical processes, the wearing away of substance through use or age" (Samson Raphael Hirsch, *The Pentateuch: Leviticus* [Gateshead: Judaica Press, 1989], 492). Thus, he describes the sins labeled *tebel* as sins that lead to a "complete degeneration."

28. Again, the pastoral implications are intriguing. Incest generates confusion, perhaps especially confusion of tongues. An incestuous family cannot communicate. Nothing means what it appears to mean. In a family where father-daughter incest has taken place, "daddy" is not daddy, mother and daughter have exchanged places, daughter has become "lover." That confusion at the heart of the family's speech overflows in confusion of speech everywhere, as well as confusion of roles and orders in the family. "My uncle-father and aunt-mother," Hamlet says, in a play full of the linguistic *tebel* of an incestuous home. Conversely, faced with a chaotic family where communication has become impossible, a pastor might begin to explore whether incest has occurred.

creatures. By using the term *tebel* to describe incest with a daughter-in-law, however, Leviticus hints at a parallel between incest with daughters-in-law and bestiality: Taking a daughter-in-law confuses categories and transgress boundaries as thoroughly as sex with a goat.

How? Why is *that* form of incest "confusion" and not other forms? How is daughter-in-law incest more confusing than incest with one's mother or one's granddaughter?

A Girardian perspective provides part of the answer.[29] A daughter-in-law or prospective daughter-in-law is *the* new woman in the family, *the* woman who comes from outside, the only woman attached to the family who has no direct flesh-relation with a husband and father. A man who has had no stirring of incestuous desire toward a daughter he has fathered, taught to read and walk, driven to school, may well be tempted by the introduction of a nubile stranger into the intimate circle of his family. As Girard's theory suggests, a man may respond to his son's desire for this new woman with mimetic desire for the same woman. In short, the introduction of the daughter-in-law has the potential to stir rivalry between father and son. Practically, a disruptive rivalry over a daughter-in-law is far more plausible than Freud's Oedipal rivalry over the mother; few sons are sexually attracted to women of their mother's generation, but many fathers lust after women of their children's age. That this scenario might produce *tebel* on a catastrophic scale is fairly obvious and is depicted in excruciating and utterly plausible detail in Louis Malle's 1992 film, *Damage*.[30]

The *tebel* of father/daughter-in-law incest is evident on another level as well: A father who seeks or seizes his daughter-in-law confuses generations. The older generation enters into competition with the younger, and the father who is supposed to direct his son forward to the future becomes instead a rival on his son's erotic playing field. This confusion of generations knots the thread of time, the thread of the future.

Knotted time is time enslaved. Above, we noted that marriage is inherently sacrificial and thus concerned with newness and fresh starts. Incest arrests that progress. More abstractly, incest arrests time. Our most explicit extra-biblical evidence for Egyptian brother-sister incest is from the Ptolemaic dynasty, and there incest expressed a political ideology committed to securing a static political and social system. Cross-generational incest, whether with a daughter or a daughter-in-law, especially retards time's progress.

Biblically, families come into being in order to die. Husbands marry wives and produce children who will leave to form families of their own. Eventually the house empties out, and in the end even the husband and wife are gone. Families are the seed cast to the ground so they can die to make room for a new family, the family of the future. Parents consecrate their children toward the future, but to do that they must be willing to assume the responsibility of the past that is passing away. Incest is an effort to keep the family from dying, to assert its immortality; it attempts to keep the family intact. Father-

---

29. Thanks to Rich Bledsoe for this suggestion.

30. The adultery in the film is not technically incestuous, since the woman is not yet married to the son. But father and son share the woman sexually.

daughter incest tries to drag the future back into the past, the new generation back into the old. The only result can be decadence and static traditionalism.[31]

If pulling the future (daughter) back into the past (father) leads to decadence, collapsing the past into the future can only create revolutionary confusion.[32] In either case, incest with a daughter or daughter-in-law confuses the deep structures of family and social life.

We may make a similar point from another angle:[33] Daughters first become prominent in the Bible in Genesis 6, in the "prophetic" stage of primeval history, after Adamic/priestly/paternal and Cainite/kingly/fraternal phases. Daughters are associated with the prophetic ministry of forming the future and are linked to the prophetic zone of life—not the sanctuary or the land but the world. Relations with the "outside" world involve giving and taking of daughters (cf. Deut 7:3; cf. Judg 3:6). Families move forward and outward through daughters. When daughters are tied up within the family, the family has no future, no witness before the world.

All these reflections only intensify the oddity of the missing daughter: If preventing father-daughter incest is a key to a family's future and its relation to the world outside, then it seems that this form of incest deserves explicit attention and severe prohibition in the law. Yet, again, the text has no prohibition at all.

We get a part of the answer when we recognize that *absence* can be a form of emphasis. Genesis, for instance, is structured by a series of *toledoth* statements ("these are the generations of . . ."), each of which introduces the descendants of the one named in the formula. Strikingly, there is no *toledoth* of Abraham; Genesis skips from the generations of Terah (11:27; the narrative of Abraham) to the generations of Isaac (25:19; the narrative of Jacob). Isaac, whose life story would dominate the *toledoth* of Abraham, is structurally expunged from the history. Similarly, 1–2 Kings introduces virtually every reign with a formulaic introduction, but the introduction is absent for the reign of Athaliah (2 Kgs 11). It is as if she never reigned at all. Leviticus 18 and 20 call attention to the prohibition of father-daughter incest precisely by *not* mentioning it: If the text included this prohibition, would commentators have puzzled over the issue as they have for millennia? Has anyone devoted the same ingenuity to explaining the prohibition of maternal incest?

Still, I submit that the rationale for this lacuna lies not primarily in the sociological but in the theological implications of the law. Highlighted by its glaring absence, father-daughter incest points to the character of Israel's God. To see how, we may begin with an apparently impious observation: Yahweh's relationship to Israel appears to be a prime example of incestuous *tebel*. Yahweh is Father to Israel, His "son" (Exod 4:23). Yet Israel (perhaps "daughter of my people," Isa 22:4), or at least Jerusalem, is also "*daughter*" (2

---

31. See Jordan, "Lot: Meditations," *Biblical Horizons* 116 (April 1999).

32. These thoughts were inspired by Eugen Rosenstock-Huessy's comments on the incest taboo in tribalism; see "Tribalism," 129–33. My comments also borrow from Rosenstock's "cross of reality."

33. This paragraph draws on the paradigm of priest, king, prophet most fully laid out in Jordan's *From Bread to Wine: Toward a More Biblical Liturgical Theology*, draft ed. 1.1 (Niceville: Biblical Horizons, 2001).

Kgs 19:21; Ps 9:14; Isa 1:8; 52:2; 62:11; Jer 4:31; 6:2; Lam 2, *passim*). Yet again, Yahweh also promises to renew covenant with Jerusalem and the land "as a young man marries a virgin" and to rejoice over her "as a bridegroom rejoices over the bride" (Isa 62:5). In the end, Jerusalem descends from heaven like a bride adorned for her husband (Rev 21:2). As bride, Jerusalem is also mother (Gal 4:26), the barren woman who rejoices over the children her husband, Yahweh, provides for her (Isa 54:1–8). The confusion becomes most pronounced in Ezekiel 16, where Yahweh tells an allegory of His love for Jerusalem: Having found her as an infant squirming in the blood of her afterbirth, He washed, clothed, and adopted her, but when she comes to puberty, He covers her with his robe to hide her nakedness and to claim her as His bride (v. 8), only to find her throwing herself to the well-hung phallic gods of the nations (cf. 23:20). In a single passage, Yahweh is adoptive Father and protective Husband to Israel, Father and Lover, while Israel fills the dual role of daughter and bride.

Leviticus 18 prepares us for these divine confusions by its silence on father-daughter incest: Yahweh never prohibits father-daughter incest, because, it would seem, He practices it Himself.

In terms of theology proper, there are two directions to go from here. The first option is voluntarist and nominalist: Perhaps, like ancient and medieval kings who violated common standards of incest, Yahweh flouts the conventions for which He condemns His people to demonstrate His *potentia absoluta*. Yahweh can do what He pleases, and no one can answer Him back. He is unbound, even by the rules He lays down for us, even though the rules He lays down reflect His own character. That line of thought is a classic expression of what Jordan has called "Islamo-Calvinist" theology. Fortunately, it is not the only option.

A Trinitarian solution is also possible and far more satisfactory: Under the Old Covenant, Israel was forced to puzzle over the revelation that Yahweh is both Father and Husband to Israel. The jarring implicit incest offered a puzzle designed to arouse Israel to consider the plurality within the life of Yahweh, the possibility of an eternal divine society. Perhaps, they would begin to suspect, Yahweh is both Father and Husband to Israel because Yahweh is Himself both Father and Son. Ultimately, the knot is undone by the gospel's fuller uncovering of Triune life, its revelation of a Father who so loves His daughter that He sends His Son to give Himself and ultimately, as Jonathan Edwards put it, to introduce her into the family of Triune life as the bride of His Son.[34]

Yahweh's glory is to conceal, but the glory of kings is to search out secrets. The missing daughter leaves a textual and legal hole that trained Israel for kingship, until, in the fullness of time, the gap was filled by the Father who sent the Son to spread the wing of His garment over Daughter Zion.[35]

---

34. Quoted in William J. Danaher, *The Trinitarian Ethics of Jonathan Edwards* (Louisville: Westminster John Knox, 2004), 87.

35. This conclusion only raises a further puzzle: If Israel is stepdaughter of the Father, how can Jesus, the "natural" Son, become her Husband (cf. Lev 20:17)? As a compliment to this book's royal readership, I leave that secret to your discovery.

PART ONE: BIBLICAL STUDIES

~

Dear Peter,

Thank you for this stimulating essay. As I have been instructed to do, I offer a few comments.

1. In footnote 21, it seems to me that Rosenstock is a bit off. Surely arranged marriages, probably the majority in history, do not begin with ecstasy that then moves into brother-sister familiarity. Moreover, since before Leviticus brother-sister marriages were allowed, and perhaps outside Israel were still all right until Acts 15, it seems to me that sisterly love often precedes marital ecstasy. In Canticles the phrase is "my sister, my bride," and in Genesis 2 Adam said, "This is bone of my bones," which is a reference to brotherly relations first of all (Gen 29:14). I think here Rosenstock's Christian romantic enthusiasm is getting the better of him.

2. In footnote 22, I would say that the sin of Ham may have been to invade his father's tent without permission, but primarily it is his telling his brothers what he saw rather than concealing it and covering for his father—all of which in context implies his desire to set up a conspiracy to seize the robe of authority from their father.

3. One difficulty with seeing the vertical relationships as always wrong from Genesis 2 forward is this: Moses' father married his aunt (Exod 6:16–20). I think it more than likely that Jochebed was the daughter of another wife of Levi, and a much later one, than was Amram's father Kohath, but it is still a vertical relationship that later was prohibited (Lev 18:12). Moreover, given the long lifespans before and after the Flood, it seems likely to me that there were many vertical marriages with aunts and uncles of various distances. It seems that only marriage to one's own father or mother, or step-parent, would have been prohibited before Sinai.

4. Girard's discussion of the father's attraction to the new woman, the younger daughter-in-law, only adds more depth to the command that a man move away from his father and mother when he marries (Gen 2:24). If this separation is necessary from the beginning in order for new cultures to be produced, how much more important is it in a world under the fall?

5. On the general matter of the absence of father-daughter incest in Leviticus 18, it seems to me that it is pretty clear from Genesis 2:24. Since the woman was taken from the man, it follows that she is included in this rule: if the man is to leave his parents, she must leave her parents also. That does not explain, of course, why the matter is not repeated and addressed in Leviticus 18.

6. Finally, I think we have to ask why brother-sister and nephew-aunt marriages were just fine and dandy before Sinai. It won't do to say they were "exceptions." My own thought is that it has to do with maturation. When the race was in infancy, marrying close relatives was proper. As we mature, God's Spirit impels outward, giving more mature people more strength, so that marriage may no longer be with close relatives. If people feel shame today about relations that were righteous and good before Sinai, that indicates that the Spirit's operation in creating the human environment has changed.

Jim

4

Holy War Fulfilled and Transformed

A Look at Some Important New Testament Texts

RICH LUSK

HOLY WAR FROM JOSHUA TO JESUS

IN THE BOOK OF Joshua, the Israelites wage war against the inhabitants of the land of Canaan. This divinely commissioned, aggressive, and total warfare is often referred to as "holy war."[1] Holy war is a major, though neglected, theme in the Scriptures. This paper will not attempt to give a comprehensive overview of the biblical doctrine of holy war since that has been done elsewhere.[2] Rather, our goal is to highlight the way several often overlooked New Testament texts help us properly understand the way in which holy war has been transformed through the coming of the Greater Joshua, Jesus Christ.[3] The New Testament uses martial imagery to portray the church's mission and, while our warfare is very different from Joshua's in many respects, understanding the relationship of Israel's conquest to the church's mission is vital to biblical theology and application.

God's commands to the Israelites were clear:

> When the LORD your God brings you into the land which you go to possess, and has cast out many nations before you, the Hittites and the Girgashites and the

---

1. Alternatively, some have referred to it as "Yahweh war" to emphasize the Lord's leading role in all holy war campaigns.

2. While the theme of holy war has not received its due in mainstream biblical scholarship, it has been a major theme in the writings of James B. Jordan. See Jordan's "The Holy War in America Today: Some Observations on Abortion Rescues," Views and Reviews: Open Book Occasional Paper 2 (Niceville, FL: Biblical Horizons, 1989). Jordan suggests holy war is one of the three major overlapping themes in the Bible: "1. The Bible is given to help us mature and grow up as images of God so that we take dominion wisely over all of life. 2. The Bible is also given, because of Satan's rebellion, to teach us holy war against principalities and powers. 3. The Bible is also given, because of Adam's rebellion, to show us the history of redemption." Cf. Jordan, "How to Do Reformed Theology Nowadays, Part 3," *Biblical Horizons* 194 (May 2007). Online: http://www.biblicalhorizons.com/biblical-horizons/no-194-how-to-do-reformed-theology-nowadays-part-3/.

3. "Jesus" is the Greek form of the name "Joshua." The name means "Yahweh saves."

PART ONE: BIBLICAL STUDIES

> Amorites and the Canaanites and the Perizzites and the Hivites and the Jebusites, seven nations greater and mightier than you, and when the LORD your God delivers them over to you, you shall conquer them and utterly destroy them. You shall make no covenant with them nor show mercy to them. . . . But thus you shall deal with them: you shall destroy their altars, and break down their sacred pillars, and cut down their wooden images, and burn their carved images with fire. (Deut 7:1–2, 5; cf. 20:16–18)

Israel's obedience to those commands was inconsistent, but when they did obey successfully, the Bible does not mince words:

> So the people shouted when the priests blew the trumpets. And it happened when the people heard the sound of the trumpet, and the people shouted with a great shout, that the wall fell down flat. Then the people went up into the city, every man straight before him, and they took the city. And they utterly destroyed all that was in the city, both man and woman, young and old, ox and sheep and donkey, with the edge of the sword. (Josh 6:20–21; cf. 8:24–29; 10:28, 40; 11:10–12, 14–15, 16–23)

We know that God does not want the church to fight this kind of violent, bloody battle against particular people groups today. Jesus did not take up the sword, but instead waged war against Satan, sin, and death throughout His earthly ministry, culminating in His sacrificial and substitutionary death on the cross. Paul said our warfare is not against blood and flesh (Eph 6:10–20) and our weapons are not carnal (2 Cor 10:4–6).[4] We know we will inherit the nations, but not through bloodshed—unless it is our own (Rev 2:26–27). The church suffers and serves her way to victory. We conquer, not by inflicting pain, but by bearing pain for the life of the world, in union with Jesus.[5]

But if we take the Scriptures seriously, and if we truly believe that all Scripture is inspired and profitable (cf. 2 Tim 3:16), we have to fit these Old Testament holy war texts into our understanding of God's purposes for His people. What, then, do we do with the holy war theme found in books like Deuteronomy and Joshua? Was the conquest an act of genocide? How do we apply these texts today? Specifically, how do we reconcile the conquest of Canaan with God's love for the world and the church's vocation to disciple the nations? How can the Warrior God also be the Prince of Peace? How do we reconcile the "furious opposites" (to use Chesterton's term) of biblical revelation? If we look at the Bible's story arc from beginning to end, we can arrive at satisfactory, albeit still mysterious, answers.

---

4. When Paul says our warfare is not against blood and flesh, he does not mean we do not have to wrestle against wicked men in various ways. We certainly do. Paul wrangled with blood and flesh when he dealt with false teachers, unjust judges, and so forth. But Paul is showing that our warfare really takes place on a different plane, with different weapons, strategies, and tactics. Paul is pointing to the war behind the war, namely our battle against Satan and false gods that enslave individuals and cultures. The "principalities and powers" are probably corporate idols and corrupt systems that twist and distort human life and society.

5. See Tremper Longman III and Daniel G. Reid, *God Is a Warrior* (Grand Rapids: Zondervan, 1995). There is still a place for the sword in the economy of the new covenant, of course. But the sword belongs to magistrates, not pastors (cf. Rom 13:1ff.).

THE CONQUEST IN CONTEXT

First, the notion that the conquest is genocidal is simply false. Morality, not race, was the key issue in the conquest. Ethics, not ethnicity, is the driving category. The Canaanites were not punished with extermination because they were Canaanites; rather, they were destroyed because they were wicked idolaters and God chose to no longer tolerate them on His earth. In other words, to call the conquest an act of "genocide" or "ethnic cleansing" is a category mistake. It would be more accurate to describe it as "idolater-cide."

God warned Israel against an attitude of racial pride from the beginning. God had already made it clear to the Israelites that they were not chosen to be His special people because they were a morally superior or numerically stronger nation in any way (Deut 7–9). Israel was specifically forbidden to assume that her possession of the land was a sign of her righteousness (Deut 9:4–6). However, there is no doubt the conquest was a judgment against Canaan's unrighteousness (Lev 18:24–25; 20:22–24; Deut 7:5; 9:5; 12:29–31; 1 Kgs 14:24; 21:26; 2 Kgs 16:3; 17:7; 21:2). This act of holy war was about divine judgment against false worship, not genocide against a particular ethnicity.

Two factors prove beyond all doubt that the conquest was not a racially motivated, genocidal attack. Note that the first Canaanite we meet, Rahab, is actually saved! This is striking: Israel has been commanded to wipe out the Canaanites because of their wickedness, and yet we are immediately introduced to a repentant Canaanite woman who fears God and shows loyalty to Israel (Josh 2:9–11; cf. Heb 11:31; Jas 2:25). As a result of her faith, her household is spared when the city of Jericho falls. The scarlet thread on her window (Josh 2:18) serves the same purpose as blood on the doorposts of Israelite dwellings in the exodus (Exod 12:22–23). Later, the Gibeonites are also spared (Josh 9), again showing that God is willing to save those under the ban if they repent and seek His favor.[6] The Gibeonites were incorporated into Israel as helpers to the Levitical priests (Josh 9:27). These instances of Gentile salvation in the midst of judgment foreshadow what is to come. Conversion, rather than conquest, will be the *ultimate* trajectory for the nations.[7] Grace for the nations will ultimately override judgment. The conquest narratives include foreshadowings of the new covenant gospel.

Also note that God threatens to treat Israel precisely the same way He treated the Canaanites if they fall into Canaanite patterns of life (Deut 9; cf. 2:1–12, 18–23). God is not partial in matters of justice (Acts 9–10; Rom 2). Israel's status before God is not an unconditional (e.g., race-based) privilege. God has already threatened to destroy Israel because of her sin (Num 14:11–25), just as He will destroy the Canaanites for their sin. The terms of the covenant threaten Israel with a Canaanite-like expulsion from the land if the nation rebels (Lev 18:28; Deut 28). Even in the books of Joshua and Judges, we find

---

6. Note that the Gibeonites, like Rahab, use righteous deception.

7. Note that those who left Egypt in the exodus were already a mixed multitude. Gentile stock was already included in the redeemed nation. During the period of wilderness wandering, the ethnic children of Abraham and these Gentile believers were woven together into one people. Surely, this is at least part of the reason why the wilderness generation was not circumcised until they were ready to enter the land (cf. Josh 5). The entire transitional forty year period was typological of the apostolic age, from AD 30–70, as we will see below.

that an Israelite individual (Achan) and a whole tribe (Benjamin) can become the objects of holy war. God will fight against His own people if they rebel. Much later in Israel's history, Israel will have done unto her what she did to the Canaanites, when God raises up the wicked empires of Assyria and Babylon to exile the nation. Israel can maintain residence in the holy land only so long as she lives as God's holy people. In short, if Israelites live like Canaanites, God treats them like Canaanites, and if Canaanites live like Israelites, they get treated like Israelites. The covenant is never absolutely tied to blood, but rather to faith. We are familiar with this as a New Testament truth, but it was already a principle in the old covenant.

Second, we need to note that the real prosecutor of holy war is not Israel, but the Lord. Indeed, this is one major distinction between "holy war" and what we could call (following Jordan) "normal war." In holy war, such as the exodus from Egypt and the conquest of Canaan, God Himself functions as chief commander (Exod 15:3; Josh 5:13–15) and combatant (Josh 23:3; Pss 44:2–3; 47:1–4) in a unique way. Holy war is total, in that everything comes under the ban (*herem* in the Hebrew) and is devoted to God, including men, women, children, and plunder (Josh 10:40–42, 11:16–20). Holy war brings an end to any future succession of the enemy and builds up God's house as the spoil is collected. Holy war is ultimately liturgical and sacrificial: the targets of this specialized form of warfare become an offering to the Lord, consumed with fire from His altar (Josh 6:24; cf. Deut 13:16).

In normal warfare, by contrast, civilian casualties and property damage were to be kept to a minimum (Deut 20; see also Num 31:7–18; Deut 21:10–14), and plunder could be kept by the people. Normal war also required Israel to pursue peaceful avenues of reconciliation before fighting (Deut 20:8) and forbade aggression on the part of Israel (Deut 17:6).[8]

The Lord authorizes and wages "holy war" as a way of administering His perfect grace and justice. The conquest is gracious because it is the way in which God gives the land He swore to Abraham to the nation of Israel. The conquest is an act of divine justice because the inhabitants of the land had filled their cup of iniquity to the brim. Several generations earlier that had not been the case, and so the gift of the land to Abraham's descendants was delayed (Gen 15:16). But when the Canaanites' wickedness had reached its full measure of maturation, God's longsuffering patience expired and the Canaanites

---

8. Jordan develops this distinction at some length in his paper "The Holy War in America Today." Jordan writes: "In the Old Covenant, after God set up the Tabernacle and constituted Israel as a nation, there were two kinds of war. The first was Holy War, and the other was what we can call normal warfare. Holy War (or *herem* warfare, as it is sometimes called, after the Hebrew for 'ban') was prosecuted in a special way, and only against certain people" (1).

Jordan goes on to demonstrate that normal warfare is never aggressive and is waged only as a last resort when peacemaking and defensive measures have failed. Because holy war finds its fulfillment in the church's ministry of the gospel, our civil magistrates must look exclusively to the Bible's teaching on normal war for guidance in prosecuting armed conflicts.

I agree with Jordan that the best treatment of the old covenant law and holy war in relation to "normal war," the so-called "culture wars," the mission of the church, and the civil magistrate is still Vern Poythress, *The Shadow of Christ in the Law of Moses* (Brentwood, TN: Wolgemuth & Hyatt, 1991), especially chapters 10–11, 16, and Appendix A.

received their just deserts. In this way, the conquest serves as sign and pointer to the final judgment and the restoration of the earth to the righteous.

It is important for us to grasp the crucial element of justice in holy war. God did *not* use Israel to invade a peace-loving, righteous people. This was not an act of oppressing the innocent. The inhabitants of the land were grossly depraved and wicked, on par with those who perished in the flood in Noah's generation. Canaanite society was filled with violence, cruelty, idolatry, and immorality. Their destruction was well deserved.

This brings us to a third point. The conquest is not inconsistent with God's love; indeed, God's love *demands* that He bring judgment on the wicked. God's anger at human cruelty and His wrath against human sin are driven by His love. Can we really say God loves if He is indifferent to the wickedness of a Hitler or Stalin? Is He loving if He lets His people suffer slander and persecution without ever doing anything to vindicate them and punish their oppressors? Is He loving if He allows the wicked to have dominion indefinitely, without ever acting against them? Consider an analogy: If I simply stand by and watch as my wife is assaulted, I do not love her. If I truly love her I will step in to defend her, even if it means using force against the one who is attacking her. The conquest shows us that God's anger is aroused by evil because evil disfigures His good creation and stands in the way of His gracious design for humanity. As a loving God, He simply has to act to defeat it. The Canaanites had come to embody evil to the fullest degree and had to be destroyed.[9]

Of course, the conquest does not reveal the whole of God's purpose for the Gentile nations. Nor should it have shaped Israel's attitude to the nations for the long run. God's law gave Israel very specific instructions for relating to aliens and strangers in the land after the conquest was over (Exod 22:21; 23:12; Lev 19:33–34; Deut 10:17–19; 14:28–29; 24:17–18; 26:12–13). Once the Israelites occupied the land, they were to show hospitality and kindness, remembering that God had showered His mercy on them.[10] The sharp distinction between the way Israelites were to treat the Canaanites during Joshua's generation and the way they were to treat Gentiles after they settled in the land is definitive proof that the conquest did not exhaust God's design for the nations outside Israel. While the conquest was a vitally important episode in Israel's history, we should keep in mind that it was also a unique event, limited in scope to a singular time and place. Even within the span of the Old Testament, the conquest hardly provided the overriding model for Israel's relationship to the other nations (cf. Exod 23:9; Jer 29:7).[11] Indeed, God's ultimate

---

9. On God's anger being driven by His love, see Miroslav Volf, *Free of Charge: Giving and Receiving in a Culture Stripped of Grace* (Grand Rapids: Zondervan, 2006), 138–39.

10. In Joshua 1, the Lord tells Joshua to walk according to the law. That law (the Mosaic *torah*) certainly included commands relating to the conquest of the land. But it also included abundant instruction about caring for the poor, the widow, the orphan, and, yes, the stranger within the gate. The apparent tensions between the conquest and the mission of God's people are not something new with the Great Commission in Matthew 28. Even in Deuteronomy, the tension is already there. Of course, the tension is resolved at least in part by placing the conquest within the wider framework of the biblical narrative and understanding it as a temporary measure.

11. This is not to say there were no further episodes of conquest/holy war after Joshua (cf. Judg; 1 Sam 15; Est 9). But it is certainly safe to say that conquest is swallowed up by mission in God's grand scheme of things.

plan is salvation for all the families of the earth (Gen 12:1–3; cf. Gal 3:8), including bringing an end to violence, as swords are beaten into plowshares and tanks into tractors (cf. Isa 2:1–4). Temporary judgments on particular nations do not negate God's overarching purpose of extending blessing to all nations in the long run.

THE TRANSFORMATION OF HOLY WAR: SEVERAL IMPORTANT NEW COVENANT TEXTS

In one sense, holy war in the new covenant remains the same as it ever was: The Lord destroys the wicked and saves the repentant. But obviously, the way this pattern of salvation and destruction unfolds is very different in the Messianic age, and so it is entirely appropriate to speak of the transformation of holy war.[12] In the new eon, we have better promises, a better method of warfare, and a better mission. Jesus clearly did not come to do literal battle with the Roman Empire, or even apostate Jews for that matter, during His earthly ministry. He came to achieve salvation for the world (cf. John 3:16–17; Luke 4:16–20). He accomplished this global salvation in His cross and resurrection. That is not to say there is no judgment reserved for the unrepentant (cf. Matt 24–25), but it is to say the accent falls in a decidedly different place in the new covenant. The conquest was primarily about the destruction of enemies, while the new covenant is primarily about the salvation and conversion of enemies.

Mark's Gospel is especially clear about the kind of warfare Jesus came to wage because of its fast pace and militant themes. Mark portrays Jesus as a new Davidic warrior king, fighting on behalf of His people. For example, when Jesus arrives on the scene, He is the Yahweh Warrior incarnate, but He has zeroed in on the true enemies of God and God's people, namely, Satan, sin, and death. In Mark's Gospel, Jesus is continually on the warpath. Through His teaching, exorcisms, healing miracles, and ultimately through His death and resurrection, "Mark seems to be portraying Jesus as the true restorer of Israel, the divine warrior reconquering holy space."[13] Mark virtually begins his Gospel with Jesus, as a freshly anointed Warrior-Priest, going into the wilderness to do battle with God's archenemy, Satan.

In Mark's Gospel, Jesus is constantly on "the way"—which is to say, He is on the warpath. Mark presents Jesus' casting out demons primarily in terms of warfare with idols, fulfilling Isaiah's promise that the gods of the nations would be toppled when the kingdom arrived. The thieving strong man has been bound so that God is now reclaiming what is His (Mark 3:20–27). Jesus even takes on a demon (or demons) named "Legion," an obvious military term (5:1–20). In 2:23–28, Jesus uses David and his band of soldiers as a paradigm for His own ministry; in other words, Jesus and His disciples are a band

---

12. In fact, the transformation of holy war had already taken place in many respects in the old covenant. The Old Testament Scriptures already revealed that God scatters His (and our) enemies primarily through faithful worship (cf. 2 Chr 20). After the destruction of the temple, it was no longer even possible to wage holy war in the sense that Joshua had because there was no longer an altar with fire to use to burn up the *herem* plunder. By the time of Daniel, it was becoming more explicitly evident that God's people would fight their battles through Spiritual means such as prayer and witness.

13. Longman and Reid, *God Is a Warrior*, 99.

of warriors on the march, as they go around teaching and healing. When Jesus sends out His disciples, they are symbolically recapitulating the exodus and conquest of the land by the twelve tribes (6:7–13). Obviously all these militant themes reach their climax towards the end of the Gospel when Jesus wins the battle by giving Himself sacrificially on the cross and rising again on the third day, as the Victim becomes the Victor, and those who see Him in His glory shake with fear (15–16). Since Mark records Jesus' Nazirite holy war vow just before He goes to the cross (14:25) and then presents a Roman soldier as the first human being to confess the divine sonship of Jesus in the Gospel (15:39), there is no question that Mark intends to highlight the *militia Christi/christus victor* theme in his gospel account. Mark shows us that Jesus has come as the Warrior God in human form to defeat His enemies and win the salvation of His people. He fights—but it is not the kind of fighting the Jews were expecting from their Messiah.[14]

The apostles pick up on this transformation of holy war. Nowhere do they call on Christians to engage in armed revolt, even when they are horribly mistreated. Instead, following the teachings of Jesus, the apostles counsel suffering Christians to be longsuffering and forgiving in the face of opposition (e.g., 1 Pet 2:13–25; cf. Matt 5:39). We are called upon to love our enemies and forgive them, rather than zealously taking up the sword against them. Christians can expect to suffer at the hands of the powers-that-be just as their Master did. But the apostles also remind the first Christians that through their faithful suffering, they are actually winning the victory. Their suffering is not in vain; rather, as they endure persecution for the sake of the kingdom, the world is defeated and brought to its knees before Christ.

Paul's way of dealing with his suffering in Acts certainly bears this out. Paul does not fight back when wrongly imprisoned; instead, he fights by singing and praying and, as a result, gets his freedom and a greater opportunity for gospel ministry (cf. Acts 16). When Paul was writing from prison to the Colossians, he did not ask them to pray that God would open the prison door, but that God would open a door for the gospel, that he might preach even in chains (Col 4:2–3). Paul knows that, as with Joseph and Job and ultimately Jesus, suffering is a prelude to glory and victory. Thus, Paul models the way we fight in the new covenant: through song, prayer, preaching, suffering, and service. Paul directs the churches to do the same, reminding them that their real battle is not against flesh and blood and does not require force of arms (Eph 6:10–20; 2 Cor 10:4), but cruciform, sacrificial living.[15] In this way, we will conquer.

That much is clear. However, there are also a number of texts in the New Testament that show us how holy war has been transformed, but because they do so in subtle ways, they often get overlooked. We will now examine a trio of key texts that through closely detailed readings further confirm and fill out this understanding of how holy war is waged in the new covenant.

---

14. For a much more extensive survey of Mark as "holy war," see ibid.

15. When Paul described the church's armor in Ephesians, he did so in a way reminiscent of the priest's vestments, connecting our warfare, priesthood, and worship in the closest possible way.

PART ONE: BIBLICAL STUDIES

Matthew 15:21–28

Virtually all serious scholars of Matthew agree that the first Gospel is deeply rooted in Old Testament themes. Matthew uses a number of complex, overlapping structures to show Jesus is the fulfillment of Israel's entire history.[16]

In Matthew 14–15, there is a clear Passover-exodus-law-conquest-feast sequence: Jesus serves a meal to a multitude in 14:13–21, then crosses the sea at night (cf. Exod 12, 14) walking on water (cf. Ps 77:19) and joining His disciples in their boat (Matt 14:22–33). Parallels with the Passover and Red Sea crossing are obvious. Next, there is a discussion of the law with the Pharisees, corresponding to the giving of the law at Sinai (15:1–20). Then Jesus engages a Gentile woman, in an episode that resonates with conquest allusions (15:21–28). Afterwards, we find Jesus healing and feeding the multitudes, providing rest and joy (15:29–39), corresponding to Israel settling in the land.

Matthew 15:21–28 is our focus because of its connections with the conquest. First, notice that Matthew describes a woman who comes to Jesus as a "Canaanite." This is striking on a number of levels, and frankly, is a dead giveaway as far as Matthew's intentions are concerned, even though most commentators either miss it or ignore it.

By the first century AD, the Canaanites had not existed as an identifiable people group for many centuries, so the label is obviously anachronistic and must tip us off to Matthew's chief concern in this pericope. Matthew's description of her as a "woman of Canaan" is also highlighted by comparison with the parallel story in Mark's gospel. Mark calls her "a Greek, a Syro-Phoenician by birth." (Mark 7:26). Mark's terminology would have certainly been regarded as more current and straightforward. For Matthew to call this woman a Canaanite would be like a modern day Frenchman calling himself a Gaul or a modern day Iraqi calling himself a Babylonian.

What, then, is Matthew doing? Matthew is sending us a theological signal. He is going to show us how the New Joshua would have His New Israel relate to "Canaanites" (that is, outsiders, outcasts, ostensible enemies) in the new age He is inaugurating. If Jesus is the New Joshua (as His very name implies), then this woman is a New Rahab (as her "Canaanite" identity implies). Jesus' ministry to her is going to challenge Israel's self-understanding and prejudices against outsiders, as well as foreshadowing the church's soon to be launched mission to the nations.

When she approaches Jesus, asking for mercy for her daughter, Jesus rebuffs her three times, reminding her that He was sent first and foremost to the covenant nation of Israel, even suggesting that she is an unclean "dog."[17] Whereas Rahab in Joshua 2 used

---

16. See Peter Leithart, "Jesus as Israel: The Typological Structure of Matthew's Gospel," available at http://www.leithart.com/pdf/jesus-as-israel-the-typological-structure-of-matthew-s-gospel.pdf. For additional helpful material on the typological themes in Matthew, see also David Holwerda, *Jesus and Israel* (Grand Rapids: Eerdmans, 1995) and C. J. H. Wright, *Knowing Jesus through the Old Testament* (Downers Grove, IL: InterVarsity Press, 1992).

17. The reference to her uncleanness is all the more interesting in light of the immediately preceding discussion with the Pharisees in which Jesus clarifies the meaning of the old covenant uncleanness laws, and then proceeds to transform, transcend, and negate them. Why does He immediately revert back to an old covenant-style way of viewing this woman immediately after overhauling the laws of uncleanness? Obviously, Jesus is up to something big.

wise deception to prove her loyalty to the true God, this woman uses her quick wits: "Yes, Lord, yet even the little dogs eat the crumbs which fall from their master's table." With these words, she acknowledges the primacy of Israel in redemptive history. The covenant is for the Jew first. But she also insists that the goodness and justice of God demand that He deal impartially with all who seek Him in faith, even if they are outside the nation of Israel. She knows Abraham received the blessing first, but also knows (possibly because she was familiar with the story of Joshua 2 the same way Rahab was familiar with the story of the exodus?) that blessing must ultimately flow out to all the families of the earth. In other words, she was a much better theologian than the scribes and Pharisees, Israel's religious leaders and supposed teachers. Because this Canaanite woman shows great faith, her household is saved, just as Rahab's family was spared by faith. She may be a Canaanite, but she acts like an Israelite, so she receives the blessings intended initially for Israel. Jesus does not wage holy war against her, but against the demon that has possessed her daughter; He does not conquer her, but conquers her oppressor, so that she is set free.

Matthew's narrative is showing us that the church will engage in a different kind of conquest of "Canaanites" (that is, outsiders/Gentiles). If we look at the wider context, we get more confirmation that Matthew has a transformed holy war theology in view in this section of the gospel. The story of the encounter with the Canaanite woman is followed by further healings, as Jesus continues His holy war against disease and sickness, and then the feeding of the four thousand with a few loaves and fish. In biblical numerology, four is the number of the world (e.g., four winds, four corners, of the earth, four faces of the cherubim representing creation, etc.).[18] Jesus' disciples collected seven large baskets of leftovers (e.g., crumbs that fell from the table; cf. Matt 15:27). When the Israelites entered Canaan, there were seven Gentile nations they were to drive out: "When the LORD your God brings you into the land you are about to enter and occupy, He will clear away many nations ahead of you: the Hittites, Girgashites, Amorites, Canaanites, Perizzites, Hivites, and Jebusites. These seven nations are all more powerful than you" (Deut 7:1–2).

The use of four and seven in close proximity to the story of the Canaanite woman point to the coming globalization of Jesus' mission. The combination of loaves and fish do as well: loaves obviously point to Jews, as the priestly nation, and fish are associated with the Gentiles.[19] Thus, the numerical and food symbolism in Matthew 15 show us that

---

Also, note the contrasting ways in which food is used in 15:1–20 and 15:21–28. In 15:1–20, we find the Pharisees are afraid that what they put in their mouths will defile them. They are obsessed with the minutiae of the law, and end up ignoring its deepest meaning. The woman, on the other hand, is happy to gobble up crumbs that fall from Jesus' table. She knows she is unclean (by Jewish standards), but also knows that if she can "eat" what Jesus offers, she and her child will be cleansed and healed.

18. Of course, most everything I know about biblical numerology, I learned from Jordan, though I cannot put my finger on where he explains the meaning of different numbers.

19. Readers of Jordan will find these symbolic connections intuitive. Bread is clearly associated with Israel in the Levitical system (e.g., the twelve loaves of showbread in the tabernacle/temple represent the twelve tribes of Israel). Fish are associated with the Gentile nations in numerous places. For example, the sea monsters represent Gentile empires. Jonah is unique in the Old Testament in featuring fish, as well as mission to a Gentile city. Jesus uses the expression "fishers of men" to describe the mission of His disciples in the new age He is inaugurating. And so forth.

PART ONE: BIBLICAL STUDIES

Jesus is putting an end to traditional boundaries between Jew and Gentile and pointing forward to the new missionary situation that will exist on the other side of Easter and Pentecost when even the "dogs" will take their place at the table (cf. Matt 8:11).[20]

Taking all these clues together, we arrive at the following: Jesus is showing that even those very peoples God once commanded to be destroyed are now to be embraced. Instead of conquering them, we are to heal them, feed them, and bless them. This is our new covenant holy war. In the new covenant, Gentiles will be invited to the covenant feast. Holy war has been transformed into mission; in the new covenant, the church will conquer her enemies unto conversion with love and mercy. Jesus does not wage war against blood and flesh, but against demonic hosts, sickness, hunger, and death—all effects of the fall.

This does not negate the theme of judgment on those who reject the word of Jesus (e.g., Matt 24–25). Jesus brings judgment, and promises to destroy His unrepentant enemies. But, compared with Joshua's day, love has replaced wrath as the leading edge of the church's ministry. The circle of grace has expanded in a radical way. In the ancient world, the greatness of a king was measured by how many people he could kill and how many nations he could conquer; in the case of Jesus, His kingly greatness is revealed in His overflowing mercy and loving service to those in need.

Acts 18:18, 20:33

The book of Acts is basically a new covenant version of Joshua.[21] The book of Acts uses Joshua as a blueprint for the church's mission. Joshua's "little commission" in Joshua 1:1–9 points to Jesus' "Great Commission" at end of the gospel narratives. Luke has very obviously constructed the early chapters of the book of Acts so that they track with the early chapters of Joshua. In other words, the church's fulfillment of her mission to the nations (Matt 28:16–20; Luke 24:46–49) is the new covenant counterpart to and fulfillment of Joshua's conquest of Canaan.

If we overlay the two books, we see that Joshua and Acts show a number of striking parallels and structural similarities:

- In each case, the leader of God's people has just left the scene (Moses in death, Jesus in His ascension).
- In the book of Joshua, Joshua is called to be Moses' successor and carry forward God's purposes in the conquest. Joshua is presented as a new Moses in a variety of ways. In Acts, the Holy Spirit comes as Jesus' alter ego to be Jesus' successor, and to carry forward the church's mission of conquest "in Jerusalem, and in all Judea and Samaria, and to the ends of the earth" (Acts 1:8).
- The Lord commands Joshua to be strong and courageous at the beginning of the book (Josh 1:1–9). At the beginning of Acts, the Lord promises power will come

---

20. The juxtaposition of Matthew 15:21–28 and 15:32–39 is very interesting. After the feeding miracle, the leftovers are gathered up so that there are no "crumbs." But perhaps this is because in the new covenant, the Gentiles "dogs" will no longer scavenge under the table but will take their place at the table.

21. Jordan, of course, is the teacher who pointed this out to me.

upon the disciples to make them strong and courageous (as seen in the sudden transformation of Peter from coward to preacher; cf. Acts 1–2).

- In Joshua, Israel is commanded to conquer the land. In Acts, the church is commanded to bear witness to the ends of the earth. The nature and scope of the conquest have been transformed and expanded.

- In Joshua, the people are led through a clear sequence of events: they cross over the Jordan in a kind of baptism (cf. 1 Cor 10:2), they get circumcised, and they celebrate Passover. In Acts, the sequence is similar: the Spirit baptizes the church, three thousand are baptized with water (the new covenant counterpart to circumcision per Col 2:11–12), and they break the bread of the Lord's Supper together (cf. Acts 2:42–46; the Lord's Supper is the new covenant fulfillment of the Passover according to 1 Cor 5:7–8).

- In both books, the first move of God's people is to invade a key city. Jericho falls by shouting and trumpeting, while Jerusalem is invaded by means of prayer and preaching. In both cases, holy war is waged by liturgical means. Jerusalem, like Jericho of old, is destined to be destroyed (cf. Matt 24; Luke 22), but those who exercise Rahab-like faith and put their faith in scarlet blood of Christ (the Greater Joshua) will be saved.

- Almost immediately in both books, we find the people of God hindered by sin in the camp: In Joshua, Achan steals booty that belongs to the Lord, and is put to death on the spot (Josh 7). Likewise, in Acts 5, Ananais and Sapphira steal from the Lord by lying about some property they had sold, and they are executed on the spot. Note the word for stealing in Acts 5:2 is a rare term, but is also used in the Greek (Septuagint) translation of Joshua 7:1. In both books, fear enters the enemies of God's people, allowing the covenant community to score significant victories (Josh 2:9–13; 5:1–2; Acts 2:2:43, 5:5, 11; 9:31; 19:17).

- In both books, we see Gentiles brought in, though with significant controversy (Josh 9; Acts 15) and attack (Josh 10; Acts 6–7).

Later on in the book of Acts, Luke chronicles Paul's missionary journeys. These journeys should be understood as holy war campaigns. Paul is invading the world in waves, going on the offensive with the gospel. Several clues indicate this truth. First, Paul takes a Nazirite vow in conjunction with his mission work, at least once, possibly twice. The Nazirite vow is preeminently a holy war vow. The person who has taken a Nazirite vow enters into special quasi-priestly status for the duration of his vow.[22] His uncut hair indicates his consecration. The Nazirite cannot drink alcohol under his vow because

---

22. Note that priests are basically full time holy warriors. When they are on the job, they are not allowed to drink alcohol, just like the Nazirites. Priests waged constant, total war by killing animals bearing the sins of the people. They destroyed the animals with sword and fire, even as holy war against the Canaanites was waged with sword and fire (cf. Judg 1:8). So the categories of Nazirite, priest, and warrior heavily overlap and interpenetrate.

such drink is given to celebrate rest and victory, which cannot happen until the holy war task is fulfilled.[23]

In Acts 18:18, Luke indicates that Paul took a Nazirite vow that ended with him cutting off his hair before he returned to Antioch, the place from which he was originally commissioned for his evangelistic work. He may have taken another Nazirite vow in Acts 21:24. While the context of the vow in Acts 21 is much more cryptic, it is still obviously tied into his missionary work. Paul, as a Nazirite, is a holy warrior, like the old covenant Nazirites who came before him. But unlike most old covenant Nazirites, the shape of his warfare is entirely missional. He wages war with the sword of the Spirit, as he preaches the gospel of Christ.

There is another clue in Acts that Paul understood his mission trips as holy war campaigns. In Acts 20:17–38, Paul makes his farewell speech to the Ephesian elders, wrapping up an extensive three year work. In Acts 20:33, he says, "I have coveted no one's silver or gold or apparel." On the surface, this is a bit odd: Other than establishing his own integrity in their eyes, why would Paul make this claim in this context? The Bible reader sensitive to intertextual echoes hears in these words an explicit repudiation of the sin of Achan.

The story of Achan is found in Joshua 7. After the Israelites defeated the metropolis of Jericho, they moved in on the tiny village of Ai. But at Ai, they experienced a stunning defeat. Joshua's account gives the clear reason for their failure in Achan's confession:

> Now Joshua said to Achan, "My son, I beg you, give glory to the LORD God of Israel, and make confession to Him, and tell me now what you have done; do not hide it from me." And Achan answered Joshua and said, "Indeed I have sinned against the LORD God of Israel, and this is what I have done: When I saw among the spoils a beautiful Babylonian garment, two hundred shekels of silver, and a wedge of gold weighing fifty shekels, I coveted them and took them. And there they are, hidden in the earth in the midst of my tent, with the silver under it. (Josh 7:19–20)

Achan confessed to having coveted and taken gold, silver, and apparel for himself. Paul confessed that he had *not* coveted these things, using virtually identical language. There is no mistaking the fact that Paul is echoing this account from the book of Joshua. Thus, Paul sees himself as a kind of anti-Achan, an Achan in reverse. Achan took from

---

23. The Nazirite vow is found in Numbers 6. But there are several other references to Nazirites in the Scriptures, which fill out our understanding of this institution. Samuel, Samson, and John the Baptist are lifetime Nazirites, each with an obvious mission to fulfill. In Judges 4–5, we find that those who went to war with Barak had taken Nazirite vows. Judges 5:2 tells us that when they went into battle, "locks hung loose"; that is, the men entered battle with uncut hair. Similarly, the holy warriors described in Revelation 9:7–8 "had hair like women's hair." Most likely, this means that in the church, all of God's people are symbolic Nazirites. We are not under the stipulations of the old covenant Nazirite vow, but we do have a holy war mission to fulfill.

Of course, the Nazirite vow is ultimately fulfilled in Christ. It is possible Matthew is using a pun to describe Jesus as a symbolic Nazirite in Matthew 2:23. Whether or not that is the case, it seems almost certain that Jesus takes a Nazirite vow just before He goes to the cross in Mark 14:25, when He promises to not drink of the fruit of the vine again until He has finished His work and brought in the kingdom (cf. John 19:28–30). For a complete discussion of the Nazirite holy war vow, see James B. Jordan, *Judges: A Practical and Theological Commentary* (reprint, Eugene, OR: Wipf & Stock, 1999), 221–27.

the spoils of war. Paul refused to do so. Instead of taking, he gave of himself and "kept back nothing that was helpful" (Acts 20:20), living according to the saying of Jesus, "It is more blessed to give than to receive" (Acts 20:35).

But this connection between Achan and Paul only makes sense if Paul saw himself as carrying on a new kind of holy war, analogous to but radically different from the holy war of Joshua. The Ephesians are his Canaanites, but instead of destroying them, he pleads and works for their salvation. He wants them to escape destruction. Instead of wrongfully claiming spoil for himself, he keeps himself pure in the sight of God.

Paul's precise choice of language shows he understood his mission work in Ephesus as a successful "holy war" campaign.[24] He expected his gospel to be victorious because he did not tolerate the sin of Achan in his war camp. Achan's coveting led to defeat for Israel; Paul's contented service will lead the church, the new Israel, to victory.

What do we learn about new covenant holy war from this intertextual fragment in Acts 20? Acts as a whole is about new covenant holy war, as the church "invades" Jerusalem, Judea, Samaria, and the ends of the earth. But the nature of her warfare has been transformed. There is a shift from killing to converting. Unlike Joshua, in the book of Acts, Paul does not inflict suffering, but bears suffering for the sake of others (Acts 20:22ff.). Paul is innocent of the blood of all men (Acts 20:26). He desires to protect rather than harm, and shows special care for the weak (Acts 20:29ff., 35). Unlike Joshua, Peter and Paul advance the kingdom through service rather than force (Acts 20:19). Unlike Joshua, Paul is not so much claiming an inheritance for himself as he is drawing others into an inheritance in God's promised new creation (Acts 20:32). However, just as with Joshua's holy war the church will only be victorious if she is first righteous.[25]

It is evident, then, that God's people no longer fight with a literal sword and fire; instead they use the sword of the Spirit (the Word of God; Heb 4:12; Eph 6:17) and witness in the fiery presence of God's Spirit (Acts 2:3). The weapons of holy war have morphed. The church can learn a great deal about her mission from the book of Joshua, but to do so she must apply Joshua's use of sword and flame in a metaphorical way, guided by Acts and the rest of the New Testament.

Hebrews 13:5

Hebrews is a book about the transition from old covenant to new covenant. That transition takes place between the death and resurrection of Jesus Christ in AD 30 and the destruction of the temple in AD 70. Hebrews is most likely written by Paul in the mid-60s to his fellow Jews who have converted to Christian faith but are finding themselves under intense pressure to turn away from Christ to avoid persecution. From the perspec-

---

24. Paul's language also echoes Samuel's speech in 1 Samuel 12. Samuel did not covet anyone's goods and led Israel in successful holy war (cf. 1 Sam 4–7).

25. This is a crucial point for pastors and elders: We are sometimes led to believe that the faithful practice of church discipline will stand in the way of church growth because the church will be perceived as harsh and unloving. This narrative shows us just the opposite is true. If the church is to be a well-heeled army, she must keep the troops in line. She will not experience true growth in the long run unless she prunes away unfruitful branches on the vine. The church is an army, and sin in the camp prevents victory.

tive of the book's original context, "the day" rapidly approaching (Heb 10:25) is the day of Jesus' coming to destroy the temple and thus end the old covenant order (cf. Matt 24). Paul calls on these believers to forsake their attachment to the earthly Jerusalem, going outside the old covenant city so that they may receive the heavenly city that is to come (Heb 13:13–14; cf. 12:22). Pastorally, Hebrews functions as an extended call to perseverance in faith, even in the face of terrible opposition and obstacles. Theologically, Hebrews demonstrates that Christ fulfills, and therefore surpasses, all the features of the old covenant age.

It is vital that we root our reading of Hebrews in the book's original historical context. While the book is most certainly applicable to the church in all times and places, in a very real sense, it is not giving us "timeless truths." Nothing in the book is abstract; it is all anchored to a specific shift taking place in the history of God's people. In order to understand the book's meaning for the church today we have to grasp what it meant for the church then. The pre-AD 70 context of the book is a vital interpretive key.

For example, in Hebrews 1, Paul says that God has spoken to us in His Son "in these last days" (1:1–2). While the "last days" may refer to the entire new covenant age, in the context of this letter, it is more likely a reference to the "last days" of the old covenant age. Hebrews is about the transition from old covenant to new covenant; as the book is being written that period of transition is drawing to a close.

Later, in Hebrews 3–4, Paul draws a typological relationship between Israel's forty year period of wilderness wandering and the church's forty year transitional period from AD 30–70.[26] Israel wandered in the wilderness for a generation, then conquered Canaan. Likewise, the church underwent a generation-long period of preparation before beginning her invasion of the nations.[27] Paul uses Psalm 95, a reflection on the wilderness period, to warn first century Christians: They must not harden their hearts and so fall short of the goal of entering the new covenant in greater fullness on the other side of AD 70. The temptations and promises for the first century church were analogous to (but much greater than) those presented to Israel under Moses.

It has been pointed out by several scholars that Hebrews is a new covenant version of Deuteronomy.[28] Just as Deuteronomy functions as a last will and testament by Moses for the people, so Hebrews is likely Paul's last epistle and therefore something of a farewell sermon. Hebrews follows the same overarching structure as Deuteronomy, quotes extensively from Deuteronomy, and like Deuteronomy, prepares a people for their coming warfare/conquest. The hearers of Deuteronomy were faced with a choice between

---

26. During Israel's wilderness wandering, the mixed multitude of Jews and (believing) Gentiles who left Egypt were assimilated into a "new Israel." The same thing is going on in the Jew-Gentile churches of the first century AD, as Paul's other epistles show.

27. Obviously, the gospel was already being preached widely before AD 70 (Col 1:24; cf. Rom 15:7–33). In fact, Paul's expansive missionary enterprise to furthest stretches of the *oikumene* (the Roman Empire) was a sign of the end of the Israel-centered old covenant (cf. Matt 24:14). The apostles who established churches throughout the world prior to AD 70 were like the spies Moses sent into the land ahead of the conquest. They laid the initial foundation for what would come in much greater fullness later on.

28. See, e.g., Douglas Wilson, *Christ and His Rivals: Hebrews Through New Eyes* (Monroe, LA: Athanasius, 2008), 13–14.

faithfulness to God, demonstrated in obedience and conquest of the land, or rebellion, curse, and loss of the land (Deut 28–30). The first readers of Hebrews were faced with a choice as well. It was a choice between Christ and apostate Judaism, between the rising glories of the new covenant and the fading glory of the old covenant. But they were also faced with a choice between two different kinds of warfare. Paul does not want them going to war with the Romans over the temple and their national independence. He knows that path is a dead end for Israel (quite literally). He does not want them to fight for a lesser altar and meal (Heb 13:10) and for a city that is going to be lost anyway (Heb 13:14). Instead, he wants them to go to war for the nations, to conquer all the families of the earth with the gospel, following the lead of the Greater Joshua, who promises an even greater rest. He wants them to give themselves to the city that is to come, the heavenly Jerusalem. He wants them to engage in a better form of sacrifice (Heb 13:15–16) and live under a better covenant (Heb 8).

The warfare/conquest theme is seen in Hebrews right out of the gate. In the first chapter, seven Old Testament texts are quoted and applied to Jesus; five of them have to do with the Christ subduing the nations to Himself. As Douglas Wilson says, "This is the great subject of the book of Hebrews. . . . All of them [that is, the Old Testament quotations in the book] fit into the story of the greater Joshua, subduing the nations of Canaan, that is, the nations of the world."[29]

All of this sets the stage for the key text we want to examine. In Hebrews 13, there is a crucial, but often overlooked Old Testament quotation that further confirms that the transformed holy war motif is at the heart of this book. Consider Hebrews 13:5: "Let your conduct be without covetousness; be content with such things as you have. For He Himself has said, 'I will never leave you nor forsake you.'"

Covetousness is at the root of all kinds of sin. In this particular situation, coveting riches would lead these Jewish believers straight back to unbelieving Judaism. If they stayed true to Christ, they could easily face the plundering of their property and the loss of wealth (Heb 10:32–34). But following on the heels of the command to resist covetousness and pursue contentment, Paul cites an Old Testament text about God's covenant faithfulness and constancy: "I will never leave you nor forsake you." Why is this text dropped into the exhortation at this point in the letter?

These words are a quotation from Deuteronomy, later repeated in Joshua (compare Deut 31:1–8 with Josh 1:1–9). The original context of the promise "I will never leave you nor forsake you" is one of preparation for battle. These are God's words of encouragement on the eve of warfare. These words are part of God's (or Moses') pre-battle pep talk to Joshua and the rest of Israel. God will be with His people as they move into battle to claim their promised inheritance.

These words function in the same way in Hebrews 13, properly understood. Times are tough for the believers addressed in this letter, but if they will hold on to God's promise with courage, He will begin to deliver the nations into their hand as an inheritance.

---

29. Ibid., 11–12.

PART ONE: BIBLICAL STUDIES

Paul is reminding them that God is with them as they move out to conquer, leaving the old covenant and its trappings completely behind.

Now that the promised Messiah, God-in-the-flesh, has come, the Lord is with us in a much greater way than He was with Joshua and the Israelites. Jesus is, after all, Immanuel. His presence with us ensures the success of our new covenant holy war campaign. The church can move forward with strength and courage to conquer the nations with the word of the gospel, which is the sword of the Spirit.

CONCLUSION

The transformation of holy war is at the heart of the coming of Jesus and His kingdom. Jesus did not come to kill like Joshua but to be killed for the sake of "Canaanite" sinners. He did not come to destroy the pagan nations but to save and convert them. He now sends His church on a mission to all the nations of the earth, but it is a mission of restoration, renewal, and healing, not a mission of destruction. This is the day of salvation for all peoples.

Furthermore, Jesus is with us to ensure the ultimate success of our holy war mission. The conquest under Joshua was not exactly a resounding success as the book of Judges reveals. But the new covenant brings greater power and greater presence to guarantee that the church will be victorious. All of this is evident if we look at the "big picture" the Scriptures give us, but also if we look at the subtle details of several New Testament texts (as demonstrated in this essay).

But that is not to say Jesus will never bring judgment, or never wage war against blood and flesh. Nor is it to say that His people may never pray for judgment against their enemies, as we see in the imprecations of David (Ps 139:19–22), Paul (1 Cor 16:22), and the saints (Rev 6:10). Judgment is the shadow that trails the gracious substance of the kingdom; it is still there, but it is not the focus as it was in the book of Joshua.

Jesus made threats against unbelieving Judaism. In AD 70, Jesus, enthroned in heaven, waged a kind of physical holy war against apostate Israel, using Rome as His instrument. He continues to bring judgments against empires, nations, and individuals in history, as He pleases. At the last day He will bring eternal destruction and damnation to those who have rejected Him and clung to idols. In other words, the holy war theme is not fulfilled by His redemptive work and the church's mission with no remainder. There are judgments in history and there is a final judgment still to come. Joshua's conquest was but a type and preview of the judgment Jesus brings and will bring against the wicked. In the end, Jesus will drive "Canaanites" who refuse to convert out of His world, destroying them and their false gods in the lake of fire forever. But the meek shall inherit the earth.[30]

---

30. It is obvious that I believe holy war is exhaustively fulfilled in Christ's work and in the church's administration of the gospel, with no remainder for the civil government. But what does this mean for the ethics of normal war? Many claim that the warfare of the Old Testament is so completely fulfilled by Christ and the church that there is no place left for Christians going to literal war on behalf of their nation, even if there is "just" cause. In other words, the church's Spiritual holy war is now the only legitimate war, and so Christians must be pacifists. This Anabaptist view is refuted easily enough by the words of Paul, speaking of

Dear Rich,

Thank you for this fine study and summary. I found your take on the Canaanite woman particularly interesting, and since I'm obliged to say something here, I'll point out that between Joshua and Jesus comes Elijah.

Elijah treats Israel as an Egypt to be plagued, but right after his attack on Israel he is sent to a Canaanite Syro-Phoenician woman (1 Kgs 17:9–24). He provides bread to her, and more than just crumbs; and he brings her dead son back to life.

Elijah is a Nazirite, a "lord [*ba'al*] of hair" (2 Kgs 1:8). Elisha is as well, it seems, for immediately after Elijah "dies very suddenly beside him" (for all intents and purposes, anyway), he is found with bald, shaven head (Num 6:9; 2 Kgs 2:11, 12, 23). This seems to be the beginning of the employment of the Nazirite vow for the prophetic side of the holy war task.

It is interesting that this is also the point in history when Yahweh begins to extend His stakes and claim other nations. Heretofore, Israel has been called to make physical holy war against the Canaanites and to bear witness to the nations. What is startling

---

the magistrate: "for he does not bear the sword in vain" (Rom 13:4). There is a legitimate use of the sword by the magistrate in punishment and protection. Paul even calls the magistrate "God's servant," opening the door to Christian participation in Caesar's administration. Caesar cannot fight a holy war, in the strict sense, but he can wage a just war, according to God's Word.

But we can go further than this and ask: If the magistrate is truly understood as God's minister, as Romans 13 indicates, does his use of the sword have any relation to the kingdom of God and the mission of the church? When Caesar converts and seeks to use the sword righteously, how can his use of the sword best further the ministry of the gospel among the nations? Even if there is no residue of holy war that sticks to the magistrate's office, even if holy war waged exclusively by the church through liturgy and ministry, does the magistrate have a role to play in the kingdom's embodiment and advancement?

To be more pointed: If we believe (with Jordan) that the gospel is theocratic, that Christendom is the outcome of the Great Commission, and that nations as nations must be discipled, can a Christianized magistrate make use of the sword in a way that serves and even expands the kingdom of God? Can the sword of the magistrate ever serve (or at least make way for) the mission of the church? Should the power of the sword be used by Christian magistrates to enforce some basic Christian/biblical morality in society? How does the church's holy war relate to our so-called culture wars against secularism, liberalism, Islam, and so forth?

We might scoff at such notions. Evangelism by the sword is one the things we most detest about Islam. We know that force of arms cannot change hearts and bring about true conversion. We know that Christian faith and practice cannot be imposed on an unwilling people without disaster for everyone involved.

But at the same time, we must recognize historically that God has used Christian magistrates to at least create space for the work of the church to grow and flourish. Many of us of European descent should be thankful that medieval Christian kings converted our ancestors, sometimes with the aid of the sword, using their office to suppress the old idolatries and support the growth of the true faith. Was that completely wrong-headed? Were medieval Christian kings wrong to use the sword to stem the brutal and bloody spread of Islam? In what way do these historical actions relate to the church's holy war, waged through prayer, preaching, discipline, service, and so on?

The church's legacy on questions of these sorts is mixed. We could point to the good that Christian magistrates have done in their attempts to assist and cooperate with the church, but we can also point to many evils and abuses that have cost lives and greatly damaged the reputation of the church and the gospel. The latter get all the attention in our day, but a balanced, informed, and wise theological and historical discussion would be very profitable, especially if carried out by a scholar of Jordan's caliber.

in the new Prophetic Covenant is the command that Hazael is to be anointed king of Aram by Elijah (1 Kgs 19:15). This is the very beginning of the "new international covenant" times, which come in their fulness with the ascension of Jesus and the destruction of the Old Creation order in AD 70. The "new model Nazirite" seems to be part of this new order.

Of course, the holy war in the New Creation era is also against principalities and powers, and the war is fought liturgically and musically. David played music to drive evil spirits from Saul, and music plays quite a role in the holy war depicted in the book of Revelation. When Jesus took the Nazirite vow at the Last Supper, He sent Judas with a message to the enemy: "Bring it on!" The same is true of our warfeast today, which has much to say about how we conduct this meal: not like a fellowship meal with the pastor politely going last in line, but as a move into battle with the local commander leading the charge—which is how the church historically has always done the Supper. I make some comments along these lines in my response to Richard Bledsoe's essay.

Well, those are some thoughts you've stimulated in me by your paper. Thank you again.

Jim

5

The Royal Priesthood in Exodus 19:6

RALPH ALLAN SMITH

IN THIS ESSAY, I argue that Exodus 19:6 has profound implications for the biblical theology of priesthood and for understanding both ancient Israel and the church. I assume Peter Leithart's definition of priest as a "household attendant" in Yahweh's house,[1] but I see complications in the era beginning with the destruction of the Garden of Eden in the Flood, for until the building of the tabernacle at Sinai, there was no house of Yahweh in which a priest could serve. In this era, therefore, the notion of priesthood must have been less developed and more vaguely defined. For example, Melchizedek is identified as a priest of the true God, even though we have no idea if he was ordained or served in a temple.[2]

I proceed in four stages. First, I briefly review John A. Davies's argument that the Hebrew expression *mamlekheth kohanim* in Exodus 19:6 should be translated "royal priesthood" and suggest some of the implications of this for biblical theology. Second, I discuss the biblical origins of covenant, priesthood, and kingship in the light of contemporary research into Old Testament backgrounds. Third, I argue that the Melchizedekian priesthood of Christ is the fulfillment of the priesthood granted to the nation of Israel. And finally, fourth, I bring these all together to reconsider the priesthood of the Christian in the new covenant.

---

1. Peter J. Leithart, *The Priesthood of the Plebs: A Theology of Baptism* (Eugene, OR: Wipf & Stock, 2003), 60. Leithart argues at length that only this definition is inclusive enough to take in the various functions of a priest.

2. In an earlier work, Leithart follows a broader definition when he speaks of Abraham and Israel. "This new human race was called, first of all, to be a nation of priests. Wherever he traveled in the land, Abraham built altars (Gen. 12:8; 13:4, 18; 22:9). Later Israel was set apart preeminently as a worshiping community, a people whose reason for being was to honor and obey the King of heaven, a people redeemed from slavery to worship the Lord exclusively (Ex. 19:1–6; 20:1–3). Like Adam, Israel's first priority was worship" (*The Kingdom and the Power: Rediscovering the Centrality of the Church* [Phillipsburg, NJ: P&R, 1993], 149–50).

PART ONE: BIBLICAL STUDIES

One question this essay seeks to answer is this: If Jesus is a priest after the order of Melchizedek, a different order from that of Aaron, why does He have to fulfill the typology of the Aaronic order? Or, stated differently, what is the relationship between the Aaronic priesthood and the Melchizedekian priesthood? The answer proposed is that the Melchizedekian priesthood was a particular expression of the priesthood inherited from Noah and Adam, the two greatest "king-priests" of the ancient world.[3] Further, the nation of Israel was called to be a nation of king-priests according to the Adamic order (Exod 19:6). The Aaronic priesthood was based upon and constituted a particularized expression of the more fundamental priesthood of the nation.[4] That is important for Christians because our priesthood is related both to the Melchizedekian priesthood of Christ (Heb 10:19ff.) and the royal priesthood of Israel (1 Pet 2:9). One question we need to consider is how it might be related to the Aaronic service.

A ROYAL PRIESTHOOD

Israel's call to be royal priests begins with the story of the Exodus, especially the call of Moses. The first verses of Exodus record Israel's remarkable growth, indicating that the Abrahamic covenant is being fulfilled (Exod 1:7;[5] cf. Gen 47:27). But the story suddenly changes. There arises a king who knew not Joseph and he oppresses the children of Israel. His murder of the male infants of Israel is both the background for the story of Moses and also the preparation for the story of the Exodus proper, which begins in chapter 3 when God calls Moses to be the liberator of His people.

When he was confronted by the burning bush, Moses was standing on Horeb, the mountain of God. The sign that he was called of God and that God would be with him was that he would bring the children of Israel to worship Yahweh at that very mountain (Exod 3:12). Thus, Exodus 19:1–6 records the climax of the story that began when God called Moses. And just as God commissioned Moses at Sinai, so also His meeting with Israel was a commission of a sort. Numerous details in Exodus 19:1–6 draw attention to the profound event transpiring.

What details? Consider, first, that in the third month of their journey Israel has finally arrived "that very day" at their destination "the mountain" (Exod 19:1–2), the

---

3. I am not suggesting they actually sat on thrones and wore crowns. But to both of them God granted authority to rule, and they both offered sacrifices—Noah after the flood (Gen 8:20) and Adam presumably after the fall. Since God clothed Adam and Eve with animal skins, animals must have died. This would seem to be the beginning of animal sacrifice. Shortly after this, when Genesis speaks of Cain and Abel offering sacrifice, there is no indication that they are beginning something new. Equally important, Adam and Noah are also each the single source of the human race, so the social institutions that developed among their descendants had their roots in Adam and Noah. See also Jordan's explanation of Ham's sin against Noah as an act of rebellion against Noah's authority (*Primeval Saints: Studies in the Patriarchs of Genesis* [Moscow, ID: Canon, 2001], 52–54).

4. My explanation of the royal priesthood of Israel and its relationship to the Aaronic and Melchizedekian priesthood differs only slightly from James B. Jordan's in *The Law of the Covenant: An Exposition of Exodus 21–23* (Tyler, TX: Institute for Christian Economics, 1984), 209.

5. Every important word in Exodus 1:7 has covenantal roots in Genesis, especially in Abraham: fruitful (1:28; 9:1, 7; 17:6; 28:3; 35:11); increased greatly (9:7); multiplied (1:28; 9:1, 7; 17:2; 22:17; 26:4, 24; 35:11; 48:4); exceedingly mighty (26:16); land filled (1:28; 9:1).

place earlier called "the mountain of God," where Moses was first called by God to free the children of Israel.⁶

Second, we are told "Moses went up to God" (19:3), rare language used especially in the context of the gift of the covenant at Sinai (cf. Exod 19:24; 24:1, 12; cf. Exod 19:22; 32:30; Deut 10:1).⁷

Third, God declares that He carried the children of Israel on "eagle's wings" and "brought you to Myself" (Exod 19:4). Though the exact wording here—"I bore you on eagle's wings"—is unique, a similar expression occurs in the song of Moses (Deut 32:11), no doubt alluding to this verse. Also, the description of God bringing Israel *unto Himself* is unparalleled, though it suggestively corresponds to the description of Moses himself going up to God.

Fourth, the literary structure of the paragraph with God's declaration to Israel is also unique. In all the Old Testament, there is no other passage that repeats its introductory formula in this manner, "Thus you shall say to the house of Jacob and tell the sons of Israel. . . . These are the words that you shall speak to the sons of Israel" (Exod 19:3, 6). As a beginning formula, something like "thus you shall say" is not uncommon, but nowhere else does a short paragraph have both an introductory and a concluding formula.

Fifth, this is the first passage in the Old Testament in which Israel is declared to be God's *segullah*, special possession. The word *segullah* is used of Israel in a few subsequent passages, which should all be understood as alluding to Exodus 19:5 (Deut 7:6; 14:2; 26:18; Ps 135:4; Mal 3:17), emphasizing the importance of the declaration here.

Sixth, remarkably this is the only passage in the Old Testament that refers to Israel as *mamleketh kohanim*, a "royal priesthood." In other words, the expression that seems to be of focal significance in the immediate paragraph—the meaning of which constitutes a profoundly important declaration of Israel's exalted status in the world—is never again repeated in the Hebrew Scriptures. Isaiah 61:6 alludes to Exodus 19:6, but the peculiar expression of privilege, *mamleketh kohanim*, is not quoted. In the New Testament, of course, Exodus 19:6 is quoted once (1 Pet 2:9) and alluded to at least three times (Rev 1:6; 5:10; 20:6).

Seventh, it is the only place in the Old Testament where Israel is called a *goy qadosh* ("holy nation" = holy *goy*).

Eighth, just as Moses saw a theophany in Exodus 3, the whole nation sees the glory cloud of God descend on the mountain and they respond, as Moses did, with fear (Exod 19:16ff.).

---

6. Jordan points out other interesting details in ibid., 55ff.

7. The exact Hebrew expression *alah el-haelohim* ("went up to God") is found only in Exodus 19:3 and 1 Samuel 10:3, but other verses in the context use similar expressions that emphasize that Moses is coming into the very presence of God. The priests and elders who go up the mountain with Moses are also said to come unto Yahweh (Exod 24:1). Expressions such as "coming unto God," "coming unto Yahweh," and "drawing near to God" are not as common in the Old Testament as one might think (Exod 19:3, 22, 24; 20:21; 21:6; 24:1–2, 12; 32:30; Deut 10:1; Judg 21:5, 8; Jer 30:21; Ezek 44:13). Note that these expressions are distinct from the verb and noun forms for offerings that bring people near to Yahweh in worship (in Lev 1:2 the same Hebrew root, *qrv*, appears in both the forms of the verb "bring near" and the noun "offering.")

Thus, the historical situation, the literary structure, the examples of unique language, the theophany, and the theological content of the central declaration by Yahweh all draw attention to the significance of the passage and call for devout attention.

The words *mamleketh kohanim* could theoretically be translated in various ways and scholars debate the possibilities. In a thorough study of the expression, John A. Davies states that scholars have suggested four, five, or even eight varying options.[8] Davies offers a different approach, analyzing the words in terms of two broader categories that hinge on "whether there is a passive or an active force to the verbal notion which underlies *mamlekheth*. Does *mamlekheth* refer to the position of the ruled or the ruler?"[9] As Davies points out, "kingdom" is the most common translation of *mamlekheth*, which suggests the passive meaning, "either the territory or the people who are its citizens."[10] In the passive view, the expressions "holy nation" and "kingdom of priests" are parallel, with the idea of "nation" and "kingdom" being basically equivalent, both pointing to the people collectively, while "priesthood" and "holy" would be the more important terms of the phrases.

The problem with the passive view according to Davies is that *mamleketh* used in construct expressions is usually a subjective genitive, "whereas the passive view requires an objective or at least an appositional genitive."[11] However, the sense of either the objective ("a body of priests subject to kingly rule"[12]) or appositional genitive ("a kingdom, that is, priests") does not fit the context well, for the nation as a whole is set apart from all the nations of the world over which Yahweh rules as King. The children of Israel are His special treasure and the implication of their being brought to Him is that they share in His kingly rule, not that they are subject to a monarchy or simply subject to God.

After an extended and careful discussion of the various alternatives for an active understanding of *mamleketh*, Davies concludes that "there are good reasons to take *mamlekheth kohanim* to mean a collective royal company consisting of 'priests.' Israel is designated as royal by one who supremely holds the position of Israel's king. It is the people of God as a whole who bear this royal dignity and honour. Individuals enjoy these privileges only insofar as they belong to the group."[13] Assuming Davies is correct and that at Sinai Israel was ordained to be God's royal priesthood, the next question is, what is the origin of the notion of a royal priesthood?

---

8. John A. Davies, *A Royal Priesthood: Literary and Intertextual Perspectives on an Image of Israel in Exodus 19:6*, Journal for the Study of the Old Testament Supplement Series 395 (London: T. & T. Clark, 2004), 68. Davies lists the options suggested by R. B. Y. Scott: "1. 'a kingdom composed of priests' (by which Scott understands those who individually have access to God as may be implied by the New Testament references); or 2. 'a kingdom possessing a legitimate priesthood'; or 3. 'a kingdom with a collective priestly responsibility on behalf of all peoples'; or 4. 'a kingdom ruled by priests'; or 5. 'a kingdom set apart and possessing collectively, alone among all peoples, the right to approach the altar of Yahweh'" (69).

9. Ibid., 69. The Hebrew of the original is here transliterated and italicized.

10. Ibid., 70.

11. Ibid., 77.

12. Ibid.

13. Ibid., 86. The Hebrew of the original is transliterated and italicized.

THE ORIGINS OF THE ROYAL PRIESTHOOD

Among scholars it is commonly assumed that Israel's institutions were borrowed from her neighbors.[14] The widespread use of similar structures and language in covenants is well known and much studied since the publication in 1954 of George Mendenhall's *Law and Covenant in Israel and the Ancient Near East*.[15] Beginning in the nineteenth century, archeology has had a major impact on Biblical studies, as scholars have learned more about the ancient Near Eastern societies that surrounded Israel. It is common knowledge now that ancient Near Eastern nations had similar institutions of priesthood and kingship, along with notions like holy places, holy times, holy things, holy people, the distinction between clean and unclean, and sacrifice. Of course, there are differences among various nations' myths, institutions, and ceremonies, but there are also apparently similar underlying beliefs, and it is at least at that level, if not at every level, that Israel is assumed to have borrowed.[16] Holy people and holy things may be defined differently but there is a broadly shared idea that some people can approach God or the gods and others cannot. That there are special times for particular ceremonies is commonly assumed, as is also the belief that one's temple is the center of the cosmos and the priest-

---

14. See, for example, Frank M. Cross, *Canaanite Myth and Hebrew Epic: Essays in the History of the Religion of Israel* (Cambridge: Harvard University Press, 1973); Walter Beyerlin, *Origins and History of the Oldest Sinaitic Traditions*, trans. S. Rudman (London: Blackwell, 1966); Albrecht Alt, *Essays in Old Testament History and Religion*, trans. R. A. Wilson (New York: Doubleday, 1968); *Essays on Ancient Israel in its Near Eastern Context: A Tribute to Nadav Na'aman* (Winona Lake, IN: Eisenbrauns, 2006); Roland de Vaux, *Ancient Israel: Its Life and Institutions*, trans. John McHugh (Grand Rapids: Eerdmans, 1961; reprint, 1997). Among the asserted borrowings, we must include the design of the temple, which Mendenhall claims is thoroughly pagan (*Ancient Israel's Faith and History: An Introduction to the Bible in Context* [Louisville: Westminster John Knox, 2001], 126). Even Israel's monotheism is interpreted in relation to the polytheism of the cultures around her, with the assumption that monotheism arises in the sixth century BC (Mark S. Smith, *The Origins of Biblical Monotheism: Israel's Polytheistic Background and the Ugaritic Texts* [New York: Oxford, 2001]).

15. Originally published in two articles in *The Biblical Archaeologist* 17.2 (1954) 26–44 and 17.3 (1954) 49–76.

16. Scholars hold differing opinions on the extent of borrowing and the exact stories, ceremonies, or institutions that were borrowed. There is no consensus. See George E. Mendenhall, *Ancient Israel's Faith and History: An Introduction to the Bible in Context*. The cover of the book tells the whole story—a picture of the statue of the goddess Diana of the Ephesians. Peter Enns, an evangelical scholar, recently wrote *Inspiration and Incarnation: Evangelicals and the Problem of the Old Testament* (Grand Rapids: Baker, 2005), in which he argues that archaeological discoveries indicate that the early chapters of Genesis borrow from ancient Near Eastern mythology. A much more radical view is espoused by Francesca Stavrakopoulou in *King Manasseh and Child Sacrifice: Biblical Distortions of Historical Realities* (Berlin: de Gruyter, 2004). Stavrakopoulou argues that child sacrifice was a common form of worship in ancient Israel in its fertility cult ceremonial, but that biblical writers have intentionally distorted the true history for ideological purposes. Chester G. Starr, formerly professor of history at the University of Michigan and a highly respected specialist on ancient history, wrote, "To modern men, who approach these early myths from a scientific point of view, the tales of the gods are neither sensible nor logical, and the view of life which they express in their repetitious verse is basically a primitive one of gross action and elemental passions. In explaining the nature of the universe men translated into divine terms their own earthly concepts of personal clash and procreation. Yet in early civilized societies these tales were so satisfying that people all over the Near East accepted them. Mesopotamian stories thus passed into the early chapters of the Book of Genesis, where they continued to answer men's curiosity about the Creation down to the past century" (*A History of the Ancient World* [New York: Oxford, 1965; reprint, 1991], 39).

king in some sense a link between heaven and earth. Every ancient culture believed that, for some reason, animals have to be sacrificed to the gods.

Having grown to nationhood in this Ancient Near Eastern context, Israel is thought to have picked up her beliefs and institutions from older and more sophisticated cultures around her. After all, Abraham came from an advanced civilization in Mesopotamia and Moses was educated as a royal son in Egypt.[17] The children of Israel lived in Egypt long enough to become so much a part of the pagan culture that they longed to return to slavery rather than serve God and fight for the land He was giving them. And even after they did enter the promised land, they repeatedly borrowed from and imitated the pagan nations around them. All of this suggests that research into Near Eastern cultures no doubt sheds light on certain aspects of Israel's language, literary conventions, theology, history, religion, and society.

However, similarities between Israel and surrounding cultures do not necessarily lead to what Peter Enns calls "the problem of the Old Testament." According to Enns, ancient Israel held a *worldview* that was essentially the same as the nations around her, which means that the Bible is not unique.[18] In his controversial work, *Inspiration and Incarnation*, Enns calls for evangelicals to adjust their doctrine of Scripture to fit new evidence brought to light by archaeology and the study of ancient history. Enns explains, "the scientific evidence showed us that the worldview of the biblical authors affected what they thought and wrote, and so the worldviews of the biblical authors must be taken into consideration in matters of biblical interpretation."[19] Again, he states that "the Genesis story is firmly rooted in the worldview of its time"[20] and that "the opening chapters of Genesis participate in a worldview that the earliest Israelites shared with their neighbors."[21]

The question of worldview is crucial, and we must turn aside from Enns's claims to consider briefly just what a worldview entails. N. T. Wright says of worldviews, "There are four things worldviews characteristically do, in each of which the entire worldview can be glimpsed."[22] According to Wright, worldviews (1) answer basic questions people ask; (2) tell a story about the world; (3) offer a symbolic system by which reality is under-

---

17. Mendenhall viewed Amorite culture as widely influential not only for ancient Israel, but for her older neighbors as well (*Ancient Israel's Faith and History*, 10).

18. "What seems to be falsely implicit in the discussion is that revelation is by its nature unique, meaning that revelation will *necessarily* be *thoroughly* distinct from the surrounding culture" (Enns, *Inspiration and Incarnation*, 42).

19. Enns, *Inspiration and Incarnation*, 6. Enns identifies three basic problems that call for a revision of the doctrine of inspiration: (1) parallels between the Old Testament and other ancient Near Eastern literature; (2) theological diversity within the Old Testament; (3) the New Testament use of the Old Testament. I address only the first of these three here. See Peter J. Leithart, *Deep Exegesis: The Mystery of Reading Scripture* (Waco, TX: Baylor University Press, 2009), 31ff. for a broader discussion of Enns.

20. Enns, *Inspiration and Incarnation*, 27.

21. Ibid., 55. Similar statements about Israel's worldview are made on 51, 52, and 53.

22. N. T. Wright, *The New Testament and the People of God*, Christian Origins and the Question of God 1 (Minneapolis: Fortress, 1992), 123.

stood; and (4) teach people how they ought to live. To state each of the four issues with a single word, worldviews involve: (1) questions, (2) stories, (3) symbols, and (4) praxis.

When Enns repeatedly claims that the Old Testament shares the worldview of the ancient Near East, he seems to be talking about the fact that everyone in the ancient world believed that the world was "created," that there was a universal flood, that society should be ruled by kings, that worship should be led by priests who offered sacrifices in temples, and so on. He sees similarities in worldview between Moses' Law and Hammurabi's Code, between the creation stories of Israel and those of the ancient Near East, and between Solomon's proverbs and the *Instruction of Amenemope*, a collection of ancient Egyptian wisdom.[23]

Since every ancient society has a worldview that provides answers to fundamental questions, stories about the world, a symbolic system, and instruction for living, superficial similarities are virtually inescapable. However, what cannot be overly emphasized is that Israel was alone in the ancient Near East in believing that the world was created from nothing by one God who has all knowledge and power. The Genesis account is unique in depicting creation from nothing by a transcendent personal God. That there is simply nothing comparable to the biblical God anywhere else in the ancient world is not merely a theological claim; it is the bold declaration of Scripture (Exod 8:10; 9:14; Deut 4:32–40; 1 Sam 2:2; Pss 89:6; 113:5; Isa 44:7; 45:5–6, 14, 21–22; 46:9; Jer 49:19; 50:44; Joel 2:27). Furthermore, every sentence of Scripture assumes or teaches this distinctly biblical theism, which means that even when a proverb of Solomon is verbally quite similar to an Egyptian proverb, the profound differences in underlying worldview give the two proverbs a fundamentally different meaning. In other words, Enns seems to miss the most important aspects of the worldview question. He seems not to take into account that the identical sentence carries two utterly different meanings depending on whether the context is polytheistic or monotheistic. In fact, the meaning would be utterly different depending on whether the context is Islamic monotheism or biblical Trinitarian monotheism.[24]

All the same, why the similarities? In considering the answer to this question, Wright may help us think through possible alternatives. He defines the requirements of a good hypothesis as the following three: (1) "it must include the data"; (2) "it must construct a basically simple and coherent overall picture"; and (3) "it must prove itself fruitful in related areas."[25] What about Enns's hypothesis? First, Enns assumes that the Old Testament shares the same basic worldview as Israel's neighbors, but this leaves out the most important data, especially data provided by the Bible about God, His law, and

23. Enns, *Inspiration and Incarnation*, 38ff.

24. Writing on the Golden Rule, Jeffrey Wattles points out that people often offer lists of various versions of the Golden Rule, assuming that various religions and philosophies share basically the same meaning. But, he says, "Under the microscope of analysis, however, things are not so simple. Different formulations have different implications, and differences in context raise the question whether the same concept is at work in passages where the wording is nearly identical" (*The Golden Rule* [New York: Oxford, 1996], 4). Though he seeks to find a common meaning for the various formulations, he also shows that Hindus, Muslims, and Christians have fundamentally different interpretations.

25. Wright, *New Testament*, 99–100.

His work in history. Second, he achieves coherence in his picture by assuming the essential validity of the modern scientific worldview, but this is at the expense of the Bible's own view of the world and its historical record. Third, a view of the Bible that radically relativizes its message is unlikely to bear positive fruit, though what fruit Enns's view will bear remains to be seen.

James Jordan offers an entirely different answer to the kind of questions Enns poses. First, Jordan recognizes that the biblical worldview is unique, not because its customs or literary forms have no parallels in the ancient world, but because the chief feature of the biblical worldview, Yahweh Himself, is utterly without parallel. Thus, biblical answers to ultimate questions are profoundly different from all ancient religions and worldviews. Second, Jordan shows how the biblical story coheres through the underlying typology and symbolism of Scripture, joining Wright's second and third points about worldview.[26] Equally important for understanding the story of the Bible is Jordan's detailed investigation of biblical chronology, for "chronology is the backbone of history."[27] Third, Jordan offers an approach to symbolism that unites Scripture from Genesis to Revelation.[28] Fourth, Jordan contributes to a biblical understanding of how Christians ought to live through his exposition of the law of God.[29] Fifth, Jordan teaches that the Bible is the key to interpreting the Bible.[30] This should be understood as an ineluctable conclusion from belief in the Bible's divine inspiration—the only book that has been revealed by God must be approached differently from all other books and interpreted in accordance with its unique nature. That does not mean that linguistic, historical, comparative religion, and cultural studies are irrelevant. Indeed they are helpful. But the ultimate standard for understanding the Bible must be the Bible itself. In fact, the Bible must be our standard for understanding extrabiblical literature, history, science, and everything else, too.[31]

How does Jordan's approach shed light on the first aspect of what Enns calls "the problem of the Old Testament"? With respect to the question of ancient parallels, Jordan offers a perspective that takes into account the kind of data that Enns disregards or downplays. I am thinking of the biblical events of Genesis 1–11, which Enns regards as myth, and biblical chronology, which he ignores.[32] In the end, Jordan offers a much more coherent picture of world history outside of the Bible also.

---

26. See James B. Jordan, *Through New Eyes: Developing a Biblical View of the World* (Brentwood, TN: Wolgemuth & Hyatt, 1989; reprint, Eugene, OR: Wipf & Stock, 1999).

27. James B. Jordan, "The Embarrassment of Biblical Chronology," *Biblical Chronology* 1.1 (Dec. 1989). All the issues of this newsletter are devoted to a study of the Bible's chronology.

28. Especially in *Through New Eyes*, but in other writings also.

29. See especially, Jordan, *The Law of the Covenant*.

30. E.g., Jordan, *Through New Eyes,* 12–17.

31. Leithart points out that the Bible gives us the guidelines for understanding extra-biblical revelation as well (*Deep Exegesis*, 39ff.). Jordan would also emphasize that the Bible can be understood only through the indwelling work of the Holy Spirit. In a way, that could be said of any book, but it is true of the Bible in a different sense. The Bible is so much the personal word of the Tri-personal God that knowing Him is prerequisite to rightly reading His word. Moreover, God is not known in isolation from other people, for He is triune. We can only know Him in His church.

32. It is ironic that Enns speaks so often of "extrabiblical evidence" that cannot be ignored, but he seems to be uninformed of the controversy surrounding ancient Near Eastern chronological studies and

If we take biblical chronology seriously and allow the Bible to provide the standards by which we evaluate ancient history, we discover that the biblical stories of the flood and the tower of Babel provide basic answers to questions about parallels. According to the Bible, after the flood, Noah and his family became the source of a new humanity. Of course, they knew the true story of creation, and they had lived in a world where men could approach near enough to the Garden of Eden to see the terrifying angels guarding its gate. Stories of creation, Eden, the cherubim (monster-like creatures that appear to be part man, part animal), the pre-flood world, and so on were passed down from the time of Adam to Noah and through Noah and his sons to the ancestors of all the ancient peoples. By the time the nations were divided at Babel, various distortions had already entered the tradition because by then mankind was in rebellion against God and His word. When they dispersed, the nations took with them their own further modified version of the stories of creation and the flood, and various symbolic expressions and institutions, including the practice of animal sacrifice and social institutions such as kingship and priesthood.

In other words, if Genesis is a true record of historical events and its chronology is trustworthy, then in the Noahic tradition and its distortion at the tower of Babel we have the common source that explains the similarities in ancient religions and societies, including the symbolic system underlying the social and ceremonial laws of Moses. From Genesis we see that there were actual events of relatively recent history[33] that the whole race had in common, which is why there are similar stories among various peoples of the world and a virtually universal tradition of the Noahic deluge.

The details of biblical chronology shed further light, as Jordan explains:

> More telling psychologically is the fact that Noah and most of his descendants would have been contemporaries of Abraham. In fact, Shem died only shortly before Abraham died, while Eber outlived him. "Eber" is cognate to "Hebrew" (Genesis 14:13). For most 20th century evangelicals this does sound strange, but for over 3000 years no one reading the text thought it odd. The strangeness comes to us because we are not used to thinking in terms of it. Why could these men not have been contemporaries?[34]

Thus not only did Noah pass down stories of the prediluvian world to the peoples who were scattered at Babel, Noah also survived almost to the time of Abraham, telling the true story of the creation and flood to Abraham's contemporaries.[35]

---

its potential for reconstruction of ancient history. See James B. Jordan, "The Egyptian Problem," *Biblical Chronology* 6.1 (Jan. 1994) and "Problems with Current Consensus Chronology," *Biblical Chronology* 6.2 (Feb. 1994). See also Peter James, et al., *Centuries of Darkness: A Challenge to the Conventional Chronology of Old World Archaeology* (London: Jonathan Cape, 1991) and online: http://www.centuries.co.uk.

33. In the biblical chronology, the flood occurred around 2350 BC and the judgment of Babel, for which we have no exact date, probably occurred some two hundred years or so later.

34. James B. Jordan, "From Creation to Solomon," Studies in Biblical Chronology 2 (Niceville, FL: Biblical Horizons, 2001), 4. Noah actually died shortly before Abraham was born, but Shem lived until after Sarah died. Cf. James B. Jordan, "The Chronology of the Pentateuch," *Biblical Chronology* 6.6 (June 1994).

35. Concerning the question of law in particular, one of Enns's concerns, Jordan writes about the Pharaoh of the Exodus: "What evidence is there that Pharaoh was operating under laws which were given

This view not only explains why the ancient Near East shares with the Bible a tradition of a flood, but also why other peoples far separated from the ancient Near East have similar traditions. Similarities that Enns regards as a challenge to the Bible's uniqueness turn out to be a confirmation of the truth of the biblical story, because on the assumption that the story in Genesis is true and biblical chronology accurate, we would expect to find flood traditions, temples, priests, and animal sacrifices all over the ancient world. The nations have distorted versions of the traditions they inherited from Noah and his sons, but their most basic institutions evolved, or devolved, from Adam and Noah, the founding fathers of kingship and priesthood. Also, the story of the tower of Babel shows us why there are not only similarities but important differences among ancient pagan societies.[36]

To bring this back where we started, then, the origins of kingship and priesthood are to be found in the Genesis story of God's creation of Adam. God commanded Adam and Eve to rule the world (Gen 1:26–28), a command that eventually led to the institution of kingship. He also commanded Adam to guard the Garden, essentially a priestly activity.[37] This is the background for what we read about Noah. When he left the ark, the first thing he did was the priestly work of offering animal sacrifices (Gen 8:20). Then God renewed the covenant with Noah that He had originally given to Adam, commanding him to rule and adding that from that point onward man would be responsible to punish murder with capital punishment (Gen 9:1ff.). Thus, like Adam, Noah functioned as king and priest. All the ancient peoples who were driven away from Babel had traditions of kings and priests because they all shared a common history in their father Noah, the new Adam of the ancient new world.

---

to God's people? Our answer is that Pharaoh's arguments with Moses make no sense unless we presuppose that he knew these laws. Remember, the exodus took place 857 years after the Flood. Shem, the Godly son of Noah, lived 502 years after the Flood. Thus there was doubtless much Godly influence all over the ancient world until well into the history of the seed people, Israel. The mixing of God's law with local customary law is called 'common law,' and considering that at the outset, right after the Flood, God's law was the only law, it is reasonable to assume that at this point in history there was still a strong common law. The law codes of the ancient world are at many places quite similar to the laws recorded in the Pentateuch—again evidence of a common source (Noah, and behind him, God). The pagans, of course, increasingly perverted and lost God's law" (*The Law of the Covenant*, 44–45).

36. Henri Frankfort observes, "But if we refer to kingship as a political institution, we assume a point of view which would have been incomprehensible to the ancients. We imply that the human polity can be considered by itself. The ancients, however, experienced human life as part of a widely spreading network of connections which reached beyond the local and the national communities into the hidden depths of nature and the powers that rule nature. The purely secular—in so far as it could be granted to exist at all—was purely trivial. Whatever was significant was imbedded in the life of the cosmos, and it was precisely the king's function to maintain the harmony of that integration. This doctrine is valid for the whole of the ancient Near East and for many other regions. But, as soon as we want to be more specific, we find that a contrast exists between the two centers of ancient civilization. Egypt and Mesopotamia held very different views as to the nature of their king and the temper of the universe in which he functioned" (*Kingship and the Gods: A Study of Ancient Near Eastern Religion as the Integration of Society and Nature* [Chicago: University of Chicago, 1948; reprint, 1978], 3).

37. "Priests, with the Levite clans, guarded the tabernacle (Num. 3:8, 38) . . ." (Leithart, *Priesthood*, 53).

In addition, the biblical story of creation and the flood contain elementary covenantal forms.[38] Covenants are part of the world of Noah even before the flood, so there is no reason to assume that Moses had to borrow the notion of covenant from the Hittites or anyone else. At the same time, since covenants and covenant forms were a common inheritance from Noah for all the tribes of man, there would have been nothing wrong with Moses learning particular literary forms for expressing the covenant relationship.[39] The point is that whoever uses covenants and covenant forms—which is everyone in the ancient world—testifies to the historical and cultural impact of Noah.

Israel's royal priesthood finds its roots in the royal priesthood of Adam and Noah. God called His firstborn son out of Egypt and set him up over all the nations of the world as a king-priest nation. The covenant given to Israel at Sinai was based upon the Abrahamic covenant, just as the Abrahamic covenant was an extension of the Noahic and the Adamic covenants. In fact, all the covenants in the old covenant era are renewals of the covenant into which Adam was created at the beginning. It is in that original creation covenant that the origins of the royal priesthood are to be found.

THE MELCHIZEDEKIAN FULFILLMENT

The book of Hebrews declares that Jesus was a priest after the order of Melchizedek, but expositors often assume that the Melchizedekian priesthood is grounded only in the explicitly cited story of Abraham together with David's prophecy in Psalm 110. I am suggesting a much broader background and one that is related to the royal priesthood of Israel. This does not diminish the importance of Melchizedek himself, but it puts the nature of his priesthood, Christ's, and ours in a new light.

To confirm this broader background and the typology of the royal priesthood, we must return to Sinai. My claim is that Israel's royal priesthood was grounded in the priesthood of Adam. If that is so, we would expect to find other creation themes in the context of Exodus 19. And we do. As in Eden, Israel makes covenant on a mountain, like the original Eden, and sees a vision of God (Exod 24:1–11). The abundance of water at Horeb may be another indication of the creation theme (Exod 17:6).[40] A large section of Exodus is written as a new creation narrative. Jordan argues that the structure of Exodus 25–40 follows the story of creation in Genesis 1,[41] so that the tabernacle is presented here

---

38. See Jordan, *Through New Eyes,* 118ff., and compare it with his *Covenant Sequence in Leviticus and Deuteronomy* (Tyler, TX: Institute for Christian Economics, 1989), 5ff. Jordan's description of the elements of a covenant corresponds closely to his exposition of the process for creation and the rite of breaking bread.

39. I am not saying that he did; I am just saying that if he did, it does not introduce a "problem."

40. "Horeb" in Exodus 17:6 seems to refer to a larger area than the mountain, but the name makes the association. Thanks to Peter Leithart for pointing out this reference.

41. "The account of the instructions for the Tabernacle is found in Exodus 25–31. It is organized as seven speeches of the Lord, 'Then the Lord spoke to Moses, saying,' or some variant of this phrase (25:1, 30:11, 17, 22, 34; 31:1, 12). Since the Tabernacle is a symbol for the world, the commands for its building could easily have been connected by God with His original commands in Genesis 1 when the physical world was built. I believe that the text gives ample evidence that this is indeed the case, and that the seven speech commands of God in Exodus 25–31 correlate with the seven Days of Genesis 1" (James B. Jordan, "The Tabernacle: A New Creation," Biblical Horizons Occasional Paper 5 [Dec. 1988; rev., June 1993], 1).

PART ONE: BIBLICAL STUDIES

as a new cosmos and Aaron is set up not as liturgical man but as cosmic man[42]—all of which confirms the picture of Israel's being set up as a new Adam in Exodus 19:6.[43]

The essential multivalence of biblical symbolism is apparent here also. The whole nation was a new Adam, Aaron was a new Adam, King David was a new Adam,[44] Ezekiel was a new Adam,[45] and of course, Christ is *the* new Adam, the last Adam. Similarly, the tabernacle as a whole testified that Israel was a God-ordained royal priesthood foreshadowing the Messiah.

> First the Tabernacle was a house for God. Second, since the universe of heaven and earth is God's house, the Tabernacle symbolized the heavens and the earth. Third, the Tabernacle was a holy mountain, specifically reproducing the configuration of Mount Sinai. Fourth, since God's house is His people, the Tabernacle symbolized the body politic of Israel at this stage of history. And fifth, since the people-house started out "in Adam" and eventually came to be "in Christ," and since Christ is the True Israel, the Tabernacle also symbolized the righteous individual person, and as such was a type of Christ.[46]

The prevalence of creation themes within the larger context of Exodus 19:6 testifies that Israel's royal priesthood was grounded in the history of Adam and Noah as king-priests and was typological of the royal priesthood of the Messiah. Since the ordination of Israel to royal priesthood at Mount Sinai was in fulfillment of the Abrahamic covenant, the clear purpose of Israel's calling was to bring Abrahamic blessing to all the nations of the world. She was to "rule," not by conquest or oppression, like the Gentiles, but by sacrifice and prayer.[47] In this, the nation as a whole was like Melchizedek, king of Salem, a king of righteousness and peace, a godly king-priest after the order of Noah, who typified the coming Messiah.[48]

---

42. "Rather, what is before us in Exodus 25–40 is the Tabernacle as Cosmos, not as Garden. Aaron is presented as the generic man of Genesis 1, the leader of creation who presides over the 'tent of meeting.' He is not at this point 'liturgical man,' who functions in the sanctuary, but 'cosmic man,' who functions in the microcosmic world of the Tabernacle. Thus, his garments are presented cosmically, in a series of seven. As we saw above, Exodus 28–29 go with the 'filling' aspect of the first day, as Exodus 25–27 go with the 'forming' aspect" (Jordan, "Tabernacle," 7).

43. Other details also confirm this view. Jordan writes of the tabernacle curtains, for example, "In view of the fact that these curtains symbolized the ranks of Israel, they also typify the nature and duty of Jesus Christ, the True Israel, in His various capacities" ("From Glory to Glory: Degrees of Value in the Sanctuary," Biblical Horizons Occasional Paper 2 [Aug. 1988; rev., Feb. 1994], 7). In *The Law of the Covenant*, Jordan argues that Israel at Sinai was constituted a new Adam (55ff.).

44. Jordan, *Through New Eyes*, 228.

45. Ibid., 244.

46. Ibid., 205–6.

47. Of course, someone might respond by saying, "Tell that to the people of Jericho!" But the conquest of Canaan was not normal warfare in ancient Israel. Canaan was under special judgment from the time of Noah (Gen 9:25). As for other nations, Israel was not permitted to engage in aggressive war. Even if another nation attacked Israel, the rules of war were different from the rules for the conquest. The judgment of Canaan was a once-for-all special commission from Yahweh.

48. There is an ancient Jewish tradition that Melchizedek was actually Shem. See M. McNamara, "Melchizedek: Gen 14,17–20 in the Targums, in Rabbinic and Early Christian Literature," *Biblica* 81 (2000) 1–31. Melchizedek may well have been a throne name, since Joshua 10:1, 3 refer to Adoni-zedek as king

To return, then, to the book of Hebrews, we are taught that Christ was a priest after the order of Melchizedek, and we also learn how He fulfilled the typology of the Aaronic order. No mention is made of Adam or Noah as priests or kings. If the exposition of the origins of priesthood offered above is correct, we must consider the relationship between the various old covenant priesthoods and the Aaronic priesthood. Why did the book of Hebrews not speak of Jesus as a priest after the order of Adam if that is most fundamental?[49] What is special about Melchizedek? Why does a royal priest in a Melchizedekian order have to fulfill the typology of the Aaronic order? The first question is complicated. To answer it, we need to consider the larger picture of royal priesthood in the light of the biblical covenants, which should also provide insight into other questions.

To begin at the beginning, Adam was created into a covenant relationship with God. He was not created into a "natural" situation and then granted a covenant afterwards, as an added feature to his relationship with God. The intratrinitarian counsel of Genesis 1:26 already defines man as God's covenantal representative and ruler of the world before Adam is created. The covenantal meaning of Adam and his race precedes the existence of Adam and already qualifies every cell in his body when God breathes into him the breath of life. His position as king over the world and priestly servant of the Yahweh in the Garden is fundamental not only for Adam, but for the whole race descended from him. The Garden is the biblical and theological starting point for royal priesthood.

The covenant given to Noah after the flood was a renewal of the covenant given to Adam. It did not replace or rescind anything in the Adamic covenant. Nor does any other covenant until the coming of Christ. Every covenant in the old covenant era—the era from Adam to Jesus—builds on the previous covenants and presupposes the original creation covenant. That means that all priesthood in the old covenant era is grounded in the royal priesthood of Adam and Noah.

---

of Jerusalem. The interpretation of Melchizedek as Shem, the priesthood of Noah, and much more have ancient Jewish roots and wide attestation. For references, see Andrei Orlov, "The Heir of Righteousness and the King of Righteousness: The Priestly Noahic Polemics in 2 Enoch and the Epistle to the Hebrews" *Journal of Theological Studies*, NS 58.1 (2007) 45–65. I disagree with Orlov's perspective, or at least his depiction of the book of Hebrews as anti-Levitical polemic, but he offers the most comprehensive bibliography available for further study and research. See also his online writings at http://www.andreiorlov.com/. Modern commentators often assume that Melchizedek is a pagan, but I think it is highly unlikely—to put it mildly—that Abraham would be offering tithes to a pagan Canaanite priest. Such an interpretation is pure speculation—or impure speculation—with no warrant in the text itself. J. A. Fitzmyer and many others not only assume that Melchizedek was a pagan priest but also that the book of Hebrews misinterprets his name (cf. J. A. Fitzmyer, "Melchizedek in the MT, LXX, and the NT," *Biblica* 81 [2000] 63–69).

49. For Orlov, the question is different: "The Epistle to the Hebrews is full of puzzles. One of the most intriguing puzzles for current research is this: why does the author never mention the name of Noah in his debates about animal sacrifices and the expiatory meaning of human and animal blood?" ("Heir of Righteousness," 59). Noah is prominent for Orlov because he believes that the use of altars for animal sacrifice began with Noah (Gen 8:20–22), though blood sacrifice itself began with Abel (Gen 4:4). However, he neglects to mention that God clothed Adam and Eve with animal skins (Gen 3:21), which clearly implies that animal sacrifice was instituted immediately after the fall. And animal sacrifice implies altars, for animals are not ritually offered on bare dirt. Abel and Seth must have had altars of some sort. For Orlov's discussion, see "Heir of Righteousness," 60–65.

PART ONE: BIBLICAL STUDIES

From the time of the flood until God gave Israel His sanctuary at Sinai, there was no central sanctuary in the ancient world and therefore no set hierarchy among godly priests of the Noahic order, though a natural hierarchy of sorts may have existed. In the days of Abraham, there may have been a number of godly priests all "ordained" in the "Noahic order." Abraham himself seems to have been some sort of priest, since he performed priestly duties presumably on the basis of the covenant that was given to him.[50] But if there was no God-ordained hierarchy among priesthoods, why should Abraham offer tithes to Melchizedek?

There may have been a number of reasons. First, Melchizedek was a godly king-priest of Jerusalem perhaps not far from the King's Valley where he met Abraham, and Abraham may have been submitting to him as the legitimate king-priest of the local area. Second, Melchizedek may have been, as the ancient Jews thought, the throne name for Noah's son, Shem. If that is the case, Abraham was submitting to a great king-priest in his own family whose authority as an elder he would accept. Third, even if Melchizedek was not Shem, he may have been a Semitic king-priest and therefore an older relative of Abraham, in which case Abraham's submission may have been related to tradition, family structure, and respect for elders. Of course, the first answer can be combined with either the second or the third.

Whatever his reasons for doing so, by offering tithes to Melchizedek Abraham recognized the king-priest of Salem as in some sense above him. Given Abraham's position as covenant-head of the new era and the one through whom the world would be blessed, it may seem odd that he would recognize another priest, unless that priest was established under the terms of a superior covenant. Melchizedek's priesthood, therefore, had to be prior to the gift of the covenant to Abraham and based upon the more fundamental Noahic covenant. Since the Abrahamic covenant is an extension of the more basic Noahic, Abraham recognizes Melchizedek's priesthood, just as Moses later recognized the priesthood of Jethro.

But the case of Moses is different. The gift of the Mosaic covenant brought a vast change to the world. From the time that God ordained Israel as a royal priesthood and gave the holy nation His sanctuary, any other godly priesthood that may have existed—Jethro's, for example—became subordinate to the royal priesthood of Israel, for God had only one sanctuary and one altar. If He accepted sacrifices and prayers from other al-

---

50. In his structural analysis of the covenants in Genesis, Jordan identifies Abraham as a prophet, the Adamic being priestly, the Noahic being kingly, and the Abrahamic being prophetic. This accords with Genesis 20:7 in which Abraham is explicitly called a prophet (Gen 20:7). However, Jordan's analysis of Genesis includes another overlapping structure, threefold sin and threefold obedience. The threefold sin is recorded in Genesis 1–6. The sin of Adam and Eve was primarily against the Father and distinctively priestly. The sin of Cain was primarily against the Brother/Son, a sin in the realm of royal authority. The sin of the sons of Seth was the sin of intermarriage, a sin against the Spirit. By contrast, Genesis 12–50 sets up Abraham, Jacob, and Joseph as men who obeyed in contrast to Adam, Cain, and the sons of Seth. In this paradigm, Abraham's obedience is specifically and especially priestly, even if Abraham is not a priest in the narrow sense of the word. See James B. Jordan, "Three 'Falls' and Three Heroes," *Biblical Horizons* 22 (Feb. 1991). Also, "God called Abraham to be a priest to the nations right after the incident at the Tower of Babel. These two events are intimately related (compare Gen. 11:4 with 12:2)" (James B. Jordan, "The Future of Israel Reexamined [Part 2]," *Biblical Horizons* 28 [Aug. 1991]).

tars—which seems certain—it was on the basis of the sacrifice offered at the central and true sanctuary. Once the tabernacle was built and Aaron was ordained as priest, it would have been inappropriate for Aaron to pay tithes to a priest like Melchizedek, though there is a sense in which he did pay tithes through Abraham in the pre-tabernacle era.

The gift of the new covenant to Israel through Moses and the establishment of Israel's tabernacle as the cosmic center redefined the world situation. The nation of Israel was God's firstborn son (Exod 4:22) and a royal priesthood, the only people who could draw near to Him in His house and bring grace and blessing to the world. The Aaronic priesthood supplemented the royal priesthood of the nation and was charged with the responsibilities of priestly service in the tabernacle, but the royal priesthood remained fundamental. The ordination of the nation preceded and provided a foundation both for the priesthood of Aaron and the later institution of kingship.[51]

Why, then, was the royal priesthood only mentioned explicitly in one verse in the Old Testament? The wrong answer to this question is that Israel lost the status of royal priest when Aaron led the children of Israel to worship the golden calf. The rebellion of Korah, together with some Reubenites, presupposes the priesthood of the nation (cf. Num 16:1–3),[52] though God's judgment against Korah emphasizes the unique privileges of the family of Aaron. There is actually one passage that clearly alludes to Exodus 19:6 and promises that Israel's status as royal priest would be internationally recognized—Isaiah 61:6. It seems, therefore, to be fundamental throughout Israel's existence. Perhaps the reason it seldom appears in the literature of the Old Testament is that Exodus 19:6 itself was so well known and important. However that may be, as the example of Melchizedek shows, it is not the only case of a profoundly important priesthood receiving scant attention.

With this background understanding of old covenant priesthood, we are ready to consider the priesthood of Christ and hopefully provide answers to the questions posed at the beginning of the section. First, Jesus was ordained as a new covenant royal priest at His baptism by John the baptizer[53] and with His baptism a new era began, though the old era did not come to a full end until the destruction of the temple in AD 70. The Messianic significance of Jesus' baptism clearly points to kingship, but priesthood is also hinted at when Luke tells us Jesus was about thirty. Also when the Spirit of God anointed the Christ to equip Him for His calling, He appeared in the form of a sacrificial animal, underscoring the priestly nature of His work. Luke also brings Jesus' baptism into rela-

---

51. Davies says, "What was in the Sinai material presented as a corporate royal status is in the Davidic covenant personified in the king, who in a sense *is* the nation" (*Royal Priesthood*, 180–81). The same thing could be said of the priesthood, for the high priest carries on his shoulders and his breastplate the names of the twelve tribes. His priestly service is performed as and for the nation. Just as the Mosaic covenant was based upon the Abrahamic (Exod 2:24; Lev 26:40–42; Deut 29:10–13), the covenants granted to the tribe of Levi (Num. 3:1–13; 18:1–20) and the family of David (2 Sam 7) were grounded in both the Mosaic and the Abrahamic.

52. See the exposition in ibid., 189ff.

53. See Ralph Allan Smith, *The Baptism of Jesus the Christ* (Eugene, OR: Wipf & Stock, 2010).

PART ONE: BIBLICAL STUDIES

tion with Adam, calling attention to the fact that in His office, He replaced the first head of the race.[54]

Jesus fulfills the typology and meaning of the royal priesthood throughout the old covenant era, beginning with Adam and including the royal priesthood of Israel. But Melchizedek has special meaning because of his relationship with Abraham. In order that he might become a type of Christ, Melchizedek was led by God to approach Abraham and bless him. David—perhaps meditating on the story in Genesis—realized that the Messiah would be a king-priest like Melchizedek because the Messiah would replace Adam as the king of the world, the firstborn son of all mankind. In effect, what David proclaims of the Messiah in Psalm 110 acknowledges that the Messiah would be not merely a king in the line of David, but something greater.

This did not, however, make the Aaronic priesthood irrelevant, for the Mosaic covenant was an advance on the Noahic, reestablishing a central sanctuary in the world. Though the nature of priestly ministry did not fundamentally change, the service of the Aaronic priests at the tabernacle and temple delineated in the Mosaic covenant constituted the most specialized and refined epitome of priestly service in the entire old covenant era. As an advanced form of the Adamic and Noahic priesthood, the Aaronic ministry provided the most exalted typological depiction of priestly labor and therefore had to be fulfilled by the Messiah, even though His priesthood was not Aaronic.

THE NEW COVENANT ROYAL PRIESTHOOD IN CHRIST

Peter Leithart's book *The Priesthood of the Plebs* demonstrates that Christian baptism constitutes the Christian as a priest. In other words, baptism is ordination to priesthood. But what sort of priesthood? The only possible answer would seem to be *Melchizedekian* priesthood, since the Aaronic order has been superseded. However, it is not explicitly stated in the New Testament that Christians are priests after the order of Melchizedek. As in many other areas, we have to make inferences based on what the Scripture teaches.

Specifically, the Christian's Melchizdekian priesthood may be concluded from at least the following three lines of inference. First, the book of Hebrews clearly associates the Christian's priesthood with that of Christ. He is the Great High Priest who opens the way for us to enter within the veil (Heb 10:19–22). Since we must be in the same priestly order as our High Priest, we are also priests after the order of Melchizedek. Second, the association of the Christian's priesthood with that of Christ can be stated more precisely: We are priests "in Christ." We not only come to God by virtue of His priestly work; we also come into the presence of God as those united to Him, one with Him, as His very body. Third, New Testament allusions to Exodus 19:6 in 1 Peter 2:9; Revelation 1:6; 5:10; and 20:6 confirm that the church fulfills the typological royal priesthood of the nation of Israel.[55] Christ is the ultimate King-Priest, the Last Adam, but His body the church also

---

54. All of these issues are discussed at some length in ibid. See also Peter J. Leithart, "Baptism into Priesthood," *Rite Reasons* 45 (May 1995).

55. A detailed exegesis of the verses in Revelation is difficult, but an allusion to Exodus 19:6 is undeniable. John seems to write that we are "a kingdom, priests," rather than saying a "royal priesthood," but it is clear that we are priests who reign (Rev 5:10; 20:6), so the use of "kingdom" here—assuming that is the

fulfills the typology of the royal priesthood of Israel, serving God as priests who occupy a royal throne (Rev 20:6).

Baptism, therefore, is ordination into a Melchizedekian priesthood. It makes Christians to be both kings and priests, opening up both the responsibilities and privileges of the royal priesthood. But where do we look to find biblical information on those privileges and responsibilities? The New Testament contains very little in the way of priestly instruction, though it does point the way. The same must be said for royal instruction. The New Testament epistles do not offer detailed instruction for kings in Christ, but the teaching it does offer suggests a broader approach.

Beginning with the royal aspect of the Christian's calling, consider how Paul instructs the churches. He deals with issues that kings and judges in the old covenant era dealt with, like marriage, business and finances, courts, interpersonal relationships, and charity. In all of these areas, as well as others, Paul constantly quotes from the books of the Old Testament and regards their instruction as authoritative, even though he also clearly teaches that Christians are not under the Mosaic covenant. In other words, the instruction and teaching of the Mosaic era is still comprehensively relevant because it is the word of God, but the way it is to be applied in the new covenant era may not be direct or simple. The church is not a national entity and as she spreads out into the world, she often finds herself in places where she is oppressed and downtrodden. In such circumstances her royal prerogatives are not in the fore. But when she grows and becomes the dominant influence in a society, the wisdom contained in the Scriptures guides her in dominion. She needs the law, the Psalms, and the prophets to guide her in judgment.

Concerning the priestly duty of the church, the situation is somewhat different. She does not have to be the dominant force in society to exercise her priestly function more or less fully. Even if it is only in secret, she can worship according to the Scriptures and intercede for the nations of the world. Her members can help one another. She can preach the Gospel to the lost world.

The question is, where does she obtain wisdom for her liturgical labors? Given the general principle that all Scripture is profitable for instruction in righteousness, it should be obvious that the book of Leviticus offers instruction that should guide Christian worship, not in the way of literal observance of Levitical rites but in the way of principles. More particularly, the fact that Paul refers to the church as God's temple (Eph 2:21) and uses sacrificial language repeatedly to describe Christian labors, self-dedication, prayer, and praise (Rom 12:1; 15:16; 1 Cor 5:7; Phil 2:17; 4:18; 2 Tim 4:6; Heb 13:15–16; 1 Pet 2:5) clearly implies that we should obtain specific instruction for our priestly duties from the

---

correct text—includes the implication that we share in God's rule. This is especially clear in Revelation 5:10, where John uses the cognate noun and verb, "You have made them *to be* a kingdom (*basileian*) and priests to our God; and they will reign (*basileusousin*) upon the earth." The Greek verb for "reign" here signifies reign by a king. Every reference to reigning in Revelation is significant (Rev 5:10; 11:15, 17; 19:6; 20:4, 6; 22:5). Kingship and rule are major themes of Revelation, with twenty-eight occurrences of cognate nouns and the verb *basileuō* in twenty-five (Rev 1:5; 5:10; 6:15; 9:11; 10:11; 11:15, 17; 15:3; 16:12, 14; 17:2, 9, 12, 14, 18; 18:3, 9; 19:6, 16, 18–19; 20:4, 6; 21:24; 22:5). The theme is further emphasized by the use of the word "throne," which occurs forty-seven times in thirty-seven verses (Rev 1:4; 2:13; 3:21; 4:2–6, 9–10; 5:1, 6–7, 11, 13; 6:16; 7:9–11, 15, 17; 8:3; 11:16; 12:5; 13:2; 14:3; 16:10, 17; 19:4–5; 20:4, 11–12; 21:3, 5; 22:1, 3).

old covenant priesthood. Of course, this is not to limit the Church to Levitical principles. The entire Bible offers instruction in wisdom to serve God. In the Old Testament, the book of Psalms especially instructs Christians in prayer, but the historical and prophetic books of the Old Testament are also replete with priestly wisdom.

CONCLUSION

I have argued here that Melchizedek's royal priesthood was grounded in the royal priesthood of Adam and Noah, that the Aaronic priesthood and the Davidic royalty were both particularized expressions of the royal priesthood of the nation, that the Aaronic priestly rites were the most refined expression of priesthood and sacrifice in the old covenant era, and that the Christian's priesthood is a royal priesthood, like the priesthood of Christ, in the Melchizedekian order. It would not be inaccurate to say that all of this is simply drawing out the implications of the New Testament teaching that Jesus is the Last Adam and that in Him the Church is a new humanity, for Adam was the first royal priest.

Even if—perhaps "even though" is the right way to say it—Christians have little understanding about the meaning of baptism as ordination into the royal priesthood and weekly worship as the communion of the royal priesthood, we still are what God has made us to be. It would be helpful to the Church of Christ if pastors explained baptism as ordination to the royal priesthood and conducted weekly worship according to the basic outline of covenant renewal that Leviticus prescribes for old covenant worship. That would be applying Leviticus to the new covenant situation so that the Church could fulfill her priestly role. As the number of Christians in a society grows, the economic and political dominion of Christian people also grows. It is not the Church as an institution that exercises economic and political dominion, though the Church is the teacher of individual, family, and civil authorities. Economic dominion is primarily the responsibility of the family. Political dominion in a Christian nation—defined here as a nation that is self-consciously following Christ as King—would be exercised by believers in Christ who seek to honor Him as leaders in civil government.[56]

The biblical vision of the kingdom of God requires Christian people to know that they are a royal priesthood and to act accordingly. Christ is Lord of lords and King of kings. Though all the world refuse to see it, His church must see the truth and rejoice in it. Our prayers and our labor must self-consciously aim for the increase of the dominion of Him who said, "All authority in heaven and on earth is mine. Go, therefore, and disciple all the nations" (Matt 28:18–20).

---

56. Leithart's *The Kingdom and the Power* offers extended and detailed discussion of what it means for the Church to live as priests and kings.

Dear Ralph,

Thank you for an essay that is both theologically acute and pastorally useful.

I'm supposed to add something, so here goes. We can say that Adam was created as priest and king, but his kingship was not to come into mature play until he acquired knowledge of good and evil and left the sanctuary garden for the wider world. This move was corrupted, of course, and it is with Noah that we come to real kingship. Adam was full priest but crown prince.

I find it interesting that it is Noah, elevated to full kingship, who plants a garden sanctuary. This sheds light on a matter you also addressed: why it is Melchizedek and not Adam who is mentioned in Psalm 110 and Hebrews. Adam was not fully king, but Jesus is.

Noah as kingly sanctuary-builder seems to be replicated in Melchizedek's giving bread and wine to Abram. Wine is the sign of Noahic kingship, and Melchizedek communicates a new "garden" to Abram. Abram/Abraham will not rule as a full king, but he will manage what Melchizedek gives him. And this Abrahamic management extends down to Aaron. Hence, as you point out, Hebrews points to Melchizedek rather than Noah in connection with the faith of Abraham and the rule of Jesus. From the stomach of Abram the bread and wine move into his body and through his loins to become Aaron's priestly bread and David's regal wine, so to speak. Hence the history of Israel flows from Melchizedek's initial gifts.

The original history is played out again in a microcosm in Israel. Aaron is priest with some slight rule in the sanctuary, and there are judges in Israel. It is when we come to Saul and then David, however, that we get real kings. Those kings build the new garden sanctuary for the priestly worship, and the faithful kings repair the Temple over and over. Hence, those kings are like Noah and Melchizedek.

Well, enough of "additions." You are certainly right that the church begins in worship and priestly service, sometimes hidden in catacombs, but that the church as God's people always matures into societal influence and kingly rule. Believers in union with the Greater Melchizedek cannot help but grow up into priest-kings. It is appalling how often this truth is denied by those claiming to represent the "Reformed faith" today.

Jim

6

Father Storm

A Theology of Sons in the Book of Job

Toby J. Sumpter

INTRODUCTION: FATHERS AND SONS

Job is a story of sons. Job is a son, the "greatest of the sons of the east" (1:3), and Job has sons, seven sons; they are princes, sons of the king. Job is a perfect and upright man, and his fear of God and shunning of evil are particularly evidenced in Job's actions as a father. Job is a perfect father who "sanctifies" his sons by offering up ascension offerings for them according to their number (1:5).

But there are other sons. There is a day in which the "sons of God" assemble themselves and stand before Yahweh (1:6). These sons stand before their Father. They were there when the foundations of the earth were fastened in place; they shouted for joy when God stretched the measuring line across the deep (38:5–7).

Thus the story of Job begins with sons and fathers, and it is the contention of this paper that the theme of sonship and fatherhood is wound through the rest of the book of Job. Far from the prologue and epilogue being in "shocking disparity"[1] to the center of the book, this motif provides a direction to which the narrative and dialogues point together, culminating in Yahweh's answer from the whirlwind and the resolution of the final chapter, offering a number of suggestions for understanding the book of Job and more importantly what it means to be a son of God and what it means for God to be our Father.

PERFECT FATHERS

It is the echo of characters in the opening narrative that invites closer study, beginning particularly with the actions of the fathers: Job and Yahweh. As we already noted, Job's

---

1. David Penchansky, *The Betrayal of God: Ideological Conflict in Job* (Louisville: Westminster John Knox, 1990), 27.

fatherly care for his sons includes the sacrifice of ascension offerings for his sons. What we find is that Yahweh's care for Job is similar. The calamity pericope in 1:13–19 forms a literary unit bound by the description of Job's sons and daughters feasting in the older brother's house (1:13, 18–19). The feasting of Job's children is the context of all the destruction reported by the messengers. The description creates a simultaneous image of the events: While the children are feasting, these disasters are falling. Furthermore, 1:13 begins with the same time stamp as 1:6, "Now there was a day . . . " (*wayhi hayom*). The day that the sons of God assemble before Yahweh corresponds to the day that Job's sons and daughters are feasting in the oldest brother's house, suggesting that the events are occurring simultaneously or should at least be understood together as a single event.[2]

The disasters themselves are described in a chiastic order with the feasting children as bookends (1:13, 18–19). Oxen and donkeys stolen and servants slain (1:14–15) are parallel to the camels stolen and servants slain (1:17). This marks 1:16 as the center of the chiasm where the "fire of God" falls and burns up the sheep and the servants and "consumes" them. The events look like this:

    A. Sons and daughters eating and drinking (1:13)
        B. Oxen and donkeys stolen and servants killed by the edge of the sword (1:14–15)
            C. Fire of God burns up the sheep and the servants and consumes them (1:16)
        B'. Camels stolen and servants killed by the edge of the sword (1:17)
    A'. Sons and daughters eating and drinking; great wind strikes house and they die (1:18–19)

Key to interpreting the rest of the events in this section is 1:16. This is the same sort of fire which burned in connection with God's presence on Mount Sinai (Deut 4:11; 9:15), and the imagery is sacrificial (cf. Lev 6:12, Neh 10:34)—which suggests that some of the other details of the calamities are, as well. Like all sacrifices, this one includes food eaten (e.g., Exod 12–13; Lev 3:11; 7:11ff.; 21:6ff.), a sword cuts up the sacrificial victims (e.g., Lev 1:6; 3:2–4; 4:4), and the fire of God consumes the offering made by fire (e.g., Lev 1:9, 13, 17).

The conclusion to the narration of the calamities is the final report concerning Job's children. A "great wind" strikes the four corners of the house they are in, it falls on his children, and they die (1:19). Here there are at least two indications that a sacrificial motif is in view. First, the great wind is of course a great *ruach*, the word for the Spirit-wind, which can refer to a more generic or natural occurrence of wind but is frequently associated with the storm presence of the Spirit of God who comes to create (Gen 1:1; 8:1; Ps 33:6) and judge (Exod 14:21; 15:8–10; Pss 18:7–15; 35:5). When Yahweh draws near to His people, He frequently comes as a great storm (Exod 19:16; 20:18), and it is this same firestorm presence of the Spirit that leads them through the wilderness and fills

---

2. Norman C. Habel, *The Book of Job* (Philadelphia: Westminster, 1985), 91.

the tabernacle (Exod 40:34–38). With the "fire of God" at the center of the calamities, this great wind should also be seen as part of the hand of God (1:11).[3]

The second indication that this great wind should be viewed in sacrificial terms is the reference to the "four corners" of the house that are struck. The most prolific use of this description of "four corners" is in the descriptions of the tabernacle in Exodus and Ezekiel's visionary temple. In Exodus it is only the bronze altar that has the same four "corners" as the house that Job's children are killed in (Exod 27:2; 38:2).[4] In Ezekiel's vision, the four corners almost exclusively are the four corners of the altar and the four corners of the temple court (Ezek 43:16, 20; 45:19; 46:21, 22). Specifically we note that the same word appears to describe the four corners of Ezekiel's altar where blood is to be smeared (Ezek 43:20; 45:19). Job's entire household is an altar, and now Job's world has been consumed by the fire of God from heaven and the blood of his children and servants is smeared on the four corners of his house.

The sacrificial imagery runs parallel to the action of Job. There are two fathers in the prologue of Job and there are at least two sets of sons. The first father is Job who is perfect and upright, who fears God and shuns evil, and he sanctifies his sons by offering up ascension offerings according to their number. Yahweh is also a faithful and perfect Father, and He is likewise concerned with sanctifying His son Job and does so by offering him up by way of the sacrificial swords and fire of disaster. In both cases there are substitutes. Presumably, Job's sons are offered up through the mediation of animals, while Job is offered up through the mediation of his entire household. As an ascension offering is cut apart and arranged on the altar and entirely consumed in the fire, so Job's household is dismembered and consumed in the fire of God. And this is why Job is left as only "dust and ashes" (2:8; 30:19; 42:6); he has been consumed on the altar by the storm of God's presence.

Several details about the ascension offering are important for understanding Job. First, the ascension offering is a foundational sacrifice in the Old Testament sacrificial system. It is the first offering described in the sacrificial manual of Leviticus, and this is because it reveals a foundational clue to all sacrifice. It establishes a central goal of every offering made by fire. When an animal without blemish is sacrificed, the perfect animal is going up to God in smoke. The fire of God consumes the offering and, through the offering, the worshiper is drawn up into the cloud-presence of the Lord. Let's consider two of these details closely.

First, we know that the sacrifice for an ascension offering must be "without blemish" (Lev 1:3). Arguably, the prologue of Job goes out of its way to emphasize and identify the sacrificial victim. Just as sacrificial animals must be *tamim*, that is, perfect, without blemish, Job is described as *tam*, perfect, blameless. And so that this is not missed, it

---

3. It is interesting that these two natural disasters are reminiscent of the life of Elijah who both witnessed the fire of God falling to consume his offering on Mount Carmel and later was taken up in the whirlwind and fire of God.

4. The altar also has four "ends" in 27:4 and again in 38:5. Different words are used to describe the four corners of the ark (Exod 25:12; 37:3) and the four corners of the table of showbread (Exod 25:26; 37:13). Literally, the ark has four "feet," while the table of showbread has four "corner-sides."

is repeated three times, once by the narrator (1:1) and twice by Yahweh (1:8; 2:3). Job himself insists that this is true, and he is criticized by his friends for it (4:6; 9:20–21). And lest we be distracted by the fact that it is all of Job's servants, animals, and children that are actually consumed, they too are described in terms of perfection, adding up to tens: seven sons and three daughters, seven thousand sheep and three thousand camels, and five hundred oxen and five hundred female donkeys (1:2–3). Job is without blemish, and his household is presented in similar fashion.

We have heard this description of perfection before: Abraham is referred to as the servant of Yahweh and called to be blameless (Gen 17:1). Noah and Jacob were also blameless before God (Gen 6:9; 25:27). That did not mean that any of them were exempt from trials and suffering. In fact, each of these men faced significant trials, struggles, and suffering, and it is the sacrificial connotations of being "blameless" that offer some helpful commentary. The description "without blemish" is used nearly thirty times in Leviticus and Numbers and always to describe the kind of animal that is eligible for sacrifice. This is because God is holy and without blemish (Deut 32:4). God is attracted to the blameless; perfection is what catches His eye. God teaches Israel to imitate Him: *Have you considered that ram of mine? Not a blemish; he would make a great sacrifice.* Of course the echo there is intentional. God takes notice of His blameless people; He is attracted to them and points them out. "Have you considered my servant Job, that there is none like him on the earth, a blameless and upright man?" (1:8).

We can take this one step further. As early as the first sin and exile from the garden of Eden, the theology of sacrifice is already set in place. Guarding the entrance to the garden are cherubim with a flaming sword, indicating how entrance back into the garden is to be obtained (Gen 3:24). The only way back into the presence of God is through the sword and fire. The way back into the garden is by being cut up by a sword and consumed in the fire.

The sacrifices of Israel all point to various aspects of this same basic principle. Going back into the garden means dealing with sin, it means having free access to God again, and it means eating and fellowshipping with God in peace. The sacrificial system is a thorough ritual education on this foundational reality. With regard to our study of Job, I want to focus particularly on the second theme which seems to be most prominent in the book, questions related to access to God. Who can stand before Yahweh? Who can enter into counsel with the Mighty One? And the beginning of the answer to this question is found in the theology of the ascension offering: Yahweh draws His blameless sons up into His presence, through the transforming storm of sacrifice. Or to put it another way, Yahweh's presence *is* a transforming storm which is frequently pictured or enacted in the ritual forms of sacrifice.

To summarize: Job opens with several categories of sons. Job has seven sons, and because he is upright and fears Yahweh, he sanctifies them with offerings made by fire to Yahweh. Job is also named a son, the greatest of the "sons of the east." Furthermore, Job is a blameless son. He is perfect, without blemish. He is sacrificial quality. Finally, there are the "sons of God" who stand before Yahweh in His presence, who bear witness to the actions of their Father, who have watched Him from the beginning (38:7), who may speak and be heard in their Father's presence. It is particularly this parallel between Job who is the greatest of the "sons of the east" and the "sons of God" who assemble before Yahweh that sets up one of the great disparities in the opening scenes of Job. Yahweh has discussed and planned events that dramatically affect the life of righteous Job, and Job was not in on the conversation. The sons of God assembled before Yahweh; they witnessed the exchange between the Accuser and Yahweh. But while Job is the greatest of the sons of the east, he is not to be found among the sons of God. Thus, we ask, "Who can stand before Yahweh? Who can enter into counsel with the Mighty One?" Our preliminary answer to this question is that the *sons of God* stand before Yahweh and enter the Mighty One's counsel. But in order to take up these questions we need to consider a little more broadly and carefully the title "son of God."

A SON OVER HIS OWN HOUSE

Adam was the first son of God. He was created in the image and likeness of God and called to continue the work of his Father (Gen 1:26). From this we conclude that there are familial and vocational elements to being a son of God. In Genesis 4:25, after Cain has murdered Abel and has been exiled from the land, Eve gives birth to a son and names him Seth. This event is elaborated in 5:3 where it states that Adam begot Seth "in his likeness and according to his image." Just as Adam was created in the image and likeness of God, so Seth was begotten in the image and likeness of Adam, which means that Seth *and* Adam were sons of God. They are family. This is clear from the family resemblance, but it is also clear from Genesis 5 that this is not primarily a biological sonship. Adam's *creation* differs from the human generation of Seth, and besides that, Adam has other "sons and daughters" (Gen 5:4). The sons of God are those chosen to carry on the seed (cf. Gen 3:15). To be a son of God in this sense is to be designated for a particular purpose in the family of God, a particular vocation.

There is a general sonship according to the "image and likeness of God" that is universal to all humanity, and there is a more specific sonship that entails the responsibility of a calling to carry on the name and mission of God. Adam was God's only son in creation to begin with and held together both of these realities. In fact, all of humanity was called to be sons of God, but because of the entrance of sin, a single line was chosen to carry out the mission until all the sons of God could be restored as mature and reconciled sons.

Nevertheless it is clear that God designated Adam for a high and glorious purpose in the world. God's image-bearing son was to have dominion over the earth, to fill the earth, and to rule it. In short, Adam, as God's son, was to be king. Adam was called to picture his Father by being this king, by carrying on the mission of his Father, by continuing to establish the Father's kingdom and rule. And the garden of Eden was significant for this task. The garden was a small picture of what God intended for the world. The garden was where Yahweh would meet with His son and teach him the wisdom he needed to rule well. By guarding that place and that privilege, Adam would be enabled to carry out the Father's will in the world. This means that the image of God and access to God are central to the calling of sons of God.

But after the Fall, as we have already noted, something significant changed. Some of that calling was lost and granted to angels (Gen 3:24). Because Adam was not a faithful son and did not guard the garden, cherubim were given the task. Angelic creatures take over as sons to watch over the work of Adam's Father. Adam must have guardians until he comes of age; the world is put in subjection to angels until he can fully rejoin his Father's presence and mission.[5] As an exiled son, Adam looks forward to regaining his place among the angels, even above the angels.

Seth, like his father, is another exiled son of God, and Genesis 5 records the genealogy of the sons of God. Even though they are outside the presence of their Father, outside their Father's house, it was at that time that "men began to call on the name of Yahweh" (4:26). While they have been driven out of the presence of their Father, they are still allowed some access. They may call on Yahweh, their Father, and He will hear and answer. He will not completely leave them; He will still lead them out of exile and teach them to be His sons.

After the Fall, the sons of God still have some access to the Father, and therefore they are still called to carry on His mission in the world as He teaches and leads them. But the sons of God intermarry with the daughters of men (Gen 6:1–4), and the flood waters of God's judgment come upon the world. But God has one perfect son, Noah, and He saves him. Noah is His blameless son, and Yahweh brings him and his family through the storm. Abram is another son of God, a descendant of Shem, the son of Noah (Gen 11:10–27). Having the names "exalted father" and "father of many nations" is ironically humiliating enough for an old, childless man. At the same time, we should not miss the greater threat that this is to God. Apart from the promised seed, *God* will have no son. God will have no firstborn to carry on His name, no Adam to carry on His mission in the world.

After Isaac, the theme of the "firstborn" comes to the fore with Esau and Jacob. The firstborn receives a double portion inheritance in order to care for his father's family and take over the household when the father is gone. The double inheritance is for a specific purpose. A younger son is not any less part of the family, nor is the firstborn necessarily a better representative. It is rather the calling to carry on the mission of the father in the world. And the inheritance is part of the means to that end. Throughout Genesis, this calling and vocation is subverted in the narratives of the brothers (and even a set of sisters). The younger sons are favored, the younger brothers are blessed, the younger brother is exalted over the older. These themes ride on the wake of the *first* firstborn son's failure. Adam fails as the firstborn son, and *his* firstborn fails just as he did. The firstborn frequently follow in their first father's steps, both highlighting his role as firstborn son and repeatedly calling into question their Father's plan to undo the evil (Gen 3:15).

Israel as a nation is the next in history to be explicitly called the firstborn son of God (Exod 4:22). When Moses is called to confront Pharaoh, the message is actually quite

---

5. I grant that man was originally created "a little lower than the angels." Angels represent something of glorified humanity from the beginning (e.g., Mark 12:25). Yet the picture in the garden is not one where man is under the rule/subjection of angels. He is under the direct tutelage of God his Father. This seems to change at the Fall.

simple: If Pharaoh will not let Yahweh's firstborn son go free, Yahweh will kill Pharaoh's firstborn son (Exod 4:23). And He does. This "firstborn" theme continues in the narrative, however, and is picked up in the Passover instructions (13:1–2). God eventually explains that in place of all the firstborn of Israel, the Levites have been chosen (Num 8:14–18). The Levites "have no inheritance" because their inheritance is in the house of God (Num 18:21ff.). Yet, because they stand for the firstborn of Israel, who is Yahweh's firstborn son, it is right to consider this as their "double portion" (cf. Deut 21:17).

The firstborn calling of the Levites is in the tabernacle, the house of God their Father. We should not forget all that we have collected so far in our theology of sons of God. The son of God is called to grow up to maturity in his Father's house, and his inheritance is a "double portion" so that he is sufficiently equipped to carry out this vocation of rule and care for his Father's estate. God's mission includes filling and glorifying the world, and the son can perform that task only as he guards his Father's house. Learning how to carry out this mission is dependent upon access to the Father. The son must serve in his Father's house in order to learn his Father's business. Being a son entails progression in maturity. The son must draw near the Father in order to be a faithful son, but he cannot enter into the fullness of being a faithful son until he has been drawn near. Thus, the progression in maturity requires that which it gives. We see this in the actual sacrificial ministry.

In particular, we need to point out that the sacrificial ministry of the tabernacle is filled with references to "sons." It is the "sons of Aaron" who repeatedly offer "sons of the herd" and "sons of the dove" for the "sons of Israel" as offerings made by fire to the Lord (e.g., Lev 1:5, 14, 4:3, 14; 5:7; 9:2–3; 12:8; 14:22). Given the clear narrative drawn from Yahweh's claim of Israel as His firstborn son, His claim of all the firstborn, the redemption of the firstborn for the tribe of Levi, and finally this repeated emphasis at the center of their calling as the firstborn son of God, it simply will not do to chalk this Levitical usage up to Hebraic idiomatic expressions. Rather, it is clear that the priestly tribe has been claimed by God in place of the firstborn sons of Israel, and the firstborn sons of Israel—as the firstborn son of God—were spared in the Passover in place of the entire nation, and this means that the "sons of the herd" and the "sons of the dove" clearly represent the sons of Israel, the son of God. This sacrificial ministry is central to what it means to be the "son of God." The imagery could not be clearer. Sons must die. In order for Israel to be the son of God, Israel must die. Blood must be shed.

When we return to the opening sequence of Job, we find that Job is not among the sons of God, and yet Job *is* a son of God. We know this because Job is an Adam. Job tends a beautiful garden, a world of blessing. Job is perfect and fears God. He has obeyed the commands of God, and he is fruitful and has multiplied. His wealth and possessions are great. He has ten children and around eleven thousand animals. Job is a king and the "greatest of the sons of the East" (1:3), like Adam who was the original prince of the East, ruling from the garden which was planted eastward in Eden (Gen 2:8).[6] But even Adam

---

6. The son of God as king motif is of course most explicit in the Davidic covenant (2 Sam 7:12–16) and is also applied to David himself in Psalm 89:20, 24–27. In the description of Job as the greatest of the "sons of the east," the word "east" may refer to antiquity and therefore wisdom (Habel, *Job*, 87). Note how

was not a *glorified* son of God. He was a perfect son who needed to learn obedience; Adam was a perfect son who needed to be *perfected*. Likewise, Job is a perfect son who needs to be perfected. Job is a blameless son who needs to be drawn up into the presence of his Father, to become a son who stands before his Father, who learns from his Father, and begins to rule with his Father so that he can carry out the mission of his Father's house in the world.

This transition from perfect to perfected, from glory to greater glory is displayed in miniature in the creation of Eve. In the narrative of Genesis 1–2, so many acts of creation are declared "good" that the declaration "not good" is startling. How can there be a "not good" in a world of perfection? But in Adam we have a righteous and blameless son whom Yahweh strikes. Adam is not good alone; he is not good in the status quo. Yahweh intends more glory for Adam, and therefore Yahweh strikes his blameless son and cuts him open. Yahweh performs the first sacrifice Himself, drawing Adam further up and further in to His glory. Job is like Adam, and after the fire of God falls and consumes him, Job tears his clothing and shaves his head and falls to the ground in a ritual enactment of what he says in the following verse (1:20). He is naked, bald, and returning to the ground out of which he was made. The particular emphasis on being naked is another parallel to Adam as is the figurative "returning to the ground." Job says, "Naked I came from my mother's womb, and naked shall I return there" (1:21).

Job is an Adam being "killed," put into a deep sleep in order to be cut so that he might be glorified. It is the Spirit-wind that hovers over the chaos at the beginning of the universe and breathes life into Adam and his new bride Eve, and it is the same Spirit-wind that strikes the house of Job to begin remaking him, transforming him from glory to greater glory. Job is a blameless Adam cut open and torn, but his suffering is a womb of new creation. He is being drawn up into his Father's presence.

A STORM OF WORDS

One of the great mistakes of many commentators is to see a radical break between chapter 2 and chapter 3 of Job. Clearly there are numerous stylistic differences between the narrative bookends and the poetic center of the book, but this does not justify ignoring the remaining continuities, which are many.

One of the continuing themes is the reoccurring *ruach*, the Spirit-wind that we have already considered in some detail. In fact, the way the book of Job is structured, readers are invited not to think of the calamities as limited to chapters 1 and 2. As the dialogue unfolds, the writer would have us understand that the calamities have actually *continued*. The Spirit-wind has struck the four corners of the house that Job's children were feasting in, but the Spirit-wind has not ceased to blow.

Frequently, the words of the rhetorical combatants are referred to as "wind." Eliphaz responds to Job's initial complaint by explaining that God does not punish the righteous;

Solomon is described as having more wisdom than any of the people of the East (1 Kgs 4:30). Thus part of the implication is that all of that wisdom is still not the same thing as being in the presence of God, having access to the Father.

He only destroys the wicked with the "wind" of his anger (4:9). Later in the same speech, Eliphaz recounts how a spirit-wind appeared to him in a dream and spoke to him (4:15). Job replies to Eliphaz by asking why he is reproving him, when his desperate words are but "wind" (6:26). Several times Job refers to his own mortality as "wind" (7:7), and the shortness of life is said to quickly blow away with the "wind" (21:18; 27:21). When Bildad joins the conversation, he asks how long Job will continue to pour forth words of "strong wind" (8:2). Eliphaz renews his accusations by asking why Job, a wise man, continues to answer with "windy knowledge" and fill himself with the "east wind" (15:2). Here we may note that "east wind" is a different word from *ruach*, but this is a similar image and several others are used throughout the book as well. "Spirit-wind" is used to describe the breath of life in man a number of times, and Eliphaz connects Job's words with the ill wind within Job that he believes has turned against God (15:13). Job turns these accusations back on his accusers in chapter 16 where he asks, "When shall the speeches of *wind* have an end?" (16:3). Zophar eventually embraces the wind imagery and explains that it is the "wind" of his understanding that causes him to answer Job (20:3).

While the "wind" plays a poetic role in the dialogues, it is also tied specifically to the argument itself. It is the words that are being exchanged which comprise the "great wind" that continues to blow on Job's house. Job describes all the terrors that have come upon him as a dark storm cloud full of "wind" driving his honor away (30:15), and arguably he is not primarily referring to the original calamities of the prologue. He is referring to the wind that has *continued* to blow in the words and accusations of his three friends. As Job closes his defense and pleas, he acknowledges that it is God who has lifted him up to the "wind" and caused him to ride in the roar of a storm (30:22). Here specifically, the words indicate a roaring, a shouting, an uproar, and this roaring storm is the storm of words that has continued to pour over Job for nearly thirty chapters. In this sense we ought to read the "great wind" of chapter 1 to be blowing throughout the rest of the dialogues. The storm of God's presence only begins in chapter 1.

When Job ends his words, Elihu steps on to the stage, and the wind gusts only increase. He says that he is "full of words" because his belly is full of "wind" (32:18). He insists that he cannot hold it in any longer, and he must find relief (32:20). The word for relief means "wide" or "spacious," but it is formed with the same letters as the word *ruach* and suggests a pun, as though Elihu's belly is about to expel all that wind! He of course claims that the wind that fills him is the "wind of God," and the breath of the Almighty is teaching him (33:4). Elihu goes on expelling that wind, and he goes on for four speeches without an answer from anyone. The words of Elihu blow and blow and blow. And the narrator seems to be subtly (or not so subtly) suggesting this when he introduces two of Elihu's speeches with the words "Elihu answered and said . . ." (34:1; 35:1). While this phrase could be read as referring more generally to the entire conversation, unlike the rest of the speeches and answers between Job and the three friends, Elihu has no immediate discussion partner. He is not really answering anyone except himself. While Elihu is a much debated character in the book of Job, these linguistic cues are at least suggestive that Elihu is not particularly different than the three older friends. The last indication of Elihu's lack of wisdom seems evident in his final comments.

PART ONE: BIBLICAL STUDIES

Elihu finishes his speech by reminding Job that God is great and mighty, and he illustrates God's greatness with the image of a terrific thunder storm (36:26—37:13). God pours out the rain (36:27–28); God spreads out the clouds and fills them with thunder and lightning (36:29–33). He speaks, thunders rumble from His mouth, and lightning streaks across the sky (37:1–15). And God is not limited to rain; He also commands the snow, and He varies the rain both heavy and gentle (37:6). He sends forth the wind both hot and cold (37:9). With His stormy breath He blows on the earth and thick clouds are all around Him (37:10–12). Elihu tells Job to consider the Storm (37:14–18): does he really think he can speak to the Storm (37:19–22)? Elihu tells Job that if he tried to talk with the Storm of God's presence, he would be swallowed up (37:20). God's lightning is too bright, too majestic, too overpowering, and Job would do well to be a little more fearful (37:21–22, 24). Elihu closes by insisting that God is a mighty storm: we cannot speak to Him and we cannot find Him (37:23). He is a righteous storm (37:24), and Elihu insists that Job cannot talk with the Storm.

And in the very next verse, the Storm bursts. But it does not destroy Job; it does not consume him. Rather, the Whirlwind *answers* Job. The Storm *talks* to Job. Elihu is wrong.

Another way to trace the themes of the prologue through the arguments of the middle of the book is by following the *words*. Matthew Lynch likewise notes that the "damage" done to Job only begins in the prologue, and the calamity continues in the form of the verbal onslaught of Job's friends. Lynch points out that "from the beginning, Job is assailed by words, by the breathless reports of his three servants, the biting words of his wife, and by his three companions." Lynch points out the repetition in chapter 1 of the phrase "while he was still speaking, another came and said. . . ."[7]

The trials of Job in some sense always come in the form of words. From the beginning, Job is pummeled with words. Before one speaker has finished, another arrives with more bad news. Just on the surface, it is interesting that there are four speeches in the prologue announcing each calamity, and there are four speakers who declare to Job their opinions regarding his complaint. Quite possibly there is another layer in the simple fact that Elihu gives four speeches as well. He piles on, and his windy words are about the equivalent of all four messengers in the first chapter.

Lynch also points out that Elihu in particular highlights the "out of nowhere" character of these word-attacks.[8] The initial calamities in chapter 1 are clearly out of nowhere; Job was not expecting them. Similarly, after the words of Job are ended in 31:40, it would read quite naturally to run right into Yahweh's response. It is also noteworthy that Yahweh never even acknowledges Elihu. Apart from the manner in which Yahweh answers, which we have already noted, Yahweh's speech picks up immediately where Job left off, and this at the very least highlights Elihu's speeches as seemingly random, out of nowhere, and in this sense very similar to the initial reports from the messenger and

---

7. Matthew Lynch, "Bursting at the Seams: Phonetic Rhetoric in the Speeches of Elihu," *Journal for the Study of Old Testament* 30.3 (2006) 348.

8. Ibid., 349.

servants. Elihu and his friends are more calamity; they continue the storm with their accusations and denunciations.

We can trace the progress of the storm through the *content* of the words as well. Job's argument has a clear trajectory. His initial plea is explicitly that he wants to die. He curses the day of his birth and wonders why he must go on in misery when he longs for death (3:20–21). Job responds to Eliphaz's initial accusations by insisting that he is innocent and once again pleads for death. This time he specifically pleads with God to "crush" him, to "loose his hand and cut" him off (6:8–9). Eliphaz's words only make him want to die more (7:13–14). It may be that Job's initial laments are just honest expressions of his pain and sorrow and loss. But as the three friends begin bringing their accusations and it becomes clear that they are not really there to comfort him, Job's complaint begins taking on more explicit characteristics of an appeal. His central complaint is that he cannot contend with God (9:3). This is first of all because God is not easily accessible (9:11), and furthermore, Job asks, "How can I answer Him and choose my words to reason with Him?" Even if he could get a hearing and was completely right, Job recognizes that he would still have to beg for mercy (9:15). And even if he did call upon God and He answered him, Job says that he would not even believe it was happening (9:16). How can he get a day in court with God (9:19)? His complaint is not merely with his circumstances but with the impossibility of taking God to court. God is not a man that Job can take to court, and there is no one who could act as a mediator between them (9:32–33).

But all of the complaints contain an implicit appeal, a request, a prayer. Job's great longing is to speak with God and receive an answer (12:4; 13:3). He says: "Though He slay me, yet will I trust Him. Even so, I will defend my own ways before Him" (13:15). Job, the son, longs to speak with his Father. He longs to enter the assembly of the sons of God and stand before Yahweh. He wants to speak with his Father about how things are going, about the three friends, about the calamities, about ruling his kingdom in such disarray.

Even Job's despairing plea for death is also related to this desire to stand before Yahweh. In chapter 14 when Job refers to the hope of a tree, he says that a tree that is cut down may die in the ground, but with a little water it will spring up out of the ground again (14:7–9). "So man lies down and does not rise. Till the heavens are no more, they will not awake nor be roused from their sleep" (14:12). But this is not nihilistic despair. Job continues, "Oh, that You would hide me in the grave, that You would conceal me until Your wrath is past, that You would appoint me a set time, and remember me! . . . You shall call, and I will answer you; You shall desire the work of Your hands" (14:13, 15).

Job's plea is to die, but to die in order that he might finally have the opportunity to stand before God, that his righteous blood may cry out for justice (16:18). Job's prayer is for something like what Adam actually endured, passing through sleep-death before being raised to the glory of a wife. Abraham also experienced a deep sleep-death where God passed before him and confirmed the covenant with him (Gen 15:12–21). What Job wants is to plead with God as a man pleads with his friend (16:21). He wants to stand as a son before his Father.

The full force of Job's argument finally bursts forth in one of the most famous passages of Job, when he proclaims, "For I know that my Redeemer lives, and He shall stand at last on the earth. And after my skin is destroyed, this I know, that in my flesh I shall see God, whom I shall see for myself and my eyes shall behold, and not another. . . . There is a judgment" (19:25–29). Job knows that there will be a final judgment, and if he cannot stand before God in the present life, he is utterly convinced that at the resurrection he will see God face to face and there finally be granted the opportunity to ask his questions and receive answers.

Again, he reiterates to his friends that what he wants is to be able to stand before God's judgment seat, to present his case before God (23:4ff.). Ultimately what Job wants is *understanding*. He knows that the search for wisdom is a worthy cause and one to which God has called man (28:1–11). It is the glory of God to conceal a matter, but it is the glory of kings to search it out (Prov 25:2). Job is in the process of searching for wisdom, but he has come to the conclusion that it is not "found in the land of the living" (28:13). "It is hidden from the eyes of all the living" (28:21). Only God has wisdom; only He has searched it out (28:27). This is why Job wants to die; he wants to die so that he can come face to face with God his Father, so that he can ask his questions and receive answers, so that he can finally understand and know wisdom. He wants to go before the Almighty and receive an answer; he wants to approach Him like a prince, like a son of God (31:35–37).

This leads us to remember the story of Jacob. His struggles all involve wrestling, culminating in a struggle with God himself, face to face.[9] This is fundamentally what Job is pleading for. But what Job may not have realized during the course of the dialogues, readers can begin to recognize for themselves. While God remains silent until the end of the story, God is preparing Job for the very thing he is asking for. Job wants an audience with God, he wants to argue his case before the Mighty One, but it is the very act of arguing with his three friends that is preparing him to do that.

Another way to look at the progression of Job is to follow the accusations. The prologue introduces the Accuser in the presence of Yahweh being granted permission to try Job's integrity, but after the Accuser leaves the stage, the accusations do not end. Job says that his counselors have turned against him (19:19), which likely refers in the first instance to his three friends. They are those whom he loved, and they have turned against him. Job refers to the "schemes" of his friends who are seeking to wrong him (21:27). In fact Job says that they have reproached him "ten times" (19:3). The accusations of his friends are a continuation of the trial that began with the Accuser in the prologue; after the Accuser has left the stage, three mini-accusers take his place. Far from being "friends," Eliphaz, Bildad, and Zophar are "little satans." Job is an Adam being tempted by three crafty serpents.

All of these elements—the wind, the words, the accusations, Job's arguing and pleading and searching for wisdom—all of these comprise the great Spirit-storm blowing over Job's life. The sacrificial storm breaks in the first chapter, but that cutting, burning, blowing storm of words has in many ways only intensified in the dialogues. This is Yahweh at

---

9. See James B. Jordan, *Primeval Saints: Studies in the Patriarchs of Genesis* (Moscow, ID: Canon, 2001), 107–16.

work as a faithful Father, sanctifying His son, drawing Job up into His presence, training and equipping him to carry out the rule and mission of his Father in the world.

THE WHIRLWIND OF YAHWEH'S WORDS

This final section seeks to fit Yahweh's answer to Job and the conclusion with the reading we have developed over the course of this paper. The Spirit-wind has blown upon Job, the wind has only increased in the dialogues, and the windstorm of words bursts out in the whirlwind answer of Yahweh (38:1).

Given all that we have noted in our study of Job, how do Yahweh's speeches fit into the overall narrative? Specifically we want to suggest a reading of all of Yahweh's questions which actually fits with the trajectory thus far. In other words, how is Yahweh's answer actually an *answer*?

Many commentators conclude that the primary aim of Yahweh's speeches is to establish His sovereignty before Job. Yahweh does all these things with wisdom and power and goodness; therefore, Job needs to calm down and trust God. The answer of Yahweh is understood on this reading as essentially rejecting Job's pleas. As Delitzsch explains, Yahweh "does not exactly do what Job wished. . . . He surprises him with questions which are intended to bring him indirectly to the consciousness of the wrong and absurdity of his challenge. . . ."[10] Yahweh's answer is an extended survey of His rule over the natural world which is intended to produce humility in Job: "Job knows even before God speaks, and yet he must now hear it, because he does not know it rightly; for the nature with which he is acquainted as the herald of the creative and governing power of God, is also the preacher of humility; and exalted as God the Creator and Ruler of the natural world is above Job's censure, so is He also as the Author of his affliction."[11]

Since Job "cannot answer a single one of those questions taken from the natural kingdom, but, on the contrary, must everywhere admire and adore the power and wisdom of God—he must appear as an insignificant fool, if he applies them to his limited judgment concerning the Author of his affliction."[12]

But there are a number of difficulties with this reading. First, it misunderstands what God is up to by not giving the prologue sufficient weight. Yahweh is a faithful Father who has used the evil intentions of the Accuser as an opportunity to "sanctify" his son Job through suffering. Yahweh's response cannot be read as though God has been wholly absent and is only now coming down to see what is going on. Rather, Yahweh answers as the faithful Father that He is, rightly challenging his son Job, but He is not merely putting Job "back in his place." Yahweh does not want Job to stay where he is. As we have seen repeatedly, the entire book up to this point has been thrusting Job forward. Job has been struck and he has suffered, but he is being made perfect through suffering. He is going from perfect to perfected. He is being drawn up into the Spirit-wind presence of his Father. The whirlwind answer is first of all an *answer*. It is Job speaking with the Lord of

---

10. F. Delitzsch, *Job*, 2 vols., trans. Francis Bolton (Peabody: Hendrickson, 1989), 2:312.
11. Ibid., 2:352.
12. Ibid., 2:353.

PART ONE: BIBLICAL STUDIES

the universe. Job has moved from being a great son in the east who was not among the "sons of God" to becoming a son who stands before his Maker and Father.

There are also broader biblical theological difficulties with this standard line of interpretation offered by Delitzsch. We can get at these from a couple of angles: While it is of course absolutely and essentially true that God's power and wisdom and goodness is on display and is rightly admired and praised, it is *not* the case that Job "cannot answer a single one of those questions." Plainly, certain of them are beyond Job's reach, but not all of them are. Job could hunt prey for lions; he could learn about the birthing habits of the mountain goats and the deer. The wild ox may be a very wild and tenacious sort of beast, but Job could probably learn a great deal about its habits and perhaps he could bring it under his rule. At one point, Yahweh asks if Job has noticed the wings and pinions of an ostrich, and whether they are like the "kindly stork's." Job may or may not know the answer at that moment, but surely he could find out. In fact, in several places Yahweh's speeches break into straightforward descriptions, lessons about creation. Surely this reveals God's great wisdom, and perhaps when it comes to the parenting habits of the ostrich Job would not have been very well studied. But when it comes to the warhorse, it would seem that Job, as a king, would be fairly familiar with many of these details. We might also point out that some of the activities Yahweh asks Job about have been done by other human beings. Eagles and hawks can be tamed by humans (39:26–27), we have begun to search the depths of the seas (38:16), and at least one man has commanded the clouds to pour water and they have obeyed (1 Kgs 17:1; cf. Josh 10:12–14). The point of Yahweh's speeches is not to emphasize the infinite divide between Creator and creature. Though this divide most certainly and absolutely exists, Job already knows this and said so explicitly much earlier in the text (9:2–9). Or if this element is present, it is not front and center.

What these observations point out, however, is that while Job and the rest of humanity with him stand back in awe at the order and beauty and complexity of creation and God's rule over it and care for it, God did not create the world merely to be *looked* at. Nor does He sustain all of nature only in order for man to be adequately humble. God created man to rule creation with Him. Even if some of the examples referred to above are debatable, at the very least we know that God created Adam to be His son, to study creation, to learn from His Father, and to rule with Him. Adam was called to rule the fish of the sea, the birds of the air, the beasts of the earth, and all of creation in wisdom. He was called to learn this wisdom from his Father so that he could carry on the mission of his Father's house in the world. In other words, according to Genesis, Job may not be able to do all those things *yet*, but he had better start learning.

But exegesis that sees only a sovereign God showing off His power and glory and leaving a humbled Job must conclude, as Michael Dick does. He says that while some biblical literature views the human being (or king) as a "viceroy of the deity," even a "co-creator of the world," and an "image of the deity himself," having "dominion over the animals of creation" to serve the "image of the divinity and to order the earth," "the author of the two YHWH speeches in the book of Job does not share this expanded view.... [U]nlike Genesis 1, here YHWH does not invite the human to participate in that domination. . . . [I]n the book of Job, humans can only marvel!"[13] Michael Dick concludes that Yahweh's speeches in Job are at odds with His words in the creation narratives in Genesis.

Given the entire book, we ought to think of God as a Father in the whirlwind, not a power-flaunting monarch. Yahweh speaks eleven poems comprising nine scenes of creation and eleven different animals (38:4—39:30). He recounts creation (38:4–11), and his first series of questions conclude with reference to the "sons of God" (38:6-7), implying that *they* know and that Job is beginning the process of learning that same wisdom. The following poems dwell on commanding, studying, dividing, and binding various aspects of creation. These scenes and the wild animals that follow picture the world in need of care, taming, and cultivation. They picture the world well cared for by the Father, and Job is invited to learn this wisdom from his Father.

Of course, Job does go speechless before Yahweh (40:4–5) just as he said he would (9:14–16). One of the hints that Yahweh means for Job to be blessed by His speeches is that He commands Job to gird up his loins, to prepare for battle. This phrase is repeated at the beginning of each speech (38:3; 40:7). Yahweh is training His son Job for battle, training His son to rule the world with Him. Likewise, what is commonly understood as a command, "I will question you, and you shall answer me" (38:3) is probably better understood as a promise. Job will learn to answer Yahweh as he stands before the whirlwind presence of his Father.

In important ways Job has already been training for this task. The entire book of Job has been a storm of words into which Job has been challenged to speak and answer. As Job answered his accusers, so Job was learning the wisdom needed to speak in the assembly of the sons of God, where accusers are wont to occasionally appear (e.g., 2:6).

But the key to the speeches of Yahweh comes in the descriptions of Behemoth and Leviathan. Specifically, Yahweh says that since Leviathan is so fierce, "Who will stand before Me?" (41:10). If you cannot stand before Leviathan, how will you stand before Me? Yahweh asks. But we know that the sons of God do stand before Yahweh. It may take a great deal of wisdom to stand before Leviathan, but he is only the king over all the "sons of pride" (41:34). Part of God's greatness and glory is the creation of man: Adam was created as a son to rule creation with his Father (Gen 1:26-28; 2:8-14, 19-20; Ps 8). Job is called to do the same.

The final proof that Yahweh really is pleased with Job's progress is the fact that Yahweh declares in the conclusion that Job is the only one who has spoken what is right concerning Him (42:7–8), and specifically, Job is granted the responsibility of praying for the three friends. Job will speak, and God promises to answer. Job no longer pleads for an audience with the King. Job stands before the King with the other sons of God assembled.[14]

---

13. Michael Dick, "The Neo-Assyrian Royal Lion Hunt and Yahweh's Answer to Job," *Journal of Biblical Literature* 125 (2006) 262–63.

14. James Jordan has pointed out that in the Bible maturity can be traced through the offices of priest, king, and prophet. Job's maturation/glorification can be seen in these categories as well. Job offers sacrifices for his sons at the beginning (priest). He struggles with wisdom throughout the dialogues as a king. And he is finally granted the prophet's mantle in the conclusion where he now sits in the counsels of God and may speak freely, offering his opinion (prayer) to the Lord of the universe.

PART ONE: BIBLICAL STUDIES

Finally, we learn that Yahweh "returns the captivity" of Job in his prayers for his friends (42:10). This means that insofar as Job was an exiled son, an Adam outside the presence of his Father, he has now been brought back into his Father's house. He has passed through the flaming sword and has been reinstated as a son, and so Yahweh re-endows him with his inheritance, giving him double what he had previously (cf. Zech 9:11–12). His eleven thousand livestock—sheep, camels, oxen, and donkeys—are doubled, and Yahweh blesses Job with twenty-two thousand livestock. This restoration from exile is a resurrection scene, and this is confirmed by the doubling of Job's children. Coming in the same numbers (seven sons and three daughters), it is difficult to miss the suggestion of resurrection (42:13). But this doubling is of course the double portion that Job receives as a firstborn son of God. This double portion is the resources he will need to carry on the mission of his Father's house in the world.

CONCLUSION

We have seen that the book of Job is concerned with a theology of sons. Principally Job is the son in the spotlight, the son who is being sanctified and drawn up into the Storm-presence of Yahweh, his Father. This process of being drawn up into the Storm is itself a storm, and in the case of blameless Job, much of the storm comes in the form of words, accusations, and denunciations.

From this survey, there are numerous connections we can make to the New Covenant and to Christ in particular. Jesus comes to be the Son of God, the perfect, blameless Son of God. He comes as the new Adam, a new Job, and He fulfills and completes what all of his predecessors only vaguely pictured. Like Job, Jesus was "made perfect through suffering," and "though He was a Son, yet He learned obedience by the things which He suffered" (Heb 2:10; 5:8). As a perfect and blameless Son, the Father was very pleased with Him. And as is the custom of the Father, He drew His perfect, blameless Son up into the heavenly presence. The Son went from the glory which He shared with the Father before the world existed to an even greater glory at the Father's right hand as the exalted King of the universe (John 17:5; 1 Pet 3:22). The way was through great suffering, but like Job, He was a faithful Son over His own house, whose house we are if we hold fast the confidence and the rejoicing of the hope firm to the end (Heb 3:6).

One of the callings of faithful sons is to sanctify more sons. Jesus came as the faithful Son to bring many sons with Him to glory (Heb 2:10). Likewise, when Yahweh blesses Job at the end of the story, even Job's daughters become sons in so far as they receive an inheritance (42:15). But this is what the New Covenant emphasizes: there is neither male nor female in Christ Jesus, and this is because all have been made heirs and joint heirs with Christ and have been given the Spirit of the Son. This Spirit is the guarantee of our inheritance, the inheritance of the Firstborn Son (Eph 1:13–14; Col 1:12–18; Heb 1:2–4). Therefore we must remember the exhortation that speaks to us as sons, "My son, do not despise the chastening of the Lord. . . . For whom the Lord loves He chastens, and scourges every son whom He receives" (Heb 12:5–6). If we are chastened as sons, then we know that the Spirit-wind is blowing over us, drawing us up into the presence of God, and we are being taught to stand before the Father and rule the world in His wisdom (Rom 8:14–17; Heb 4:14–16).

∽

Dear Toby,

Thank you for this excellent essay. I've never done intensive work with Job, and this was very eye-opening. Since I'm supposed to make comments, here are just a couple.

In footnote 5 you state that Adam was under the direct tutelage of God his Father. I question that. It appears to me that it may partly be true: certainly Yahweh gave the initial commands to Adam, and perhaps further instruction would have come from Him on the Sabbath had Adam not sinned. It is the serpent, however, that is brought in from the field, as the wisest of the field creatures, to tutor Adam and Eve in field-wisdom. They are babies in the kinder-Garden, and must learn wisdom to go out into the field area, where new kinds of food, such as grains, must be worked with to be eaten. Behind this serpent-as-teacher is the principle of angelic tutelage during the childhood of humanity. Lucifer's fall and his attempt to corrupt humanity meant that the Second Person of God came in his stead as the Angel/Messenger of Yahweh. Anyway, I believe that angels were the Father's assistants in tutoring unfallen humanity, and in that sense we were under the angels until the resurrection of Jesus.

I was struck by the "wind" theme in Job, which I had not really noticed. I want to compare it with the "mist" theme in Ecclesiastes. I understand the four wisdom books as follows: Proverbs shows us the strength of wisdom; Canticles shows us the love of wisdom, as political eros displaying the love of the wise king for his people; Ecclesiastes shows us the limitations of wisdom, that what we do is good but misty and temporary; and Job shows us the complete failure of wisdom in ultimate situations—Job's Friends say wise things, but they are irrelevant. The "wind" sweeps away all "mist," and before the Wind one can operate only by faith alone.

Which brings me to Elihu, "My Mighty One is Yah." Elihu is the big question mark in Job, and you take him as another windy attack. I still take him as a windy anticipation of Eloah's (God's) Wind. From his name I'm inclined to see Elihu as an Israelite priest/pastor in King Job's court. He waits until the three political cornerstones have finished and then bursts with the wind of God, just as Eloah Himself will do. As you say, Elihu says that one has to trust God and that one cannot talk with the Storm. You say that Elihu was wrong, but it appears to me he is correct. Yahweh talks to Job, and Job says he repents and has nothing to say to Yahweh. Elihu does not claim that God never speaks to man (cf. Job 33:14), only that before God man is not in a position to demand anything—and Job twice agrees (40:3–5; 42:1–6).

Like Elihu, Yahweh has four speeches, after all. It appears to me that Yahweh starts off in His first speech with exactly what Elihu has just said: that God's greatest works are beyond the ken of man. Elihu's admonition to "stand and consider the wonders of God" (Job 37:14) seems to be just what God is saying throughout, especially with the descriptions of animals. Hence, Yahweh has no need to acknowledge Elihu because Elihu has anticipated what He Himself will say.

Elihu is, however, a debatable character, and I won't be terribly surprised to find out in heaven that you are right and I was wrong.

You are certainly right to criticize Delitzsch for saying Job is called upon to confess ignorance and submit to God's sovereignty. No, what Yahweh says to Job is "I made all these things and I love all these things. And I love you, Job. Trust Me." It's all about God's love.

I cannot forbear noting that Job begins with 11,000 livestock and ends with 22,000. Twenty-two is, of course, the number of letters in the Hebrew alphabet, and this number occurs many times in the Former Scriptures as a number of completeness and totality. Job now has a full alphabet of livestock, from Aleph to Tav, from Urim to Thummim, from Alpha to Omega.

Also, after death and resurrection comes the glorification of the Bride. Women are glorified after the death and resurrection of Israel in the wilderness, being included in the new census of Numbers 26, being allowed to inherit (the daughters of Zelophehad), and being elevated in the new version of the Tenth Word in Deuteronomy 5. Similarly, here at the end, Job's daughters are named, said to be beautiful, and given inheritance.

Jim

PART TWO

Liturgical Theology

7

On Earth as It Is in Heaven

The Pastoral Typology of James B. Jordan

BILL DEJONG

IN STATING HIS PURPOSE for writing *Through New Eyes: Developing a Biblical View of the World*, James B. Jordan expresses succinctly what is arguably his vocational *raison d'etre*: "to get into the Bible and become as familiar as possible with the Bible's own worldview, language, and thought forms" in order to "see the world through new eyes—through Bible eyes."[1] Unhappy that the Bible's message is so often communicated in the analytical language of philosophy and science, Jordan has devoted much of his career to understanding, and then presenting, the message of the Bible in its own language, "the language of visual imagery (symbolism) and repeated patterns (typology)."[2]

Typological interpretation, therefore, lies at the heart of Jordan's biblical hermeneutic. Though often mistaken for utilizing the same methodology, typological interpretation must be carefully distinguished from allegorical interpretation. Whereas the objective of allegorical interpretation is to uncover timeless truths in Scripture (usually of a moral or philosophical nature) without concern for historical factuality, typological interpretation locates the meaning of the text in the historical character and progress of revelation.[3] The differences between allegorical and typological interpretation are reproduced in the differences between "exemplary" (*exemplarisch*) and "redemptive-historical" (*heilshisto-*

---

1. James B. Jordan, *Through New Eyes: Developing a Biblical View of the World* (Brentwood, TN: Wolgemuth & Hyatt, 1988; reprint, Eugene, OR: Wipf & Stock, 1999), 4.

2. Ibid., 3.

3. Helpful discussions of this distinction can be found in Patrick Fairbairn, *The Typology of Scripture* (New York: Funk & Wagnalls, 1900; reprint, Grand Rapids: Baker, 1975) 1–9; Jean Daniélou, *From Shadows to Reality: Studies in the Biblical Typology of the Fathers*, trans. Don Wulstan Hibberd (Westminster, MD: Newman, 1960), 57–65;131–49; Leonard Goppelt, *Typos: The Typological Interpretation of the Old Testament in the New,* trans. Donald H. Madvig (Grand Rapids: Eerdmans, 1982), 50–51; and Cornelis Trimp, *Preaching and the History of Salvation*, trans. Nelson D. Kloosterman (Scarsdale, NY: Westminster Discount Book Service, 1996), 28–34.

risch) approaches to preaching historical texts.[4] Whereas "exemplary" preaching abstracts persons and events from their historical contexts and presents them as timeless examples to be emulated or avoided, "redemptive-historical" preaching locates the significance of biblical persons and events in their historical contexts and in their relation to the progress of redemption, especially the coming of Christ.

Though valued for the insights of their panoramic perspective, typological interpretation and redemptive-historical preaching are often criticized for their apparent irrelevance. Hendrik Krabbendam captures the sentiment: "Indeed, preaching in the redemptive-historical tradition is often comparable to a ride in a Boeing 747 high above the landscape, with its hot deserts, its snowpeaked mountains, its wide rivers, its dense forests, its open prairies, its craggy hills and its deep lakes. The view is panoramic, majestic, impressive, breathtaking, and always comfortable. But there is one problem. The Christian is not "above" things. He is in the middle of things. He is trekking through the landscape."[5]

Many who employ typological interpretation and preach in a redemptive-historical manner are content to connect the dots between the types of the old covenant and their fulfillment in the new covenant without much reflection on their ongoing relevance for Christian praxis today. For Jordan, however, identifying the relevance is a necessary interpretative step, which is why I have dubbed Jordan's approach "pastoral typology."[6]

My intent in this essay is to provide an introduction to the meaning of the word *typos* in Scripture, summarize Jordan's view of typology, illustrate it in terms of his fascinating treatment of the overarching temple motif in the Bible, and conclude by showing the value of Jordan's typology for the preacher and the church.

THE MEANING OF *TYPOS*

Greek lexicographers generally agree that *typos* derives from the Greek verb *typō*, "to strike," and that very early on it communicated the idea of "form," "mold," "impression," or "stamp" (i.e., the result of a blow).[7] The word eventually could refer to (a) the matrix

---

4. For a discussion of these terms as they surfaced in a mid-twentieth century Dutch controversy, see Sidney Greidanus, *Sola Scriptura: Problems and Principles in Preaching Historical Texts* (Toronto: Wedge, 1970).

5. "Hermeneutics and Preaching," in *The Preacher and Preaching*, ed. Samuel T. Logan, Jr. (Phillipsburg, NJ: Presbyterian & Reformed, 1986), 235.

6. Jordan insists that his four-fold method for interpreting the laws of Moses applies equally to typological interpretation: "To expound the law adequately, we have to ask what this law meant to the people of that time, in terms of the horizon of the Mosaic covenant as a package affair. Then we have to ask how this law was fulfilled by Christ. Then we have to ask how the Church, in union with Christ, manifests the fulfillment of this law. And fourthly and finally, we ask what possible *relevance* this law may have for believers in the new covenant situation" (emphasis mine). He then adds, "I believe this same four-fold method is very important in dealing with symbolism and typology, as in the Tabernacle and sacrificial system" ("Apologia on Reading the Bible," *Contra Mundum* 3 [Spring 1992], 29).

7. See Richard M. Davidson, *Typology in Scripture: A Study of Hermeneutical ΤΥΠΟΣ Structures* (Berrian Springs, MI: Andrews University Press, 1981), 116–19. Cf., Leonard Goppelt, "τυπος," in *Theological Dictionary of the New Testament*, ed. G. Kittel and G. Friedrich, trans. G. W. Bromiley, 10 vols. (Grand Rapids: Eerdmans, 1972), 8:246–47.

that leaves an impression, (b) the impression left by the matrix, or (c) the matrix that is at the same time the impression.[8]

In Acts 7:43–44 we find the word used first in the sense of "impression" and then in the sense of "matrix." Stephen says, "'You took up the tent of Moloch and the star of your god Rephan, the images (*typous*) that you made to worship; and I will send you into exile beyond Babylon.' Our fathers had the tent of witness in the wilderness, just as he who spoke to Moses directed him to make it, according to the pattern (*typon*) that he had seen." In the first instance, in verse 43, *typous* denotes the graven images formed as representations of pagan gods and has the sense of the impression left by the matrix. In the second instance, in verse 44, *typon* refers to the model or pattern according to which Moses had to construct the tabernacle and has the sense of the matrix that leaves the impression.

It is especially instructive to consider New Testament passages that involve the interpretation of the Old Testament and employ the term *typos*.[9] Most of these passages involve linear or horizontal typological structures, relating the old and new covenants: 1 Corinthians 10:1–13, for instance, where Israelite baptism in the Red Sea and partaking of the spiritual food and drink correspond to Christian baptism and the Lord's Supper; Romans 5:12–21, where Adam corresponds to Christ; and 1 Peter 3:18–21, where flood-salvation corresponds to baptism-salvation. Other hermeneutical *typos* passages, however, involve vertical typological structures, relating heaven and earth: Hebrews 8:5 and Hebrews 9:24, where the earthly tabernacle corresponds to the heavenly sanctuary (cf. Exod 25:40 LXX). In passages involving horizontal typological structures, *typos* denotes an Old Testament shadow that finds a New Testament fulfillment; conversely, in passages involving vertical typological structures *typos* denotes a New Testament reality (i.e., the heavenly sanctuary) that looks back to an Old Testament shadow. The functional movement of typology from old covenant type to new covenant fulfillment is present, however, in all of these *typos* passages.[10]

TYPOLOGY THROUGH JORDAN'S EYES

In *Through New Eyes*, Jordan indicates that the Greek word *typos* denotes an image pressed onto something else, like a seal impressed on wax.[11] In terms of the specifically biblical worldview, Jordan contends, the type refers to heavenly patterns that God wants to imprint on earth. He appeals to Acts 7:44 (quoted above) where Stephen tells his hostile Jewish compatriots that God directed Moses to construct the tabernacle according to the pattern (*typon*) of the heavenly blueprint God had shown him (cf. Heb 8:5).[12] This commission to Moses is representative for Jordan of humanity's calling to take the patterns of heaven and push them down to the earth, to "heavenize" the earth, as expressed

---

8. Davidson, *Typology*, 185.
9. Davidson discusses these instances in ibid., 191–397.
10. Ibid., 406.
11. Jordan, *Through New Eyes*, 49.
12. Ibid., 29.

in the third petition of the Lord's prayer, "Your will be done on earth, as it is in heaven."[13] History, therefore, is the progressive impression of a heavenly blueprint on earth and of the heavenly Man, Jesus Christ, on His people through the processes of sanctification and glorification.[14]

It is clear, therefore, that Jordan understands typology primarily in terms of vertical (heaven/earth) structures. This in itself is quite remarkable since a cursory glance at definitions in homiletic literature indicates that the focus is almost exclusively on the horizontal structures.[15] Jordan's conception of typology as primarily vertical is an important dimension to his worldview, the fundamental premise of which is that the world in its diversity is a revelation of God in his infinity (Ps 19:1-2; Job 12:7-9).[16] Jordan's typology does not neglect the horizontal dimension, however, since earthly imprints of heavenly patterns often appear in a linear succession of increasing glory, such that the Solomonic temple, for example, is more glorious than the Mosaic tabernacle. Typological interpretation, in Jordan's view, involves studying these imprints, understanding how they are transformed into more glorious equivalents, and determining what meaning these different stages have in God's economy. Typological interpretation therefore shows us, Jordan contends, that history is both (a) *teleological*, designed for humanity to mature into the full likeness of God as He transforms us by His Spirit, and (b) *rhythmic*, involving patterns that repeat, with variations, as time moves to the realization of God's plan.[17]

THREE HEAVENS

How heaven can function as a blueprint for earth requires an investigation of Genesis 1. The "heaven" of Genesis 1:1 is, for Jordan, the "highest" or "third" heaven, the special throne-house of God (Isa 66:1; cf. Ps 11:4), which exists in another dimension from earth and must be distinguished from the "firmament" that God created on the second day and also called "heaven" (Gen 1:8).[18] The blue sky of the firmament-heaven (Gen 1:8), stretched out above like a "tent curtain" (Isa 40:22), is, in Jordan's conception, a symbolic boundary between the waters above and the waters below, an image of the highest heaven (which has the same name) and of the heavenly sea before the Throne

---

13. James B. Jordan, *The Sociology of the Church: Essays in Reconstruction* (Tyler, TX: Geneva Ministries, 1986; reprint, Eugene, OR: Wipf & Stock, 1999), 32, 86.

14. Jordan, *Through New Eyes*, 51.

15. See, for example, Trimp, *Preaching*, 66; Bryan Chapell, *Christ-Centered Preaching*, 2nd ed. (Grand Rapids: Baker, 2005), 281-88; and Sidney Greidanus, *Preaching Christ from the Old Testament: A Contemporary Hermeneutical Method* (Grand Rapids: Eerdmans, 1999), 212-20, 254. Even Leonhard Goppelt (*TDNT*, 8:258-59) insists that vertical typology in Hebrews is "merely an aid to the presentation and characterization of the horizontal" and reflective of the "mythical cosmic analogy thinking of antiquity."

16. Jordan, *Through New Eyes*, 21.

17. Ibid., 169.

18. The three "heavens" are discussed in Jordan, *Through New Eyes*, 41-48. Jordan acknowledges indebtedness to Meredith Kline for some of these ideas. See Kline, *Images of the Spirit* (Grand Rapids: Baker, 1980; reprint, Eugene, OR: Wipf & Stock, 1998), 15-26 and his lecture syllabus published as *Kingdom Prologue: Genesis Foundations for a Covenantal Worldview* (reprint, Eugene, OR: Wipf & Stock, 2006), 22-33.

(Rev 4:6; cf. Exod 24:10; Ps 19:1; Dan 12:3).[19] The blue sky—which represents the heavenly ocean, the waters above—looks like the waters below, the earthly seas and oceans. The phenomena found in the firmament-heaven (e.g., stars and birds) symbolize things found in the highest heaven (e.g., angels; cf. Job 38:7; Rev 12:4; 18:2). A similar vertical typology relates clouds to God's glory-cloud, rainbows to the rainbow around His throne, and the sun to Christ (Rev 1:16b).[20]

The hovering Spirit of Genesis 1:2 corresponds, in Jordan's understanding, to the hovering cloud-chariot of God elsewhere in the Bible (e.g., Deut 32:10–11; cf. Ezek 1) and represents God's portable heaven.[21] With the creation of light, the Spirit manifested God's presence as a cloud of glory, also called Shekinah Glory. This glory was reproduced in the firmament-heavens or the sky that God created on the second day. When people saw the glory-cloud, they were seeing heaven, or at least a type of heaven in the world.[22] In order to do God's will on earth as it is done in heaven, therefore, we must "see" heaven. Though the Bible occasionally affords us glimpses of heaven, as in Ezekiel's visions of the divine Glory (e.g., Ezek 1:1ff.; 3:12ff.; 10:1ff.), we see models of God's heavenly house especially in the successive sanctuaries for Israelite worship.[23] These sanctuaries, Jordan contends, do not function merely as an illustration of a Scriptural type, but as the fundamental, overarching, unifying type in Scripture.

In what follows, we will trace the contours and uncover the insights of Jordan's tabernacle-temple typology, using as a foil G. K. Beale's recent study of the temple.[24] Though their understanding of the temple's evolution and architecture is remarkably similar, Beale and Jordan reach different conclusions about the relevance of the temple, which illustrate the uniquely pastoral dimension to Jordan's typology.

THE GARDEN-SANCTUARY IN EDEN

The garden in Eden, according to Jordan, was the sanctuary where Adam would meet with God.[25] Through this garden flowed a river that then divided into four rivers to bring humanity to the four corners of the world (cf. Ezek 7:2; Rev 20:8).[26] Since rivers flow downhill, Eden was located on a mountain, nearest to heaven, a place where people can meet God.[27] "In the Bible, God frequently meets with men on mountaintops. We can think of Mount Moriah, where Abraham offered Isaac; Mount Sinai, where God met with Moses and the elders of Israel; Mount Zion, where God built His City; Mount

19. Jordan, *Through New Eyes*, 46.
20. Ibid., 46.
21. Ibid., 43–44, 48.
22. Ibid., 43.
23. Ibid., 42.
24. *The Temple and the Church's Mission: A Biblical Theology of the Dwelling Place of God* (Downers Grove, IL: InterVarsity, 2004).
25. Jordan, *Sociology*, 87, 153; similarly, Beale: "The Garden of Eden was the first archetypal temple in which the first man worshipped God" (*Temple*, 66). Where subsequent parallels with Beale are observed I will cite only the source and not Beale's exact formulation.
26. Jordan, *Through New Eyes*, 147–48.
27. Ibid., 155–59; similarly, Beale, *Temple*, 147.

PART TWO: LITURGICAL THEOLOGY

Carmel, where God defeated the prophets of Baal; the Mount on which Jesus preached His great Sermon; and Calvary Hill, where Jesus was elevated as dying King."[28]

The garden is the sanctuary and the outlying areas or the lands downstream, Havilah, Cush and so forth, would be the location of man's labors and raw materials, not least among them precious stones (Gen 2:10–12).[29] Adam's descendants, Jordan argues, were to move to these downstream lands and trade with those still in Eden, sending back precious stones to Eden to adorn the sanctuary.[30] Eventually Adam's sons who moved downstream would set up their own garden-sanctuaries, though the Edenic sanctuary would remain central.[31]

In the center of the Edenic sanctuary were sacramental trees, often associated in the Bible with appearances of God.[32] Abraham often met God near trees (Gen 12:6; 13:18; 14:13; 18:1), and Moses, of course, had a dramatic encounter with God at the burning bush (Exod 3:1–5). Much like mountains, trees are biblical images of ladders to heaven (Dan 4:11–12).[33] In this garden-sanctuary Adam was the priest whose task it was to recognize the boundaries of the garden (cf. Ezek 40) and protect it against invasion (i.e., to tend and to guard the garden).[34] Adam however admitted the enemy serpent and passively stood by Eve, allowing her to fall when the devil tempted her (Gen 3:6). Because Satan was given access to the Garden, as a seducer and an enemy, Adam and Eve were disqualified from guarding it and new cherubic guardians were set up in their place (Gen 3:24).[35]

THE GARDEN-OASIS SANCTUARIES OF THE PATRIARCHS

Worship during the patriarchal era often occurred at garden-oasis sanctuaries.[36] The river that flowed through the Edenic garden had, in Jordan's view, been cut off after the fall and so the patriarchs, to locate water, dug wells deep into the ground.[37] Moreover, they built altars—mini-mountains—in grove settings (tree and altar, Gen 12:7; 13:8; 14:13; 18:4, 8; 21:33; 23:17; 35:4–8; tree, well and worship, Gen 21:30–34; altar and well, Gen 26:23–25, 32–33).[38]

Patriarchal altars were probably just pillars constructed of stone and earth, but what they symbolized is set out in an important vision in Ezekiel 43 where Ezekiel describes an altar in the form of a stepped pyramid with its top section called "the mountain of

---

28. James B. Jordan, *Primeval Saints: Studies in the Patriarchs of Genesis* (Moscow, ID: Canon, 2001), 16. See also Jordan, *Through New Eyes*, 156–57 and Beale, *Temple*, 73, 145.

29. Much of the information in this section is gleaned from Jordan, *Through New Eyes*, 143–63. See also Jordan, *Sociology*, 88.

30. Jordan, *Through New Eyes*, 73; similarly, Beale, *Temple*, 73.

31. Jordan, *Sociology*, 86–89; similarly, Beale, *Temple*, 149.

32. See Jordan, *Through New Eyes*, 81–93; similarly, Beale, *Temple*, 103.

33. Jordan, *Through New Eyes*, 87ff.

34. Ibid., 136; similarly, Beale, *Temple*, 68.

35. Jordan, *Sociology*, 91; similarly, Beale, *Temple*, 70.

36. Jordan, *Through New Eyes*, 189–90; similarly, Beale, *Temple*, 97.

37. Jordan, *Through New Eyes*, 249.

38. Ibid., 189–90; similarly, Beale, *Temple*, 102.

God."[39] Pillars themselves became important in the patriarchal era as symbols of God's holy mountain, the true ladder to heaven.[40] Twice Jacob set up a pillar of stone in the places he named Bethel, meaning "house of God" (Gen 28:18–19; 35:13–15). The patriarchs met with God, not in buildings, but in open-air, garden-oasis sanctuaries. Though the imagery is Edenic, the garden-oasis sanctuaries of the patriarchs, unlike the Garden in Eden which was planted by God, were established by men.[41]

THE MOSAIC TABERNACLE

In the Mosaic era, worship occurred at the tabernacle, a centralized sanctuary which, unlike the patriarchal garden-oasis sanctuaries, was constructed at God's express command to His specific design and located precisely by the movement of His glory-cloud.[42] The tabernacle recalled the garden-oasis sanctuaries in that the altars, trees, and wells of the patriarchs were woven into its architecture and structure.[43] The inner chamber of the tabernacle, called the Most Holy Place, was God's throne room, which symbolized the highest heaven, the ultimate throne of God.[44] There God sat enthroned on the outstretched wings of two golden guardian cherubim with His feet resting on the mercy seat atop the ark of the covenant (Exod 25:10–22; 37:1–9), a chest constructed of wood, recalling the Edenic grove.[45]

A beautiful inner veil embroidered with cherubim (Exod 26:31–33), barring the way into God's presence (cf. Gen 3:24), separated the Most Holy Place from the immediately adjacent, larger, and less lavish room called the Holy Place, which represented the firmament-heaven.[46] Both the highest heaven and the firmament-heaven are called tents or tabernacles of God in the Bible (Job 36:29; Pss 18:11; 19:4; 104:2; Isa 40:22). The Holy Place contained the golden lampstand (Exod 25:31–40; 37:17–24) recalling the tree of life.[47] Moreover, there was a dinner table with "the bread of the Presence" on it (Lev 24:5–9; Exod 25:23–30) and an altar of incense (Exod 30:1–5; 37:25–29) which produced glorified, aromatic air symbolizing God's glory-cloud, as it appeared in the firmament-heavens (Exod 19:18).[48]

Beyond the blue curtain of the Most Holy Place (Exod 26:36–37), representing the blue sky of the firmament-heaven, one would find the courtyard, a small replica of earth.[49]

---

39. Jordan, *Through New Eyes*, 190; similarly, Beale, *Temple*, 100.

40. Jordan, *Through New Eyes*, 191; similarly, Beale, *Temple*, 102; cf. 98–107.

41. Jordan, *Through New Eyes*, 193.

42. Surprisingly, Beale devotes considerable space to the garden-sanctuary in Eden and the patriarchal garden-oasis sanctuaries, but virtually ignores the tabernacle that immediately preceded the temple.

43. Jordan, *Through New Eyes*, 203; similarly Beale, *Temple*, 97.

44. Jordan, *Through New Eyes*, 207; similarly, Beale, *Temple*, 32–33. Cf. Vern Poythress, *The Shadow of Christ in the Law of Moses* (Brentwood, TN: Wolgemuth & Hyatt, 1991), 15.

45. Jordan, *Through New Eyes*, 172.

46. Ibid., 207; similarly, Beale, *Temple*, 34, 35. Cf. Poythress, *Shadow of Christ*, 16.

47. Jordan, *Through New Eyes*, 87; similarly, Beale, *Temple*, 325.

48. James B. Jordan, "Thoughts on Jachin and Boaz," Biblical Horizons Occasional Paper 1 (Aug. 1988), 14 and *Through New Eyes*, 212; similarly, Beale, *Temple*, 35.

49. Jordan, *Through New Eyes*, 207; similarly, Beale, *Temple*, 33, 38.

PART TWO: LITURGICAL THEOLOGY

Among the furniture of the courtyard there was a bronze altar—a mini-mountain—for sacrifice (Exod 27:1–8; 38:1–7; 43:16) and a bronze laver for cleansing (Exod 30:17–21; 38:8), which was a small basin of water elevated above the earth. Unlike the wells dug in patriarchal sanctuaries, the raised laver called to mind the heavenly sea, water above the firmament-heaven and the waters of Eden.[50] Recalling the Edenic sanctuary, the tabernacle was a more glorious and organized form of the garden-oasis sanctuaries, which symbolized the nature and glory of the Mosaic covenant.[51]

Eventually God tore the Mosaic tabernacle apart (1 Sam 4) and it was never put back together again as such. During David's reign, the Mosaic tabernacle, minus the ark, functioned alongside the Davidic tabernacle on Mount Zion, where the ark was (1 Sam 6; 1 Chr 15–16). When at last, under Solomon, God had one house again in Israel, it was not a tabernacle but a temple, an even more glorious house than before.[52]

THE SOLOMONIC TEMPLE

The Hebrew word for temple also means "palace," and thus the central sanctuary for the worship of God in Israel became less tent-like and more house-like.[53] Just as the Mosaic tabernacle featured gold and gems gleaned from Egyptian spoil (Exod 12:35–36), so the Solomonic temple was adorned with gold and gems from other downstream lands (2 Sam 8:11; 1 Kgs 7:51; 9:28; 10:11).[54]

Yet virtually every aspect of the Solomonic Temple complex was an enhancement or glorification of some aspect of the tabernacle complex.[55] The dimensions of the Most Holy Place were doubled, for example, which made it eight times as large as the tabernacle. Similarly, the number of cherubim was doubled, as God "sat" on the wings of two cherubim, but the wings of two others now overshadowed the throne.[56] The Holy Place, similarly, was twelve times as large as it was in the tabernacle. Instead of a little altar, there was a massive mountain-like bronze altar fifteen feet high and thirty feet wide (2 Chr 4:1). Instead of the small laver of cleansing out in the courtyard, there was a huge bronze "sea" with twelve thousand gallons of water (1 Kgs 7:23–26; 2 Chr 4:2–5). There were now, in addition to the arboreal lampstand from the tabernacle, ten golden lampstands in the Holy Place, with silver lampstands in the courtyard to give light at night (1 Chr 28:15). There were also ten water "chariots" in the courtyard (1 Kgs 7:27–39).

---

50. Jordan, *Through New Eyes*, 161, 207. Cf. Kline, *Images*, 41.

51. Jordan, *Through New Eyes*, 205.

52. "I believe that the rending of the Tabernacle should be associated with the rending of the animal in the sacrificial system. It is a picture of death, and the building of the Temple is a picture of the resurrection" (Jordan, *Through New Eyes*, 224–25). For a discussion of the rending of the Mosaic tabernacle and of the tabernacle of David, see Peter J. Leithart, *From Silence to Song: The Davidic Liturgical Revolution* (Moscow, ID: Canon, 2003).

53. Jordan, *Through New Eyes*, 222.

54. Ibid., 158.

55. Much of what follows is from ibid., 231–34.

56. Ibid., 231.

These new features were not simple extrapolations of tabernacle symbolism, but radical transformations of it.[57]

Moreover, there were some new architectural features evident in the Temple, not least the two massive freestanding bronze pillars flanking the open porch outside the Temple, the one on the north called "Boaz" meaning "Strength" and the one on the south "Jachin" meaning "Established" (1 Kgs 7:21; 2 Chr 3:17).[58] They were made like giant lilies, topped with a lily blossom, along the sides of which dangled one hundred Edenic pomegranates (cf. Jer 52:23), about the size of apples, which struck the hollow columns and rang a rich sound when the wind blew, heralding the majesty of God and the glory of His presence.[59] Jordan contends that one of these pillars represented the king and the other represented the High Priest: Boaz, the most famous of David's ancestors and Jachin, one of the chief priests in charge of the twenty-first order (1 Chr 24:17). They stood on either side of the door to guard the entry to God's house and were indicative of the new monarchical phase of Israel's history.[60] The Solomonic temple, for Jordan, symbolized the nature and the glory of the Davidic covenant.[61]

EZEKIEL'S AND ZECHARIAH'S VISIONARY TEMPLES AND THE POST-EXILIC TEMPLE

Ezekiel receives a vision of a new temple, described in chapters 40–48, which is so vast that it could never realistically be built.[62] Jordan contends that this visionary temple symbolized the nature and the glory of the post-exilic restoration establishment.[63] It is striking that instead of a laver or "sea" in this temple, there is an out-flowing river (Ezek 47). Jordan interprets this to mean that the bronze ocean has been "tipped over" so that temple water can now flow outward.[64] Previously in Israel's history the water always stayed in the land, in the tabernacle and in the temple, and the nations came to it. This, in Jordan's view, is indicative of pre-exilic centripetal evangelism when the nations came to Israel at the center of the world, as the Queen of Sheba came to Solomon. The water in Ezekiel's visionary temple flows outward (albeit in one direction and not to the ends of the earth) indicating, Jordan argues, that in the post-exilic, pre-New Testament world evangelism was increasingly centrifugal as the Jews would begin to move out from

---

57. Ibid., 222.

58. The meaning of these pillars is investigated in Jordan, "Jachin and Boaz," 15. Cf. Jordan, *Through New Eyes*, 231.

59. Jordan, "Jachin and Boaz," 6; similarly, Beale, *Temple*, 71.

60. Jordan, *Through New Eyes*, 222, 231.

61. Ibid., 234.

62. Ibid., 246; similarly, Beale, *Temple*, 335–54.

63. Jordan, *Through New Eyes*, 242. Cf. Beale who argues that this visionary temple refers not to the glory of the post-exilic Israelite community, but to "a heavenly temple linked to a non-architectural earthly reality"—namely, the eschatological people of God (*Temple*, 340).

64. Jordan, *Sociology*, 90.

PART TWO: LITURGICAL THEOLOGY

Palestine as missionaries, so that by New Testament times there would be synagogues and Gentile converts in all the world.[65]

The historical post-exilic temple built by Ezra was a small affair (Ezra 3:12; Hag 2:3) which thus symbolized the nature, but not the glory of the restoration covenant.[66] God similarly gave Zechariah night visions in which he assured him that though the rebuilt temple did not look like much, one could see with the eyes of faith that the seven-fold lampstand had now become a lamp with forty-nine branches and forty-nine lights on it (Zech 4:1–14).[67]

THE NEW TEMPLE IN JESUS

The apostle John says in his Gospel that the Word became flesh and tabernacled among the disciples who saw his glory (John 1:14). Jesus is the ultimate fulfillment of the tabernacle and his glory recalls the glory-cloud that filled the tabernacle.[68] What follows in John's gospel, Jordan proposes, is a literary tour through the tabernacle/temple.[69] At his ascension, Jesus passed through the firmament-heavens and became the first man in history to enter the highest heavens (Heb 9:24; cf. Rev 4–5), from which Satan is cast out (Rev 12). There in heaven Jesus sets up an even more glorious temple than ever before—namely, the church, not made with hands, but made of people and organized by the Spirit. What came down upon the disciples at Pentecost, Jordan insists, was God's glory-cloud, old covenant architectural models of which are found in the tabernacle and Temple. The descent of the New Jerusalem from heaven that John sees in Revelation 21 is a picture of what happened in Acts 2. "The heavenly cloud-pattern typologically imprinted itself on the house, creating a new world, and also upon the individuals in the house, filling them with the Spirit (Acts 2:4) and creating a new humanity."[70] The Spirit present among the believers, according to Paul, constitutes the church as the temple

---

65. Jordan, *Through New Eyes*, 249. My own view here is that Ezekiel's visionary temple coalesces with the prophecies about the end of exile (both geographical and theological), the coming of YHWH as king and the restoration of Jerusalem, the fulfillment of which is inaugurated with the first advent of Christ. See N. T. Wright, *The New Testament and the People of God*, Christian Origins and the Question of God 1 (Minneapolis: Fortress, 1992), 264; see also 299–338. Cf. Beale, who argues that the absence of the bronze sea in this visionary temple points to the absence of the sea in Revelation 21 and the "radical change in the future cosmos" (*Temple*, 361).

66. Jordan, *Through New Eyes*, 246.

67. Ibid., 252.

68. Ibid., 267. Cf. Kline, *Images*, 16.

69. After presenting the Lamb (John 1), John begins where the priest would have, with the laver of cleansing, where the priest would wash himself and also the sacrifice before offering it. We discern references to water in John 1:18–34 (baptism of John); John 2:1–11 (water for purification rituals turned into wine); and so forth. John then turns his attention to the table of showbread, and we find allusions to eating and drinking in John 6 (Jesus is the bread of life) and John 7 (Jesus is the drink of life, recalling the libations that went with the showbread and meal offerings). Next we encounter the lampstand in John 8 (Jesus is the light of the world) and so forth. See Jordan, *Through New Eyes*, 267–69; cf. Poythress, *Shadow of Christ*, 18–25, and Beale, *Temple*, 195ff.

70. Jordan, *Through New Eyes*, 274; similarly, Beale, *Temple*, 204.

(1 Cor 3:10–17).[71] Similarly, because the Spirit dwells in them, individual believers are temples that must not be polluted from the outside (1 Cor 6:19–20; cf. Eph 2:19; 4:1–9).[72]

Through his work Christ has introduced "a new heavens and a new earth" (Rev 21:1), a phrase that refers not exclusively to the final eternal state but also, in some sense, to the time inaugurated by Christ's ascension.[73] The leaves of the trees in the New Jerusalem exist, after all, for something not needed after the last judgment—namely, the healing of the nations (Rev 22:2). Moreover, people are invited to wash their robes and enter the gates (22:14) and the Spirit and bride summon outsiders to come in (22:17); such evangelism, however, will not occur after the last judgment.[74] As the writer to the Hebrews argues, we have already come to the New Jerusalem (12:22). Paul teaches that believers are seated with Christ in heavenly places. The church, in some sense, is positioned in heaven, which is why ministers of the Word, in the book of Revelation, are called stars (e.g., Rev 1:16, 20) and angels (e.g., Rev 2–3).[75]

THE VALUE OF JORDAN'S TYPOLOGY

How exactly are the types we observe in the Bible relevant for the Christian life? In the minds of many contemporary interpreters and homileticians the purpose of typology is simply to point people to Christ.[76] The relevance of temple typology, in particular, even in studies devoted to worship in the Old Testament, is often limited to theological conclusions about the work of Christ (e.g., Christ offers the final bloody sacrifice on the cross) and to spiritual applications (e.g., we offer incense through prayer).[77] For James B. Jordan, the relevance of the typological temple transcends these general conclusions and applications and extends to specifics of contemporary Christian worship and praxis.

This pastoral feature of Jordan's temple typology becomes especially apparent in comparison with the conclusions of G. K. Beale, whose commentary on the evolution and architecture of the temple is strikingly similar to Jordan's. Though both trace the development of temple motif back to the patriarchal garden-oases and beyond to the Edenic garden and though both see the temple as a cosmic house representing the highest heavens (the most holy place), the firmament-heavens (the holy place), and the earth (courtyard), Beale and Jordan part company in their conclusions about the relevance

71. Jordan, *Through New Eyes*, 77, 144, 213.

72. Ibid., 216, 265.

73. Beale sees the emphasis in Revelation 21 on the new cosmos and the terminus of God's temple-building activity (*Temple*, 369). Jordan argues that history involves a sequence of new heavens and new earth that corresponds roughly to the sequence of covenants (e.g., Adamic, Noahic, Abrahamic), such that following the flood, for example, God created a new heaven and a new earth (2 Pet 3:5–6). See Jordan, *Through New Eyes*, 175, 197, 227, 243ff. Cf. Beale, *Temple*, 25: "'Heaven and earth' in the Old Testament may sometimes be a way of referring to Jerusalem or its temple, for which 'Jerusalem' is a metonymy."

74. Jordan, *Through New Eyes*, 269–70.

75. James B. Jordan, "The Revelation of Jesus in Revelation 1:12b–16 and Its Relation to the Structure of the Book of Revelation," Biblical Horizons Occasional Paper 33 (Feb. 2003), 21.

76. E.g, Greidanus, *Preaching Christ*, 259–60.

77. E.g., Tremper Longman III, *Immanuel In Our Place: Seeing Christ in Israel's Worship* (Phillipsburg, NJ: P & R, 2001).

PART TWO: LITURGICAL THEOLOGY

of the temple today. Beale's "practical reflections" on the temple's significance revolve around our identity "with Jesus through the Spirit as part of the end-time temple" and our calling as "spiritual Levitical priests" to keep the order and peace of "the spiritual sanctuary" and offer sacrifices in "the spiritual temple's liturgy."[78] Though sound, these applications restrict the relevance of the temple to an ethereal sphere and betray a fundamental difference between Jordan and Beale in terms of their typological interpretations.

As indicated earlier, typology for Jordan shows that history is both teleological and rhythmic. This is true of the temple in terms of the evolution (teleology) of an increasingly glorious sanctuary and the varied repetition (rhythm) of certain sanctuary motifs (e.g., the motif of Edenic water is repeated in patriarchal oasis and then in tabernacle laver, temple sea, and Ezekiel's visionary river). Because we do not yet see the complete coalescence of cult and culture of the eschaton and we continue to distinguish, as the Israelites did in the old covenant, special times (Lord's Day), places (worship facilities), and people (office-bearers) from ordinary times, places, and people, this story of temple progress and repetition, Jordan contends, continues in the church today.[79]

Beale's temple typology, by comparison, is full of the teleological, but void of the rhythmic. This in turn means that the accent in Beale's "practical reflections" falls on the eschatological trajectory of temple worship and therefore the dissimilarity and discontinuity between old covenant worship and worship today.

Whereas Beale makes the general application, for example, that all believers are priests who must "keep the order and peace of the spiritual sanctuary," Jordan underscores that some are special priests who have been given special stewardship of the keys of the kingdom (Matt 16:19) and are special guardians of the sanctuary.[80]

Whereas for Beale the water-motif of the temple has been so fulfilled by Jesus that the earthly element seemingly disappears in new covenant temple worship, Jordan insists that to enter into God's presence we must pass through the waters of baptism, just as the priests had to be washed with water from the laver of cleansing (tabernacle) or the bronze ocean (temple).[81] The waters of baptism descend from "the waters above," represented by the laver of cleansing, and thereby indicate for Jordan that the only appropriate mode for baptism is sprinkling or affusion and not immersion.

Whereas Beale argues that "we also continually offer sacrifices in order to keep the order of the spiritual temple's liturgy," Jordan insists that the temple liturgy can and ought to inform the liturgical order of corporate worship today.[82] The sequence of sacrifices in

78. Beale, *Temple*, 398.
79. Jordan, *Through New Eyes*, 271.
80. Beale, *Temple*, 398; Cf. Jordan, *Through New Eyes*, 264, 272; Jordan, *Sociology*, 39.
81. Beale, *Temple*, 196–97; Jordan, *Sociology*, 114.
82. Beale, *Temple*, 398. The case for seeing the roots of Christian liturgy in the temple and not the synagogue is also made by Peter Leithart, "Synagogue Or Temple? Models for The Christian Worship," *Westminster Theological Journal* 64.1 (Spring 2002) 120–33. See also Jeffrey J. Meyers, *The Lord's Service: The Grace of Covenant Renewal Worship* (Moscow, ID: Canon, 2003), 55–229; Michael Farley, "Reforming Reformed Worship: Theological Method and Liturgical Catholicity in American Presbyterianism,1850–2005" (Ph.D. diss., Saint Louis University, 2007), 264–335; and Michael Farley, "What Is 'Biblical' Worship? Biblical Hermeneutics and Evangelical Theologies of Worship," *Journal of the Evangelical Theological Society* 51.3 (2008) 591–613.

the temple liturgy (Lev 9) can and should still be followed—namely, the sin offering (v. 15; confession of sin) first, then the whole burnt or ascension offering (v. 16; consecration of life) attended by the grain or tribute offering (v. 17), and finally the peace offering (v. 18; communion with God and others).[83] Liturgical worship today should follow the same basic sequence: cleansing through corporate confession of sin and God's declaration of forgiveness, then consecration through the proclamation of the Word, and finally communion through the celebration of the eucharist. The consecration through the proclamation of the Word is in view in, for instance, Hebrews 4:12 which pictures the word of God as a sword that pierces to "the division of soul and of spirit, of joints and of marrow, and discerning the thoughts and intentions of the heart." References to bones and marrow being cut by a double-edged sword do far more than provide a vivid description of the power of the word; they also place us in the realm of sacrificial imagery. We are dismembered in worship by the cutting word so that we may offer ourselves as sacrifices in praise, gratitude, and prayer.[84]

The rhythmic narrative of temple progress continues in the church today such that the patterns of contemporary Christian worship should follow the patterns of old covenant temple worship. Herein lies the value of Jordan's typology: we are enabled to apply the Word of God to contemporary situations.[85] Because the patterns in the narrative of Scripture continue to repeat in post-canonical history, we can make connections—through a Christological grid to be sure—between events then to events today. "We can draw parallels," Jordan writes, "between our present churches and civilization to specific times in the Old Covenant, analogies that will help us understand our present predicament."[86]

According to George Lindbeck, this was exactly the thrust of pre-modern typological exegesis:

> Typology was used to incorporate the Hebrew Scriptures into a canon that focused on Christ, and then, by extension, to embrace extrabiblical reality. King David, for example, was in some respects a typological foreshadowing of Jesus, but he was also, in Carolingian times, a type for Charlemagne and, in Reformation days, as

---

83. James B. Jordan, *Theses on Worship*, rev. ed. (Niceville, FL: Transfiguration Press, 1988), 30, 84–93. Jordan also argues (*Theses*, 81–82) that this order is present already in the Garden of Eden where, on the day of rest (the day of the Lord's rest), God comes to call Adam and Eve to appear before Him (Gen 3:9), to proclaim His Word to them (Gen 3:14-19), to feed them (cf. Gen 3:22), and then to dismiss them to carry out the mandates He has given them (Gen 3:24). Each of these elements, however, is twisted because of Adam's sin. God summons Adam forcefully, does not proclaim Adam's sins forgiven because Adam has not yet confessed them, preaches a largely negative sermon of judgment (though each of the three points ends up with good news for Adam and Eve), withholds the food he had prepared (Gen 3:22), and then drives Adam and Eve out of the garden instead of dismissing them for service.

84. Jordan, *Theses*, 85.

85. Jordan is insistent that the Bible does not give us a code and therefore rejects, for example, interpretations of Revelation that link "beast" with Nero in particular, or worse, Hitler or Saddam Hussein (*Through New Eyes*, 15). The controls on Jordan's exegesis are nicely summarized by R. S. Clarke, "The Maximalist Hermeneutics of James B. Jordan," *Ecclesia Reformanda* 1.1 (2009) 23–27.

86. Jordan, *Through New Eyes*, 278. Cf. Henk de Jong, "All Under One Head: Christ," *Pro Rege* (Dec. 1990) 25: "My impression is that biblical history is a paradigm of history as such. In European history, for instance, there has also been a development comparable with that of the Bible."

> even Protestants said, for Charles V in his wars against the Turks.... It is important to note the direction of interpretation. Typology does not make scriptural contents into metaphors for extrascriptural realities, but the other way around. It does not suggest, as is often said in our day, that believers find their stories in the Bible, but rather that they make the story of the Bible their story. The cross is not to be viewed as a figurative representation of suffering nor the messianic kingdom as a symbol of hope in the future; rather, suffering must be cruciform, and hopes for the future messianic.[87]

Jordan is not content merely to tell us the alluring story of worship sanctuaries in redemptive history; he is intent on situating us as characters in that story who in the progress of redemption must learn the patterns of the past in order to repeat them in the future.

Typological interpretation is often applauded for its panoramic insightfulness and chastised for its apparent irrelevance. James B. Jordan's typological interpretation of the temple invites the applause and escapes the chastisement. Not only does Jordan interpret the rich symbolism and meaning of the temple architecture and unveil the glorious evolution of the temple sanctuary with tremendous acumen, he shows us the relevance of temple worship as a whole. Far from being limited to an ethereal dimension in which "spiritual" priests offer "spiritual" sacrifices in a "spiritual" sanctuary, the relevance of the temple today extends to the task of the office-bearers of the church, for example, and the sequence of the worship liturgy. The church in Jordan's typology, to borrow Krabbendam's terminology, is not "above" things, but in the middle of things, trekking through the landscape, en route to yet a better sanctuary that will encompass the entire earth.

∼

Dear Bill,

Thank you for this nice treatment of my work. I certainly hope that my pastoral intent is clear to all who read what I've written. God's goal, after all, is new people, and the highest form of theology is pastoral theology. All other departments of theology are at the service of pastoral theology, of glorifying His bride.

Your essay took me back. I read Greidanus's *Sola Scriptura*, on the controversy between exemplary and redemptive preaching in the Netherlands, back in 1972, and it formed my thinking ever since. Also in that same year I met Hendrik Krabbendam, and in conversation with him I learned the danger of flying in an airplane from the beginning to the end of the Bible without also walking slowly on the way. I suppose it's the musician in me that began to see that a way out of the difficulties was to hear that many melodies repeat in the Bible, with variation, and that this kind of "typology" undergirds the "slow walk" through Bible history.

Jim

---

87. *The Nature of Doctrine: Religion and Theology in a Post Liberal Age* (Philadelphia: Westminster, 1984), 117–18. Peter Leithart writes, "The answer to the charge of irrelevance is that typology is the only basis for making the Bible practically relevant. Only if there are correspondences between events—that is, only if one event may be a 'type' of a future event—can the Bible be relevant, since the Bible obviously does not speak about our circumstances directly" (*A Son To Me: An Exposition of 1 & 2 Samuel* [Moscow, ID: Canon, 2003], 23).

8

Why Don't We Sing the Songs Jesus Sang?

The Birth, Death, and Resurrection of English Psalm Singing

DUANE GARNER

JAMES JORDAN TELLS A story about the ordination examination of a Reformed Episcopal pastoral candidate. The old bishop, whose approval was necessary in order for the candidate to pass his exam, asked the prospective pastor, "If you are going to be a pastor, what would you say is the most important book of the Bible for counseling people and addressing their emotional and spiritual problems?" The candidate replied, "I would say the Book of Psalms. The psalms are at the center of biblical counsel." The bishop agreed, then asked, "If you are going to be a pastor, and lead in worship, what is the most important book of the Bible for learning about worship, and for leading people in the worship of God?" The younger man replied again, "That would also be the Book of Psalms."

Continuing, the bishop asked, "So the Book of Psalms is the most important book for you to know as a pastor for counseling and for worship, is that correct?" The candidate answered, "Yes, I think it is."

"Well then," the bishop replied, "beginning with Psalm 1, go through the book and give me the gist of every psalm, and don't stop until you get to Psalm 150." The candidate began to do just that, but faltered somewhere around Psalm 11 and couldn't continue. The bishop then told him, "You aren't ready to be a pastor yet. Come back when you can do them all."

While that examination question might worry even the best Bible scholars, it is no doubt an important question—one we might consider including in future ordination exams—and a question we all ought to be confronted with ourselves. If the Book of Psalms is indeed as vital as the bishop suggested, then what is our excuse for not knowing the Psalter thoroughly enough to be able to provide a quick summary of all 150 psalms?

The fact that most of us do not have this level of familiarity with the psalms indicates that we do not regularly use the psalms in our churches as they were intended. The Psalter is God's holy, inspired hymnal, given to His people to use in worship; He commands us to sing them (Eph 5:19; Col 3:16). He likes to hear the psalms sung. They are

His favorite songs. He wrote them. He likes to hear the other songs we have written, He wants to hear new songs, but He especially wants to hear the psalms.

We do not know the psalms because we have not sung them as we have been commanded. We have not grown up singing all of them, in their entirety, regularly, throughout our whole lives, and so we do not know them nearly as well as we know other newer hymns and songs. We have not sung the psalms because we apparently do not think that they are as important or as relevant as the gospel songs written 150 years ago or the praise and worship songs written ten or twenty years ago. Rather than purposely and primarily singing the songs that God has expressly commanded us to sing, the Church has gotten into the habit of singing songs about personal experiences, rather than psalms that recount God's mighty acts in history.

It has not always been this way, however. The predominant use of extra-biblical hymn sources in worship over the past couple hundred years is something of an anomaly when you study the history of Church music. The psalms have always been the starting point for Christian worship; it is impossible to overstate their usefulness or their importance. They have been the foundation and source of all faithful hymnody throughout the centuries. The Christian who ignores the psalms does so to his own hurt. The hymn writer or musician who ignores the psalms will inevitably engage himself in the making of music that draws the Church away from Jesus rather than pointing her to Him. As one writer states, "The psalms are the womb of Church music. They are not only the hymnal of the Old Testament and the songs of Israel, they are the voice of the Church."[1] No congregation can honor God or be entirely obedient to Him in worship so long as it fails to use the psalter regularly.

Psalm-singing develops a distinct church culture, a "strong, militant, and bold spirituality."[2] The introduction to the *Trinity Psalter* reads:

> Calvinism produced what Roland Bainton called "a race of heroes," and Psalm-singing had no small part in bringing this about. These are the songs of the *church militant*. The Huguenots in their struggle against the French monarch, the Dutch in their fight for independence from the Spanish Empire, and the Parliamentary armies in their civil war against the Stuart monarchy all sang the Psalms into battle, often against overwhelming odds. The 68th, "Let God arise," is known as the battle Psalm of the Huguenots. Our Reformed forefather's favorite metaphor for the Christian life was that of warfare. Nearly every Psalm refers to the conflict between the righteous and the wicked (148 of 150 by one count), a theme which is almost nonexistent in modern hymns. One author has said, "When iron was in men's souls, and they needed it in their blood, they sang Psalms." The Psalms will stiffen a church accustomed to accommodation and compromise with the world.[3]

It is precisely this strong, militant, and bold spirituality which the Church in the West has lacked over the past couple centuries, and which Jordan throughout his teaching and writing ministry has sought to restore to her. Arguably, some of his most impor-

---

1. Paul Westermeyer, *Te Deum: The Church and Her Music* (Minneapolis: Fortress, 1998), 23.
2. "Why the Psalms?" in *Trinity Psalter*, ed. Terry Johnson (Pittsburgh: Crown & Covenant, 1994), vi.
3. Ibid.

tant work has been translating the psalms and setting them to hearty, vibrant music, as well as exhorting pastors and churches to rediscover the psalms and use them in worship. It is precisely those exhortations I wish to echo here. Let us explore some of the reasons why Protestants have forgotten the psalms, and why we must work diligently to reclaim them.

SOME COMMON ARGUMENTS AGAINST PSALM-SINGING[4]

Nothing can reform the Church quite like the singing of psalms publicly in corporate worship. Not only can we be sure that we are singing songs devoid of heresy, but in singing the Psalms we also have songs that are full of substance and balance and mature subject matter. Not only are we avoiding the vacuous, disposable lyrics supplied by the Christian pop music industry, but we are also being obedient to the Lord, albeit in this simple way. Obedience is the beginning of revival and reformation. We have countless examples in the Scriptures of how the Lord visits His people with favor and delivers them from their oppressors when they obey. Without the psalms at the center of our liturgies, prayers, and lives, we can never honestly expect any form of reformation.

Nevertheless, the overseers of the Church today prefer leading her in worship that is most often characterized by the cooing of sickly-saccharine platitudes softly into a microphone, and then repeating these a few dozen times. Even in Presbyterian and Reformed churches, where historically there is a stronger tradition of psalm-singing, the Psalter is often neglected while ten-year-old folk ditties are preferred. It is no wonder that the Church is weak and effete and feckless against her enemies, given her refusal to sing the war chants she was given. The Church has become more like the silly girl writing fabulously bad poetry in the attic who dots her i's with a heart and less like the warrior princesses of the Bible—Deborah and Miriam and Hannah and Mary—who all composed and sang rich, pithy songs recounting Yahweh's mighty acts through history, rejoicing in the destruction of His enemies.

Granted, this neglect of the Psalter for most Christians is, more often than not, a sin of ignorance rather than a high-handed refusal to do what the Bible says. Most simply never have been confronted with the idea of psalm-singing. The few that have been exposed to the idea and yet still reject it do so based on the commonly-heard arguments that the psalms are too militant, too Jewish and too Old Covenant to be relevant for the Church today. On an ideological level, these objections are the product of a confused eschatology and a timid ecclesiology together with a dash of Marcionism. But when you really get down to it, on a practical level, the lyrics "O daughter of Babylon, who are to be destroyed, Happy the one who repays you as you have served us! Happy the one who takes and dashes your little ones against the rock" (Ps 137) do not sound so good when accompanied by a Hammond organ or a soft-rock praise band.

---

4. These arguments are summarized from countless discussions with pastors, musicians, music ministers, and congregants over the course of my personal wanderings through evangelical, fundamentalist, and charismatic circles.

PART TWO: LITURGICAL THEOLOGY

However, let us take just a moment to think through these commonly-heard objections seriously. Truly, the psalms are militant, but there is no dissonance between the militancy of the psalms and the commands of Jesus to love your neighbor and your enemy. The New Testament is not devoid of militant language; Jesus said, "I did not come to bring peace but a sword" (Matt 10:34). In Revelation 6, John describes Jesus sitting on a white horse, with a bow, "and he went out conquering and to conquer" (Rev 6:2).[5]

Faithful students of the Bible recognize that all of the militaristic themes of the Old Testament point forward to the warfare of the Church in the world with Jesus as our new Joshua, our new General. The conquest of Canaan and the warfare of Israel are types and shadows of the continuing conflict between the Seed of the Woman and the seed of the Serpent (Gen 3:15).

Of course, we are not commissioned by Jesus to spread the gospel by the sword of iron, but by the Sword of the Spirit, which is the Word of God. This does not mean, however, that the Church's warfare is anything less than a real war. Jesus is still a man of war just like His Father (Exod 15:3). His sword is that Sword of the Spirit which kills the old man under Adam and resurrects him to new life under the Second Adam. His sword cuts up men disfigured by sin and rearranges their features, conforming them to the image of Christ. So the most loving thing that you can do for your neighbors, your enemies, and their little ones is to "dash them" against the Rock who is Jesus.

We lose all of these important emphases if we neglect the Psalter. If "worship is warfare,"[6] as Peter Leithart has put it, then we need not be embarrassed by battle language in our songs. Psalm 144 begins "Praise be to Yahweh my Rock, who trains my hands for war, my fingers for battle." The battle that David is doing with his fingers is the plucking of the psaltry—his stringed instrument—and singing the inspired songs of holy warfare. Remember that when the enemies of Yahweh threaten Israel throughout the Scriptures, and the people cry out in prayers and songs for Him to help, the Lord responds by bringing the plans of the oppressors and aggressors to nothing. A faithful Israel's first line of defense against the enemy is worship, and the Lord fights her battles (2 Chr 20). In other accounts such as the Battle of Jericho and Gideon's conquest of the Midianites, Israel defeated her enemies time and again by carrying out a liturgy of worship to the Lord of Hosts on the battlefield. Yes, the psalms are militant. That is a good thing, and we ought to sing them unapologetically.

What of the argument that the psalms are "too Jewish" and thus not relevant or meaningful for Western Christians? If by "Jewish" we mean "Hebraic" or "pre-Messianic," then they certainly are that, but so is the rest of the Old Testament and we still read that big section of the Bible in our churches and even preach out of it on occasion. But if by "Jewish" we are saying that the psalms belong to that group of people who today still hold to a form of the religion of the first-century Jews, then this thinking is seriously flawed. The psalms don't really mean anything to those who still hold to the Jewish religion,

---

5. For a full treatment this theme in the book of Revelation, see James B. Jordan, *The Vindication of Jesus Christ: A Brief Reader's Guide to Revelation*, 3rd ed. (Monroe, LA: Athanasius, 2009).

6. Peter J. Leithart, "Worship Is Warfare," *Credenda/Agenda* 13.2:17.

because all of the psalms are about Jesus and His people. The Jews may still use them now, but they do so in ignorance of their true meaning.

A pastoral candidate was once asked in his ordination exam to name all of the "Christological psalms," and the examiner was expecting to hear an answer along the lines of "Psalm 22, Psalm 24, Psalm 110. . . ." However, the candidate began his answer, "Psalm 1, Psalm 2, Psalm 3, Psalm 4. . . ." His point was that all the psalms are Christological. Try to find one that does not talk about Jesus.

Therefore, in rejecting Jesus, the Jews have rejected the very substance of the psalms. The psalms do not belong to the Jews, they belong to the Church. They are our songs, and they are the best representation of our faith in a God who sends the Messiah He has promised, and the worship of a Messiah who has sat down at Yahweh's right hand until all His enemies are made His footstool. These are not the songs of a people who are waiting on a nationalistic messiah-state that will never come.

Turning to the last argument—that the Psalms are too Old Covenant for use in New Covenant worship—one only has to read the New Testament to see how often the psalms are quoted. The psalms are carried forward into the New Testament in the heads and hearts of Jesus and the apostles, quoted over 140 times throughout the Gospels and epistles. If the apostles, through the use of the books of Moses and the prophets, confirm them, then why not the psalms as well? Certainly, we sing them today knowing the fullness of the revelation that is the Lord Jesus Christ in a way that David or the sons of Korah could not. This doesn't mean that they are less helpful to us than they were to them; rather, the psalms are even more helpful and appropriate for us, now that we know more fully the Lord of whom they speak.

When you scratch the surface, then, you see that the common objections to using the psalms in worship have not been well thought out, but are only defenses frantically tossed up against the idea of singing things so different from what we have grown accustomed to singing. At heart, the issue is whether we are going to pretend to know more than Jesus—who sang the psalms—and whether we think we are holier than the Holy Spirit who wrote them.

Only a minority of Christians today would even get this far into the discussion. As stated, most congregations do not sing the psalms because it has never crossed their minds to do so. They simply have never taken Paul's repeated instruction to "sing the psalms" to mean, literally, "sing the psalms." The great majority of evangelicals have never seen all the psalms put with music, printed and bound all together in a single book. Though they may have sung a stray verse or two in a praise chorus, they have never heard them sung in their entirety. The psalms have largely disappeared from the fabric of Christian worship in North America.[7] How did we get to this point?

---

7. The scope of this chapter is narrowly focused on the slow death of psalm singing in English-speaking Protestant churches over the last three hundred years or so. The psalms have been in perpetual use in other branches of the church all over the world. As is the case in so many areas, we are the exception here, not the rule.

PART TWO: LITURGICAL THEOLOGY

THE BIRTH OF THE ENGLISH PSALTER

Any time we ask the question "Why are things the way they are today?" we have to look for the answer in history. Nothing in human culture generates spontaneously out of a void. Everything has a history—a story of its development—a trajectory, and thus, a future. So the Church did not simply decide collectively on some slow Tuesday afternoon sometime in the early nineteenth century that she was going to forsake the psalms. The widespread usage of the psalms ground to a halt slowly over the space of a couple hundred years as a result of a number of influences and currents. However, before we can understand the story of how the Church in English-speaking countries went from psalm-singing to not-psalm-singing, we must first look briefly back to the time of the English Reformation when the practice of singing the psalms in English began, as the congregation was readmitted into participation in the liturgy.

When the waves of the Reformation hit the shores of England, it took on a different form and flavor than the Reformation currents on the European continent. With their reforming efforts, the churches of England sought to present what is commonly referred to as the "middle way" between both the superstitions and excesses of Rome and what was perceived, by some of them, to be the overly zealous iconoclastic Continental Reformers. The criticism often made of England's Reformation is not only that it was primarily the product of King Henry VIII's marital problems, but also that it had no great theological giant or prophetic voice like Calvin or Luther. One response to that criticism is that the prevailing spirit of the English Reformation was that the Christian faith is to be "prayed" before it is "thought."[8] Certainly the legacy of this sentiment is represented in the one great product of the English Reformation—the *Book of Common Prayer*.

Thomas Cranmer (1489–1556), archbishop of Canterbury, was the man primarily responsible for the *Book of Common Prayer*, which has not only been a helpful influence on liturgical and prayer language throughout the past few centuries but has also had a profound impact on the very English language itself. Cranmer had a remarkable mastery of the tongue as well as an ability to craft English phrases for worship, producing prayers with a style marked by both a beauty and an economy of words that has gone quite unmatched in history. The first *Book of Common Prayer* appeared in 1549 and was revised in 1552 as Cranmer came to understand more of Calvin's teaching on communion and amended his language to better reflect the Reformed perspective. This openness on Cranmer's part both to be taught and to receive the very best of what other church traditions had to offer is reflected in the composition of his prayer book. For the prayers and the forms of the *Book of Common Prayer* he drew from his own vast ecumenical liturgical knowledge and included elements and forms from the Eastern Church and the Lutherans, as well as from Martin Bucer's liturgies from Strasbourg. He combined all these influences into a very serviceable and catholic prayer book. Sadly, in 1556, shortly after French Catholic Mary Tudor came to the throne, Cranmer was burned at the stake

---

8. Westermeyer, *Te Deum*, 165. Westermeyer quotes Cyril Richardson who puts it more strongly: for Anglicans, "Christianity is not to be thought, but to be prayed."

for heresy. His prayer book lived on and has remained in use since, going through revisions three more times in 1662, 1928, and 1979.

Most germane to our study here, though, is the fact that contained in the *Book of Common Prayer*, along with the table of Scripture readings for both Sunday and daily use, was a prescribed cycle of psalms translated into English to be sung, in worship, by the congregation between Scripture readings. All 150 psalms were arranged in such a way that through morning and evening prayers every day, the entire Psalter would be sung over the space of one month.

In 1550, musician John Merbecke built on Cranmer's work and composed the *Book of Common Prayer Noted* (that is, "with musical notation"), putting the prayers and orders, and especially the psalms of the prayer book, to music. Merbecke was a church organist who had his own run-in with the Roman Catholic magistrates in 1543 over his Calvinist leanings, and for publishing the first concordance of the English Bible. He was so influenced by John Calvin that when he began setting the psalms for singing, he drew from Calvin's own work in Geneva. Calvin, together with composer Louis Bourgeois, had recently produced the Genevan Psalter, arranging all 150 psalms metrically in French. Merbecke borrowed the Genevan Psalter's general approach to the psalms, arranging them metrically,[9] assigning every syllable a note just as Bourgeois had done. Where he could, he borrowed Bourgeois' tunes. In other parts of his book the musical settings were plainsong chants, but the finished product was a singable, functional English Psalter for congregational use.

Mary Tudor's ascent to the throne in 1553 silenced Merbecke's work but when the crown was restored to the Protestant Elizabeth I in 1558, English congregations took up the singing of psalms with a vengeance. Psalm-singing became the "principle form of congregational song, becoming normative for the next three hundred years."[10] English Psalters were produced at an incredible rate; one of the most popular went through sixty-five editions between 1560 and 1599. Throughout the sixteenth and seventeenth centuries, English composers, poets and churchmen—such as John Milton and Richard Baxter—set the psalms to music and produced a profuse number of Psalters in varying degrees of quality. In 1560, John Jewel, the Anglican Bishop of Salisbury, in a piece of correspondence describing the excitement and fervor surrounding the practice of Psalm singing in London, wrote: "For as soon as they had once commenced singing in public, in only one little church in London, immediately not only the churches in the neighbourhood, but even the towns far distant, began to vie with each other in the same practice.

---

9. Metrical psalm-singing, referenced throughout this chapter, is the term used for the practice of dividing up the text of a psalm into stanzas and rearranging the words and phrases in order to fit the meter of a particular tune. The Anglo-Genevan Psalter features metrical psalms exclusively. This is different from chanting the psalms or arranging them by "through-composition," which are efforts to preserve the text intact and to cause the music to serve the text rather than forcing the text to conform to the music.

10. Robin Leaver, "British Hymnody from the Sixteenth Through the Eighteenth Centuries," in *The Hymnal 1982 Companion*, ed. Raymond Glover, 4 vols. (New York: Church Hymnal Corporation, 1990), 1:369.

You may now sometimes see at St. Paul's cross, after the service, six thousand persons, old and young, of both sexes, all singing together and praising God."[11]

As the Reformation incorporated the people in the pew back into worship the music of worship became the music of all of life. Four-part singing of the psalms in homes and among young people became as popular a form of recreation as watching a movie or playing a card game would be for us today. Bible, prayer book, and Psalter were commonly published together in one volume, creating a single book around which all of life revolved. Not all the psalm translations and tunes in use at the time were perfect, but people were singing the psalms and, in the process, memorizing significant portions of Scripture. Most everyone from the youngest to the oldest could have answered the old Reformed Episcopal bishop's question confidently and would probably even have sung parts of their answer because they knew the Psalter.

ENTER THE PURITANS

The Puritans arrived on the scene in the 1570s, during the reign of Queen Elizabeth I. They began as staunch Reformers who wished to get on with the business of reforming the English church the way the church was being reformed on the European Continent, and they sought to work that reformation from within. They regarded the English church's stance as a "middle way" between Rome and the Reformation as nothing more than a halfway-house between the two. After some time, a significant number of Puritans grew dissatisfied with the hope of ever seeing real reform in the Anglican church. They called the established English clergy "dumb dogs" and, separating from the church, became known as "Separatist" Puritans. Those who chose to remain in communion with the main body of the church in England became known as the "Non-Separatists."[12]

The Separatist Puritans, then, founded the earliest "independent" Protestant churches, the source from which we can trace the Baptist, Congregationalist, and other independent church bodies. The Non-Separatists were the fathers of Presbyterian branch of the Church. Separatist Puritans, as we would expect, were uncomfortable with set liturgies, written prayers, and pretty much anything else that reminded them of the church they had left. They stripped down the set order of worship, yet for a time they held on to the psalms. The ideal Separatist liturgy eventually consisted of an introductory prayer followed by Scripture readings, a sung psalm, prayers, a lengthy sermon, more prayers, the collection of alms, another sung psalm, and a benediction. Gone was weekly communion. There were no responses or set forms of prayers, nor was there weekly communion, but early on they were still ardent psalm-singers, singing English metrical psalms in harmony, even without choirs or instruments. They were apparently so vigorous and

---

11. Bishop Jewel to Peter Martyr, London, March 5, 1560, in *The Zurich Letters, or, The Correspondence of Several English Bishops and Others*, trans. and ed. Hastings Robinson, 2nd ed. (Cambridge: Cambridge University Press, 1846), 90.

12. For a more detailed treatment of the story of the Puritans and their influence upon English psalm-singing, see Westermeyer, *Te Deum*, ch. 12.

unreserved in their singing that one contemporary of the Separatists remarked on the "Puritans that have sore throats with overstraining."[13]

Before long, however, what we have come to regard as the stereotypical Separatist Puritan traits of morose gravity, pietism, and fear of anything remotely "popish" all became factors in dragging down even the most lively psalm-singing congregations. One retarding influence was the practical necessity of lining out the psalms sung in rural congregations. The Separatist movement was more popular in rural than urban settings, and at the time, in those rural congregations, there were fewer readers and fewer Psalters to go around than in the city churches. So in Separatist churches, the worship leader would typically read a line of the psalm and the congregation would sing it back to him. Line by line, they would do this, all the way through the entire psalm. This was either tedious and tiresome or a glorious meditation and dwelling on the text of the psalm, depending on whose account you want to believe. The truth was probably somewhere in between, but before long psalm-singing became nearly unbearable both to hear and to participate in.

Separatists began commenting on how the psalms should sound and how they should be sung, over against the way that they were performed by the choirs and congregations of the Non-Separatist and English churches. One music historian remarks on the Separatist psalm settings of the time and how they should be performed authentically. "They should not be sung like modern Hymn tunes, but slowly, with grave dignity, not neglecting the proper pause for breath at the end of each line."[14] Imagine singing the joyful Psalms 24, 108, 148, or 150 "slowly and with grave dignity," pausing to take a breath at the end of each line.

The influential Puritan John Cotton said about the psalms that God allows us "to sing them in any such grave, and solemn, and plain tunes as do fitly suit the gravity of the matter, the solemnity of God's worship and the capacity of a plain people."[15] While the texts of some psalms demand grave and solemn singing, many of the psalms do not. Lost in the perspective of Cotton and his contemporaries is the militant, hearty, vigorous, spirited singing that suits the content of a great number of the psalms and that was characteristic of that early psalm-singing age.

A growing number of the Separatists began to question the practice of singing Psalms altogether toward the end of the sixteenth century, mocking the singing of the Cathedral Churches where "the service of God is grievously abused by piping with organs, singing, ringing, and trowling of Psalms from one side of the choir to the other."[16] In defiance of the manner in which the English mainline church sang the psalms, and in their suspicion of just about everything that might possibly be tainted by Rome, Congregationalists stopped singing altogether. Some rejected singing metrical psalms because group singing required a set form and because singing a metrical psalm was, to them, an unaccept-

---

13. Cited in ibid., 181.

14. Winfred Douglas, *Church Music in History and Practice* (New York: Scribner, 1937), 221.

15. John Cotton, *Singing of Psalms a Gospel Ordinance* (London, 1650), 56.

16. *A Parte of a Register* (London, c. 1590), quoted in Horton Davies, *The Worship of the English Puritans* (Westminster: Dacre, 1948), 168.

able alteration of the words and thoughts of Scripture. Congregationalist Robert Brown condemned congregational psalm singing as vanity and "gaming" in worship.[17]

John Smyth, the Baptist pastor of the Gainsborough Separatists who fled England to go to Amsterdam in 1603, wrote that very same year: "We hold that the worship of the New Testament properly so-called is spiritual, proceeding originally from the heart and that reading out of a book (though a lawful ecclesiastical action) is no part of spiritual worship. . . . We hold that singing a psalm is part of spiritual worship, therefore it is unlawful to have the book before the eye in time of singing a Psalm."[18]

Smyth went on to argue that the psalms were given as the Holy Spirit gave utterance, and thus the Holy Spirit must give men the unction to sing them, not in a compulsory way, directed by a form or liturgy, but voluntarily, without human mediator. He rhetorically asked whether men had the authority to tie the words of Scripture to meter and rhythm and tune, and whether setting the psalms to specific tunes was not a quenching of the Spirit.

Following Smith's reasoning, a Separatist woman named Katherine Sutton wrote a tract, published in 1663, titled *Christian Womans Experiences of the Glorious Workings of Gods Free Grace,* in which she indicates the importance of "immediate experience," which to her meant the practice of extemporaneous singing. She includes some of the hymns that she wrote extemporaneously in her booklet and concludes with the words, "I assure you courteous reader, these are not studied things, but are given immediately."[19]

In the Baptist and Congregationalist churches that agreed with Smith's and Sutton's position, one would think that at least spontaneous singing by individuals would be permitted and encouraged, but the most common result was that there was no music at all. Having rejected the supposedly awful things that the Metrical Psalters had done to the Scriptures and the vain way in which the psalm-singing churches were singing, and not having the skill or the resources to produce music they found suitable, they were left with nothing.

Still other Separatists argued that the psalm-singing commended by Paul in Colossians and Ephesians was specifically that sort of singing that one does to himself, pointing out that in both passages, Paul makes mention of "singing in your heart" (Eph 4:19; Col 3:16) and thus there was no need to sing the psalms out loud. In response to that, we can point out that, while it is certainly proper and commendable to meditate on the psalms, the language of the psalms themselves necessitates and directs the making of sounds and the articulation of words, the playing of loud instruments, cymbals, and trumpets, and even dancing. It is impossible to pluck a stringed instrument or blow a trumpet inside your heart. Moreover, the singing of a psalm in your heart in no way precludes actually singing it out loud at the same time. In Ephesians, Paul emphasizes "speaking to *one another* in psalms, hymns and Spiritual songs." Moreover a better translation of the Ephesians passage—"making melody in your heart to the Lord"—might be

---

17. Attributed to Robert Brown, *A True and Short Declaration* (1583) in Westermeyer, *Te Deum*, 183.

18. Westermeyer, *Te Deum*, 184.

19. Katherine Sutton, *Christian Womans [sic] Experiences of the glorious working of Gods [sic] free grace* (Rotterdam: Henry Goddaeus, 1663), quoted in Westermeyer, *Te Deum*, 183.

"psalming *from* your heart," with the word "psalming" being a specific reference to that plucking of the stringed instrument that originally accompanied the singing of psalms. Paul certainly did not intend for his readers to come away with the impression that he was commending the private murmuring of the psalms to one's self, excluding all outward forms of music. This interpretation, however, was enough to keep many congregations from singing psalms out loud.

The practice of printing Psalters with the text and music together became a matter of contention for some New England Puritans. They asserted in their journals that "the names of the notes were blasphemous"; that it was "popish"; that the printing of Psalters was a contrivance to get money; that it would bring musical instruments into the churches; and that "no one could learn the tunes anyway." A writer in the *New England Chronicle* wrote in 1723, "Truly I have a great jealousy that if we begin to sing by rule, the next thing will be to pray by rule and preach by rule and then comes popery."[20] It seems these fellows believed that you could simply call the view you disdained "popery" and your argument was won.

The strong repulsion against the singing of psalms exhibited by these Separatists for all these spurious reasons gradually grew, and by the end of the seventeenth century a flurry of treatises flew back and forth between the two factions of Puritans regarding the singing of psalms. While the aforementioned Separatist John Cotton ended up on the side of those who encouraged psalm-singing, he still took the opportunity in his papers to remind his readers of the solemn and grave manner in which he thought all the psalms should be sung. He even produced something of an apologetic for that practice of "lining out," suggesting that it served a didactic purpose; for in both *saying* and *singing* the psalm, each psalm was better learned. Even in arguing in favor of the psalms, he argued for the most tedious method of singing them.

In the aftermath of the controversy, few heirs of the Separatist Puritan movement sang the psalms as energetically or as profusely as the churches of the English Reformation did before the controversy. Though some psalters, such as the famous *Bay Psalm Book*, were still in use in the early days of the American colonies, the psalm settings that continued in popular use were largely bland and plain. Most of the independent churches hardly sang at all, and the malaise spread even to those non-Separatist and Anglican churches. After a steady and gradual decline of psalm-singing over the next one hundred years, the days that Bishop Jewel described were long gone. Rather than continuing the Reformation's emphasis on psalm-singing and improving upon the way that psalms were composed and sung, the music of the most populated branches of the church from the eighteenth century through the present day has been in a state of constant regression.

The musical vacuum that remained among the Baptists, Congregationalists, and independents would be filled in the nineteenth century by perhaps the most maudlin, sentimental, gnostic, saccharine music the church has ever known.[21] These controversies

---

20. Alice Morse Earle, *Sabbath in Puritan New England* (part 3 of 4). Online: http://www.fullbooks.com/Sabbath-in-Puritan-New-England3.html.

21. For an excellent survey of the hymns of the nineteenth century, see Ann Douglas, "The Domestication of Death: The Posthumous Congregation," in *The Feminization of American Culture* (New York: Noonday, 1977), ch. 6.

largely ruined psalm-singing for two hundred years and turned the attention of musicians and congregants to music written for parlors and tent revivals, with themes and emphases vastly inferior to the texts of the psalms.

Essentially, one generation very piously and self-righteously rejected something good and holy and beneficial, under the influence of threadbare logic and reactionary hysteria, and deprived subsequent generations of the opportunity to build upon a sure foundation. The Puritan psalm-singing controversy, then, is not the only reason churches do not sing the psalms today, but it played a significant role in the death of this most important, vital practice, especially in America and among evangelicals.

PSALM-SINGING TODAY

Happily, because of the work of James Jordan and others whom he has influenced, as well as the work of countless other musicians, poets, and translators across North America, psalm singing in worship is in a period of recovery. Like the Church at the beginning of the English Reformation, branches of the Church today are rediscovering the psalms and learning how to enjoy and utilize them as God intended. Young people are singing and memorizing the psalms in their homes, at schools, camps, and college ministries.

For older generations unaccustomed to singing the psalms—much less the practice of chanting or keeping up with the odd cadence of the Genevan tunes—adopting the psalms into worship is a greater challenge. It is much more comfortable to use the revival songs and praise choruses of the past century. Those more familiar songs have significance for people and they bring back memories of important, special events, and many do not see the need to put forth the effort to make such difficult strides or to do the hard work necessary to learn the psalms. In answer to this, Jordan has often asked the questions, "What songs do we want our children pairing with important events in their lives? What songs do we want to become special to them? What better songs can we give them than the psalms?"

Moreover, what songs does the Church need to be singing in a day when she is threatened by oppressors from without and heresies and schisms from within? What songs will put iron in men's souls as they face the increasing encroachment of Islam, secularism, and wicked magistrates? What songs make the devils shake in fear?

The cooing and warbling of praise ditties does not scare the Devil. Islam will not find anything to fear in revival songs about going to heaven. The tyrant is not offended by "In the Garden." There is a reason, though, that tyrants such as Mary Tudor do not like the psalms. Despots and oppressors do not fare so well in the texts of the psalms.[22] The psalms are the Church's arsenal against the enemies of the Lord. The Lord hears these sung prayers, and He delivers and defends His people.

In a sermon delivered in February 2007, James Jordan asked, "What can we do to change the situation in Darfur?"[23] For the past ten years or so, Christians in the south

---

22. See Psalms 83 and 135, for example.

23. James B. Jordan, "What We Can Do to Change the Situation in Darfur?" (sermon delivered at Auburn Avenue Presbyterian Church, Monroe, Louisiana, 4 February 2007). Cf. James B. Jordan, "How to Stop the Killing in Darfur," *Rite Reasons* 92 and 93 (Jan. and April 2007).

part of the Sudan have been tortured and massacred by Muslims and have been driven into the western region, known as Darfur. This situation has received a great deal of press, but celebrities and politicians have been able to accomplish very little, no matter the amount of money or "awareness" they have been able to raise.

Jordan suggests that if the Church of Jesus Christ would employ her "secret weapons"—the psalms—the situation would change considerably. He points out that just as Israel was a kingdom of priests who stood as mediators bringing their sacrifices to God on behalf of a world that would not and could not present their own sacrifices, the Church today worships on behalf of others. With regard to Israel's priesthood, the world at that time was estranged from God and did not know how to pray, so the priests and the nation of Israel were to pray and to worship not only for themselves, but for many who were not there. In like manner, the Church today brings her sacrifices of prayer and worship and song to the altar on behalf of others who are not there, praying for all the people who do not know how to pray, representing them before the throne of God. Just as the High Priest appeared before the very presence of God in His throne room, in the Holy of Holies, so the Church now has been invited into that place where real change happens, where God listens to His people and forgives sin, with Jesus as the new mercy seat.

So given this invitation and opportunity that the Church has been granted, what kind of prayers ought God's people be praying, and what sort of songs ought they to sing? How do we best pray for our brothers and sisters suffering in difficult, heartbreaking situations around the globe? Even as you sit reading this, Christian women and girls are being raped by Muslims in the Sudan, Christian men and boys are being beheaded by Muslims in Iran, parents are being killed in front of their children, and children are being forced into slavery. Their property is being plundered and their places of worship are being bombed. What are we going to do about it?

Turning to Luke 18, Jordan points to Jesus' parable as an example of what is expected of us: "In a certain town there was a judge who neither feared God nor cared what people thought. And there was a widow in that town who kept coming to him with the plea, 'Grant me justice against my adversary.' For some time he refused. But finally he said to himself, 'Even though I don't fear God or care what people think, yet because this widow keeps bothering me, I will see that she gets justice, so that she won't eventually wear me out with her coming!'" (Luke 18:2–5 NIV). And then Jesus comments on his own parable, saying, "Listen to what the unjust judge says. And will not God bring about justice for his chosen ones, who cry out to him day and night? Will he keep putting them off? I tell you, he will see that they get justice, and quickly. However, when the Son of Man comes, will he find faith on the earth?" (Luke 18:6–8 NIV).

The widow relentlessly presented herself before the unjust judge, pleading for justice and for the quelling of the adversary. The judge heard her and delivered her. If that is the way an unjust judge responds, how will the Just Judge respond to His chosen ones who cry out to Him day and night? Our Christian brothers who are being tormented by tyrannical oppressors need for us to be praying the same way the widow prayed, and immature choruses and eighteenth-century romantic hymns are not going to cut it. They are not war songs. They do not mention the reality of the Lord's adversaries and plead that they be destroyed. Those songs are not built for battle. Most of them are not even prayers, and they are just not up to the task. They do not change anything and are hollow comfort for our brothers experiencing persecution in Darfur and Iran and China.

We need songs that will change the world when we come, singing them, into the Lord's presence. Other songs can be good and serve a purpose in worship, but only psalms truly call on God to move in such a way that He changes men and nations, squashes the oppressors and delivers His people. Jordan concludes that sermon: "From everything I can tell the Bible teaches us that we are all priests. Priests are people who get to come into God's presence. And what they get to do is sing the psalms, as they are written, with enthusiasm and with musical instruments in a way that will change the world. That's what it means to be a priest, and to be part of the priesthood of all the believers."

The most significant thing the Church can do for her oppressed brothers around the world is to step into the throne room of God week after week and sing the psalms. If we share James Jordan's enthusiasm for the singing of psalms and see with him the vital need for their widespread use today, then we can join him by placing the Psalter centrally in our public worship and private devotion. We can not afford to bring up the silly protests and arguments and the excuses that have failed the church before. The church must instead encourage the work of those men and women who are producing better English translations and more suitable tunes, and devote resources to the production of new Psalters—lots of them.[24]

Christians ought to include the singing of psalms in their daily routines and in their homes to such an extent that all of us from the least to the greatest would pass the old bishop's test with ease. Most importantly, congregants must be flexible and patient enough to learn how to sing—and even chant—the psalms, and to use them abundantly in worship, in order that the Church might once again pick up where she left off. She must move the work of reformation forward, witnessing the defeat of the Lord's enemies and pressing the crown rights of King Jesus into every sphere. Reformation will not take place without the revival of psalm-singing. The Church of the Lord Jesus Christ is indebted to James Jordan and his passion to see her sing the songs her Lord gave her to sing.

Dear Duane,

Thank you for your encouraging paper. You've summarized my intentions perfectly.

I'll add something, since I'm supposed to. I have come to think more and more that "typology" has its origins, as it must of course, in the Triune life of God. The Spirit brings the impress of the Father's life upon the Son. And as the creation is made as a Daughter

---

24. No one composer or translator is going to be able to produce final, best versions of all 150 psalms, but each might be able to do two or three fine ones. The work of putting together the best arrangements of all the psalms for use in worship is a collective effort, over many generations, and will most certainly be an ever-changing project for many thousands of years to come. So rather than shooting for one perfect authoritative Psalter in our day, we ought to encourage the work of many to put together the best arrangements they can, and to use the best of what is available to us now.

of the Father and a Bride for the Son, the Spirit brings the impress of the Father progressively on the creation, bringing her to maturity and beyond. Hence, the progressive ouranification (heavenization) of all things eventually leads us to the Father (1 Cor 15:24).

As we see the diversity of heaven-forms in history, we can see that becoming more like God has an infinity of flavors. Each human being is uniquely being imprinted with the life of God and will manifest that life in ever more particular ways. The same is true of cultures. The same is true in churches, as we see in the diverse churches of Revelation 2 and 3.

It is this that we celebrate in liturgy. God brings His typological impress upon us in a variety of ways as we hear the Word, sing the Word, eat the Word in the Supper, and so forth. And we respond in a variety of ways. In the liturgy, and then in the outflow into life, as we one-another one another, we bring the impress of the life of God more fully to one another.

Well, those are just some musings that come after reading your essay, Duane. Thanks again for it.

Jim

9
Psalm 46

William Jordan

Psalm 46

for my brother, James Jordan

William Jordan

164

Dear Brother Bill,

Thank you for honoring me with this piece. Here we are: You the composer with an interest in the Bible and theology, and me the theologian with an interest in music. I guess that's how we grew up, hearing religion discussed in the home and hearing phonograph records of Beethoven symphonies, Chopin piano music, Bach passions, and lots of Lully, Couperin, Charpentier, DeLalande, Marais, and all the rest of the French baroque. Surely it also helped us to grow up in the Lutheran Church of America at the time when the service music by Regina Fryxell was full, glorious, and enthusiastic. It has a way of staying with you, doesn't it?

 Thanks again, so much.

Jim

PART THREE
Theology

10

A Pedagogical Paradigm for Understanding Reformed Eschatology

With Special Emphasis on Basic Characteristics of Christ's Person[1]

C. KEE HWANG

DISCUSSIONS OF ESCHATOLOGY HAVE generally been one-sided, focused on end-times considerations. However, the heart of eschatology is the doctrine of God's Kingdom and is not a question of *when* or *what* but rather *who*. It is not a schedule or a plan, but the Person of Jesus Christ. As the God-man, our Lord Jesus Christ represents both the whole Church and *panta* (all). Because He represents the whole church (including the invisible church), His people have already died and risen again with Him (Eph 2:5–6). Likewise, His death and resurrection have already transformed *panta* (all) beyond the cosmic scope. Thus, His death and resurrection indicate that the old creation, or "this age," has passed away; the new creation, or "the age to come," has been inaugurated in Christ.

The redemptive-historical event on the cross has already transformed His people as well as all things (*panta*), but this great transformation has not yet been realized and will be completed with His final coming. Therefore, Jesus Christ's exodus from Jerusalem (Luke 9:31) realized the coming of His kingdom. The destruction of the temple and Jerusalem in AD 70 should be understood as the end of the old Jewish age, that is, the covenant judgment of God upon His people of Israel due to the destruction of His body, the true temple, on the cross. The church consists of God's people upon whom the ends of both the old and new order have already arrived (1 Cor 10:11). With His final advent, all (*panta*) will be transformed into a new heaven and a new earth.

As such, the foundation and center of biblical eschatology is not time but the Person of Jesus Christ. A proper Christocentric eschatology frees the believer from end-time

---

1. This essay originated in a visiting lecture presented at Redeemer University College on November 15, 2001. It is printed here with modifications and the addition of footnotes.

PART THREE: THEOLOGY

related worries like man-made or natural disasters. Rather, all believers are to be faithful to their daily services (Rom 12:1) and the corporate worship of the Lord.

INTRODUCTION

As a token of esteem and affection for my dear colleague and fellow Westminster Seminary alumnus James B. Jordan, I dedicate to him the present work, the result of a renewed attempt to understand a Reformed eschatology with special emphasis on basic characteristics of Christ's Person, and I pray the Lord's blessing for his continued well-being. Dr. Jordan has been a prolific writer in the field of biblical theology with special interest in Christocentric perspectives.

With respect to transformation according to the Person of Jesus Christ, this essay is written for the pedagogical purpose of teaching Christians what Jesus Christ has already accomplished: how they have become God's children and enjoy His blessings here and now in this world.[2] On the one hand, I hope to thwart perspectives with time-bound eschatology, while on the other hand I hope to stress the notion that the death and resurrection signify the transformation of all (*panta*) based on His Person. I also hope to engage with "basic and decisive considerations already realized in the present identity ... of the Christian, and so too in the present life and mission of the church."[3]

The prevailing characteristic of biblical-theological eschatology has been a focus on the issue of time. There has been strong interest among Christians in the time of the second advent of Jesus, in terms of the linear progress of time—creation, fall, redemption, and the Second Advent of Jesus. This near-obsession with time has caused a stir in society as some cults have persuaded their members to abandon their everyday lives in order to "prepare" for Jesus' Second Advent. Some have even committed suicide.

However, biblical eschatology focuses on the Person of Jesus rather than on the time of His second coming. The crux of eschatology is not when or what but who Jesus is. The Gospels do not give us a blueprint of the future, but they connect all things to the Person of Jesus. There are several foci of biblical eschatology: covenant, redemptive history, and God's victory. All these focus on transformation according to the Person of Jesus Christ. In other words, we have experienced the transformation of all things through Jesus' life, death, and resurrection but we still wait for the great transformation of the cosmos along with His Second Advent.

The "already" dimension of what Jesus Christ accomplished is my emphasis. For example, concerning the concept of regeneration (Tit 3:5), we ignore the fact that "the foundation of regeneration in the Bible is first of all eschatological and cosmic rather than being focused on individual salvation."[4] In fact, a lot of theological concepts have

---

2. Richard B. Hays takes important notice of this: "Paul seeks *to teach his readers to read Scripture eschatologically*, mindful of God's final judgment of every human thought and action, while also looking forward in hope to God's final reconciliation of all things to himself" (*The Conversion of the Imagination: Paul as Interpreter of Israel's Scripture* [Grand Rapids: Eerdmans, 2005], xvi, emphasis mine).

3. Richard B. Gaffin, Jr., "The Usefulness of the Cross," *Westminster Theological Journal* 41 (1979) 228–46.

4. "Regeneration," in *The Eerdmans Bible Dictionary*, ed. Allen C. Meyers (Grand Rapids: Eerdmans, 1987), 877–78.

paid little attention to the Whole Church Person, which I will explain later, focusing too much attention instead on our individual responsibilities as Christians. First, let us observe the distinctiveness of Jesus Christ's Person as the Bible suggests.

THE UNIQUENESS OF CHRIST'S PERSON[5]

In order to know a person, we must look at what that person has done and what effect his works have had. To perceive the Person of Christ, we must examine His works and the changes effected by them. Christ's works establish the foundational characteristic of the Gospel on the basis of His Person.

Christ's Characteristics in the Gospel[6]

I begin this discussion with 1 Corinthians 15:1–5, in which the Apostle Paul defines the Gospel through Jesus' works.

> Moreover, brethren, I declare to you the gospel which I preached to you, which also you received and in which you stand, by which also you are saved, if you hold fast that word which I preached to you—unless you believed in vain. For I delivered to you first of all that which I also received: that Christ died for our sins according to the Scriptures, and that He was buried, and that He rose again the third day according to the Scriptures, and that He was seen by Cephas, then by the twelve.

In this passage Paul summarizes the gospel he preached to the Corinthian church and explains how this gospel caused the transformation of believers. Verses 3–5 establish what Paul preached as the gospel. Some theologians say that the gospel consists of four verbs without interpretation.[7] The author of the Gospel of John sees Jesus' dying, being buried, rising, and appearing as the *journey* of the Son of God and interprets the cross using a journey motif (Jesus' coming from and returning to the Father). In other words, these four events can be seen as part of the Christological movement.[8] The Bible refers to them—to this Christological movement—as the gospel. How are we to understand this gospel? We must look to the works of Jesus to discover the basic aspects of His Person.

The Believers' Eschatological Transformation

In verse 1, Paul says to the believers of the Corinthian church, "I declare to you the gospel which I preached to you, which also you received *and in which you stand*" (*en hō kai hestēkate*). And verse 2 refers to this gospel as that *"by which also you are saved* (*di' hou kai sōzesthe*), if you hold fast that word which I preached to you—unless you believed in vain." Though these words first apply to the Corinthian church, they then bring the

---

5. C. Kee Hwang, *Jesus, the Church and I: A Redemptive Historical Interpretation of the New Testament in the Light of the Person of Jesus Christ with Indications for Homiletical Application* (Seoul: Sung Kwang Publishing, 1988), 17–20, 232–35, 268–83. This book is in Korean.

6. Ibid., 257–62.

7. J. Gresham Machen, "What is the Gospel?," *Union Seminary Review* 38 (1927) 164.

8. Joel B. Green, "Death of Jesus," in *Dictionary of Jesus and the Gospels*, eds. Joel B. Green, et al. (Downers Grove, IL: InterVarsity Press, 1993), 162.

transformation to all who read and believe in them. These transformations that apply to believers living on any part of the earth are based solely on the redemptive work of our Lord Jesus Christ accomplished on the cross in Jerusalem. As such, the events of the Gospel must be so unique that they transform all believers regardless of the boundaries of time and space.

Understanding this transformation of believers requires an eschatological reasoning.[9] By *eschatological* I mean nothing having to do with the end time, but everything to do with Christ's redemptive work. While redemption has already been accomplished on the cross, its application, the redemption of our body, has not yet been completed. A believer must understand that he or she has already been saved by the grace of Jesus Christ and is also *being* saved, and that the redemption of the body will be completed at Christ's second coming (Rom 8:23).[10] The *being saved*—that is, the present aspects of a believer's transformation—means that we as believers are being transformed into the image of Jesus through the Spirit of the Lord (2 Cor 3:17–18).

The Uniqueness that Transcends Time and Space

As Jesus dies and lives again, believers also die and live again with Him, transformed to be seated with Him in the heavenly realm (Rom 6:3–9; Eph 2:5–6).[11] This phenomenon provides a living hope for those yet unborn at the time of Jesus' death and resurrection. "According to His great mercy, He has caused us to be born again to a living hope through the resurrection of Jesus Christ from the dead" (1 Pet 1:3 NASB). Here Peter insists that God the Father has given His elect, who are "strangers in the world" (1 Pet 1:1 NIV), new birth through Christ's resurrection although they have not seen Jesus Christ. So Christ is not confined to the New Testament. Moses believed in Christ (Heb 11:26). Christ is both David's son and David's Lord (Ps 110:1; Matt 22:44; Acts 2:34–35).

How can such paradoxes be? How do we understand Jesus Christ who was revealed in the Scripture? Who is this Jesus, that His redemptive work done in first-century Palestine allowed the Corinthian church to "stand" (1 Cor 15:1) in Macedonia? Jesus died, was buried, rose on the third day, and appeared to people in Jerusalem. How is it that by these events, the Corinthian church, far away from Palestine both chronologically and geographically, was saved (1 Cor 15.2)? Who is Jesus Christ that those who received the first epistle of Peter in Asia Minor did not even see Jesus but were born again and transformed (1 Pet 1:1–8)?[12]

---

9. Hays, *Conversion of the Imagination*, 11.

10. Three tenses are found in 2 Corinthians 1:10 "who *delivered* us from so great a death, and *does deliver* us; in whom we trust that He *will still deliver us*."

11. G. R. Beasley-Murray, "Dying and Rising with Christ," in *Dictionary of Paul and His Letters*, eds. Gerald F. Hawthorne, et al. (Downers Grove, IL: InterVarsity Press, 1993), 218–22.

12. No other person able to do such work has existed in the history of mankind. For example, Lazarus (John 11) was also a person who experienced the works done by "four verbs without interpretation." Lazarus also died, was buried, rose, and appeared to people. However, believing in the person of Lazarus and his work does not result in the believer's transformation. Koreans undoubtedly believe that King Seh-Jong created and spread the use of "Han-geul," the written Korean language; we do not deny that General Lee, Soon-shin, built the Turtle Ship (an ironclad war ship) that brought great victory against the Japanese invasion of Korea in 1592. However, our belief and certainty that these events occurred do not transform us.

Transformation happens only when one believes Jesus' works of salvation. Nothing like the work of Jesus has ever been or ever shall be. Jesus' works are not limited to the time in which they happened nor are they limited by location. Jesus' life, death, and resurrection are not confined to the first century and the region of Palestine. The effect of His redemptive work transcends time and space. However, most people understand Him simply as a historical figure.

The gospel consists of four events: Jesus' (1) dying, (2) being buried, (3) rising and (4) appearing. Inasmuch as these movements were horrific and shocking, they cause a miraculous transformation in believers. The Person of Jesus, the subject of the four verbs that make up the Gospel, merits further investigation. However, the gospel has seldom been explained with respect to the Person of Jesus. Rather, the Gospel has been understood with regard to His works accomplished on the Cross. In other words, the Gospel of redemption has been applied in light of His works rather than His Person. Lacking a biblical concept of Christ's Person, sermons from pulpits have degenerated into moral and ethical lessons, at least in Korea where Confucianism and Buddhism, along with other folk beliefs like Shamanism, have been predominant. Korean churches are drowning in various practices of syncretism.

CHRIST'S WHOLE CHURCH PERSON[13]

Jesus Christ is not an ordinary person. Let us consider how the Scriptures describe the Person of Jesus Christ (cf. Rom 1:3–4). His Person should not be considered in terms of His divinity and humanity as described in systematic theology, but rather with redemptive-historical perspectives as revealed in biblical theology. I contend that this perspective of the Person of Jesus Christ is the heuristic lens for understanding all of the major doctrines of biblical theology. Such a thesis may serve a pedagogical purpose by introducing Reformed eschatology into Korean churches.

> Now when they had departed, behold, an angel of the Lord appeared to Joseph in a dream, saying, "Arise, take the young Child and His mother, flee to Egypt, and stay there until I bring you word; for Herod will seek the young Child to destroy Him." When he arose, he took the young Child and His mother by night and departed for Egypt, and was there until the death of Herod, that it might be fulfilled which was spoken by the Lord through the prophet, saying, "Out of Egypt I called My Son." (Matt 2:13–15)

After an angel of the Lord appeared to Joseph in a dream, he took Mary and Jesus down to Egypt to escape Herod, and they stayed there until Herod died. According to the gospel of Matthew, this happened so that a prophecy could be fulfilled. Instead of simply quoting Hosea 11:1, Matthew writes: *"that it might be fulfilled* which was spoken by the Lord through the prophet, saying, 'Out of Egypt I called My Son'" (2:15).

---

13. I coined this term to mean that Christ is representative of the whole invisible church since Adam and Eve, up to His Second Advent, including the New Jerusalem Church in heaven.

PART THREE: THEOLOGY

In this way, Matthew relates Jesus' deliverance from Egypt to the fulfillment of Hosea 11:1,[14] in which Hosea recounted how God had faithfully brought Israel out of Egypt in the exodus under Moses' leadership. Matthew is comparing God's "son" Israel to Jesus, the One who will be revealed as God's true Son.[15] As Moses was rescued from Pharaoh's edict to kill the Israelites' baby boys (Exod 1:15—2:10), Jesus is spared from the slaughter of the innocents in Bethlehem.[16] In fact, this infancy narrative points to Jesus as a new Moses.[17]

It is important to note that Jesus' exodus and the Israelites' exodus (including at least 600,000 soldiers) are treated *identically*, which signifies that even though Jesus is but one Person, His Person is *identical* to the entire nation of Israel. Further identifying Christ with many saints, following Matthew's testimony in 27:51b–53, D. C. Allison states that "Jesus was not the only one to rise from the dead: so did many saints. Thus the Messiah's vindication cannot be viewed in isolation. Rather, Jesus' resurrection inaugurated the general resurrection."[18]

Later in chapter 2, Matthew again identifies Jesus with Israel:

> Then Herod, when he saw that he was deceived by the wise men, was exceedingly angry; and he sent forth and put to death all the male children who were in Bethlehem and in all its districts, from two years old and under, according to the time which he had determined from the wise men. Then was fulfilled what was spoken by Jeremiah the prophet, saying: "A voice was heard in Ramah, lamentation, weeping, and great mourning, Rachel weeping for her children, refusing to be comforted, because they are no more." (Matt 2:16–18)

The *Reformation Study Bible*'s note on Matthew 2:18 provides this explanation:

> The writer of Matthew cites Jeremiah 31:15, a verse taken from the middle of a prophecy about the return of Israel from exile. Rachel, the matriarch, represents Israel in her weeping, and the departure of the Lord's Christ to Egypt is like the departure of Rachel's sons Joseph and Benjamin to Egypt in Genesis. The citation in Matthew thus connects the sorrow preceding the exodus from Egypt with the sorrow in Babylon prior to the return and with Israel's sorrow at this time in Christ's life.[19]

In addition, we ought not to miss that the writer of Matthew identified the children of Israel in Jeremiah's prophecy with Jesus. According to the authors of the *ESV Study Bible*, Matthew interprets the horrible killing of babies in Bethlehem as follows: "Jeremiah used the personification to describe the mothers of Israel (Rachel) mourning for their chil-

---

14. R. T. France, *Matthew: Evangelist and Teacher* (Grand Rapids: Zondervan, 1989), 168.

15. *ESV Study Bible*, ed. Lane Dennis (Wheaton, IL: Crossway, 2008), 1823.

16. Craig L. Blomberg, "Mathew," in *Commentary on the New Testament Use of the Old Testament*, eds. G. K. Beale and D. A. Carson (Grand Rapids: Baker, 2007), 7. See also Raymond E. Brown, *The Birth of the Messiah: A Commentary on the Infancy Narratives in the Gospels of Matthew and Luke* (Garden City, NY: Doubleday, 1977), 214–16.

17. Blomberg, "Matthew," 8.

18. D. C. Allison, Jr., "Eschatology," in *Dictionary of Jesus and the Gospels*, 208.

19. *NIV Spirit of the Reformation Study Bible* (Grand Rapids: Zondervan, 2003), 1546.

dren who had been removed from the land and carried off into exile, leaving Israel no longer a nation and considered dead (Jer 31:35). Like the exile, the *attempt on Jesus' life was intended to wipe out the chosen one of God.*"[20]

The Person of Jesus is not only to be understood as a historical figure who lived and died in the land of Palestine during the first century, but also as a corporate Person whose body now expands without limit through time and space.

> As he journeyed he came near Damascus, suddenly a light shone around him from heaven. Then he fell to the ground, and heard a voice saying to him, "Saul, Saul, why are you persecuting Me?" (Acts 9:3, 4; cf. Acts 22:7; 26:14)

Saul went to the high priest and asked for letters to the synagogues in Damascus so that if he found any of the Lord's disciples, he might take them as prisoners to Jerusalem. When Jesus speaks to Saul, He does not say, "Why do you persecute my disciples?" but rather, "Why do you persecute *Me*?" thus *identifying* Himself with His disciples. To persecute Christians is to persecute Christ.[21] Matthew 25:45 (cf. also v. 40) may be interpreted similarly as Jesus *identifying* Himself with His people. "Then He will answer them, saying, 'Assuredly, I say to you, inasmuch as you did not do it to one of the least of these, you did not do it to Me.'"

Later, Paul speaks of Christ this way:

> For the love of Christ compels us, because we judge thus: that if One died for all, then all died; and He died for all, that those who live should live no longer for themselves, but for Him who died for them and rose again. (2 Cor 5:14–15)

What does the *all* refer to in these verses? What is its significance in this sentence? "One died for all, then all died." *All* refers to all of us who died in Christ and now live in Him (see vv. 15–17; cf. 4:10–14), that is, all believers.[22] We must remember that all who trust in Him comprise the Body of Christ, including those who are yet unborn, that is, the invisible Church.[23]

There is no doubt that these words bear a substitutionary force. Philip E. Hughes writes:

> For this conclusion cannot be valid except on the understanding that Christ died in the stead of all, as their substitute. On this ground alone is there justification of speaking as Paul does here of a logical *identification of all with Christ* in His death.[24]

Athanasius also clearly writes with this passage in mind: "The death of all was consummated in the Lord's body, and both death and corruption were utterly destroyed

---

20. *ESV Study Bible*, 1823, emphasis mine.
21. Ibid., 2098.
22. *NIV Spirit of the Reformation Study Bible*, 2230.
23. In spite of the strangeness of the term "invisible Church," pointed out by Douglas Wilson, "The Church: Visible or Invisible," in *The Federal Vision*, eds. Steve Wilkins and Duane Garner (Monroe, LA: Athanasius Press, 2004), 263–69.
24. Philip E. Hughes, *Commentary on the Second Epistle to the Corinthians*, New International Commentary on the New Testament (Grand Rapids: Eerdmans, 1962), 193, emphasis mine.

PART THREE: THEOLOGY

through the Word who was present in it."[25] So also here, Jesus' Person that encompasses the Whole Church of both the old and new covenant is reconfirmed. He represents the Whole Church Person. "Now to Abraham and his Seed were the promises made. He does not say, 'And to seeds,' as of many, but as of one, 'And to your Seed,' who is Christ" (Gal 3:16).

With this passage from Galatians in mind, consider the following: Abraham's descendants who came out of Egypt numbered over 600,000 people. Despite this enormous number, all Israel is called *one*. Israel is progressively reduced to a remnant,[26] then to the "Servant of Yahweh" in Isaiah 40–66, then to the "Son of Man" in Daniel 7:13–14,[27] and finally to One Person, Jesus Christ.[28] Finally redemptive history has reaches its center. After Christ's death and resurrection an important change appears within redemptive-historical progression.

Second, redemptive history after the time of Jesus no longer leads from the many to the One as in the old covenant period, "but on the contrary *from the One, in progressive advance, to the many*."[29] Now the procession advances from Christ to those who believe in Him—to the apostles, to the seventy disciples, to the one hundred twenty disciples on whom the Holy Spirit was poured out at Pentecost, and so on. The number of believers increased so rapidly that many thousands of Jews came into the Church (Acts 21:20). For pedagogical purposes, the Body of One, Christ, may be understood by its chronological progress in history: the first century Church, the fifth century Church . . . the eighteenth century church . . . the twenty-first century Church, and so on, up to His second coming.

Similarly, Peter J. Leithart recognizes that N. T. Wright "finds support in the use of 'sperma' in the LXX of Genesis 15:13; 17:7–8; 22:17–18, and in the light of 1 Corinthians 12:12, the Christ of Galatians 3:16 could refer to the *totus Christus*, Head and body."[30] N. T. Wright observes that "in the LXX 'sperma' in the singular, when referring to human offspring, is in fact almost always collective rather than singular."[31] He also insists that Paul uses of "Christ" in a representative or corporate sense:

> Paul understands "Christ" as "Messiah," carrying the significance of the one "in whom" the people of God is summed up precisely as the people of God; and Galatians 3:23–9 is in fact one of the most important bits of evidence of this. Many of Paul's frequent "incorporative" expressions cluster together in verses 26–29, in

---

25. Quoted in Hughes, *Second Epistle to the Corinthians*, 195.

26. Since the Israelites, as the covenantal people of God, were not faithful to the mission assigned to them, there next appears a "remnant" as representative of the people, of which the prophets speak.

27. That "Son of Man" represents the saints is shown in James B. Jordan, *The Handwriting on the Wall: A Commentary on the Book of Daniel* (Powder Springs, GA: American Vision, 2007), 395, 406–8.

28. Oscar Cullmann, *Christ and Time*, trans. Floyd V. Filson, rev. ed. (Philadelphia: Westminster, 1964), 115–16.

29. Ibid., 117, emphasis mine.

30. Peter J. Leithart, *The Priesthood of the Plebs: A Theology of Baptism* (Eugene, OR: Wipf & Stock, 2003), 200–201.

31. N. T. Wright, *The Climax of the Covenant: Christ and the Law in Pauline Theology* (Minneapolis: Fortress, 1993), 158.

just that passage where the worldwide church is affirmed to be "one" and therefore to be "the seed of Abraham."[32]

Third, Abraham's descendants consist not only of his physical bloodline but also of those who believe in the Lord (Gal 3:7, 26, 29). Therefore, all believers under both the old covenant and new covenant are sons of Abraham who belong to the One, Jesus Christ, the representative and head of the invisible "Church as the Whole Church including those who are yet unborn."[33] According to Galatians 3:7, 26, and 29, the invisible Church as the Whole Church may be summed up this way: in the Old Testament the many are narrowed down into One, and in the New Testament, the One broadens out to become many.[34]

In summary, there is an invisible church that consists of all God's people in the Old Testament and all believers in the New Testament, including those who are in Christ and yet unborn. The Whole Church is covered within the "One Person of Christ." Therefore, the Lord's Whole Church of the old and new covenant must be *identified* with the Person of Jesus Christ. In other words, the Church, the body of Christ, is regarded as the corporate solidarity of those who "have been united with him in a death like his, and united with him in a resurrection like his" (Rom 6:5 NIV). Those whose old selves have been crucified with Him have also done away with "the body of sin" (Rom 6:6), that is, the kingdom of darkness or "humanity outside Christ."[35]

All believers are mysteriously united with Jesus Christ. They died with Him, were buried with Him (Rom 6:4–6), were raised up together with Him, and are seated with Him in heavenly realm (Eph 2:5–6, Col 2:12–13). He is the representative of the Whole Church Person, including the heavenly Jerusalem Church (Heb 12:22). Therefore, it can be said that believers' eschatological transformation is enabled because of the Person of Jesus. The principle of both representative and Immanuel can be understood in a concrete and reasonable way through His Person.

CHRIST'S *PANTA* PERSON[36]

The Person of Christ is bigger than the universe; it extends into *panta* (all things). Let us closely examine this aspect of our Lord's Person. "And He put all things under His feet, and gave Him to be head over all things to the church, which is His body, the fullness of Him who fills all in all" (Eph 1:22–23).

As the italicized phrases indicate, Christ is the head of the church, which is above all (*panta*). As when we speak of a present-day head of government, the term "head" points

---

32. Ibid., 165.

33. The phrase "those who are yet unborn" refers to those who will be future Christians as God's elect.

34. Ibid., 117–18.

35. Tom Holland, *Contours of Pauline Theology: A Radical New Survey of the Influences on Paul's Biblical Writings* (Fearn, Ross-shire: Christian Focus, 2004), 85–110, 288.

36. I coined this term to mean that Christ is the representative of all creatures without exception: things in heaven and on or under earth, visible and invisible, things of past, present, and future. However no pantheistic connotation is intended by this term.

PART THREE: THEOLOGY

to Christ's preeminence as Lord. Thus, Christ is the head of all (v. 22) and simultaneously the head of the church. Peter J. Leithart explains the dual meaning of Christ's headship:

> Headship implies authority and rule. Christ is also said to "fill all things (*panta*) in every way"; in fulfillment of God's command to Adam, He "fills" the whole creation with His presence. At the same time, the church is called the "fullness" of Christ (1:23). Christ is present among His people in a way that He is not present in the whole creation, and His headship over the church is different from His headship over all things. There is a headship over the church, and there is a headship over the world; there is a filling appropriate to the church, and a filling appropriate to the creation as a whole. We distort the Scriptures if either of these truths is denied, or if either is subordinated to the other.[37]

Considering these two implications of Christ's headship, we must recognize that no authority can be allowed above the Church in this world. God set Christ as the head *over all things* (*hyper panta*) to the church.[38] Christ has so identified Himself with His church that she, filled by Christ,[39] may fill all creation as Christ's representative (Eph 1:23).[40]

> For by Him all things were created that are in heaven and that are on earth, visible and invisible, whether thrones or dominions or principalities or powers. All things were created through Him and for Him. And He is before all things, and in Him all things consist. And He is the head of the body, the church, who is the beginning, the firstborn from the dead, that in all things He may have the preeminence. (Col 1:16–18)

In the expression "He [Jesus Christ] is the head of the body, the church,"[41] the church is included in what is called "the body," and this body includes "all" in verses 16 and 17. The definition of "all" can be found in verse 16: all "that are in heaven and that are on earth, visible and invisible, whether thrones or dominions or principalities or powers."

Therefore, all (*panta*) is included in the body of Christ, the Church. There is nothing that is not included in the church, the body of Christ.[42] The "holy world," the church, or the body of Christ, has a larger dimension than the whole universe and yet no less dimension than all (*panta*). Therefore, the Person of Christ may be called the *Panta* Person.

We therefore draw the following conclusion: Christ is the *Panta* Person as well as the Whole Church Person who transcends time and space. Time and space are mere components of His creation. Nevertheless, the Creator, our Lord Jesus Christ, has been conceived as a figure bound by time, space, and His created order. Such a formulation of

---

37. Peter J. Leithart, *The Kingdom and the Power: Rediscovering the Centrality of the Church* (Phillipsburg, NJ: P&R, 1993), 62.

38. *Kai auton edōken kephalēn hyper panta tē ekklēsia* (dative: "to the church, for the church").

39. *ESV Study Bible*, 2264.

40. This issue is beyond the scope of this paper. I only state the truth that Christ, as the head of the Church, may be conceived as the *Panta* Person.

41. *Hē kephalē tou sōmatos tēs ekklēsias*. The second genitive in this phrase is to be construed as a genitive of apposition. Cf. Maximilian Zerwick, *Biblical Greek*, trans. Joseph Smith (Roma: Editrice Pontifico Istituto Biblico,1994), 17.

42. A. T. Robertson, *Word Pictures in the New Testament*, vol. 4: *The Epistles of Paul* (Grand Rapids: Baker, 1931), 478–80.

the Person of Christ is a minimalist understanding, especially in contrast with the view that the Person of Jesus Christ is the Creator who contains the entire universe and is not bound by time and space. Understanding of the Person of Jesus Christ in this way has pedagogical value for the Church.[43]

By overlooking the *Panta* Person of Christ, theologians in recent times have erred in most theological disciplines, especially biblical eschatology. Eschatological subjects have been obsessed with end-time considerations like the timing of Jesus' second coming and its related phenomena. In addition, influential scholars focus especially on the atoning nature of Christ's death and resurrection without due regard for its eschatological ramifications.

ESCHATOLOGICAL TRANSFORMATION

How should we conceive of the eschatological transformation in relation to His death and resurrection? As observed above, Jesus Christ represents both the Whole Church Person and the *Panta* Person. The transformation of *panta* (all) has already been initiated. However its completeness will be finally realized upon His second coming.[44] We should examine the dimensions of both individual believers and *panta* (all).

The Believers' Eschatological Transformation

By Christ's death and resurrection, a new creation came into being. All believers mysteriously united with Him are transformed into the same image of Jesus Christ by the Spirit of the Lord (2 Cor 3:17–18). Therefore, this transformation based on the Whole Church Person or the *Panta* Person of Jesus Christ may be no less than a pneumatological transformation. It is the passing away of the old, condemned person and the restoring as new in the eschatological transformation. It has already been granted to every believer in accordance with His death and resurrection.

All believers must firmly believe that they should enjoy their abundant heavenly graces, here and now, in Christ. Many biblical passages testify that we, as believers, are in His kingdom:

> He [God] has delivered us from the domain of darkness and transferred us to the kingdom of his beloved Son, in whom we have redemption, the forgiveness of sins. (Col 1:13–14 ESV)

> Truly, truly, I say to you, whoever hears my word and believes him who sent me has eternal life. He does not come into judgment, but has passed from death to life. (John 5:24–25 ESV)

---

43. It is my hope that this paper serves to correct the minimalist's understanding of the Person of Jesus Christ as one bound by the constraints of time and space.

44. Albert Wolters, "Living the Future Now: The Earthliness of Our Eschatological Task" (paper presented at the opening lecture of the first semester of Kosin University in 1999), 1–10. Cf. Sinclair Ferguson's insistence that "The vision of the future in Romans 8:20–21 anticipates the liberation and renewal, not the destruction and re-creation *ex nihilo*, of the universe" (*The Holy Spirit*, Contours of Christian Theology [Downers Grove, IL: InterVarsity, 1996], 254).

PART THREE: THEOLOGY

This transformation is tangibly enacted through baptism and the sacraments.[45] The Bible also teaches both definitive and progressive sanctification of all believers even though many struggle with sufferings and difficulties for His sake. The following are graces often unrealized by believers.

One Who is Seated in the Heavenly Places

"Even when we were dead in our trespasses, [God] made us alive together with Christ—by grace you have been saved—and raised us up with him and seated us with him in the heavenly places in Christ Jesus" (Eph 2:5–6 ESV). Being "made alive together with Christ" (v. 5) means that this transformation is a work of the Spirit. In 1 Corinthians 15:45, this Spirit is called "a life-giving Spirit." That "the last Adam became a life-giving Spirit" is a redemptive-historical transformation from the first Adam,[46] by which all believers are also being transformed into His likeness (2 Cor 3:17–18). Christians are enthroned in heaven because they are in Christ.[47]

One Who Has Two Lives

All believers have a life aside from the physical life (*psychē*) that unbelievers have,[48] for we have eternal life (*zoē*) which "is in His Son" (1 John 5:11; John 1:4). Article 35 of the Belgic Confession says, "Now those who are born again have *two lives* in them. The one is physical and temporal—they have it from the moment of their first birth, and it is common to all. The other is spiritual and heavenly, and is given them in their second birth; it comes through the Word of the gospel in the communion of the body of Christ; and this life is common to God's elect only" (emphasis mine).

Jesus Christ says that "everyone who lives and believes in me shall never die" (John 11:26 ESV). The main verb, "die," is used in future tense in English translation. However, in reality it refers to the present. Leon Morris writes,

> It means that the moment a man puts his trust in Jesus he begins to experience that life of *the age to come which cannot be touched by death*. Jesus is bringing Martha *a present power, not the promise of a future good*. . . . [When He says that everyone who lives and believes on Jesus will never die,] Jesus does not of course mean that the believer will not die physically. . . . He means that he will not die in the sense in which death has eternal significance. He will not die with reference to the age to come. He has eternal life, *the life of the age to come*.[49]

---

45. Beasley-Murray, "Dying and Rising with Christ," 218–22.

46. Richard B. Gaffin, Jr., *The Centrality of the Resurrection* (Grand Rapids: Baker, 1978), 78–97.

47. Leithart, *Kingdom and Power*, 68.

48. I refer to life (*psychē*) as the regular manifestation of the whole person, both physical body and soul. See also E. Schweizer, "ψυξή," in *Theological Dictionary of the New Testament: Abridged in One Volume*, ed. Gerhard Kittel and Gerhard Friedrich, trans. Geoffrey W. Bromiley (Grand Rapids: Eerdmans, 1985), 1347.

49. Leon Morris, *The Gospel according to John*, New International Commentary on the New Testament (Grand Rapids: Eerdmans, 1971), 350–51, emphasis mine.

Stanley E. Porter also comments on the use of future tense in English versions: "The context shows that a Future verb need not necessarily implicate future reference. Rather, Jesus seems to be using it as an emphatic contrast to the Aorist Subjunctive (*apothanē*)."[50]

One Who Is Victorious Over the World

First John 5:4–10 reveals that everyone born of God overcomes the world. To be victorious over the world means being victorious over darkness, sin, Satan's rule, and death. There are three that bear witness: the Spirit, the water, and the blood, and the three are in agreement (1 John 5:7–8). "Overcoming the world" is not to be construed to mean that all believers will avoid facing difficulties. But we will overcome them rather than fall before them because God never allows us to be tempted beyond what we are able to bear (1 Cor 10:13). How many among us are boldly enjoying the victorious life?

One Who Has the Power of the Resurrection

Believers already have the power of the resurrection. In his fourth prayer in the Epistle to the Ephesians (1:15ff.), Paul prays "that you may know . . . his incomparably great power for us who believe" (NIV). Paul hopes for the believers of the Church of Ephesus to know just *what* the mighty power is (v. 19).[51] According to Paul, that mighty power is the power of Jesus Christ's resurrection, "which He worked in Christ when He raised Him from the dead and seated Him at His right hand in the heavenly places" (v. 20). This verse lays bare the truth that the power of the resurrection already exists in the believer. However, most do not seem to realize that they possess this wonderful gift.

One Who is Greater than John the Baptist

Believers dwelling in Christ's Kingdom are already greater than John the Baptist. Matthew 11:11 reads, "Assuredly, I say to you, among those born of women there has not risen one greater than John the Baptist; but he who is least in the kingdom of heaven is greater than he." Are we able to find anyone who is not born of woman? In other words, John the Baptist must be the greatest man among all humanity. However, we who are already in His kingdom are greater than John the Baptist. Of course, the concept of being "great" is not defined by a popular scale, but rather by the values of His Kingdom (Matt 20:26; Luke 22:26).

One Who Fulfilled the Law

Believers have fulfilled all requirements of the Law (Rom 8:4). Romans 10:4 says, "For Christ is the *end of the law* for righteousness to everyone who believes." Here, "the end of the law" does not necessarily mean it is finished, but rather that it is the goal and aim. The demands of the law can be only satisfied by the work of Jesus on the cross. "For what

---

50. Stanley E. Porter, *Verbal Aspect in the Greek of the New Testament, with Reference to Tense and Mood* (New York: Lang, 1989), 425

51. *Kai ti to hyperballon megethos tēs dynameōs autou eis hēmas tous pisteuontas* ("and what is the exceeding greatness of His power toward us who believe"). Paul did not ask them to check *whether* the power of resurrection exists, but to find out *what* sort of power they already have in them. In verse 19, the interrogative pronoun *ti* ("what") assumes that all believers have the power of resurrection in them.

the law could not do in that it was weak through the flesh, God did by sending His own Son in the likeness of sinful flesh, on account of sin: He condemned sin in the flesh, that the righteous requirement of the law might be fulfilled in us who do not walk according to the flesh but according to the Spirit" (Rom 8:3–4).

Jesus came to this world to accomplish this goal. Preachers are to proclaim that the believers must regard themselves as having already fulfilled the righteous requirements of the law. In appreciation for His accomplishment, every believer must make every effort to achieve God's will according to the law.

Other Graces Given to Believers

The following benedictions have also been directed toward all believers: righteous one, saint (1 Cor 1:2), true worshiper (John 4:23), perfect one (Col 1:28), God's son (Eph 1:5), royal priesthood (1 Pet 2:9), and so forth. These titles are eschatological blessings. We have already tasted heaven (Heb 6:4–6), the wedding banquet of the Lamb (1 Cor 10:16; Rev 19:6). Every Christian, as the wife of the Lamb, is already in the city of the living God (the Holy City), New Jerusalem (Heb 12:18–24; Rev 21:9), which is a new heaven and a new earth (Rev 21:1; 22:15). All of these are due to the redeeming work on the cross of Jesus who is both the Whole Church Person and the *Panta* Person. All believers already have been blessed with such special privileges here and now as mentioned above, but all will be brought to completion through Jesus' Second Advent. The Church should put an emphasis on these graces given to all believers so that they may have an assurance of their salvation and enjoy themselves as Christians in this world.

Eschatological Transformation of All (Panta)

Jesus' redemptive work of dying on the cross and rising again transformed not only the individual believer but also all things (*panta*). The transformation extends beyond the Whole Church or the whole cosmos. It has occurred in every realm—in all (*panta*).

New Creation in Christ

> Therefore, if anyone is in Christ, he is a new creation; old things have passed away; behold, all things have become new. Now all things are of God, who has reconciled us to Himself through Jesus Christ, and has given us the ministry of reconciliation. (2 Cor 5:17–18)

Here Paul explains that believers do not live for themselves but for Jesus Christ who died and was raised again (v. 15). The result of these pivotal events of Christ's life, death, and resurrection is in verse 16: "Therefore, from now on, we regard no one according to the flesh. Even though we have known Christ according to the flesh, yet now we know Him thus no longer." A radical change is necessary for Christian fellowship as members of the "one new man" in Christ (Eph 2:15). There is no place for nepotism and favoritism in Christian fellowship.

Verse 17 declares that there is transformation of all (*panta*) through Jesus' death and resurrection. Being created anew as a man-in-Christ is part of the eschatological transformation into the new heaven and the new earth. At first glance, verse 17 may be read as having to do with a subjective experience, but in reality it deals with eschatological newness.[52] In other words, this expression reveals that a new eschatological development, not only for believers but for all (*panta*), has been unfolded through the coming of Christ.

God's Reconciliation with All (*Panta*)

God's reconciliation with the world is described in 2 Corinthians 5:18–19. The object God's reconciliation is "us" in verse 18. Verse 19 repeats the preceding verse, but the "us" of verse 18 is magnified as "world" in verse 19.[53] The relationship between "in Christ" and "God was reconciling" in verse 19 has been long debated, and therefore it is difficult to come to any definite interpretation here.[54] However, it is clear that the author emphatically explains God's reconciliation of the world to Himself.

This verse implies that the effect of reconciliation is on a scale beyond a cosmic level because it is applied through man. Just as man's sin brought the fall of all (*panta*), by restoring man, all the cosmos will be restored. A similar description of cosmic reconciliation is found in Colossians 1:19–20.

The Passing of the Old

Paul contrasts the old and the new in 2 Corinthians 5:17. He explains that the old is changed into the new. The transformation began with Jesus' death and resurrection. G. K. Beale insists on the following: "Christ's death was the beginning of the end of the old creation and the inauguration of a new creation. . . . Christ's death is not just any death, but it is the beginning of the destruction of the entire world."[55]

We must not limit Jesus Christ to the first century and to Palestine, ignoring both His Whole Church Person and the *Panta* Person.

"The old has gone" means that sin (1 John 3:5), Satan (1 John 3:8), and death have passed away. Therefore, Jesus' death and resurrection inaugurate the end of darkness, the end of sin, the end of Satan, and the end of death. They also mean the end of bondage and of this Age because Jesus has appeared at the end of the world (Heb 9:26). In this sense, believers are those "upon whom the ends of the ages have come" (1 Cor 10:11).

---

52. George E. Ladd, *A Theology of the New Testament*, rev. ed. (Grand Rapids: Eerdmans, 1993), 521.

53. C. K. Barrett writes, "The absence of the article (*kosmon katallassōn*) has the effect of the object of emphasizing the nature rather than the particularity of the objects of the verb—it was a whole world he reconciled" (*The Second Epistle to the Corinthians* [New York: Harper & Row, 1973], 177). I have transliterated and italicized the Greek phrase in this quotation.

54. For two different views about the way of God's reconciliation, cf. Hughes, *Second Epistle to the Corinthians*, 207.

55. G. K Beale, "The Eschatological Conception of New Testament Theology," in *Eschatology in Bible and Theology: Evangelical Essays at the Dawn of a New Millennium*, eds. Kent E. Brower and Mark W. Elliot (Downers Grove, IL: InterVarsity Press, 1997), 19.

PART THREE: THEOLOGY

Rethinking Jesus' Death and Resurrection

We need a renewed understanding of Jesus' death and resurrection. "We can think of Christ's life, and particularly death and resurrection, as a diamond which represents the new creation."[56] His resurrection represents the general resurrection and the beginning of the new world. His death, the death of the true Temple (John 2:21), portends the destruction of Herod's temple built of stones. Furthermore, His death also represents the destruction of the old *panta*. Therefore, the catastrophic destruction of the Jerusalem temple in AD 70 represents the end of old Judaism. James B. Jordan explains: "At the destruction of Jerusalem, the Jewish sun went into black eclipse, mourning in sackcloth, and the Jewish moon went into red eclipse, the blood-red of sacrifice. Immediately after the destruction of Jerusalem, God began shaking down the nations, darkening their suns and moons, and replacing them with the light of the Sun of Righteousness, whose rising brings healing in His wings (Mal 4:2).[57]

Jesus' death is the "judgment of this world" (John 12:31), the casting out of the demons (John 16:11), and the destruction of the doomed (John 17:12; 2 Thess 2:3). Jesus Himself is both the end (*eschaton*) and its content.

CONCLUSION

The Person of Christ unites two distinct natures: divinity and humanity. He is both fully God and fully man in one Person. Furthermore, this Person is the Whole Church Person. All saints of the old covenant beginning with Adam and all saints of the new covenant beginning with Jesus have been included in Christ. All saints are included in Christ, both the true saints of the contemporary church and those who are not yet born. These saints have already died and risen again with the Lord. All the saints of the old covenant—Adam, Noah, Abraham, Moses, David, Ezra, Nehemiah—and all the saints of the New Testament (including all the saints of the last two millennia and those not yet born) died with Him, rose with Him, and ascended into heaven with Him. The Christ's movement in life, death, and resurrection transcends time and space. Therefore, biblical eschatology is not time-centered but is centered on Christ's Person.

Jesus Christ, as the Whole Church Person, is also the *Panta* Person. He created all and in Him are all things (*panta*). He embraces all things on earth, all angels in heaven, the visible and invisible, the things in the past and in the present, and the things that will appear in the future. With His death and resurrection, all (*panta*) has been restored as New Creation. The destruction of the whole universe and the advent of the new heaven and the new earth have already been inaugurated with the death, the resurrection, and the ascension of Jesus Christ. Its complete realization will be accomplished with His second coming. The passing of the old world (this age) and the presence of the new world (the age to come) are embodied by the death and resurrection of Jesus Christ.

---

56. Beale, "Eschatological Conception," 23.

57. James B. Jordan, *Through New Eyes: Developing a Biblical View of the World* (Brentwood, TN: Wolgemuth & Hyatt, 1988; reprint, Eugene, OR: Wipf & Stock, 1999), 66–67.

Dear Kee,

Thank you very much for this thought-provoking paper. You have put your finger on a most important issue, that the core history of the universe is "in Christ Jesus" and therefore that eschatology is "in Christ Jesus."

Before Jesus' resurrection, the promised Seed of the woman remained centered on a world navel: the garden of Eden, Abraham's altars, the tabernacle, Jerusalem, and finally Jesus Himself. Similarly, the corporate biography of that Seed is carefully recorded in the chronology of the Bible, a chronology always tied to the center, a chronology that spiraled down to the three years of Jesus' earthly ministry.

Now, however, in the glorious resurrection of Jesus the Transformed Seed is centered in heaven and thus wherever on earth the saints are gathered. And now, in the new age, all of history is drawn into the original olive tree history (Rom 11) and is moving toward universal history for the whole of the human race. All nations are being drawn in, and we are still at the beginning of this age of triumph.

And indeed, as you have insisted, the universe itself is being renewed. The universe is the garment of humanity, which is her captain, and renewed humans take dominion and make the world a better and better place. Here again, the kingdom of Christ has only begun to renew the face of the earth.

So again, I thank you for drawing these things together and giving us much to think about.

Jim

11

Light and Shadow

Confessing the Doctrine of Election in the Sixteenth Century

JEFFREY J. MEYERS

JOHN CALVIN HAD FRIENDLY relations with Luther and the early "Lutherans." It is not difficult to demonstrate that Calvin looked up to and learned from Luther as the "pathfinder" of the Reformation.[1] Nor is it difficult to show that Calvin accepted the Augsburg Confession, possibly even subscribing to it.[2] Even during his debates with Westphal and Hesshusius, Calvin was deeply concerned about Lutheran-Reformed relations; he argued that his treatises against "fanatics" like Westphal were not intended to be attacks on Lutherans as such.[3] Calvin was convinced that there was essential continuity between

---

1. For Calvin's evaluation of Luther, see B. A. Gerrish, "John Calvin on Luther," in *Interpreters of Luther: Essays in Honor of Wilhelm Pauck*, ed. Jaroslav Pelikan (Philadelphia: Fortress, 1968), 67–96.

2. In August 1556, Calvin wrote to John Laski explaining his controversy with Westphal. In that letter he appealed to the Augsburg Confession: "The fact is, and it is useful to recognize this in the first place, that there is nothing in the Augsburg Confession which is not in agreement with our own teaching" (*Ioannis Calvini opera quae supersunt omnia*, ed. G. Baum, et al., 59 vols., *Corpus Reformatum* [Brunswick: Schwetschke, 1863–1900], 16:263; hereafter = CO. See also W. Nijenhuis, "Calvin and the Augsburg Confession," in *Ecclesia Reformata: Studies on the Reformation* [Leiden: E. J. Brill, 1972], 97–114).

Not only did Calvin endorse the Augsburg Confession, he also appears to have signed it. In a letter to Schalling he says that he actually "signed" (*subscripsi*) the Augsburg Confession (Calvin to Martin Schalling, March 25, 1557, CO 16:430). Nijenhuis understands "signed" figuratively as "agreeing with" or "subscribing to," but Calvin himself, after his return from Strassburg, urged Jean Garnier, who took his place as pastor to the French congregation, to *sign* the Augsburg Confession: "I do not see why you hesitate to sign the Augsburg Confession" (Dec. 10, 1554; CO 15:336). Calvin certainly signed the Wittenberg Concord (which included an explicit declaration of loyalty to the Invariata [!] and the Tetrapolitan Confession) when he assumed his pastoral duties in Strassburg. Calvin even attended the ecumenical colloquies at Hagenau, Worms, and Regensburg (1540–1541) as a *Lutheran* Representative (at Worms his status was changed from the Strassburg to the Duke of Lüneburg delegation). Ernst Bizer notes that during Calvin's Strassburg pastorate (1538–1541) Calvin was able among the Lutherans "to pass for one of themselves" (Ernst Bizer, *Studien zur Geschichte des Abendmahlsstreits im 16. Jahrhundert* [Darmstadt: Wissenschaftliche Buchgesellschaft, 1962], 244–47).

3. See Wulfert de Greef, *The Writings of John Calvin: An Introductory Guide*, trans. Lyle D. Bierma (Grand Rapids: Baker, 1993), 190–93.

PART THREE: THEOLOGY

his theological program and that of Luther and Melanchthon. He believed this to be true, despite differences of emphasis in each community's theological program.[4] My purpose in this essay is to investigate the similarities between the way the Lutheran and Reformed churches confessed the biblical teaching on election in the sixteenth century.

The Lutheran churches of the sixteenth century offered no explicit treatment of the doctrine of election in their confessional documents until Article XI in the Formula of Concord (1577). Reformed churches, on the other hand, began incorporating this doctrine in their confessions and catechisms early on. The First Confession of Basel (1534) was the earliest Reformed symbolic document to give the doctrine of election a separate treatment—more than forty years before the Formula of Concord (1577). This temporal discontinuity, however, may not be all that doctrinally significant. Although it is true that early Lutheran symbols find no separate place for the doctrine of election, this fact might be little more than an accident of history. Reformed churches experienced controversy over this doctrine from the start and so tended to include explicit articles on election in their confessions and catechisms. Lutherans also looked to the Augsburg Confession (1530) as a model confession, while the Reformed churches had no similar authoritative model to establish the basic outline of articles to be confessed. Furthermore, the influence (and authorship!) of Calvin and Luther on the shape and content of the confessions emerging in their respective communions cannot be overlooked. Luther does not give the doctrine of election the kind of systematic weight that Calvin does. None of these considerations, however, necessarily implies that the sixteenth-century Lutheran and Reformed churches were fundamentally at odds over the confessional doctrine of election.

It is that last point that I wish to address here. When the Lutheran church did come to confess election in 1577, was it substantially different from the Reformed confessional understanding of the doctrine? How do the two ways of confessing the doctrine of election compare? Specifically, are the concerns of the Formula's Article XI properly

---

4. After Calvin's death, Reformed and Lutheran theologies begin to diverge. The reasons for this parting are complex and demand much more scholarly attention. See Jill Raitt, *The Colloquy of Montbeliard: Religion and Politics in the Sixteenth Century* (Oxford: Oxford University Press, 1993); Jill Raitt, "Probably They are God's Children: Theodore Beza's Doctrine of Baptism," in *Humanism and Reform: The Church in Europe, England, and Scotland, 1400-1643*, ed. James Kirk (Oxford: Blackwell, 1991); Lewis W. Spitz and Wenzel Lohff, *Discord, Dialog, and Concord: Studies in the Lutheran Reformation's Formula of Concord* (Philadelphia: Fortress, 1977); and Mark D. Tranvik, "Jacob Andreae's Defense of the Lutheran Doctrine of Baptism at Montbeliard," *Lutheran Quarterly* 6 (1992) 425–37. I believe that there is a profound connection between the obvious embarrassment of later Reformed theologians with respect to Calvin's positive evaluation of Luther and his theology and their gradual abandonment of Calvin's hearty sacramental theology. Gerrish points out that even as early as Beza we discover something of a mild annoyance with Calvin's sacramentalism. As the editor of Calvin's correspondence, Beza "censored" certain portions of Calvin's correspondence that seemed to him to be evidence of too much compromise with Luther (B. A. Gerrish, *The Old Protestantism and the New: Essays on the Reformation Heritage* [Edinburgh: T. & T. Clark, 1982], 32, 285). In addition to this, under Beza's leadership Calvin's doctrine of predestination takes a more central, defining place within Reformed theology. This may have precluded later Reformed theology from fully utilizing Calvin's robust theology of sacramental instrumentality. A modified Zwinglian view, which is more compatible with a centralized doctrine of predestination, seems to make headway in the late sixteenth century. At any rate, the fascinating question of the relationship between later Reformed theology's doctrine of election and its understanding of the sacraments remains to be investigated.

directed at the Reformed confessions and catechisms? Without conducting a detailed historical investigation into the actual intentions of the Formula's authors (whether they had Reformed theologians and/or symbolic documents in mind), we might nevertheless profitably ask if the pastoral and theological concerns addressed by the Lutherans in Article XI apply to the Reformed church's way of *confessing* predestination and election. Answering this question would necessarily involve a careful examination of the texts of the Reformed symbolic documents in the light of the concerns articulated in the Formula of Concord. This essay attempts to do just that. I will examine the doctrine of election as confessed in the Reformed symbolic documents of the sixteenth-century confessions and catechisms in order to determine continuities and discontinuities between the Lutheran and Reformed ways of confessing election.

My thesis is that there was no substantial difference in theological content between the way these two Reformation communities publicly confessed the doctrine of election in the sixteenth century.[5] Reformed confessions and catechisms treat the doctrine of election positively as the light that illumines the reality of the experience of salvation, thereby grounding the Reformation doctrine of justification *sola gratia* in God's eternal counsel.[6] The shadow of reprobation, however, finds little or no place in the Reformed church's public confession of the gospel. The truth of God's election might have any number of minor uses or functions within the system of Christian doctrine; nevertheless, its fundamental *confessional* function involves illuminating and thereby anchoring the central Reformation confession of salvation in God's eternal purpose. Election is confessed

---

5. After quoting the Formula of Concord's fundamental concern—that the preaching of the gospel not lead to either despair or false assurance (Solid Declaration [hereafter SD] XI, 91–92)—Karl Barth notes: "This could not be said against Calvin and the Calvinists except through misunderstanding, or with reference to certain inferences which seriously embarrass their teaching. The Calvinists themselves might well wish that they had done so more emphatically in order that misunderstanding might have been avoided" (Karl Barth, *Church Dogmatics*, vol. 2, part 2, *The Doctrine of God*, eds. G. W. Bromiley and T. F. Torrance, trans. G. W. Bromiley [Edinburgh: T. & T. Clark, 1957], 15; hereafter = CD). However many discontinuities may have existed between the way Lutheran and Reformed theologians taught this doctrine in books, tracts, lectures, and disputations, they do nothing to damage my central thesis concerning the essential theological unity of confessional substance. Reformed communities did emphatically link their doctrine of election with the gospel in their public confessional articles. Any "embarrassment" that might have resulted from their other more philosophical, polemical, or scholastic works does not concern us here. It does not lie within the scope of this essay to examine the entire debate between Lutheran and Reformed theologians concerning predestination and election.

6. All of the Reformed confessions and catechisms conceive of predestination in the light of justification; election is expounded as the objective ground for the material principle of the Reformation. See Matthias Schneckenburger, *Vergleichende Darstellung des lutherischen und reformirten Lehrbegriffs*, ed. Eduard Güder, vol. 1 [Stuttgart: J. B. Metzler, 1855], 32). "Schneckenburger argues that the Reformed doctrine of predestination cannot be conceived as a consequence of the idea of God and his attributes since the characteristic of Reformed systematics is not the objective determination of the doctrine of predestination but the personal assurance of election by the grace of God. . . . Schneckenburger finds a continuity throughout the Reformed systems of the sixteenth century in this conception of predestination as the result of justification, the subjective or material principle of the Reformation, seeking out its objective ground" (Richard A. Muller, *Christ and the Decree: Christology and Predestination in Reformed Theology from Calvin to Perkins* [Durham, NC: Labyrinth, 1986], 4).

PART THREE: THEOLOGY

in both Lutheran and Reformed communions as the flip side of *sola gratia*, or better, election is a way of confessing the gospel of grace from the perspective of eternity.

The analysis will proceed in three stages. First, I will expound the fundamental concerns of Article XI of the Formula. Second, the sixteenth-century Reformed Confessions and catechisms must be analyzed carefully to discover the shape and content of the doctrine of election as *confessed* by Reformed churches. Finally, I will compare and contrast the Formula's Article XI with the confessional doctrine of election discovered in the Reformed symbolic documents, highlighting areas of continuity and discontinuity between the Lutheran and Reformed way of confessing the doctrine of election.

THE BURDEN OF THE FORMULA OF CONCORD ON ELECTION

The Formula offers four *stated* reasons for including this article. First, the doctrine of election "has become the occasion of very serious controversies at other places and has involved our people also" (Solid Declaration [hereafter SD] XI, 1).[7] It is not entirely clear what these "other places" are. There may not have been any "public dissension" on this article among the theologians of the Augsburg Confession (SD XI, 1), but there was at least one not entirely private dispute between Luther and Amsdorf.[8] Amsdorf taught a rather symmetrical version of "double predestination," which Luther and others rejected. In addition to this, we do know of at least three general disputes over the doctrine of election in "other places" that might qualify as illuminating background for the content of this article. Surely the synergistic controversy with the so-called Philippists is one dispute that underlies the concern in this article to deny any determinative role to human choice in one's salvation (Epitome [hereafter EP] XI, 5, 15, 20; SD XI, 23, 30, 31, 43–44).[9]

Moreover, the various tract wars fought by Calvin, Beza, and other Reformed theologians against such dissenting voices as Bolsec and Pighius may also have been in view. Calvin published his *Consensus pastorum Genevensis ecclesiae* in 1552, an extensive exposition of his doctrine of election that culminated a decade or so of debate with Pighius, Bolsec, and Georgius.[10] These debates were surely known among the Lutheran theologians. Calvin's own *Institutes* had gone through six editions, the last published in

---

7. Theodore G. Tappert, ed. and trans., *The Book of Concord: The Confessions of the Evangelical Lutheran Church* (Philadelphia: Fortress, 1959), 661. All English references to Lutheran confessional or catechetical documents, unless otherwise noted, are from the Tappert edition.

8. Robert Kolb, "Nikolas von Amsdorf on Vessels of Wrath and Vessels of Mercy: A Lutheran Doctrine of Double Predestination," *Harvard Theological Review* 69 (1976) 325–43.

9. See Robert A. Kolb, "Historical Background of the Formula of Concord" in *A Contemporary Look at the Formula of Concord*, eds. Wilbert Rosin and Robert D. Preus (St. Louis: Concordia, 1978), 29–33, 53–56.

10. CO 6:225–404; John Calvin, *Calvin's Calvinism: Treatises on the Eternal Predestination of God and the Secret Providence of God*, trans. Henry P. Cole (Grand Rapids: Baker, 1987). For a discussion of the literature in these tract wars, see De Greef, *Writings*, 149–93. In the dedication to the *Consensus pastorum Genevensis ecclesiae* Calvin reminds the reader that assurance of salvation can be found only in Christ. We should fix our gaze upon Christ, since only in Him is eternal life revealed and offered to us. One should not attempt to pry into the hidden decrees of God. Nevertheless, the one who embraces the promise of the gospel will recognize that God's grace and mercy are rooted in his eternal decree since it is He who opened our eyes and elected us in Christ before we were conceived in the womb.

1559, and contained a full exposition of his doctrine of election.[11] In addition to this, Jacob Andreae and Calvin's successor Theodore Beza had faced off at the colloquy of Poissy in 1561. The doctrine of predestination was not really an issue at Poissy, but as Jill Raitt notes, "From this point on Andreae and Beza became more and more inimical, especially through the battle for the Palatinate. . . ."[12]

We should take note, however, that the Formula makes no explicit mention of Calvinism or Reformed theology, so one must be careful about identifying the precise objects under attack. Three of the four antitheses, however, in the Formula's Epitome reject some form or another of soteriological particularism (EP XI, 17–19; cf. SD XI,), so it is reasonable to assume that the predestinarian particularism of Calvinism (at least as it was perceived by the authors of the Formula) provides the background for these passages that highlight God's universal will and grace. Nevertheless, my investigation in this essay will seek to determine whether the public, ecclesiastical Reformed confessions and catechisms in particular might have been in view. Would the way in which the doctrine of election was confessed in these Reformed symbolic texts lead to the kind of polemical statements that we find in Article XI of the Formula?

Finally, Strasbourg is another one of these "other places" where controversy broke out over this issue. Just a little more than a dozen years before the Formula was written a serious dispute over predestination broke out between the Reformed theologian Jerome Zanchi and the Lutheran pastor Marbach. This particular theological altercation focused on Zanchi's scholastic doctrine of predestination, which Marbach found particularly destructive to pastoral care. This bitter debate ended with the Strasbourg Concord (1563), a document written in part by Andreae and Brenz, which Zanchi signed with serious reservations. This incident no doubt alerted the Lutheran theologians to the potential pastoral problems associated with an errant or even a badly skewed doctrine of election.[13]

The other three reasons stated for the inclusion of this article are the desire (1) to standardize theological terminology among Lutheran theologians, (2) to make

---

11. Calvin, *Institutes of the Christian Religion* (1559 Edition), ed. John T. McNeil, trans. Ford Lewis Battles (Philadelphia: Westminster, 1960), 3.21–24 (hereafter = *Inst*).

12. Raitt, *Colloquy of Montbéliard*, 45. See also Donald Nugent, *Ecumenism in the Age of the Reformation: The Colloquy of Poissy* (Cambridge: Harvard University Press, 1974).

13. Zanchi's predestinarian theology was largely dependent on Thomistic philosophical and metaphysical categories. The principle of causality plays a large part in his doctrine of God, indicating that he appropriated scholasticism's ontological and epistemological presuppositions as well as its form and method. Zanchi's doctrine of predestination, however, does not compare to Beza's supralapsarianism, since he views man as *creatus et lapsus* under the decree.

For more on Zanchi's theology see Christopher Burchill, "Girolamo Zanchi: Portrait of a Reformed Theologian and His Work," *Sixteenth Century Journal* 15.2 (1984) 185–207; John Patrick Donnelly, "Calvinist Thomism," *Viator* 7 (1976) 441–55; John Patrick Donnelly, "Italian Influences on the Development of Calvinist Scholasticism," *Sixteenth Century Journal* 7 (April 1976) 81–101; Otto Gründler, *Die Gotteslehre Girolamo Zanchis und ihre Bedeutung für seine Lehre von der Prädestination* (Neukirchen-Vluyn: Neukirchener, 1965); Richard A. Muller, *Christ and the Decree*, 110–25; and Joseph N. Tylenda, "Girolamo Zanchi and John Calvin," *Calvin Theological Journal* 10 (1975) 101–41. For an account of the debate between Zanchi and Marbach, see James M Kittelson, "Marbach vs. Zanchi: The Resolution of Controversy in Late Reformation Strasbourg," *Sixteenth Century Journal* 8.3 (1977) 31–44.

the church's position on election public and explicit "so that all men may know what we teach, believe, and confess in this article" (SD XI, 2), and (3) to set forth the true biblical doctrine: "precisely in order to avert such misuse and misunderstanding, we must set forth the correct meaning on the basis of Scripture" (SD XI, 3).

Underlying each of these four expressed reasons stands the deep pastoral concern that pervades the Formula's careful treatment of this doctrine. The Formula's treatment is more concerned with outlining a basic evangelical and pastoral shape or context for the doctrine of election than with articulating a definitive body of teaching on the subject. Summarizing the content of this article will reveal the depth of this pastoral concern.

First, Article XI traces the outlines of an important distinction between God's Lordship over evil and his gracious election of his people (EP XI, 1–4; SD XI, 4–7). Although God is Lord over all that happens, including good and evil, He does not *originate* or *cause* evil and wickedness as He does the salvation of his people in Christ. Sin is not produced or authored by God (EP XI, 3; SD XI, 79–86). This accounts for the concern to distinguish between foreknowledge and predestination as an explanation of God's asymmetrical relation to damnation and salvation (EP XI, 2–5; SD XI, 4–8). The Formula does not even attempt to explicate a more comprehensive "general" doctrine of predestination. The article is silent about the cosmological or philosophical possibilities in this doctrine.

The fundamentally asymmetrical nature of God's work can also be seen in the strong language used in Article XI to describe the proper positive doctrine of the Christian's eternal election. Referencing Matthew 6:18, John 10:20, and Acts 3:48, the Solid Declaration ascribes to the positive doctrine of election unto salvation everything it denies to reprobation: "God's eternal election, however, not only foresees and foreknows the salvation of the elect, but by God's gracious will and pleasure in Christ it is also a cause [*eine Ursach*] which creates, effects, helps, and advances our salvation and whatever pertains to it" (SD XI, 8).[14]

Theologically, then, God's dealings with man are fundamentally asymmetrical. Because God does not work evil desires in man in the same manner (*eodem modo*) as He works salvation in His people, the church's doctrine of election must not press logical connections in order to arrive at a nice symmetrical doctrine of predestination. The Formula eschews all attempts to penetrate or concatenate the various disparate elements so evident in the Scriptural expression of this doctrine. The church's confession of election will always manifest the paradox of this doctrine's inherent mystery, the inexplicable *cur alii, alii non*.[15]

Second, in light of this emphasis on directing Christians to the revealed will of God in the gospel of Christ, Article XI warns against speculative forays into the "secret

---

14. Hans Lietzmann, et al., eds., *Die Bekenntnisschriften der evangelisch-lutherischen Kirche*, 11th ed. (Göttingen: Vandenhoeck & Ruprecht, 1992), 1066, 21–22 (hereafter = BS; throughout I cite page number followed by line numbers). All German references from the Formula of Concord are taken from this book.

15. See Preus, "Predestination and Election," in Preus, ed., *A Contemporary Look*, 277; and J. A. O. Preus, *The Second Martin: The Life and Theology of Martin Chemnitz* (St. Louis: Concordia, 1994), 321–25.

and inscrutable counsel of God" (EP XI, 5–7; SD XI, 9). The example given makes God's will intolerably arbitrary, like a "military muster," choosing one person and passing by another. Line up humanity and count them off; every one with an even number will be saved. This reduces God's eternal counsel to a mathematical or statistical nightmare. This one shall be saved, that one shall be damned, this one shall persevere, that one shall not persevere.

> Hence if we wish to think or speak correctly and profitably about eternal election or about the predestination and ordering of the children of God to eternal life, we should accustom ourselves not to speculate concerning the absolute, secret, hidden, and inscrutable foreknowledge of God. On the contrary, we should consider the counsel, purpose, and ordinance of God in Christ Jesus, who is the genuine and true "book of life" as it is revealed to us through the Word. (SD XI, 13)

This means that we should keep together the "entire teaching" (*die ganze Lehre*) concerning the purpose, counsel, will, and ordinance of God relating to our redemption, just as Paul does in Romans 8 and Ephesians 1.[16] Our thinking about election should be organized around the eight points of doctrine outlined in SD XI, 15–22. It is only in this "light" that the doctrine of election should be considered (SD XI, 24). The solution to man's tendency to reduce God's eternal mind and will to man's puny proportions through fruitless speculation is always to think of the entire doctrine of God's purpose and counsel (predestination) Christologically and soteriologically.

Third, Article XI eschews all formulations of the doctrine of election that would evacuate its ability to comfort *individual* Christians concerning God's gracious and infallible will concerning their salvation (SD XI, 23, 43–49, 91–93). Thus, God's eternal purpose is not merely to make salvation possible or to make it available to all in general; on the contrary, He has specifically "elected to salvation each and every person among the elect" (SD XI, 23).[17] The question of the identity of the elect must be carefully considered. Since the doctrine of election ought to comfort the elect, the questions "who are the elect?" and "wherefrom and whereby can and should one discover [one's election]?" become acute. The Formula answers these questions by warning against making judgments based on the law, reason, or outward appearance, and especially any attempt "to investigate [*forschen*] the secret and hidden abyss of divine foreknowledge [*den heimlichen, verborgenen Abrund götlicher Vorsehung*]" (SD XI, 26).[18]

Rather than leading us into the dark, hidden depths of God's being, the doctrine of election *stands behind* the revealed will of God in Christ (Eph 1:9, 10). Therefore, assurance of our election comes through the call of the gospel (SD XI, 27–29). For this reason, the Formula is concerned to direct believers to the "revealed will of God" for certain knowledge of his will. If believers cannot trust God's intentions in the gospel, then God must be deceiving us or contradicting himself (SD XI, 34–35). Both possibilities are intolerable. God's intention is accurately revealed in his Word and Sacrament.

---

16. SD XI, 14; BS, 1068, 28.
17. BS, 1070, 9.
18. BS, 1070, 44–46.

If God has two wills, two intentions, one secret and one revealed, how will we know with "absolute certainty" that God loves us in Christ (see EP XI, 17–19)? There can be no deception in God's gospel call: it goes out freely and sincerely to all. The elect are those, according to God's decree, who "hear the Gospel, believe on Christ, pray, give thanks, are sanctified in love, have hope, patience, and comfort in afflictions (Eph. 1:11, 13; Rom. 8:25)" (SD XI, 30).

Fourth and finally, the Formula makes it abundantly evident that the doctrine of election is a corollary to and ground for the mercy of God in Christ revealed in the gospel. The doctrine of election can be understood only as an evangelical doctrine. In paragraphs 43 through 51, the Formula outlines four major and two minor "uses" for the doctrine of God's eternal foreknowledge or election. There is a nice *inclusio* in paragraph 51 that ties these six "uses"—altogether eight paragraphs—together: "Thus it is possible to use the teaching in this article in a profitable, comforting, and salutary way" (SD XI, 51).[19]

First, God has revealed the mystery of foreknowledge as powerful support for the central article of justification by grace through faith. Citing Ephesians 1:4, Romans 9:11, and 2 Timothy 1:9, the Formula explains that election "is indeed a useful, salutary, and comforting doctrine, for it mightily confirms the article that we are justified and saved without our works and merit, purely by grace and solely for Christ's sake" (SD XI, 43).[20]

Second, the doctrine of election overturns all false doctrines about "the powers of the natural will" (SD XI, 44).[21]

Third, this doctrine is designed to afford "beautiful and glorious comfort" to individual Christians. They can know that nothing will separate them from the love of God in Christ (Rom 8:35), since God has ordained their salvation in his eternal purpose even before the foundation of the world.

Fourth, this doctrine helps a Christian find assurance and comfort, especially during times of trial and affliction. Here the Formula derives a very practical use from the Christological orientation of election. Referencing Romans 8, the doctrine of election ought to comfort us in our trials, reminding us that we are "predestined to be conformed to the image of his Son," persevering through cross and affliction as He did.

Fifth, the doctrine of election assures us that the Church of God will endure against all odds and in spite of "the outward prestige of the false church" (SD XI, 50).

A sixth use is noted, but not explained. The article of election, according to such passages as Luke 4:24; 7:30; and Matthew 22:14, "contains strong admonitions and warnings" (SD XI, 51).[22]

In outlining these six uses of the doctrine the Formula intends to highlight the inseparable organic relationship between the doctrine of election and the foundational doctrine of the justification. Any use of election that strays from its connection with the gospel becomes an improper and dangerously unbiblical use.

19. BS, 1078, 44–45.
20. BS, 1076, 36–38.
21. BS, 1077, 5–6.
22. BS, 1078, 35–36.

We can conclude our review of Article XI's chief concerns with eight summary points. In confessing the biblical teaching of election the Formula seeks to

1. provide the outline of a biblical and pastorally sensitive doctrine of election;

2. champion the gospel context and ground of the doctrine of election as a objective substructure of justification and *sola fide*;

3. guard the asymmetrical character of God's dealings with men;

4. repudiate God's causal complicity with sin and evil by denying that God is the *author* of evil or the *cause* of damnation;

5. explain election as God's gracious, eternal choice of individuals for salvation in Christ in such a way that would comfort Christians in times of doubt and temptation;

6. uphold the sincerity and universality of God's love for all mankind, Christ's atonement, and the gospel's free offer of salvation;

7. deny any contribution to salvation from man's works or will (contra synergism); and

8. warn against speculative investigations into God's will outside of Christ and his revealed Word.

These eight points must now be turned into questions and directed to the sixteenth-century Reformed confessions and catechisms. Do the Reformed symbolic documents exhibit the same considerations when confessing the doctrine of election? Do they ignore or possibly violate any of the Formula's evangelical concerns? Do they confess a doctrine of election that is fundamentally at odds with the shape and content of the doctrine summarized in the Formula? Is election cut loose from Christology and justification in the Reformed symbols? The texts of these pre-Concord, sixteenth-century symbolic documents must now be examined and analyzed.

ELECTION AS CONFESSED IN THE REFORMED SYMBOLIC DOCUMENTS

In this essay I am not particularly interested in each of the Reformers' "extended" or "general" doctrine of election, but rather in the evangelical publication of the doctrine *as it is confessed in their ecclesiastical confessions and catechisms*. Our goal is to ascertain the way in which the doctrine of election was *publicly confessed* by the Reformed church, not how it was *taught* or *argued* in the schools. Consequently, we will avoid detailed analyses of each particular Reformer's doctrine of election as he might have expounded it in lectures, books, or polemical tracts apart from the churchly confessions and catechisms. For our purposes, these works will be used only occasionally to help illumine otherwise opaque passages in the symbolic texts. Our method will be to introduce each confession or catechism briefly, cite all the relevant passages that touch on the doctrine of the elec-

PART THREE: THEOLOGY

tion, and make expository comments relevant to our goal of comparing the Lutheran and Reformed ways of confessing election.[23]

The first distinctively "Reformed" confessions begin with the symbolic works of Zwingli and those allied with him in the Swiss Reformation. None of Zwingli's four ecclesiastical writings, however, give election any special prominence, and no extended treatment is given to explicating that doctrine. Allusions to the reality of election do appear in the later two larger works (*Fidei ratio* [1530] and *Expositio fidei christianae* [1531]), especially in connection with the treatment of the fall, redemption, and the nature of the church—sensitive topics central to Zwingli's apologetic battle with Rome. But even here election is primarily discussed using the terminology of Scripture, with little or no explicit theological exposition.

In 1530, Zwingli presented a confession to the emperor at the Diet of Augsburg. He sent his *Fidei ratio* to Charles V as a concise summary of the Zurich church's confession of faith. The doctrine of election finds no separate treatment in this document. The first mention of foreordination is found in connection with his article on God.

> I know that that Supreme Divinity who is my God has freely made appointment concerning all things, so that his counsel does not depend on the occasioning of any creature, since it is peculiar to marred human wisdom to reach a decision because of a preceding discussion or example. But God, who from eternity to eternity knows all that is with a single and simple regard, has no need of any ratiocination, or expectation of acts, but, equally wise, prudent, and good, freely determines and disposes concerning all things [*libere constituit ac disponit de rebus universis*]—seeing that all that exists is His. Therefore, though He knowingly and purposefully in the beginning made the man who should fall, He yet equally determined to clothe His own Son in human nature, that He might repair the fall.[24]

What at first glance looks like a general, cosmological doctrine of predestination actually turns out to be an expression of the believer's personal trust in a gracious Father to order [*constituere*] all things, especially (note the connecting "therefore" in the last sentence) his determination of the incarnation of his Son to repair the fall of man. Zwingli does not speak of God's determining [*constituere*] the fall of man, but of his "knowingly and purposefully [*sciens ac prudens*] making the man who should fall." God is not the

---

23. I am relying on the common distinctions between what is believed, taught, and confessed by the church. "Without setting rigid boundaries, we shall identify what is 'believed' as the form of Christian doctrine present in the modalities of devotion, spirituality, and worship; what is 'taught' as the content of the word of God extracted by exegesis from the witness of the Bible and communicated to the people of the church through proclamation, instruction, and churchly theology; and what is 'confessed' as the testimony of the church, both against false teaching from within and against attacks from without, articulated in polemics and in apologetics, in creed and in dogma" (Jaroslav Pelikan, *The Christian Tradition: A History of the Development of Doctrine*, vol. 1, *The Emergence of the Catholic Tradition (100–600)* [Chicago: University of Chicago Press, 1971], 4). I will not, however, examine polemical and apologetical documents in expounding the Reformed churches' public, ecclesiastical confession of the doctrine of election. I will confine myself to sixteenth-century symbolic documents used by the various churches to give form to their public confession of faith.

24. Hermann A. Niemeyer, ed., *Collectio Confessionum in Ecclesiis Reformatis Publicatarum* (Leipzig: Iulii Klinkhardti, 1840), 18.

cause of man's fall; rather, his determination comes in as consequence of the fall in order to repair it. This is how Zwingli puts it elsewhere:

> Then, when the time came to reveal his goodness, which he had determined from eternity to display no less than his justice, God sent his Son to assume our nature in every part, except as far as it inclined to sin, in order that, being our brother and equal, he could be a mediator, to make a sacrifice for us to divine justice, which must remain holy and inviolate, no less than his goodness. Thereby the world might be sure both of the appeasing of the justice and the presence of the goodness of God. For since he has given his Son to us and for us, how will he not with him and because of him give us all things? What is it that we ought not to promise ourselves from him, who so far humbled himself as not only to be our equal but also to be altogether ours? Who can sufficiently marvel at the riches and grace of the divine goodness, whereby he so loved the world, that is, the human race, as to give up his Son for its life. This I regard as the heart and life of the Gospel [*hos Evangelii fontes ac venas esse duco*]; this is the only medicine for the fainting soul, whereby it is restored to God and itself. For none but God himself can give it the assurance of God's grace.[25]

This paragraph outlines a thoroughly Trinitarian and evangelical doctrine of God's "determination" from all eternity. Zwingli stresses the riches of God's goodness such that his justice serves his beneficent design for human nature. The overflow of his goodness resulted in his determination to send his Son to be our "brother and equal." The Christological matrix of Zwingli's doctrine of God's eternal determination stands out from the outset. God has, from all eternity, determined to send his Son to save the world. As the next paragraph proves, the election of God serves the doctrine of *sola gratia* and *sola fide*:

> Hence there is left neither justification nor satisfaction based on our works, nor any expiation nor intercession of the saints, whether on earth or in heaven, for those who live by the mercy of God. For this is the one sole mediator between God and men, the God-man Christ Jesus. The election of God, however, stands and remains firm, since those whom He elected before the constitution of the world He so elected as to choose to himself through his Son; for he is holy and just as he is good and merciful. All his works therefore savor of mercy and justice. Election therefore properly savors of both. It is of his goodness that he has elected whom he will; but it is of his justice that he has adopted his elect to himself and joined them to him through his Son as a victim offered to satisfy Divine justice for us. . . .[26]

Election is single. God has elected us before the constitution of the world "through his Son" as an expression of his holiness, justice, goodness, and mercy. There is no hint of a decree of reprobation or an ordination unto wrath. Election serves to heighten and objectify the grace of God and ground the sacrifice of the cross in his eternal counsels. Election is expounded in terms of Christology since it is understood as the gracious activity of God in Christ.

---

25. Ulrich Zwingli, *On Providence and Other Essays*, ed. William John Hinke (Durham, NC: Labyrinth, 1983 [1922]), 39; Niemeyer, *Collectio*, 19.

26. Zwingli, *Providence*, 39–40; Niemeyer, *Collectio*, 19–20.

PART THREE: THEOLOGY

Finally, Zwingli's *Ratio Fidei* also briefly treats election in the course of explaining the nature of the church. Here again, election is single, not symmetrically double—unto salvation without mention of any causal determination to damnation. We should also note that, according to Zwingli, one comes to the assurance of one's election by faith. One may not always be sure about another's election, but one can be certain that he is elected by God through the ministry of the Spirit who enables us to call upon God as our Father. There is nothing speculative, philosophical, or deterministic about Zwingli's doctrine. Neither does it immobilize anyone by causing him to doubt his election. Believe and you may be certain of your election.

> Of the Church, then, we think as follows: The term Church is variously used in Scriptures. For those elect ones whom God has destined to eternal life. It is concerning this Church that Paul speaks when he says that it has no spot or wrinkle. This Church is known to God alone; for he only, according to the word of Solomon, knows the hearts of the sons of men. But, nevertheless, those who are members of this church know themselves, since they have faith, to be elect and members of this first Church; but they are ignorant with regard to other members. For it is thus written in the Acts: "And as many as were ordained to eternal life believed" [Acts 13:48]. Those, then, who believe are ordained to eternal life. But who truly believes no one knows but the one who believes. He then is certain that he is elected of God. For according to the word of the Apostle, he has the Spirit as a pledge, by whom he is sponsored and sealed, and knows himself to be free and made a son of the family and not a slave. For that Spirit cannot deceive. As He declares God to be our Father, we call upon Him as Father with assurance and boldness, being firmly persuaded that we shall obtain eternal inheritance because we are sure that the Spirit of God has been poured out into our hearts. It is certain, then, that we shall obtain an eternal inheritance because we are sure that the Spirit of God has been poured out into our hearts; for those who believe are ordained to eternal life.[27]

Telling references to election appear in connection with Zwingli's treatment of good works in his posthumously published, semi-symbolic confession *Expositio fidei christianae* (1531). The Reformation conviction of *sola gratia* must be defended against every foreign incursion of merit, especially in the church's doctrine of good works. Here election functions as a safeguard against any possible synergistic misunderstanding. In his article "On faith and works" he writes:

> It is therefore by the grace and goodness of God alone, which He has abundantly poured out on us in Christ, that eternal bliss is attained. What, then, shall we say of the passage of Scripture adduced above, in which a reward is promised for a draught of cold water and the like? This to wit: That the election of God is free and gratuitous [*Electionem dei liberalem esse ac gratuuitam*]; for He elected us before the constitution of the world, before we were born. God therefore did not elect us on account of works, but he elected us before the creation of the world. Our works therefore have no merit. But when he promises a reward for works it is after the manner of human speech; "for," says Augustine, "what wilt Thou, O good God,

---

27. Zwingli, *Providence*, 43–44; Niemeyer, *Collectio*, 22–23.

remunerate except Thine own work? For since it is Thou that workest in us both the willing and the doing, what is left for us to claim for ourselves?"[28]

Bucer, aided by Capito and Hedio, in great haste produced the so-called Tetrapolitan Confession of 1530 as an expression of the faith of the four imperial cities (Strasbourg, Constance, Memmingen, and Lindau) to be presented at the Diet of Augsburg. The document seeks a *via media* between Luther and Zwingli. It is the first attempt by Bucer to compose an "evangelical union symbol."[29] In its twenty-three chapters only once (Art. IV, Of Good Works) is mention made of foreknowledge and predestination, and there it is merely a conflated quotation of Romans 8:29 and Ephesians 2:9. Nevertheless, in Article III (Of Justification and Faith) the gospel is given a firm grounding in the work of the Father's drawing, the Son's revealing, and Holy Spirit's regenerating. The words foreknowledge, election, and predestination are not mentioned, but the evangelical understanding that "salvation is of the Lord" is prominent.

> For since it is our righteousness and eternal life to know God and our Savior, Jesus Christ; and it is so impossible for this to be the work of flesh and blood that it is needful for it to be born anew; and we cannot come to the Son except by the Father's drawing, nor know the Father except by the Son's revelation; and Paul has written so expressly that it is not of us nor of works—it is evident enough that our works can help nothing toward our becoming righteous from the unrighteous ones which we were born; because as we are by nature the children of wrath, and on this account unrighteous, so we are unable to do anything just or pleasing to God. But the beginning of all our righteousness and salvation must proceed from the mercy of the Lord, who from his own favor and the contemplation of the death of his Son first offers the doctrine of truth and his Gospel, those being sent forth who are to preach it; and, secondly, since "the natural man receives not the things of the Spirit," he causes a beam of his light to arise at the same time in the darkness of our heart, so that now we may believe his Gospel preached, being persuaded of the truth thereof by his Spirit from above, and then, relying upon the testimony of this Spirit, may call upon him with filial confidence and say, "Abba, Father," obtaining thereby sure salvation, according to the saying: "Whosoever shall call upon the name of the Lord shall be saved."[30]

The First Confession of Basel (1534) was the first Reformed confession to contain a separate paragraph on election. This confession was published by the Council of Basel with a preface by the bürgermeister on January 21, 1534. It is essentially the work of Oecolampadius, being revised upon his death in 1531, by his successor, Oswald Myconius. The confession consists of twelve short articles in the following order: God, Man, God's Care for Us, Christ, the Church, the Lord's Supper, Excommunication, Church Polity, Faith and Works, Judgment Day, Adiophora, and Against the Error of the Anabaptists.

---

28. Zwingli, *Providence*, 266; Niemeyer, *Collectio* 58.

29. Philip Schaff, ed., *The Creeds of Christendom*, vol. 1, *The History of Creeds* (New York: Harper & Brothers, 1931; reprint, Grand Rapids: Baker, 1990), 529.

30. Arthur C. Cochrane, ed., *Reformed Confessions of the 16th Century* (Philadelphia: Westminster, 1966), 58; E. F. Karl Müller, ed., *Die Bekenntnisschriften der reformierten Kirche: In authentischen Texten it geschichtlicher Einleitung und Register* (Leipzig: Deichert, 1903), 57, 23–46 (hereafter = BSR).

PART THREE: THEOLOGY

The first article (Of God) contains a single sentence paragraph confessing the doctrine of election:

> We believe in God the Father, God the Son, God the Holy Spirit, one holy, divine Trinity, three Persons and one single, eternal, almighty God, in essence and substance, and not three gods. We also believe that God has created all things by His eternal Word, that is, by his only begotten Son, and preserves and strengthens all things by his Spirit, that is by his power; and therefore, God sustains and governs all things as he created them.
>
> Hence we confess that before he created the world God elected all those whom he willed to bestow the inheritance of eternal salvation [*Dannenhar bekennend wir das Gott vor und ee er die welt erschaffen, alle die erwölt habe, die er mit dem erb ewiger seligkeit begaben will*]. Scripture texts: Rom 8:29, 30; 9:11–13; Eph 1:4–6.[31]

Since this offers little more than a restatement of key biblical phrases, it cannot possibly be misunderstood as setting out a deterministic conception of God—even if the doctrine is subsumed under the article on God. Election is not confessed here philosophically or cosmologically. Neither does it flow out of the doctrine of God as a metaphysical, logical deduction as in some forms of medieval and seventeenth-century Reformed scholasticism. On the contrary, it is interesting to note that it is directly tied to the Trinitarian confession that precedes it. The Triune God himself is the God who elects to bestow eternal salvation. The same Father who created through his Son and preserves and sustains all things by the Spirit—this God has elected from all eternity the inheritors of eternal salvation. Eternal salvation is thereby anchored in the gracious freedom of the Triune God of creation. No mention is made of reprobation or damnation. The soteriological purpose of the doctrine of election is prominent.

The First Bohemian Confession (1535), authored by John Augusta (d. 1572) and revised at Luther's suggestion, was presented to King Ferdinand. Although he rejected it, this confession became the symbolic formula for the Polish Calvinists and the exiled Bohemian Brethren in Poland (1555).[32] The article defining justification (Art. VI) briefly denies the possibility that "one can have this faith by his own power, will or choice; since it is the gift of God who, where and when it seems good to Him, works it in man through the Holy Spirit."[33] Predestination and election are not discussed in this confession.

At a diet held in Prague in 1575, a second Bohemian Confession was presented to Emperor Maximilian II (1564–1576), who thereupon promised the Lutherans, Calvinists, and Brethren religious liberty. McNeill describes this document as "Melanchthonian rather than typically Calvinist."[34] Nevertheless, the Bohemian Calvinists received it as an accurate statement of faith. The people of God are designated "elect" in the Second Confession in connection with the discussion on the nature of the Church. The elect children of God are those "true and faithful Christians, all of whom as a whole and with-

---

31. Cochrane, *Reformed Confessions*, 91; BSR, 95, 14–15.
32. John T. McNeill, *The History and Character of Calvinism* (London: Oxford, 1954), 283–84.
33. Niemeyer, *Collectio*, 793; see also Benjamin B. Warfield, "Predestination in the Reformed Confessions," in *Studies in Theology* (New York: Oxford University Press, 1932), 153.
34. McNeill, *History and Character*, 284–85.

out exception are holy with a holiness imputed in Christ and begun in them by the Holy Spirit; and these only God deigns to call his sheep...."[35]

What we now call the First Helvetic Confession of 1536 has also been called the Second Confession of Basel. The Confession was written by the committee of Bullinger, Grynaeus, Myconius, Judae, and Megander appointed by the conference of Swiss Reformed delegates who met at Basel on January 20, 1536, in order to prepare for the Pope's own announced general council scheduled to meet in Mantua in 1537. Bucer and Capito, although not part of the committee, assisted in the composition of the twenty-seven articles of the confession, especially the article on the Lord's Supper. These two especially had high hopes to further doctrinal concord between Luther and the Swiss churches and so were anxious to frame a confession that would unite the churches in their common faith. Articles 9–11 of the First Helvetic Confession are relevant to our investigation.

> Article 9. Free Will. We ascribe free will to man because we discover (*experimur*) in ourselves that we do good and evil knowingly and deliberately. We are able to do evil of ourselves but we can neither embrace nor fulfill the good unless we are illumined, quickened and impelled by the grace of Christ. For God is the one who effects in us the willing and the doing, according to his good pleasure. Our salvation is from God, but from ourselves there is nothing but sin and damnation (*us gott ist unnser heyl, us uns aber jst nüt dann sünd und verdampnus*).[36]

While synergism is denied in this article, a radical monergism that traces back to God every act of man, including his sin and evil, is also definitively denied. The doctrine of man's will is treated in an evangelical way. Man is responsible for his own acts, while God is solely responsible for man's salvation. No attempt is made logically to penetrate philosophical and cosmological questions about causality that might arise because of this paradoxical way of confessing God's free agency in salvation.

> Article 10. How God has saved man through his eternal counsel [*durch sin Ewigen Ratschlag*]. Although man through his own guilt and transgression justly incurs eternal damnation and has come under the righteous wrath of God, yet God, the gracious Father, has never ceased to be concerned about him. We can perceive and understand this sufficiently, clearly and plainly from the first promise and from the whole law by which sin is awakened though not wiped out, and from Christ the Lord who was appointed and given for that purpose.[37]

This article introduces the "eternal counsel" of God for man's salvation. Man is *saved* through God's eternal counsel. In the First Helvetic Confession election is not expounded as a separate article or doctrine, nevertheless, it clearly undergirds the evangelical theology of the Confession. What else does election mean but that "our salvation is from God" and that "from ourselves there is nothing by sin and damnation"? Therefore, we can only be saved "through the eternal counsel" of God "the gracious Father," who in

---

35. Warfield, "Predestination," 153.
36. Translation slightly modified from Cochrane, *Reformed Confessions*, 102. BSR, 103, 2–3.
37. Translation slightly modified from Cochrane, *Reformed Confessions*, 102–3. BSR, 103, 5–12.

spite of man's incursion of eternal damnation, "has never ceased be concerned about him." The First Helvetic Confession evidences no interest in the question of reprobation. The counsel of God is confessed as the eternal *ground* of the Christian's salvation, not as the origin of a causal series that embraces all men's destinies. Furthermore, man incurs eternal damnation "through his . . . guilt and transgression." He will be damned of his own fault even though "the gracious Father has never ceased to be concerned about him." Christ, therefore, has been given for the "purpose" of fulfilling God's *promise* to mankind. He is preeminently the elect one, who took on our human nature in order that we might inherit eternal life:

> Article 11. Concerning Christ the Lord and what we have through him. This Lord Christ, a true Son of God, true God and man, assumed a true human nature, with body and soul, in the time thereto appointed by God from eternity [*hat jnn der zyt, die got von Ewygkeyt har darzu bestimpt*]. He has two distinct, unmixed natures in one single, indissoluble Person. The assumption of human nature took place in order that He might quicken us who were dead and make us joint heirs of God. This also is the reason He has become our brother. . . .[38]

> Article 12. The Purpose of Evangelical Doctrine. Consequently in all evangelical teaching the most sublime and the principal article [*das höchst und fürnempst houptstück*] and the one which should be expressly set forth in every sermon and impressed upon the hearts of men should be that we are preserved and saved solely by the one mercy of God and by the merit of Christ. . . .[39]

The doctrine of election does not occupy the "central" or "principle" article in this Reformed confession. That position is clearly reserved for the gospel of the mercy of God. No theological or metaphysical deductions are made from the doctrine of election. God's eternal counsel, determining that Christ should take on human flesh for the salvation of man, stands behind this gospel as the guarantor of its eternal efficacy. The doctrine of election, when discussed in isolation from Christology and soteriology (as it tended to be treated in post-Reformation, seventeenth-century dogmatics), is often carried out in such a way that the electing God is not understood seriously as the one who elects in Christ. Instead, theologians degenerate into speaking of "the will of God" and the "decree of God" (*decretum Dei*) in such a way that erects a *Deus nudus* or *Deus exlex* "behind" or "back of" Christ. In contrast, Article 11 of the First Helvetic Confession speaks of the eternal election or determination (*bestimmen*) by God of the humanity of Christ. By means of Jesus Christ God enacts in history his eternal counsel to save mankind. The doctrine of election is confessed in the First Helvetic Confession in a Christological, soteriological matrix that guarantees its pastoral value for the assurance of doubting souls.

---

38. Cochrane, *Reformed Confessions*, 103; BSR, 103, 13–20.
39. Cochrane, *Reformed Confessions*, 104; BSR, 104, 1–9.

CALVIN AND THE SYMBOLS OF THE GENEVAN CHURCH

Two symbolic documents were produced in the early years of the Reformation in Geneva: the Lausanne Articles and the Geneva Confession of 1536. The Lausanne articles, although never official adopted by Geneva, were propounded by its pastor Guillaume Farel at the Lausanne disputation of October 1, 1536. They were delivered as representative of the core theological theses of the Reformation of French-speaking Swiss cantons. These articles contain no discussion of election or predestination. Once Calvin had joined Farel in Geneva, he produced a brief confession of faith that would summarize the evangelical doctrines outlined in the first edition of his *Institutes of the Christian Religion* (1536). The Genevan Confession (1536) contains twenty-one articles. The only article that even hints at election is Article 10, "All Our Good in the Grace of God," which immediately precedes the article on faith:

> Art. 10. In order that all glory and praise be rendered to God (as is his due), and that we be able to have true peace and rest of conscience, we understand and confess that we receive all benefits from God, as said above, by his clemency and pity, without any consideration of our worthiness or the merit of our works, to which is due no other retribution than eternal confusion. . . .[40]

Calvin's treatment of election in his 1536 *Institutes* occurs in chapter 2 as a part of his exposition of the "fourth part" of the Apostles' Creed ("I believe in the Holy Catholic church). There is no discussion of reprobation or any symmetrically conceived double decree. The doctrine of election is given an explicitly Trinitarian and Christological shape in this early exposition.

> But those who, not content with Christ, strive to penetrate more deeply, arouse God's wrath against themselves and, because they break into the depths of his majesty, from his glory cannot but be oppressed. For since Christ our Lord is he in whom the Father, from eternity has chosen those he has willed to be his own and to be brought into the flock of his church, we have a clear enough testimony that we are among God's elect and of the church, if we partake in Christ. *Then, since the very same Christ is the constant and unchangeable truth of the Father, we are by no means to doubt that his word truly proclaims to us the Father's will as it was from the beginning and ever shall be.* When therefore by faith we possess Christ and all that is his, it must certainly be established that as he himself is the beloved Son of the Father and heir of the kingdom of heaven, so we also through him have been adopted as children of God, and are his brothers and companions in such a way as to be partakers of the same inheritance; *on this account we are also assured that we are among those whom the Lord has chosen from eternity*, whom he will ever protect and never allow to perish.[41]

---

40. Cochrane, *Reformed Confessions*, 122.

41. John Calvin, *Institutes of the Christian Religion: 1536 Edition*, trans. Ford Lewis Battles (Grand Rapids: Eerdmans, 1986), 60 (*Inst.* 2.24); *Joannis Calvini opera selecta,* eds. Peter Barth, et al. (Munich: Kaiser, 1926–1952), 1: 88 (hereafter = OS).

PART THREE: THEOLOGY

Calvin's *Catechismus ecclesiae Genevensis* (1545) was dedicated to the "faithful ministers of Christ who preach the pure doctrine of the Gospel in East Friesland."[42] In the dedication Calvin says that his burden in writing this catechism was the unity of the churches. The catechism was written as an expression of the pure doctrine upon which the Reformed churches were founded. The doctrine of election is expressed in six different questions (Q. 27–29, 93, 96, and 100). Calvin divides his exposition of the Apostles' Creed into four parts: "The first refers to God the Father; the second concerns his Son Jesus Christ, and also includes the entire sum of man's redemption. The third part concerns the Holy Spirit; the fourth the Church and the divine benefits vouchsafed to it" (Q. 18).[43] The first occurrence of the doctrine of election is found in questions 27–29, which conclude Calvin's catechetical exposition of the first article of the Apostles' Creed.

> Q. 27. Why then do you call God merely creator, when it is much more excellent to defend and preserve creatures in their being, than once to have made them? A. This term does not merely imply that God so created his works once that afterwards he took leave of them [*ut illorum postea curam abiecerit*]. Rather, it is to be held that the world, as it was once made by him, so now is preserved by him, and that similarly both the earth and all other things persist only in so far as they are sustained by his virtue and as it were his hand. Besides, since he has all things under his hand, it also follows from this that he is the supreme ruler and lord of all. Hence from his being Creator of heaven and earth, we are to understand that it is he only who with wisdom, goodness and power rules the whole course and order of nature; who is the author of both rain and drought, hail and other storms, as also of serenity; who fertilizes the earth of his beneficence, or again renders it sterile by withdrawing his hand; from him also both health and disease proceed; to whose power finally all things are subject and at whose nod they obey [*cuius denique imperio subiaceant omnia et nutui obsequantur*].[44]

Question 27 does not actually mention election or predestination, but rather focuses on God's wise and good providential control over his creation. Calvin uses biblical language and imagery to convey the truth that God's Fatherly care and control extend over all of creation. He has not absented (*abeo*) himself from his creation, but takes personal, detailed interest in it. Calvin's last comment that all things are "subject" to God and "obey" his command surely is not meant to establish a species of metaphysical determinism. Calvin goes on in the next question to discuss God's control over evil:

> Q. 28. Now what shall we say of wicked men and devils? Shall we say that they too are subject to him? A. Although he does not govern them by his Spirit, yet he checks them by his power, as with a bridle, so that they are unable even to move unless he permits them to do so. Further, he even makes them ministers of his will, so that

---

42. Calvin had produced earlier catechisms to train the youth of Geneva and Strasbourg (see De Greef, *Writings*, 132–33), but his 1545 catechism culminates his own catechetical efforts.

43. "The Catechism of the Church of Geneva," in *Calvin: Theological Treatises*, ed. and trans. J. K. S. Reid (Philadelphia: Westminster, 1954), 93. The Latin text of the Catechism is found in OS, 2:59–157. That Latin edition is later than the French, incorporating Calvin's own emendations and corrections to the original document.

44. Calvin, *Theological Treatises*, 94; OS, 2:78:1–17.

they are forced, unwilling and against their inclination, to effect what seems good to him.[45]

Calvin affirms the biblical truth that Satan and his fallen angels are "subject" to and "governed" by God, but he does not here confess that their wicked deeds are predestined by God such that their wickedness and rebellion is directly *caused* by God. God does not govern them "by his Spirit" in the same way that He does the good angels and his people. Here we see Calvin's concern to articulate the fundamental asymmetry in God's dealings with men and angels. Although He works in us all faith, righteousness, and every good thing, God "checks" and "permits" and "forces" wicked men and devils "against their inclination, to effect what seems good to him." And Calvin confesses this not because he is interested in establishing some abstract idea of God's absolute power or fill out his "system" by drawing out as many logical implications of predestination as he can.[46] On the contrary, he has a pastoral concern, as we discover in the next question.

> Q. 29. What benefit accrues to you from the knowledge of this? A. Very much. For it would go ill with us, if anything were permitted wicked men and devils without the will of God; then our minds could never be tranquil, for thinking ourselves exposed to their pleasure. Only then do we safely rest when we know them to be curbed by the will of God and, as it were, held in confinement, so that they cannot do anything but by his permission, especially since God himself undertakes to be our guardian and the captain of our salvation.[47]

It is God the Father as the "guardian and captain of our salvation" that insures that wicked men and devils are "permitted" to do nothing against his own will. Such knowledge strengthens the weak and faltering soul who may be buffeted by the persecutions of evil men and the temptations of Satan. The knowledge that God's enemies can do nothing "but by his permission" insures that nothing in the universe can threaten the salvation of the one who trusts in the Father. There is no evidence here of philosophical or metaphysical determinism or of an overly curious mind that delights in prying into God's secret counsel. Calvin's expounds these truths in the context of the gospel as pastoral assurance to his flock that nothing can separate them from the love of God in Christ (Rom 8:39).

Three more questions on the church also briefly describe the doctrine of election:

---

45. Calvin, *Theological Treatises*, 94; OS, 2:78, 18–23.

46. Barth draws out the implications of Calvin's refusal: "We must resist the temptation to absolutize in some degree the concept of choosing or electing. We must not interpret the freedom, the mystery and the righteousness of the election of grace merely as the definitions and attributes of a supreme form of electing posited as absolute. We must not find in this supreme form as such the reality of God. Otherwise we shall be doing what we ought not to do. We shall be forging and constructing (out of this very characteristic) a supreme being. And it is difficult to imagine how the description of the activity of this being can ever become a Gospel. If the distinctive and ultimate feature in God is absolute freedom of choice, or an absolutely free choice, then it will be hard to distinguish His freedom from caprice or His mystery from the blindness of such caprice" (CD II/2, 25).

47. Calvin, *Theological Treatises*, 94; OS, 2:78, 24–32.

PART THREE: THEOLOGY

> Q. 93. What is the Church? A. The body and society of believers whom God has predestined to eternal life.
>
> Q. 96. In what sense then do you call the Church holy? A. In this sense, that all whom God chooses he justifies, and remakes in holiness and innocence of life (Rom. 8:29), so that in them his glory may be displayed. This is what Paul intends, when he affirms that Christ sanctifies the Church which he redeemed, that it might be glorious and free from all stain (Eph. 5:25).
>
> Q. 100. But is it possible to know this Church other than by the faith with which it is believed? A. There is indeed also a visible Church of God, which he has described to us by sure signs and marks. But strictly this question concerns the company of those who, by secret election, he has adopted for salvation; and this is not always visible with the eyes nor discernible by signs.[48]

The fact that Calvin does not treat the doctrine of predestination as a corollary to his doctrine of God's transcendence or as a logical deduction from any of his attributes, but subsumes his only explicit mention of predestination under the doctrine of the church and her justification and sanctification, leads to the conclusion that he is confessing this doctrine an evangelical way. This fact becomes even clearer when we consider the French Confession of Faith.

The origins of the *Confession de foy* (1559) are complex. From the beginning of the Reformation in France, the churches were liable to severe persecution. The Genevan church in French-speaking Switzerland served both as refugee camp and headquarters for the often-underground church in France. Various confessions came out of the Reformed churches in France, but the last and enduring confession was composed from a draft written by Calvin and revised at a secret meeting of the French church in Paris in May, 1559. It was presented to King Francis II with a new preface in 1560, and at the colloquy of Poissy (1561) it was offered by Beza to Charles IX as *the* Reformed confession of faith. Although the details of its origin and use in the Reformed churches cannot concern us here,[49] it should be noted that the confession gained explicit approval from Calvin, Beza, and other key leaders in the Reformed churches. The doctrine of election is confessed in three separate articles.

> Art. VIII. We believe that he not only created all things, but that he governs and directs them, disposing and ordaining by his sovereign will all that happens in the world [Eph 1:11; Prov 16:4]; not that he is the author of evil, or that the guilt of it can be imputed to him, as his will is the sovereign and infallible rule of all right and justice; but he has wonderful means of so making use of devils and sinners that he can turn to good the evil which they do, and of which they are guilty [Acts 2:23; 4:27]. And thus, confessing that the providence of God orders all things, we humbly bow before the secrets which are hidden to us, without questioning what is above our understanding [Rom 9:19–20]; but rather making use of what is revealed to

---

48. Calvin, *Theological Treatises*, 102–3; OS, 2:88, 23–24; 89, 11–16; 90:4–9.

49. See Schaff, *Creeds of Christendom*, 1:490–98; Brian G. Armstrong, "Semper Reformanda: The Case of the French Reformed Church, 1559–1620," in *Later Calvinism: International Perspectives*, ed. W. Fred Graham, Sixteenth Century Essays and Studies 12 (Kirksville, MO: Sixteenth Century Journal, 1994), 119–38.

us in Holy Scripture for our peace and safety, inasmuch as God, who has all things in subjection to him, watches over us with a Father's care, so that not a hair of our heads shall fall without his will. And yet he restrains the devils and all our enemies, so that they can not harm us without his leave [Matt 10:30; Job 1:12; 2:6; Matt 8:31; Jer 19:11].[50]

Here again, as in Calvin's Genevan Catechism, the doctrine of providence contains a confession of God's "disposing and ordaining by his sovereign will all that happens in the world." Once again, also, one must carefully note the purpose or use of the confession of this certainty—to assure the Christian that God's Fatherly care and concern for him is no mere wish or impotent desire on God's part. God even makes use of devils and evil deeds in order to turn to good the evil that they perform in defiance of God. Thus, the article very carefully describes God's providential work so as to insist that God is not the author of evil since "his will is the sovereign and infallible rule of all that is right and just." This may seem paradoxical to the creature. Nevertheless there is one will of God, which is "the sovereign and infallible rule of all right and justice." There is no dark, capricious God "behind" the Father. He has revealed his will for our salvation in Christ. Thus, the confession forbids curious minds from prying into "secrets which are hidden from us" and "questioning what is above our understanding." The next article moves from God's providential will to his eternal counsel of grace in Christ.

> Art. XII. We believe that from this corruption and general condemnation in which all men are plunged, God, according to his eternal and immutable counsel, calls those whom he has chosen by his goodness and mercy alone in our Lord Jesus Christ, without any consideration of their works [Rom 3:2; 9:23; 2 Tim 2:20; Titus 3:5, 7; Eph 1:4; 2 Tim 1:9], to display in them the riches of his mercy [Ex 9:6; Rom 9:22]; leaving the rest in this same corruption and condemnation to show in them his justice. For the ones are not better than the others, until God discerns them according to his immutable purpose which he has determined in Jesus Christ before the creation of the world. Neither can any man gain such a reward by his own virtue, as by nature we can not have a single good feeling, affection, or thought, except God has first put it into our hearts [Jer 10:23; Eph 1:4–5].[51]

Article XII confesses the evangelical doctrine of election unto salvation. Five important points should be noted. First, supralapsarianism is ruled out in this article. God elects men to salvation as *homo lapsus*, that is, "from this corruption and general condemnation in which all men are plunged." There is no doctrine of reprobation, but rather of God's *preterition*, his "leaving the rest in this same corruption and condemnation." Second, God's election proceeds "by his goodness and mercy alone in our Lord Jesus Christ." The "alone" is significant. There is no other basis or motive in God's election of sinners other than his "goodness and mercy." The confession avoids the specter of an arbitrary selection based on some dark, hidden purposes known only to God. It also does not speak of predestination or election unto damnation. Third, not only is election motivated by the love of God, but He has chosen us "in our Lord Jesus Christ" and

---

50. Cochrane, *Reformed Confessions*, 147; OS, 2:312, 24—313, 19.
51. Cochrane, *Reformed Confessions*, 148–49; OS 2:314, 19–36.

his immutable purpose is determined "in Jesus Christ." God predestines *in Christ*. There is no evidence that the doctrine of election has been cast in terms of a deterministic logico-causal nexus; instead we have a clear confession of election as a corollary to the gospel of the grace of God in Christ. Fourth, not only does God's election originate in his mercy and grace, but his declared *end* in electing his people is to "display the riches of his mercy." Finally, even though the confession does not use the language of causality, it does clearly state that the wicked are not made wicked by God, but "left" in the corruption and condemnation that they justly deserve. The question of the relation of God's eternal counsel to the fall and the origin of evil is left an unaddressed mystery.

The two articles that follow Article XII speak to the question of God's universal salvific will.

> Art. XIII. We believe that all that is necessary for our salvation was offered and communicated to us in Jesus Christ. He is given to us for our salvation, and "is made unto us wisdom, and righteousness, and sanctification, and redemption": so that if we refuse him, we renounce the mercy of the Father, in which alone we can find a refuge.
>
> Art. XVI. We believe that God, in sending his Son, intended to show his love and inestimable goodness towards us, giving him up to die to accomplish all righteousness, and raising him from the dead to secure for us the heavenly life [John 3:16; 15:13].[52]

The dogmatic doctrine of election has its ground in the proclaimed and believed gospel of God's freely granted grace in Jesus Christ. The doctrine of election must be understood and articulated as another form of the proclamation of the gospel. The dogmatic, confessional presentation of the gospel ought not to lead us to raise questions that take us behind or beyond the will of God expressed in the gospel. Commenting on John 6:40, Calvin warns, "And if God's will is that those whom He has elected shall be saved by faith, and He confirms and executes his eternal decree [*aeternum suum decretum*] in this way, whosoever is not satisfied with Christ but inquires curiously about eternal predestination desires, as far as lies in him, to be saved contrary to God's purpose. The election of God in itself is hidden and secret. The Lord manifests it by the calling with which He honors us."[53]

---

52. Cochrane, *Reformed Confessions*, 149, 150; OS 2:315, 1–6; 316, 1–5.

53. Comm. on John 6:40 (CO, 47, 147); cf. *Inst.* 3.21.1. Calvin is willing to formulate the problem of God's will in reprobation as a paradox unavailable to the creature's reasoning power. "Although to our apprehension the will of God is manifold, yet he does not in himself will opposites, but according to his manifold wisdom (as Paul calls it, Eph. 3:10), transcends our senses, until such time as it shall be given to us to know how he mysteriously wills what now seems to be adverse to his will" (*Inst.* 3.24.17; cf. 1.18.3; 3.20.43). The advent of Christ will reveal God's one will to save mankind, but until then, for the mind of the time-bound creature, God *appears* to have two wills. Commenting on Matthew 23:37, Calvin notes: "... we fully believe that his *will* is simple and one; but as our minds do not fathom the deep abyss of secret election, in accommodation to the capacity of our weakness, the *will* of God is exhibited to us in two ways" (John Calvin, *Commentary on a Harmony of the Evangelists, Matthew, Mark, and Luke*, vol. 2, trans. William Pringle (Grand Rapids: Baker, 1981), 109; CO 83, 644).

When he expounds passages such as 1 Timothy 2:4f. and 2 Timothy 2:19, Calvin is not shy about articulating God's universal salvific will. "By exhibiting to all the Gospel and Christ the Mediator God shows that

Art. XXI. We believe that we are enlightened in faith by the secret power of the Holy Spirit, that it is a gratuitous and special gift which God grants to whom he will, so that the elect have no cause to glory, but are bound to be doubly thankful that they have been preferred to others. We believe also that faith is not given to the elect only to introduce them into the right way, but also to make them continue in it to the end. For as it is God who has begun the work, he will also perfect it.[54]

This is the last reference to election in the French Confession of Faith. Election is clearly expounded as a corollary of the Reformation doctrine of grace, a guard against Pelagian and synergistic errors and a confirmation of our trust, but as such it is secondary, not primary. In the French Confession of Faith, then, the doctrine of predestination emerges in connection with God's providence as comfort for the believer (Art. VIII), but finally, the definitive doctrine of election is confessed as the eternal backdrop of God's gracious justification of sinners in Christ (Arts. XII, XIII, XVI, and XXI).

TWO ENGLISH CONFESSIONS

The reign of "Bloody Mary" in England forced many who confessed the Reformation faith into exile. Fleeing to the cities of the Continent where they sought freedom to confess the gospel, about 18,000 found refuge principally in Strasbourg, Frankfurt, Emden, Zurich, and Geneva. There they organized their own English-speaking congregations. In 1555, the city of Geneva granted the English exiles the privilege of citizenship and then found them a suitable place of worship. The congregation chose John Knox and Christopher Goodman as pastors. The small congregation had great influence on the future direction

---

he wishes all men to be saved" (CO 80, 246). "The fruit of the sacrifice by which he made atonement for sins extends to all" (CO 80, 268). "The mystery is that 'souls' perish who are bought by the blood of Christ" (CO 82, 165). God's perfect will to bring light and life to all through Christ is fully revealed in the gospel; so much so that his judgment must be an *accidental* (or alien) characteristic of God's action. Calvin explains 2 Corinthians 3:7: "It happens *accidentally* that the Gospel is the source of death, and accordingly is the occasion of it rather than its cause, inasmuch as it is in its own nature salutary to all" (CO 78, 42).

Whatever else Calvin teaches about the reality of reprobation, it cannot be conceived of on the same level as or symmetrical with election to salvation. Not the Word, the gospel, nor the sacraments minister judgment *per se* but *per accidens*. With regard to the difficult saying of Jesus in Mark 4:11–22, Calvin explains: "The doctrine is not strictly speaking or by itself, or in its own nature, but by accident (*per accidens*), the cause of blindness. . . . When the Word of God blinds or hardens the reprobate, it belongs truly and naturally to themselves, but it is accidental as respects the Word" (CO 83, 361). The gospel *binds* and *looses*, as Jesus says in Matthew 16:19, but the latter "does not belong to the nature of the Gospel, but is *accidental* (*accidentale*)" (CO 83, 475). Again: "The Gospel is preached for salvation. This is what properly belongs to it, but believers alone are partakers of that salvation. In the meantime, its being an occasion of condemnation to unbelievers—that arises from their own fault. Thus Christ came not into the world to condemn the world (John iii.17,), for what need was there of this, inasmuch as without him we are all condemned? Yet He sends his apostles to bind, as well as to loose, and to retain sins as well as to remit them (Matt. xviii:19; John xx:23). He is the light of the world (John viii:12,) but He blinds unbelievers (John ix:39). He is a rock, for a foundation, but He is also to many a stone of stumbling (Isaiah viii:14). We must always therefore distinguish between the proper office of the Gospel and the accidental one (so to speak), which must be imputed to the depravity of mankind, to which it is owing that life to them is turned into death" (Comm. on 2 Cor 2:15; John Calvin, *Commentary on the Epistles of Paul the Apostle to the Corinthians*, trans. William Pringle (Grand Rapids: Baker, 1981), 161; CO 78, 34).

54. Cochrane, *Reformed Confessions*, 151; OS 2:317, 12–20.

of the Reformed church. The scholars and pastors of the 186-member church produced a church order and service book that became a standard for later Reformed worship, a metrical version of the Psalms that was widely used in England and Scotland, and a translation of the Bible—the Geneva Bible (1560)—that served as the standard Reformed Bible well into the next century.

They also produced a Confession of Faith (1560), the authorship of which is uncertain. Although it was probably the work of Whitingham, it certainly received Knox's approval and the early editions also bore the statement: "and approved by the famous and godly learned man, John Calvin."[55]

The four articles of this confession follow the pattern of Calvin's fourfold exposition of the Apostles' Creed (Father, Son, Holy Spirit, and Church). References to election occur in Articles III (Holy Spirit) and IV (Church).

> Art. III. Moreover, I believe and confess the Holy Ghost, God equal with the Father and the Son, who regenerates and sanctifies us, rules and guides us into all truth, persuading us most assuredly in our consciences that we are the children of God, brethren to Jesus Christ, and fellow-heirs with him of life everlasting. Yet notwithstanding it is not sufficient to believe that God is omnipotent and merciful, that Christ has made satisfaction, or that the Holy Spirit has this power and effect, except we do apply the same benefits to ourselves who are God's elect.

> Art. IV. I believe therefore and confess one holy Church which (as members of Jesus Christ the only Head thereof) agree in faith, hope, and love, using the gifts of God, whether they be temporal or spiritual, to the profit and furtherance of the same. This Church is not visible to man's eye but only known to God, who of the lost sons of Adam has ordained some as vessels of wrath to damnation [Rom 9:21-22], and has chosen others as vessels of his mercy to be saved [Rom 9:23; Eph 1:4-6, 11-12]. In due time he also calls them to integrity of life and godly conversation, to make them a glorious Church for himself. . . .[56]

This confession contains the only explicit reference to an ordination unto damnation. One should note, however, that the word "ordained" is the only extra-biblical word used; the language used in the confession is taken largely from the text of Romans 9. Moreover, the "double ordination" of Article IV cannot be construed as a reference to a supralapsarian doctrine of double predestination. The prepositional phrase "of the lost sons of Adam" warns against such a reading. Neither does the text construct a causal tree whereby man's lostness can be traced back to its root in God's absolute power or will. God's ordination of some as vessels of wrath presupposes their lost condition. Rigid logical and determinist lines of thought cannot be imputed to the confession's brief statement. The references to election do not proceed from a logicized conception of God's transcendence, but rather, occur within the discussion of the application of salvation and of the constituency of the Church of Jesus Christ.

This Confession of Faith was brought back and used in Scotland for a few years in the late 1550s as the leaders of the evangelical movement there labored for the legaliza-

---

55. Cochrane, *Reformed Confessions*, 129.
56. Ibid., 133-34.

tion of the Reformation church. But in 1560, the Reformation Parliament approved a new confession, known as the Scots Confession, drawn up by John Knox and his colleagues.[57] The Confession is composed of twenty-five articles, only two of which make any reference to the doctrine of election. The Scots Confession stands out among the Reformation symbolic documents for its decidedly Trinitarian, theocentric, and therefore evangelical shape and content. This is particularly true of the way in which the doctrine of election is Christologically confessed. At the heart of the mystery of election is the wondrous conjunction of God and man in Christ. Christ is the elect one. Only in him may we contemplate our election. Chapter VII ("Why the Mediator had to be true God and true man") is very short, but wonderfully placed after the doctrine of the incarnation and before the chapter on election: "We acknowledge and confess that this wonderful union between the Godhead and the humanity of Christ Jesus did arise from the eternal and immutable decree of God from which all our salvation springs and depends."[58] The eternal and immutable decree of God has to do *first* with the Son's incarnation in history. Our salvation "springs and depends" upon the execution of *this* decree of God. The next chapter on election unpacks this relationship.

> Chapter VIII. Election. That same eternal God and Father, who by grace alone chose us in His Son Christ Jesus before the foundation of the world was laid, appointed Him to be our head, our brother, our pastor, and the great bishop of our souls. But since the opposition between the justice of God and our sins was such that no flesh by itself could or might have attained unto God, it behooved the Son of God to descend unto us and take himself a body of our body, flesh of our flesh, and bone of our bone, and so become the Mediator between God and man, giving power to as many as believe in Him to be the sons of God; as he himself says, "I ascend to My Father and to your Father, to my God and to your God." By this most holy brotherhood whatever we have lost in Adam is restored to us again. Therefore we are not afraid to call God our Father, not so much because he has created us, which we have in common with the reprobate, as because he has given unto us his only Son to be our brother, and given us grace to acknowledge and embrace Him as our only Mediator. Further, it behooved the Messiah and Redeemer to be true God and true man, because He was able to undergo the punishment of our transgression and disobedience, and by death to overcome him that was the author of death. But because the Godhead alone could not suffer death, and neither could manhood overcome death, he joined both together in one person, that the weakness of the one should suffer and be subject to death—which we have deserved—and the infinite and invincible power of the other, that is, of the Godhead, should triumph, and purchase life, liberty, and perpetual victory. So we confess, and most undoubtedly believe.[59]

The most significant fact about this article on election in the Scots Confession has to be the explicitly Christological, even Trinitarian, matrix of the doctrine. The reality of election is set out and explained in terms of the gracious purposes of the Father and the

---

57. See "Scots Confession" in *Dictionary of Scottish Church History and Theology*, ed. Nigel M. de S. Cameron (Downers Grove, IL: InterVarsity Press, 1993), 751–52.
58. Cochrane, *Reformed Confessions*, 168.
59. Ibid., 169.

PART THREE: THEOLOGY

Son toward sinful humanity. According to the Scots Confession, the hypostatic union between God and man occupies the heart of the mystery of election. The election of the humanity of Christ unveils the pattern of our election in Christ. Christ is himself the elect one, and in him our election is certain because of his atoning mediation. No evidence can be found in this confession of an arbitrary election or determination that takes place apart from Christ or behind his back (so to speak), since Christ himself is the true image of God's character and purposes.[60] Perhaps the majesty of this Trinitarian and soteriological confession of election can be appreciated only against the tendency of later seventeenth-century Reformed confessions to "abstract" the doctrine of election and predestination from its proper Trinitarian, Christological, and therefore evangelical context. The Westminster Confession of Faith (1647), for example, expounds the doctrine of God's decree with noticeably different concerns. Consider the first four paragraphs of Westminster's chapter "Of God's Eternal Decree":

> 1. God, from all eternity, did, by the most wise and holy counsel of his own will, freely, and unchangeably ordain whatsoever comes to pass: yet so, as thereby neither is God the author of sin, nor is violence offered to the will of the creatures; nor is the liberty or contingency of second causes taken away, but rather established.
>
> 2. Although God knows whatsoever may or can come to pass upon all supposed conditions, yet hath he not decreed anything because he foresaw it as future, or as that which would come to pass upon such conditions.
>
> 3. By the decree of God, for the manifestation of his glory, some men and angels are predestined unto everlasting life; and others foreordained to everlasting death.
>
> 4. These angels and men, thus predestined, and foreordained, are particularly and unchangeably designed, and their number so certain and definite, that it cannot be either increased or diminished.[61]

In contrast to the way of Westminster, the Scots Confession expounds election in terms of Christology from the start. Election can only be understood as the eternal activity of God *in Christ*. God has chosen us in Christ before the foundation of the world (Eph 1:4). But Westminster's treatment of predestination is abstracted from Christology and the Trinity. Thus, the church's understanding of the ultimate character of God himself is impoverished and ultimately imperiled. The Westminster tradition gives the distinct impression of a predestination or eternal purpose of God that takes place apart from Christ or "outside of" and "before" Christ.

---

60. In the same year, in addition to this confession, Knox also published a lengthy doctrinal treatise on election: "An answer to a great number of blasphemous cavillations written by an Anabaptist, and adversarie to God's eternal Predestination" (*The Works of John Knox*, ed. David Laing, 6 vols. [Edinburgh, 1846–1864], 5:19–468). Knox argues that without this doctrine of election Christians would not fully appreciate their utter dependence upon God's unbounded mercy and grace in Christ. For Knox, the doctrine of election is the corollary to *sola fide*; in defending the doctrine, one defends the utter freedom and unconditional nature of God's grace in Jesus Christ and his gospel.

61. *The Westminster Confession of Faith* (1647; reprint, Edinburgh: Free Presbyterian Publications, 1976), 28–29.

Furthermore, the order is different in the Scots Confession. In the Scots Confession Christ is determined before the foundation of the world "to be our head, our brother, our pastor, and the great bishop of our souls." Christ is the predestined one (*prädestinatio christi*) and our election is consummated when we are given to partake of the "most holy brotherhood" restored to us through Christ. This constitutes a thoroughly evangelical way of confessing the doctrine of election, a confession without any hint of philosophical baggage or interest in cosmological/metaphysical questions of causality and freedom.

THE HEIDELBERG CATECHISM AND BELGIC CONFESSION

What we have discovered so far concerning the fundamental soteriological confession of the doctrine of election in the sixteenth-century Reformed symbolic documents will also characterize the next two confessional documents. The Heidelberg Catechism was composed by Heidelberg's professor of theology, Zacharius Ursinus (d. 1583), and the city's main pastor, Caspar Olevianus (d. 1587). The first edition was published by Fredrick III in the Palatinate on January 19, 1563.[62] It was intended as a summary of the best of Lutheran and Reformed theology to instruct simple Christians in the evangelical way of the Reformation.[63]

The doctrine of election cannot be said to occupy a central or defining place within this catechism's system of doctrine since it is mentioned in only three questions (Q. 31, 52, and 54). The first two references occur as part of the explanation of the second article of the Apostles' Creed.

> Q. 31. Why is he called Christ? A. Because he is foreordained [*verordnet*] by God the Father, and anointed with the Holy Spirit, to be our chief Prophet and Teacher, who fully reveals to us the secret counsel and will of God concerning our redemption; and our only high priest, who by the one sacrifice of his body has redeemed us, and ever lives to make intercession for us with the Father; and our eternal King, who governs us by his Word and Spirit, and defends and preserves us in the redemption obtained for us.[64]

> Q. 52. What comfort is it to you that Christ shall come again to judge the quick and the dead? A. That in all my sorrows and persecutions, with uplifted head, I look for the very same One who has before offered himself for me to the judgment of God, and removed from me all curse, to come again as Judge from heaven; who shall cast all his and my enemies into everlasting condemnation, but shall take me, with all his chosen ones to himself [*mich aber sampt allen außerwehlten zu jm*], into heavenly joy and glory.[65]

---

62. Mark A. Noll, ed., *The Confessions and Catechisms of the Reformation* (Grand Rapids: Baker, 1991), 133–36.

63. See Christopher J. Burchill, "On the Consolation of a Christian Scholar: Zacharias Ursinus (1534–1583) and the Reformation of Heidelberg," *Journal of Ecclesiastical History* 37 (1986) 568–83; and Derek Visser, ed., *Controversy and Conciliation: The Reformation in the Palatine, 1559-1583* (Alison Park, PA: Pickwick, 1986).

64. Translation slightly modified from *Creeds of Christendom*, 1:317–18; BSR, 690, 32—691, 2.

65. Translation slightly modified from *Creeds of Christendom*, 1:323–24; BSR, 696, 6–15.

PART THREE: THEOLOGY

The same pattern emerges here as in other Reformed confessions. The explanation of election is placed in connection with the doctrine of Christ and salvation. As in the Scots Confession, Christ is the preeminent elect one. *He* is the one "ordained by God the Father." Furthermore, God's purpose in foreordaining Christ was so that he might be "our chief Prophet and Teacher" and unveil for us the "secret counsel and will of God concerning our redemption." The secret counsel and will of God here does not function as a dark, unknown purpose hidden in the arcane will of a capricious God behind Christ; rather, the work of God "fully reveals" what was secret and hidden before Christ. God's will in Christ is for our redemption. God's electing will and his saving work in Christ are inseparably conjoined.

> Q. 54. What do you believe concerning the holy catholic Church? A. That out of the whole human race, from the beginning to the end of the world, the Son of God, by his Spirit and Word, gathers, defends, and preserves for himself unto everlasting life, an elect communion [*eine auserwählte Gemeine*] in the unity of the true faith; and that I am, and forever shall remain, a living member of the same.[66]

This last reference to election helps explain the meaning of the Church. Heidelberg has expanded on Luther's explanation of the third article of the Apostles' Creed in his Small Catechism. The "elect communion" is composed of those of true faith that are gathered, defended, and preserved by the Son of God unto everlasting life. Since these three questions represent the entire substance of the doctrine of election as confessed by the Heidelberg Catechism, there can be no denying that predestination does not function in this document as a central dogma or as the logical construct of logico-causal theological deduction. The gospel context is foundational for Ursinus and Olevianus when confessing the doctrine of election.

During the Spanish inquisition in the Lowlands, the need arose for a definitive statement of faith that would unite Reformed Christians. Guido de Bres (1522–1567) and colleagues composed what is called the Belgic Confession, the first draft (1559) of which was sent to Calvin, who approved it.[67] The Belgic Confession is modeled after the French Confession (1560) so that it contains thirty-seven articles in the same order. The doctrine of election is confessed in Article XII (Of Divine Providence) and Article XVI (Of Eternal Election).

> Art. XIII. Of Divine Providence. We believe that the same God, after he had created all things, did not forsake them, or give them up to fortune or chance, but that he rules and governs them, according to his holy will, so that nothing happens in this world without his appointment [*ut nihil in hoc mundo absque ipsius ordinatione eveniat*; twenty-five separate Scripture passages are cited as proof–JM]; nevertheless, God neither is the author of, nor can be charged with, the sins which are committed [*quamvis tamen Deus peccatorum quae fiunt neque autor neque reus sit*]. For his power and goodness are so great and incomprehensible, that he orders and executes his work in the most excellent and just manner even when the devil and wicked men act unjustly [Matt 8:31–32; John 3:8]. And as to what he does

---

66. Translation slightly modified from *Creeds of Christendom*, 1:324–25; BSR, 696, 30–36.
67. *Creeds of Christendom*, 1:502–8.

surpassing human understanding we will not curiously inquire into it further than our capacity will admit of; but with the greatest humility and reverence adore the righteous judgments of God which are hid from us [Rom 11:33–34], contenting ourselves that we are disciples of Christ, to learn only those things which he has revealed to us in his Word without transgressing these limits. This doctrine affords us unspeakable consolation, since we are taught thereby that nothing can befall us by chance, but by the direction of our most gracious and heavenly Father, who watches over us with a paternal care, keeping all creatures so under his power that not a hair of our head (for they are all numbered), nor a sparrow, can fall to the ground, without the will of our Father, in whom we do entirely trust; being persuaded that he so restrains the devil and all our enemies that, without his will and permission, they cannot hurt us. And therefore we reject that damnable error of the Epicureans who say that God regards nothing, but leaves all things to chance.[68]

The "same God" refers to the Holy Trinity as confessed in the preceding articles, not to some vague, undefined natural notion of God.[69] The Father orders all things for the sake of his Son by means of the Holy Spirit. God's ordination of all things finds its place here in the chapter on providence, not because of the logical constraints of a deterministic system of doctrine, but because Christians need consolation: "we are taught thereby that nothing can befall us by chance, but by the direction of our most gracious and heavenly Father." The Christian ought to be certain that his "most gracious and heavenly Father" has control of all things—that *nothing* happens apart from his appointment.

This comprehensive ordering of all things, however, does not mean that God directly *causes* all things. God "orders and executes" his own works according to justice even as "the devil and wicked men *act* unjustly." God cannot "be charged with the sins which are committed," and so can never be guilty as the author of sin and evil. His work with reference to evil is characterized as "restraining the devil and all our enemies that, without his will and permission, they cannot hurt us." He is not the author of sin and evil.[70] Consequently, the Belgic Confession's article on providence directs doubtful and

---

68. Cochrane, *Reformed Confessions*, 197; BSR, 237, 1–19.

69. Although less well known, the Hungarian Confession (Peter Mélius Juhász, 1570), also contains a very Trinitarian-shaped confession of election: "Out of the Word of God we call Him Father, God, and Jehovah, having life in himself, existent from none, wanting all beginning, who from eternity without any beginning or change begot out of his own Person as it were the character and splendor of his glory, the only begotten Son—through whom He from eternity foreknew and disposed all things, and in the beginning created, and conserves them, and saves his elect by justifying them, but condemns the impious" (Warfield, "Predestination," 155). Here, in this late Reformed confession, even after the strong influence of Beza on Peter Mélius Juhász, its author, the doctrine of election has a very decidedly Trinitarian, soteriological, and therefore pastoral shape. Although numerous local confessions were framed as the Reformation moved into Hungary in the sixteenth century, the *Confessio Catholica* (also known as the *Confessio Debreciensis* or *Agrovallensis*) is one of the last and most well known of the Reformed Hungarian confessions (being published in the *Syntagma confessionum*). For the full text see BSR, 265–376. On the origin and development of Reformed theology in Hungary, see David P. Daniel, "Calvinism in Hungary: The Ecclesiastical Transition to the Reformed Faith," in *Calvinism in Europe: 1540-1620*, eds. Andrew Pettegree, et al. (Cambridge: Cambridge University Press, 1994), 205–30; and Kálmán D. Tóth, "The Helvetic Reformation in Hungary," in *John Calvin: His Influence in the Western World*, ed. W. Stanford Reid (Grand Rapids: Zondervan, 1982), 155–60.

70. The Hungarian Confession also contains a powerful paragraph denying God's complicity in evil. "As it is altogether impossible that things that are in direct repugnance to one another and are mutually

PART THREE: THEOLOGY

troubled Christians to the will of their all-powerful Father in heaven, who orders all things, including Satan, demons, and wicked men, so mysteriously and perfectly that "they can not hurt us." The pastoral purpose of this article is evident.

The Belgic Confession contains one brief, very precisely worded article on election unto salvation:

> Art. XVI. We believe that all the posterity of Adam, being fallen into perdition and ruin by the sin of our first parents, God then did manifest himself such as he is; that is to say, MERCIFUL AND JUST: MERCIFUL, since he delivers and preserves from this perdition all whom he, in his eternal and unchangeable council, of mere goodness has elected in Christ Jesus our Lord, without any respect to their works [*pro gratuita sua bonitate in Jesu Christo Domino nostro elegit et selegit, absque ullo operum eorum respectu*]: JUST in leaving others in the fall and perdition wherein they have involved themselves [*reliquos in lapsu et perditione, in quam sese praecipitaverant, relinquendo*].[71]

Rather than finding a rationalistic predestinarian system grounded on a speculative doctrine of the will of God, we discover a Christocentric confession of election emphasizing soteriology not causality. God's election takes place against the backdrop of the fall. The fallen posterity of Adam are mercifully elected out of God's mere goodness in Christ Jesus the Lord. Logical symmetry does not enter the picture. God's relation to those outside of Christ is not described with the language of foreordination, predestination, or election; rather, God "leaves others in the fall and perdition wherein they have involved themselves."[72] Damnation is justly meted out, but remains the shadow, the fearful antipode against which the Christian's election stands out in sharp relief. The light of God's mercy shines in his deliverance of the elect in Christ Jesus, without any respect to their works. The Christian's salvation must be traced back solely to God's grace and mercy apart from works. At the center of the Belgic Confession's theological concern is the confession of God's mercy in Christ. The doctrine of election serves to ground the gospel in God's eternal and unchangeable council, not as the foundation of a theological system-building project that serves logically to tie everything together in the will of God.

---

destructive can be the efficient and formal cause of their contraries; as light is not the cause of darkness, nor heat of cold (Psalms 5, 46, 61, 66, 80, 84, 114, 135); so it is impossible for God, who is Light, Righteousness, Truth, Wisdom, Goodness, Life, to be the cause of darkness, sin and falsehood, ignorance, blindness, malice, and death; but Satan and men are the cause of all these. For God cannot *ex se* and *per se* do things that He prohibits and on account of which He condemns" (Warfield, "Predestination," 155).

71. Cochrane, *Reformed Confessions*, 199–200; BSR, 238, 43—239, 3.

72. The Hungarian Confession makes explicit what is only implicit here in this confession. God's election is not arbitrary or capricious: "As he who justly renders to those who work equally an equal reward, and who gives to the undeserving, out of grace and voluntarily, what he will, is not a respecter of persons; so God would have acted justly, if out of debt, according to justice and his own law, he had rendered death and condemnation as the stipend of sin to all who deserve it. And, on the other hand, when for the sake of his Son, out of the plenitude of his grace and in his freedom of will, he gives to the undeserving righteousness and life, this is not *prosopoliptis*, that is, he is not a respecter of persons, as it is said. . . . [quoting Matt 20]" (Warfield, "Predestination," 155–56).

THE SECOND HELVETIC CONFESSION

The last Reformed work to consider is the Second Helvetic Confession (1566). It will serve well to introduce our conclusions, since the doctrine of election receives a much fuller treatment—one that gathers together and confirms everything we have been observing about the fundamental shape and content of this doctrine according to the churchly Reformed documents. The Second Helvetic Confession was written by Heinrich Bullinger (d. 1575) as a filling-out of the First Helvetic Confession. Even though this confession was the work of a single author and not commissioned by any one church, it became one of, if not the most widely respected Reformed confessions.

The first mention of election is found in Chapter VIII (Of Man's Fall, Sin and the Cause of Sin). After paragraphs outlining the fall of man, the nature of sin, the curse of death, and original sin, the confession devotes one paragraph to explain that "God is not the author of sin, and how far He is said to harden [*Deus non est author peccati, et quantenus indurare dicatur*]." This paragraph is especially interesting in light of the Formula of Concord's explicit discussion of God's hardening (SD XI, 39–41, 57, 84, 85). The Second Helvetic Confession begins by citing Scripture references that deny God's complicity in evil and sin:

> It is expressly written: "Thou art not a God who delights in wickedness. Thou hatest all evildoers. Thou destroyest those who speak lies" (Ps. 5:4ff.). And again: "When the Devil lies, he speaks according to his own nature, for he is a liar and the father of lies" (John 8:44). Moreover, there is enough sinfulness and corruption in us that it is not necessary for God to infuse into us a new or still greater perversity. *When, therefore, it is said in Scripture that God hardens, blinds, and delivers up to a reprobate mind, it is to be understood that God does it by a just judgment as a just Judge and Avenger.* Finally, as often as God in Scripture is said or seems to do something evil, it is not thereby said that man does not do evil, but that God permits it and does not prevent it, according to his just judgment, who could prevent it if he wished, or because he turns man's evil into good, as he did in the case of the sin of Joseph's brethren, or because he governs sins lest they break out and rage more than is appropriate. St. Augustine writes in his *Enchiridion*: "What happens contrary to his will occurs, in a wonderful and ineffable way, not apart from his will. For it would not happen if he did not allow it. And yet he does not allow it unwillingly but willingly. But he who is good would not permit evil to be done, unless, being omnipotent, he could bring good out of evil." Thus wrote Augustine.[73]

This paragraph is self-explanatory. God is not the cause of sin or evil. He does not harden morally "neutral" men. His hardening is a just judgment, not an arbitrary selection of some for damnation. The Formula of Concord makes the same point: "On the contrary, as God has ordained in his counsel that the Holy Spirit would call, enlighten, and convert the elect through the Word and that he would justify and save all who accept Christ through true faith, so he has also ordained in his counsel that he would harden, reject, and condemn all who, when they are called through the Word, spurn the Word and persistently resist the Holy Spirit who wants to work efficaciously in them through

---

73. Cochrane, *Reformed Confessions*, 236–37, emphasis mine; BSR, 178, 5—179, 22.

PART THREE: THEOLOGY

the Word" (SD XI, 40). The Second Helvetic Confession concludes this chapter on man's fall and the cause of sin with a warning against illegitimate speculative inquires:

> Curious questions. Other questions, such as whether God willed Adam to fall, or incited him to fall, or why he did not prevent the fall, and similar questions, we reckon among curious questions (unless perchance the wickedness of heretics or of other churlish men compels us also to explain them out of the Word of God, as the godly teachers of the Church have frequently done), knowing that the Lord forbade man to eat of the forbidden fruit and punished his transgression. We also know that what things are done are not evil with respect to the providence, will, and power of God, but in respect to Satan and our will opposing the will of God [*sed et mala non esse quae fiunt, respectu providentiae Dei, voluntatis ac potestatis Dei, sed respectu satanae et voluntatis nostrae, voluntati Dei repugnantis*].[74]

The Second Helvetic Confession directs men to the Word of God for access to God's will for man. Disputations and investigations into the relationship between predestination and the fall of man are profitless. It is enough to know that God forbade man to eat of the tree and that man rebelled against God's explicit will. This is the origin of evil. The Second Helvetic Confession does, however, make a telling concession in passing. Sometimes it is necessary that heretics and other churlish men (e.g., Erasmus, Pighuis) be answered, and this may require theologians and pastors (e.g., Luther, Calvin) to write, lecture, or preach on this subject. Nevertheless, such questions as God's causal connection with the fall are not normally proper subjects for Christian preaching and confession. The Second Helvetic Confession seems to allow that such polemic works have a different function than ecclesiastical confessions.

Chapter X (Of the Predestination of God and the Election of the Saints) contains the longest treatment of this subject in any of the sixteenth-century symbolic texts.

> 1. God has elected us out of grace [*Deus elegit nos ex gratia*]. From eternity God has freely, and of his mere free grace, without respect to men, predestined or elected the saints, whom he wills to save in Christ [*Deus ab aeterno praedestinavit vel elegit libere et mera sua gratia, nullo hominum respectu, sanctos, quos vult salvos facere in Christo*], according to the saying of the apostle, "God chose us in him before the foundation of the world" (Eph 1:4). And again: "Who saved us and called us with a holy calling, not in virtue of our works but in virtue of his own purpose and the grace which he gave to us in Christ Jesus ages ago, and now has manifested through the appearing of our Savior Christ Jesus" (2 Tim 1:9).

> 2. We are elected or predestined in Christ [*In Christo electi vel praedestinati sumus*]. Therefore, not without means [*non sine medio*], though not according to any merit of ours, but in Christ and according to Christ [*in Christo et propter Christum*], has God elected us; even those who are grafted in Christ by faith [*ut qui jam sunt in Christo insiti per fidem*], these he has elected; truly the reprobate are those outside of Christ [*reprobi, vero, qui sunt extra Christum*], according to the word of the apostle, "Examine yourselves to see whether you are situated in [the] faith . . ." (2 Cor 13:5).

---

74. Cochrane, *Reformed Confessions*, 237, and Warfield, "Predestination," 157; BSR, 179, 20–22.

> 3. We are elected to a definite end [*Electi sumus ad finem certum*]. Finally, the saints are chosen in Christ by God for a definitive purpose, which the apostle himself explains when he says, "He chose us in Him for adoption that we should be holy and blameless before him in love. He destined us for adoption to be his sons through Jesus Christ that they should be to the praise of the glory of his grace" (Eph 1:4ff.).[75]

Predestination properly evidences the free grace of God in Christ, not the transcendent power or will of God. God's gracious will is revealed in Christ. The Second Helvetic Confession contains no doctrine of reprobation such that God's predestination forks off in two directions to create some for damnation and others for eternal life. The doctrine present here is radically asymmetrical. Furthermore, God has not merely predestined the means whereby men can save themselves if they so choose, but He has elected them to a "definite end."

> 4. We should have a good hope for all [*Bene sperandum de omnibus*]. And although God knows who are his, and here and there mention is made of the small number of the elect, yet we must hope well of all, and not rashly judge any man to be a reprobate. For Paul says to the Philippians, "I thank God for you all" (now he speaks of the whole church in Philippi), "because of your fellowship in the Gospel, being persuaded that he who began a good work in you will bring it to completion at the day of Jesus Christ. It is also right that I have this opinion of you all" (Phil. 1:3ff.).
>
> 5. Whether few are elect [*An pauci electi*]. And when the Lord was asked whether there were few that should be saved, he does not answer and tell them that few or many should be saved or damned, but rather he exhorts every man to "strive to enter the narrow door" (Luke 13:24): as if he should say, It is not for you curiously to inquire about these matters, but rather to endeavor that you may enter into heaven by the straight way.[76]

The confession warns against questioning whether one is elect or not. It cites Paul's own practice of treating entire churches as elect. All things considered, the community of Christians must be considered the elect of God.

> 6. What is to be condemned in this matter. Therefore we do not approve of the impious speeches of some who say, "Few are chosen, and since I do not know whether I am among the number of the few, I will enjoy myself." Others say, "If am predestined and elected by God, nothing can hinder me from salvation , which is already certainly appointed for me, no matter what I do. But if I am in the number of the reprobate, no faith or repentance will help me, since the decree of God cannot be changed [*Si vero sum de reproborum numero, nulla me vel fides vel poenitentia iuvabit: cum definitio Dei mutari non possit*]. Therefore, all doctrines and admonitions are useless." Now the saying of the apostle contradicts these men: "The Lord's servant must be ready to teach, instructing those who oppose him, so that if God

---

75. The first and third paragraph are my modification of the translation in Cochrane, *Reformed Confessions*, 240, and the second paragraph is my own translation, drawing from both Cochrane and Warfield, "Predestination," 157; BSR, 181, 29–39.

76. Apart from a slight change in the title of paragraph 4, this is the translation in Cochrane, *Reformed Confessions*, 240–41; BSR, 181, 40—182, 4.

should grant that they repent to know the truth, they may recover from the snare of the devil, after being held captive by him to do his will" (2 Tim 2:23ff.).

7. Admonitions are not in vain because salvation proceeds from election. Augustine also shows that both the grace of free election and predestination, and also salutary admonitions and doctrines are to be preached (*de Dono Perseverantiae*, chapt. 14).

8. Whether we are elected. We therefore find fault with those who outside of Christ ask whether they are elected from eternity [*qui extra Christum quaerunt, an sint ab aeterno electi*]. For what has God decreed for them from all eternity [*statuerit Deus*]? For the preaching of the Gospel is to be heard, and it is to be believed; and it is to be held as beyond doubt that if you believe and are in Christ, you are elected [*et pro indubitato habendum, si credis ac sis in Christo, electum te esse*]. For the Father has revealed unto us in Christ the eternal purpose of his predestination [*Pater enim praedestinationis suae aeternam sententiam*], as I have just now shown from the apostle in 2 Tim 1:9–10. This is therefore above all to be taught and considered, what great love of the Father toward us is revealed to us in Christ. We must hear what the Lord himself daily preaches to us in the Gospel, how He calls and says: "Come to me all who labor and are heavy-laden, and I will give you rest" (Matt 11:28). "God so loved the world, that He gave his only Son, that whoever believes in him should not perish, but have eternal life" (John 3:16). Also, "It is not the will of my Father that one of these little ones should perish" (Matt 18:4). Let Christ, therefore, be the looking glass, in whom we may contemplate our predestination [*Christus itaque sit speculum, in quo praedestinationem nostram contemplemur*]. We shall have a sufficiently clear and sure testimony that we are inscribed in the Book of Life if we have fellowship with Christ, and He is ours and we are his in true faith.

9. The temptation with reference to predestination [*Tentatio praedestinationis*]. With regard to the temptation associated with predestination—there is hardly any more dangerous—we are confronted by the fact that God's promises apply to all the faithful [or all those who possess faith; *quod promissiones Dei sunt universales fidelibus*], for He says: "Ask, and everyone who seeks, shall receive" (Luke 11:9f.). This finally we pray, with the whole church of God, "Our Father who art in heaven" (Matt 6:9), both because by baptism we are ingrafted into the body of Christ, and we are often fed in his church with his flesh and blood unto life eternal. Thereby being strengthened, we are commanded to work out our salvation with fear and trembling, according to the mandate of Paul.[77]

One can hardly fail to notice the similarities between the Second Helvetic Confession and the Formula of Concord's Article XI. The Formula warned that an errant doctrine of election might lead to soul-destroying questions that could never be answered as well as faith-quenching doubts that might lead to despair.[78] Paragraphs 6–7 in the Second

---

77. Translation slightly modified from Cochrane, *Reformed Confessions*, 241–42; BSR, 182, 5–43.

78. "Such a view, however, leads many to draw and formulate strange, dangerous, and pernicious opinions and causes and fortifies in people's minds either false security and impenitence or anxiety and despair. As a result they trouble themselves with burdensome doubts and say: 'Since God has foreordained his elect to salvation "before the foundations of the world were laid" (Eph 1:4) and since God's foreknowledge can never fail and no one can ever change or hinder it (Isa 14:27; Rom 9:19, 11), therefore if I have been foreknown to salvation, it will do me no harm if I live in all kinds of sin and vice without repentance, despise Word and sacraments, and do not concern myself with repentance, faith, prayer, and godliness.

Helvetic Confession warn against similar "logical" deductions in the Christian life. Paragraph 8 squelches another "curious question" fully in accord with the Formula. Man may be tempted to believe that he can intrude into God's beyond in order to obtain some answer about his destiny. But the effort is futile. In effect, such a search would have to be conducted outside of Christ and his Word, since according to the gospel, all who trust in Christ have been drawn by the Father and can be assured of their election. The Second Helvetic Confession understands election only "in Christ," that is, only as a corollary to the gospel. Furthermore, election is understood in tandem with God's revealed will and not as some secret or hidden will that might be ascertained apart from the gospel. The "book of life" faithfully mirrors the faithful fellowship a Christian experiences with Christ by faith. The *speculum* of election is Christ as he is revealed in the gospel.

CONCLUSIONS

Having examined the specific content of the Lutheran and Reformed ways of confessing the doctrine of election, we are now in a position 1) to summarize and characterize the Reformed confessional doctrine of election, and 2) to compare and contrast the Reformed and Lutheran confessional traditions in the sixteenth century. As we summarize the doctrine of election in these Reformed texts, we cannot help but do so with the pastoral concerns of the Formula's Article XI in the background. All along in our exposition of the Reformed confessions and catechisms we have been looking for similarities and dissimilarities between the two approaches. Two lists will suffice to summarize our findings in the light of the Formula's concerns.

First, according to the symbolic documents surveyed in this paper, the sixteenth-century Reformed confessional and catechetical content of the doctrine of election shows *no* evidence of:

1. Originating in extra-biblical reasoning (cf. EP XI, 16; SD XI, 1–3).[79] The Reformed confessions and catechisms have been careful to use biblical phraseology as far as possible, explicitly grounding the confessed doctrine in biblical truth.

2. Being framed, explained, or "captured" by philosophical (Aristotelian, Stoic, Ramist, etc.) or metaphysical categories and terminology (cf. SD XI, 3). This follows from the first point but ought to be made explicit. There is no evidence of the Reformed doctrine having taken its shape from pressure from any supposed logical, theological, or philosophical "system." The doctrine of predestination is not subjected to alien philosophical pressure in these symbols.

3. Overburdening the doctrine of election with overly subtle distinctions and overextending the biblical doctrine with illegitimate logico-deductive implications. The documents surveyed here have not introduced scholastic distinctions and metaphysical subtleties. On the contrary, they have confessed rather simply the pro-

On the contrary, I shall and must be saved since God's foreknowledge must be carried out. But if I am not foreknown, then everything is in vain, even though I were to hold to the Word, repent, believe, etc., since I cannot hinder or alter God's foreknowledge'" (SD XI, 10).

79. References to Article XI of the Formula appear in parenthesis as references to parallel concerns.

found doctrine of God's merciful election in Christ as a corollary to and defense of *sola gratia*. The Reformed symbols invent no new doctrine of predestination unknown in the catholic tradition of the Western church, nor do they inaugurate a new Reformed "scholasticism."

4. Being characterized by or preoccupied with speculative "prying" into God's secret counsels apart from the gospel of Christ (cf. EP XI, 6; SD XI, 9, 33, 89). The Reformed confessions and catechisms that have provided a fuller treatment of the doctrine have all warned against "curious questions" as a temptation attending the high doctrine of predestination (see especially Second Helvetic Confession VIII and X, 6–8).

5. Functioning as a "central" dogma, from which other doctrines are systematically deduced such that the result is a rationalizing, predestinarian system of theology.[80]

6. Being grounded in an abstract, speculative doctrine of the will or Power of God (as in Nominalism). The Reformed confessions, therefore, do not even hint at a terrifying, incapacitating conception of God as arbitrary and capricious (cf. SD XI, 9, 91). Election does not mean that God wields some dark, irrational power of *potentia absoluta*.

7. Constructing a symmetrical, supralapsarian *predestinatio gemina* such that God is efficient cause of sin, evil or damnation as (*eodem modo*) He is the absolute, efficient cause of righteousness and salvation (cf. EP XI, 3; SD XI, 6–7, 79–82).[81]

8. Identifying God as the *cause* of sin. Nothing in these Reformed symbols would lead one to conclude that God is the cause or author of the fall, sin, or unbelief (cf. SD XI, 7–8, 62–64, 79–81). On the contrary, this is explicitly and forcefully denied in almost every Reformed confession and catechism.

9. Establishing a causally deterministic understanding of the relationship between God and the universe that results in a metaphysical determinism in terms of a *necessitas rerum* that cannot be changed under any circumstances.

10. Bifurcating the will of God such that a Christian is confronted with a secret, hidden will of God that is in contradiction to his revealed will in Christ and in the gospel. The Reformed confessions betray no hesitation in proclaiming God's genu-

---

80. Muller has put to rest the caricature that Reformed sixteenth-century Orthodoxy developed a theological method that sought to deduce an entire theological system from a single principle or dogma. These are not deductive systems teased out of a central dogma of predestination. See Richard A. Muller, "Calvin and the 'Calvinists': Assessing the Continuities and Discontinuities Between the Reformation and Orthodoxy," *Calvin Theological Journal* 30 (1995) 345–75 and part two, *Calvin Theological Journal* 31 (1996) 125–60.

81. According to Barth, the doctrine of election's "content is instruction and elucidation, instruction and elucidation which are to us a proclamation of joy. It is not a mixed message of joy and terror, salvation and damnation. Originally and finally it is not dialectical but non-dialectical. It does not proclaim in the same breath both good and evil, both help and destruction, both life and death. It does, of course, throw a shadow. We cannot overlook or ignore this aspect of the matter. In itself, however, it is light and not darkness. We cannot, therefore, speak of the latter aspect in the same breath" (CD II/2, 13). Barth's comments serve as an accurate appraisal of the doctrine of election in these Reformed confessions.

ine and serious intention that all men come to repentance and believe the gospel (cf. EP XI, 10, 12, 13, 17–18; SD XI, 17–18).

11. Being overburdened with polemics that have no impact on the simple Christian's full apprehension of the gospel of God's unconditional grace in Christ (cf. EP XI, 13, 16, 22; SD XI, 91, 93).

12. Embracing any form of synergism. The Reformed confessions and catechisms allow no *decretum conditionatum* ordained by God *intuitu fidei* or contingent on anything in man (*aliquid in homine*) (cf. SD XI, 88, 89).

13. Denying or compromising the universality of God's grace in Christ or the genuine offer of Christ in the gospel to all men (cf. SD XI, 28–32, 34–36).

14. Insensitivity to the pastoral needs of tender consciences who need the assurance of God's gracious eternal counsel in Christ toward them (cf. SD XI, 45–47, 90–93).

15. Attempting to *explain* God's causal relationship to the fall, sin, and damnation using an extra-biblical distinction between *praescientia* and *praedestinatio* or *electio* (contra EP XI, 1–5; SD XI, 4–6).

This last denial calls for some explanation, since this is the one place that the Reformed and Lutheran ways appear to diverge. The Reformed documents examined here show no evidence of making a systematic distinction between foreknowledge and predestination as a way to *explain* the difference between God's relation to damnation and salvation. If the distinction between foreknowledge and predestination is offered by the Formula as a rational solution to the problem of the origin and cause of evil, then it is an extrabiblical one at best. The Bible itself does not offer this solution.[82] It may appear to exonerate God from any complicity in evil, but at what cost? The Formula utilizes the concept of *vorsehung* as *praescientia* to describe God's relation to evil and unbelief (SD XI), even though the Bible never speaks this way. As Preus notes, in the Formula's discussion of election, "Foreknowledge is usually spoken of in an unbiblical and ecclesiastical sense, meaning that God knows in advance all that occurs but is not necessarily the cause of such events and occurrences."[83]

---

82. Furthermore, once this all-important terminological distinction is made, it is almost immediately ignored—the term *vorsehung* is used as a synonym for election (SD XI, 10, 12)!

83. Robert Preus, "Predestination and Election," 272. We might also wonder about the lurking imperialism of *praescientia*. It seems that wherever the idea of prescience has gained admittance as a solution, it has grown in power and has finally broken through the boundaries to which it was at first confined. The distinction between "knowing" and "election" seems to have been refined later on such that the *voluntas universalis antecedens* (over all men) was followed via prescience by the *volutas consequens* in connection with the faith that had been foreseen by God. For example, Schmid understands that salvation is intended for everyone, according to *voluntas universalis*, but that the actual decision of salvation embraces only part of mankind. God's foreknowledge embraces "who these will be, and this foreseeing is then the basis upon which the counsel of God, encompassing only a certain number of people, is an eternal counsel" (Heinrich Schmid, *Die Dogmatik der evangelisch-lutherischen Kirche*, 7th ed. [Gütersloh: Bertelsmann, 1893], 193–95).

See also Gerhard's view that Christ is the *causa electionis* and *etiam fidei intuitum decreto electionis esse includendum*. Only those are elected whom God has foreseen that they would truly believe and would

PART THREE: THEOLOGY

The biblical testimony, however, mostly connects God's foreknowledge (*proginōskō; prognōsis*) with his special love for his people (Rom 8:29; 11:2; 1 Pet 1:2, 20), not with his advance *knowledge* of historical events. These passages do not say that God foreknew "faith" or foresaw some human activity; rather, He foreknew certain people. "Knowing" is used here in the strong Hebraic sense of intimate love. "Those whom He foreknew" (Rom 8:29) means "Those whom He fore-loved." From all eternity God has fore-loved, that is, foreknown his people.

The one place in the New Testament where we might allow that *proginōskō* is used in the sense of *praescientia* (Acts 2:23) will nevertheless permit no separation of divine foreknowledge from divine foreordination. Peter uses one definite article in the phrase "the fixed purpose and foreknowledge of God" in order to connect these two nouns in the closest possible way. God's foreknowledge of Christ's death included his planning and willing it to occur. It was God's fixed (*hōrismenē*; settled, determined) purpose. God predestined the most wicked act ever perpetrated by mankind—Christ's death. "Herod and Pontius Pilate . . . have assembled . . . to accomplish whatsoever your hand and purpose predestined (*proōrizō*) to occur" (Acts 4:27–28).[84]

The Formula at its best recognizes the inexorably paradoxical, mysterious nature (*Geheimnis*) of this question for human reason (SD XI, 52, 55, 64).[85] Read in the best light, the Formula's foreknowledge/predestination distinction might be treated as a manifestation of the concern to avoid any hint of determinism that might indict God as the author of evil (*auctor mali*), not as a rational explanation of the mystery of evil. Clearly,

---

persevere in that belief till the end. See Johann Gerhard, *Loci Theologici*, ed. Edward Preuss, vol. 3 (Berlin: Gustav Schlawitz, 1865), 86. Gerhard rejects faith as a *causa meritoria* or *efficience electionis*, since God has not elected us *propter fidem*; nevertheless, He does elect us *intuitu fidei* in Christ. Gerhard represents the systematization of the synergistic potential in the foreknowledge/predestination distinction. Thus, once foreknowledge is introduced into the theological system in the extra-biblical sense of *praescientia*, even single predestination is gobbled up and lost.

Even though the Word of God does not allow for a symmetrical doctrine of predestination, one should be careful that a criticism of symmetry does not degenerate into a denial or limitation of the counsel of God over all things. Paul Althaus notes that in later Lutheran theology "election" as God's gracious freedom towards man tends to be relativized by an emphasis on God's "foreknowledge" of man's proper use of the objective means of grace. "In the doctrine of predestination of non-Thomist and Old Lutheran-Orthodox dogmatics, this independence (of the divine will from the human posture) is transformed into its precise opposite, the essential dependence of the decisive divine salvific will on the human posture. It is not necessary to state that this theory represents a deterioration away from the New Testament and from the theology of the Reformers. The idea of predestination is perverted and falsified" (Paul Althaus, *Die Christliche Wahrheit: Lehrbuch der Dogmatik*, vol. 2 [Gütersloh: Bertelsmann, 1949], 435).

84. S. M. Baugh, "The Meaning of Foreknowledge" in *The Grace of God, The Bondage of the Will*, eds. Thomas R. Schreiner and Bruce A. Ware (Grand Rapids: Baker, 1995), 183–200. The translation here is Baugh's.

85. "Since the sinner cannot believe by his own power but, on the contrary, faith is created by the Holy Spirit through Word and Sacrament; since, moreover, not all who hear the Gospel and receive the sacraments are saved but only those who believe, no solution remains in the final analysis but to find the difference between the saved and the lost sinners in God's action and therefore also in God's counsel. Nevertheless it is striking that the twofold predestination, though never denied in the Augsburg Confession, is peculiarly passed over in silence, and the same is true of the Apology, the two Catechisms, and the Smalcald Articles" (Edmund Schlink, *The Theology of the Lutheran Confessions*, trans. Paul F. Koehneke and Herbert J. A. Bouman [Philadelphia: Fortress, 1961], 290).

this is the use to which the Formula puts the distinction, and this is fully consistent with the Reformed way of confessing predestination unto salvation while remaining silent about the relation between God's eternal counsel and the origin and existence of evil. If the Reformed symbolic texts do not explain the asymmetry of election and damnation by means of the distinction between *praescientia* and *predestinatio*, they nevertheless do not thereby deny asymmetry in favor of a full-blown determinism traced back to the transcendence of God. They merely refuse to penetrate the mystery.

Second, having listed our conclusions negatively above—what the Reformed confessions do *not* say—we now complement this with a positive statement of the shape and content of the doctrine of election in these symbolic texts. The doctrine of election as confessed in these sixteenth-century symbolic documents

1. Shows abundant evidence for its foundational kerygmatic, evangelical orientation. The doctrine of election is presented as a powerful support and ground for the biblical doctrine of justification (cf. SD XI, 14–24).[86]

2. Carefully maintains biblical language in its exposition and avoids philosophical terminology and categories.

3. Faithfully teaches that God has elected *individual* Christians to eternal salvation and rejects any kind of "general election" of the means of salvation (cf. SD XI, 21–23).

4. Explains election as the eternal ground and guarantee of *sola gratia* and justification by faith. The doctrine of election is nothing else but God's absolute and efficient causality in salvation (cf. EP XI, 12; SD XI, 14, 43). All forms of synergism are excluded.

5. Consistently presents election as "in Christ" (Eph 1:4) and often grounds the Christians election in a *praedestinatio Christi*. (cf. EP XI, 6, 13; SD XI, 25–26, 65–67).

6. Provides a Trinitarian context that avoids any hint of an abstract, hidden predestinating God that exists "behind" or "back of" Christ—a *decretum absolutum* abstracted from Christ and the gospel. Jesus Christ is the only true *speculum* or "book of life" in which one can know God's gracious will (cf. EP XI, 6; SD XI, 13, 26, 52, 65, 89).

7. Consistently speaks of gaining assurance of one's election through faith in Christ as He is faithfully revealed in the gospel as it is communicated in Word and Sacrament. Nothing in these creeds is calculated to leave Christians in despair about their salvation because they do not have access to the eternal counsel of God. In Christ and the gospel everyone has access to the will of God (cf. EP XI, 9, 13; SD XI, 76–77).

8. Indicates the variety of ways in which Reformed communities placed the doctrine

---

86. "The primary ground of the doctrine of predestination, of the emphasis on God's absolute and efficient causality in salvation, and of the stress on the doctrine of God and his decree is justification by faith alone" (Muller, *Christ and the Decree*, 5).

PART THREE: THEOLOGY

in the order of confession. Some set the doctrine in the context of God and Trinity or providence. Others place it after sin or within a discussion of justification. Still others subsume it under the doctrine of Christ or within a discussion of conversion or the church. Nevertheless, the doctrine always serves the needs of the individual believer in his relationship with God and the world.

9. Gives no encouragement or comfort to men who might presume on their election apart from faith in Christ and a diligent use of the "means of grace" (cf. EP XI, 14; SD XI, 10, 21).

10. Affords the believer assurance that there is no force or person (angelic or human) that can thwart God's absolute decree to save all those who sincerely repent and trust in Christ for eternal life (cf. EP XI, 13; SD XI, 20, 50).

11. Shows the kind of pastoral sensitivity in framing the doctrine that the Formula of Concord requires (cf. EP XI, 1, 16, 22; SD XI, 1–3, 10–13, 45–49, 68–77, 89–95).

The Reformed symbols faithfully communicate the biblical and evangelical doctrine of election in so far as they do not make divine preterition part of their explicit teaching (the Confession of the English Congregation in Geneva, 1556, being the sole exception).[87] Using Berkouwer's metaphor, for the biblical writers as well as for the Reformed confessions the *light* of God's gracious election of his people in Christ must be publicly confessed and believed and the *shadow* of God's justice in passing by others must never be elevated to the same status and place in the confession of the church. The American Princeton Reformed scholar B. B. Warfield made a similar observation about the sixteenth-century Reformed Confessions and Catechisms. He observes how carefully the sixteenth-century Reformed symbolic documents maintain a soteriological emphasis. So much so that the doctrine of "sovereign preterition" is not explicitly defined and receives "merely incidental treatment." Warfield, however, turns this universal omission into a positive statement: "Clearly the omission of allusion to reprobation is not to be interpreted in such instances as arguing any chariness as to the doctrine: it may rather be supposed to be omitted just because it is so fully presupposed."[88] That may be one way to interpret the evidence, but is certainly less than "clear."

It is much more likely, as Berkouwer notes, that the early Reformed symbolic documents outline "the essential structure of the doctrine of election."

> From a deterministic point of view one would have to speak simultaneously of election and rejection. The *necessitas* of determinism does not permit a single preference or variation or emphasis or a "more or less," and it does not allow to speak

---

87. Kolb's characterization does not appear to accurately describe the doctrine of election as *confessed* in the Reformed symbols: "While Reformed orthodoxy agreed that sinners are responsible for their own sin, it also taught that God had predestined the reprobate to hell. Reformed theologians put the Evangelical doctrine of election into a more rigid, logical, systematic framework and accorded predestination a much more important part in their doctrinal system than did the Lutherans" (Kolb, "Nikolas von Amsdorf," 326). Indeed, one might question whether such a statement accurately captures the genuine heart of the Reformed doctrine of election as the sum of the gospel.

88. Warfield, "Predestination," 223.

of election as being primary. But in the light of Scripture, the "disturbed" balance in the Confessions is not only understandable but completely legitimate. For the Confessions did not mean to give an explanation of how everything, in the same causal manner, is derived from God. When they spoke of the light of election they also spoke of the shadow, but never with any trace of parallelism.[89]

Surely this explains the emphasis in the Reformed confessions, even if it does not answer other questions about the shape and content of the doctrine of election in non-confessional contexts.[90] Such questions, however, take us beyond the scope of our present study. Whatever validity these charges (in our first list above) might have against later seventeenth-century school-based Reformed theology or even against sixteenth-century non-symbolic Reformed documents, they hardly apply to the churchly confessions under consideration here.

Why do later Reformed confessions show evidence of a more school- or academy-oriented construction? The sixteenth-century documents are ecclesiastical, pastoral, confessional, and soteriological in content, shape, and scope. The seventeenth-century documents tend to be more school-oriented, institutional or clerical, polemical, and cosmological.[91] What accounts for this shift? Do the seventeenth-century confessions and catechisms trace their roots back along the trajectory established in extra-ecclesiastical dogmatics among sixteenth-century theologians?

In conclusion, both in the Lutheran and Reformed *confessional* symbols of the sixteenth century the doctrine of election had its ground in the restored gospel of God's freely granted grace in Jesus Christ. The doctrine of election was consistently *confessed* in

---

89. G. C. Berkouwer, *Divine Election*, trans. Hugo Bekker, Studies in Dogmatics (Grand Rapids: Eerdmans, 1960), 194–95.

90. See Lynne Courter Boughton, "Supralapsarianism and the Role of Metaphysics in Sixteenth-Century Reformed Theology," *Westminster Theological Journal* 48 (1986) 63–96. Also, Richard Muller notes the rich variety of ways that Reformed theologians had of articulating the doctrine of election: "An examination of the sixteenth-century systems and, indeed, of the seventeenth-century systems written before 1630, reveals a variety of structures and several different placements of the doctrine of predestination. Heppe, unfortunately, adopted an arrangement of doctrine quite atypical of the sixteenth century and not even representative of the theology of Beza: he even cites Calvin on predestination under the doctrine of God and Trinity. Several important theologians—Polanus, Trelcatius the younger, Gomarus, Maccovius, Zanchius—did indeed set the decree into the context of the doctrines of God and Trinity, and, alone among the writers of his time Maccovius chose to place the decree above the doctrine of the Trinity in the *locus* concerned with the divine essence and attributes. Calvin, however, had stated the doctrine of predestination in the context of faith and justification. He was followed by Bucanus. A similar soteriological interest is also evidenced by the placement of predestination in the systems of Vermigli, Musculus, and Ames. Others, influenced perhaps by the powerful ecclesiology of Calvin, discussed predestination as part of the doctrine of the church: Ursinus, Danaeus, Perkins. Others still, sensible of the bond between the causality of election and the historical work of Christ, discussed the doctrine of predestination in association with their Christological exposition: Keckermann, Walaeus, the 'Leiden Synopsis,' Downham" (Muller, *Christ and the Decree*, 3–4).

91. Lutheran seventeenth-century systematics, of course, are not altogether free from similar problems, even if their scholasticism seems to have followed a different trajectory. See Robert Preus, "The Doctrine of Election as Taught by the Seventeenth Century Lutheran Dogmaticians" *Quartalschrift* 55.4 (1958) 229–61, and Rune Sönderlund, *Ex praevisa Fide, Zum Verständnis der Prädestinationslehre in der lutherischen Orthodoxie*, Arbeiten zur Geschichte und Theologie des Luthertums, New Series, vol. 3 (Hannover: Lutherisches Verlagshaus, 1983).

both confessional traditions as another form of the proclamation of the gospel. Schlatter's observation serves well as a conclusion to our study: "We express once again the whole gracious gift of God, the whole Gospel, when we state: God has elected us."[92]

The evidence has shown that none of these dogmatic, confessional presentations of the eternal gospel tempted simple Christians to raise questions that take them behind or beyond the gospel—no more so than the biblical revelation of election itself. The sixteenth-century Lutheran and Reformed churches' confession of election avoided all "vulgar" philosophical constructions of time, causality, anthropology, and so forth. No independently fabricated concept of God (e.g., one speculatively deduced from his omnipotence or omni-causality) was allowed to determine the church's confession of election.

The doctrine of election, therefore, emerges in these documents as a corollary of the gospel and not of some universally conceived ontological ideas about God, man, or the cosmos. The recovery of the gospel most certainly impacted the sixteenth-century theologians' understanding of these cosmological realities, and we have abundant evidence of confessional theologians in both camps that sought to work out the scholarly implications of God's eternal counsel for cosmological questions. Even so, the sixteenth-century church managed to keep its own confessional documents free of school-based metaphysical and cosmological speculation. These academy-oriented issues were not allowed to disfigure the *church's public confession* of God's gracious electing love in Christ. Throughout the sixteenth century, the public, ecclesiastical confessions of the churches continued to remain faithful to the truth that "The doctrine of election is the sum of the Gospel."[93] Barth's two criteria for "full publicity" of the doctrine of election agree with the Formula of Concord and are met by the sixteenth-century Reformed confessional documents:

> The basic demand by which any presentation of the doctrine must be measured, and to which we ourselves must also conform, is this: that (negatively) the doctrine must not speak of the divine election and rejection as though God's electing and rejecting were not quite different, as though these divine dealings did not stand in a definite hierarchical relationship the one with the other; and that (positively) the supremacy of the one and subordination of the other must be brought out so radically that the Gospel enclosed and proclaimed even in this doctrine is introduced and revealed as the tenor of the whole, so that in some way or other the Word of free grace of God stands out even at this point as the dominating theme and the specific meaning of the whole utterance. It is along these lines that it will be proved whether or not the doctrine is understood in conformity with the Bible and therefore with divine revelation. Only if understood in this way can it lay claim to the full publicity within the church defended by Calvin. If not understood in this way, then even as a secret wisdom for theologians it can have no real significance, or rather it can have only a very dangerous significance.[94]

---

92. Adolf Schlatter, *Das christliche Dogma* (Stuttgart: Calwer, 1923), 518.
93. Barth, CD II/2, 34.
94. Barth, CD II/2, 18. One ought to be able to appreciate Barth's criteria for "full publicity" without buying into his own peculiar doctrine of election and reprobation.

Dear Jeff,

Thank you for the gift of this essay. I certainly don't have anything to add to your research!

I do have one observation. It seems to me that what the Westminster Confession does is not entirely unpastoral. After the Arminian controversy it was likely necessary to say something more about the absolute sovereignty of God, to make sure that the God we worship in the church is the Creator and not Zeus. The Creator of space and time is perforce the Creator of all events in that space and time, and that is ultimately what is meant by general predestination.

I tend to agree, however, that the additional statements in the Westminster Confession about election to salvation might better have been placed later in the Confession. After the work of Cornelius Van Til on the Creator/creature distinction, it is easier to see that general predestination is an aspect of creation, while election to salvation and glory is a different though related matter.

Jim

PART FOUR

Culture

12

James Jordan, Rosenstock-Huessy, and Beyond

RICHARD BLEDSOE

If anything whatever is common to all believers, and even to many unbelievers, it is the sense that in the Gospels they have met a personality. There are characters that we know to be historical but of whom we do not feel that we have any personal knowledge—knowledge by acquaintance; such are Alexander, Attila, or William of Orange. There are others who make no claim to historical reality but whom, none the less, we know as we know real people: Falstaff, Uncle Toby, Mr. Pickwick. But there are only three characters who, claiming the first sort of reality, also actually have the second. And surely everyone knows who they are: Plato's Socrates, the Jesus of the Gospels, and Boswell's Johnson.

—C. S. Lewis, *Modern Theology and Biblical Criticism*[1]

Hence, the third article of the Creed is the specifically Christian one: from now on the Holy Spirit makes man a partner in his own creation. In the beginning God had said, "Let us make man in our image" (Gen. 1:26). In this light, the Church Fathers interpreted human history as a process of making Man like God.... Christ, in the center of history, enables us to participate consciously in this man-making process and to study its laws.

—Eugen Rosenstock-Huessy, *The Christian Future*[2]

---

1. C. S. Lewis, *Christian Reflections* (Grand Rapids: Eerdmans, 1967), 156.

2. Eugen Rosenstock-Huessy, *The Christian Future: Or the Modern Mind Outrun* (New York: Scribner, 1946; reprint, New York: Harper & Row, 1966), 108.

PART FOUR: CULTURE

> God's intentions for man are set out in Genesis 2:15, "Then the Lord God took the man and put him into the Garden of Eden to cultivate (serve) it and to guard it." There are two tasks here, and we shall call them man's kingly (or basilic) and priestly (or hieratic) tasks.... Man's understanding of these two duties was to be progressive. Though made "like God," man was to become more and more like God through a process of growth and maturation in His image.
>
> —James Jordan, *Through New Eyes*[3]

LEWIS, IN THE ABOVE quotation, notes the intense and felt reality that the personality of Jesus presses upon us. There is something I have termed "the Emily Dickinson effect." What I mean by this is that her poetry (and other great poetry as well, but she is a particularly good subject) illustrates the paradox that poetic illumination of the smallest fact, the slightest reality, the tiniest event, creates with readers a reverberation that is more universal than all of the philosophy of, say, German Idealism, which was aiming to be universal and an explanation of everything.[4]

In my own personal experience as a pastor and preacher, when I would preach a sermon that would touch the largest number of people in the deepest possible way, when I would preach a sermon that appeared to speak "universally" across all boundaries, it was invariably one that grew out of some previous dealing with some individual about some highly particular life issue. And the more particular and even rarified the issue, the better. The lessons or the Gospel cure that would be biblically applied to that highly particular difficulty would evoke a nearly universal response on the part of the congregation. By contrast, sermons that grow out of a general exegesis or systematic theology are broad and general in content. That sort of sermon rarely hit a target at all, let alone what might be termed a "universal" target.

The paradox being illustrated here is this: the most rarified particular is often the most universal thing there is. A description by Emily Dickinson of a grain of sand can be larger than whole theoretical galaxies. The application here is that the incarnation of Jesus as one particular individual in one particular place in one particular time is more universal than all of the broad and universal pantheisms or general theisms in the entire world. Jesus is truly what Hegel termed "a concrete universal." This is the scandal of Christianity.

In some sense, Jesus seems to be all men (and women) in one, and yet He is entirely Himself.

Here is an exercise that one can do. A number of years ago, a spate of books were written concerning "temperament types." Most of these books had a "counseling" flavor about them. Each of the four temperament types, first recognized and sketched by the Greeks (sanguine, choleric, phlegmatic, and melancholy) has strengths and also weakness. The point of these books was to help Christians to recognize their potential

---

3. James B. Jordan, *Through New Eyes: Developing a Biblical View of the World* (Brentwood, TN: Wolgemuth & Hyatt, 1988; reprint, Eugene, OR: Wipf & Stock, 1999), 133–34.

4. For example, Emily Dickinson, "The Sky Is Low," in Oscar Williams, ed. *The Pocket Book of Modern Verse: English and American Poetry of the Last Hundred Years from Walt Whitman to Dylan Thomas*, rev. ed. (New York: Washington Square, 1958), 85.

strengths and weaknesses as fallen creatures and to be able to strengthen and correct themselves under the power of the Holy Spirit.

Here is a place where the particularity of Jesus seems to express itself in a universal way. Many Bible characters have been identified by these writers as either predominantly one or a combination of temperaments. John is predominately melancholy, while Peter is clearly sanguine. Abraham seems to be mostly phlegmatic, while Paul has large quantities of choleric (with a dash of melancholy). But what temperament type is Jesus? I defy anyone to identify Him as one or as a usual mixture. He is somehow, in perfection, all of them. He seems to be all and yet beyond them all. He has the unflappable unhurriedness of the phlegmatic, the rich poetic nature of the melancholy, the strength and intensity of the choleric, and the playfulness of the sanguine. He simply cannot be identified within typical and usual parameters. It is a very odd reality. He cannot be cast as one or the other: He is all, and yet He is entirely luminous in His individuality. I know of no other human person of whom such a thing could be said.

Again, Jesus is the fulfillment of all types and symbols of what came before Him, and in this way expresses His universality as a particular man. He is the fulfillment of Israel itself, and all of Israel was reduced to one man in Him as He fulfilled Israel's mission, which Israel itself was incapable of finally or adequately fulfilling. In the temptations in the desert, He resisted all satanic temptation in a way that Israel was not able to. He gathers to Himself twelve new "sons" as disciples, becoming the new Jacob, the new Israel, who had wrestled with God on numerous occasions before appearing before the new Esau in the person of Herod.

In every sense, He fulfills Israel. He is the new Abraham in His faithfulness, the new Isaac in being offered up as sacrifice, the new Jacob as the new Israel, and the new Joseph as the new Nazarite,[5] and He is the new Samson as He lifts the gates of hell and carries them away. He is the new David as the new king, the new Solomon in His demonstration of Solomonic wisdom (Matt 22:23–45). He is the second Isaiah in His calling (Matt 13:14–15) and the second Jeremiah as the one who is the final fulfillment of "the Suffering Servant," of which Jeremiah was the first.

But He is more universal than the New Israel. He is the fulfillment of all types before Israel, beginning with the borderline figure of Abraham, who as Paul tells us, was the father of both Jewish and Gentile believers (Rom 4:9–12). He is the new Noah as the one who built an ark, which is the type of the church (1 Pet 3:18–22). He is the savior of both clean and unclean (Jews and Gentiles) just as clean and unclean animals were all put on the ark together. And beyond even that, Jesus is the New Adam (Rom 5:14). Having returned all the way to the foundation of the world in Adam, Jesus represents all that is human and is universally the new beginning and the new universal man.

Paul takes note of Jesus as the new Israel and the new Adam, but even beyond that, He expands these types to become cosmic. Jesus is the "cosmic Christ." Paul says in

---

5. Joseph was the first Nazarite, as Genesis 49:26 tells us: "They shall be upon the head of Joseph, and a crown of the head of him who was separate (*nazarite*d) from his brothers." Jesus was from Nazareth, which Matthew takes note of in this connection (Matt 2:23). He was likewise "separated from his brothers" and with double *entendre* is thus a "son of Joseph" (John 6:42; 7:5).

PART FOUR: CULTURE

Colossians first that He is the type even of God. He is "the image of the invisible God" and one who is universal even beyond what Adam has represented before. He is the "firstborn of all creation." Hence, He is an Adam who is even before Adam. It is through Him that the whole created order came to be as all created authorities and powers were "created through Him and for Him" (Col 1:16). And in the book of Ephesians, He becomes the cosmic David as He is "seated at the right hand" of the Father, "far above all rule and authority and power and dominion" (Eph 1:20–21). And likewise, both epistles emphasize that the church is His Bride, as He fulfills all biblical marriages, and this has cosmic dimensions as the church is now to be the co-ruler with Him in the heavenly places as His bride (Eph 2:6; Col 3:1–4).

There are many more types of which Jesus is the fulfillment, but this short list is adequate to demonstrate how Jesus is both particular in fulfilling each type but also universal in fulfilling them all.

Jesus is also the only wholly persuasive picture of goodness that has ever been given us in all of literature of either real or fictitious characters.

Much of the debate surrounding John Milton's *Paradise Lost* swirls around the question: Just what role does Satan play? Is he the hero of the poem or the villain? Many of the Romantic critics surmised (with great scandal) that Satan was the hero of the poem. They surmised this, because he clearly is the most interesting and heroic character in the entire epic. He seems to have Milton's sympathy.

There are several things that can be said about this. First, an evil Satan may well be the most luminous character in the entire epic, not because he is the one who has the largest draft of Milton's sympathy, but because we all know far more of evil than we know of goodness and depicting it exhausts even the greatest of genius. Milton simply knew more about highly developed sinfulness than he did about perfect goodness.[6]

The same can be said of Dante's *Divine Comedy*. The *Paradisio* is not the least real and the most icy of the three poems because Dante has more of a brief for hell and purgatory than he does for heaven, but because, as a fallen man, he understands the environments and realities of sin and sinful places far better than he does perfect goodness. Likewise, in the novels of Dostoevsky, Ivan Karamazov—the sinner—is more luminous and real than Prince Mishkin is. The only place where we meet completely real and convincing goodness is the Jesus of the Gospels.

There is a great deal being made now about "narrative," about story. The story of every human life is of infinite importance. This cannot be so when either the tacit and oblique or the unequivocal background is one of monism or pantheism. For any pantheism, there is no final story, but only a final absorption of all particularity, of all plots, of all denouements. The Bible, unlike even the theistic but unitarian Qur'an or the holy books of the East (such as the Bhagavad Gita), is a story. It is not just a subplot that is finally

---

6. There is a great deal to be said in favor of Stanley Fish's Reader Response Theory, in which the reader is suppose to become aware of his own sinfulness by responding to the beauty and persuasiveness of Satan in much the same way that Adam and Eve did. The reader thus replicates the fall in his own experience. But it is doubtful that Milton could have equally created the same response to the perfection, beauty, and goodness of God since we are so much less well acquainted with it. See Stanley Fish, *Surprised by Sin: The Reader in Paradise Lost*, 2nd ed. (Cambridge: Harvard University Press, 1998).

absorbed in a blank of unitarian glory or of monistic oneness; its story of the creation and redemption of the human race retains a Trinitarian diversity.

Jesus, who is the infinite personhood, becomes the paradox of Donne's great Christmas poem regarding His mother, "Immensity cloister'd in thy dear womb." He is the most intense particularity who is infinity Himself, confined to one womb, one family, one town, one carpenter shop, one cross, one tomb, which becomes an empty tomb. He is universality itself, who is as particular as one grain of sand on one beach next to one ocean in one world. He is the author of story and enters His own story and then becomes the co-author of a thousand million other stories in His own people and His own church. Each one is not absorbed into infinite plasma, but each one becomes more gloriously himself, and yet each one also reaches out to become more and more universal. As C. S. Lewis remarked, "How monotonously alike all the great tyrants and conquerors have been: how gloriously different are the saints."[7]

These are all literary exercises of imagination that I invite my readers to try. In all cases, the uniqueness of Jesus quickly establishes itself.

Jesus is the complete concentration of all of human nature. He is the grain of sand more universal than all of German Idealism. He is, to quote Paul, where "the whole fullness of deity dwells bodily" (Col 2:9 ESV). As the second head of humanity, Jesus is not only the fullness of deity but also the fullness of human nature. He is all of "mature manhood . . . the measure of the stature of the fullness" (Eph 4:13 ESV). The theology of Paul in Ephesians seems to indicate that it will eventually require all of the fullness of the church to be the expression of His fullness. The revelation of the whole Bible, which is finalized in the capstone of the New Covenant, is an extremely concentrated document which will require all of history to unfold and apply.

THE UNIVERSAL MAN OF THE CHRISTIAN ERA

The beginning of the fulfillment of the church and individual believers as themselves types of Christ is perhaps visible through the whole of the Bible, but one can see this with great clarity in the early Apostles and with great visibility in the Apostle Paul.

Paul is Jewish to his cuticles. He describes himself as one who was "circumcised on the eighth day, of the people of Israel, of the Tribe of Benjamin, a Hebrew born of Hebrews; as to the law a Pharisee" (Phil 3:5 RSV). And yet this man, particular to the point of being tribal, became in Christ more cosmopolitan and universal than any man of his time.

---

7. C. S. Lewis, *Mere Christianity* (New York: Macmillan, 1960), 190. The entire last section of the chapter from which the above quotation is taken says a great many of the same things I am trying to say in this essay. Here is one more quotation: "The more we get what we now call 'ourselves' out of the way and let Him take us over the more truly ourselves we become. There is so much of Him that millions and millions of 'little Christs,' all different, will still be too few to express Him fully" (189). Eugen Rosenstock-Huessy, the great German born Christian historian, wrote an 800-page book (*Out of Revolution: The Autobiography of Western Man* [Norwich, VT: Argo, 1969; reprint, Providence, RI: Berg, 1993]) to elucidate how this reality has worked itself out in a thousand years of western history. James Jordan's entire theological project has done much to undergird Rosenstock-Huessy's treatment of history with a biblical foundation.

PART FOUR: CULTURE

In one sense, he threw over his intensely particular Jewishness, all of the privileges that came to him as a Jew, and all pretense of righteousness through his Jewish privileges: "I count them as refuse." Yet, in another equally important sense, he kept it all. Paul's entire calling was the calling of transforming the particular Hebrew revelation and Hebrew privilege into a revelation and privilege for the entire world, for all peoples, nations, and tribes. In this calling, he was called to bring this revelation to the whole of the "ecumene," the world conquered and established by Rome. He was called to bring this revelation "before the Gentiles and kings and the sons of Israel" (Acts 9:15). We are led to believe that he eventually brought the revelation before even Caesar himself, who was in his person, the very embodiment of the cosmopolitan. But Paul stood before him as one more universal, far more universal, than he.

ROSENSTOCK-HUESSY AND UNIVERSAL HISTORY

Hence, all of history following the coming of Christ is this unfolding of "particular universal" types. The Holy Spirit begins to develop a humanity that progressively reveals the fullness of the humanity that is found in Christ. Eugen Rosenstock-Huessy has perhaps disclosed this better than anyone with his development of a "universal history" that develops and unfolds this fullness of Christ as a personality in a series of "types" and "characters" that are released into history by revolutions ignited by the Christian revelation.

He is concerned with the revolutionary character of the western world and western history since the coming of Christ. Just as one must navigate one's way through space if one is to be an explorer, even more central is the fact that one must navigate one's way through time. Apart from Christ, it is impossible to navigate through time. Greek thought is extensively interested in the visual and hence in space. It is Hebrew and biblical thought that makes time the primary interest.

He likewise believes that western Christian history has developed through a series of explosions that have resulted from pressures that have built themselves up in various areas of the world through either response or reaction to the Gospel message. Some revolutions have been explicitly anti-Christian, such as the French or the Russian Revolution, but no matter. The prime force behind these explosions has inescapably been the Gospel message and reception or reaction to it. According to John, "anti-Christ" is a substitute for Christ, and one cannot have substitutes until the original is in place. Many of the revolutionary ideas of the modern world have had the character of a substitute for Christ and the new world that He has brought. But even in reaction, it is only possible to imitate what He has initiated. The limitations of the ancient and pagan world have be been removed. Human nature was fixed in ways that we no longer consider to be so.

In a subsection entitled "Let Us Make Man" in the essay "Creed of the Living God," Rosenstock-Huessy gives us a number of examples of the creation of new types of men in the Christian era. He calls this "anthropurgy": "as metallurgy refines metal from its ore, anthropurgy wins the true stuff of Man out of his coarse physical substance. Christ, in the center of history, enables us to participate consciously in this man-making process and to study its laws."[8]

---

8. Rosenstock-Huessy, *Christian Future*, 108.

He gives several examples:

> Christian astronomers, chemists, doctors, preachers, missionaries, painters, masons have populated the earth. Anticipating a Last Judgment over our corruptible flesh, they have come into the flesh out of the Spirit, achieving a tempestuous resurrection from the dead in the name of the new life. The Chaldean astrologers of antiquity came to life as modern astronomers. The Hippocratean doctor, in whose tradition Socrates asked that a cock be sacrificed at his death, came to life as the modern scientific doctor, in the name of the Living God, uncorrupted by local prejudice. In the light of the central dogma of a final resurrection, we have seen many partial resurrections accomplished, and this and nothing else is the Great Economy of our destiny.[9]

Paul is a kind of first fruit of this "particular universality." Eugen Rosenstock-Huessy has traced this ongoing process through western history. Western history could be seen through the lenses of the unfolding "particular universality" in the ongoing revelation of Jesus Christ in His church and people.

Rosenstock-Huessy conceived of his great book, *Out of Revolution: Autobiography of Western Man*, as a re-telling of the story of the five great total revolutions that have formed our modern world. Each revolution has produced a new kind of man and another side of Christian character. These five great total revolutions are Gregory VII and his opposition to the emperor and the kings of his time; Luther who proclaimed that the just shall live by faith; Cromwell, who led the revolution of the English gentleman against the Royal House; *Liberty, Fraternity, and Equality*, on the part of the Enlightened French populace against the old and rotten Royal Establishment; and the Russian uprising of the Proletariat against the Czarist order. The American Revolution is termed a "half revolution" by Rosenstock-Huessy because it lacked the completeness and the originality of the total revolutions and partook of the elements of both Cromwell and his re-institution of Common Law and the French Revolution's lifting up of the "natural" against the corrupting civilized pretensions of those times.

These revolutions unfolded by moving *backward* through the Bible. The first revolution, that of Gregory VII, was inspired by the Last Judgment, and the last, the Russian Revolution, moved back to Genesis 1:2.

THE INVESTITURE CONTROVERSY

Hildebrand, who adopted the name Gregory VII, in the solitariness of his monkish cell represented a revolution as total as the one instituted by Lenin involving the millions and the masses, according to Rosenstock-Huessy.[10] Gregory represented the complexity and contradictoriness of the prism when it breaks into manifold parts the singularity of the brilliant white sunshine. He represented the "groanings" that Paul speaks of that can only be translated and understood by God Himself. These "groanings" represent what seem to be contradictory strands of human experience that need to be held in tension

---

9. Ibid., 110.
10. Rosenstock-Huessy, *Out of Revolution*, 530.

PART FOUR: CULTURE

and not entirely torn apart and yet need to be separated out as strands that have their own individuality.

The foundations of what we know today as "Europe" were laid by the determination of Gregory VII to resist the power of emperor and king to have the right to ordain priests in the church:

> The clergy mutinied against its dependence on the palace. This mutiny is called by historians the struggle over investiture. Investiture was the appointment of a bishop or abbot by a royal order from the king's palace or chapel. During the struggle this privilege of the emperor was contested by the pope. But in so doing the pope was acting as the trustee of all Christendom against imperialism. The Papal Revolution was as complete in social depth as any modern "revolt of the masses." The popes emancipated the whole spiritual army, from primate and archbishop down to chaplain and parish priest. The papacy cut the direct and domestic relation between throne and altar in every manor or palace, and claimed the right to be guardian and spokesman for every local representative of the spirit. The vicar of St. Peter, to whom the most distinguished Cathedral in Christendom was given, now claimed to represent every pulpit or cathedral before the emperor.[11]

Rosenstock-Huessy goes on to say, "The threat of a Caliphate was not fictitious in the Western civilization of the eleventh century. It was necessary that this fatal course be eschewed by the new emancipation of the clergy."[12] The great weapon of Hildebrand in this battle was the imposition of clerical celibacy, which had never been a requirement until this time. With this imposition, the possibility of every lord of every manner having a priest in the pocket through the marriage of the priest to his own daughter was averted. An independent clergy and independent church was secured.

If this had not happened, the west too would have suffered the fate of Byzantium and the Orthodox churches, and the church would have continued to be a department of the state. If the royal houses of the west had not endured this unhappy quarrel with the church, both church and state would have suffered and the great individuality and national characters of Europe would never have been emancipated. It was not only nations that were emancipated, but personality and individuality. The ongoing quarrel of church and state, of king and priest in the West created a new kind of unity, a unity of the one and many rather than simply the dominance of the one as a continuation of the wearisome ontocracy fostered in all of paganism.[13]

Edwin Friedman says that "huddling together" is the cure for anxiety that all dysfunctional families practice. Almost all dysfunctional families are close, too close. There is no flowering as personalities as the individual is smothered under family together-

---

11. Ibid., 529.
12. Ibid., 532–33.
13. Ontocracy is the term coined by Arend Theodoor van Leeuwen. He means by this that the state was the all-absorbing reality of the ancient empires and was the primary idol behind all other idols. The state was essentially a divine order of which king and emperor were the principle and divine representatives. Cf. Arend Theodoor van Leeuwen, *Christianity in World History: The Meeting of the Faiths of East and West* (London: Edinburgh House, 1964), 165–73.

ness.[14] The entire world was "dysfunctional" in this sense until the release of the nations because of Gregory's revolt against royal control.

Gregory asserted a universal church over against a universal emperor. Petty kingdoms began to show their outlines and gradually the nations of modern Europe emerged. Each nation was a part of Christendom by virtue of one church and one faith that united them. But each nation developed its own character and, in the confines of what is known today as "Europe," more united diversity of more national types emerged in a comparatively small area than anywhere on earth.

This let loose a torrent of creative energies over the next five hundred years, and it is impossible to do any more than glance at what might be termed "underrevolutions" in that orb of influence.

G. K. Chesterton, in his beautiful book on Francis of Assisi, describes him as "a character."[15] In his companion volume on Thomas Aquinas, he compares and contrasts Thomas and Francis in the first chapter.[16] It is a fascinating comparison because he demonstrates that Thomas was as much a "character" as Francis, but utterly different. They were both doing the same thing and, according to Chesterton, they were both singing the song of nature's liberation from the bondage of the ancient world. Just as the nations were called forth and liberated because of Gregory's revolution, so finally in the thirteenth century, nature herself was called forth to a new independence under God, and what and who she was were seen for the first time by civilized men.

Under Francis, as both Rosenstock-Huessy and Chesterton remind us, nature ceased to be our mother and became our sister. The Church became our mother.[17]

The early medieval world found itself most completely, in the narrative of the biblical text, in the Last Judgment. This seed germinated between 1200 and 1300 and blossomed most completely in Dante's *Divine Comedy*. The Pope (and the Emperor) identified themselves as judges who viewed the world from the end of time. They themselves were an eschatological appearance.

This is significant because history to this time had been experienced as cyclical. With the introduction of the end of time, there is an escape from the pagan cycle and the linear enters history. History as a possibility, first disclosed by Augustine, could now begin to be experienced as such. The emphasis on the Last Judgment might appear to limit history as a possibility if the end is immanent. However, the Papacy elongated time with its understanding of the "anti-Christ." The end could not come until the anti-Christ appeared. But the anti-Christ could not appear as long as the papacy was vigilant, be-

---

14. Edwin H. Friedman, *A Failure of Nerve: Leadership in the Age of the Quick Fix* (New York: Seabury, 2007), 54, 66–75. This is an overstatement to make a point. Tribalism, which is the form of life that Hildebrand emancipated us from, is not really "dysfunctional" any more than a large family with small children is dysfunctional when all of the children have an almost unified collective psyche. One only becomes dysfunctional if one attempts to revert to this unity and sameness after reaching adolescence and adulthood. This is then the shrinking back from the difficulties of individuation. Hildebrand brought the world into adolescence, and brought about the birth of individuals.

15. G. K. Chesterton, *St. Francis of Assisi* (Garden City, NY: Doubleday, 1957), 83.

16. G. K. Chesterton, *Saint Thomas Aquinas* (Garden City, NY: Doubleday, 1956), 19–48.

17. Rosenstock-Huessy, *Out of Revolution*, 581ff.; Chesterton, *St. Francis of Assisi*, 87.

PART FOUR: CULTURE

cause the Pope was the guard against his appearance. He could not come if the Pope was on the watch.

Carl Schurtz noted that in all of Homer, there are no descriptions of landscapes.[18] The beauty of the earth was not seen by pagan man. It is noted and seen in the Psalms, but is only called forth for all to see by Francis and Thomas in the thirteenth century. "Nature" was a mere subsection of the monism of all of ancient paganism. The energies and powers of nature were especially subsumed under the greatest expressed power of nature in the late, decadent Roman Empire, and that power was the power of sex.

The church fled to the desert and became ascetic and world-denying in its attempt to cleanse itself from the pagan sex obsession that was the final expression of undifferentiated monism in that dying world.[19] By the thirteenth century, according to Chesterton, the cleansing was complete, and nature was now to be freed. The sometimes alleged pantheism of Francis was no such thing. His personalized interaction with the entirety of nature could happen only as each being was recognized by him as God's creature, and addressed and named by him. "The birds of the air," so called by Jesus, came to hear sermons from Francis, and the sun and the moon were named and experienced as "brother, sister." Each element of the world was liberated with its own personality under him.

Thomas was the philosophical corollary, as he freed that great generic rubric of "being" from the monism of the entire Classical and pre-Classical world, to become the order of God, fresh from His hand, upheld by Him at every second, and giving testimony in its own contingency to the upholding reality of the personal Father. Thomists see "being" as it is expressed in every pebble, fly, tree, or any other thing, as an expression of God Himself, not part of a monistic goo, but an individual expression, each known, addressed and named in its individuality by and under the God of the Bible. Being was freed from Aristotle's pagan blindness.

LUTHER

Luther renewed both the universal and the particular. Luther took upon himself a particular yoke by declaring his loyalty to the German Prince. He also renewed the universal by declaring himself and the entire congregation as the new priesthood.

A whole series of elements that we regard as "normal" were established as the rights of all persons in Christendom by Luther and his revolution. Because of Luther, we today enjoy the right of choice of profession, the right to marry, the right to write and establish one's own will.

---

18. Carl Schurtz, *Reminiscences*, cited in Eugen Rosenstock-Huessy, *Out of Revolution*, 578.

19. I once encountered a devotee of Trungpa Rinpoche, an exiled Buddhist teacher from Tibet who found a great following in the United States, as he was inebriating himself into a drunken stupor. His rationale for pursuing drunkenness, which he said he had learned from Trungpa (and Trungpa's dissolute lifestyle would lend credence to this claim) was that it was in both drunkenness and orgasm that the boundaries of the ego collapsed and one could find "oneness" with all. Trungpa's personal pursuit of both drunkenness and promiscuous orgasm were legendary. This would seem a corollary to the decadence of the late and collapsing Roman Empire.

Luther appeared as the representative of Paul and the Pauline doctrine. However, Paul was the great anti-type of the Old Testament prophet. The Hebrew prophet spoke to the king. He both instructed and warned him. Paul is always ultimately moving toward Rome, and his final calling is to speak to the Caesar. All through the book of the Acts, he is constantly speaking to magistrates and thus begins to fulfill the prophesy of Jesus, "They will drag you before kings and magistrates, where you will offer witness to me" (Luke 21:12–13). Luther thus represents the Old Testament prophets who speak to kings and magistrates. At one point, Fredrick the Great (who never met Luther) offered Luther protection. Luther refused, offering instead to give his protection to Fredrick.

Now the papacy claimed that the end could not come as long as the Papacy was doing its job and protecting the world against the anti-Christ. But Luther brought the world to an end when he announced that indeed the anti-Christ had appeared and the anti-Christ was the Pope himself. Each revolution brings the world to an end and begins it all over again. Luther brought this end, and the world began again.

CROMWELL

Cromwell renewed the universal and particular. Cromwell established the centrality of the seas. By becoming Lord Protector in 1644, he inaugurated the next great revolution. Cromwell and his Roundheads committed regicide. By committing this act, they radicalized what Luther had done. Luther called the church to prophesy to the king. Cromwell brought the gentry forward and gave government to the under-magistrates, while renewing Common Law, which was in large measure, biblical law. Cromwell eliminated the king, and thus moved behind the prophets and the kings in the Bible to the time of the Judges.

The British are famously "repressed," understated, and hypocritical. Rosenstock-Huessy tells us why. It is because of Oliver Cromwell. The British in fact owed their national and world greatness to Cromwell. He was the man who put Britain on the map, so to speak, who enabled the British to conquer the world in their relatively benign way and to have a good Christian conscience about ruling many and diverse people. But the British could never acknowledge the source of their greatness because Cromwell committed the unthinkable crime. Cromwell is the Oedipus of Britain. He may not have married his mother, but he did murder his father. Cromwell committed regicide. The history of the English is a "detective history."[20]

Rosenstock-Huessy chronicles, as did no one before him, how in examining British history from Cromwell's time on we always see an exaggeration of Cromwell's crimes and a diminution of the crimes of those who followed him and who reproduced so many of his policies.

William II in 1688 brought about the so-called "Glorious Revolution" and did not shed a drop of blood. He restored the rights of Englishmen and the rights of Common Law, and he did so peacefully. Cromwell, on the other hand, was a "usurper" and committed great and terrible revolutionary crimes. But, says Rosenstock-Huessy, this way of

---

20. Rosenstock-Huessy, *Out of Revolution*, 257–62.

telling the story is an exaggeration and a repression. William was not so peaceful as he is made out to be, and Cromwell not so criminal and violent. The scar on the English soul is the execution of the King by Cromwell. But William was really restored as a lifelong "Protector," not a king with the rights of an inheritable throne.[21] He was very unlike a king and very much like Cromwell.

Furthermore, Cromwell was the revenge of the Lord Chancellor. Henry VIII executed his Chancellor, Sir Thomas More. But, as a result of Cromwell's action, the king was permanently demoted and the Chancellor became the Prime Minister.[22] The realm became the realm of the Gentleman, the Christian, the Puritan Gentleman. The Whigs, who became the conservatives and conquered the planet with the British flag, were a result of Oliver Cromwell. But the execution of the king is too much to bear and remember, so it is suppressed or repressed.[23]

Psycho-analysis was later invented in Vienna, but it was really invented for the English and their heirs, the Americans. Peoples on the Continent do not suffer from repressions in the way the English do. They have no Oedipus in their histories. All nations have great crimes in their pasts and have invented mythologies to cover the crimes. But the British mythologies are a source of peculiar shame and even embarrassment, and, as a result, the British foundation—a Puritan past—is elaborately hidden.

THE FRENCH REVOLUTION

The French Revolution was preceded by the French Enlightenment, and the Revolution unveiled the truth that French reasonableness was a *drive* and a *passion*. The desire for autonomy was as fraught with emotion and was as passionate as the Church she sought to replace.

Much of what has been given to western character through the French Revolution is negative and anti-Christian. The French Revolution wanted Liberty, Equality, and Fraternity. It is true that these ideals could never have been coined in a non-Christian world. They are borrowed from the Christian world. But they are borrowed on the basis of an innocent Adam who was driven from the Garden by a tyrant God who did not want a thinking and independent creature to deal with. He rather wanted a perpetual child who was unseasoned, unthinking, and subservient. Maturity—and beyond that, heroism—is only gained in the fall. The fall was not a fall into sin, but into heroism and character. All that could be interesting in him was a result of revolt and rebellion and the establishment of autonomy. The greatest enemy to man's own development was God.

What the French Revolution clarifies for us is its great wrongheadedness. Autonomy is not the pathway to maturity, adulthood, and freedom, even though these are the desired ends. Paradoxically, surrender is the pathway. This paradox needs to be developed. Alcoholics Anonymous has done as much to clarify this as anyone. Our problem is not weakness of will but strength of autonomous will, self will, which curiously leads to

---

21. Ibid., 332–42.
22. Ibid., 280–84.
23. Ibid., 301–5.

enslavement. And what is true on an individual level is also true on a collective level. When previously Christianized man declares himself a god, he discovers that his entire claim to now "be in charge" is overturned. His will will now become the slave of his passions. The modern "addictive personality" has its origins in the French passion for autonomy. The reasonableness of the Enlightenment was overturned with the passions of the Revolution. The higher self was enslaved by the lower self.

Likewise the Chestertonian commentary on the French Revolution is a very conservative and optimistic one and shows how a Christian can bring renewal to what was initially anti-Christian. He transmuted the Revolution into something positive. He did not react to its leveling tendencies in the way Edmund Burke did, for example, seeing its destructive side, but he transformed it into something else. He did what Burke did but in the terms of the Revolution itself. The Revolution was not radical enough in its democratizing tendencies. He extended them considerably beyond them to include the largest block of the disenfranchised. He included the dead. He describes "tradition" as "the democracy of the dead."[24] He re-includes the past, tradition, privilege, and precedent, just as Burke did, but as a democratic rather than aristocratic inclusion.

Alcoholics Anonymous and the Chestertonian re-interpretation of the Revolution are both examples of the anti-Christian being transformed into the Christian.

THE RUSSIAN REVOLUTION

The Russian Revolution ushered in an era beyond that of the French. It ushered in the man of resentment—of *ressentiment*, to use the term coined by Nietzsche.[25] The man of the Left is the man whose identity is one of resentment over perceived victimhood and attainment of power on that basis.

Nietzsche, from a profoundly anti-Christian perspective, spoke of a "transvaluation of values."[26] His claim was that Christianity universalized and further developed what he saw as the perversions of Hebrew "slave mentality" and morality.

Nietzsche was a truly profound interpreter of the Classical world. His admiration of Greek and Roman Classical culture was quite revolutionary and is still appreciated. In his work, the *Birth of Tragedy*,[27] he argued against the prevailing German intellectual ethos of the time and gave a new interpretation of the development of Greek art. It was commonly argued that the breathtaking beauty and freshness that was created was because the Greco world was the nursery of humanity. It was the freshness and precociousness of the world's childhood. Greece represented the child prodigy of humanity and she created with unconscious effortlessness. Nietzsche challenged this and said that Grecian art was not a result of a precocious child but rather was the result of those who summoned all

---

24. G. K. Chesterton, *Orthodoxy* (New York: Image Books/Doubleday, 2001), 39.
25. Friedrich Nietzsche, *On the Genealogy of Morals and Ecce Homo* (New York: Vintage, 1967), 37–39.
26. Ibid., 33–34.
27. Friedrich Nietzsche, *The Birth of Tragedy and Genealogy of Morals* (Garden City, NY: Doubleday, 1956).

of their powers and became "overmen" or "supermen,"[28] overcoming the terror inspired by the cosmic chaos.

The Greek metaphysic was based on an ontological dualism of form and matter. Form represented order imposed from the realm of the intellect onto the formless and chaotic matter of the world. Homer's *Odyssey* and *Iliad* represented the two classic forms of heroes battling the two great primordial kinds of chaos and imposing order or form upon them. The *Odyssey* represented the sea with all of its formless terror, and the *Iliad* was the great story of the battlefield and of the chaos of war threatening the city. The city-state represented the Greek masterpiece of ideal political order imposed on barbarian chaos by enlightened leaders and philosopher kings. Art and politics were closely intertwined. Art, particularly the sculpting arts, represented the imposition of form upon the chaos. The city-state was the human ethical form of statuary.

The power and terror of chaos cannot be overstated. The recent tsunami illustrated the power to destroy civilization and order with peculiar clarity. Order is rare and unnatural. For the Greeks, in common with modern Darwinism, the chaos is ultimate, and order within the cosmic chaos is but a speck, an island, imposed momentarily by the gods and by men who are heroes. Ultimately, the chaos will triumph, and there is no final hope. But momentarily, the heroes construct a dike and impose an order that is beautiful, orderly, and symmetrical. To do this is the ultimate ideal.

Christianity then came along and attacked and undermined the ideal of the hero, and even saw it as the quintessence of evil and sin. The Greek hero is the incarnation of pride, which is the heart of original sin, according to Augustine. Christianity attacked Classical excellence and exalted the mediocrity of the slave, and the weakling.

Classicism produced excellence, and this human excellence was very well portrayed by Aristotle in his *Nicomachean Ethics*,[29] which was intended to be a portion of his *Politics*.[30] The excellent man, the magnificent man, who is also the proud man, is a man of beautiful form, and is the ideal citizen of the city state.

Christianity, according to Nietzsche, exalted the weakling, the underling, the mediocre man, over against this magnificent man. It caused the slave to resent his superior, to envy him, and to wish to overthrow him with his own inferiority. Christianity exalted the sniveling victim and gave honor to criminals, prostitutes, beggars, and the worthless throw-aways who clearly were enemies of the perfect order of the city-state. Christianity was the ally of chaos and a new class of underling barbarians who lacked both the strength and the intelligence to create anything beautiful or worthy.

Nietzsche noticed certain things in his own nineteenth century Europe that he attributed to Christianity and that he saw Christianity as sanctioning and promoting. He saw the rise of the envy of excellence, and the resentment of greatness by the small-minded. He used the French form of the English word resentment—*ressentiment*—because the French word carries with it subtle undertones of persistent hatred rooted in a feeling

---

28. Nietzsche, *Genealogy of Morals*, 39–43.

29. Aristotle, *The Basic Works of Aristotle,* ed. Richard McKeon (New York: Random House, 1970), 984–1002.

30. Ibid., 935–36.

of impotence that the English does not quite convey. This thesis has been very broadly explored and adopted by a number of thinkers, because it so clearly portrays very obvious realities in the modern world. Several of these thinkers are very profound and are themselves Christians. While Nietzsche attributes these modern realities to Christianity in a most complete way, one can as a Christian thoroughly appreciate his psychological and cultural perceptiveness and yet in a modified and more indirect way relate these things to Christianity.

Max Scheler quotes Goethe as early as 1787 raising these cultural phenomena:

> Christian "mercy" (note the force and spirit of this old fashioned word) is replaced by the feeling expressed in the statement "it arouses my pity." As early as 1787, Goethe could question the kind of "humanism" *(Humanitat)* Herder preached under Rousseau's influence: "Moreover . . . I think it is true that humanism will triumph at last; only I fear that the world will at the same time be a vast hospital, where each will be his fellow man's humane sick-nurse."[31]

My own interpretation of the phenomena of *ressentiment* is that it is indeed a side effect of Christianity. There is little or no evidence of such psychic processes in the ancient world. Manfred Frings, in his introduction to Scheler's very profound volume *Ressentiment*, says that such feelings and emotion do not exist "when individuals freely accept the social stations they are born in and where there is little or no competition." He goes on to say,

> The pervasive slavery of ancient Rome, for example, apparently did not generate ressentiment to speak of against Roman masters. To be born a slave at the time was felt to be a natural state. Neither Aristotle in *Nicomachean Ethics,* nor Plato in his *Republic* perceive an omen of possible upheavals when they touch upon the theme of social classes. Accepting the social bed one was born in was, right or wrong, was the order of the day, and contributed to some communal feelings of solidarity which modern societies are not prone to develop.[32]

On the deepest level of spiritual existence there is a transformation of fallen man's sense of sinful rivalry with God. In the ancient, pre-Christian world, God is experienced as *the Almighty, the Powerful One*. The act of creation is an act of infinite power. Even in the crass idolatry of animism, or in the idolatry of monistic or pantheistic religions, the experience of the gods is one of terrible power. Therefore man, either in imitation or in rivalry of God or the gods, is animated primarily by this sense of power. The ancient world everywhere idolized the mighty warrior. We see evidence of this very early in the Old Testament prior to the flood when there were giants and mighty men who filled the earth with violence (Gen 6:4, 13) Even earlier, Lamech boosts of his prowess by boasting that he kills for being wounded or hurt, and that he shall seek revenge seventy seven fold for all offenses against him (Gen 4:23–24). This is the *gibbor*, the mighty and fearful warrior. This is the hero who is animated by pride and is in rivalry with the power of God.

---

31. Max Scheler, *Ressentiment* (Milwaukee: Marquette University Press, 1994), 97.
32. Frings, introduction to Scheler, *Ressentiment*, 17.

PART FOUR: CULTURE

But in the New Covenant, God comes in a different way. He comes not as the Mighty Warrior, but as the Humble and Meek One who is finally victimized in every way. Paul's profound poem of the Kenotic Christ in Philippians 2 tells us of this strange redeeming God who is so different from the ancient terrible warrior. He becomes of no reputation, becomes a slave, and dies a horrible death on a gibbet. He is a victim. Therefore, just as ancient men came into rivalry with God by becoming powerful oppressors and creating victims, modern man comes into rivalry with God by becoming a false Christ and transforming himself masochistically into a victim.

Now this is precisely the phenomena that Nietzsche noticed and wrote upon and protested so violently. The tantalizing new possibility that did not exist in the ancient world, and still does not exist in non-Christianized parts of the world is the new possibility of the weak persecuting the strong by assuming the role of victim. The modern neurotic is a backwards upside-down Christ. He is in effect, an anti-Christ. He is a mockery, an imitation of Christ. "If I cannot be happy, if I cannot actualize my fantasies, my hopes, if I cannot achieve or be given my utopia, my New Jerusalem, then it is the fault of the strong, the rich, the powerful, the excellent, the talented. I am victimized by them, I am made powerless by them, I am placed on a Cross by them, and it is their fault."

The degree of suffering that can be inflicted on others in this way is not to be minimized. Let me here quote Karl Stern:

> Now there are living in our midst thousands and thousands of people (there is a strong possibility that they form the majority of mankind in our present civilization) who suffer, or produce suffering among those around them, in a most puzzling manner. They live in mortal anxiety, or they are unable to hope, or they are entangled in a mysterious hatred, they are out to destroy that which would give them happiness, they are incapable of trusting, or they are being oppressed by something which is best called insatiable remorse. They form a huge army of suffering, dissatisfaction, frustration, and assault. . . . If an observer could, at one glance, behold all the neurotic suffering and entanglement in the world today, he would get the impression of something quite infernal. Infernal is a good word for it. Many of our neurotic patients express the thought literally: "this is hell on earth." Those who live with them often say: "Life with that person is hell on earth."[33]

Infliction of such suffering may be as terrible and as much an oppression as the old-fashioned tyranny of the powerful. And the phenomena of *ressentiment* greatly complicates judging the case of many peoples in the modern world. Many minority groups who have been historically powerless enter modernity and the possibilities that modern equalities afford. Their case then becomes a complex and sometimes indiscernible combination of being oppressed and victimized, and at the same time learning the powerful possibilities of assuming the role of victim and using this as a means of inflicting suffering on the older and established classes and groups. The persecuted become persecutors.

It has been noted by various thinkers that destructive revolution almost always happens, not when people are at the nadir of being oppressed, but rather as oppression is

---

33. Karl Stern, *The Third Revolution: A Study in Psychiatry and Religion* (Garden City, NY: Image Books, 1961), 10–11.

lifting and rising expectations give birth to hope. In the time prior to the revolution in 1917, Russia had freed the peasants and had a rapidly expanding economy with more possibilities for upward mobility than anywhere in Europe at the time. The peasantry owned 80% of the arable land, while in Britain more than half the fertile soil was owned by large estates. "Life in Siberia around 1900 was no worse than in North Dakota or Saskatchewan at that time."[34] And yet the revolutionaries paid back in misery many times over those they deemed their oppressors.

I have heard similar things in regard to the precursors of the French Revolution. Likewise, feminism did not arise in, say, Islamic areas where brutal oppressions of women exist but amongst the best educated and relatively wealthy women in the United States and Europe. A resentful feeling of oppression was the very strongest amongst the freest women in all of the world or all of history.

All of this is the psychic and spiritual background of Marxism and the Soviet Revolution. Nietzsche is the greatest excavator of this background, which prepared the world's soil. The Soviets identified themselves with Genesis 1:2, "the darkness and the void." They identified with the chaos and harnassed all of the power of *ressentiment* transforming it into the great revolutionary engine. But the whole of the twentieth century has identified with the chaos and has lived in the great hope that a dip into the chaos by means of revolution would rejuvenate the world.

TODAY

The revolutionary temper of the Soviet is now everywhere upon us. This universalized revolutionary temper shares in common the absolute religious conviction that chaos and destruction will give way to a rebirth. This is not necessarily untrue. Genesis 1:2 has two clauses. The first, which affirms that the cosmos was "without form and void," is followed by the second half that reminds us that the "Spirit of God was hovering, moving, brooding over the face of the chaos." It is the presence of the Spirit that creates and recreates out of chaos. But the revolutionary is not watching for that. He believes in the power of chaos to produce order of its own accord. It is divorced from God. The modern Leftist temperament is a post-Christian rebirth of ancient sensibilities. It is a rebirth of magic as opposed to sovereign power of the Triune God. The rituals of the tribe and the emperor's statist powers are able to manipulate the chaos and recreate utopian order.

The old Byzantine Eastern Orthodox only blessed, and they only blessed and praised like a child. They did not bless against the background of the fallenness of the fallen world. They did not praise God as the persecuted, as the warriors, as the reformers, but only as those escaping the world and all of its woes. Hence, the Bolshevik in reaction only learned to curse, to hate, to revile all of the existing order.

The Christian is called to bless and to curse. Cursing is an essential side of being a Christian. If curses are not uttered against the rottenness of the existing order, then there is no condemnation of that which ought to be condemned. If there is no blessing, then

---

34. Erik von Kuehnelt-Leddihn, *Leftism: From De Sade and Marx to Hitler and Marcuse* (New Rochelle, NY: Arlington House, 1974), 146.

there is no new order to come. *Ressentiment* is the culmination of curses with no blessing, and these curses are uttered wholly from the foundation of the autonomous self. All ought be cursed and damned. Nihilism is only a universal curse of all, the murder of all. Leftism does not bring the judgment of God, a judgment of justice, but the universal judgment of resentment, the desire to see all reduced to rubble or blotted out. This is the same "being," existents, things, that Francis and Thomas called forth from pagan darkness, named, and blessed. For the new underman—whether Marxist, Fascist, city gang member, protesting world youth—it is all to be cursed.

THE NEW WORLD OF PRE-HISTORY

We have entered the era of the pre-linguistic, when the irrational, the primitive, and the ahistorical animal spirit of man have come to full expression. In the arts, jazz and primitivism in painting had their source in the tribal and primitive regions of the earth. These may all become highly developed art forms, but they were originally intended to represent the pre-historical, the primitive. Jazz was originally referred to dismissively and insultingly as "jungle music." The story of Paul Gauguin (1848–1903), loosely retold in novelistic form by Somerset Maugham in *The Moon and Sixpence,* briefly represents this retreat from the civilized to the primitive.[35] In our own time, heavy metal rock gives a fair representation of the power and dominance of chaos in contemporary youth culture.

This retreat began much earlier and was found already in concentrated form in Rousseau. Rousseau rebelled against all citification and imagined that "original sin" and a fall from virtue was to be found in the civilizing of man. Virtue could be regained by retreating to the stage of the "noble savage." But Nietzsche had fathomed that by his own time the ideal of the primitive had devolved from a noble savage to an "underman." The underman is suffused with a "slave mentality" and is ruled by resentment and hatred of anything that is superior to him. His primary drive is to overturn and destroy. All of this inarticulate violence and resentment were harnessed by nineteenth and twentieth century theorists and leaders. An era of "permanent revolution" was introduced and was the hidden center and ideal of all Leftist movements.

Neurosis is the individual and family equivalent of the political revolutionary. Neurosis is self-sabotage and family sabotage. To be *scandalized* is an age-old category. It means literally "to be caused to stumble," and it is to have a stumbling stone placed before one by another. It is to be offended by the actions or behavior of others. But neurosis is the desire to be constantly offended and to seek that as a permanent state. It is to place stumbling stones before oneself but then to blame others for the offense. It is to be the master of "the double bind" so that, no matter what others do, one has positioned oneself to always be offended. Neurosis is private, permanent revolution. Leftism is political neurosis.

The last two great revolutions were anti-Christian in nature but are still a part of the Christian era. This entire era is in the "Age of ages" and is the era of Jesus Christ, and that is so regardless of how the world responds or reacts to Him. He is now inescapable,

---

35. W. Somerset Maugham, *The Moon and Sixpence* (New York: Pocket Books, 1967).

either to be loved or hated. So whether the last revolutions are anti-Christian or not is irrelevant to their being a part of His era. Sometimes reaction to the era of Jesus Christ is reaction to the rottenness of the church and the visible expression of His Kingdom, and even unconsciously reacts only with attempts (however perverse or inadequate) to replace false representations with true. So it is clear that the French Revolution was in large measure a reaction to a rotten aristocratic class and royal house that had lost contact with the broader life of the nation and had resisted renewal and reformation. And the Bolshevik Revolution was in large measure a revolt against the unhistorical character of Orthodoxy, its lack of fight and prophetic office, and against its childish religion of pictures and icons.

It is arguable that in either Revolution the revolutionary child succeeded no better than the aged parent. It is a truism that when the child hates the parent, he is doomed to repeat the very folly that is reacted against. Only love and forgiveness enable true transcendence over the past and repentance for past sins.

But even if the original revolutionaries did not do better than the parents (and in many cases, worse), each revolution is universal in nature, and it is the calling of the worldwide church as the nursery of the Kingdom of God to overcome what has been reacted against. The Pentecostal is the Kingdom's answer to the pre-historical, tribal, primitive underman who spawned perpetual revolution.

Rosenstock-Huessy contends that we have entered the era of dumbness, of complete inarticulateness. He speaks of the death of the theater. A few expletives are adequate for modern man to express the little he has to express.

The Pentecostal is both the end and the beginning of language. What needs to be said is what cannot be said. Modern man needs to speak but cannot. He needs articulation but has none. For the first time in Western history, there is no bard. Rather, there is the Pentecostal. But the Pentecostal is not only the end but also the beginning. Language must be reborn, and the beginnings of this are not in the academy or the theater but in the church.

In the ancient world, there was a gradual emergence from shame and glory cultures to ethical cultures. Ethical cultures are indeed a step up from shame cultures but also are built on the foundation of shame cultures. The achievements of the earlier are purified and taken up in the later. In Genesis, shame comes before guilt. Adam and Eve felt ashamed ("I knew I was naked, and I was ashamed") before they knew that they were guilty. God dealt with their shame before He dealt with their guilt, at least in their own consciousness.

The ancient world gradually emerged from shame and glory cultures to ethical cultures. Greece and Rome were perhaps the first, and perhaps the only, ethical cultures in the ancient world, outside of Israel. I think it fair to say that Confucius dealt primarily with the questions of shame and honor and not with right and wrong. But Plato's Socrates, and then following him, Aristotle, dealt primarily with ethical questions, perhaps for the first time in an extensive way in the world (again, outside of the Bible.).

Rosenstock-Huessy says that in the rediscovery of the Classical world, after the collapse of the Roman Empire, it was recovered backwards. First the West recovered interest in Julius Caesar, and gradually Western thinkers moved back through the Roman Republic to its origins and beginnings. After that, the Greek world was recovered with Aristotle, then later, Plato. Then the great earlier playwrights of Athens were recovered, and eventually we moved back to Homer. Since the 1930s, we are moving behind Homer to the ancient empires and to the tribes.[36]

The church has done the same. The church began in the Roman Empire, and its consciousness has very slowly moved backward. Hence, the church, as it moved forward out of empire with the collapse of Rome, left a world of ethics and encountered the tribes, and in the tribes again encountered shame and glory cultures that were devoid of legal and ethical development. Initially, it taught the tribes what an ethical world was by teaching them the moral law of God. We have been dominated by the teaching of the moral law ever since. Luther's gospel was a gospel that dealt with moral guilt and ethical incapability, and that gospel was the result of teaching the tribes the law of God for nearly a thousand years. The law began as a great illumination to the tribes and was a great advance as it enabled the tribes to move from being only shame and honor cultures to being ethical cultures as well. But eventually, the law ceased to be good news and became bad news as it was discovered that the law unveiled and revealed a sinful nature that in the end was incapable of ethical uprightness. Luther's gospel brought a cure to European man who was crushed by his sinfulness.

But as civilization has continued to move forward through time, we have continued to move backward in our consciousness, and this has set up a paradox. As initially the western world moved out of empire and into tribe, the church carried an ethical and legal mentality from the previous empire into the tribes. But then as the tribes slowly became nations and then empires—and now in the twentieth and twenty-first century we have become a global economic empire—we have slowly lost our tribal memories and our tribal roots. It is important for white, Anglo/Germanic/Gaelic peoples of European extraction to remember that our ancestry is as tribal as the Apache or the Sioux. But we have long since lost this element in our awareness. As a result, we have slowly lost our tribal consciousness of glory.

This is an important point. The tribes were pre-prepared for the ethical teaching of the law of God on the part of the monks because they were already glorious as proud warrior peoples. This element of tribal gloriousness has slowly evaporated, and now we have almost no sense of honor or glory. We are a deglorified people and, as a deglorified people, we struggle extensively with shame and what can only be identified as a deep sense of uncleanness and a growing and pervasive sense of being filled with death. Modern depressiveness and feelings of meaninglessness are struggles with death consciousness, which is what uncleanness is.

In consciousness, we are moving back to the tribal and early empire phase. But as we come to this old, but now new, continent of consciousness, we are still trying to deal with it in the categories of ethics and righteousness and it is not hitting the mark. Just as we now in our theological curriculum have classes that deal with ethics, we may need

---

36. Eugen Rosenstock-Huessy, "Lecture 6" (lecture given at Dartmouth College, March 2, 1954), 1, in *Universal History—1954* (transcript), Eugen Rosenstock-Huessy Lectures, vol. 12 (Essex, VT: Argo, 1997).

classes that deal with clean and unclean, shame and glory. The books of Leviticus and Numbers and Exodus and Deuteronomy may be becoming far more culturally relevant. As we move into tribal and early empire consciousness, we are dealing not only with a consciousness of right and wrong, guilt and righteousness, but also of shame and honor, shame and glory.

Let us identify three principal traits of the tribesman that set him off from his modern counterpart. First, he is possessed of an immense verbal inventiveness, and the part of speech that is dominant is the proper noun. He has a genius for naming. Tribes have a capability of inventing and reinventing languages almost overnight. Secondly, he wears the tribal tattoo. The tribal tattoo is a symbol that is etched into the body. It essentially tells the tribal story, which therefore identifies the tribesman. It is a narrative of who he is. And thirdly, each tribesman is a warrior, and it is in this that he is victoriously glorious.

On the contrary, his late decadent empire counterpart does not have language. Expression can be reduced to a few expletives. There is no shared literature or symbol system. What language he does have is abstract and stiff and is the weakest at the point of the noun and proper noun. Modern man has little facility for naming, and the particular is largely replaced with broad abstraction. He is himself nameless. Modern names, unlike tribal names, are almost never badges of descriptive identity. And poetry as a cultural form has largely disappeared.

Secondly, he is deficient in terms of narrative and autobiographical narrative. He has no story. The birth of psychoanalysis was the rebirth of the shaman who enabled those who come to him to rediscover a personal narrative. Freud reinterpreted Greek myth as a larger story that would enable his patients to rediscover a personal narrative within that larger narrative stream. Current counseling of all sorts is a continuation of the renewed quest for a personal story.

And finally, the last thing a modern man is is a warrior. In this way, he is particularly naked and ashamed and has lost glory. He is inarticulate, has no story, and is not a warrior. Identity is problematic. Shame is inescapable because modern man is psychically naked and is therefore prone to self-hatred as he projects hatred on all that is around him.

We now are dealing everywhere with shame and honor. Inner city gangs, which are modern tribal rebirths, are struggling with honor, not with guilt. Feminism likewise is an attempt to deal with shame and a feeling of having no glory. Ethical consciousness does not loom large on the screen in such venues. Until the shame of young men and young women is dealt with, it is not very fruitful to attempt to deal with the ethical. They need to be re-clothed with glory before they can deal adequately with the issues of guilt.

Feminist crusaders and boys running in gangs are all overwhelmed with a feeling of uncleanness and shame and are trying to rid themselves of these. They all have death and shame on them and all need to be cleansed. But to accomplish this purification this we need the codes of clean and unclean that are prior to the ethical consciousness of the Ten Commandments. We need Leviticus, we need Exodus, and we need Numbers. This is now what we need from the Old Testament. We need corollary volumes to our volumes that deal with ethics to deal with clean and unclean and with shame and glory. And just as theonomy has struggled with the application of Old Testament Law to modern civil codes, similar grappling needs to happen in the application of the ritual codes of the Law of Moses.

We tend to think of glorification as the capstone of righteousness, something that comes later, because our theology believes in an *ordo salutis* that sees glory as that which follows after justification (Rom 8:29–30) and usually, in the next life. But I am not sure this is right. It may be that glory sometimes comes first before righteousness because it deals with shame and glory is the cure for shame. It is only after shame is dealt with that it is possible to deal with guilt. Adam and Eve are aware of shame before they are aware of being guilty.

Glory does not necessarily follow righteousness. Even for the Apostle Paul, glory is not just a future category but also a present one. Paul declares that we are now beholding the glory of Christ and are being "transformed . . . from one degree of glory to another" (2 Cor 3:18 ESV), and he says that the very preaching of the gospel in an evangelistic way is the shining of the glory of Christ on unbelievers (2 Cor 4:4). It is also the case that for Paul, to be "glorified" is in the same tense as "to be justified" (Rom 8:30). It is not wholly future nor necessarily in a linear progression of events. Likewise, in the creation account, nascent glory precedes full righteousness. Yahweh breathes life into Adam, places him in the Garden as its keeper and guardian (warrior), and gives him the task of being the namer, where he displays the verbal facility with the proper noun that the tribesman later inherited. He is then given the woman who is his glory (1 Cor 11:7).

It is only the glorious man and woman who can be clothed with full righteousness. Adam is created as "Earth"; he is made from the dust of the earth. Even this is glorious. But he is then further glorified. When Eve is taken from his side and he awakens, as a bard he sings the world's first love poem:

> This is now bone of my bones
> And flesh of my flesh,
> She shall be called Woman,
> Because she was taken out of Man. (Gen 2:23)

Man is *Ish* and woman is *Ishshah*, which, loosely translated, mean "flame" and "flamette."[37] Eve is Adam's fire. She is what heats him. She is Adam's glory. Earth has been transformed into fire. Adam has been glorified in Eve, and she is glory.

All of this happens before they are tested at the Tree of Knowledge. The Tree of Knowledge is, among other things, the tree of ethical decision. When Adam and Eve do partake of it, it is too soon. The clear implication of this is that glory precedes righteousness, at least in consciousness. It may be that the crowning of righteousness implies further degrees of glory, but glory is already in bloom before real ethical consciousness has budded.

---

37. The Hebrew word for "woman" is *Ishshah*. The Hebrew word for "sacrifice by fire" is *Ishsheh*. This word play would have been heard and noted by the native Hebrew ear, and makes the meaning of "man" and "woman" a double *entrendre*. This wordplay was noted by James Jordan in a lecture at the Biblical Horizons Conference in July, 2009. He credited Dr. Rob Maddox for first noting this connection.

The extensive concern of the Old Testament—and particularly the books of the law in Exodus, Leviticus, Numbers, and Deuteronomy—with the concept of "flesh" are illuminated by the creation account. If the human race is not re-glorified after the fall, it then reverts to being only "flesh," living dirt, and exists in a state of uncleanness, which means it is filled with death. Glory is what is needed, and this glory is only available in God's presence. Uncleanness makes one unable to be in His presence. Leviticus tells us in veiled gospel form how we become clean and thereby enter God's presence to be glorified. Jesus has fulfilled the meaning of Leviticus. This we must understand if we are to win our deglorified world back to the gospel.

Adam and Eve were glorified *before* they began their trek to confirmed righteousness. They were about to *begin* to learn out of obedience. Out of obedience, they would be educated about justice and equity. They would then be sealed and given a further growth in righteousness to become wise and also be given a further degree of glory. We grow from one degree of glory to another. The first time this happened, they would eat fruit from the Tree of Knowledge. Eventually, they would sit and drink wine. Wine is *fire water* and is filled with glory, and it makes one more glorious when drunk at the bequest of God but foolish and stupid when drunk apart from His direction.

The Nazarite fulfilled his vow, and only at the end of that vow did he drink and then evaluate the work accomplished while in the state of the Nazarite warrior.

When this tree is participated in, the effect is *to open the eyes*. The opening of the eyes means that one has become like God, *knowing* good and evil. The emphasis here is on *knowing*. It involves that odd and wonderful human capability not only of knowing, but of being self-aware in the act of knowing. It is a state of knowing that I know and of evaluating and then of evaluating my evaluations. It is a state of self-consciousness. It means that one is capable of determining worth in the same way that God determined worth after each creation day when He offered a pronouncement on His own work. He declared on five occasions that it was "good" and, on the sixth, that it was "very good."

If one eats before one ought, before one has been given adequate degrees of glory, then one becomes a judge and one is destroyed by one's own judgments. Adam and Eve became self-evaluators before they ought to have. They now turned eyes inward and discerned that they were naked. The result was deglorification, which leads to, or perhaps is, shame. They became judges before they ought to have and were destroyed by their own judgment.

The entire Cartesian project, which the western world has tried to make its cornerstone, is the project of the unhappy child prodigy. The true child prodigy happily, and without effort or thought, creates. But the unhappy child prodigy "thinks before he has lived" and judges before he knows. He tries to understand and evaluate knowledge. He judges before he has played. He judges before he is thankful. It reverses the order of the trees. He was first to have eaten of the tree of life, which is a tree of eucharist, a tree of gratitude and thanksgiving and of joy. And then at the appropriate time, he is given the tree of knowledge in which he evaluates.

If one evaluates, judges, has the eye opened and becomes a critic *before* one has become grateful and joyful, then one is on the road to self-destruction and the destruction of everything that is gazed upon by the judging eye. One becomes the *ressentiment*-filled, self-pitying, brat adolescent Leftist that the western world is now being destroyed by. It is the state of mind described by Jacques Maritain concerning the entire Kantian project. Maritain very aptly says that the Kantian critiques do critique of knowledge before anything is known.[38] Epistemology precedes ontology, advanced judgment precedes naive knowledge and this leads to mental anorexia since the knowing mind has nothing to feed on, and judgment and critique can only lead to the nakedness of everything that is seen. Everything is "seen through" and, as C. S. Lewis has said, "To 'see through' all things is the same as not to see."[39] This is a terrible state and is the state of hell. Hell is a critical self-awareness, an awareness that pitilessly judges everything in a final and eternal deglorification. The Kantian and Cartesian man is already in the suburbs of hell. No wonder the last century was such an unhappy one.

Just as the Lutheran and Reformation era could preach the Gospel to that ethics-hungry era, that guilt-ridden era, with a Law / Gospel dichotomy, so now we perhaps need a Death / Gospel or Unclean / Clean or Flesh / Glory dichotomy to reach our own age. We must recover a full glory and recover a tribal Gospel. The tribesman is principally a warrior, and it is in this that he experiences his glory. Modern people are losing capacity for war and are replacing it with psychic masochism and projected hatred which is sadism. We must become new warriors. But the new enemy is not the "other" in other tribes, but the world, the flesh, and the devil, who is the prince of the principalities and powers. It is only in this way that all of the tribes can be united under one great Emperor, Jesus, and humanity can reach its glory.

The new warrior must likewise regain the joy of the tribes. Modern man must overcome *ressentiment* with thanksgiving. He must truly become the eucharistic being, the new man of gratitude and joy.

And finally, he must recover the reality of *Ish* and *Ishshah*. The meaning of being, in gender, as beings of fire has obvious erotic overtones. Our oversexed age is also curiously, an age of slavering impotence.[40]

The sight of Eve makes Adam "hot." In his heat, he sets Eve on fire, and the fact that she is heated further heats Adam. This is an obvious description of sex, but it has applica-

---

38. Jacques Maritain, *Distinguish to Unite: Or, Degrees of Knowledge* (New York: Scribner, 1959), 74.

39. C. S. Lewis, *The Abolition of Man, or, Reflections on Education with Special Reference to the Teaching of English in the Upper Forms of Schools* (New York: Macmillan, 1955), 91.

40. A number of years ago, the feminist, Naomi Wolf, published an article lamenting the sexlessness and impotence of our era ("The Porn Myth," *New York Magazine* [20 Oct. 2003]). She recounts how, when pornography was initially becoming easily available, it was feared that its easy availability would transform every man into a rapist. In actual fact, the result has been the exact opposite. Men are bored, sated, and sexually un-ignitable. And, ordinary and real women cannot compete with the airbrushed models that will satisfy every male urge and desire for every perversion. She recounted her own envy of an Israeli friend of hers who lived on a kibbutz and lived a life of immense sexual conservatism with her husband. The only man who ever saw her hair, which was otherwise covered, was her husband, and the mere sight of her hair let down was enough to ignite his passion. Ms. Wolf opined that she envied the sexual power and confidence that her friend had with her husband and compared that with the sense of helplessness and frigidity along with the relative impotence that she was only too acquainted with in her cultural configuration in the "liberated" United States.

tion to every realm of life. She is his inspiration, and by being inspired, he inspires her. When she is inspired, it further inspires him, and she then accommodates that inspiration with further inspiration. The loss of monogamous marriage under God means quite simply that men and women go back to being dirt, and little more, and they will treat each other as such.

Just as the sight of the Woman, the *Ishshah*, inspired Adam as one who named and as a poet and bard, so now the same fire of language needs to be reborn. The tribal Pentecostal is the first stage of rebirth as language is reborn at the level of "unknown utterances," and then it can rise up in the whole of the Psalter as it is sung as our new war songs. From there, the whole of the Scripture becomes our new narrative within which we find ourselves and our whole identity.

As a civilization, our fire has gone out. It needs to be re-lit. James Jordan has understood this as no one else that I know. His theology has laid the groundwork for this new way, this new path, for preaching the Gospel to our naked, shamed, and deglorified age.

Hail to my friend, James Jordan!

∼

Dear Rich,

This is wonderful stuff. I particularly liked your discussion of shame and uncleanness. Shame is a sense of powerlessness and exposure, and of death. It is interesting that in recent years the fact that Jesus was "raised for our justification" has come into more prominent notice. I think you are onto something in suggesting that new life from death—glorification in a sense—is underneath justification, at least as we experience it. I think that God's order is to clear us from liability before glorifying us, but I suspect that we experience things in a rather different order—at least sometimes.

Since glory is social—we get glory when "our team" wins—modern man's loss of glory is linked with his loss of connections. Loneliness, anomia, futility—all these are answered by glorification into the Society of the Trinity as that Society is extended into the community of the Church. What that means, though, is that local churches must revive community and tribality by vigorous singing of psalms (not goofy, dripping, torch songs for Jesus), weekly communion with alcohol, and the like.

The Christian warfare is holy war, and it is liturgical war. We can no longer be contented with mere hymns and metrical psalms that seek merely the ideas of the psalms but ignore their shape and form—a tiny bit of gnostic influence in our midst. We need to be singing both the psalms in their lined shape and vigorous sermonic metrical paraphrases of the psalms. In fact, worship needs to be mostly sung throughout, kicked up a notch from mere talking. Singing knits people together in one s/Spirit.

We need to sense that we are not just "called to worship" but called to a Feast. Let the pastor and the distributors sit around a table and pass the loaf hand to hand, eating as they go, before taking out large portions to be passed among the people. Similarly, let the pastor drink the death+glory blood+wine first and pass a chalice around the table to the distributors, and then let it flow out like a river into the congregation. Let the warfeast be a warfeast. Let the unit commander lead his people into battle, as Jesus does at the feast (Rev 19:7–16).

A final observation. Once upon a time, when Thomas and Luther were around, a university education took place within the multiform cultures of biblical and Christian history and milieu. The biblical historical narrative was taken as "our" story and was not questioned. Science and art took place within this world, which is the real, true world. All was seen as exploration and glorification of the real world.

The modern university—and to an extent the theological seminary, including "conservative" ones—exists for the purpose of tearing young people away from their story context. It seeks to castrate them from history and make them question everything from a "neutral" standpoint that is actually a void. This is "modernity," and so-called postmodernism is simply modernity with a vengeance.

Did your pastor tell you God made the world in six days only a few thousand years ago? That there was a world-wide Flood? That the Nile turned to blood? Bosh. That's for children. Now you are a grown-up "Reformed" theologian you can know that these are just myths designed to give out ideas and notions. Did your mommy and daddy tell you sex outside of marriage is wrong? Baloney. You can have sex with anyone; as long as she, he, or it consents, no harm is done.

The secular university has gradually grown from a largely Christian to a semi-Christian and now to an anti-Christian establishment. And because of the anti-glories of universal education, the entire Western world is a castrated academe. The world of modernity is an unreal world, a world of complete fantasy, with a billions-year old universe and other insupportable folly. It is cultivated insanity, education out of reality into insanity. After over a decade of world-wide cooling, the insane crow louder than ever about man-made global warming. After a century of the failures of fascist economics, the Democrat party and half the Republicans advocate it more than ever. As the "Reformed" churches grow weaker and weaker as they pursue praise chorus worship, the response is the promotion of ever more "relevant" impotence, while those who advocate a return to the powerful worship of the Reformation are forced out.

Jim

13

Theology of Beauty in Evdokimov

BOGUMIL JARMULAK

> God is beautiful. His throne is set in glory and beauty, and He commanded that His Temple and His priests be garbed in glory and beauty. Gold, fine linen, beautiful colors, precious stone, careful architectural lines, orchestras of professional musicians, trained choirs—all of these things we find in the Bible's description of God's house and His worship.
>
> —James B. Jordan[1]

> Beauty will save the world.
>
> —Fyodor Dostoevsky, *The Idiot*

THE GOAL OF THIS essay is to present the theology of beauty in the works of Paul Evdokimov (1901–1970), a Russian Orthodox theologian who left Russia after the Revolution and settled down in Paris. His last publication, *The Art of the Icon: A Theology of Beauty*,[2] deals with this subject. Evdokimov first presents his theology of beauty and art and then shows how they are related to the sacred, especially to liturgy and the icon. After the presentation, an evaluation of it will be provided, based on the writings of Jacques Ellul, a French Reformed theologian, and James B. Jordan.

BEAUTY

The point of departure for Evdokimov's theology of beauty is the biblical description of the week of creation. The Greek text says that at the end of each day of creation God "saw that it was beautiful."[3] For Evdokimov, this is a justified interpretation since the Hebrew word used here means both good and beautiful. But the created world was not

---

1. James B. Jordan, "Arts and Play (III)," *Open Book* 7 (Jan 1992).
2. Paul Evdokimov, *The Art of the Icon: A Theology of Beauty* (Redondo Beach, CA: Oakwood, 1990).
3. Ibid., 2.

only beautiful. It was also to become more and more beautiful as a result of cooperation between God and man. The perfect beauty will be called the Kingdom of God.

Evdokimov calls the Third Person of Trinity "the Spirit of Beauty,"[4] who not only manifests the Word in the world but also overcomes the chaos and ugliness. This means that a perception of beauty is a perception of God's dealings in the world. There is a connection between an aesthetic and a religious experience. Nevertheless beauty can also deceive, especially when man ignores the metaphysical aspect of beauty, because "true Beauty is not found in nature itself but rather in the epiphany of the Transcendent. This epiphany transforms nature into a cosmic place of its radiance."[5]

For Evdokimov beauty is never an abstraction, precisely because it reveals the nature of God in His creative and salvific actions. This is why Evdokimov criticizes abstract art: It has no place for the Word that became flesh but only for general ideas. For the same reason he advocates the use of chants, icons, incense, bread and wine in the liturgy, which give the matter its original sense and status as a tool of the Spirit. The connection between aesthetics and religion was broken by sin, but the incarnation of Christ reconnected the two. To prove this Evdokimov quotes 1 John 1:1–3:

> That which was from the beginning, which we have heard, which we have seen with our eyes, which we looked upon and have touched with our hands, concerning the word of life—the life was made manifest, and we have seen it, and testify to it and proclaim to you the eternal life, which was with the Father and was made manifest to us—that which we have seen and heard we proclaim also to you, so that you too may have fellowship with us; and indeed our fellowship is with the Father and with his Son Jesus Christ.

As Bruno Forte, an Italian Roman-Catholic theologian and archbishop, puts it, "Since God entered history—to the point of pouring himself out entirely in the Incarnation of the Son and his paschal mystery—the visible has offered the invisible a home, even if without taking the invisible prisoner, in a way at least analogous to how human words have been inhabited by the Word of God."[6]

Noteworthy is the visual character of beauty emphasized by Evdokimov. He admits that in the Old Testament Israel was a people of hearing, but in the New Testament the situation is changed. The Bible does not deny the value of seeing but "the word and the image are in dialogue.... The word tends to establish the truth of something, prove it through speech and the image tends to show that truth, to make it visible."[7] Of course, not all images show the truth, but only those that reflect the word of truth. Again, true beauty has to be connected with God and stay in accordance with His dealings in the world. This is why Christians cannot go back to the Old Testament religion with its emphasis on hearing. Christian liturgy, in particular, has to reflect the fact of the incar-

---

4. Ibid.
5. Ibid., 24.
6. Bruno Forte, *The Portal of Beauty: Towards a Theology of Aesthetics* (Grand Rapids: Eerdmans, 2008), 68.
7. Evdokimov, *Art*, 33.

nation, for it is a presentation of the biblical story. A rejection of an image in liturgy is "a regression to the pre-iconographic period of the Old Testament."[8]

After establishing a case for a liturgical use of images, Evdokimov goes back to his discussion of beauty, and especially of its ambiguity. He quotes the famous words of Dostoevsky—"Are you aware that mankind can do without the English, that it can also do without Germany, that nothing is easier for mankind than to do without the Russians, that it can live without science or even bread? Only beauty is absolutely indispensable, for without beauty there is nothing left in the world worth doing. Here is the entire secret; all of history, right in a nutshell"[9]—only to point to the danger of "an aesthetic utopia, that is, the idolatrous belief in the theurgic power and magic of art."[10] The truth is that beauty is not always true. The evil one tries to imitate God by clothing himself in beauty in order to deceive man and make him indifferent to good and evil. The evil one presents beauty as a mere aesthetic phenomenon that pleases the desires of man and promises to lead him back to the lost soul's homeland. Man is easily deceived by beauty because it inflames his strongest desires and touches his deepest longings.

Because of the disintegration of beauty, truth, and goodness we cannot agree with Dostoevsky's statement that "beauty will save the world." If beauty is to be able to save the world, it has to be reintegrated with truth and goodness of God. This is an eschatological task and can happen only in the cult of the Church, which reconnects beauty with its transcendental source. As Milica Bakic-Hayden put it, "The main problem Evdokimov sees with the beauty of the world is in the separation of aesthetic principle from ethical and ultimately religious principle; in other words, in the separation of beauty from the mystery of life as liturgy."[11]

This reconnection is important for, among other things, the right self-understanding of man. Evdokimov points to the fact that even the greatest atheists do not deny the similarity between God and man, which can be seen in such characteristics of man as intelligence, liberty, creativity, and prophetic clairvoyance. Of course, they do not attribute them to *imago Dei*, but nevertheless they use them to define a human person. "For whatever point of view, man thinks of himself in relation to the Absolute, and to understand man is to explain this relation."[12] The main question to be answered is: Who creates whom?

The likeness of God seen in man is a precondition for revelation because it institutes a compatibility between divine Logos and human logos. Man is a creator and a poet as long as he resembles God, or, precisely speaking, Christ. In fact, God created man in the image of the Son with the incarnation in mind. This, however, is not the end of the story, because God not only became man but man also can become god if he is born not only

---

8. Ibid., 35.

9. Ibid., 37.

10. Ibid.

11. Milica Bakic-Hayden, "The Aesthetics of Theosis: Uncovering the Beauty of the Image," in *Aesthetics as a Religious Factor in Eastern and Western Christianity*, ed. Wil van den Bercken and Jonathan Sutton (Dudley, MA: Peeters, 2006), 31.

12. Evdokimov, *Art*, 45.

of woman, but also of water and the Holy Spirit. Then, besides being an earthly man, he becomes a heavenly man too. This does not mean, though, that he is "different from the world; he is simply the world's truth and is thereby responsible for its destiny."[13]

This responsibility cannot express itself in taking dominion of the world by force, because any good that violates human conscience turns into evil. Christians should not turn the world into the Church but rather saturate the world with deifying energies and turn it into God's Temple. For this reason Christ became not only a priest, but also a lay person. He took a worldly calling so that man may glorify the world through any profession. This glorification is not a simple re-creation of the world, but a bringing of it to its fullness, which is possible through the purification of man from every evil seed so that the paradisiacal seed may grow and bring forth its fruit. Here again, Evdokimov brings together cult and culture: cult shapes culture, and culture reconstitutes cosmic liturgy. In other words, culture shaped by true cult "becomes a ministry in the service of the Kingdom of God, it justifies history, man, and his priesthood in the world."[14]

So the culture is not an aim in itself. It leads to a greater goal.

> In fact, culture never has an infinite development. It is not an end in itself. When it becomes self-conscientious and objectified, culture turns into a system of constraints. In any case, when it is enclosed in its own limits, the problem of culture has no solution. Sooner or later, thought, art, social life reach their own limits, and at that moment, a choice must be made: either dig into the vicious infinity of its own immanence and get drunk on its own emptiness; or go beyond the choking limits of culture and, in a transparence like clear water, reflect the transcendent. This is the way God wanted it, for His Kingdom is only accessible through the chaos of this world. The Kingdom of God is not a transplant foreign to this world but the revelation of the hidden, numenal depth of this very world.[15]

On the other hand, art that breaks with liturgical tradition and symbolism becomes autonomous and lacks the breath of the transcendent. It no longer communicates the truth of God, but only describes the world perceived by human senses. According to Evdokimov, this is the problem of western art, which, being alienated from the liturgy of the Church, is also alienated from the universe and, instead of pointing to relations between created things, it disintegrates the reality. Analysis destroys synthesis:

> Every artist has the terrible liberty of representing the world in the image of his own devastated soul, and this tendency by no means excludes even the vision of a gigantic latrine in which dismembered monsters squirm around. . . . The modern artist . . . questions his own soul, then looks at the world and applies his disintegrating vision to things. He thus becomes an accomplice to the ancient rebellion which tries to get free from every meaning, from every preexisting and normative principle.[16]

---

13. Ibid., 55.
14. Ibid., 59.
15. Ibid., 65.
16. Ibid., 78.

This has to happen when man rejects an all-encompassing ontological and uniting foundation of things. The result of this rejection is abstract art that denies any resemblance and reality. It lacks the cosmic context and meaning. All that is left are "geometrical figurations" and "play with colors."[17] And because of the rejection of an uniting foundation of reality, abstract art cannot help nor comfort man; it can neither please the eyes nor enlighten men's spirit.

THE SACRED

The second part of Evdokimov's book deals with the sacred. He starts with the creation of the world. The original calling of man was to cultivate nature, to humanize the rest of creation. But the fall changed things. Because of man's sin, nature lost its original norm and orientation. This had important consequences for science, too.

> The Fall also affects science's capacity to perceive and study nature in its secret undergirding or foundation. Brought face to face with this secret and irreducible substructure of nature, science is forced to multiply "antinomical points of view." This is why the methods and means of understanding nature depend on an unavoidable abstraction because science studies a nature whose mystic heart has been cut out of it.[18]

The secret undergirding of nature, although not seen by science, does exist. It is a necessary outcome of creation. The Creator assures the unity of different realms of reality and makes them into one Whole. The unity of reality means that the spiritual and the material also are closely related. The same can be said about time that has its beginning and end. That is why the Kingdom is not a regained Paradise lost but a fulfillment and a perfection of the creation.

This unity of creation necessitates its concreteness. The language of the Bible is not abstract but poetic and rejects any dualism. We can describe and understand the world because it was created by the Word. The unity of creation means also that what can be known by human senses is not just an instrument or stage for the heavenly powers. Sensible things are symbols of the invisible things. "The Kingdom of Heaven is symbolized by the most day to day earthly realities, even the most fleshly ones: a sower who smells of the good open earth, a woman who puts yeast in the dough, a grain of wheat, the vine, the fig tree. The world of senses carries in itself all that is necessary for teaching the most profound mysteries of the divine creation."[19]

Because there is a real connection between a symbol and the symbolized, a symbol is never accidental. "The earth and the heavens do not just prefigure the new heavens and the new earth of the Kingdom, but they are substructure of the forthcoming change."[20] The same can be said about the Eucharistic elements.

17. Ibid., 77.
18. Ibid., 100.
19. Ibid., 106.
20. Ibid.

PART FOUR: CULTURE

Evdokimov once again states that man's calling is to "cultivate the earth in paradise, reunite the earth and heaven."[21] When man rejects this task, he becomes a slave of the world and an idolater. This reversal of relations introduces a lying spirit into the world. It does not mean that nature becomes evil; it means that it loses its original purpose and function. It does not mean that man is no longer an image of God; it means that he loses the actualization of the image, which in the Orthodox tradition is the likeness of God.

The lack of actualization of the image of God in man has important consequences for the rest of the world, because man was created as a king and a priest of the world. This "gives an ecclesiological accent to biblical cosmology."[22] According to St. Maximus the Confessor, the world is a "cosmic temple." The role of the Church, whose roots go back to Eden, is, among other things, to heal the world, to energize and to unite it with God.

The healing of the world occurs by the means of "deprofaning" and "devulgarizing," which means through sacraments and sacramentals. The Church sanctifies the world because "everything is destined for a liturgical use. . . . The liturgy integrates the most elementary actions of life: drinking, eating, washing, speaking, acting, communing . . . . It restores to them their meaning and true destiny, that is, to be blocks in the cosmic temple of God's glory."[23] But this is not a one-way street. Man in liturgy not only brings the profane things of the world to the Church to sanctify them, but he also integrates the Church with the history of the world.

> With Constantine, the cultic building began to be part of the social structure of the city, the Day of the Lord coincided with man's day of rest, and the temple offered the image of the organized cosmos. The Church's liturgy is not simply a copy of the heavenly liturgy but is rather an eruption of the heavenly into history: God descends and sanctifies not only souls but the whole of nature and cosmic space. In the same way, the Church's calendar and the cycle of offerings sanctify and fill with meaning the elements of time and the march of history. It is man's task to grasp and extend these transcendent measures over human time and space.[24]

In other words, the reconnection with the Holy One, which takes place in liturgy, makes things holy.

One of the redeemed things is time. In Christ, time finds its axis. It is no longer Chronos eating its own children, it is not even an historical time running to its final point, but it is time which stops the decay of created things and brings the seeds of creation to their fulfillment. The other redeemed thing is space, which "does more than just bring about the simple coexistence of two things side by side. Sacred space makes us 'one' in Christ."[25] A church building is a special space. It is "the earthly heaven." Unfortunately, says Evdokimov, contemporary church buildings became anthropocentric in an attempt to adapt to modern mentality. Originally church buildings were "theocentric in their

21. Ibid., 110.
22. Ibid., 114.
23. Ibid., 117.
24. Ibid., 120.
25. Ibid., 139.

attempt to express God's descent into His creation."[26] That does not mean that new forms are to be rejected. The problem with modern forms is their lack of biblical symbolism. They are purely utilitarian and pragmatic. Christian church buildings should resemble the Temple in the New Jerusalem. An architect cannot just express himself but has to follow the heavenly patterns.

A church building has to be first of all an *imago mundi* as the Jerusalem Temple was. According to Josephus, "it was situated in the 'Center of the World,' Jerusalem, and it sanctifies the cosmos and time. The courtyard represented the sea; the sanctuary, the earth; and the Holy of Holies, heaven. The twelve loaves of bread on the table stood for the twelve months of the year, and the seventy branch candelabra represented the decans of the zodiac."[27] In other words, a church building resembles the structure of the world. It is a microcosm.

But man is also a microcosm. So a church building shows what man is to become. "It ardently calls all men to become 'living stones' of the cosmic church in which 'everything that has breath sings God's praises.'"[28] One of the symbolical aspects of a church building is its placement of the altar on the eastern wall. God planted the Garden east of the land of Eden where He met with Adam and Eve. Also, at his second coming, Christ will appear in the east. At the other end, on the western wall of Orthodox church buildings, we find a painting of the Last Judgment and a door leading outside to the not yet evangelized lands. The east-west axis defines also a direction of man's life: man meets God first in the East, in His Sanctuary, and then moves westwards to fill the Earth with the glory of God.

THE ICON

The third part of Evdokimov's book on theology of beauty deals with the theology of the icon. He starts his deliberation with the so-called Seventh Ecumenical Council, which condemned iconoclasm as "heretical compendium" because in a docetical way it attacks the reality of the Incarnation and the ability of the sacred to transform nature. The iconoclasts rejected the notion that a symbol is not a mere sign that just informs and teaches, because it

> contains in itself the presence of what is symbolized. It fulfills the function of revealing a meaning and at the same time it becomes an expressive and effective container of the "presence." Symbolic knowledge is always indirect. It appeals to the contemplative faculty of the mind, to the real imagination, both evocative and invocative. In this way, symbolic knowledge decodes the meaning and message of the symbol and grasps its epiphanic character, a character which shows forth a figured, symbolized but very real presence of the transcendent.[29]

---

26. Ibid., 143.
27. Ibid., 145.
28. Ibid., 148.
29. Ibid., 167.

PART FOUR: CULTURE

Evdokimov calls the icon a means of grace.[30] Evdokimov criticizes the western tradition for reducing the function of sacred art to a mere didactic one: it can inform us about a thing but cannot communicate the transcendental dimension of the object. The difference between western religious paintings and eastern icons is this: "A 'religious' painting represents man but intends that the faithful see and understand the God-Man. The icon represents the Hypostasis of the Word and shows God in Man."[31] So for Luther a religious painting is but an illustration, and for Calvin the only artistic decoration of a church building can be a reproduction of the Word of God.

For the East, the icon is "the vehicle for a person's presence."[32] The Seventh Ecumenical Council stated that we can remember and enter into the presence of biblical prototypes, not only through the Scriptures, but also through the icon. The Council of 860 added that "what the Gospel says to us in words, the icon announces to us in colors and makes it present to us."[33] Although the icon in itself is just a piece of wood, it draws its theophanic value through participation in the "wholly other" and it give us "an experience of the invisible."[34] Evdokimov not only explains the icon but also gives a biblical argument for the icon. The Old Testament prohibition of making images of God was for him "the purification of a waiting period; it was a prophecy of the coming of the icon in Christ."[35] But even in the Old Testament, man was to represent the heavenly realm, although it had to be limited to the angelic world.

Summing up Evdokimov's theology of beauty, Bruno Forte states that he "is an outstanding witness to how passionately the Orthodox East longs for the last things as they are anticipated and promised in the revelation of the crucified Lord."[36] The last things shine forth a light that can be seen by the eye of faith and that enables man to perceive the world in the context of the life of the Trinity, the source and guardian of all existing things. This means that it is not knowledge that creates the light, but it is the light that enables man to truly know anything. The ultimate light that brought us knowledge is Christ, because in Him both truth and beauty dwell harmoniously.

ELLUL'S CRITIQUE OF EVDOKIMOV

Jacques Ellul, in *The Humiliation of the Word*,[37] deals with the role of images in modern society. Images force out words, and their popularity is a sign of our laziness in pursuance of spiritual maturity. This, in turn, produces problems with communication as well as a problem of perspective. We prefer sight to hearing, because it enables us to "catch"

---

30. Ibid., 210.
31. Ibid., 169.
32. Ibid., 178.
33. Ibid.
34. Ibid., 179.
35. Ibid., 190.
36. Forte, *Portal*, 66.
37. Jacques Ellul, *The Humiliation of the Word* (Grand Rapids: Eerdmans, 1985).

the space around us and make it our own. It puts us in the center of the world. "My sight constructs a universe for me."[38] It establishes spatial relations.

It is not the same with hearing. Noises come to us, even if we are not looking for them. They are much more independent from us than images. We can close our eyes and stop seeing, but it is much harder to close our ears and stop hearing. Images form a panorama, but noises do not. They make us feel uneasy. There is a special kind of noise, namely human words. According to Ellul, the main difference between seeing and hearing is that humans are just one of many kinds of things that we can see, but spoken words come only from other humans. Besides, we do not need much time to see an image, but much time and attention is required to hear a story. Last but not least, while images establish spatial relations, words establish personal relations. In this context it is notable, says Ellul, that God's main means of communication with man is speech. Ellul also reminds us that the Bible strongly opposes seeing and hearing, quoting such passages as Exodus 33 and Judges 13. "God cannot be seen, but he can be heard."[39]

Further he writes that "the prohibition against portraying God . . . amounts to a prohibition against attributing to tangible and visible matter what belongs only to the creator of heaven and earth, and who therefore does not belong to the earthly order."[40] Protestant, and especially Reformed, theology strongly underlines the distinction between the Creator and the creation.

And so Ellul's main criticism of Evdokimov's theology of beauty is that, although he mentions other arts, he concentrates on visual art, and especially on the icon:

> At the outset it is significant and basic to note that for the author, beauty relates only to the icon. He constructs his theology of beauty, in general, only on the basis of objects that are seen—painted objects. Everything related to music, poetry, the beauty of language and rhetoric, of taste and odors, is forgotten. Only one of the senses is given special status: sight, which grants a person access to the contemplation of the invisible.[41]

For Orthodox Christians, the icon is special because it leads man beyond itself to the indescribable. "The Word is not enough. . . . The icon alone enables a person to participate in the indescribable."[42]

Ellul goes further in his criticism of Evdokimov. He points to the fact that most of Evdokimov's argument is based on the Greek Fathers, and biblical argumentation "amounts to two pages and seven quotations."[43] The argument from the Incarnation does not take into account the unfulfilled aspect of eschatology. For Evdokimov, everything is established; man is deified and reestablished in his former dignity. The "not yet" is almost not present in his eschatology.

38. Ibid., 6.
39. Ibid., 93.
40. Ibid., 94.
41. Ibid., 102.
42. Ibid., 103.
43. Ibid., 104.

PART FOUR: CULTURE

Another weak point of his theology is his conception of the image of God in the Creation. "The image of God is the materiality of visible humanity. This concept tries to place humanity permanently on the mount Tabor. . . . That corresponds exactly to the error of the disciples who accompanied Jesus and who wanted to set up tents in order to remain permanently in the Transfiguration."[44] In spite of the genuine effort of Orthodox theologians, Christianity turns out to be a way of escape from the present world in popular belief. Besides, common people often do not grasp the subtleties of the theology of the icon and its differentiation between symbol and symbolized reality, and they treat symbols as reality.

When it comes to the Incarnation, Ellul admits that because of it the Word could be seen. But that was the only such case in the history of mankind, and this was a temporary situation, at least so far. This is why John says: "Blessed are those who have not seen and yet believe" (John 20:29). After the Ascension, just as before the Incarnation, faith and sight are in contradiction. "Faith comes from hearing" (Rom 10:17).

Nevertheless Ellul does not reject icons fully.

> Icons remain false in their pretention to be symbolically shown reality. But they are acceptable as the recall of a promise and as a reference to the reconciliation of sight and word not yet accomplished, but simply announced. They are acceptable on the condition that they remain at the level of recall and reference, that is, with no reality, no liturgical role, without attracting piety or prayer (but this is precisely what they have not done!). They must be simply a signpost we consult to know in what direction God is leading us. But no one meditates on a signpost: we continue on our way![45]

JORDAN ON ART AND THE ICON

One of James B. Jordan's main fields of interest is Christian worship, and particularly Covenant Renewal Worship, in which God renews His covenant with His people: cleanses them from their sins, consecrates them with His Word, and communes with them at His table. During this time God also bestows on His people three gifts: glory, knowledge, and life. But at the end of the worship service God commands His people to go back to their everyday duties and impose on earth the same patterns they saw in heaven. But what do we see when we are lifted up to the heavenly temple? According to Psalm 27:4, it is first of all the beauty of God that we see in the House of the Lord: "One thing have I asked of the LORD, that will I seek after: that I may dwell in the house of the LORD all the days of my life, to gaze upon the beauty of the LORD and to inquire in his temple."

A few conclusions follow from these observations. First of all, the worship of the Church should be beautiful. Second, our engagement in the world should reveal the beauty of God. Like Israel of old, we need to bring our best to the House of the Lord. This includes our tithes, which represent the fruit of our work. We are to come near to God in special, holy clothes, singing beautiful songs. As we read in Revelation 22:24–26, we are

---

44. Ibid.
45. Ibid., 242.

to bring the glory of our nations and offer it to our Lord. But apart from beautifying the worship, we need to beautify the world, too. In other words, we are to fill the earth with the beauty and glory of God. God beautifies us so that we may shine forth His glory into the world.

One of the sources of inspiration for Jordan's theology of worship is Alexander Schmemann, an Orthodox theologian. In *The Sociology of the Church*,[46] we find a longer quotation from *For the Life of the World*, where Schmemann states that although the beauty of the liturgy may seem unnecessary, it is an expression of love and "joy which alone is capable of transforming the world."[47] In other words, we beautify the worship of the Church because we love and enjoy the Kingdom of God, which is "the perfection of beauty" (Ps 50:2). It is exactly this vision of the beautiful Kingdom that drives us to work in the world and change it from glory to glory.

Nevertheless, one can find a great amount of critique of Orthodox theology, and especially of the icon, in Jordan's writings. In his exposition of the Second Commandment he, in a way similar to Ellul's, talks about the opposition of sight and vision, which in his opinion is grounded in the invisibility of God: "Visibility is not an attribute of God. God makes Himself visible, but in Himself He is invisible. On the other hand, God is Pure Language. Language or Wordness is an attribute of God; indeed, so much so that the Second Person of the Godhead is the Word of God. . . . This is why the revelation and worship of God is verbal, not visual, and why adoring things made by human hands is forbidden in the Second Word."[48]

But sinful man prefers seeing to hearing because sight turns persons into objects, which we can control. They do not talk back but only reveal our preconceived ideas. They neither challenge nor judge us. It is much easier to close the eyes and stop the flow of visual information than to close the ears and stop the flow of verbal information. But sight is neither very accurate nor relational. It is only by listening to a person that we can get to know him or her better. If we only look at a person and do not want to listen to him or her, we tell ourselves our story of the person. The same is true of God. This is why liturgy has to be based on the revealed Word of God and not on our ideas about God.

This does not mean that all visual art is evil. And this is not what the Second Commandment states. It does not even say that no picture of God may be made. "What it says is that no image of anything can be set up as an avenue of worship to God and the court of heaven."[49] Yes, the Tabernacle and Temple were full of images of plants and animals, but they did not serve as an avenue of worship and nobody worshiped nor adored them. They were symbols of heavenly and earthly things but not places of accumulation of divine energy. Their function was for decoration and education.

---

46. James B. Jordan, *The Sociology of the Church: Essays in Reconstruction* (Tyler, TX: Geneva Ministries, 1986; reprint, Eugene, OR: Wipf & Stock, 1999), 172.

47. Alexander Schmemann, *For the Life of the World: Sacraments and Orthodoxy* (Crestwood, NY: St Vladimir's Seminary Press, 1973), 30.

48. James B. Jordan, "The Second Word I: Seeing & Hearing," *Rite Reasons* 33 (June 1994).

49. James B. Jordan, "The Second Word II: Seeing & Hearing; Exposition," *Rite Reasons* 34 (Aug 1994).

This has not changed with the coming of the Son of God in the flesh. Yes, Christ was God's voluntary self-representation, but He went to heaven and said: "It is good for you that I go away" (John 16:7). So we still have to wait patiently to see God and not follow Adam and Eve in their premature seizing of what was not yet given to them. For Jordan, any attempt to use a visual thing as an avenue to God is a rejection of personal maturity and a sign of dissatisfaction with God that is connected with "lack of eschatological awareness . . . a failure to keep a clear distinction between the Kingdom now and the Kingdom to come."[50] Both Christ's local presence and a transformed, glorified world await us in the future. We will see Christ face to face at the end of history, which has not come yet.

The rejection of personal maturity is connected with an unbiblical view of the relation between man and his works. "Men believe that their own priestly manipulation of the creation serves to mystify the creation and suck divine energy into it. As a result, the works of men's hands become mysterious, and technology and art are aborted in their development. Men see themselves as under their works, not over them."[51] In other words, when man tries to raise the created things up by merging them with divine energies, then sooner or later he starts to serve and worship them. On the other hand, the merging of the divine with the created blurs a distinction between Creator and creature. James Jordan, following Eugen Rosenstock-Huessy, reminds us that the Second Commandment is a very strong "No!" to any attempt to confuse the two. At stake here is a clear distinction between the works of God and the works of man.

Man, in his artistic enterprise, imitates God who is the Great Artist. Nevertheless, even the greatest human artist remains a man and his works are only mere creations. "For the ancients, however, the visual arts were ways in which man participated mystically in the divine. Inspired by a god or spirit, a man would make a painting or a statue, and that painting or statue would then house that spirit or god or divinity in some sense."[52] The Reformation and the Renaissance helped to separate astronomy from astrology, chemistry from alchemy, and art from mysticism. No man-made object houses any aspect of divinity. Even sacral art is symbolic and not divine and "represents man before God, not God before man."[53] It is praise offered to God but not a means of ascending to heaven. Jordan writes,

> Art is glory. It is man's labor to continue God's original work of bringing light, form, and filling to the world. . . . Glory is not, however, the place where God meets man; and this is what the Orthodox semi-Christians forget or do not admit. Glory is an outflow of God's relationship with man—apart from God men tend to "uglify" rather than glorify the cosmos. God meets man in language, in personal discourse. Music may glorify that conversation—and it should do so in worship—but God does not meet man in music. Nor does He meet man in visual art of any sort. He

---

50. James B. Jordan, *The Liturgy Trap: The Bible versus Mere Tradition in Worship* (Niceville, FL: Transfiguration Press, 1998), 47–48.
51. James B. Jordan, "The Second Word IV: Implications," *Rite Reasons* 36 (Dec. 1994).
52. James B. Jordan, "The Second Word V: On Images and Art, Part 1," *Rite Reasons* 57 (May 1998).
53. Ibid.

meets man in the Word of God, in language; and because God is incorporeal, He meets man in language alone.[54]

In other words, God meets us through His Son in our sin and weakness. Our glory, as well as our good works and maturity, is an outcome of this meeting, and not a foundation of our relationship with God. This is why worship has to start with confession of sins and absolution, with no musical elements: they restore in us the glory of God, of which we fell short because of our sins.

If this is the case, then beauty cannot save the fallen world. It is a gift of God for the saved ones and not a vehicle of the saving grace. Sinful man rejects the beauty of God, but apart from God there is no beauty. Whatever beauty man can produce, it is always a consequence of his personal encounter with God, and this may happen only through the Word. This is just another reason why the icon is a very bad choice for a meeting place with the divine. But the same can be said about music, which plays the role of the icon in many modern churches. It stimulates man on his way upwards to heaven. But both visual art and music are only human answers to the divine Word. They cannot lead us to God nor reconcile us with Him, even though they should be our sacrifice of worship offered to God.

CONCLUSION

In conclusion, we can say that practically all Christians agree that God is beautiful and the source of beauty. His House is beautiful and so His people are to be so. One of the main tasks for Christians is to beautify the world, transforming it from glory to glory according to heavenly patterns. The point of disagreement is how it has to happen. Orthodox theologians believe that God's beauty is revealed in the icon and is an energetic force that raises the creation up to be deified and saved. Reformed theologians believe that God's beauty is an inspiration for Christians to transform the creation to the glory of God and according to heavenly, or Trinitarian, patterns as revealed in the Word of God.

The difference comes from different understanding of the Incarnation. For Orthodox theologians, the Incarnation brought an end to a religion that emphasized hearing and initiated a religion that emphasizes seeing. This change was later reinforced by the coming of the Spirit who infuses divine energies into creation. This is why the icon is not only a symbol of divine things but also a means of grace, a place of theophany and revelation, a heavenly gate through which deifying energies flow to creation.

On the other hand, Reformed theologians emphasize that there is only one source of revelation, which is the Word of God. All arts, as well as all other human works, are just human responses to the Word. The primacy of the Word is preserved even after the Incarnation, because the Incarnate Word of God left us and went up to heaven and sent the Spirit, who now speaks the Word into the world rather than infusing divine energies into the world. He communicates heavenly patterns and creates new relations in the world, which leads to the transformation of the world according to the will of God. This creates beauty.

54. James B. Jordan, "The Second Word VII: On Images and Art, Part 3," *Rite Reasons* 59 (Sept 1998).

PART FOUR: CULTURE

Beauty is not a matter of energy but of relations. This is why the New Testament has so much to say about ethics but not so much about visual art. The work of the Spirit is reconciliation and cooperation. Peaceful and fruitful relationship between once hostile people is beautiful. This is what Psalm 133 states: "Behold, how good and pleasant it is when brothers dwell in unity!" It is noteworthy that the word "good" can also be translated as "beautiful." It can be found, among other places, in Genesis 1:4, the verse that Evdokimov cites to prove that the world was not only good but also beautiful when it was created by God. If this is the case, then we should not be surprised that the beauty of the Temple communicates ethical principles. In Ezekiel 43:10 God says to the prophet: "Describe to the house of Israel the temple, that they may be ashamed of their iniquities." The architectural design, the paintings on the walls, as well as the flow of liturgy were "sermons" and communicated to the worshiping people of God, how they were to live to shine forth the beauty of God. This beauty can be seen in the interpersonal relations between Father, Son, and the Spirit.

∼

Dear Bogumil,

Thank you for this excellent essay. What struck me as I read the first part, summarizing Evdokimov on beauty, was how much of this I learned from Rousas J. Rushdoony years ago when reading various things he wrote. There is a lot of profound reflection here, which obviously is or should be common to all Christian creational thinking. Sadly, Evdokimov and all Eastern Orthodox writers move in the wrong direction from these insights.

I really don't have anything to add. I hope that readers will take to heart what you've written here, because it is a continuing problem in the Church. We must not join Orthodoxy and reproduce the sin of Adam by grasping for things we are not yet supposed to have.

Jim

14

Empire, Sports, and War

Douglas Wilson

INTRODUCTION

THE GAME OF LACROSSE was called "little brother of war" by the Iroquois, whose magnificent game it was. Now compared to some subjects, the Bible has little to say about lacrosse (and other modern sports), but it does have a great deal to say about war and about empire—and about what ought to be the Church's relation to both. Moreover, there are a surprising number of biblical references to some of the ancient sports and some interesting connections that we can make from those references. In this spirit, the title of this essay should be considered something of an enthymeme, with the essay itself being an attempt to fill in at least some of the gaps.

It can also be considered part of a discussion arising from one aspect of Jim Jordan's provocative challenge to Western civilization. I take Jim's central point as given—the necessity of a thoroughly biblical education—but also believe there is more that can be said than in what follows:

> Biblical manhood is not connected with hunting or with sports. The great men of the Bible were not hunters but accountants; contrast Jacob and Esau. There is nothing wrong with hunting, but it has nothing to do with manhood one way or another. There is nothing wrong with many sports either, but we should note that while sports were an important part of Greek education, they play no part in Biblical training at all. Biblical manhood is connected, however, with martial skills. At the age of 20, every man was enlisted in the militia (Numbers 1). When the trumpet was blown, every man was expected to show up to fight.[1]

---

1. James B. Jordan, "The Case Against Western Civilization (7), Part 5: Laying New Foundations in a Dying World (continued)," *Open Book* 42 (Oct 1998).

PART FOUR: CULTURE

In response, the argument of this essay is neither complicated nor profound—but for various reasons the argument might be easy to overlook. I want to suggest that there is a clear connection between sports and warfare in Scripture. And if we think about it carefully, we should see a straight line connection between sports and warfare, and then from warfare to empire (at least for those who are good at warfare). Because the scriptural attitude to empire, hegemony, or superpower status—whatever you want to call it—is not a simplistic one, we should find ourselves at the end of the day with a similar, hedged appreciation of sports—an appreciation coupled with and tempered by suspicion. Not surprisingly, a biblical position can consistently maintain a balance between the separatists and the sell-outs. The separatists reject any activity with a ball in it as "worldly," an error that Jim rejects above, and the sell-outs are not nearly as wary as they should be when it comes to the rank idolatry that takes place in the modern commercialization of sports.

AGONISTIC SPORTS IN THE BIBLE

It is quite true that Scripture says *comparatively* little about sports. There is still more scriptural data than many might assume, and what we do find is distinctively related to the larger questions of war (and therefore empire). Therefore, a view on any one of these subjects will bring with it views on the others, and we find the traffic goes both ways. We should not be surprised, when we get into it, that these are subjects that tend to generate simplistic pros from the supporters (of empire, sports, and war) and simplistic cons from the opponents (of empire, sports, and war). It is not a coincidence that those who have a visceral dislike of a popular high school quarterback are also the ones who have the same kind of visceral dislike of someone who flies jet planes off aircraft carriers.

There is a deep connection here, but apart from an ultimate reference point in Christ, the division between the hippies and the jocks is still "under the sun," and winning that particular debate is yet another attempt to shepherd the wind. Both sides should be reminded that their dispute is like what Senator Eugene McCarthy once said about being a senator—he said it was a lot like being a football coach in that you had to be smart enough to follow the game and dumb enough to think it was important. We will attempt to be a bit more nuanced than that and will try to connect these things to what really matters.

Athletic competitions should be understood as structured, artificial conflicts, with varying degrees of hostility present. At one end is staged conflict that is entirely friendly, with the competitors having a beer together afterwards, and at the other end we find barely controlled and thinly disguised hostility—war without funerals afterwards. Rachel describes her competition with her sister as a *wrestling* (Gen 30:8), and she was not talking about a wrestling match held for purposes of entertainment. And Jacob wrestled with God until dawn at Peniel (Gen 32:24). These were genuine struggles—they were not arranged for purposes of entertainment or amusement. At the same time, they are spoken of (at least) under an athletic metaphor.

In other portions of Scripture, we see an athletic event mentioned to illustrate a principle, and then a military image is immediately evoked to do the same thing. Athletics and war belong side by side as illustrations together. This is a point we will see a number of times later on in the New Testament. Take this example from Ecclesiastes: "I returned, and saw under the sun, that the race is not to the swift, nor the battle to the strong, neither yet bread to the wise, nor yet riches to men of understanding, nor yet favour to men of skill; but time and chance happeneth to them all" (Eccl 9:11).

The race and the battle run along the same lines, and sometimes there is the same kind of surprise or twist at the end. The swift sometimes stumble, the tortoise sometimes beats the hare, and there have been more than a few times when an overconfident army gets shellacked. The point here, of course, is that sometimes the unexpected happens (as with poor men of understanding, and unfavored men of skill), but it is still notable that the mind moves naturally from an athletic competition to a battle.

It is difficult to read the accounts of warfare in ancient Israel without recognizing that Samson and Achilles lived and fought in the same kind of world. The weapons and tactics are similar, and the presence of great champions is another common element. And in the same way, although athletic games do not have the same (recorded) prominence among the Hebrews as among the Greeks, they are still present—an example of which we can see in Psalm 19: "There is no speech nor language, where their voice is not heard. Their line is gone out through all the earth, and their words to the end of the world. In them hath he set a tabernacle for the sun, which is as a bridegroom coming out of his chamber, and rejoiceth as a strong man to run a race. His going forth is from the end of the heaven, and his circuit unto the ends of it: and there is nothing hid from the heat thereof" (Ps 19:3–6).

In this great poem by a Hebrew warrior and king, the sun is compared to a champion athlete, exhilarated by the challenge of the race he is appointed to run every day. The practice was common enough that David could feel free to use the comparison without fear of confusing anyone. Just as his reference to a bridegroom coming out of his chamber presupposes a common cultural knowledge of bridegrooms and their chambers, so also a strong man running a race would have been well understood.

There are times when the tournament teeters on the very edge of war, as when the young men "play" before Abner and Joab: "And Abner said to Joab, Let the young men now arise, and play before us. And Joab said, Let them arise" (2 Sam 2:14). The word for *play* here is perhaps better rendered as *compete*, but the sense is still clear. Aristotle once said that an adroit use of metaphor was the mark of genius—but this particular connection, this metaphor comparing one kind of struggle to another, doesn't take a genius to see.

The bloodshed that followed does more to reveal the common agonistic nature of athletics and warfare than it represents an unfortunate intrusion of one kind of event into an entirely dissimilar event. Many years ago, I learned this lesson from my father, a man with acute Girardian instincts. We had gone to a football game, and when we entered the stadium the crowd was already in full swing, whooping and hollering, and

PART FOUR: CULTURE

doing the kind of things that a happy football crowd always likes to do. "Well," my father said. "It's better than a public hanging."

Athletics are controlled and sublimated violence, and this can be good or terrible, depending. One scholar, Johan Huizinga, notes the similarity in language: "Ever since words existed for fighting and playing, men have been wont to call war a game. . . . Language everywhere must have expressed matters in that way from the moment words for combat and play existed."[2]

By the time of the New Testament, the Isthmian games in Corinth were held every other year, and so it is quite possible that the apostle Paul was there for the grand event. "And he continued there a year and six months, teaching the word of God among them" (Acts 18:11). But whether he was there or not, he was certainly quite familiar with the realm of athletics, and illustrations from these sorts of competitions came to him readily. Most Bible students have a general awareness of Paul's use of athletic metaphors, but when you string them end to end it starts to look as though he might well have had a subscription package with ESPN.

> Know ye not that they which run in a race run all, but one receiveth the prize? So run, that ye may obtain. And every man that striveth for the mastery is temperate in all things. Now they do it to obtain a corruptible crown; but we an incorruptible. I therefore so run, not as uncertainly; so fight I, not as one that beateth the air: But I keep under my body, and bring it into subjection: lest that by any means, when I have preached to others, I myself should be a castaway. (1 Cor 9:24–27)

Of course the point is not that the use of one metaphor sanitizes everything. Christ is returning like a thief in the night, but not in order to steal something. But Paul uses athletic metaphors clustered with other metaphors, and in a way that suggests that the callings involved are all honorable. In 2 Timothy, we see the close and natural connection between the conflict of sports and the conflict of war: "No man that warreth entangleth himself with the affairs of this life; that he may please him who hath chosen him to be a soldier. And if a man also strive for masteries, yet is he not crowned, except he strive lawfully. The husbandman that laboureth must be first partaker of the fruits. Consider what I say; and the Lord give thee understanding in all things" (2 Tim 2:4–7).

The verb that is translated twice as *strive* here in verse 5 is *athleō*. Paul uses three illustrations, back to back. The first is the vocation of warrior, the second is that of an athlete, and the third is that of a farmer. All of these callings require hard, *physical* discipline. They are the kind of pursuits that require a man to have the ability to tell his body *no*—and, as it turns out, this is just the kind of character that is necessary in Paul's mind for true ministry. A farmer is not just a businessman; he is the kind of businessman who has to have discipline over his *body*, just as warriors and athletes do. This is actually something we are desperately short of in the modern Church. We need more men in ministry who did their stint in the military, or who played defensive tackle, or who have done some hardscrabble farming.

---

2. Johan Huizinga, *Homo Ludens: A Study of the Play-Element in Culture* (Boston: Beacon, 1950), 89.

A bookish man can follow Paul's metaphors here, but someone who has "been there" will understand him at a deeper level. Men who have learned discipline in the military, or on the playing field, or in a southern cotton field, are men who know the value of hard work in ministry as well. We exclude from this, of course, those who simply want to read fine theology in air-conditioned comfort—those who want an indoor job with no heavy lifting. As one wit once pointed out, a hot sun and a slow mule have been responsible for many a call to the ministry. There is difference between transferring discipline from one realm to another, as Paul did, and seeking to avoid the hot discipline, as some have wanted to do.

It would not be too much to say that athletic illustrations provided one of the controlling (and obviously recurring) metaphors of Paul's life, and that they were at the very center of his self-awareness. These passages from 2 Timothy and Philippians provide some more good examples:

> For I am now ready to be offered, and the time of my departure is at hand. I have fought a good fight, I have finished my course, I have kept the faith: Henceforth there is laid up for me a crown of righteousness, which the Lord, the righteous judge, shall give me at that day: and not to me only, but unto all them also that love his appearing. (2 Tim 4:6–8; cf. 1 Pet 5:4)

> Brethren, I count not myself to have apprehended: but this one thing I do, forgetting those things which are behind, and reaching forth unto those things which are before, I press toward the mark for the prize of the high calling of God in Christ Jesus. (Phil 3:13–14; cf. 2:16)

Because of how common this is with him, it is likely that when Paul refers generally to "running" in the context of his ministry, he is likely referring to the structure of an athletic competition and not to more of a random situation, like running from a bear or something. This is what we see in Galatians: "And I went up by revelation, and communicated unto them that gospel which I preach among the Gentiles, but privately to them which were of reputation, lest by any means I should run, or had run, in vain" (Gal 2:2).

When Paul thinks of running, he is including the idea of prizes and the playing of national anthems. And if Hebrews is from his pen, as I think it is, we also have the additional idea of an amphitheater and a sold-out crowd:

> Wherefore seeing we also are compassed about with so great a cloud of witnesses, let us lay aside every weight, and the sin which doth so easily beset us, and let us run with patience the race that is set before us, Looking unto Jesus the author and finisher of our faith; who for the joy that was set before him endured the cross, despising the shame, and is set down at the right hand of the throne of God. For consider him that endured such contradiction of sinners against himself, lest ye be wearied and faint in your minds. Ye have not yet resisted unto blood, striving against sin. (Heb 12:1–4)

And notice how the struggle of athletic competition moves naturally and easily to the related question of "resisting unto blood." The *agōn* of athletic striving is right next

PART FOUR: CULTURE

door to the *agōn* of warfare. So when we put all these together, what lessons may we draw from it?

> Athletic images conjure up a number of stimulating associations, including rigorous training or exercise (1 Cor. 9:25; 1 Tim. 4:7-8), singleness of purpose (1 Cor. 9:26), delayed gratification (1 Cor. 9:25), streamlining for maximum performance (Heb. 12:1), self-control (1 Cor. 9:27), perseverance (Heb. 12:2) and endurance (1 Tim. 4:8). Athletic endeavor also involves intense competition with lofty objectives (1 Cor. 9:24) and high stakes (Eph. 6:12), and it requires faithful adherence to a prescribed set of rules to avoid disqualification (2 Tim. 2:5; 1 Cor. 9:27). In spite of all the hard work, the end result is transitory fame. But for the Christian the crown to be won is imperishable (1 Tim. 4:8; 1 Cor. 9:25).[3]

The famous wrestling (*palē*) mentioned in Ephesians 6:12 either *is* warfare or it morphs into a warfare image by the next verse. Our English translations usually have the word rendered as a verb ("we wrestle not"), but in the Greek it is a noun ("the wrestling"). You could paraphrase it as "we are not in the ring with flesh and blood, but are matched up against principalities and powers." "Paul more often uses the terms *struggle* (*agōnizomai*) and *strive* (*athleō*)—derived from the context of athletic events—to symbolically represent the efforts of Christians on behalf of the gospel."[4]

The games are an *agōn*, and so is war. And so, as it turns out, is our spiritual war. So what do we have thus far? Sports metaphors are common in Scripture, and they are overwhelmingly a *positive* metaphor. The disciplines and virtues that pertain to sports pertain to Christian living as well. The same goes for military metaphors, and these are also commonly used in the Bible as illustrations of that same Christian life. Further, the characteristics that these illustrations point to are often the same—discipline, sacrifice, hard work, focus, intensity, and so on.

EMPIRE NEITHER HERE NOR THERE

I am using the word *empire* here in both a broad and narrow sense. In the narrow sense, you have a powerful nation that subdues other nations and accepts tribute from them. In the broad sense, you have a powerful nation that is far more influential than the others and that usually gets its way. In the former sense, Rome and Persia were empires, and America is not. In the latter sense, all of them are.

Either way, biblical Christians are ambivalent about the empires of men. On the one hand, they are not dazzled by them, and on the other, they are not freaked out by them. Consistent believers should be more than willing to defy emperors as necessary or to work for them as necessary. They avoid the errors of hangers-on, courtiers, and climbers of silver ladders, who want to flatter their way to the top, and they also avoid the errors

---

3. "Athletics," in *Dictionary of Biblical Imagery*, ed. Leland Ryken, et al. (Downers Grove, IL: InterVarsity Press, 1998), 54.

4. "Wrestling," in *Dictionary of Biblical Imagery*, 974. Cf. Colossians 1:29; 4:12.

of *soi disant* prophets, who want to speak truth to power on the condition that the power agrees beforehand never to listen to them.[5]

Our task is to take the entire Bible together. Factions and sects like to cherry-pick certain passages and build a theology on them, with other inconvenient passages assuming the office of "problem passages." Their theological opponents do the same thing, only with the favored passages and problem passages reversed. And so we have some Christians who think that empires are savage and bestial, of necessity, all the time and in every respect, and other Christians who assume that the king is always kind and benevolent, of necessity, and what could *ever* go wrong? But the scriptural data won't let us do this. Joseph, Daniel, Esther, and Nehemiah all had positions of (uncompromised) influence in great empires, and yet anyone who took the mark of the Roman beast was headed for Hell (Rev 14: 9–11). This calls for wisdom, and not a cookie cutter wisdom either.

As much as we would like to remain in the simplicity of immaturity, God has determined to govern history in a very messy way. When we are overwhelmed by the messiness, we are frequently tempted turn back to a mythic past, instead of trusting God in our present the same way our fathers trusted God in *their* present. Jim Jordan points out how our current cultural structure is falling apart:

> The Spirit creates bonds. The more the Spirit is free to work among men, the more bonds He creates. These bonds become wider and wider, as tribes bond to form nations, and nations bond to form an oikumene. We have grown up in a large bonded oikumene, commonwealth, or cosmopolitan order called Western Civilization. Most of us have also grown up in the United States of America. We have had a sense of "belonging" to these large groups. But that sense of "belonging" is collapsing today, and for the simple reason that the Spirit has been quenched and grieved for a long time and the bonds are disintegrating.[6]

But this is happening because something else will replace it. One of the things that the Spirit is doing in history is creating a breed of Christian that is mature enough to roll with it. This "rolling with it" should not be confused with the compromises of the zeitgeistians, who are always ready to sign up for whatever the secularists are currently doing—they always take the glossy promises that are printed in the devil's brochures at face value ("No, we really are in a *post*-modern era. It *said*."). The fact that the Spirit directs history should not be taken as evidence that every new development is healthy or good. But wise Christians understand that there really are some deep transformations under way, and they bring a thoroughly biblical understanding of those transformations to bear.

Cultural engagement is not capitulating to the current confusions that a lost world generates—whether those confusions come from the entertainment world, the political world, the academic world, or the world of athletics. If the Spirit is directing the unfolding of human history from within (a doctrine distinct from and consistent with God's

---

5. A hilarious example of this can be found dissected in Peter Leithart's *Against Christianity* (Moscow, ID: Canon, 2003), 135.

6. James B. Jordan, *Crisis, Opportunity, and the Christian Future* (Niceville, FL: Transfiguration Press, 1994), 33.

sovereignty *over* all of it), then it makes sense that He will be leading, teaching, directing Christians within the course of that history. They are fully engaged with the course of history, but they are not possessed by that history—they are owned by Christ. Another way of putting this is that they maintain perspective.

They may work for the president or emperor, but they understand the relative importance (or lack of it) in everything they do. In the same way, they undertake to train people to do what they are doing, and this training follows the standard "best practices." But the one who is Spirit-led in this does not have the tunnel-vision that an idolater has. The idolater thinks that nothing is more important than the preservation of Rome, or the Holy Roman Empire, or the British Empire, or the America of fifty years ago. In a similar way, when that idolater was being (athletically) trained for service to the empire, it is likely that he thought that absolutely nothing is more important than getting the ball into the end zone. *Nothing*. People who have perspective on the playing field are more likely to have perspective later. People who lose perspective whenever a ball is involved are unlikely to have perspective elsewhere.

In this, we can gather some lessons for the next three generations by looking at the last three generations. Anyone who has coached young men (as I have) knows that there is a certain kind of competitive edge that good athletic training is designed to get rid of. The competitive focus that gets sucked into competition for its own sake is a terrible thing—for teams and for nations. If what matters for Christians is a right attitude and understanding of the empires they find themselves in, then it should also be true that what matters for us with regard to sports is the same thing.

FOOTBALL EXPLAINING AMERICA

Now what the biblical writers saw as a common element in sports, war, and ministry, secularists have noticed as a common element between sports and war and their empires. For just one example, Sal Paolantonio refers to the "profound influence that places such as West Point and Annapolis have had on the American game of football."[7] One of his illustrations was the contribution of Douglas MacArthur, who after World War I was given the task of cleaning up and reforming West Point:

> Naturally, MacArthur started with the athletic department.
>
> > *Upon the fields of friendly strife*
> > *Are sown the seeds*
> > *That, upon other fields, on other days*
> > *Will bear the fruits of victory.*
>
> He wrote the quatrain and ordered it carved on the stone passageway leading to the West Point gym.[8]

Charles Beard once laconically observed that empires are not built in fits of absent-mindedness. Those who do this kind of thing know what they are doing. More to the

---

7. Sal Paolantonio, *How Football Explains America* (Chicago: Triumph Books, 2008), xx.
8. Ibid., 76.

point, when they are on top of their game, they really know *how* to do it. Men study what works, and they know how to prepare and train young men for what works. Brian Kilmeade has compiled an impressive list of cultural leaders—from Jack Welch to George Bush—whose first significant accomplishments were in the realm of sports.[9]

The Duke of Wellington was famously credited with saying that "the battle of Waterloo was won on the playing fields of Eton," which he probably didn't say and which wouldn't have been true about organized sports at Eton if he *had* said it, but a kernel of truth remains in the comment nonetheless. The saying was not attributed to Wellington until three years after his death, and there weren't any organized sports at Eton in time enough to have helped out at Waterloo at all. But the kernel of truth is that discipline is discipline, and that the right kind of discipline transfers. Whatever the realities of Waterloo, this has certainly been true in the American experience.

So a clear connection remains between sports and war (and the concomitant rise of nations and empires). The transformation that has occurred in warfare as a result of the Industrial Revolution has *not* created a gap between these two, and this is because sports have been transformed by that same Industrial Revolution, and in the same direction. Both sports and warfare have been affected by the same logic coming from their surrounding environment. There has been a shift from the directly agonistic sports (racing, wrestling, or trials of strength) to the disciplined choreography of team sports. "There are, however, other forms of contest that develop of their own accord into 'sports.' These are the ball-games."[10]

In the American context, one of the interesting things is the role that Christians had in adjusting sports to fit with the new world. "As the United States was developing into a world political power, as industry boomed, and as the frontier closed, muscular Christians oversaw the development of modern sport."[11]

Football reflects, among a number of other things, the American sense of gaining and holding territory. The ball is not so much a mere ball (as it is in tennis or basketball) as it is a territorial marker. Manifest Destiny, working from east to west, looked a lot like a sustained Elway drive.

And then there is the huddle. Someone once defined a football game as committee meetings punctuated by violence, and there is something to that. What other game has *huddles*? The man who popularized the huddle—Amos Alonzo Stagg—was a devout Christian who had once studied for the ministry. And it showed: "Stagg viewed the huddle as a vital aspect of helping to teach sportsmanship. He viewed the huddle as a kind of religious congregation on the field, a place where the players could, if you will, minister to each other, make a plan, and promise to keep faith in that plan and one another."[12] "The world's a tough place, guys." "Yeah, I screwed up on that one. My bad. We'll get

---

9. Brian Kilmeade, *The Games Do Count: America's Best and Brightest on the Power of Sports* (New York: HarperCollins, 2004).

10. Huizinga, *Homo Ludens*, 196.

11. Tony Ladd and James Mathisen, *Muscular Christianity: Evangelical Protestants and the Development of American Sport* (Grand Rapids: Baker, 1999), 18.

12. Paolantonia, *Football*, 41.

it next time." But if your mistake was really egregious, you could find yourself excommunicated to the bench. In short, our sports are not disconnected from the rest of our lives. And if football explains America, soccer explains the world, as a recent book put it.[13] And the traffic goes both ways—with our lives informing the sports and the sports forming our lives. A third distinctively American characteristic in football is the leadership style of the quarterback—part strategist, part gunslinger, part hot dog. We cultivate this spirit on the field because this is what we want in our military and cultural leaders.

If the Spirit is driving history, and things like the Industrial Revolution or the Cyber Revolution are not accidents or flukes, then the re-formation of sports in a way comparable to the re-formation of warfare should not be surprising. We should not expect our sports to stay limited to the ancient agonistic forms, any more than we expect our modern infantrymen to know how to use a spear. Although we do retain those sports, it is striking that they are hardly the most popular sports. Something has shifted. The shift from the popularity of the ancient Olympian sports to the modern team sports is the result of a profound shift in the world.

I recall a number of years ago, while I was in the control room of a nuclear submarine at battle stations, realizing how much warfare had changed over the centuries. We were in a darkened compartment full of blinking computer lights, and we were busy at our stations doing math problems. If this had been an actual battle situation, we could have ended the event just as dead as Hector, but the run-up to that death would have been very different. In the same way, a well-executed football play is not at all like two ancient wrestlers grappling in the ring—and yet . . . it is still the same kind of thing.

IN SUM

Some colleges and universities have been destroyed by their athletic programs. A wild lack of any sense of proportion has made chasing a ball far more important than chasing wisdom. And that, of course, is bad. But this is something that is commonly understood as a problem, even when it is not adequately addressed on a practical level. Everybody understands that a twenty million dollar athletic center and a $500,000 dollar library tells you *something*.

At the same time, we should at least consider other possible problems. How many Reformed seminaries have been destroyed because they *didn't* have a football program? How many denominations have gone liberal because they did not require their future ministers to go to seminary on a football scholarship? As might be imagined, such (admittedly whimsical) questions are easier to ask than answer, but it could still be edifying to ask them anyway. Reformed Christians don't like being reminded that they have bodies, and nothing reminds you of the presence of your body so much as throwing up on the sidelines. But *we* tend to think we have bodies because God wanted us to have some kind of vehicle that could walk our brain to church.

---

13. Franklin Foer, *How Soccer Explains the World: An Unlikely Theory of Globalization* (New York: Harper, 2004).

A well-understood athletic program is a mild form of military training, one that is suitable for boys. If I were asked to compare and set side-by-side two experiences in my life that were supposed to be (on paper) dissimilar, but that *felt* very similar, the two experiences I would pick would be three-a-day high school football practices in August and my time in boot camp. Not only did the former prepare me for the latter, but it prepared me by being very much the same kind of thing.

Athletics prepare for full military training, and military training prepares for cultural and political leadership. But this is not automatic. As one coach put it, "Practice doesn't make perfect. Perfect practice makes perfect." Many have learned all the wrong lessons on the field of play and on the field of battle. This is why we have been historically interested in maintaining a civilian leadership for our nation. But from George Washington on, many of our presidents have proven themselves in battle first. When it is done well, nations and civilizations are greatly benefited—as far as it goes. I say "as far as it goes" because this is all still horizontal, under the sun.

So what about the kingdom of God? It is not the case that the lessons learned only transfer horizontally, from one worldly agonistic struggle to another more important agonistic struggle. Just as a nation is benefited when its young people grow up learning discipline, sportsmanship, and so forth, so the Church also benefits when Christians transfer what they have learned into the service of the Church. I have seen many young men in classrooms who desperately needed to learn lessons that *could* not be taught to them in a classroom. Their understanding of Paul's metaphors, to the extent they understood them at all, was an academic understanding. "One should keep on going when the cause is right, even if one doesn't feel like he can." That is simple enough to understand, but it is extremely hard to *do*. These lessons could certainly be imparted through formal military training, or martial arts classes, but my argument here has been not that modern sports can be substituted in for military training, but rather that they *are* a form of military training. Moreover, such sports are a kind of military training better suited for modern warfare than some of the ancient sports.

~

Dear Doug,

Well, first, I repent in dust and ashes. Your paper really does correct some of my "first impressions" from life. I grew up in a university town with my father as head of the Foreign Languages Department. I grew up in a situation where football was virtually a religion, one that a student of comparative religions might well analyze: agonistic contest, festival consumption of special foods and much alcohol, yelling and dancing, song, and an aftermath of joy or rage.

I had two reactions. As a musician and liberal arts person, I felt that the measurably vaster money given to sports was money given to children's games stupidly perpetuated into adulthood. And, as a Christian, I sensed a competitive religion. I mention this to explain the disparaging view of sports that I have held.

Until now, of course.

PART FOUR: CULTURE

I'd like to add a few comments, since that's what I'm supposed to do. First, musical instruments are weapons of holy war in the Bible. David was trained at both war and music (Ps 144:1 + 9), and we need to recover a sense of the liturgical war.

Second, it has been observed that team sports is like the development of orchestras and of polyphonic music in Western Christendom. In all such things men and women need to learn to yield to one another, to allow each player to take his or her turn in the sun, to submit intelligently to a director. Neither the ancient cultures nor the Islamic ones ever develop any such Trinitarian societal forms. There were no team sports in the Olympic Games.[14]

I conclude with a note to the reader: Doug cites Huizinga's *Homo Ludens*. This is one of those must-read books that any person seeking a broad understanding of culture needs to digest. I highly recommend it.

Jim

14. Rudimentary "team sports" like lacrosse were more like stylized battles. (And David Brin's famous attack on *Star Wars* was just along these lines. In *Star Wars* the hero has superhuman powers and acts alone. By contrast, in *Star Trek* no one has superhuman powers and all must act as a team. Cf. Brin, "'Star Wars' Despots vs. 'Star Trek' Populists." Online: http://www.salon.com/entertainment/movies/feature/1999/06/15/brin_main).

Afterword

JOHN M. FRAME

I'M VERY HAPPY FOR the opportunity to salute Jim in this volume. His friendship over the years has been one of God's best blessings to me, and his writing a constant edification.

Jim studied with me at Westminster Seminary in Philadelphia in the late 1970s. He was always brilliant in his coursework and in his dealing with questions in and out of class. He had been a student of Greg Bahnsen at Reformed Theological Seminary in Jackson, Mississippi, and at first I saw him as one of the group that was working through the implications of the Bahnsen/Rushdoony theonomy, the view that the Old Testament civil law (including the specific penalties for transgressions) must be incorporated into present-day legal systems. After his graduation, however, it became evident that he was after something more than theonomy—a whole fresh way of interpreting the Bible, in accord with the patterns of symbolism running through the text.

Jim saw his hermeneutic—unhelpfully called by some "interpretive maximalism"—as an expansion of the old Reformed principle of comparing Scripture with Scripture. But he carried it to lengths that aroused controversy. The Rushdoony group banished him for agreeing with Gary North's suggestion that Rahab's scarlet cord (Josh 2:18) represented, in addition to Passover blood, a legal token of her lost virginity (cf. Deut 22:13–21), and therefore a model of salvation, also implied in 2 Corinthians 11:2. Jim's background in literature led him naturally to search the Scriptures for such correlations, but not all were sympathetic to his project.

In time, Jim's theological writing left me in the dust. I always found his work fascinating, but he would come up with new ideas before I was able to adequately think through the old. He built large theological structures, one floor upon another, while I was still examining the entryway. Normally, theologians work much slower. They submit each idea to a "refereed journal," and if their idea survives that (often hostile) exposure, they go on to publish a sequel the following year. But Jim worked in a theological culture outside the academic mainstream, one that eagerly awaited each of his new contributions. This is not, of course, to suggest that he faced no hostile criticism along the way; he has endured more than his fair share of that. Nor is it to suggest that he failed adequately to think his ideas through, only that he thought faster than most of us.

Sometimes I have wished that he had written in a more traditional theological climate and had dealt more with critics. But in the end I have concluded that there are too many people in the standard academies already, and Reformed theology deeply needs to be challenged from outside the traditional circles. Creative thinkers like Van Til and Jordan need to be able to work outside the mainstream if they are to meet their full potential.

I wrote the Introduction to Jim's early book *The Law of the Covenant: An Exposition of Exodus 21–23*.[1] I hope that Jim has forgiven my comparisons there between him, Pat Buchanan, and J. R. Ewing, which, especially in retrospect, appear pretty silly and inappropriate. But in that Introduction I noted distinctive features of Jim's work that have continued over the years:

1. Though theoretically sophisticated, his work is highly practical. He is interested in economics, politics, church worship, family life. He has distanced himself somewhat from theonomic politics over the years and has become more focused on the centrality of the church for human culture. But he still sees the Scriptures as having a bearing on all human life and culture.

2. He gets into the life-situations of the biblical writers, showing how they thought about things, how they connected one idea to another. His wonderful *Through New Eyes*[2] continues this theme from *The Law of the Covenant*, building piece-by-piece our understanding of the biblical worldview. "Worldview" has become something of a cliche now. Usually writers like myself identify it with the Creator-creature distinction and other metaphysical basics of theism. But for Jim, worldview is a fuller concept, including the world of symbolism, the world as God's house, the heavenly lights, rocks, gold, and gems, trees and thorns, birds and beasts, angels, five-fold and six-fold patterns, breaking bread as transformation, man as king, Eden as the world of transformation, the tabernacle, temple, and so on.

3. Jim still stands, then, in the great tradition of Reformed writers who have tried to think comprehensively about the great plan of our sovereign God, like Calvin, Bavinck, Kuyper, Schilder, Dooyeweerd, Van Til, Rushdoony, Runner, Hebden Taylor, and Singer. I was deeply moved by his essay, "The Closing of the Calvinistic Mind,"[3] in which he cited many of those great thinkers and then asked what has happened to that tradition in our own time. Few Calvinistic writings are published today that have such intellectual and theological rigor, breadth, and depth, and that interact with the full range of historical and modern thought. This tradition

---

1. James B. Jordan, *The Law of the Covenant: An Exposition of Exodus 21–23* (Tyler, TX: Institute for Christian Economics, 1984).

2. James B. Jordan, *Through New Eyes: Developing a Biblical View of the World* (Brentwood, TN: Wolgemuth & Hyatt, 1988; reprint, Eugene, OR: Wipf & Stock, 1999).

3. *Biblical Horizons* 177 (Aug. 2005). Online: http://www.biblicalhorizons.com/biblical-horizons/no-177-the-closing-of-the-calvinistic-mind/.

saw the Reformed faith, not just as a group of confessions, but also as a dynamic movement to bring all areas of life subject to the sovereignty of Christ.

Jim analyzes the present problem in terms of the recent controversy over the "Federal Vision," a movement in which his own formulations have been influential:

> The controversies over the so-called "federal vision" and "new perspective on Paul" are but two examples of the closing of the Calvinistic mind, at least in many parts of the Reformed world. Men with little knowledge of history, evidently incapable of thinking presuppositionally, and sometimes (not always) rather obviously motivated by political concerns (if not by sheer envy), have not hesitated to distort and even lie about this thing called "federal vision" (which, as they discuss it, is largely a product of their own minds).
>
> With minds like steel traps, these critics insist that "shibboleth" be pronounced their way, on pain of expulsion. Indeed, those who try to reason within the great Reformed tradition—the tradition reflected by the list of books above—have been called "heretics" because they don't say "shibboleth" rightly.

Although I differ at points with the Federal Vision, I agree emphatically that the debate has not represented Reformed thought at its best. As Jim says, "Once upon a time, a man being examined for presbytery could take issue with Calvin or the Westminster Standards, defend himself from the Bible and Reformed theology, and have a conversation." Indeed, that is true (as I can testify, being a bit older than Jim), and this openness and flexibility have often been replaced by a rather mechanical "strict constructionist" appeal to the confessions, governed more by a theological tradition than by an honest reading of the confessions, properly subordinating them to Scripture. (Thankfully, there are exceptions, such as the presbytery in which I live and work.)

I'm not yet ready to say with Jim that "the Protestant age is coming to an end." But I very much hope that the Protestant world will give heed to Jim's alarms. And I hope that they will join his positive program: "We must take all the great gains of the Calvinistic heritage and apply them with an open Bible to the new world in which we are now living. We must be aware that there is far more in the Bible than the Reformation dealt with, and that many of our problems today are addressed by those hitherto unnoticed or undeveloped aspects of the Bible."

May God give Jim many years of health and strength to develop this program and many readers willing to join him.

The Writings of James B. Jordan, 1975–2010

<hr>

COMPILED BY JOHN BARACH

<hr>

FOR SEVERAL DECADES, JAMES Jordan has been a prolific writer. He began writing for publication while he was still in college, though those essays are not listed here. Since 1975, he has produced a steady stream of newsletters, essays, and books. By the time this volume is published, this bibliography will no longer be up to date.

I have attempted to include everything that Jim has written and published since 1975, in several languages and in various formats,[1] but I am sure that there have been a few lapses. If you find something that should have been included, please let me know so that I can improve this list.

I wish that I could have included all of Jim's recorded lectures and sermons, but it would not have been possible to establish the exact dates—let alone locations—on which they were given. Most of them are available from *Biblical Horizons* (http://biblicalhorizons.com), Auburn Avenue Media (http://www.auburnavenuemedia.org/), or WordMP3.com, but you can find others online.[2]

It is customary for a bibliography in a Festschrift to be in chronological order. In Jim's case, however, it is particularly profitable to pay attention to chronology.

First, to borrow Raymond Chandler's phrase, Jim frequently cannibalizes his earlier writings. Many of his newsletter essays are "works in progress," intended to become chapters in a longer work. Sometimes this reworking is obvious. For instance, the various essays entitled "Advice from a Sojourner" became the monograph by the same name. In such cases, I have not indicated which essay became which chapter. In other cases, I have. For example, several of the chapters of *The Sociology of the Church* are revised versions of essays originally published in various journals and newsletters. But it would be

<hr>

1. In many cases, I have provided the web addresses at which these essays can be found online. But to keep the list a little briefer, I did not provide those addresses for the many newsletters available at the Biblical Horizons website (http://biblicalhorizons.com).

2. For instance, several lectures or sermons can be found at http://christthekingkirk.com/audio/ (2007); www.covenantpca.org/templates/default.asp?id=28679&PID=327270 (1992 and 2002); http://crecsermons.wordpress.com; http://www.reformalt.hu/audio; http://reformationcovenant.org/sermons.asp (1992, 1993, 1995, 1999, 2003, 2006, 2010); and http://stmarkreformed.org/sermons/ ("Living as the Church 2010 Conference").

cumbersome to track down every republication or extended quotation from Jim's earlier works in his later ones.

Second, Jim has often revisited the same topics or passages of Scripture. His later writings supplement and sometimes supplant the earlier ones. So if you are reading something more recent, you might find that Jim uses terminology you are unfamiliar with (e.g., bread as Alpha food and wine as Omega food) or assumes things that you are not yet persuaded of (e.g., that "lip" in Genesis 11 refers, not primarily to language, but to religious confession). In such cases, Jim is often building on things he has discussed in earlier writings. If you come late to the conversation, you will not understand as much as you would if you start at the beginning. On the other hand, if you are reading Jim's earlier material, you will often find him assuming or even defending positions and views that he no longer holds and you should bear in mind the possibility that a later document or lecture will correct or revise the one you are currently reading.

It is my hope that this bibliography will help readers by allowing them to trace the development in Jim's thought and that readers will bear in mind what Jim himself has so often said about his works: they are not intended to be the final word but are presented with the hope that they will be a *helpful* word.

FORMAT

As much as possible, I have listed Jim's writings in chronological order. In each year, I list first the documents for which I know (or can roughly guess) the month of publication and then, in alphabetical order, the various other books or monographs or essays that Jim published that year (including newsletters for which I could not guess a more specific date).

In each month, I list the documents alphabetically by the title of the monograph or the title of the newsletter or journal in which an essay was published (e.g., *Biblical Horizons*, *Calvin Speaks*, *Council of Chalcedon*). If more than one item appeared in the same issue of a newsletter or journal, I list them in the order of publication because in some cases the second of two essays expands on something in the first.

1975

"The Love Feast in the Early Church." Reprinted in *The Love Feast in the Early Church*. Niceville, FL: Biblical Horizons, 1991.

1976

"A Survey of Southern Presbyterian Millennial Views Before 1930." *The Journal of Christian Reconstruction* 3.2 (Winter 1976–1977): 106–21. Reprinted: Views and Reviews: Open Book Occasional Paper 9.

1977

Review: Edmund S. Morgan, *The Puritan Family*. *Journal of Christian Reconstruction* 4.2 (Winter 1977–1978): 170–72.
Van Til and the Greeks. Published in 1991.

1978

"Calvinism and the 'Judicial Law of Moses': An Historical Survey." *The Journal of Christian Reconstruction* 5.2 (Winter 1978–1979): 17–48.

"Anti-Utopianism in Modern Conservative Thought: Some Criticisms of Thomas Molnar and Eric Voegelin." Published in January 1991.

1979

"Sons of Issachar." *Presbyterian Heritage* 1.1.

"Thornwell's Theocracy." *Presbyterian Heritage* 1.1.

"Those Foolish Young Men." *Presbyterian Heritage* 1.2.

"Social Security and the Christian—Part 1." *Presbyterian Heritage* 1.2. Though this says "Part 1," there does not appear to have been a "Part 2."

"The Presbyterian Presuppositions. No. 1: The Trinity." *Presbyterian Heritage* 1.2.

"Introduction to William Symington's *Messiah the Prince*." *Journal of Christian Reconstruction* 6.1 (Summer): 195.

"Some Observations on Physical Education." *The Biblical Educator* 1.1 (October): 3. Reprinted: *Baptist Reformation Review* 10.1 (Spring 1981): 13–15. Spanish: "Algunas Observaciones sobre la Educación Física." Trans. Donald Herrera Terán. Online: http://www.biblicalhorizons.com/espanol-files/Educ_Fis.pdf.

"Foreign Languages in the Christian Schools." *The Biblical Educator* 1.2 (November): 3.

"Singing—Part 1." *The Biblical Educator* 1.3 (December): 2.

"The Biblical Chronology Question: An Analysis [Part 1]." *Creation Social Sciences & Humanities Quarterly* 2.2 (Winter): 9–15. Reprinted in Views and Reviews: Open Book Occasional Paper 10.

"Puritanism and Music." *The Journal of Christian Reconstruction* 6.2 (Winter 1979–1980): 111–33. Reprinted: Views and Reviews: Open Book Occasional Paper 5.

1980

"Singing—Part 2." *The Biblical Educator* 2.1 (January): 3.

"What Is a Theonomist?" *Presbyterian Heritage* 1.3

"Was Calvin a Bibliocrat?" *Presbyterian Heritage* 1.3.

"The Presbyterian Presuppositions 2: The Covenant." *Presbyterian Heritage* 1.3.

"The Biblical Chronology Question: An Analysis [Part 2]." *Creation Social Sciences & Humanities Quarterly* 2.3 (Spring):17–26. Reprinted in Views and Reviews: Open Book Occasional Paper 10.

"Are Christian Schools the Best Answer?" *The Biblical Educator* 2.4 (April): 1–2.

Slavery in Biblical Perspective. Westminster Theological Seminary, ThM Thesis (April).

"Home Education and Christian Music." *The Biblical Educator* 2.5 (May): 1–3.

"The Motive Goal and Standard in Education: The Van Til Prospective." *The Biblical Educator* 2.6 (June): 1–3. [The title appears this way in the original, with no punctuation.] Spanish: "El Motivo, la Meta y el Estándar en la Educación." Trans. Donald Herrera Terán. Online: http://www.biblicalhorizons.com/espanol-files/MME_Educ.pdf.

, ed. "The Execution of Rebellious Children (Part 1)." *Calvin Speaks* 1.1 (July). The *Calvin Speaks* newsletter printed sermons by John Calvin, with updated English, some light editing, and explanatory footnotes by James Jordan. Many of these sermons were reprinted in *The Covenant Enforced* (1990).

, ed. "The Execution of Rebellious Children (Part 2)." *Calvin Speaks* 1.2 (August).

, ed . "The Death Penalty Is Not Optional (Part 1)." *Calvin Speaks* 1.3 (September).

, ed . "The Death Penalty Is Not Optional (Part 2)." *Calvin Speaks* 1.4 (October).

"The Bible and Modern Science." *The Biblical Educator* 2.11 (November): 2–3.

, ed. "The Court of Final Appeal (Part 1)." *Calvin Speaks* 1.5 (November).

, ed. "The Court of Final Appeal (Part 2)." *Calvin Speaks* 1.6 (December).

"Christianity and the Calendar, Part 1: The Rhythmic Creation." *Chalcedon Report* 184 (December).

"Forerunners of Reformation Sacramental Theory: Ratramnus of Corbie and Berengarius of Tours." Reprinted in *Christ in His Supper: Two Essays*. Niceville, FL: Biblical Horizons, January 1991.

"The Presence of Christ in the Eucharist: Thoughts Arising from Nevin's *The Mystical Presence*." Reprinted in *Christ in His Supper: Two Essays*. Niceville, FL: Biblical Horizons, January 1991.

1981

, ed . "Christian Rulers (Part 1)." *Calvin Speaks* 2.1 (January).
"No Close Encounters: A Christian Looks at UFOs." *The Council of Chalcedon* 2.11 (January): 4–8. Reprinted in *Journal of Christian Reconstruction* 7.2 (Winter 1981): 231–36.
, ed. "Christian Rulers (Part 2)." *Calvin Speaks* 2.2 (February).
"Christianity and the Calendar, Part 2: Sunrise." *Chalcedon Report* 186 (February)
, ed. "Rules for Rulers." *Calvin Speaks* 2.3 (March).
"Christianity and the Calendar, Part 3: Sunrise and the Seasons." *Chalcedon Report* 187 (March).
"Calvin's Incipient Postmillennialism." *The Council of Chalcedon* 3.1 (March): 4–7.
"The Christian and Tax Strikes: Pros and Cons." *Biblical Economics Today* 4.2 (April–May).
, ed. "Adultery and Its Penalty." *Calvin Speaks* 2.4 (April).
"Christianity and the Calendar, Part 4: The Regulative Principle of Worship." *Chalcedon Report* 188 (April).
, ed. "The Sanctity of Marriage (Part 1)." *Calvin Speaks* 2.5 (May).
"Joseph's Job." *Christian Reconstruction* 5.3 (May–June).
"The Mosaic Head Tax and State Financing." *Biblical Economics Today* 4.3 (June–July).
, ed. "The Sanctity of Marriage (Part 2)." *Calvin Speaks* 2.6 (June).
"Calvin and the Mosaic Judicials." *Calvin Speaks* 2.6 (June).
"Christianity and the Calendar, Part 5: Lord of the Calendar." *Chalcedon Report* 190 (June).
"The Future of Capitalism." *The Council of Chalcedon* 3.4 (June): 14–15.
, ed. "The First Sermon on the History of Melchizedek (1559) (Part 1)." *Calvin Speaks* 2.7 (July).
"Christianity and the Calendar, Part 6: Day-Keeping." *Chalcedon Report* 191 (July).
"Daniel's Job." *Christian Reconstruction* 5.4 (July–August).
"Theses on Tithing." *Biblical Economics Today* 4.4 (August–September).
, ed. "The First Sermon on the History of Melchizedek (1559) (Part 2)." *Calvin Speaks* 2.8 (August).
"Whole Men and Cheap Shortcuts." *The Council of Chalcedon* 3.6 (August): 8–9.
, ed. "The Second Sermon on the History of Melchizedek (1559) (Part 1)." *Calvin Speaks* 2.9 (September).
, ed. "The Second Sermon on the History of Melchizedek (1559) (Part 2)." *Calvin Speaks* 2.10 (October).
"Play in Christian Perspective." *The Biblical Educator* 3.11 (November): 1–2.
, ed. "The Third Sermon on the History of Melchizedek (1559) (Part 1)." *Calvin Speaks* 2.11 (November).
"The Geocentricity Question." *The Biblical Educator* 3.12 (December): 1–4. Reprinted with slight revisions in *Contra Mundum* 7 (Spring 1993) and *Open Book* 46 (June 1999).
, ed. "The Third Sermon on the History of Melchizedek (1559) (Part 2)." *Calvin Speaks* 2.12 (December).
"God's Hospitality and Holistic Evangelism." *The Journal of Christian Reconstruction* 7.2 (Winter): 87–113. Reprinted, with significant revisions, as ch. 11 of *The Sociology of the Church* (1986).

1982

"Biblical Perspectives on the Arts." *The Biblical Educator* 4.1 (January): 2–3.
, ed. "Altars and Ensigns (Part 1)." *Calvin Speaks* 3.1 (January).
"Christianity and the Calendar, Part 7: The Sabbath: A Permanent Ceremonial Law." *Geneva Papers* 1 (January): 2–3 .
Review: Martha Zimmerman, *Celebrate the Feasts (of the Old Testament in Your Own Home or Church)*. *The Biblical Educator* 4.2 (February): 3–4.
, ed. "Altars and Ensigns (Part 2)." *Calvin Speaks* 3.2 (February).
"Christianity and the Calendar, Part 8: The Old Covenant Sabbath." *Geneva Papers* 2 (February): 4.
, ed . "Blessings and Curses (Part 1)." *Calvin Speaks* 3.3 (March).
"Christianity and the Calendar, Part 9: The New Covenant Sabbath." *Geneva Papers* 3 (March): 4.
Review: Robert E. Webber, *The Secular Saint: A Case for Evangelical Social Responsibility*. *Westminster Theological Journal* 44.1 (Spring): 198–202.
, ed. "Blessings and Curses (Part 2)." *Calvin Speaks* 3.4 (April).

"Christianity and the Calendar, Part 10: The Sacramental Sabbath." *Geneva Papers* 4 (April): 2–3.
, ed. "Secret Sins (Part 1)." *Calvin Speaks* 3.5 (May).
"Christianity and the Calendar, Part 11: Dimensions of the Sabbath." *Geneva Papers* 5 (May): 2–3.
, ed. "Secret Sins (Part 2)." *Calvin Speaks* 3.6 (June).
"Pies, Docs, Kuyps, and Lits." *Geneva Papers* 6 (June): 1.
"Christianity and the Calendar, Part 12: The Sabbath and the Dietary Laws." *Geneva Papers* 6 (June): 4.
, ed. "The Curse and Justification (Part 1)." *Calvin Speaks* 3.7 (July).
"Christianity and the Calendar, Part 13: The Sabbath, Labor, and the Death Penalty." *Geneva Papers* 7 (July): 2–3.
, ed. "The Curse and Justification (Part 2)." *Calvin Speaks* 3.8 (August).
"Christianity and the Calendar, Part 14: The Sabbath and Authority." *Geneva Papers* 8 (August): 4.
, ed. "Promise, Obedience, Blessing (Part 1)." *Calvin Speaks* 3.9 (September).
"Christianity and the Calendar, Part 15: The Alternate Sabbath." *Geneva Papers* 9 (September): 2–3.
, ed. "Promise, Obedience, Blessing (Part 2)." *Calvin Speaks* 3.10 (October).
, ed. "Blessing and Affliction (Part 1)." *Calvin Speaks* 3.11 (November).
"Note on Pessimism and Optimism in Calvin's Thought." *Calvin Speaks* 3.11 (November).
"Christianity and the Calendar, Part 16: The Sabbath and Culture." *Geneva Papers* 11 (November): 2–3.
, ed. "Blessing and Affliction (Part 2)." *Calvin Speaks* 3.12 (December).
"Christianity and the Calendar, Part 17: The Sabbath and Debts." *Geneva Papers* 12 (December): 3–4.
ed., *The Failure of the American Baptist Culture*. Christianity and Civilization 1. Tyler, TX: Geneva Divinity School.
"Editor's Introduction." In *The Failure of the American Baptist Culture*, ed. James B. Jordan, v–xv. Christianity and Civilization 1. Tyler, TX: Geneva Divinity School.
"The Moral Majority: An Anabaptist Critique." In *The Failure of the American Baptist Culture*, ed. James B. Jordan, 77–93. Christianity and Civilization 1. Tyler, TX: Geneva Divinity School. A review of Robert E. Webber's *The Moral Majority: Right or Wrong?*
"Theses on Paedocommunion." *Geneva Papers*, special edition.

1983

, ed. "Separation unto Blessing (Part 1)." *Calvin Speaks* 31 (January).
"Christianity and the Calendar, Part 18: Repetition, Variation, and Development." *Geneva Papers* 13 (January): 3–4.
"Abortion: Its Cause and Cure." *Phineas Report* 7 (January).
, ed. "Separation unto Blessing (Part 2)." *Calvin Speaks* 32 (February).
"Some Thoughts on E.T." *The Council of Chalcedon* 4.12 (February): 2–5.
"Christianity and the Calendar, Part 19: Three Types of Religious Calendars." *Geneva Papers* 14 (February): 3–4.
Review: Mircea Eliade, *Ordeal by Labyrinth: Conversations with Claude-Henri Rocquet*. *Geneva Review* 1 (February): 1.
Review: Mircea Eliade, *Tales of the Sacred and the Supernatural*. *Geneva Review* 1 (February): 1.
Review: Norman Girardot and Mac Linscott Ricketts, eds. *Imagination and Meaning: The Scholarly and Literary Worlds of Mircea Eliade*. *Geneva Review* 1 (February): 1–2.
, ed. "God's Threats (Part 1)." *Calvin Speaks* 33 (March).
"Christianity and the Calendar, Part 20: Rationalism and Reductionism." *Geneva Papers* 15 (March): 3–4.
Review: Rupert Sheldrake, *A New Science of Life: The Hypothesis of Formative Causation*. *Geneva Review* 2 (March): 1–2.
, ed. "God's Threats (Part 2)." *Calvin Speaks* 34 (April).
"Christianity and the Calendar, Part 21: The Moon." *Geneva Papers* 16 (April): 3–4.
"*Baptist Reformation Review*: What Next?" *Geneva Review* 3 (April): 2.
Review: G. W. Ahlstrom, *Royal Administration and National Religion in Ancient Palestine*. *Geneva Review* 3 (April): 2.
Review: R. P. C. Hanson, *The Life and Writings of the Historical Saint Patrick*. *Geneva Review* 3 (April): 2.
, ed. "God's Plagues (Part 1)." *Calvin Speaks* 35 (May).

"Christianity and the Calendar, Part 22: The Calendar Before Sinai, Part I." *Geneva Papers* 17 (May): 3–4.

, ed. "God's Plagues (Part 2)." *Calvin Speaks* 36 (June).

"Christianity and the Calendar, Part 23: The Calendar Before Sinai, Part II." *Geneva Papers* 18 (June): 2–3.

Review: *Something Wicked This Way Comes* (film). *Geneva Review* 4 (June): 1. Reprinted in *The Council of Chalcedon* 5.6 (August): 24.

Review: Josephus, *The Jewish War*, trans. and ed. Gaalya Cornfield. *Geneva Review* 4 (June): 1–2.

Review: Keith L. Sprunger, *Dutch Puritanism: A History of English and Scottish Churches of the Netherlands in the Sixteenth and Seventeenth Centuries*. *Geneva Review* 4 (June): 2.

Review: Giordano Bruno, *The Ash Wednesday Supper*, trans. and ed. Stanley L. Jaki. *Geneva Review* 4 (June): 2.

, ed. "God's Anger (Part 1)." *Calvin Speaks* 37 (July–August).

"Christianity and the Calendar, Part 24: The Calendar Before Sinai, Part III." *Geneva Papers* 19 (July–August): 3–4.

, ed. "God's Anger (Part 2)." *Calvin Speaks* 38 (September).

"Christianity and the Calendar, Part 25: The Calendar at Sinai." *Geneva Papers* 20 (September): 3–4.

, ed. "The Peril of Apostasy (Part 1)." *Calvin Speaks* 39 (October).

"Liturgical Notes No. 1: A Liturgy of Malediction." *Geneva Papers* 21 (October): 1–2. Reprinted as ch. 13 of *The Sociology of the Church* (1986).

"Christianity and the Calendar, Part 26: The Third Day." *Geneva Papers* 21 (October): 4.

Review: Mircea Eliade, The Old Man and the Bureaucrats. *Geneva Review* 5 (October): 1.

Review: Moises Silva, *Biblical Words and Their Meaning: An Introduction to Lexical Semantics*. *Geneva Review* 5 (October): 1.

Review: Gordon J. Wenham, *Numbers*, and A. Noordtzij, *Numbers*. *Geneva Review* 5 (October): 1–2.

Review: John Platt, *Reformed Thought and Scholasticism: The Arguments for the Existence of God in Dutch Theology, 1575–1650*. *Geneva Review* 5 (October): 2.

Review: Rousas J. Rushdoony, *By What Standard? An Analysis of the Philosophy of Cornelius Van Til*. *Geneva Review* 5 (October): 2.

, ed. "The Peril of Apostasy (Part 2)." *Calvin Speaks* 40 (November).

"Liturgical Notes No. 2: A Liturgy of Healing." *Geneva Papers* 22 (November): 1–3. Reprinted as ch. 14 of *The Sociology of the Church* (1986).

Review: *Tender Mercies*. *Geneva Review* 6 (November): 1. Reprinted in *The Council of Chalcedon* 5.10 (December): 18–20.

, ed. "Signs and Wonders of Wrath (Part 1)." *Calvin Speaks* 41 (December).

"Liturgical Notes No. 3: The Petitioner and the Circularizer." *Geneva Papers* 23 (December): 1.

Review: Douglas F. Kelly, ed., *The Journal of Christian Reconstruction: Symposium on the Media and the Arts* 10:1 (1983). *Geneva Review* 7 (December): 1–2.

"Pacifism and the Old Testament." In *The Theology of Christian Resistance*, ed. Gary North, 77–93. Christianity and Civilization 2. Tyler, TX: Geneva Divinity School Press. Reprinted: Views and Reviews: Open Book Occasional Paper 6. Review of four books: Peter C. Craigie, *The Problem of War in the Old Testament*; Jacob C. Enz, *The Christian and Warfare: The Roots of Pacifism in the Old Testament*; Vernard Eller, *War and Peace, from Genesis to Revelation*; Millard C. Lind, *Yahweh Is a Warrior: The Theology of Warfare in Ancient Israel*.

Review: John H. Yoder. *Nevertheless: The Varieties and Short-Comings of Religious Pacifism*. In *The Theology of Christian Resistance*, ed. Gary North, 333–35. Christianity and Civilization 2. Tyler, TX: Geneva Divinity School Press.

Review: Werner O. Packull. *Mysticism and the Early South German-Austrian Anabaptist Movement 1525–1531*. In *The Theology of Christian Resistance*, ed. Gary North, 336–37. Christianity and Civilization 2. Tyler, TX: Geneva Divinity School Press.

"Rebellion, Tyranny, and Dominion in the Book of Genesis." In *Tactics of Christian Resistance*, ed. Gary North, 38–80. Christianity and Civilization 3. Tyler, TX: Geneva Divinity School Press. Reprinted: Views and Reviews: Open Book Occasional Paper 21.

"Tithing: Financing Christian Reconstruction." In *Tactics of Christian Resistance*, ed. Gary North, 355–70. Christianity and Civilization 3. Tyler, TX: Geneva Divinity School Press.

1984

, ed . "Signs and Wonders of Wrath (Part 2)." *Calvin Speaks* 42 (January–February).
"Christianity and the Calendar, Part 27: Is the Church Calendar Desirable?" *Geneva Papers* 24 (January): 1–2.
"Liturgical Notes No. 4: How Biblical Is Protestant Worship? (Part 1)." *Geneva Papers* 25 (February): 1–4. Reprinted as part of ch. 10 of *The Sociology of the Church* (1986).
, ed. "God Is Our Fortress (Part 1)." *Calvin Speaks* 43 (March).
"Liturgical Notes No. 5: How Biblical Is Protestant Worship? (Part 2)." *Geneva Papers* 26 (March): 1–2. Reprinted as part of ch. 10 of *The Sociology of the Church* (1986).
"Christianity and the Calendar, Part 28: The Calendar in Outline." *Geneva Papers* 25 (March): 3–4.
Review: Word Biblical Commentaries. *Geneva Review* 8 (March): 1.
Review: Enrique T. Rueda, *The Homosexual Network: Private Lives and Public Policy*. *Geneva Review* 8 (March): 2.
Review: Lynn R. Buzzard and Laurence Eck, *Tell It to the Church: Reconciling Out of Court*. *Geneva Review* 8 (March): 2.
Review: Howard Galley, ed., *Morning and Evening Prayer, with Selected Psalms and Readings for the Church Year*. *Geneva Review* 8 (March): 2.
, ed. "God Is Our Fortress (Part 2)." *Calvin Speaks* 44 (April).
"Christianity and the Calendar, Part 29: Advent, Christmas, and Epiphany." *Geneva Papers* 27 (April): 4.
"Popular Fictional Literature." *Geneva Review* 9 (April): 1–2.
, ed. "A Plethora of Plagues (Part 1)." *Calvin Speaks* 45 (May).
"Symbolism: A Manifesto." *Geneva Papers* 28 (May): 1–4. Online: http://www.biblicalhorizons.com/pdf/Symbolism-A-Manifesto.pdf. Polish: "Symbolizm: manifest." Trans. Bogumil Jarmulak. *Reformacja w Polsce* 7.4 (December 2005). Online: http://www.reformacja.pl/index.php/artykuly-autorzy/83-james-b-jordan/479-05-04-2005.
"Old Testament Ethics." *Geneva Review* 10 (May): 1.
"Short Notes." *Geneva Review* 10 (May): 2.
, ed. "A Plethora of Plagues (Part 2)." *Calvin Speaks* 46 (June).
"Jerry Falwell and the Heresy of Christian Zionism." *Geneva Review* 11 (June): 1–3. Reprinted as "Christian Zionism and Messianic Judaism," ch. 8 of *The Sociology of the Church* (1986).
"Should Churches Incorporate?" *Geneva Papers* 30 (July–August): 1–4. Reprinted as ch. 9 of *The Sociology of the Church* (1986).
"Gold, Silver, and Precious Stones." *Biblical Economics Today* 7.5 (August–September). Online: http://biblicalhorizons.wordpress.com/2009/05/18/gold-silver-precious-stones/.
"The Three Faces of Protestantism." *Geneva Papers* 31 (September): 1–4. Reprinted as ch. 4 of *The Sociology of the Church* (1986).
"Recent Old Testament Commentaries." *Geneva Review* 13 (September): 1–2.
"Triumphalistic Investiture." Presbyterian Heritage 4 (September). Reprinted as ch. 12 of *The Sociology of the Church* (1986).
, ed. "Exodus Undone (Part 1)." *Calvin Speaks* 47 (October).
Review: *Red Dawn*. *The Council of Chalcedon* 6.8 (October): 23–24.
"How to Be an Effective Roger Williams" [by "Robin Williams"]. *Presbabterian Heritage* 1 (October). Reprinted as "The Effective Church Splitter's Guide," ch. 6 of *The Sociology of the Church* (1986).
, ed. "Exodus Undone (Part 2)." *Calvin Speaks* 48 (November).
"*Greystoke*: *Chariots of Fire* II?" *The Council of Chalcedon* 6.9 (November): 18–20.
"Conversion." *Geneva Papers* 33 (November): 1–4. Reprinted as ch. 5 of *The Sociology of the Church* (1986).
"Einstein Beached; or Canterbury Cant, Cacophonous Caterwauling, and Christian Counterpoint." *Presbabterian Heritage* 2 (November).
"The Menace of Chinese Food: Observations on Christmas and Christmas Trees." *Presbyterian Heritage* 5 (December). Online: http://www.biblicalhorizons.com/pdfs/chinese.pdf. Polish: "Jeszcze raz o swietach." Trans. Bogumil Jarmulak. *Reformacja w Polsce* 10.3–4 (October 2008). Online: http://www.reformacja.pl/index.php/artykuly-autorzy/83-james-b-jordan/502-04-03-04-2008. The Polish article is only a portion of the original.
"Crossfire." *Presbyterian Heritage* 5 (December).

"Introduction." In Duane E. Spencer. *Holy Baptism: Word Keys Which Unlock the Covenant*, vii–xii. Tyler, TX: Geneva Ministries.

The Law of the Covenant: An Exposition of Exodus 21–23. Tyler, TX: Institute for Christian Economics. Chapter 5 has been translated into Spanish: "La Esclavitud (Éxodo 21:2–11)." Translated by Donald Herrera Terán. Online: http://www.biblicalhorizons.com/espanol-files/Cir_oido.pdf.

Sabbath Breaking and the Death Penalty: An Alternate View. Tyler, TX: Geneva Ministries.

"Study Guide for Alexander Schmemann's *For the Life of the World*." Unpublished document, written circa 1984. Online: http://www.exodusbooks.com/Samples/SVP/5334SG.pdf.

"William Kirk Kilpatrick's *Psychological Seduction*." *Preface* 10:1–4.

1985

"Interpreting the Historical Books of Scripture." *Geneva Papers* 35 (January): 1–4.

Review: Duane E. Spencer, *Holy Baptism: Word Keys Which Unlock the Covenant*. *Geneva Review* 16 (January): 1.

Review: David Chilton, *Paradise Restored: An Eschatology of Dominion*. *Geneva Review* 16 (January): 1–2.

"Joseph's Enslavement of the Egyptians: Fair or Foul?" *Geneva Papers* 36 (February): 1–4.

"Eastern Orthodoxy: The Current Interest." *Geneva Review* 17 (February): 1–3.

"Recent Bible Study Materials." *Geneva Review* 17 (February): 3–4.

"Workshop on Church Law and Government." Supplement to *Geneva Review* (February).

"Some Encouragements Toward an Evangelical Doctrine of the Deification of Man." Paper presented at the Regional Meeting of the Evangelical Theological Society, Dallas, TX (March 2). Published on microfiche: Portland: Theological Research Exchange Network, 1987.

"The 'Reconstructionist Movement.'" *Geneva Review* 18 (March): 1–4.

"*King David*: A Film Review." *The Council of Chalcedon* 7.3 (May): 23–24.

"Misleading Analogies: Roadblocks to Reconstruction." *Geneva Review* 19 (June): 6–7.

"Biblical Church Government Part 1: The Council and Its Membership." *Presbyterian Heritage* 6 (June).

"Studies in Genesis One: Six Days." *Geneva Review* 20 (July): 3–4.

"Catholics and Protestants." *Geneva Review* 20 (July): 6.

"Liturgical Renewal Resources." *Geneva Review* 20 (July): 6–7.

"Studies in Genesis One: God's Rite for Life." *Geneva Review* 21 (August): 3.

"Biblical Church Government Part 2: Conciliar Hierarchy—Children and Women." *Presbyterian Heritage* 7 (August).

"Christian Piety: Deformed and Reformed." *Geneva Papers* 2.1 (September). Included as an appendix in *From Bread to Wine* (2001).

"Studies in Genesis One: The Structure of Genesis." *Geneva Review* 22 (September): 4–5.

"Extending the Stakes: Alexander Schmemann." *Geneva Review* 22 (September): 7.

"Studies in Genesis One: Outline and Structure." *Geneva Review* 23 (October): 5–6.

"Ziklag Bivouac." *Presbyterian Heritage* 8 (October). Reprinted as the introduction to Part II of *The Sociology of the Church* (1986).

"Studies in Genesis One: An Infinity of Time." *Geneva Review* 24 (November): 6–7.

"Recent Bible Study Aids." *Geneva Review* 24 (November): 7–8.

"Star Over Bethlehem: A Snapshot of Dominion." *Geneva Review* 25 (December): 1–2.

Review: *1918*. *Geneva Review* 25 (December): 7.

"An Outline of the Book of Malachi." *Geneva Review* 25 (December): 8.

"The Israelite Militia in the Old Testament." In *The Militia in Twentieth Century America: A Symposium*, ed. Morgan Norval, 23–29. Falls Church, VA: Gun Owners Foundation. Reprinted in *Safeguarding Liberty: The Constitution and Citizen Militias*, ed. Larry Pratt, 237–50. Franklin, TN: Legacy Communications. Reprinted: Views and Reviews: Open Book Occasional Paper 23.

Judges: God's War Against Humanism. Tyler, TX: Geneva Ministries. Reprinted as *Judges: A Practical and Theological Commentary*. Eugene, OR: Wipf & Stock, 1999.

ed., *The Reconstruction of the Church*. Christianity and Civilization 4. Tyler, TX: Geneva Ministries.

"Editor's Introduction." In *The Reconstruction of the Church*, ed. James B. Jordan, vii–xiv. Christianity and Civilization 4. Tyler, TX: Geneva Ministries. Included in Views and Reviews: Open Book Occasional Paper 8.

"The Church: An Overview." In *The Reconstruction of the Church*, ed. James B. Jordan, 1–21. Christianity and Civilization 4. Tyler, TX: Geneva Ministries. Included in Views and Reviews: Open Book Occasional Paper 8.

"Church Music in Chaos." In *The Reconstruction of the Church*, ed. James B. Jordan, 241–65. Christianity and Civilization 4. Tyler, TX: Geneva Ministries. Reprinted: Views and Reviews: Open Book Occasional Paper 7.

"Song at the Red Sea (Exodus 15)." Music (ca. 1985).

Studies in Genesis: Class Syllabus. Notes, charts, and essays to accompany the "Studies in Genesis" lectures.

1986

"Tough Talk." *Geneva Review* 26 (January): 1–2.

"Studies in Genesis One: Heaven and Earth." *Geneva Review* 26 (January): 6.

"Fat Christians in an Age of Anorexia." *Geneva Review* 26 (January): 8.

"An Invitation to Attend the Fourth Annual Geneva Reconstruction Conference: 'Workshop on Church Law and Government.'" *Geneva Review* 26 (January). This invitation is a three-page long essay.

"Biblical Church Government Part 3: Conciliar Hierarchy—Elders and Bishops." *Presbyterian Heritage* 9 (January).

"Books of Note." *Reformed Heritage* 1 (January).

"An Open Letter to Morton Smith." *Geneva Review* 27 (February):1–2.

"Studies in Genesis One: Formless and Empty." *Geneva Review* 27 (February): 7.

"Studies in Genesis One: Angels and Men." *Geneva Review* 28 (March): 7–8.

"Books of Note." *Reformed Heritage* 2 (April).

Sabbath Breaking and the Death Penalty: A Theological Investigation. Geneva Papers 2.3–6 (June).

"Where is Bill Gothard Going?" *Geneva Review* 29 (June): 3, 8.

"The Origin of 'Evil' (Studies in Genesis One)." *Geneva Review* 30 (July): 1–2.

Review: George Grant, *The Dispossessed*. *Reformed Heritage* 3 (July).

Review: Rousas John Rushdoony, *Christianity and the State*. *Reformed Heritage* 3 (July).

Review: Cordwainer Smith, *Quest of the Three Worlds*. *Reformed Heritage* 3 (July).

"Paper Money." *Biblical Economics Today* 9.5 (August–September).

"The Heavenly Blueprint (Studies in Genesis One)." *Geneva Review* 31 (August):1, 6.

"Good Night (Studies in Genesis One)." *Geneva Review* 32 (September): 2–3.

Review: Graydon F. Snyder, *Ante Pacem: Archaeological Evidence of Church Life Before Constantine*. *Geneva Review* 32 (September): 6.

"Recent Old Testament Commentaries." *Geneva Review* 32 (September): 6–7.

"One in the Spirit." *Presbyterian Heritage* 10 (September).

"Daylight [Studies in Genesis One]." *Geneva Review* 33 (October–November): 3.

"Christian Reconstruction: A Definition," *Journey* 1.6 (November–December): 8–9.

"Farewell to Eden: A Review of *The Trip to Bountiful*." *Geneva Review* 34 (December): 1, 5. This issue of the Geneva Review was wrongly numbered as 33 instead of 34, and the first page dates it as October–November.

"Christianity in the Science Fiction of 'Cordwainer Smith.'" This essay is already mentioned as available for sale in *Reformed Heritage* 3 (July 1986), so it must have been written prior to this date. Reprinted in *Contra Mundum* 2 (Winter 1992): 34–38.

"Foreword." In George Grant. *The Dispossessed: Homelessness in America*, xi–xiv. Ft. Worth: Dominion Press. Since Jordan reviewed this book in July, it must have been published early in the year.

"Understanding the Story of the Gerasene Demoniac." In George Grant. *The Dispossessed: Homelessness in America*, 243–49. Ft. Worth: Dominion Press.

The Sociology of the Church: Essays in Reconstruction. Tyler, TX: Geneva Ministries. Reprinted: Eugene, OR: Wipf & Stock, 1999.

1987

"The Firmament-Heaven: Studies in Genesis One." *Geneva Review* 35 (January–February): 3, 7.
"*On Valentine's Day*: A Film Review." *Geneva Review* 35 (January–February): 5, 4.
"The Separated Waters: Studies in Genesis One." *Geneva Review* 36 (March): 5.
Review: Gordon MacDonald, *Ordering Your Private World*. *Geneva Review* 36 (March): 8.
"Holy Rain: Studies in Genesis One." *Geneva Review* 37 (April): 4, 11.
"Music and Life: The Benefits of Psalm Singing." *Geneva Review* 37 (April): 9–10.
"Dr. Cornelius Van Til: 1895–1987." *Geneva Review* 38 (May): 3, 11.
"The Ethics of Surrogate Motherhood." *Geneva Review* 38 (May): 4, 5.
"Music and Life: Minimalism in Music." *Geneva Review* 38 (May): 10, 9.
"Land and Sea: Studies in Genesis One." *Geneva Review* 39 (June): 5, 9.
"Saul: A New Adam for Israel." *Geneva Papers* 2.9 (July). Reprinted as part of "King Saul: A New Adam and a New Fall," which is listed now in the Biblical Horizons catalog as "King Saul: A Study in Humanity and the Fall." *Geneva Papers* 2.9 & 11.
"Plants Seeding Seed: Studies in Genesis One." *Geneva Review* 40 (July–August): 6–7.
Review: *Mosquito Coast*. *Geneva Review* 41 (September): 7, 12.
"Creation and Covenant Making, Part One [Studies in Genesis One]." *Geneva Review* 42 (October): 4–5.
"Creation and Covenant Making, Part Two: Studies in Genesis One." *Geneva Review* 43 (November): 8.
"Incentive Dynamics in the Tabernacle Corporation." *Biblical Economics Today* 11.1 (December–January).
"Starry, Starry Night: Studies in Genesis One." *Geneva Review* 44 (December): 4.
Review: Gary North, *Healer of the Nations: Biblical Blueprints for International Relations*. *Geneva Review* 44 (December): 8.
"Christian Zionism and Messianic Judaism." Appendix B in David Chilton. *The Days of Vengeance: An Exposition of the Book of Revelation*, 612–21. Fort Worth, TX: Dominion Press. Reprinted from *The Sociology of the Church*.

1988

"Abraham's Astral Prophecy: Studies in Genesis One." *Geneva Review* 45 (January): 5, 8.
"The Twelve 'Stars': Studies in Genesis One." *Geneva Review* 46 (February): 4, 8.
"Prophetic Stars: Studies in Genesis One." *Geneva Review* 47 (March): 5.
"The End of the World: Studies in Genesis One." *Geneva Review* 48 (April): 4–5.
"Fish and Fowl: Studies in Genesis One." *Geneva Review* 49 (May): 4, 7.
"No Longer Strangers, But Still Heretics: A Report on 'Pentecost 1988: A Gathering of Christians.'" *Christian Reconstruction* 12.4 (July–August).
"Saul: A Study in Original Sin: An Examination of 1 Samuel 13–15." *Geneva Papers* 2.11 (July 1988). Reprinted as part of "King Saul: A New Adam and a New Fall," which is listed now in the Biblical Horizons catalog as "King Saul: A Study in Humanity and the Fall." *Geneva Papers* 2.9 & 11.
"Thoughts on Jachin and Boaz." Biblical Horizons Occasional Paper 1 (August).
"From Glory to Glory: Degrees of Value in the Sanctuary." Biblical Horizons Occasional Paper 2 (August; revised February 1994).
"The Death Penalty in the Mosaic Law: Five Exploratory Essays." Biblical Horizons Occasional Paper 3 (August; revised January 1989).
"Swarming and Crawling: Studies in Genesis One." *Geneva Review* 50 (August): 3–4.
"Dinosaurs: Studies in Genesis One." *Geneva Review* 51 (September): 5.
"Reconsidering the Mosaic Law: Some Reflections—1988." Biblical Horizons Occasional Paper 4 (October). 2nd ed., May 1989.
"Cattle and Beasts: Studies in Genesis One." *Geneva Review* 52 (November): 7.
"A Letter on Paedocommunion." *Journey* 3.6 (November–December): 8–10.
"The Tabernacle: A New Creation." Biblical Horizons Occasional Paper 5 (December; revised June 1993).
"Symbolism and Worldview." *Geneva Review* 53 (December): 1–5.
"The Abomination of Desolation: An Alternative Hypothesis." Appendix A in Gary DeMar, *The Debate over Christian Reconstruction*, 237–43. Ft. Worth: Dominion Press / Atlanta: American Vision. Online: http://www.preteristarchive.com/Modern/1988_jordan_abomination.html.

The Bible and the Nations: A Syllabus. Niceville, FL: Biblical Horizons.
Christianity and the Calendar: A Syllabus. Niceville, FL: Biblical Horizons.
Drawing Near: An Overview of Leviticus. Niceville, FL: Biblical Horizons. Syllabus to accompany lectures.
From Slavery to Sabbath: An Overview of Exodus. Niceville, FL: Biblical Horizons. Syllabus to accompany lectures.
Old Gold: An Overview of Deuteronomy. Niceville, FL: Biblical Horizons. Syllabus to accompany lectures.
Primeval Saints: Studies in the Patriarchs of Genesis. Draft version. Niceville, FL: Biblical Horizons. Revised and reprinted: Moscow: Canon, 2001.
"A Review of H. Wayne House and Thomas Ice, *Dominion Theology: Blessing or Curse? An Analysis of Christian Reconstructionism*." Views and Reviews: Open Book Occasional Paper 1.
Sand Trek: An Overview of Numbers. Niceville, FL: Biblical Horizons. Syllabus to accompany lectures.
Through New Eyes: Developing a Biblical View of the World. Brentwood, TN: Wolgemuth & Hyatt. Reprinted: Eugene, OR: Wipf & Stock, 1999. Korean: Seoul, Korea: Logos Publishing, 2002. Russian: St. Petersburg, RU: Reformatskaya Teologicheskaya Seminaria, 2005. The introduction is available in Spanish: "Introducción a 'Con Nuevos Ojos.'" Trans. Donald Herrera Terán. Online: http://www.biblicalhorizons.com/espanol-files/Int_NuevOjos.pdf.

1989

"The Mosaic Law and Social Issues." *Biblical Horizons* 1 (January).
"Who Were the Angels of Jude 6?" *Biblical Horizons* 1 (January).
"The Battle of Gog and Magog." *Biblical Horizons* 2 (February).
"'Do This!'" *Rite Reasons: Studies in Worship* 1 (March).
"The Beginning of Tyranny." *World* 3.37 (March). This essay is included in "Elijah's War with Baal." *Biblical Horizons* 5 (July 1989).
"The Son of Joseph." *Biblical Horizons* 3 (April).
"The Problem of Psalm 137." *Biblical Horizons* 3 (April). Polish: "Psalm 137." Trans. Bogumil Jarmulak. *Reformacja w Polsce* 6.2–3 (June 2004). Online: http://www.reformacja.pl/index.php/artykuly-autorzy/83-james-b-jordan/475-07-02-03-2004.
"Advice from a Sojourner, Part 1." *Biblical Horizons* 4 (May).
"The Beatitudes and Woes." *Biblical Horizons* 4 (May).
"The Son of Joseph, Revisited." *Biblical Horizons* 4 (May).
"The Love Feast." *Rite Reasons: Studies in Worship* 2 (June).
"Elijah's War with Baal." *Biblical Horizons* 5 (July). Polish: "Eliasz kontra Baal." Trans. Bogumil Jarmulak. *Reformacja w Polsce* 6.1 (March 2004). Online: http://www.reformacja.pl/index.php/artykuly-autorzy/83-james-b-jordan/474-06-01-2004.
"An Antidote for Yuppie Postmillennialism." *Biblical Horizons* 6 (August). Polish: "Antidotum na postmilenijnych japiszonow." Trans. Sebastian Smolarz. *Reformacja w Polsce* 10.2 (May 2008). Online: http://www.reformacja.pl/index.php/artykuly-autorzy/83-james-b-jordan/497-12-02-2008.
"The Law of Forbidden Mixtures." Biblical Horizons Occasional Paper 6 (August).
"An Introduction to the Mosaic Dietary Laws." *Studies in Food and Faith* 1 (August).
"Observations on the Bible and Health." *Studies in Food and Faith* 2 (August).
"On Boiling Meat in Milk." *Studies in Food and Faith* 3 (August).
"The Approach of the Church Fathers to the Dietary Laws of Moses." *Studies in Food and Faith* 4 (August).
"Interpretation of the Mosaic Dietary Laws: A Survey." *Studies in Food and Faith* 5 (August).
"Theses on Worship, Part 1." *Rite Reasons: Studies in Worship* 3 (September).
"The Embarrassment of Biblical Chronology." *Biblical Chronology* 1.1 (October). Polish: "Klopoty z biblijna chronologia." Trans. Bogumil Jarmulak. *Reformacja w Polsce* 6.4 (November 2004). Online: http://www.reformacja.pl/index.php/artykuly-autorzy/83-james-b-jordan/476-04-04-2004.
"Advice from a Sojourner, Part 2." *Biblical Horizons* 7 (October).
"The Tragedy of the Reagan Years." *Biblical Horizons* 7 (October).
"Thoughts from Nadia Boulanger." *Biblical Horizons* 7 (October).
"The History of Biblical Chronology." *Biblical Chronology* 1.2 (November).
"Advice from a Sojourner, Part 3." *Biblical Horizons* 8 (November).

"The Theology of Biblical Chronology." *Biblical Chronology* 1.3 (December).
"Theses on Worship, Part 2." *Rite Reasons: Studies in Worship* 4 (December).
Covenant Sequence in Leviticus and Deuteronomy. Tyler, TX: Institute for Christian Economics.
"The Holy War in America Today: Some Observations of Abortion Rescues." Views and Reviews: Open Book Occasional Paper 2.
"Should Christians Be 'Pro-Life'?" Included in Views and Reviews: Open Book Occasional Paper 2, but obviously photocopied from some other magazine which has not been identified.

1990

"The Capitulation of Biblical Chronology." *Biblical Chronology* 2.1 (January).
"What is 'Interpretive Maximalism'?" *Biblical Horizons* 9 (January).
"*Foucault's Pendulum*: A Book Note." *Biblical Horizons* 9 (January).
"Theses on Worship, Part 3." *Rite Reasons: Studies in Worship* 5 (January).
"Animals and the Bible." Studies in Food and Faith 6 (January).
"The Meaning of Eating in the Bible." Studies in Food and Faith 7 (January).
"Diet from Adam to Moses." Studies in Food and Faith 8 (January).
"The Tabernacle and the Dietary Laws." Studies in Food and Faith 9 (January).
"The Meaning of Clean and Unclean." Studies in Food and Faith 10 (January).
"The Meaning of the Mosaic Dietary Laws." Studies in Food and Faith 11 (January).
"The Mosaic Dietary Laws and the New Testament." Studies in Food and Faith 12 (January).
"An Exposition of Leviticus 11." Studies in Food and Faith 13 (January).
"Groping through the Gaps." *Biblical Chronology* 2.2 (February).
"Advice from a Sojourner, Part 4." *Biblical Horizons* 10 (February).
"Sidetracked by the Septuagint." *Biblical Chronology* 2.3 (March).
"Theses on Worship, Part 4." *Rite Reasons: Studies in Worship* 6 (March).
"The Second Cainan Question." *Biblical Chronology* 2.4 (April).
"Advice from a Sojourner, Part 5." *Biblical Horizons* 12 (April).
"The Arphaxad Connection." *Biblical Chronology* 2.5 (May).
"Advice from a Sojourner, Part 6." *Biblical Horizons* 13 (May).
"Theses on Worship, Part 5." *Rite Reasons: Studies in Worship* 7 (May).
"The Abraham Connection." *Biblical Chronology* 2.6 (June).
"Advice from a Sojourner, Part 7." *Biblical Horizons* 14 (June).
"The Moses Connection." *Biblical Chronology* 2.7 (July).
"The Dominion Trap." *Biblical Horizons* 15 (July).
"Theses on Worship, Part 6." *Rite Reasons: Studies in Worship* 8 (July). Polish: "Psalmy w nabozenstwie." Trans. Bogumil Jarmulak. *Reformacja w Polsce* 10.3–4 (October 2008). Online: http://www.reformacja.pl/index.php/artykuly-autorzy/83-james-b-jordan/501-06-03-04-2008.
"The Temple Connection." *Biblical Chronology* 2.8 (August).
"The Evangelical Cocaine Lobby." *Biblical Horizons* 16 (August).
Review: Cornelis van der Waal, *The Covenantal Gospel*. *Biblical Horizons* 16 (August).
"The Mysterious Numbers of Edwin R. Theile." *Biblical Chronology* 2.9 (September).
"The Unjust Steward Revisited." *Biblical Horizons* 17 (September).
"The Liturgy Trap (Part 1)." *Rite Reasons: Studies in Worship* 9 (September).
Review: Gregory Palamas. *The One Hundred and Fifty Chapters*. *Westminster Theological Journal* 52.2 (Fall): 394–96.
"Confusion among the Kings." *Biblical Chronology* 2.10 (October).
"Advice from a Sojourner (Part 8)." *Biblical Horizons* 18 (October).
"The Liturgy Trap (Part 2)." *Rite Reasons: Studies in Worship* 10 (October).
"The Babylonian Connection." *Biblical Chronology* 2.11 (November).
"Who Rules the Land? The Meaning of the Noahic Covenant (Part 1)." *Biblical Horizons* 19 (November).
"The Liturgy Trap (Part 3)." *Rite Reasons: Studies in Worship* 11 (November).
"Daniel's 70 Weeks." *Biblical Chronology* 2.12 (December).

"Who Rules the Land? The Meaning of the Mosaic Covenant (Part 2)." *Biblical Horizons* 20 (December). There is a mistake in the title: "Mosaic" should be "Noahic."

"The Liturgy Trap (Part 4)." *Rite Reasons: Studies in Worship* 12 (December).

Edited: John Calvin, *The Covenant Enforced: Sermons on Deuteronomy 27 and 28*. Tyler, TX: Institute for Christian Economics.

"Editor's Introduction." In John Calvin, *The Covenant Enforced: Sermons on Deuteronomy 27 and 28*, xxvii–xxxvii. Tyler, TX: Institute for Christian Economics.

Witness or Perish: Studies in the Book of Esther. Niceville, FL: Biblical Horizons. Syllabus to accompany lectures.

1991

"Whom Shall We Believe?" *Biblical Chronology* 3.1 (January).

"The Dominion Church." *Biblical Horizons* 21 (January).

"Advice from a Sojourner (Part 9)." *Biblical Horizons* 21 (January).

"Understanding Russia." *Open Book* 1 (January). Review of Ewa Majewska Thompson: *Understanding Russia: The Holy Fool in Russian Culture*.

Anti-Utopianism in Modern Conservative Thought: Some Criticisms of Thomas Molnar and Eric Voegelin. Niceville, FL: Biblical Horizons, January. Originally written in 1978.

Christ in His Supper: Two Essays. Niceville, FL: Biblical Horizons, January. Includes "Forerunners of Reformation Sacramental Theory: Ratramnus of Corbie and Berengarius of Tours" and "The Presence of Christ in the Eucharist: Thoughts Arising from Nevin's *The Mystical Presence*," both originally written in 1980.

The Love Feast in the Early Church. Niceville, FL: Biblical Horizons, January. Originally written in 1975.

"The Chronology of Ezra & Nehemiah (I)." *Biblical Chronology* 3.2 (February).

"Three 'Falls' and Three Heroes." *Biblical Horizons* 22 (February).

"Theosniglets & Theoneologisms." *Biblical Horizons* 22 (February).

"Theses on Worship, Part 7." *Rite Reasons: Studies in Worship* 13 (February).

"The Chronology of Ezra & Nehemiah (II)." *Biblical Chronology* 3.3 (March).

"The Whole Burnt Sacrifice: Its Liturgy and Meaning." Biblical Horizons Occasional Paper 11 (March).

"The Chronology of Ezra & Nehemiah (III)." *Biblical Chronology* 3.4 (April).

"Advice from a Sojourner (Part 10)." *Biblical Horizons* 24 (April).

"Advice from a Sojourner (Part 11)." *Biblical Horizons* 24 (April).

"Chariots of Water: An Exploration of the Water-Stands of Solomon's Temple." Biblical Horizons Occasional Paper 12 (April).

"Chariot of Fire: The Ordination of Ezekiel." Biblical Horizons Occasional Paper 13 (April).

"Theses on Worship, Part 8." *Rite Reasons: Studies in Worship* 14 (April).

"The Chronology of Ezra & Nehemiah (IV)." *Biblical Chronology* 3.5 (May).

"Advice from a Sojourner (Part 12)." *Biblical Horizons* 25 (May).

"The Abomination of Desolations Part 1: An Overview." *Biblical Horizons* 25 (May). Reprinted with revisions in *Studies in The Revelation* 0 (January 1997).

"The Framework Hypothesis." *Biblical Chronology* 3.6 (June).

"The Abomination of Desolation Part 2: The Man of Sin." *Biblical Horizons* 26 (June). Reprinted with revisions in *Studies in The Revelation* 0 (January 1997).

"The Abomination of Desolation Part 3: An Overview of the Pattern." *Biblical Horizons* 26 (June). Reprinted with revisions in *Studies in The Revelation* 0 (January 1997).

"Theses on Worship, Part 9." *Rite Reasons: Studies in Worship* 15 (June).

"What About the 'Seventh Ecumenical Council?'" *Rite Reasons: Studies in Worship* 15 (June).

"Deuteronomy." *Tabletalk* 15.6 (June): 28–29.

"Chronologies and Kings (I)." *Biblical Chronology* 3.7 (July).

"The Future of Israel Reexamined (Part 1)." *Biblical Horizons* 27 (July).

"Chronologies and Kings (II)." *Biblical Chronology* 3.8 (August).

"The Future of Israel Reexamined (Part 2)." *Biblical Horizons* 28 (August).

"Chronologies and Kings (III)." *Biblical Chronology* 3.9 (September).

"The Future of Israel Reexamined (Part 3)." *Biblical Horizons* 29 (September).
"Symposium on a Christian Political Party." *The Christian Statesman* 134.5 (September–October).
"Arts & Play (I)." *Open Book* 5 (September). Polish: "Sztuka i zabawa, cz.1." Trans. Bogumil Jarmulak. *Reformacja w Polsce* 9.3 (September 2007). Online: http://www.reformacja.pl/index.php/artykuly-autorzy/83-james-b-jordan/492-07-03-2007.
"Solomon's Disastrous Geopolitics (Chronologies and Kings IV)." *Biblical Chronology* 3.10 (October).
"What About Boycotting?" *Biblical Horizons* 30 (October).
"Testimonies of Two Witnesses (Chronologies and Kings V)." *Biblical Chronology* 3.11 (November).
"The Abomination of Desolation Part 4a: Abominable and Detestable." *Biblical Horizons* 31 (November). Reprinted with revisions in *Studies in The Revelation* 0 (January 1997).
"Arts & Play (II)." *Open Book* 6 (November). Polish: "Sztuka i zabawa, cz.2." Trans. Bogumil Jarmulak. *Reformacja w Polsce* 9.4 (December 2007). Online: http://www.reformacja.pl/index.php/artykuly-autorzy/83-james-b-jordan/495-04-04-2007.
"The Formation of the Remnant (Chronologies and Kings VI)." *Biblical Chronology* 3.12 (December).
"The Original Low-Down Filthy Male Chauvinist Pig-Dog." *Biblical Horizons* 32 (December).
"The Abomination of Desolation Part 4b: Abominable and Detestable." *Biblical Horizons* 32 (December). Reprinted with revisions in *Studies in The Revelation* 0 (January 1997).
Ezekiel: Eighteen Lectures. Niceville, FL: Biblical Horizons. Syllabus to accompany lectures.
Van Til and the Greeks. Niceville, FL: Biblical Horizons. Originally written in 1977.

1992

"The Assyrian Eponym Canon (Chronologies and Kings VII)." *Biblical Chronology* 4.1 (January).
"Thoughts on Euthanasia and Suicide." *Biblical Horizons* 33 (January).
"Christianity in the Science Fiction of 'Cordwainer Smith.'" *Contra Mundum* 2 (Winter): 34–38. This is a reprint of an essay already mentioned as available for sale in *Reformed Heritage* 3 (July 1986) and obviously written prior to that.
"Arts & Play (III)." *Open Book* 7 (January). Polish: "Sztuka i zabawa, cz.3." Trans. Bogumil Jarmulak. *Reformacja w Polsce* 10.1 (February 2008). Online: http://www.reformacja.pl/index.php/artykuly-autorzy/83-james-b-jordan/496-10-01-2008.
"Ahab and Assyria (Chronologies and Kings VIII)." *Biblical Chronology* 4.2 (February).
"The Resurrection of Peter and the Coming of the Kingdom." *Biblical Horizons* 34 (February). Polish: "Zmartwychwstanie Piotra i nastanie Krolestwa." Trans. Sebastian Smolarz. *Reformacja w Polsce* 7.1 (February 2005). Online: http://www.reformacja.pl/index.php/artykuly-autorzy/83-james-b-jordan/477-01-01-2005.
"Advice." *Rite Reasons: Studies in Worship* 19 (February).
"Jehu, Hazael, and Assyria (Chronologies and Kings IX)." *Biblical Chronology* 4.3 (March).
"Words and Glory." *The Christian Statesman* 135.2 (March–April): 26–27. Reprinted in *Open Book* 21 (1994).
"Apologia on Reading the Bible." *Contra Mundum* 3 (Spring): 28–36. Reprinted: Views and Reviews: Open Book Occasional Paper 11. Polish: "Apologia czytania Biblii." Trans. Bogumil Jarmulak. *Reformacja w Polsce* 12.1-2 (November 2010): 5–26. Online: http://www.reformacja.pl/nr-2010-1-2/apologia-czytania-biblii-james-b-jordan.html.
"Arts & Play (IIII)." *Open Book* 8 (March). Polish: "Sztuka i zabawa, cz.4." Trans. Bogumil Jarmulak. *Reformacja w Polsce* 10.2 (May 2007). Online: http://www.reformacja.pl/index.php/artykuly-autorzy/83-james-b-jordan/498-09-02-2008.
"Jehoram of Judah (Chronologies and Kings X)." *Biblical Chronology* 4.4 (April).
"Tentmaking." *Biblical Horizons* 36 (April).
"The Knots of II Kings 11–14 (Chronologies and Kings XI)." *Biblical Chronology* 4.5 (May).
"Wars and Rumors of Wars (Chronologies and Kings XII)." *Biblical Chronology* 4.6 (June).
"A Letter on Paedocommunion." *Rite Reasons: Studies in Worship* 21 (June).
"The End of the Kingdom of Judah (Chronologies and Kings XIII)." *Biblical Chronology* 4.7 (July).
"The Lamb of God (Part 1)." *Biblical Horizons* 39 (July).
"Eve as Artist." The Christian Statesman 135.4 (July–August): 46–48. Reprinted as "The Bride as Artist." *Open Book* 21 (1994).

"A Summary of Old Testament Chronology." *Biblical Chronology* 4.8 (August).
"Robert E. Dwelle." *Biblical Horizons* 40 (August).
"The Lamb of God (Part 2)." *Biblical Horizons* 40 (August).
"*Worship in the Presence of God*: A Review (Part 1)." *Rite Reasons: Studies in Worship* 22 (August). These essays were collected in the book *Liturgical Nestorianism* (1994).
"Meredith G. Kline and the Myth of the Old Testament." *Biblical Chronology* 4.9–10 (September–October).
"The Firstborn Son's Double Portion." *Biblical Horizons* 42 (October).
"Entropy and Depravity." *Biblical Horizons* 42 (October). Polish: "Entropia i deprawacja." Trans. Bogumil Jarmulak. *Reformacja w Polsce* 9.3 (September 2007). Online: http://www.reformacja.pl/index.php/artykuly-autorzy/83-james-b-jordan/493-06-03-2007.
"*Worship in the Presence of God*: A Review (Part 2)." *Rite Reasons: Studies in Worship* 23 (October).
"Bridging the Last Gap: Daniel's Seventy Weeks Revisited." *Biblical Chronology* 4.11 (November).
"Leviticus 27." *Biblical Horizons* 43 (November).
"The Enoch Factor." *The Christian Statesman* 135.6 (November–December): 23–24. Reprinted in *Open Book* 21 (1994).
"Sophomoric Theologians Versus the Mystery of Art (Part 1)." *Open Book* 12 (November).
"Chronology of the Gospels." *Biblical Chronology* 4.12 (December).
"The Restrainer." *Biblical Horizons* 44 (December). Polish: "Strofowanie." Trans. Bogumil Jarmulak. *Reformacja w Polsce* 7.2–3 (August 2005). Online: http://www.reformacja.pl/index.php/artykuly-autorzy/83-james-b-jordan/478-02-02-03-2005.
"*Worship in the Presence of God*: A Review (Part 3)." *Rite Reasons: Studies in Worship* 24 (December).
"Gene Wolfe Interview." Online: http://mysite.verizon.net/~vze2tmhh/wolfejbj.html. Reprinted in *Shadows of the New Sun: Wolfe on Writing / Writers on Wolfe*, ed. Peter Wright, 101–31. Liverpool Science Fiction Texts and Studies. Liverpool: Liverpool University Press, 2007.
Pig Out? 25 Reasons Why Christians May Eat Pork. Niceville, FL: Transfiguration Press. 2nd ed., slightly revised,1998.

1993

"Problems with New Testament History." *Biblical Chronology* 5.1 (January).
"On Blood Transfusions and Organ Transplantations." *Biblical Reflections on Modern Medicine* 41 (January): 6–7. This is a titled and lengthy letter to the editor.
"Sophomoric Theologians Versus the Mystery of Art (Part 2)." *Open Book* 13 (January).
"Jubilee, Part 1." *Biblical Chronology* 5.2 (February).
"The 'Seven-Point Covenant Model': Notes on Work in Progress (Part 1)." *Biblical Horizons* 46 (February).
"*Worship in the Presence of God*: A Review (Part 4)." *Rite Reasons: Studies in Worship* 25 (February).
"Jubilee, Part 2." *Biblical Chronology* 5.3 (March).
"The 'Seven-Point Covenant Model': Notes on Work in Progress (Part 2)." *Biblical Horizons* 47 (March).
"The Geocentricity Question." *Contra Mundum* 7 (Spring): 28–32. Reprinted, with slight revisions, from *The Biblical Educator* 3.12 (December 1981):1–4. Reprinted again in *Open Book* 46 (June 1999).
"666: Deciphered at Last!" [by "Metron V. Nodrojianishvili."] *The BEAST Report* 1 (April 1).
"Jubilee, Part 3." *Biblical Chronology* 5.4 (April).
"The 'Seven-Point Covenant Model': Notes on Work in Progress (Part 3)." *Biblical Horizons* 48 (April).
"*Worship in the Presence of God*: A Review (Part 5)." *Rite Reasons: Studies in Worship* 26 (April).
"The 'Seven-Point Covenant Model': Notes on Work in Progress (Part 4)." *Biblical Horizons* 49 (May).
"On the Making of Books (Part 1)." *Open Book* 15 (May).
"The 'Seven-Point Covenant Model': Notes on Work in Progress (Part 5)." *Biblical Horizons* 50 (June).
"A Note on Exodus 22:31." *Biblical Horizons* 50 (June).
"Pro-Life Rhetoric and Tactics: A Critical Reassessment." *Contra Mundum* 8 (Summer): 34–40. Views and Reviews: Open Book Occasional Paper 12.
"*Worship in the Presence of God*: A Review (Part 6)." *Rite Reasons: Studies in Worship* 27 (June).
"On the Making of Books (Part 2)." *Open Book* 16 (July).
"Observations on the Covenant of Works Doctrine." *Biblical Horizons* 52 (August).
"*Worship in the Presence of God*: A Review (Part 7: The Psalter)." *Rite Reasons: Studies in Worship* 28 (August).

"1994?—Not! (Part 1)." *Biblical Chronology* 5.5 (September).
"Thoughts on the 'Covenant of Works' (Part 2)." *Biblical Horizons* 53 (September).
"The Bible and Family Planning: An Answer to Charles Provan's *The Bible and Birth Control*." *Contra Mundum* 9 (Fall): 2–14. Also: Views and Reviews: Open Book Occasional Paper 13.
"Returning to The Village." *Open Book* 17 (September). Review of Matthew White & Jaffer Ali, *The Official Prisoner Companion* and Dean Motter, *The Prisoner* (graphic novel).
Review: *Metropolis*. *Open Book* 17 (September).
"1994?—Not! (Part 2)." *Biblical Chronology* 5.6 (October).
"The Woman's Head Covering in 1 Corinthians 11:2–16." *Biblical Horizons* 54 (October).
"*Worship in the Presence of God*: A Review (Part 8)." *Rite Reasons: Studies in Worship* 29 (October).
"Anglicanism." *Rite Reasons: Studies in Worship* 29 (October).
"The New Earth." *Tabletalk* 17.10 (October): 13–15.
"1994?—Not! (Part 3)." *Biblical Chronology* 5.7 (November).
"Born from Above." *Biblical Horizons* 55 (November).
"The Trinity Review." *Biblical Horizons* 55 (November).
"Graphic Novels." *Open Book* 18 (November). Review of Frank Miller, *The Dark Knight Returns*; Alan Moore & David Gibbons, *Watchmen*; and Timothy Truman, *Hawkworld*.
"Egypt in Biblical History." *Biblical Chronology* 5.8 (December).
"The Production of the New Testament Canon: A Revisionist Suggestion." *Biblical Horizons* 56 (December). Online: http://biblicalhorizons.wordpress.com/2008/02/14/an-older-essay-on-the-gospel-order/.
"The Peril of Weekly Communion." *Rite Reasons: Studies in Worship* 30 (December).
Advice from a Sojourner: Humility and Dominion in Proverbs 30. Niceville, FL: Transfiguration Press.

1994

"The Egyptian Problem." *Biblical Chronology* 6.1 (January).
"*Through New Eyes*, Volume II." *Biblical Horizons* 57 (January).
"The Jubilee and Biblical Chronology." Biblical Horizons Occasional Paper 16 (January).
Review: *Greystoke*. *Open Book* 19 (January).
"Two by Hitchcock." *Open Book* 19 (January). Review of *I Confess* and *Rope*.
Review: *2001: A Space Odyssey*. *Open Book* 19 (January).
"Problems with Current Consensus Chronology." *Biblical Chronology* 6.2 (February).
"*Through New Eyes*, Volume II (conclusion)." *Biblical Horizons* 58 (February).
"The First Word." *Rite Reasons: Studies in Worship* 31 (February).
"The Chronology of the Pentateuch (Part 1)." *Biblical Chronology* 6.3 (March).
"*Shadowlands*: Afterthoughts." *Open Book* 20 (March).
"The Chronology of the Pentateuch (Part 2)." *Biblical Chronology* 6.4 (April).
"PROLIFISM: A New Humanism." *Biblical Horizons* 60 (April).
"The New Age Food Threat." [by "Merri Perrier."] *The FEAST Report* 1 (April 1).
"The First Word (conclusion)." *Rite Reasons: Studies in Worship* 32 (April).
"Not in '94!" Biblical Horizons Occasional Paper 17. No date is given for this paper, but it must have been published between January (when Occasional Paper 16 was published) and August (when Occasional Paper 18 was published).
"The Chronology of the Pentateuch (Part 3)." *Biblical Chronology* 6.5 (May).
"Thousands of Generations." *Biblical Horizons* 61 (May). Polish: "Tysiace poloken." Trans. Bogumil Jarmulak. *Reformacja w Polsce* 9.3 (September 2007). Online: http://www.reformacja.pl/index.php/artykuly-autorzy/83-james-b-jordan/494-03-03-2007.
"Broadening Our View of the Trinity." *Biblical Horizons* 61 (May).
"Words and Glory." *Open Book* 21 (May).
"The Bride as Artist." *Open Book* 21 (May).
"The Enoch Factor." *Open Book* 21 (May).
"The Chronology of the Pentateuch (Part 4)." *Biblical Chronology* 6.6 (June).
"Thinking About Church History." *Biblical Horizons* 62 (June).
"Daniel 12:2." *Biblical Horizons* 62 (June).

"The Second Word I: Seeing and Hearing." *Rite Reasons: Studies in Worship* 33 (June).
"The Chronology of the Pentateuch (Part 5)." *Biblical Chronology* 6.7 (July).
"Human Life in Four Directions." *Biblical Horizons* 63 (July).
"A Short Survey of Good Fantasy and Science Fiction for Christian Schools and Home Schools." *Open Book* 22 (July).
"The Chronology of the Pentateuch (Part 6)." *Biblical Chronology* 6.8 (August).
"The Grape Harvest of Revelation 14:17–20." *Biblical Horizons* 64 (August). Reprinted with revisions in *Studies in The Revelation* 0 (January 1997).
"The Future of Israel Reconsidered: A Preterist View of Romans 11." Biblical Horizons Occasional Paper 18 (August).
"The Second Word II: Seeing and Hearing; Exposition." *Rite Reasons: Studies in Worship* 34 (August).
"Covenants and Dates." *Biblical Chronology* 6.9 (September).
"The Kings from the East." *Biblical Horizons* 65 (September). Reprinted with revisions in *Studies in The Revelation* 0 (January 1997).
"An Apology Concerning YWAM." *Biblical Horizons* 65 (September).
"Genesis 5 & 11: Theological Reflections." *Biblical Chronology* 6.10 (October).
"The Seven Thunders: An Interpretive Suggestion." *Biblical Horizons* 66 (October). Reprinted with revisions in *Studies in The Revelation* 0 (January 1997).
"The Last Eight Visions of Revelation." *Biblical Horizons* 66 (October). Reprinted with revisions in *Studies in The Revelation* 0 (January 1997).
"The Second Word III: Exposition; Implications." *Rite Reasons: Studies in Worship* 35 (October).
"Genesis 5 & 11: Chronological-Theological Reflections (Part 2)." *Biblical Chronology* 6.11 (November).
"Daniel: Historical & Chronological Comments (I)." *Biblical Chronology* 6.12 (December).
"Peter as High Priest." *Biblical Horizons* 68 (December).
"Jesus' Burial Clothes." *Biblical Horizons* 68 (December).
"The Girding of Peter." *Biblical Horizons* 68 (December).
"The Second Word IV: Implications." *Rite Reasons: Studies in Worship* 36 (December).
Crisis, Opportunity, and the Christian Future. Niceville, FL: Transfiguration Press. 2nd ed., slightly revised, 1998. 3rd ed., Monroe, LA: Athanasius Press, 2009.
Liturgical Nestorianism and the Regulative Principle: A Critical Review of Worship in the Presence of God. Niceville, FL: Transfiguration Press. 2nd ed., slightly revised, 2000. Reprints *Rite Reasons* 22–29.
The Liturgy Trap: The Bible vs. Mere Tradition in Worship. Niceville, FL: Transfiguration Press. 2nd ed., slightly revised, 1998. 3rd ed., slightly revised, Monroe, LA: Athanasius Press, 2008.
A Preliminary Commentary on the Book of Daniel. Niceville, FL: Biblical Horizons. The actual title on the document itself is *A Preliminarie Chronological, Historical, Literary, & Theological Commentarie Vpon the Booke of the Prophecies of Daniel, to which are appended various Tables and Chartes shewing the times in which the Prophet lived & of which hee spoke*.
Revelation Chapter 1: A Preliminary Commentary. Syllabus to accompany lectures.
Theses on Worship: Notes Toward the Reformation of Worship. Niceville, FL: Transfiguration Press. 2nd ed, slightly revised, 1998. Reprints *Rite Reasons* 3–8, 13–15.

1995

"Daniel: Historical & Chronological Comments (II)." *Biblical Chronology* 7.1 (January).
"Triune Revelation and Through New Eyes Volume 2." *Biblical Horizons* 69 (January).
"Mansions in the Sky: The Meaning of the Tabernacle." *Biblical Horizons* 69 (January).
"The Angels of Revelation." *Biblical Horizons* 69 (January). Reprinted with revisions in *Studies in The Revelation* 0 (January 1997).
"Eugen Rosenstock-Huessy: A Brief Introduction." *Open Book* 25 (January).
"Belling *The Bell Curve*." *Open Book* 25 (January).
"Sex and Power." *Open Book* 25 (January). [Note that there is a correction to this article in *Open Book* 26 (April 1996).]
"Daniel: Historical & Chronological Comments (III)." *Biblical Chronology* 7.2 (February).

"The Angels of Revelation (continued)." *Biblical Horizons* 70 (February). Reprinted with revisions in *Studies in The Revelation* 0 (January 1997).
"The Angelic Triads in Revelation." *Biblical Horizons* 70 (February). Reprinted with revisions in *Studies in The Revelation* 0 (January 1997).
"Daniel: Historical & Chronological Comments (IV)." *Biblical Chronology* 7.3 (March).
"The Angels in Revelation (Addendum)." *Biblical Horizons* 71 (March). Reprinted with revisions in *Studies in The Revelation* 0 (January 1997).
"The Hymn of the Revelation." *Rite Reasons: Studies in Worship* 38 (March).
"Daniel: Historical & Chronological Comments (V)." *Biblical Chronology* 7.4 (April).
"The Seven Seals of Revelation." *Biblical Horizons* 72 (April). Reprinted with revisions in *Studies in The Revelation* 0 (January 1997).
"Daniel: Historical & Chronological Comments (VI)." *Biblical Chronology* 7.5 (May).
"And the Holy of Holies Became Flesh." *Biblical Horizons* 73 (May). Polish: "Sanktuarium cialem sie stalo." Trans. Bogumil Jarmulak. *Reformacja w Polsce* 10.3–4 (September 2008). Online: http://www.reformacja.pl/index.php/artykuly-autorzy/83-james-b-jordan/503-02-03-04-2008.
"Are Not All These Galilaeans?" *Biblical Horizons* 73 (May).
"A Correction on Daniel 7." *Biblical Horizons* 73 (May).
"Who Were the Firstborn Sons?" *Biblical Horizons* 73 (May).
A Chronological and Calendrical Commentary on the Pentateuch. Biblical Horizons Occasional Paper 22 (May). Reprinted as Studies in Biblical Chronology 3 (October 2001).
"Behind the Scenes: Orientation in the Book of Revelation." Biblical Horizons Occasional Paper 19 (May). 2nd ed., May 1999.
"Eldership and Maturity (Part 1)." *Rite Reasons: Studies in Worship* 39 (May).
"Understanding the Mosaic Law: The Law's Multiple Dimensions." *Tabletalk* 19.5 (May): 8–10.
"Daniel: Historical & Chronological Comments (VII)." *Biblical Chronology* 7.6 (June).
"The Great Hangover (Part 1)." *Biblical Horizons* 74 (June).
"Daniel: Historical & Chronological Comments (VIII)." *Biblical Chronology* 7.7 (July).
"The Great Hangover (Part 2)." *Biblical Horizons* 75 (July).
"Eldership and Maturity (Part 2)." *Rite Reasons: Studies in Worship* 40 (July).
"Daniel: Historical & Chronological Comments (IX)." *Biblical Chronology* 7.8 (August).
"Daniel: Historical & Chronological Comments (X)." *Biblical Chronology* 7.9 (September).
"The Triune Office Reconsidered." *Rite Reasons: Studies in Worship* 41 (September).
"Daniel: Historical & Chronological Comments (XI)." *Biblical Chronology* 7.10 (October).
"Getting the Translation Right." *Biblical Horizons* 78 (October).
"Daniel: Historical & Chronological Comments (XII)." *Biblical Chronology* 7.11 (November).
"At the Center of the Book of Kings." With Peter J. Leithart. *Biblical Horizons* 79 (November).
"Dynastic Aspirations in the Book of Judges." *Biblical Horizons* 79 (November).
"Doing the Lord's Supper." *Rite Reasons: Studies in Worship* 42 (November).
"Daniel: Historical & Chronological Comments (XIII)." *Biblical Chronology* 7.12 (December).
"Rethinking the Order of the Old Testament." *Biblical Horizons* 80 (December).
Esther in the Midst of Covenant History. Niceville, Florida: Biblical Horizons. 2nd ed., slightly revised, 2001. The title on the document itself is *Esther in ye Midst of Couenant Historie (Being an Argvment that ye Booke of Esther is not a mere Side Light in ye Historie of GOD's Couenantal & Redemptiue Work, byt is an Indispensable Link in that Gloriovs Chaine; & that Darivs ye Greate is ye KING in Esther, being himself a newe Solomon; & inclvding a Briefe Commentarie vpon ye Whole)*.
"Psalm 150." Translation and music (ca. 1995).

1996

"Cosmos Constructors: An Investigation of the Tabernacle-Building Labors of Merari, Gershon, and Kohath as Recapitulations of Genesis One." Biblical Horizons Occasional Paper 24 (January).
"Daniel: Historical & Chronological Comments (XIV)." *Biblical Chronology* 8.1 (January).

"Concerning Contracts and Covenants." *Biblical Horizons* 81 (January). The newsletter has it as "by Eugen Rosenstock-Huessy and James B. Jordan," but the Rosenstock-Huessy contributions consist of some extended quotations.

"Hermeneutical Polytheism." *Biblical Horizons* 81 (January). Polish: "Hermeneutyczny politeizm." Trans. Bogumil Jarmulak. Online: http://jarmulak.com/?p=168.

"The Beasts of Revelation." *Studies in The Revelation* 1 (January).

"The Date of Revelation." *Studies in The Revelation* 1 (January).

"Daniel: Historical & Chronological Comments (XV)." *Biblical Chronology* 8.2 (February).

"Jesus at Belshazzar's Feast: Being an Explanatory Disquisition on an Aspect of the Story of the Woman Taken in Adultery." *Biblical Horizons* 82 (February).

"Like a Dove." *Biblical Horizons* 82 (February).

"What Is God?" *Biblical Horizons* 82 (February). Polish: "Jaki jest Bog?" Trans. Bogumil Jarmulak. Online: http://jarmulak.com/?p=222.

"The Beasts of Revelation (2)." *Studies in The Revelation* 2 (February).

"The Earthquakes of Revelation." *Studies in The Revelation* 2 (February).

"Esther: Historical & Chronological Comments (I)." *Biblical Chronology* 8.3 (March).

"A Letter on Geocentricity." *Biblical Horizons* 82 (March).

"Genesis 1 and Genesis 8." *Biblical Horizons* 83 (March).

Review: John Owen, *Biblical Theology*. *Biblical Horizons* 83 (March).

"The Beasts of Revelation (3)." *Studies in The Revelation* 3 (March).

"That You May Live Long." *Tabletalk* 20.3 (March):11–13. Reprinted in *Family Practice: God's Prescription for a Healthy Home*, ed. R. C. Sproul, Jr., 77–81. Phillipsburg: P&R Publishing, 2001.

"Esther: Historical & Chronological Comments (II)." *Biblical Chronology* 8.4 (April).

"Christ in the Holy of Holies: The Meaning of the Mount of Olives." *Biblical Horizons* 84 (April).

"The Beasts of Revelation (4)." *Studies in The Revelation* 4 (April).

"Esther: Historical & Chronological Comments (III)." *Biblical Chronology* 8.5 (May).

"Some Observations." *Biblical Horizons* 85 (May).

"The Beasts of Revelation (5)." *Studies in The Revelation* 5 (May).

"Men as Jews in Revelation." *Studies in The Revelation* 5 (May).

"Tribes, Tongues, Peoples, Nations." *Studies in The Revelation* 5 (May).

"Esther: Historical & Chronological Comments (IV)." *Biblical Chronology* 8.6 (June).

"Jesus and Amalek." *Biblical Horizons* 86 (June).

"Jephthah's Daughter." *Biblical Horizons* 86 (June).

Review: Isaac E. Mozeson, *The Word: The Dictionary that Reveals the Hebrew Sources of English*. *Open Book* 27 (June).

"The Beasts of Revelation (6)." *Studies in The Revelation* 6 (June).

"Jerusalem: From Old to New (1)." *Studies in The Revelation* 6 (June).

"Esther: Historical & Chronological Comments (V)." *Biblical Chronology* 8.7 (July).

"Concerning Colors, Architecture, and Sacraments." *Rite Reasons: Studies in Worship* 46 (July). This newsletter was misdated as July 1995.

"Jerusalem: The Old and New (2)." *Studies in The Revelation* 7 (July).

"The Oikumene." *Studies in The Revelation* 7 (July).

"Esther: Historical & Chronological Comments (VI)." *Biblical Chronology* 8.8 (August).

"Concerning Halloween." *Open Book* 28 (August). Reprinted as "Halloween: A Distinctively Christian Holiday: A Discernment Exercise." *Critique* 1 (2000). Online: http://www.ransomfellowship.org/articledetail.asp?AID=370&B=James%20Jordan&TID=8. Polish: "Odnosnie Halloween." Trans. Bogumil Jarmulak. *Reformacja w Polsce* 8.2–3 (September 2006). Online: http://www.reformacja.pl/index.php/artykuly-autorzy/83-james-b-jordan/482-08-02-03-2006.

"Concerning Unicorns." *Open Book* 28 (August).

"Fun Reading." *Open Book* 28 (August). Review of Harry Turtledove & Richard Dreyfuss, *The Two Georges* and Richard Garfinkle, *Celestial Matters*.

"The Bowls of Revelation (1)." *Studies in The Revelation* 8 (August).

"The Financial Metaphor in Revelation." *Studies in The Revelation* 8 (August).

"Countdown to Exile. I. Political Conservatives Versus the Christian Right." *Biblical Chronology* 8.9 (September).
"The Bowls of Revelation (2)." *Studies in The Revelation* 9 (September).
Review: Arthur M. Wainwright, *Mysterious Apocalypse: Interpreting the Book of Revelation*. *Studies in The Revelation* 9 (September).
Review: Archbishop Averky, *The Apocalypse of St. John: An Orthodox Commentary*. *Studies in The Revelation* 9 (September).
"Countdown to Exile. II. Rebellion Against God's Order." *Biblical Chronology* 8.10 (October).
"Jeremiah 52:28–30." *Biblical Horizons* 88 (October).
"Concerning the Nations." *Open Book* 29 (October).
"The Day of the Lord and Its 24 Hours." *Studies in The Revelation* 10 (October).
"Countdown to Exile. III. Warnings Against False Hopes." *Biblical Chronology* 8.11 (November).
"Music and Hermeneutics." *Biblical Horizons* 89 (November). Online: http://biblicalhorizons.wordpress.com/2008/04/05/music-and-hermeneutics/. Polish: "Muzyka i hermeneutyka." Trans. Bogumil Jarmulak. *Reformacja w Polsce* 9.2 (June 2007). Online: http://www.reformacja.pl/index.php/artykuly-autorzy/83-james-b-jordan/491-04-02-2007.
"Babylon and the Babel Project (1)." *Studies in The Revelation* 11 (November).
"Countdown to Exile. IV. Ezekiel and the Structure of History." *Biblical Chronology* 8.12 (December).
"The Oddness of the Feast of Booths." *Biblical Horizons* 90 (December).
"A Note on Matthew." *Biblical Horizons* 90 (December).
"Beginning and New Beginning in Luke." *Biblical Horizons* 90 (December).
"Twelve Fundamental Avenues of Revelation (Part 1)." *Open Book* 30 (December).
"Babylon and the Babel Project (2)." *Studies in The Revelation* 12 (December).
"For My Life." In *The Promise: Study Edition: Contemporary English Version*. Atlanta: Thomas Nelson. Brief comments on each chapter of the New Testament. Jordan's comments were shortened but are substantially what he wrote.
Samson the Mighty Bridegroom. Niceville, FL: Biblical Horizons. Syllabus to accompany lectures.

1997

"Countdown to Exile. V. The Destruction of Jerusalem." *Biblical Chronology* 9.1 (January).
"In the Fish; or, The Church as Tomb." *Biblical Horizons* 91 (January).
"Squaring Off and Crossing Up." *Biblical Horizons* 91 (January).
"The Angels of Revelation." *Studies in The Revelation* 0 (January). Reprinted with revisions from *Biblical Horizons* 69–71 (January–March 1995).
"The Seven Seals of Revelation." *Studies in The Revelation* 0 (January). Reprinted with revisions from *Biblical Horizons* 72 (April 1995).
"The Grape Harvest of Revelation 14:17–20." *Studies in The Revelation* 0 (January). Reprinted with revisions from *Biblical Horizons* 64 (August 1994).
"The Kings from the East." *Studies in The Revelation* 0 (January). Reprinted with revisions from *Biblical Horizons* 65 (September 1994).
"The Seven Thunders: An Interpretive Suggestion." *Studies in The Revelation* 0 (January). Reprinted with revisions from *Biblical Horizons* 66 (October 1994).
"The Last Eight Visions of Revelation." *Studies in The Revelation* 0 (January). Reprinted with revisions from *Biblical Horizons* 66 (October 1994).
"Studies in the Abomination of Desolation." *Studies in The Revelation* 0 (January). Reprinted with revisions from *Biblical Horizons* 25–26, 31–32 (May–June, November–December 1991).
"Babylon and the Babylon Project (3)." *Studies in The Revelation* 13 (January).
"Meredith G. Kline Strikes Back." *Biblical Chronology* 9.2 (February).
"A Blossom of Yahweh's Field." *Biblical Horizons* 92 (February).
"The Allegory of Susanna." *Biblical Horizons* 92 (February).
"Twelve Fundamental Avenues of Revelation (Part 2)." *Open Book* 31 (February).
"Babylon and the Babel Project (4)." *Studies in The Revelation* 14 (February).
"Meredith G. Kline Strikes Back, Part 2." *Biblical Chronology* 9.3 (March).

"Bathsheba: The Real Story." *Biblical Horizons* 93 (March). Polish: "Batszeba—jak bylo naprawde?" Trans. Bogumil Jarmulak. *Reformacja w Polsce* 5.4 (December 2003). Online: http://www.reformacja.pl/index.php/artykuly-autorzy/83-james-b-jordan/473-10-04-2003.
"An Alphabetical Psalm." *Rite Reasons: Studies in Worship* 50 (March).
"Babylon and the Babel Project (5)." *Studies in The Revelation* 15 (March).
"John Sailhamer Weighs In (I)." *Biblical Chronology* 9.4 (April).
"Toward a Chiastic Understanding of the Gospel According to Matthew (Part 1)." *Biblical Horizons* 94 (April). Reprinted in "Structures of the Gospel According to Matthew." Biblical Horizons Occasional Paper 38 (December 2010).
"Twelve Fundamental Avenues of Revelation (Part 3)." *Open Book* 32 (April).
"Jesus' First Eschatological Discourse (1)." *Studies in The Revelation* 16 (April).
"John Sailhamer Weighs In (II)." *Biblical Chronology* 9.5 (May).
"Toward a Chiastic Understanding of the Gospel According to Matthew (Part 2)." *Biblical Horizons* 95 (May). Reprinted in "Structures of the Gospel According to Matthew." Biblical Horizons Occasional Paper 38 (December 2010).
"Jesus' First Eschatological Discourse (2)." *Studies in The Revelation* 17 (May).
"John Sailhamer Weighs In (III)." *Biblical Chronology* 9.6 (June).
"The Sin of Ham and the Curse of Canaan (Part 1): An Exposition of Genesis 9:20–27." *Biblical Horizons* 96 (June).
"Twelve Fundamental Avenues of Revelation (Part 4)." *Open Book* 33 (June).
"Jesus' First Eschatological Discourse (3)." *Studies in The Revelation* 18 (June).
"John Sailhamer Weighs In (IV)." *Biblical Chronology* 9.7 (July).
"The Sin of Ham and the Curse of Canaan (Part 2): An Exposition of Genesis 9:20–27." *Biblical Horizons* 97 (July).
"Countdown to Exile: The End of the Kingdom of Judah." Biblical Horizons Occasional Paper 26 (July).
"Jesus' First Eschatological Discourse (4)." *Studies in The Revelation* 19 (July).
"Studies in the 'Abomination of Desolation' [chs. 5–6]." *Studies in The Revelation* 19 (July). The first four chapters of this essay were published in *Studies in The Revelation* 0 (January 1997).
"The Anthropomorphic Days of C. John Collins (I)." *Biblical Chronology* 9.8 (August).
"The Sin of Ham and the Curse of Canaan (Part 3): An Exposition of Genesis 9:20–27." *Biblical Horizons* 98 (August).
"Twelve Fundamental Avenues of Revelation (Part 5)." *Open Book* 34 (August).
"Jesus' First Eschatological Discourse (5)." *Studies in The Revelation* 20 (August).
"Studies in the 'Abomination of Desolation' [ch. 7]." *Studies in The Revelation* 20 (August).
"The Anthropomorphic Days of C. John Collins (II)." *Biblical Chronology* 9.9 (September).
"Psalms for Exile: The Narrative Progression in the Fifth Book of the Psalter." *Rite Reasons: Studies in Worship* 53 (September). Polish: "Piata ksiega Psalmow." Trans. Bogumil Jarmulak. *Reformacja w Polsce* 10.3–4 (October 2008). Online: http://www.reformacja.pl/index.php/artykuly-autorzy/83-james-b-jordan/500-07-03-04-2008.
"Studies in the Abomination of Desolation [ch. 8]." *Studies in The Revelation* 21 (September).
"The Sequence of Events in the Creation Week (I)." *Biblical Chronology* 9.10 (October).
"Cracking Up the 'Bible Code.'" *Open Book* 35 (October).
"*The Empire Strikes Back*: Some Notes." *Open Book* 35 (October).
"The Case Against Western Civilization Part 1: Introduction." *Open Book* 36 (October).
"Studies in the Abomination of Desolation [ch. 8, cont'd]." *Studies in The Revelation* 22 (October).
"Jesus' First Eschatological Discourse (6)." *Studies in The Revelation* 22 (October).
"The Sequence of Events in the Creation Week (II)." *Biblical Chronology* 9.11 (November).
"The Structure of the Psalter: Some Observations." *Rite Reasons: Studies in Worship* 54 (November).
"The Coming of the Son of Man (1)." *Studies in The Revelation* 23 (November).
"The Sequence of Events in the Creation Week (III)." *Biblical Chronology* 9.12 (December).
"The Case Against Western Civilization Part 2: The Enoch Factor; Part 3: Philosophy." *Open Book* 37 (December).
"The Coming of the Son of Man (2)." *Studies in The Revelation* 24 (December).
"Jesus' First Eschatological Discourse (7)." *Studies in The Revelation* 24 (December).

ed., *Christendom Essays*. Niceville, FL: Transfiguration Press. This is also *Biblical Horizons* 100 (December).

"The Fourth Book of the Psalter." In *Christendom Essays*, ed. James B. Jordan, 136–73. Niceville, FL: Transfiguration Press.

1998

"Waltke on Genesis One." *Biblical Chronology* 10.1 (January).
"A Brief Reader's Guide to Revelation, Part 1." *Biblical Horizons* 101 (January).
"A Visionary Liturgy (Part 1)." *Rite Reasons: Studies in Worship* 55 (January).
"The Gates of Nehemiah's Holy City." *Studies in The Revelation* 25 (January).
"Jesus' First Eschatological Discourse (8)." *Studies in The Revelation* 25 (January).
"Dr. Waltke on Genesis One, Concluded." *Biblical Chronology* 10.2 (February).
"A Brief Reader's Guide to Revelation, Part 2." *Biblical Horizons* 102 (February).
"The Case Against Western Civilization Part 3: Philosophy (continued)." *Open Book* 38 (February).
"Proleptic Consummation." *Studies in The Revelation* 26 (February).
"Jesus' First Eschatological Discourse (9)." *Studies in The Revelation* 26 (February).
"Stanley Jaki on Genesis One." *Biblical Chronology* 10.3 (March).
"A Brief Reader's Guide to Revelation, Part 3." *Biblical Horizons* 103 (March).
"A Visionary Liturgy (Part 2)." *Rite Reasons: Studies in Worship* 56 (March).
"Studies in the Abomination of Desolation [ch. 9]." *Studies in The Revelation* 27 (March).
"Jesus' First Eschatological Discourse (9 [cont'd])." *Studies in The Revelation* 27 (March).
"Seely on the Waters." *Biblical Chronology* 10.4 (April).
"A Brief Reader's Guide to Revelation, Part 4." *Biblical Horizons* 104 (April).
"The Case Against Western Civilization Part 4: The Nephilim Factor." *Open Book* 39 (April).
Review: *Gattaca*. *Open Book* 39 (April).
"Jesus' First Eschatological Discourse (10)." *Studies in The Revelation* 28 (April).
"Studies in the Abomination of Desolation [ch. 10]." *Studies in The Revelation* 28 (April). This essay is also part of "Jesus' First Eschatological Discourse (10)." The two series of essays overlap here.
"Chronology and Gnosticism." *Biblical Chronology* 10.5 (May).
"A Brief Reader's Guide to Revelation, Part 5." *Biblical Horizons* 105 (May).
"The Second Word V: On Images and Art (1)." *Rite Reasons: Studies in Worship* 57 (May).
"The Destruction of Jerusalem: A Comparative Chronology." *Studies in The Revelation* 29 (May).
"Jesus' First Eschatological Discourse (11)." *Studies in The Revelation* 29 (May).
"The Moses Connection." *Biblical Chronology* 10.6 (June).
"A Brief Reader's Guide to Revelation, Part 6." *Biblical Horizons* 106 (June).
"The Case Against Western Civilization Part 5: Laying New Foundations in a Dying World." *Open Book* 40 (June).
"Jesus' First Eschatological Discourse (12)." *Studies in The Revelation* 30 (June).
"Puzzling Out the Era of the Judges." *Biblical Chronology* 10.7 (July).
"The Framework Hypothesis: A Gnostic Heresy." *Biblical Horizons* 107 (July).
"Re-creation in the Ascension Offering." *Biblical Horizons* 107 (July).
"The Second Word V: On Images and Art (2)." *Rite Reasons: Studies in Worship* 58 (July).
"Jesus' First Eschatological Discourse (13)." *Studies in The Revelation* 31 (July).
"The Problem of Saul's Reign." *Biblical Chronology* 10.8 (August).
"Patriarchal Dominion." *Biblical Horizons* 108 (August).
"The Case Against Western Civilization Part 5: Living in a Dying World (continued)." *Open Book* 41 (August).
"Jesus' First Eschatological Discourse (14)." *Studies in The Revelation* 32 (August).
"The Seven Letters as Anticipations of the Book of Revelation as a Whole." *Studies in The Revelation* 32 (August).
"The Date of Creation, Chapter 1, Part 1: Ancient World Chronology and the Bible." *Biblical Chronology* 10.9 (September).
"Crisis Time: Patriarchal Prologue (1)." *Biblical Horizons* 109 (September).
"The Second Word V: On Images and Art (3)." *Rite Reasons: Studies in Worship* 59 (September).
"Ten Historical and Prophetic Charts." *Studies in The Revelation* 33 (September).

"The Date of Creation, Chapter 1, Part 2: Conclusion (Sothic Dating)." *Biblical Chronology* 10.10 (October).
"Crisis Time: Patriarchal Prologue (2): Abraham and Joshua." *Biblical Horizons* 110 (October).
"The Case Against Western Civilization (7) Part 5: Laying New Foundations in a Dying World (continued)." *Open Book* 42 (October).
"Jesus' First Eschatological Discourse (15)." *Studies in The Revelation* 34 (October).
"The Date of Creation, Chapter 2: The Embarrassment of Biblical Chronology." *Biblical Chronology* 10.11 (November).
"Crisis Time: Patriarchal Prologue (3): Jacob and Solomon." *Biblical Horizons* 111 (November).
"The Third Word." *Rite Reasons: Studies in Worship* 60 (November).
"Jesus' First Eschatological Discourse (16)." *Studies in The Revelation* 35 (November).
"The Date of Creation, Chapter 3: The Departure from Biblical Chronology." *Biblical Chronology* 10.12 (December).
"Crisis Time: Patriarchal Prologue (4): Joseph and Esther." *Biblical Horizons* 112 (December).
"Buchanan and Free Trade." *Open Book* 43 (December).
Review: David Gress, *From Plato to NATO: The Idea of the West and Its Critics*. *Open Book* 43 (December).
"Jesus' First Eschatological Discourse (17)." *Studies in The Revelation* 36 (December).
Psalter Book 3. Privately distributed.

1999

"The Date of Creation, Chapter 4, Part 1: Covenants and Dates, Part 1." *Biblical Chronology* 113 (January).
"Crisis Time: Patriarchal Prologue (5): Moses and Jesus." *Biblical Horizons* 113 (January).
"The Date of Creation, Chapter 4, Part 2: Covenants and Dates, Part 2." *Biblical Chronology* 114 (February).
"Additional Notes on Musical Instruments." *Biblical Horizons* 114 (February).
"Neo-Tribalism and the Kosovar Situation." *Open Book* 44 (February).
"The Date of Creation, Chapter 5: Chronology and Gnosticism." *Biblical Chronology* 115 (March).
"An Additional Note." *Biblical Horizons* 115 (March).
"Baptismal Rain and the Feast of Booths." *Biblical Horizons* 115 (March).
"The Revelation of Jesus in Revelation 1:12b–16 (Part 1)." *Studies in The Revelation* 37 (Spring).
"Jesus' First Eschatological Discourse (18–19)." *Studies in The Revelation* 37 (Spring).
Review: R. C. Sproul, *The Last Days According to Jesus*. *Studies in The Revelation* 37 (Spring).
"The Date of Creation, Chapter 6: The Days of Genesis One." *Biblical Chronology* 116 (April).
"Lot: Meditations." *Biblical Horizons* 116 (April). Polish: "Lot." Trans. Bogumil Jarmulak. *Reformacja w Polsce* 8.4 (December 2006). Online: http://www.reformacja.pl/index.php/artykuly-autorzy/83-james-b-jordan/488-02-04-2006.
"Five Cities and Isaiah 19." *Biblical Horizons* 116 (April).
"Creation With the Appearance of Age." *Open Book* 45 (April). Polish: "Pozornie stare stworzenie." Trans. Bogumil Jarmulak. *Reformacja w Polsce* 8.4 (December 2006). Online: http://www.reformacja.pl/index.php/artykuly-autorzy/83-james-b-jordan/487-06-04-2006.
"The Date of Creation, Appendix B: When Was the Turn of the Year?" *Biblical Chronology* 117 (May).
"Call Me Ishmael (1): Meditations." *Biblical Horizons* 117 (May).
"The Date of Creation, Chapter 7, Part 1: The Chronologies of Genesis 5 & 11, Part 1." *Biblical Chronology* 118 (June).
"Call Me Ishmael (2): Meditations." *Biblical Horizons* 118 (June).
"The Geocentricity Question." *Open Book* 46 (June). Originally published in *Biblical Educator* 3.12 (December):1–4, and, with slight revisions, *Contra Mundum* 7 (Spring 1993).
"Jesus' First Eschatological Discourse (20)." *Studies in The Revelation* 38 (Summer).
"The Revelation of Jesus in Revelation 1:12b–16 (Part 2)." *Studies in The Revelation* 38 (Summer).
"The Date of Creation, Chapter 7, Part 2: The Chronologies of Genesis 5 & 11, Part 2." *Biblical Chronology* 119 (July).
"Daniel 1: The Victory of the Sacred Vessels, Part 1." *Biblical Horizons* 119 (July).
"The Date of Creation, Appendix C: Theological Observations on Genesis 5 & 11." *Biblical Chronology* 120 (August).
"Daniel 1: The Victory of the Sacred Vessels, Part 2." *Biblical Horizons* 120 (August).

"The Apocrypha." *Open Book* 47 (August).
"The Date of Creation, Chapter 8: Was There a Second Cainan?" *Biblical Chronology* 121 (September).
"Daniel 1: The Victory of the Sacred Vessels, Part 3." *Biblical Horizons* 121 (September).
"The Revelation of Jesus in Revelation 1:12b–16 (Part 3)." *Studies in The Revelation* 39 (Autumn).
"The Date of Creation, Chapter 9: The Arpachshad Connection." *Biblical Chronology* 122 (October).
"Daniel 1: The Victory of the Sacred Vessels, Part 4." *Biblical Horizons* 122 (October).
"The Apocrypha: Bel and the Dragon: Commentary." *Open Book* 48 (October).
"The Prayer of Manasseh." *Open Book* 48 (October).
"The Date of Creation, Chapter 10: From Adam to the Flood." *Biblical Chronology* 123 (November).
"A Canonical Investigation (Part 1)." *Biblical Horizons* 123 (November).
"The Date of Creation, Chapter 11: The Moses Connection." *Biblical Chronology* 124 (December).
"A Canonical Investigation (Part 2)." *Biblical Horizons* 124 (December).
A Brief Reader's Guide to Revelation. Niceville, FL: Transfiguration Press. Reprinted, slightly revised, as *The Vindication of Jesus Christ: A Brief Reader's Guide to Revelation*. Monroe, LA: Athanasius Press, 2009.
Creation in Six Days: A Defense of the Traditional Reading of Genesis One. Moscow: Canon. Includes a lot of the material relating to Genesis in *Biblical Chronology* 9 & 10.
"An Exposition of the Book of Revelation: Lecture Notes."

2000

"A Canonical Investigation (Part 3)." *Biblical Horizons* 125 (January).
"How to Chant the Psalms." *Rite Reasons: Studies in Worship* 61 (January).
"A Canonical Investigation (Part 4)." *Biblical Horizons* 126 (February).
"From Bread to Wine: Toward a More Biblical Liturgical Theology I." *Rite Reasons: Studies in Worship* 62 (February).
"A Canonical Investigation (Part 5)." *Biblical Horizons* 127 (March).
"God's Life and Our Lives: Toward a More Biblical Liturgical Theology II." *Rite Reasons: Studies in Worship* 63 (March).
"A Canonical Investigation (Part 6)." *Biblical Horizons* 128 (April).
"From Three to Five: Toward a More Biblical Liturgical Theology III." *Rite Reasons: Studies in Worship* 64 (April).
"A Canonical Investigation (Part 7)." *Biblical Horizons* 129 (May).
"From Three to Five (concluded): Toward a More Biblical Liturgical Theology III." *Rite Reasons: Studies in Worship* 65 (May).
"Covenant Renewal: Toward a More Biblical Liturgical Theology IV." *Rite Reasons: Studies in Worship* 65 (May).
"Was Job an Edomite King? (Part 1)." *Biblical Horizons* 130 (June).
"Toward a More Biblical Liturgical Theology V." *Rite Reasons: Studies in Worship* 66 (June).
"Death and New Life." *Rite Reasons: Studies in Worship* 66 (June).
"Was Job an Edomite King? (Part 2)." *Biblical Horizons* 131 (July).
"The Seven Edomite Kings." *Biblical Horizons* 131 (July).
"Death and New Life (concluded): Toward a More Biblical Liturgical Theology VI." *Rite Reasons: Studies in Worship* 67 (July).
"On Not Yoking an Ox and an Ass Together." *Biblical Horizons* 132 (August). Spanish: "Sobre No Enyugar Juntos al Buey y al Asno." Trans. Donald Herrera Terán. Online: http://www.biblicalhorizons.com/espanol-files/Yugo_BAss.pdf.
"Repeating the Ritual: Toward a More Biblical Liturgical Theology VII." *Rite Reasons: Studies in Worship* 68 (August).
"Hath God Said?" *Tabletalk* 24.8 (August): 9–12, 56–57.
"153 Big Fish." *Biblical Horizons* 133 (September).
"Abram's 318 Men." *Biblical Horizons* 133 (September).
"The Places of Trial and Suffering: Toward a More Biblical Liturgical Theology VIII." *Rite Reasons: Studies in Worship* 69 (September).
"The Return of Hamor." *Biblical Horizons* 134 (October).

"Journey to Maturity 1: Leaving Home: Toward a More Biblical Liturgical Theology IX." *Rite Reasons: Studies in Worship* 70 (October).

"Concerning the Giants." *Biblical Horizons* 135 (November). Polish: "O olbrzymach." Trans. Bogumil Jarmulak. *Reformacja w Polsce* 8.1 (February 2006). Online: http://www.reformacja.pl/index.php/artykuly-autorzy/83-james-b-jordan/481-04-01-2006.

"Some Notes on Genesis 46:8–17." *Biblical Horizons* 135 (November).

"Journey to Maturity 2: Mid-Life Crisis (I): Toward a More Biblical Liturgical Theology X." *Rite Reasons: Studies in Worship* 71 (November).

"Thirty-Eight Years by the Sheep Pool." With Jeffrey J. Meyers. *Biblical Horizons* 136 (December). Polish: "38 lat przy owczej sadzawce." Trans. Sebastian Smolarz. *Reformacja w Polsce* 8.2–3 (September 2006). Online: http://www.reformacja.pl/index.php/artykuly-autorzy/83-james-b-jordan/485-03-02-03-2006.

"Journey to Maturity 2: Mid-Life Crisis (II): Toward a More Biblical Liturgical Theology XI." *Rite Reasons: Studies in Worship* 72 (December).

"Psalm 119." *Rite Reasons: Studies in Worship* 72 (December).

"Psalm 7." Translation and music.

"Psalm 25." Translation and music.

"Psalm 118." Translation and music.

2001

"Daniel 2: God's New Kingdom, Part 1." *Biblical Horizons* 137 (January).

"Journey to Maturity 3: Becoming Prophets: Toward a More Biblical Liturgical Theology XI." *Rite Reasons: Studies in Worship* 73 (January). This article should have been XII. All the subsequent essays in this series are misnumbered accordingly.

"Daniel 2: God's New Kingdom, Part 2." *Biblical Horizons* 138 (February).

"Genesis 1 and Biography: Toward a More Biblical Liturgical Theology XII." *Rite Reasons: Studies in Worship* 74 (February).

"Daniel 2: God's New Kingdom, Part 3." *Biblical Horizons* 139 (March).

"Genesis 1 and Biography [continued]: Toward a More Biblical Liturgical Theology XIII." *Rite Reasons: Studies in Worship* 75 (March).

"Daniel 2: God's New Kingdom, Part 4." *Biblical Horizons* 140 (April).

"Genesis 1 and Ritual (Part 1): Toward a More Biblical Liturgical Theology XIV." *Rite Reasons: Studies in Worship* 76 (April).

"Life from the Dead." *Biblical Horizons* 141 (May).

"Is Abraham's Life a Type?" *Biblical Horizons* 141 (May).

"Genesis 1 and Ritual (Part 2): Toward a More Biblical Liturgical Theology XV." *Rite Reasons: Studies in Worship* 77 (May).

"Psalm 119 (continued)." *Rite Reasons: Studies in Worship* 77 (May).

"Leviticus 1:1–2." *Biblical Horizons* 142 (June).

"Swaddling Clothes and Paedocommunion." *Rite Reasons: Studies in Worship* 78 (June).

"Leviticus 1:2." *Biblical Horizons* 143 (July).

"Introduction to the Ascensions." *Biblical Horizons* 143 (July).

"Leviticus 1:3–4, 10." *Biblical Horizons* 144 (August).

"The Ten Words and Their Liturgical Usage." *Rite Reasons: Studies in Worship* 79 (August).

"Leviticus 1:4–5, 11." *Biblical Horizons* 145 (September).

"Leviticus 1:5, 11." *Biblical Horizons* 146 (October).

"Toward a Biblical Theology of the Church Year, Part 1." *Rite Reasons: Studies in Worship* 80 (October).

"The Theology of Biblical Chronology." Studies in Biblical Chronology 1 (October).

"From Creation to Solomon." Studies in Biblical Chronology 2 (October).

A Chronological and Calendrical Commentary on the Pentateuch. Studies in Biblical Chronology 3 (October). This is a reprint of Biblical Horizons Occasional Paper 22 (May 1995).

"Harold Camping on Genesis 5 and 11." Studies in Biblical Chronology 4 (October).

"Darius, Artaxerxes, and Ahasuerus in the Bible." Studies in Biblical Chronology 5 (October).

"Leviticus 1:5–8, 11–12." *Biblical Horizons* 147 (November).

"Leviticus 1:8–9, 12–13." *Biblical Horizons* 148 (December).

"Toward a Biblical Theology of the Church Year, Part 2." *Rite Reasons: Studies in Worship* 81 (December).

From Bread to Wine: Toward a More Biblical Liturgical Theology. Draft ed., 1.1. Niceville, FL: Biblical Horizons. Includes much of the material published in *Rite Reasons* 62–77 (February 2000—May 2001).

Primeval Saints: Studies in the Patriarchs of Genesis. Moscow: Canon. Original "draft version" available in photocopy form since 1988. Polish: *Pradawni swieci. Studium pierwszej ksiegi Pisma Swietego*. Trans. Iwona Zydek. Wroclaw: Ewangeliczny Kosciol Reformowany, 2007. Korean: Trans. Jung Jin Ahn. Seoul: Christian Literature Crusade, 2009.

"That You May Live Long." In *Family Practice: God's Prescription for a Healthy Home*. ed. R. C. Sproul, Jr., 77–81. Phillipsburg: P&R Publishing. Reprinted from *Tabletalk* 20.3 (March 1996): 11–13.

2002

"The Fowl Ascension: Leviticus 1:14." *Biblical Horizons* 149 (January).

"1. What Is Meant by Biblical Theology?" *Biblical Theology Basics* 1 (January). Spanish: "Puntos Básicos de la Teología Bíblical." Trans. Donald Herrera Terán. Online: http://www.biblicalhorizons.com/espanol-files/Teo_Biblica.pdf.

"2. What Is the Covenant? [Part 1]." *Biblical Theology Basics* 1 (January).

"The Scandal of Christian Worship." *Rite Reasons: Studies in Worship* 82 (January).

"Leviticus 1:15–17." *Biblical Horizons* 150 (February).

"2. What Is the Covenant? (continued)." *Biblical Theology Basics* 2 (February).

"Aaron's Sons the Palace Servants: A Postscript to Leviticus 1." *Biblical Horizons* 151 (March).

"3. Covenant Maturation." *Biblical Theology Basics* 3 (March).

"Spiritual Worship." *Rite Reasons: Studies in Worship* 83 (March).

"The Gospel: Glorification by Faith." *Biblical Horizons* 152 (April).

"4. The Three Faces of the Covenant." *Biblical Theology Basics* 4 (April).

"No Circumcision in the Wilderness." *Biblical Horizons* 153 (May).

"5. Priest, King, and Prophet." *Biblical Theology Basics* 5 (May).

"The Allegory of the Biblical Rituals, Part 1: Replaying Genesis." *Rite Reasons: Studies in Worship* 84 (May). Reprinted in "The Allegory of the Levitical Rituals." Biblical Horizons Occasional Paper 37 (January 2010).

"No Circumcision in the Wilderness [Part 2]." *Biblical Horizons* 154 (June).

"An Introduction to the Seven-Fold Covenant Model, With Notes on the Five-Fold Covenant Model." Biblical Horizons Occasional Paper 29 (June).

"A Canonical Inquiry: An Investigation of Two Possible Canonical Structures of the Books of the Bible." Biblical Horizons Occasional Paper 30 (June).

"6. Covenant Phases in the Bible." *Biblical Theology Basics* 6 (June).

"Of Lads and Bears." *Biblical Horizons* 155 (July).

"The Touch of Affliction: The 'Plague' of 'Leprosy' in Leviticus 13." Biblical Horizons Occasional Paper 31 (July).

"7. The Literary Shape of the Covenant, Part 1." *Biblical Theology Basics* 7 (July).

"The Allegory of the Biblical Rituals, Part 2: Journey to Peace." *Rite Reasons: Studies in Worship* 85 (July). Reprinted in "The Allegory of the Levitical Rituals." Biblical Horizons Occasional Paper 37 (January 2010).

"7. The Literary Shape of the Covenant, Part 2." *Biblical Theology Basics* 8 (August).

"8. The Literary Shape of the Whole Bible." *Biblical Theology Basics* 8 (August).

"9. A Text for Chanting." *Biblical Theology Basics* 9 (September).

"10. A Text with Shape and Flow." *Biblical Theology Basics* 10 (October).

"11. An Introduction to Chiasm." *Biblical Theology Basics* 11 (November).

"12. Chiasm and Life." *Biblical Theology Basics* 12 (December).

"Psalm 136." Translation and music.

Psalm translations for chanting in *Cantus Christi*. Moscow: Canon. The *Cantus Christi* mistakenly attributes Psalm 94 ("O LORD God, to Whom Vengeance Belongeth") to Jordan.

- "The Heavens Are Declaring the Mighty One's Glory (Psalm 19)." Translated in 2000.
- "Ascribe to Yahweh, Sons of Mighty Ones (Psalm 29)." Translated in 2000.
- "Yahweh Reigns! Let the Land Rejoice! (Psalm 97)." Translated in 1997.
- "Of Lovingkindness and Justice Will I Sing (Psalm 101)." Translated in 2000.

Studies in the New Testament. Seoul: Grisim Publishing. Selections from *Biblical Horizons* in Korean.

"Vespers Service, Preces, Kyrie, and Sanctus." "Sanctus" online: http://biblicalhorizons.files.wordpress.com/2009/05/jordan_sanctus.pdf.

2003

"Thoughts on Sovereign Grace and Regeneration: Some Tentative Explorations." Biblical Horizons Occasional Paper 32 (January).

"13. The Menorah Chiasm." *Biblical Theology Basics* 13 (January).

"Was Moses a Murderer?" *Biblical Horizons* 158 (February).

"The Revelation of Jesus in Revelation 1:12b–16 and Its Relation to the Structure of the Book of Revelation." Biblical Horizons Occasional Paper 33 (February).

"14. Comments on *The Covenantal Gospel* by Cornelis van der Waal." *Biblical Theology Basics* 14 (February).

"The Three Babylons and the Confusion of Tongues." *Biblical Horizons* 159 (May).

"The Memorial of Cornelius." *Biblical Horizons* 160 (June).

"Leviticus 1: Translation and Commentary." Biblical Horizons Occasional Paper 34 (June).

"Cyrus and Daniel." *Biblical Horizons* 162 (October).

"Toward a Theology of Nehemiah." *Biblical Horizons* 163 (November).

"The 2300 Evening-Mornings of Daniel 8." *Biblical Horizons* 164 (December).

"Some Moments with the Magus: An Interview with Gene Wolfe." With Nick Gevers and Michael Andre-Driussi. *Infinity Plus*. Online: http://www.infinityplus.co.uk/nonfiction/intgw.htm. Reprinted in *Shadows of the New Sun: Wolfe on Writing / Writers on Wolfe*, ed. Peter Wright, 184–89. Liverpool Science Fiction Texts and Studies. Liverpool: Liverpool University Press, 2007.

Studies in the Old Testament. Seoul: Grisim Publishing. Selections from *Biblical Horizons* in Korean.

2004

"The Beatitudes as Kingdom Announcement." *Biblical Horizons* 165 (January).

"Misusing the Westminster Confession." *Biblical Horizons* 166 (February).

"The First Phase of the New Covenant, Part 1." *Biblical Horizons* 167 (March).

"The First Phase of the New Covenant, Part 2." *Biblical Horizons* 168 (April).

"The 'Ungodly King' of Daniel 11:36–45: Implications of the Herod Identification, Part 1." *Biblical Horizons* 169 (May).

"Liturgical Man, Liturgical Women—Part 1." *Rite Reasons: Studies in Worship* 86 (May). Polish: "Mezczyzna i kobieta w liturgii, cz. 1." Trans. Sebastian Smolarz. *Reformacja w Polsce* 8.1 (February 2006). Online: http://www.reformacja.pl/index.php/artykuly-autorzy/83-james-b-jordan/480-06-01-2006.

"The 'Ungodly King' of Daniel 11:36–45: Implications of the Herod Identification, Part 2." *Biblical Horizons* 170 (June).

"Liturgical Man, Liturgical Women—Part 2." *Rite Reasons: Studies in Worship* 87 (June). Polish: "Mezczyzna i kobieta w liturgii, cz. 2." Trans. Sebastian Smolarz. *Reformacja w Polsce* 8.2–3 (September 2006). Online: http://www.reformacja.pl/index.php/artykuly-autorzy/83-james-b-jordan/483-06-02-03-2006.

"Ecological Sin in a Difficult Passage: 2 Kings 3." *Biblical Horizons* 171 (July).

"From Glory to Glory." *Biblical Horizons* 171 (July).

"'LORD' or 'Yahweh'?" *Biblical Horizons* 171 (July).

"Jesus' Representative and His Assistants: Worship in Revelation." *Rite Reasons: Studies in Worship* 88 (July).

"Defiled and Holy Houses: Luke 11:14–52." *Biblical Horizons* 172 (August).

"The Son of Man in Daniel 7, Part 1: Ezekiel (begin)." *Biblical Horizons* 173 (September).

"The Son of Man in Daniel 7, Part 2: Ezekiel (end)." *Biblical Horizons* 174 (October).

"The Son of Man in Daniel 7, Part 2: Leviticus 16." *Biblical Horizons* 175 (November).

"Merit Versus Maturity: What Did Jesus Do For Us?" In *The Federal Vision*, eds. Steve Wilkins and Duane Garner, 151–200. Monroe, LA: Athansius Press.

Studies in the Psalter 1. Niceville, FL: Biblical Horizons. Originally published as a series of essayletters sent to donors in 2004.

"A Survey of the Apocrypha and the Intertestamental Period: Lecture Notes."

2005

"Posture at the Table and the Hermeneutics of Ritual." *Rite Reasons: Studies in Worship* 89 (January). This issue is wrongly dated 2004 instead of 2005.

"The Census of Caesar Augustus." *Biblical Horizons* 176 (March).

"Proleptic Exodus." *Biblical Horizons* 176 (March).

"Strange and Glorious New Rites." *Rite Reasons: Studies in Worship* 90 (July). This issue is wrongly dated 2004 instead of 2005.

"Eating and Drinking Together." *Rite Reasons: Studies in Worship* 90 (July). This issue is wrongly dated 2004 instead of 2005.

"The Closing of the Calvinistic Mind." *Biblical Horizons* 177 (August).

"FV, NPP, PCA, AAPC, Etc." *Biblical Horizons* 177 (August).

"The End of the World (Ezekiel 32:17–32)." *Biblical Horizons* 178 (September).

"The Test-Temptations of Jesus, Part 1: Introduction." *Biblical Horizons* 179 (October). Polish: "Kuszenie Jezusa, cz. 1." Trans. Bogumil Jarmulak. *Reformacja w Polsce* 9.1 (March 2007). Online: http://www.reformacja.pl/index.php/artykuly-autorzy/83-james-b-jordan/489-03-01-2007.

"The Test-Temptations of Jesus, Part 2: The Tempter." *Biblical Horizons* 180 (November). Polish: "Kuszenie Jezusa, cz. 2: Kusiciel." Trans. Bogumil Jarmulak. *Reformacja w Polsce* 9.2 (June 2007). Online: http://www.reformacja.pl/index.php/artykuly-autorzy/83-james-b-jordan/490-06-02-2007.

"The King Must Die." *Biblical Horizons* 180 (November).

"The Test-Temptations of Jesus, Part 3: Matthew, Introduction." *Biblical Horizons* 181 (December).

Studies in the Psalter 2. Niceville, FL: Biblical Horizons. Originally published as a series of essayletters sent to donors in 2005.

Trees and Thorns: Studies in Genesis 2–4. Draft edition 1.1. Niceville, FL: Biblical Horizons. Originally published in the *Trees and Thorns* essayletter sent to donors, 1991–2003.

2006

"The Test-Temptations of Jesus, Part 4: Matthew, Stones into Loaves." *Biblical Horizons* 182 (January).

"The Test-Temptations of Jesus, Part 5: Matthew, Conclusion; Mark's Account." *Biblical Horizons* 183 (February).

"The Test-Temptations of Jesus, Part 6: Luke, Introduction and First Temptation." *Biblical Horizons* 184 (March).

"The Test-Temptations of Jesus, Part 7: Luke, Second and Third Temptations." *Biblical Horizons* 185 (April).

"The Test-Temptations of Jesus, Part 8." *Biblical Horizons* 186 (May).

"How Matthew Came to be Written." *Biblical Horizons* 187 (June). Online: http://biblicalhorizons.wordpress.com/2008/03/20/how-matthew-came-to-be-written/.

"How Mark Came to be Written." *Biblical Horizons* 188 (July). Online: http://biblicalhorizons.wordpress.com/2008/03/24/how-mark-came-to-be-written-2/. Polish: "Jak napisano Ewangelie Marka." Trans. Bogumil Jarmulak. *Reformacja w Polsce* 8.2-3 (September 2006). Online: http://www.reformacja.pl/index.php/artykuly-autorzy/83-james-b-jordan/484-05-02-03-2006.

"A Review of *Cantus Christi*." *Rite Reasons: Studies in Worship* 91 (September).

"Narrative and Supernarrative." *Biblical Theology Basics* 15 (November). Polish: "Narracja i metanarracja." Trans. Bogumil Jarmulak. *Reformacja w Polsce* 8.4 (December 2006). Online: http://www.reformacja.pl/index.php/artykuly-autorzy/83-james-b-jordan/486-09-04-2006.

"Children and the Religious Meals of the Old Creation." In *The Case for Covenant Communion*, ed. Gregg Strawbridge, 49–68. Monroe, LA: Athanasius Press.

Studies in the Book of Revelation. Seoul: Grisim Publishing. Selections from the *Studies in The Revelation* newsletter in Korean.

Studies in the Psalter 3. Niceville, FL: Biblical Horizons. Originally published as a series of essayletters sent to donors in 2006.

2007

"Should Anyone Trust the Orthodox Presbyterian Church?" *Biblical Horizons* 191 (January).

"Ecclesiastes: Notes, Outline, and Translation." Biblical Horizons Occasional Paper 36 (January).

"How to Stop the Killing in Darfur, Part 1." *Rite Reasons: Studies in Worship* 92 (January).

"How To Do Reformed Theology Nowadays, Part 1." *Biblical Horizons* 192 (February).

"How To Do Reformed Theology Nowadays, Part 2." *Biblical Horizons* 193 (April).

"How to Stop the Killing in Darfur, Part 2." *Rite Reasons: Studies in Worship* 93 (April).

"How To Do Reformed Theology Nowadays, Part 3." *Biblical Horizons* 194 (May).

"Justification and Glorification." Blog entry (May 21). Online: http://www.leithart.com/archives/003032.php.

"How To Do Reformed Theology Nowadays, Part 4." *Biblical Horizons* 195 (June).

"How To Do Reformed Theology Nowadays, Part 5." *Biblical Horizons* 196 (July).

"How To Do Reformed Theology Nowadays, Part 6." *Biblical Horizons* 197 (August).

"Worship Music: Worship in Spirit, Part 1." *Rite Reasons: Studies in Worship* 93 (September). Note that this issue should be 94, not 93; subsequent issues are also misnumbered.

"Worship Music, Part 2: Musical Instruments." *Rite Reasons: Studies in Worship* 94 (October).

"Worship Music, Part 3: Weapons of Worship." *Rite Reasons: Studies in Worship* 95 (November).

"Leviticus in Outline." *Biblical Horizons* 198 (December).

The Handwriting on the Wall: A Commentary on the Book of Daniel. Powder Springs, GA: American Vision. 2nd ed., 2010. The second edition corrected many typos, has the appendices numbered correctly, and includes an index.

"Song at the Red Sea (Exodus 15)." Translation and music (ca. 2007).

Studies in the Psalter 4. Niceville, FL: Biblical Horizons. Originally published as a series of essayletters sent to donors in 2007.

2008

"Music and Typology." *Biblical Theology Basics* 16 (March).

"Worship Music, Part 4: An Army of Lions." *Rite Reasons: Studies in Worship* 96 (March).

"Exile or Ark?" (April). Online: http://biblicalhorizons.wordpress.com/2008/04/10/exile-or-ark/.

"The Offertory." *Rite Reasons: Studies in Worship* 97 (May).

Polish: "Typy i symbole w Ew. Jana." Trans. Bogumil Jarmulak. *Reformacja w Polsce* 10.2 (May). Online: http://www.reformacja.pl/index.php/artykuly-autorzy/83-james-b-jordan/499-05-02-2008. This is a portion of *Through New Eyes*.

"Ritual Versus Christianity." (August). Online: http://biblicalhorizons.wordpress.com/2008/08/18/ritual-versus-christianity/.

"Evil Empire?" *Biblical Horizons* 199 (September).

"Worship Music, Part 5: The House of God." *Rite Reasons: Studies in Worship* 98 (September).

"Ritual and Typology." (October). Online: http://biblicalhorizons.wordpress.com/2008/10/29/ritual-and-typology/.

"The Great Antiphons." *Studies in the Psalter* (December). This is an introduction to the "Great Antiphons," originally published as the monthly donors' essayletter (though the essayletter itself has the wrong month: November instead of December). It is not included in *Studies in the Psalter* 5 with the rest of the 2008 newsletters.

"Q&A." In *Love the Lord with Heart and Mind*, eds. Steve Hays and James Anderson, 99–102. N.p., 2008. 2nd ed., 2009. Online: http://www.triapologia.com/hays/Love_the_Lord.pdf.

Studies in the Psalter 5. Niceville, FL: Biblical Horizons. Originally published as a series of essayletters sent to donors in 2008.

2009

"The Gospel." *Biblical Horizons* 200 (January).
"Psalms 23–29." (January 19). Online: http://biblicalhorizons.wordpress.com/2008/01/19/psalms-23-29/.
"A Reply on the Nature of the Psalter." (January 21). Online: http://biblicalhorizons.wordpress.com/2008/01/21/a-reply-on-the-nature-of-the-psalter/.
"Let Each Esteem the Other Better." (January 23). Online: http://biblicalhorizons.wordpress.com/2008/01/23/let-each-esteem-the-other-better/.
"Handraising in Worship: Questions." (January 28). Online: http://biblicalhorizons.wordpress.com/2008/01/28/handraising-in-worship-questions/.
"Evil Empire: Retractions and Extra Considerations." *Biblical Horizons* 201 (February).
"Jesus' Baptism and Ours." (February 8). Online: http://biblicalhorizons.wordpress.com/2008/02/08/jesus-baptism-and-ours/.
"Problems with Church History Studies." (February 26). Online: http://biblicalhorizons.wordpress.com/2008/02/26/problems-with-church-history-studies/.
"Getting Real with the Patriarchs." *Biblical Horizons* 202 (March). This issue came out in August. It clearly follows "Getting Real in Genesis" (see below), but is dated and numbered before it.
Polish: "Nabozenstwo jako odnowienie przymierza." Trans. Bogumil Jarmulak. *Reformacja w Polsce* 11.1–2 (March 2009). This is a section of *Theses on Worship*. Online: http://www.reformacja.pl/index.php/artykuly-autorzy/83-james-b-jordan/504-05-01-02-2009.
"Rainbow Coalition?" (March 2). Online: http://biblicalhorizons.wordpress.com/2009/03/02/rainbow-coalition/.
"Obama as Fool." (March 3). Online: http://biblicalhorizons.wordpress.com/2009/03/03/obama-as-fool/.
"Romans 7" (April). Online: http://biblicalhorizons.wordpress.com/2009/04/19/romans-7/.
"Worship Music, Part 6: Contra Goudimel." *Rite Reasons: Studies in Worship* 99 (April).
"Getting Real in Genesis." *Biblical Horizons* 203 (May).
"The Pastoral Function." (May). Online: http://biblicalhorizons.wordpress.com/2009/05/16/the-pastoral-function/.
"Did God Speak Hebrew to Adam?" *Biblical Horizons* 204 (June).
"Rome? Why Bother?" (July). Online: http://biblicalhorizons.wordpress.com/2009/07/14/rome-why-bother/.
"How to Talk in Worship." *Rite Reasons: Studies in Worship* 100 (August).
Polish: "Czlowiek—narzedzie transformacji." Trans. Bogumil Jarmulak. Online: http://jarmulak.com/?p=986. This is a section from *Through New Eyes*.
"Getting Real with the Gospels." *Biblical Horizons* 205 (October).
"The Amazing Adventures of Myrtle Morningstar, Part 1: Introducing Our Heroine." *Biblical Horizons* 206 (November).
"Concerning BMEV." (November 12). Online: http://biblicalhorizons.wordpress.com/2009/11/12/concerning-bmev/.
"More Thoughts on BMEV." (November 26). Online: http://biblicalhorizons.wordpress.com/2009/11/26/more-thoughts-on-bmev/.
"Protestants and BMEV." (November 27). Online: http://biblicalhorizons.wordpress.com/2009/11/27/protestants-and-bmev/.
"John Calvin and the Reformation of Psalmody: Overcoming Liturgical Heresy." In *Revisiting John Calvin*. Seoul: Baekseok University Theological Seminary, 2009. In Korean. And in *Calvin and Heresy*. Busan: Korean Institute for Reformed Studies, Kosin University, 2009. In English and Korean.
Studies in the Psalter 6. Niceville, FL: Biblical Horizons. Originally published as a series of essayletters sent to donors in 2009.

2010

"The Allegory of the Levitical Rituals." Biblical Horizons Occasional Paper 37 (January). Reprint of "The Allegory of the Biblical Rituals, Part 1: Replaying Genesis." *Rite Reasons: Studies in Worship* 84 (May 2002) and "The Allegory of the Biblical Rituals, Part 2: Journey to Peace." *Rite Reasons: Studies in Worship* 85 (July 2002).

"The Astonishing Adventures of Myrtle Morningstar, Part 2: Introducing the King." *Biblical Horizons* 207 (February).

"What's Wrong with N. T. Wright?" (February). Online: http://biblicalhorizons.wordpress.com/2010/02/12/whats-wrong-with-n-t-wright/.

"The Astounding Adventures of Myrtle Morningstar, Part 3: Introducing the Troublemaker." *Biblical Horizons* 208 (March).

"The Sin of Ham Revisited." (May). Online: http://biblicalhorizons.wordpress.com/2010/05/15/the-sin-of-ham-revisited/.

"The Awestriking Adventures of Myrtle Morningstar [Part 4]: A Perfect Kingdom (1:1)." *Biblical Horizons* 210 (June).

"Monocovenantalism." (June 5). Online: http://biblicalhorizons.wordpress.com/2010/06/05/monocovenantalism/.

"'Imputation of Active Obedience'—Some Notes." (June 8). Online: http://biblicalhorizons.wordpress.com/2010/06/08/imputation-of-active-obedience-some-notes/.

"The Sensational Adventures of Myrtle Morningstar [Part 5]: A Kingdom at Peace (1:1-4)." *Biblical Horizons* 211 (July).

"The Stunning Adventures of Myrtle Morningstar [Part 6]: An Endless Festival (1:3-6)." *Biblical Horizons* 212 (August).

"The Spectacular Adventures of Myrtle Morningstar [Part 7]." *Biblical Horizons* 213 (October).

"The Stupendous Adventures of Myrtle Morningstar [Part 8]." *Biblical Horizons* 214 (November).

"The O Antiphons (Part 1)." *Studies in the Psalter* (November). This essay was published as the monthly donors' essayletter. It is not included in *Studies in the Psalter 7* with the rest of the 2010 newsletters.

"The Startling Adventures of Myrtle Morningstar [Part 9]." *Biblical Horizons* 215 (December).

"Structures of the Gospel According to Matthew." Biblical Horizons Occasional Paper 38 (December 2010). Reprint of *Biblical Horizon* 94 and 95.

"The O Antiphons (Part 2)." *Studies in the Psalter* (December). This essay was published as the monthly donors' essayletter. It is not included in *Studies in the Psalter 7* with the rest of the 2010 newsletters.

Studies in the Psalter 7. Niceville, FL: Biblical Horizons. Originally published as a series of essayletters sent to donors in 2010.

Additional Notes

From 1989 to 1993, James Jordan worked for Ligonier Ministries, preparing daily devotional meditations for *Tabletalk*. Most of these meditations were drawn from lectures by R. C. Sproul and rewritten and edited to fit into the devotional format, though some were mainly Jordan's own work. Several of these devotional meditations were later published in book form:

R. C. Sproul, *Before the Face of God, Book 1: A Daily Guide for Living from the Book of Romans*. Grand Rapids: Baker, 1992. This book is adapted from the 1989 *Tabletalk* devotionals, and Jordan thinks he wrote all the meditations that were later published in this book.

———, *Before the Face of God, Book 2: A Daily Guide for Living from the Gospel of Luke*. Grand Rapids: Baker, 1993. This book is adapted from the 1990 *Tabletalk* devotionals; most (if not all) of all of these meditations would have been prepared by James Jordan.

———, *Before the Face of God, Book 3: A Daily Guide for Living from the Old Testament*. Grand Rapids: Baker, 1994. This book is adapted from the 1991 *Tabletalk* devotionals and includes material written by Jordan himself. A note at the front says, "Contributing material for studies on Ruth, Chronicles, Proverbs, and portions of the Minor Prophets were Robert F. Ingram, Michael S. Beates, Frederic C. Putnam, and James B. Jordan, respectively."

———, *Before the Face of God, Book 4: A Daily Guide for Living from Ephesians, Hebrews, and James*. Grand Rapids: Baker, 1994. This book is adapted from *Tabletalk* devotionals. Ephesians appeared in *Tabletalk* in July 1992 as well as in April–September 1993, Hebrews in October 1992 and also April–September 1993, and James in October–December 1993. It seems likely that at least the 1992 material was prepared

THE GLORY OF KINGS

by James Jordan, though it is impossible to tell exactly which devotionals he worked on, let alone how much was his own writing as opposed to adaptation of material drawn from R. C. Sproul's lectures. This volume does not indicate who contributed material; instead, by mistake, it includes exactly the same note that appeared in the previous volume.

www.ingramcontent.com/pod-product-compliance
Lightning Source LLC
Chambersburg PA
CBHW080407300426
44113CB00015B/2428